The
Shape
of
Fiction

# The Shape of Fiction

SECOND EDITION

## ALAN CASTY
Santa Monica College

D. C. HEATH AND COMPANY
Lexington, Massachusetts / Toronto / London

# Acknowledgments

"A Tree of Night," copyright 1945 by Truman Capote. Reprinted from *A Tree of Night and Other Stroies*, by Truman Capote, by permission of Random House, Inc.

"The Chrysanthemums," from *The Long Valley* by John Steinbeck. Copyright 1937, 1965 by John Steinbeck. Reprinted by permission of The Viking Press, Inc.

"The Country Husband," reprinted from *Stories* by John Cheever, by permission of Farrar, Straus & Giroux, Inc. Copyright 1954 by *The New Yorker Magazine, Inc.* Copyright © 1966 by Farrar, Straus & Giroux, Inc.

"The Face Within the Face," by Mark Schorer, reprinted by permission of Brandt & Brandt. Copyright © 1949 by *The New Yorker Magazine, Inc.*

"Suicides," by Cesare Pavese, from *Stories of Modern Italy*, edited by Ben Johnson. © Copyright 1960 by Random House, Inc. Reprinted by permission.

"Four Summers," reprinted from *The Wheel of Love* by Joyce Carol Oates by permission of the publisher, Vanguard Press, Inc. Copyright, © 1970, 1969, 1968, 1967, 1966, 1965, by Joyce Carol Oates.

"In Search of a Missing IUD," by Anne Higgins. Reprinted by permission of John Cushman Associates. Inc. Copyright © 1972 by Anne Higgins. First published in *New American Review.*

"Son in the Afternoon," by John A. Williams. Reprinted by permission of the author.

"Gold Coast," from *Hue and Cry,* by James Alan McPherson. Copyright © 1968, 1969 by James Alan McPherson. Originally appeared in *The Atlantic.* Reprinted by permission of Little, Brown and Co. in association with The Atlantic Monthly Press.

"Cutting Edge," by James Purdy, from *The Color of Darkness.* Copyright © 1957 by James Purdy. Reprinted by permission of New Directions Publishing Corporation.

"The Rapids," copyright 1941 by Walter Van Tilburg Clark. Reprinted from *The Watchful Gods and Other Stories,* by Walter Van Tilburg Clark, by permission of Random House, Inc.

"A Worn Path," copyright, 1941, renewed, 1969, by Eudora Welty. Reprinted from her volume *A Curtain of Green and Other Stories* by permission of Harcourt Brace Jovanovich, Inc.

# PREFACE

In this second edition I have included nine new stories; doing so has of course caused the omission of some of the selections in the original edition. Some readers may regret—as I do—the loss of a favorite or two; all will, I believe, find the new additions interesting and valuable. The premise for the selection of new materials has been a strengthening of the book's representation of contemporary trends in fiction—in terms of types of writers and subject concerns that have been receiving increased attention since the first edition and in terms of the current flexibility in approaches to the form and style of the story. These trends are reflected in the new pieces by Oates, Higgins, Lessing, and Mansfield, Williams and McPherson, Purdy, Vonnegut, and Monroe.

I have also made adjustments in some of the pairings of stories, providing fresh and provocative perspectives for approaching some of the pieces retained from the first edition. Otherwise, the premises for the selection and organization of the material remain the same.

I have first of all demanded of the stories that after many readings they still move me. The stories have been picked not only for their enduring literary value, but also for their strong dramatic and emotional impact. To use a theatrical term, they *act*—whether through the tensions of plot action or the intensity of emotional crisis; they do not merely reflect precious minor moods or evanescent shifts of being. While their surface impact is direct, these stories demonstrate the subtle powers of fiction to catch the human situation in all its complexity.

These are, then texts which capture life within the conventions of an art, within the cage of form. It is part of the design of this book to enlarge the possibilities of the student's response to the varieties, methods, and pleasures of these conventions, with materials that provide a cross-section in time—from Hawthorne and Poe to Malamud and Oates—as well as a cross-section in approaches, types, methods, lengths, and styles.

The central teaching design of the book is that of comparison—connection and opposition, unity and distinction. The ability to establish connections and relationships, to shape categories and the complementary ability to make distinctions are central to the learning process. And they are especially appropriate and effective in teaching the understanding of literature. For whether we stress theme or structure, symbolic statements or devices, we are basically trying to get the student to establish the connections within a story that produce its statement and then by extension, to perceive the connections between stories. These further connections not only reveal the traditional themes and conventions of the form, but project in even stronger light the means and meanings of individual stories. For these reasons, I have selected the stories on the basis of the provocative, creative connections that can be established between them. In Part Two, the stories are grouped into eleven pairs so that the interrelationships—of both content and form—within each group can direct and assist the reader's responses. These groups are not deadened by such labels as *Love* or *Death* and are susceptible of a number of interpretations of their connections. Each story, of course, can also be valuably assigned and studied on its own. In Part Three the stories are not grouped, but they have been selected with an eye to their possible connections to the pairs in Part Two and to their possible bases of grouping among themselves.

The book offers several other tools for study. Its two explanatory sections have been sharpened and amended in light of responses to their use in the first edition. The introduction defines in concrete detail both the elements of the short story and the techniques of the attentive, responsive reader. The postscript on writing papers explains both the general purposes and strategies of the literary paper and the tactics and techniques for completing fifteen specific types of assignments, including examinations. These typical assignments can serve as the basis for interpretive approaches to the stories in the book.

New to this edition are five, full-length essays that not only serve to indicate ways of approaching eight of the book's stories, but also provide models for carrying out several different types of writing assignments.

All of the stories in Part Two are followed by questions that are designed to lead the reader to establish the connections among the specific details and aspects of the stories. The stories in Part Three are free of questions.

A.C.

*Santa Monica, California*

# CONTENTS

## Part Three
### Stories—For Further Comparison   329

## Part Four
### Writing about Fiction   423

# Part Five
## Assignments in Criticism
### —Five Models    449

# PART ONE

*The Shape of Fiction and
the Cage of Form:
An Introduction*

*It is the one orderly product which our muddling race has produced. . . .*
E. M. FORSTER

*. . . a clarification of life, not necessarily a great clarification, such as sects and cults are founded on, but a momentary stay against confusion . . .*
ROBERT FROST

*The writer's task is to cleanse, to organize, to articulate the substance of life. . . .*
HUGO VON HOFMANNSTHAL

*. . . not the power of drawing out in black and white the explanation of the mystery of the universe, but the power of so dealing with things as to awaken in us a wonderfully full, new, and intimate sense of them. . . .*
MATTHEW ARNOLD

*Taking his position at the hub of things, the writer contemplates the mystery of the universe . . . and traps Heaven and Earth in the cage of form. . . .*
LU CHI

Such phrases, in their resonances and implications, can provocatively suggest the nature of literature. But here, at the beginning of our study, we will have to push on to translate those echoes into more precise, if also more plodding, analytical terms. The purpose of this analytical indirection, however, is to bring the reader back to a more direct encounter with the echoes and resonances of the work of fiction; so that (to paraphrase the British writer T. S. Matthews) when the person on one end of the circuit that is fiction shouts, "My God, I'm alive! You're alive!", the reader on the other end, face to face and open to the work before him, is prepared to receive the message and say, "My God, you're right! We're both alive!"

To begin our translation of what literature means and does when it shares this news with its readers, we can see it as attempting to capture and control three entrances into the awareness that we are, indeed, all alive. These three doorways to fuller consciousness can be termed the complexity in unity of being alive, the intensity of feeling

3

of it, and the meaning and value of it. The three are inseparable in the artistic, and personal, control of life; but we will plod on and separate them, for the moment.

Literature—like magic, dreams, and the games of children—is a rebellion against being merely human and thus subject to forces beyond our control. And it is an assertion of being fully human and thus able to control the uncontrollable—if only in the emotions and the mind, if only in myth, legend, and story. It controls by imposing shape on the shapeless, form on the formless, and thus meaning on the meaningless. It controls, primarily, by means of connections and symbols.

Literature seeks to control by maintaining the fullest complexity of things within the connections of its organic unity. When any one thing —a person, a place, a tree, a dog—is reduced from its full complexity of being so that it can fit into the pattern of unity imposed, the value and accomplishment of the work of literature is reduced accordingly. Rather, the tensions, the oppositions, must be kept, even while the connections are being established. The writer seeks the connections in the fabric of being alive. He sees correspondences, similarities, comparisons, harmonies, relationships, syntheses, fusions, combinations; yet he doesn't blink away differences, contradictions, competitions, oppositions, discords. He sets limits, but at his best maintains the sense of something unlimited, unknown or unknowable, something open and beyond. And when, as James Joyce has said, he has maintained the uniqueness and complexity of an object but has adjusted it in what Joyce calls an "exquisite" relationship with the other parts of the patterned whole, "we recognize . . . its soul, its *whatness.*"

This same mixture of connection and opposition is inevitable as well to the second means of control—symbols. Literature, first of all, is a verbal art and must use as its basic tools words which are symbols, which *stand for* something else, whether concrete like *tree* or abstract like *democracy.* There is a connection between the word "tree" and the thing *tree,* but there is also a difference, a separateness, a gap between the world and words. From this unalterable limitation of language arise many of the complex devices of verbal art. In surmounting the paradox of its limitations, literature is a dramatizing and illustrating art. It evokes its meanings by indirection, by dramatizing or illustrating them with concrete symbolic details rather than directly stating them in generalizations. These selected, illustrative, symbolic details—whether a single image of a flower or a long, complicated story of a war—establish connections between the selected formal unity of the pattern and the living complexity that overlaps beyond. They show the significance of what has been selected, they *stand for* what is too complex for direct statement—what always loses something in the translation.

Too often discussion of a literary work ignores the dramatic intensity of feeling that can be developed with the writer's resources of shaping and symbolizing—the power of literature to move us. The experience of reading a work of literature is both emotional and intellectual; the work's ideas emerge through its emotions. But since the emotional effect is difficult to define—except in the reductive terms of "I liked it" or "I didn't like it"—this primary experience is often not analyzed. What exactly are the subtleties and complexities of the emotions of the characters in a story? What is the unique nature, the combination of feelings in the total experience of the story? What are the emotions aroused in the reader? What kind of pleasure —both intellectual and sensory—is produced? These questions must be pursued and analyzed if we are to form any ideas about a literary work.

The intellectual intent of a literary work, its moral and ethical implications, the values it tries to convey, are conveyed with the special impact of dramatized emotion, so that the significance of the work is always more than intellectual. The characters, events, places, and emotions that a writer selects and shapes have, for him, a resonating significance. They cast shadows, create echoes. The writer's subjects are, for him, important because they represent something beyond themselves. With them he examines his life and ours, comments on its truths and untruths, criticizes, sympathizes, evaluates, explores the meaning of being alive; and when the creative act of writing fuses with a creative act of reading, the reader is led to do the same. In this way, as commentators from Aristotle and Plato onward have agreed, literature can enlarge and expand our intellectual views and our sympathies, open the mind and liberalize the sentiments, illuminate and strengthen the spirit, and thus influence the feelings and actions of men, and the moral and social life of communities.

In a poem about a broken and yet still beautiful statue of the Greek god Apollo, the German poet Rainer Maria Rilke has caught the essence of this kind of creative interchange, this connection between the work of art and its audience. When he has fully perceived and fully responded to the statue's form, he realizes that not only is he looking at it, demanding something of it; it is looking at him, demanding something of him: " ... for there is no point that does not see you. You must change your life."

## The Reader of Fiction

*A thing becomes beautiful because it promises to remove some of my helplessness before the chaos of my experience.* ARTHUR MILLER

*What literature can do is to take this unmeaning, haphazard show of life, that means nothing to you, and arrange it in such a way as to make*

*you think very much more deeply about it than you ever dreamed of thinking about actual incidents that come to your knowledge.*

GEORGE BERNARD SHAW

*Here is a verbal contraption; how does it work? And what kind of a guy inhabits it?*    W. H. AUDEN

What is the nature of the reader of fiction who can respond openly, actively, and accurately to an encounter with a work of art? What does he do? What do *you* do?

Good reading is a creative act, and like other creative acts it is improved and perfected both by intuition and training. Leaving the intuition to fend for itself, let us look at the demands and methods of training for creative reading.

We can begin by establishing a connection of our own. The work of fiction sets up a paradox: a logical, meaningful unity of the whole that still maintains the complex freedom and independence of its parts. In a like manner, the reader of fiction must approach the work in a paradoxical manner: with the accuracy and logic of intellectual analysis and the complex freedom of imagination. And, in a further paradox, both parts of the approach can be trained, even the imagination.

The reader's job is to perceive the unity—the distinctive pattern— of the work before him. To create this synthesis, he must perceive and respond to the various relationships, the connections, established in the work: between its concrete details and its abstract emotions and ideas, between its parts and its whole, between one and another of its parts. What, for example, is the relationship in a story between what a character does and the kind of person he is, the kind of conflicts he undergoes? What is the relationship between what a character does on one page and what he does on another page? Or the relationship between a character's physical traits and his personality, between one character and another, between a part of the setting and character, an action, an emotion? It is the sum of such relationships that is the unity of the work.

To connect the work's unity to its meaning, the reader must repudiate literalness and free his imagination, must adjust to the symbolic nature of literature that is both precise and suggestive at the same time. Our emotional life, no less than our intellectual life, is often lived in terms of stereotypes; it is the job of the creative reader to train his responses to get beyond these stereotypes, meet the work of art on its own ground.

In doing his job, the reader can be guided by the following general suggestions.

*Get the facts first.*    Accurately understand the literal surface sense of a story before developing a fuller response to it: understand the sequence of actions and of time, the emotions of characters, the meanings of words.

*Notice particularly* the typical devices and key elements of stories, elements which will be discussed in the following sections.

*Be alert for repetitions or contrasts.* Often a pattern will be aided or developed by the repetition of words, thoughts, descriptions of things or actions at certain points or throughout a story or by the contrasts of these things with their opposites.

*Read for emphasis.* In addition to repetitions and contrasts, emphasis can be shown by correlation. An element—say the conditions of the weather—that is closely correlated with something that is clearly climactic in a story is probably important itself. Details at the beginning and ending of a story will usually also have special significance. This is particularly true of endings, since in one sense the whole story is written to enable the writer to arrive at the ending.

*Recognize direct statements.* Although fiction is an art of indirection, there are a number of ways in which an author emphasizes certain ideas by direct statements. These significant statements of philosophic, moral, or psychological content may appear in the dialogue of characters (where, of course, the personality and evaluation of the character speaking has to be taken into account) or in the midst of descriptive or narrative passages.

*Follow transitions closely.* Shifts in time, place, point of view, for example, must be noted and the relationships between the parts or sections of a work examined.

*Consider the title.* Titles are carefully chosen and often contain clues to the proper perspective from which to approach the story, and to the best emphases to keep in mind. Notice that many titles are allusions to or excerpts from other pieces of writing, literary or popular.

*Estimate the author's intention.* It is usually not possible or necessary to define the author's intention or purpose with any great precision, but some consideration of his probable concern and emphasis or even some consideration of the fact that he thought *something* was significant can prove of value.

*Establish the connections,* the synthesis of the surface details of the pattern.

*Connect the concrete,* symbolic details of the synthesis with the abstract emotions and meanings of the work. Create a hypothesis—tentative and undoubtedly partial—about the whole.

## The Nature of the Short Story

*... a special distillation of personality, a unique sensibility ... which orders all.*                    SEAN O'FAOLAIN

*For within our whole universe the story only has authority to answer
that cry of heart of its characters, that one cry of heart of each of
them:* "Who am I?"                                    ISAK DINESEN

*. . . some glowing center of action from which past and future will be
equally visible.*                                    FRANK O'CONNOR

Like all fiction, the short story is a narrative of certain interrelated
events (psychic and physical) which involves a significant conflict and
resolution and leads us to ponder its comment on human feelings,
conduct and beliefs. But it is a *short* story, and the fact of its length
has produced in it a set of traditions and conventions that give it
certain distinguishing characteristics. Distinguishing, but not completely distinct. For it is a genre that encompasses many variants and
mavericks, a genre whose distinctions are best seen as a matter of degree, not of kind.

The first significant result of its length is its *compression*. It must
make every stroke, every touch count. It must start fast: introduce,
orient, and get the conflict going all at once. It must be dense in detail, thick in texture, complex in interrelationships. Its ending must
carry a great weight of meaning and implication, must, as Sean
O'Faolain has said, "avoid the sense of a bump," yet order a final
vision of past, present, and future.

Its compression leads to its strong *symbolism*. Novels, of course, are
symbolic, too, but not so tightly, pervasively, demandingly, not always
with so central, so well defined, so all-encompassing a pattern. In this
it joins the complex, multileveled use of details of the poem with the
basic narrative approach of the novel.

Its compression leads, as well, to a typical emphasis on one central
action, within a limited span of time, "the single incident," as Henry
James called it. This emphasis, and its difference from the novel, can
be illustrated by the way in which two works reveal the tragic and
destructive core of the life of a slum boy in Chicago. In Nelson Algren's short story, "A Bottle of Milk for Mother," the details of only
one incident are selected: Lefty Bruno Bicek's confrontation with the
police sergeant and the resultant thoughts, fantasies, and statements;
the revelation of the murder he has committed; the final effect of the
confrontation on his awareness of his plight as he is returned to his
cell. Yet from the details of this one incident, Algren produces a brief
and emotional insight, a suddenly lighted opening, one quick, sure
probe into the wound that is the life of Lefty and others like him. Not
in all of its details, but in its essence. On the other hand, in a novel
like James T. Farrell's *Studs Lonigan* the truth of the life of a similar
boy is slowly and gradually documented through the many facets of
his whole short span of life: his childhood and his dreams; his rel-

tionship to his fellows, to girls, to his parents, to his church, to his school; the world of his work and lack of work; his later and changing relationships to his fellows, girls, parents, church and city; the final days of his disintegration.

There is, of course, a good deal of variation in the degree to which this emphasis on the single incident is employed in a short story. In some cases, through the use of flashback or narrative summary, the writer includes other events besides and before the central and climactic action. In some cases there may well be a sequence of several equal events. In others—and this is one of the most important directions the modern short story has taken—there is the exclusion of any central climactic action at all. Rather, the story focuses on the internal events—in the emotions and thoughts, the spirit—of the character, and intentionally avoiding an emphasis on plot, produces a sudden moment of illumination into the true inner condition of the life of the character as he takes part in or responds to an event or action that is not climactic or significant in itself at all.

And, finally, whether plotted or anti-plotted, whether comprising a single action, several actions, or none at all, the short story is distinguished by what Edgar Allan Poe called its *unity of effect*. However, whereas Poe theorized about a unified *emotional* effect, modern practitioners of the story (as well as Poe himself, for that matter) have aimed for understanding as well as sensation, have attempted to combine emotional with intellectual or thematic effect. However the story may be shaped, some organizing and controlling effect should be recognized as the typical basis of selection of the varied details that form the unified pattern of the modern short story.

## The Elements of the Short Story

*. . . to imagine, to invent and select and piece together the situations most useful and favorable to the sense of the creatures themselves, the complications they would be most likely to produce and feel.*

HENRY JAMES

*Location pertains to feelings—feelings are bound up in place.*

EUDORA WELTY

*. . . its method is metaphor, saying one thing and meaning another, saying one thing in terms of another.* ROBERT FROST

*. . . a focus of relationship. . . .* GEORGE WHOLLEY

In translating the reading of a short story into a learning process, in analyzing and explicating, the reader needs to sharpen his powers (intellectual and emotional together) of connecting, discriminating, and even noticing. To do this he must coldly find out how the thing works: he must isolate and examine certain of the typical devices and key elements of the story (which it shares, to some degree, with all forms of literature). But he should not forget to put the pieces back together again.

*1. Conflict and Resolution.*    It would be rather difficult to write a story about a man who wanted nothing, felt no desires, stresses, anxieties or tensions, who was so perfectly in equilibrium that he was merely content to just sit there, just as he was and always would be. For the essence of story telling is some jarring, even staggering of the state of equilibrium. Without tension—which is thus a kind of suspense—there is no movement; and without movement—whether internal or external, subtle or extreme—there is no story. The tension of a conflict is what makes a story move, and the ability to recognize, discriminate, and understand the great variety of conflicts possible is the necessary first step in understanding and appreciating the art of the short story.

Any conflict must have at least two sides, two forces or poles. There must be a desire and something that counters that desire. At the most obvious, and easiest, end of the spectrum of conflicts, there is the overt physical desire (and consequence action) of one character blocked by another or others. The young advertising salesman wants the position of account executive, but he is blocked by an unscrupulous older salesman. The secret agent wants to steal the plans, and the other agents block him; the cavalry wants to wipe out the enemy (or the enemy the cavalry) and the others fight back; the lover wants to win the girl, and she, her mother, her social class don't want him to, or at least are not sure they want him to. Boy loves girl, boy loses girl, boy gets girl. These *external conflicts* can also get more sophisticated, and thus more meaningful. For a number of reasons (or desires), a complex man like Macbeth wants to rule the kingdom, and for a number of reasons there are many who want to block him. Or a man wants to feel a greater dignity, or value, or freedom, and the complex forces of his society, his government, his family, or the very nature of life itself throw up counters to his desire.

As the external conflict becomes more complex and meaningful, it often fragments into a number of related conflicts; and often some of these are internal. A man can desire one thing and yet realize he also desires something else that runs counter to it. He wants that promotion to account executive, but he also wants integrity, and he is afraid that the job, and the means he might have to use to get it, will jeopardize that integrity. There are pressures, forces, within the character (as well as within his antagonists) that produce a tension, an *internal conflict,* which in turn adds other, and deeper, dimensions to the external conflict. Even a secret agent story develops this greater complexity when the secret agent recognizes the tension produced within himself by having to kill to do his job, or the cavalry man the conflicts that are developed by his job of killing soldiers.

In the modern serious short story the focus is often primarily on the internal conflicts. With this emphasis, the external clashes become merely the means of dramatizing the mental, moral, and spiritual tensions within the human being, the reasons for and significance of his desires. With this emphasis, too, the nature of the desires is often more complex, a welter of intangible impulses, emotions and ideas. On the other hand in many modern anti-plot stories, the conflicts are completely internal and subtle, their external manifestations minor or even non-existent.

Besides discerning the different *kinds* of conflicts in a story, the reader must recognize the *levels* of conflict involved. What are the connections and symbolic implications of the literal conflicts? In William Carlos Williams' "The Use of Force" (and notice the clues conveyed by the title) a doctor wants to examine a little girl's throat for diphtheria, and she fights back wildly to prevent him, until he loses his temper and cruelly forces her to defeat. What, then, is *represented* by this conflict? *Why* did the author find it significant? These are the questions the reader should ponder, and in this case he is led to consideration of a constellation of more abstract conflicts: the tension within the doctor between reason and irrationality, between social consciousness and selfishness; the tensions in the girl between a kind of wild freedom and the practical demands of fear; the wider clash between force and freedom, adults and children, society and the individual.

Consideration of this same story can lead us to the other end of the line—the final resolution of the tensions of the conflict. On one level the story is resolved by the conquest of the girl, and the discovery that, yes, she does have the disease. But William Carlos Williams is concerned with more than that, more than resolving just that particular mystery. He is concerned with the discovery that the doctor makes about himself, about the kind of disease of irrationality that exists in men of good will like himself—even under the banners of the noblest of causes. He is concerned with the less intellectually defined discovery that the girl makes about the nature of her life and freedom. He is concerned with the discovery the reader makes about the existence of the complex conflicts revealed in the story. The focus of concern is their existence, not their solutions. For, except at the least sophisticated levels of storytelling, a resolution is not necessarily a solution. It is a coming to rest of tensions—at least for the moment. It is a fuller, more complete sense of order that includes—even though it may not solve—the tensions released in the story. And in stories where the consciousness of the human being about the nature of himself and his life is at stake, the resolution is, finally and most fully, a matter of greater *awareness*.

This increase in awareness can be examined further in terms of both the characters of a story and the reader. In a character it can, on the one hand, take the form of growth. Through his experiences he has been led to a fuller understanding of himself and his desires, and to a finer sense of moral evaluation of his life and relations to others, and finally, to an awareness of the possibilities of changing his life. On the other hand, the increase in awareness may be a more limited kind of solidification. That is, he may be forced to the brink of awareness and yet balk before a full intellectual or emotional acceptance of what he has fleetingly experienced, and so merely be subtly hardened in his ways. Or he may come to recognitions which he nonetheless knows he cannot act upon, and thus be sealed even more tragically within the dilemmas that are too much for him. The possibilities and variations are many.

Equally important is the increase in the awareness of the reader. When the character undergoes a positive growth, the reader's response of course may parallel this growth. But, as is the case in many contemporary stories, when the resolution is more limited and complicated, the reader's relation to the final position of the character changes. For it is often the aim of the structure and content of a story to lead the reader to a greater, more complete awareness than the characters themselves are able to experience. In these cases it is the reader's consciousness that experiences the full meaning of the resolution, not the character's. At the extreme of this type of story is the ironic treatment of a character who believes he is right, has grown, does understand enough, but whose limitations and errors are made quite apparent to the reader by the construction of the story. A less extreme example is the case of the character who is a victim, who means well, knows he is erring, and yet can do nothing about it. Here, too, the reader can be made more aware of the truths of this kind of being alive, even though he is shown no way to solve or surmount the situation. Again, the possible variations are as numerous as the many ways of looking at the often painful truths of being alive.

Whatever the particular variation or combination of awareness in character and reader, the reader should push on to the symbolic level of the surface plot resolutions and consider them in terms of their significance.

*2. Point of View.* The sequence followed here is not necessarily the order in which the elements of a story should always be examined; an analysis of a story's elements must vary according to its particular contents and emphasis. One element that is often a valuable first entrance into a story (and yet at other times is not particularly significant) is *point of view.* In the study of literature this term does not refer to someone's opinions or views; rather it refers to the point of consciousness and observation from which we perceive and are told the events of the story. From just what position (inside or outside a character, close or distant) and on just whose authority (a character's or the author's) we get the facts are matters of central consideration to the modern story writer. Point of view is more than a mere technical device. It is part of the modern writer's concern with the consciousness of human beings and with the philosophical and psychological questions of truth as, at least in part, a matter of somebody's way of seeing and shaping his reality. In examining this important convention, we will set up three basic points of view and look at their variations, and the advantages and disadvantages of their effects.

The *omniscient* point of view was for a long time the traditional mode of storytelling for the writer posing as all-knowing author. The "author" speaks to us directly, commenting at will on the characters and their actions and often digressing to give what passes as his own view of things. While this method has the advantage of the clarity and strength of the author's explicit statements on the matters of his tale, in mediocre writing it can lead to an excess of abstract summary and judgment, an intrusion upon our sense of the free dramatic flow of the story and our sense of participation in its aliveness. A mediocre author too often may *tell* us what is true, rather than *show* us, or, if he does both, the summary still may reduce the effectiveness of the showing. He might directly tell us, for example, that Sam Crosswell is a man who is actually insecure under a surface veneer of bravado and thus is quick to turn cruel when he feels he is being put into question. Even if he then gives us an example or two of this as well, he might have been just as effective if he had merely shown us the symptoms and let us make the summary diagnosis for ourselves.

The border line between this omniscient point of view and the viewpoint in *third person narration* is crossed so often, either by the "author" or narrating character, that it is a kind of no man's land. For third person narration, involving the use of third person pronouns, establishes the point of consciousness in one or another of the characters, usually one at a time. Thus, the omniscient narrator may often come down from his heavenly heights and let us perceive some of the story from the closer viewpoint of a character or two. On the other hand, the third person narrator may move around to so many characters that he practically becomes an omniscient storyteller anyway. A basic difference between the two approaches is likely to be the degree and relative importance of the "author's" generalized summary and evaluation of the characters and their actions. A third person narration usually gives relatively little generalized commentary, and that is ordinarily confined to the more limited viewpoint we would expect from participating characters.

In analyzing the point of view for stories with a third-person narration, it may help to see a graduated scale: At one end would be a fairly diffused or scattered "roving" point of view, with the story told from time to time by different characters, each with vision restricted to what he might reasonably know, see, or understand at that moment. The scattered point of view lets the reader see a number of sometimes conflicting views in the course of a story, but the process of switching viewpoints can become intrusive or confusing if used inexpertly, to the point of cluttering the pattern of meaning. At the center of the scale would be the point of view of the limited third person, the most frequently used in modern writing. Here the author stays with the consciousness and perspective of one character throughout, though he may vary tremendously in the closeness or distance he permits us with this character, depending on whether he reproduces the character's words and thoughts concretely, or gives us a more general summary of the character's view in the "author's" words. Whatever the variation, this method has the advantage of maintaining the dramatic vitality of the story, letting the reader identify with the character, and letting the character's narration clarify the focus and meaning of the story. At the other end of the scale would be the objective, or effaced-author, style of narration, with the author acting somewhat as a dramatist, limiting his comments to stage directions, dialogue, and narrative at the most concrete level. The impact of the action is thus delivered as directly and impersonally as possible, though there is less variety of emphasis and little chance to identify with the fate of any of the characters.

A method that establishes immediacy and emotional involvement and yet allows for a good deal of focusing, shaping, and even authoritative commenting is the *first person narrative*. The first person ($I$) narrator can be a direct and central participant in the story or an observer on its perimeter, but in either case it is important that he be fully developed as a person (and not just a storyteller) so that the full effect of his relationship can be achieved. It is equally important that the reader keep in mind that any narrator *is* a specific, limited person and not necessarily the spokesman for the author. Only when this is recognized, is the full truth of what is being narrated kept in view. For particularly when the narrator is one of the central characters, his view and version of the truth may not *be* the whole truth or the only version of the truth. In fact, in satirical narration, the voice of the character or even of the supposed "author" has been set up to state the opposite of what the writer wants the reader to believe; the contrast between the evident truth of the action and the "truth" according to the narrating voice is so great that we usually end up believing the exact reverse of his statements, judgments, or values.

A careful look at the point of view of narration in any story may be one of the best ways to determine its direction, for it is one of the author's central devices for focusing and stressing his material, controlling the reader's response, and maintaining dramatic vividness.

*3. Character.* As it turns out, the term *character* has two aspects and meanings: (1) an individual who appears in a story and (2) the combination of emotions, beliefs, values, attitudes, desires, ideas that an individual (in a story or out) is or has. In fact, one of the most significant parts of the content of the modern short story is its characterization; most of a story's action (as we shall pursue it in the next section) may be considered as the extension and dramatized result of character. Thus, some of the most crucial questions we can ask are these: What kind of people inhabit this story? How do we *know* what kind of people they are? Why do they do what they do? How are we to respond to and judge what they are and do? Why is their character and action important to the author? What do they represent or signify? These are the questions that carry us furthest in our attempts to understand the meaning of the pattern an author has imposed on the flux of being alive.

To combine the first two, how does the author let us know what kind of people inhabit his story? He can, first of all, tell us directly— either with the complete summary statements of the omniscient narrator or the more circumspect placement of a few choice descriptive adjectives or even nouns. But more likely he will show us by more indirect methods. He can use physical descriptions of the character himself—his dress, his little mannerisms, his residence as an indication of some aspect of character and personality. He can also use the way the character reacts to other people and their actions, to certain places or things. Or he may use his actions generally as a revelation of what the person is.

In characterization there is a two-way movement: What the person is causes his actions; conversely, what he does reveals what he is. In talking about what actions reveal, we should notice particularly the more constant conditions of a character's kind of relationships to other people. A character's dialogue, too, is a kind of action, and an author can reveal much about the person through his own statements. This applies also to the total narration, if the first person narrative is used. Of course, the character's thoughts and feelings—whether caught in concrete terms by the author or in more general summaries—are indicators of the man, and so are the opinions about a character, comments on him, and interpretations and judgments of him that are made by other characters in the story. However, the reflections of other characters are often *not* the opinions, interpretations, and judgments of the author, since they are being made and contributed by people in the story whose own characters—what *they* are—may be producing distortions that are part of the author's pattern.

If the author has used his methods of character revelation skillfully, the result is a pattern of character, a coherent and unified set of traits that *is* the reality of the person. But the kind of coherence and unity created can vary greatly. On the one extreme we have the creation of flat characters or types, even stereotypes and caricatures, who have been too neatly summarized and classified. In a stereotype a central trait or traits is so strongly defined (and dramatized) as the key to the person that he loses the three (or actually four) dimensional complexity of reality, and becomes a puppet or pasteboard figure. The stereotypes of popular entertainment, which fit so effortlessly into standard categories, are often idealizations of characteristics that unthinking audiences find it all too easy to identify with—as in the fast and tough spy hero, the heroic mother or laughable and good-natured father, the mechanized and sadistic villain, or the uninhibited sex-queen heroine. However, serious writers as well as entertainers may go beyond a straightforward presentation of stereotypes to "play games" with a caricature, making a kind of joking parody of the type that has been built up over the years, as in recent treatments of comic-book and spy-thriller caricatures. Readers should keep alert for the reaction that seems to be expected to typed characters.

In the middle ground of approaches to characterization is the more rounded character, who is developed in the kind of depth that lets us see contrasting and even contradictory features in conflict within him, such as loyalty with rebelliousness. Often this conflict of opposing features is the dominant emphasis given to his character, and hence perhaps to the conflict of plot and theme for an entire story. For this rounded, many-dimensional kind of character, the focus of interest is on the pattern of conflict and stress of opposing traits that the author has developed.

At the other extreme, we have the contemporary tendency (the result of current philosophical and psychological beliefs) to maintain as much as possible the elusive inner condition of humanity, capturing the many facets of a person without the kind of final classification or definition of traditional literature. This kind of character may be the hardest for the reader to respond to appropriately, but in the mixture of order and ambiguity that is his pattern, the reader also may be provided the deepest insight.

The connection between character and action—*why* a man does what he does—is in some ways the most important aspect of characterization in a story; and in this depiction of motivation, the same variety of approaches to character can be seen. This variety would range here from the obvious definitions of motive in character, through the competing inner pressures of the rounded character, to the more dynamic cluster of motive and impulse in what we might call the "open end" character. As one illustration, a striking uniqueness in the latter type of character might be noted: the presence of the irrational. In many cases—although certainly not in all—an act cannot be traced, or can be traced only in part to some definable motive; it has to be seen as the result of the irrational, impulsive dimension of human character. This refusal to clearly define motive may be thought to be an evasion of imposing order on the material; but it is not. Rather, it is the imposing of a more subtle order on the undiminished fullness of the human experience.

The reader's response to character is the key factor in his understanding and appreciation of a story. The people are what he must feel, comprehend, what he must connect with. But on the terms that the author has set, and with the clues that the author has provided. The reader must get outside and beyond his own preconceptions and stereotypes, the reductions of his habitual (and often conditioned) clichés of emotion, classification and judgment. This openness to the full reality of the characters is important because the characters, and their constellations of traits, are the most important symbolic connections to the significance of the story. For we are concerned, most deeply of all, with what the author thinks of and feels about his people. Does he judge, and if so, how? Does he judge and sympathize, judge and hate? What is his full attitude toward these people and what they do? What are the moral, religious, psychological, social, economic, philosophical implications of what they are and do? What do they *mean* to him? And thus to us? Answers to questions like this take us close to the heart of fiction.

*4. Plot.*    The kind of balance that a story maintains between plot and character makes an interesting measure for classifying it within the range of fiction. At the slick, commercial, and consequently bland end of the scale, we have the complete emphasis on action (as the old Hollywood formula had it: ODTAA—One Damned Thing After Another) and suspense, with only the minimal bow necessary to simplified and stereotyped character. At the other end of the scale, we can find the intentional reduction, even outright avoidance, of action, with maximum emphasis on the delineation of the emotions and thoughts of the character. Yet a serious and significant story need not avoid action and suspense, or the emotional involvement of the reader in these pleasures of storytelling. In the vast middle ground of storytelling there is plenty of room for a variety of combinations, which, to one degree or another, use the dramatic actions of a plot as the extension, result, and revelation of people whom we have been led to care about as people, not just as pawns in the action. In this view, then, the plot and its incidents, and the emotions that they produce in the reader, are seen as the triggers that explode some insight into human beings and the condition of their lives. Or, to change the metaphor, character may be the main road to understanding in the short story; but plot is, for most readers, the vehicle that is going to get them interested in traveling along that road.

Even at its simplest levels, a plot is a means of ordering happenings, a selection and then arrangement of incidents into a sequence. And whether the purpose of this sequence is thrills or insight, all good plots will have a central organizing factor in common: causality. It is the cause and effect relationships between the events that produce the pointed, ordered pattern of a plot. To use one of E. M. Forster's examples, "The King dies; the Queen dies," is not a plot. But, "The King died; because she could not bear to live without him, the Queen died," is at least the start of a plot. And, "The King died; because she could not bear to live with her guilt, the Queen died," is the start of another. It is not then the incidents themselves, but the relationships established between them that create the plot. This definition does not exclude accidental or irrational events, as long as these events are clearly used to illustrate the relationship of accidental and irrational events to other events. Even a mystery thriller, however, is weakened when it has too many loose ends, too many incidents that do not seem inevitable, either in a direct causal relationship or in the believable relationship to other incidents that accidents can have.

Besides causality, there are other factors that plots have in common. If a plot is to *move*—that, is proceed into and through its network of relationships—its incidents must first initiate and then continue to be moved by a conflict. It is in setting the terms of this conflict (or conflicts) that the opening of a short story achieves its compressed complexity and density. The opening must quickly suggest the surroundings and the backgrounds of the characters, begin to delineate their traits, plunge us into the tensions of the actions, and from these factors begin to build the basic conflict of the story.

The middle stages of a story usually then consist of a series of further minor conflicts, or complications—its turns and counterturns —that produce its suspense and development. While most readers can recognize the actual physical actions and events that produce the story's complications, they are sometimes not aware enough of the way in which the dialogue between characters (and even the thoughts and emotions within a character) not only reveals character traits but moves the plot through its complications. Take, for example, a

Hemingway story called "Hills Like White Elephants" in which a crisis between a man and a woman (centering on his insistence that she undergo an abortion, but throwing into question the whole basis of their relationship) is revealed, moved through its complications, and ambiguously resolved, almost completely through dialogue. Only by a careful reading and accurate response to the characters' statements can the reader understand these people and their situation, or even the specific content of their conflict.

The climax of a plot is reached when the conflict has been brought to the final and complete stage of the crucial central incident, when the crucial conflict must be faced directly, and decided one way or another or (in some cases) not exactly decided at all. This climactic sequence often involves a major turning or reverse—either in the character's fortunes or his attitude toward those fortunes (that is, in the latter case, he may get what he wanted, but find he doesn't really want it, at least not quite in that way). Whether there is a full reversal or not, the action of the climax leads into a resolution, which (as we have indicated before) produces a final and more complete ordering of events and particularly a more complete awareness of the significance of the events on the part of the character, reader, or both. This resolution can vary in length, though in short stories it tends to be relatively brief and may even be mainly implied by a final symbolic action or descriptive detail.

One other kind of order or arrangement in a story's plot needs to be mentioned, and that is the use of time. The sequence of events may be ordered by simple, forward-moving chronology, by the interruption of the forward chronology by a flashback, by the constant paralleling of present events with past events, or by variations in the amount of space and detail devoted to the narration of an event. The story can present a brief summary of actions that occurred over a longer time period, or deliberately build a detailed scenic development of events that occurred over a shorter time span. Different patterns will produce different effects on the reader, and may well show in crucial differences in the significance of the events.

It is, finally then, not only *what*, but *why* that concerns us, not only what happens, but why it happens. There are two kinds of *why's* to be considered: *why* the character did it and *why* the author had him do it. The reader must connect the character of the actor with his actions to determine his motivations; at the same time he must also connect this combination of elements with their possible thematic implications. In the interpretation of plot actions, the method of presenting a given event makes a great difference: a death portrayed in shocking detail affects us far differently than a death, even a murder, portrayed calmly, passed over hurriedly, or built up humorously. The narrative facts are no more important than their emotional impact; both intellectual and emotional elements contribute to the symbolic effect of a plot.

5. *Structure.* In a broader view, the chronological patterns, the suspense patterns, the cause-and-effect patterns of plot are but one type of organizing principle by which the details of a story can be given a meaningful structure. The others might be termed rhetorical principles, in contrast to the chronological principles, not unlike the means by which exposition and argument can be organized. Especially in contemporary stories, other methods of organization may be at work along with plotting, or instead of plotting.

Here are a few of the possibilities. The events or scenes of a story might be selected to establish parallels, so that even when they seem to take random leaps or are not tied to each other by cause-and-effect relationships, they are establishing the repetition of some type or situation of human behavior. These parallels can be seen as variations on a theme. Sometimes, instead of parallels, the principle is contrast, an alternating sequence of opposites. These parallels might ultimately be shaped into a circular structure, in which later echoes repeat earlier events, in which a never-ending cycle, even a relentless sense of a trap can be conveyed. The associations between events might also have the freer, wilder kinds of connections of dreams, or nightmares; they may, in another variation, be moored to the suggestiveness of language itself—a word in one sequence, for example, triggering an imaginative leap into the next.

With or without plotting, contemporary writers often play on mythic patterns; that is, they shape their events to echo or play provocative variations on traditional stories and figures, materials that have long-established significance. Whether drawing parallels with Greek myths like that of Prometheus, American myths like that of Horatio Alger or contemporary popular culture myths like that of Humphrey Bogart, the writer may be indicating the continuing validity of the myth or exposing its illusions. This use of myth places special emphasis on the device of allusions—references to historical, cultural or literary materials with which the reader is expected to have some familiarity. But of course allusions—and their attendant problems for the reader —are a frequent part of conventional storytelling as well. The reader must sometimes seek help in tracking down the significance of literary allusions, but quite often there are enough contextual details present to make that significance available within the story itself.

6. *Setting.* In all honesty, we should admit that many descriptive passages, filling in the setting, deserve our unfortunate habit of skip-

ping past them to get on with the action. In much inferior modern writing, and to some extent in the conventions of pretentious older writing, description of the setting seems to come as a ponderous inter-ruption, a pompous pause while the scene-painter puts up an elab-orate backdrop, much as he might construct a travelogue scene. But any skillful author's description of setting has a more valuable func-tion. Especially in the short story, the setting is not a large block of inert descriptive detail, but an active part of the story and its sig-nificance. Within the compressed unity of the modern short story, every detail counts, and in many stories none to greater effect than the details of the setting.

The details of setting are those that describe the natural, man-made, and social background against which and out of which the action de-velops. The accuracy of the depiction of this background—the place, the time, the season, the weather, the furniture of the scene—is one of the prime means of producing a sense of reality in the work. As part of the story's revelation of life by suggestive detail, the setting becomes an active part of the story because of its dynamic interaction with other parts of the story.

This interaction may take three forms, which in a story may all be operating at the same time, though we may analyze them separately. There is, first of all, the direct effect and influence of the setting on a character's emotions and ideas: the way in which he is immediately affected by a forest, or a slum tenement, by a black rainy night, or heavy fog, or smog, or blazing sun; the way in which his emotions and actions are shaped by a long association with some setting, or how a change of setting affects him. Closely related to these direct plot-level effects are the symbolic effects on the reader, the suggestive associations created by the setting or its relationship to a character. In John Steinbeck's "Flight," for example, the limited perspective and understanding of the boy Pepe is determined by his life in a primitive mountainous setting, which he has never left. At the same time, the location of his home, clinging precariously to the side of a great cliff that rises above the ocean, suggests also the kind of natural, innocent, primitive life and freedom which he represents. As the plot unfolds and he must flee for instinctively killing a man who he felt had put into question his dignity and honor, the wilderness he travels through takes its physical toll on him, but also symbolizes his progressive return to a primitive, almost animal-like existence. At the conclusion, the cruel rocky peak on which he is trapped saps his final strength, but also provides an emotional parallel or correlation for the cruel harsh-ness, the desolation of the final destruction of his life. Finally, the total effect of the *atmosphere* of the setting produces an emotional effect on the reader, a particular *mood*—oppressive, free, irritated—and this may affect a reader's emotional approach to the story quite differently than would some consciously grasped association for a specific symbolic detail.

In addition to the broader aspects of environment, specific single objects—props, in the terminology of the theatre—can have meaningful relationships with the people who use them. They too can become a part of the way the author draws out the human feelings and meanings that reside for us in the physical things of this world.

*7. Style.*    One aspect of style is the tone established by the texture and manner of the language of a story, by the context of emotional connotations beyond and around the literal information conveyed by that language. This style is more than a conscious technical selection of words and structures; it is the result of and embodiment of a way of looking at things. It results in a characteristic sound or tone that expresses an attitude of the reader.

Some of the more striking styles may clearly typify the writer's approach to his material and his art. There is the disciplined, understated, aggressively simple style of Ernest Hemingway—with its concrete words, short, direct sentences, heavy use of compound parallel structure. This style has as much to tell the careful reader about the meaning of the events depicted as the events themselves. At the opposite extreme, there is the complex, often tortuously dense style of Henry James or William Faulkner, so similar in their long, convoluted sentence structures—constantly interrupted by modification and qualification—yet so different in final tone because of Faulkner's more emotional, even sensational, choice of words, or diction. Similar to Faulkner's high, rhetorical style, yet differentiated by a less tragic and anguished, a more exhuberant and innocent, diction is that of Thomas Wolfe. Here, to indicate two extremes of style and effect are paragraphs from climactic moments in stories by Faulkner and by Hemingway.

*The cow now stood in the centre of the yard. She and the mule faced one another a few feet apart. Motionless, with lowered heads and braced forelegs, they looked like two book ends from two distinct pairs of a general pattern which some one of amateurly bucolic leanings might have purchased, and which some child had salvaged, brought into idle juxtaposition and then forgotten; and, his head and shoulders projecting above the back-flung slant of the cellar entrance where the scuttle still sat, Snopes standing as though buried to the armpits for a Spanish-Indian-American suttee. Only again it did not take this long.*

*The major came very regularly to the hospital. I do not think he ever missed a day, although I am sure he did not believe in the machines. There was a time when none of us believed in the machines, and one day the major said it was all nonsense. The machines were new then and it was we who were to prove them. It was an idiotic idea, he said, "a theory, like another." I had not learned my grammar, and he said I was a stupid impossible disgrace, and he was a fool to have bothered with me. He was a small man and he sat straight up in his chair with his right hand thrust into the machine and looked straight ahead at the wall while the straps thumped up and down with his fingers in them.*

Not all styles of course, are so different or distinctive, or so easy to characterize. A particularly interesting stylistic effect can be achieved by the frequent use of the first person narrator. The narrating "author" assumes the voice and language of a character in the story, who may be somewhat like himself, or, more often, very different. In so doing the writer can use a distinctively colloquial, informal style that often produces a great sense of immediacy and reality, as well as, in many cases, humor. The impact of the language in a first-person style is often heightened and made more meaningful by the way it reveals the character of the person narrating. The idiom and point of view can be used to produce sympathy or distaste for the speaker, as in the sympathetic treatment of Holden Caulfield in J. D. Salinger's *A Catcher in the Rye* or the mocking treatment of the narrow, selfish boasters and braggarts in the stories of Ring Lardner.

The Lardner stories and other first-person narratives show a good example of an author's satirical or ironical attitude concealed behind the "tone of voice" of the narrating character. We may speak of the character's *tone,* in the sense that his tone of voice conveys a certain attitude toward his listeners or readers (with the Lardner characters, a hypocritical attitude, asking that we believe the narrator and overlook his cruelties and crudities). At the same time, behind the narrating voice, we can speak of the *author's tone,* the attitude of the author toward his audience, as conveyed ironically by the contrast the author creates between what the narrating character says and what he actually seems to have done or condoned. In all literature, the relationship between author and reader is basically regulated by the tone of a speaker, whether character or narrating author, in showing such attitudes as closeness, sincerity, moral loftiness, superiority, condescension. Of course the variety of possible attitudes is nearly infinite, and the difference between the voice of the narrating character and the implied "voice" of the author behind him may make the relationship quite complex. But it is through the medium of tone that fiction expresses much of its vitality.

The use of irony as a contributing part of the author's tone or attitude makes an important element in many stories. A discussion of an ironic tone is worthwhile in itself, and it serves to illustrate how tone can contribute to the total emotional and intellectual meaning of a work.

*Irony* is a special way of connecting related elements in a pattern. It involves posing opposites together and against each other, juxtaposing them. In most instances, these opposites present a clash between false appearance and reality, and thus the connections created are not to be taken at face value, or at least not only at face value. Irony brings a stronger emotional charge to the intellectual or informative content of the material.

The most obvious degree of irony involves a complete reversal. You say something that is the opposite of what you mean, as in the sarcasm of the expression "big deal!"; or you may do something opposite to what is expected in the situation, as in a forced smile or gracious gesture to someone who has just made a hateful remark. The reverse reaction can be a strong way of exposing how far the provocative event falls short of what was expected. Thus the sour remark is shown up as bad taste with an elaborated sweet-tempered reply, opposite of what it deserved, and a parody of the politeness that should have been expected.

A less blatant degree of irony is the *incongruity,* the juxtaposition of apparently incompatible statements, events, or situations that reflect on each other, not with direct opposition or exact reversal of meaning, but with deliberately disturbing contrast in significance. An example is Poe's story, "A Cask of Amontillado," in which the victim's jolly attitude, symbolized by his masked-ball clown suit, contrasts vividly with the evil intent of his killer, the tinkling bell of the clown hat and forced laughter incongruously ringing with the sounds of the man's destruction. The effect, again, is to intensify the significance of the main event (the killing) by contrast with the emotions that might have been conveyed (convivial mirth and friendship).

A frequently used form of ironic incongruity is the understatement or overstatement. Intense, important, or even horrifying events may be presented in a matter-of-fact style, either by the narrator or by the conversation of a character, giving a startlingly understated effect which may highlight the horror or lighten it humorously, depending on the details of the situation. Most commonly used for humorous effect is the irony of overstatement, the satirical reporting of trivial events in overblown style as if they were momentous.

A more subtle degree of irony occurs with an author's deliberate creation of accidental or coincidental incongruities, or incongruous parallels, usually in the form of unexpected twists in the action of the story. The result may be a startling, apparently unintended moment of recognition of a major theme in the story, as in the prophetic but apparently random ravings of a fool and a madman in Shakespeare's *King Lear,* or, in Crane's *Red Badge of Courage,* the frequent accidental placement of the cowardly Henry in the role of courageous soldier, a role that he eventually justifies. The accidents of such ironic events, seemingly not logical or inevitable developments in the action, can often give us a sudden new perspective on the story, catching the theme by surprise.

The various degrees of irony can appear in two forms, or a mixture of these: as *verbal irony,* or *irony of statement* (from the narrating author, character, or from dialogue); or as *irony of situation* or *dramatic irony* (from interplay of characters and plot). The bragging, self-justifying statements of a first person Ring Lardner narrator are examples of extended verbal irony, to which the reader responds in just the reverse of the way the narrating speaker would expect, but, of course, in just the way the author intends. Dramatic irony of situation occurs in great works as well as trivial: Sophocles' King Oedipus seeks the evildoer who has brought the plague on Thebes, doggedly pursuing his course until he discovers that *he* is the evildoer, and that, unknown to them all, he has killed his father and married his mother. Similarly, the criminal in a mystery story may find it is just that thing that he has always wanted—the money, the jewels, the girl—that trips him up in the end. A combination of verbal and dramatic irony can be cited from a routine of the comedian Bob Newhart: he tells the story of the two German soldiers who have been hiding out for years without hearing that World War II is over; the climax is reached when they see an American family drive up in a car, a Volkswagen. In great joy, the Sergeant shouts, "You see that, Schultz, you see? We've won! We've won!"

Irony often results in humor, and often in a subtle mixture with other emotions. With or without humor, it can be used at the expense of the characters, in satirical, sarcastic mocking of them; or it can be rueful and sympathetic, embittered at the turns of the world, not the characters.

Beyond tone, another aspect of style may be even more important in developing one's skill as a reader or member of the audience. And that is the overall approach in using the materials and elements of the story. If style is the embodiment in form of a way of seeing and thinking about life, then it obviously is more than a matter of choice of language. It is the total manner of expression, the manner in which all the elements of the art, of both technique and content, are used, and fused, together. It is a way of giving an external form to an internal sense of what life is. As feelings about the world change (as feelings about what art is and should do change), so do the approaches to an art and the forms that result.

What this means most specifically to the reader of short stories is the need to recognize and adjust to (and gain pleasure from) the demands of other styles beyond that of the conventional realistic story (or play, or film, or painting, or sculpture, for that matter). The realistic style seeks to represent—to mirror accurately and imitate the literal objective surfaces of the world and human life, the ordered patterns of the inner life. It uses the elements of the story accordingly —accurate psychological characterization, credible plot actions and cause-and-effect relationships.

Other overall approaches do not seek this same kind of accurate rendering of the plausible and ordinary; these non-realistic styles include expressionistic, surrealistic, epic, and absurd approaches. They aim at the essence, rather than the literal facts, of experience, the way things subjectively *feel,* rather than the way they objectively *are.* They involve distortions, exaggerations, hyperboles, allegories, myths; their use of such elements as characterization or plotting or tone will thus not follow the conventions of realistic applications of these materials.

*8. Symbolism.*    This section can serve as a reemphasis of what we have noted on every page: the short story is a symbolic experience. It is initiated by the author's symbolic cast of mind: he sees connections, he sees that things can stand for, signify, something beyond themselves. And it is created by the author's use of symbolic forms that reveal these connections, these pointings beyond.

At the broadest level, a story is symbolic when the author feels that the people in it and what they experience are important. When they and their actions mean something to him, he writes about them to reveal what they represent, what is significant for all of us in the lives that he is depicting.

At a more specific technical level, a story contains particularized individual symbols, but in most stories these symbolic details are not coldly and mechanically placed to form a little puzzle for the reader. Rather, the symbolic objects, words, or events are part of the literal emotional depiction of the situation first and begin to take on their added dimensions, their resonance and echoes (possibly even in the author's mind) as the pattern of their connections takes shape. And so the symbolic events should be responded to by the reader in this same way, as parts of a story that is being told, not as a kind of shorthand code that only serves to lead us to something else.

For a story is not a coded version of another, more abstract or philosophical statement; it is the simultaneous statement of the concrete and the abstract together in a single re-creation of experience. A story is not its abstract thematic statement, it is the *way* that statement is given body, dramatic form, and life. The scene in which the Doctor in William Carlos Williams' story finally forces open the mouth of the child is not moving and memorable because it leads us to ideas about the meaning of force. Because it puts us through the Doctor's experience, it is moving and memorable in itself *and* in the meanings it leads us to ponder—all at the same time. What happens when the significance of a story is pinpointed symbolically has been translated into critical language by Robert Penn Warren: "A symbol serves to combine heart and intellect, making a welter of experience manageable, graspable." At the same time the symbol takes part in the vivid reality of that welter of being alive.

A comparison of our own can further demonstrate this point, a comparison of the difference between the process of allegory and the process of symbolism. Allegory begins with an abstract meaning and seeks an example, a proof, in the concrete. It subordinates the imagination to the intellectual, produces a precise system of equivalents to prove its point. "The greedy destroy themselves" might be an allegorist's abstract premise, and so he creates a figure to illustrate the components of greed and creates a situation to demonstrate the destruction they produce. On the other hand, the symbolist (among others, the short story writer) begins with the actual, the concrete, even if he is working with fantasy. He seeks to make as compelling and vivid as possible the tangible, complex details of his actual vision, and as he does so his imagination deepens and widens the pattern of the details into a pattern of significance as well. His meaning rises from the concrete details; his concrete details do not merely drop from an abstract premise. He is a juggler, keeping aloft and in balance the concrete and the abstract, not forsaking either. And the reader must be at least an apprentice juggler, too.

Two further considerations can help a reader learn this imaginative juggling. One is *context,* the other *emphasis.* In isolation a potentially symbolic detail can point in many directions; its implications or abstract equivalents would be difficult to determine. Take *rain.* If, in the manner of a free association test, we asked, "What does rain mean?", each respondent might come up with a different equivalent, depending on the association he has built up around the word: freshness, freedom, darkness, isolation, growth, or even death. Too many readers respond to the details of a story in just this way, on the basis of their own random associations, as though the story were a free-association test. It is not. The direction of the implications of a symbolic detail is not left free and random; it is shaped by the context of its surroundings, by the whole situation or background, the pattern, out of which it rises. The reader is not given a free choice; he must respond in the same way that he must respond to a word in the context created by its surrounding words. Take *rain,* again. In Hemingway's *A Farewell to Arms,* rain occurs a number of times at the same time that violent, painful and destructive events occur. In this way, the symbolic implications of the descriptions of rain are given shape and direction by their constant connection to tragic events, and by the time we reach the last line of the book, following the death of Lt. Henry's wife, "I walked back to the hotel in the rain," this climactic reference to rain not only reminds us of the other times it rained, but shapes as well our final response to the symbol: the gloom, destruction, fated injustice, and defeat that the figurative rain of the world brings down upon us.

This example also illustrates the use of emphasis in establishing the symbolic patterns of the story. Here, both the repetition of the rain and its conspicuous position at the very end of the book illustrate two of the frequent devices of emphasis. Details of action and setting that occur at the beginning or ending of stories, or at obvious moments of crisis and climax, are likely carriers of symbolic associations. So are details of action and setting that figure more than once in the course of a story—either in direct repetition, or variation (like the rain), or in a striking opposite form: a character refuses to get out of bed at the beginning; he gets out of bed at the end. The meaningful repetitions of key events or things are called motifs.

*9. Statement.*   We arrive now at the end of the line of the reader's responsibility to pull together a synthesis of the separate elements that he has perceived and analyzed, and from that synthesis to develop a theory about the total statement of the story. The broader and more ambiguous term *statement* is more useful here than the more frequently used *theme,* for the total communication of a work is not necessarily a program, a solution, or even necessarily a judgment, nor is it purely an intellectual concept or opinion. It is a combination of the concrete details of the work, the emotions they involve and engender, the emotional attitude of the author toward them, and the intellectual abstractions to which they are connected. When we translate all of this into the valuable and necessary words of a theme, we must remember what is lost in the translation: the essence of the story itself, the *way* in which the theme is given concrete form.

It is the process of defining a work's theme—how we go about fully and accurately connecting various parts of the story to a generalization about it—that we are usually most concerned with in the study of literature. But too often our efforts to define this theme are led astray by a failure to take into account and accurately respond to the emotional patterns of the action, people and events, and the author's emotional attitude toward them. A good case in point is Hemingway's *The Sun Also Rises.* From this book students often extract a pattern of facts—all of which are in the book—that add up to a generalization about the depressing and sordid life of a bunch of drunken and promiscuous people. They then go on to apply a judgment from their own frame of reference, as though the book were a collection of data from the police blotter. But in so doing they have ignored a number of other facts of the book because they have not responded to its subtle emotional mixtures, its emotional context or ambience. There is much despair in the book, but there is also a good deal of delight—even joy —derived from certain basic and simple pleasures, whatever the reader might think of these pleasures. The reader's job is to note these joys and their combination with despair, note Hemingway's attitude toward them, his suggestions as to the reasons for the particular patterns of pleasures and pains in the book. Only then can a thematic statement about the *whole* of the book be created.

Strangely enough, the very popular *A Catcher in the Rye,* by J. D. Salinger, has often been distorted by readers in a similar way. Extracting certain surface facts from the book, students determine that it is about an obnoxious, selfish, snobbish brat who exaggerates everybody else's faults and pays no attention to his own. While this judgment might become a part of someone's broader conception of the book, it is not the whole of the book or its major direction of meaning because it ignores, again, the emotional life of the book, in this case, the book's insight into the importance of the emotions in life. Salinger's attitude toward his creation must be taken into account (although it might then be criticized) : he seems to sympathize with, nay, love Holden *because* of the intensity of his responses and feelings, the depth of his sensitivity and concern—even if Holden does exaggerate.

Of course, even when the emotional life, the surface facts, and the intellectual conceptions of a book are all taken into account, there is still no one all-inclusive and definitive theme to be extracted from a work. Literature is not mathematics or physics, and it doesn't intend to be; its models are not $2 + 2 = 4$ or $E = mc^2$. It breeds on the intangible, and thrives on the intangible; it cannot be reduced to absolute formula.

But that doesn't mean it's always open season on answers: $2 + 2$ doesn't equal any old thing somebody wants it to equal. There may not be only one right answer to a question about what a story means; there are still plenty of wrong answers. As it turns out, in most instances the many different definitions of the theme of a work do not actually contradict each other: If definition A is true, it in no way demands that definition, B, C, or D thus be untrue. Many definitions merely emphasize or select different and separate aspects of a work for consideration and thus can be seen to actually complement each other rather than contradict. And many definitions of a theme are merely different ways of saying (translating) the same thing, but couched in the different languages of the different ways of looking at things. As an example, the intense emotional relationship between Paul Morel and his mother in D. H. Lawrence's *Sons and Lovers* could be approached from a number of different perspectives: social history, philosophy, ethics, psychology, sociology, economics, anthropology, religion, science. These different approaches would result in different definitions of what the book's relationships and the book mean; but on closer analysis one could probably see that they are not in contradiction, but are merely different ways of talking about the same thing.

Still, for the beginner, there are certain helpful guidelines that can be thrown down to hasten his arrival at a likely and probable *thematic hypothesis*. The thematic hypothesis, like any hypothesis, is designed to provide a generalization that will best account for a number of separate elements—for example, the hypothesis determined by a detective to best account for the various clues at the scene of a murder. It should take into account the largest number of details possible. It need not use all the details in its development, but it should not ignore prominent details that contradict it—in the same way that a detective cannot ignore the unwieldy fact that his favorite suspect was 3,000 miles away from the scene of the crime. In other words, it must be consistent with all the details and connections of the story, though it need not refer to all of them. It must be consistent with them individually and consistent with any connections or patterns between them. This is the logical doctrine of completeness of a hypothesis of any sort.

On the other hand, a thematic hypothesis should be as simple and specific as possible, while still being complete enough. You should not seek the broadest, highest level of generality you can find, but the narrowest, most limited, most pointed generality that still accounts for the evidence. Rather than deciding that a story illustrates the relationships between love and money, decide that it illustrates how the pressures of a value system based on money affect a man's ability to fulfill a relationship of love. Rather than deciding that a story illustrates the possible dangers of innocence, decide that it illustrates the way in which an unworldly, extreme innocence leaves a man unable to cope with evil and so liable to commit it himself.

Thirdly, your hypothesis about a story's meaning should follow inevitably and relevantly from the concrete details of the material. Don't leap to farfetched theories that drag in God or the evils of Communism when there are no details in the story that open those directions of meaning. This is the logical doctrine of probability.

Further, the hypothesis should attempt to take into account the author's probable intentions and evaluation of the people and events, although these can then be criticized. You may be right in deciding that the story depicts the life of people without hope, but you need to go further in the direction of what his attitude toward that life and those people then is. Does he condemn them or sympathize with them, does he suggest the causes of such a condition, does he imply an alternative?

It is, of course, helpful to know as much about an author and his work as you can, although you can usually reach some kind of valid interpretation on the evidence of a story alone. Too careless a use of background material, however, is often distorting, leading to a mistaken attempt to jam a story into the pattern of a generalization that may not apply to it, *or* to apply far too vague a generality (this story is concerned with the problems of love) that would apply to any of the author's works but doesn't capture the uniqueness of the story under consideration.

As noted earlier, a focus on the characters in a story is often the best way to gain an understanding of its themes, although an emphasis on some other element of the story—the point of view, the style, the title —can be equally valuable as a starting point.

As a final clue to the nature of statement and theme in a story, we might note the remark attributed to the unique American writer Gertrude Stein. Just before dying, Miss Stein was reported to have looked up and said, "What is the answer to it all? No, no, what are the *questions?*"

## Some Comparative Connections

We have been concerned up to this point with the connections established within a single work of fiction—the means used in establishing them and the unity of beauty, emotion and meaning created by them. The study of literature, however, is also concerned with the interpretive and critical connections that can be established between two or more works of fiction—either by the same author or different authors. As you may already have noticed, one of the bases of organization of this book is to place stories together in provocative and enlightening combinations so as to guide you in this next step of establishing the connections between two or more short stories.

The first main purpose of establishing these further connections may at first seem paradoxical. It is that by comparing two or more stories the reader can increase his understanding of each story individually. There are several reasons for this. For one thing, the new combination creates a broader context of stimuli or clues in which to reconsider each story. Details that may not have been noticed become more noticeable and meaningful when they are related to similar details in another work. There are, in a sense, more clues to alert the reader to emphases and connections, whether they be plot actions, character traits, stylistic characteristics, tone, point of view, etc. Similarly, the elusive significance of the pattern of one story can be better brought under interpretive control with the additional stimuli and clues provided by the similar (yet never identical) pattern of another story. This additional practice of establishing different kinds of connections also furthers the reader's ability to make connections within single stories. The more kinds of connections he works on, the more does he gain insight into the process of connecting itself. It is a generally acknowledged educational maxim that learning consists of the extension of the ability to establish connections and relationships to larger and larger classifications and of the complementary ability to make distinctions within the unifying classifications established. This applies as well to learning to read short stories.

But besides enabling the untrained reader to better understand a single story, the comparison of stories—even for the trained and professional reader—can help cast further light on the central subjects and concerns of a writer by comparing how these concerns were treated in several of his works, or by comparing his treatment with the treatment of similar subjects and concerns in the work of another writer. In the same way that it can produce a better understanding of a single writer's insights and meanings, this process of comparison can also produce a greater understanding of the subjects themselves. To take a common literary subject—our understanding of what is really involved when people love someone or something is deepened by seeing how two or more writers approach and develop material that can be related to this general subject. Thus, comparison helps both to sharpen our hypotheses about a single writer and to build larger hypotheses on the connections between the works of two or more writers. And, finally, it can sharpen our understanding of some of the methods and devices of fiction, too, as we connect similar or contrasting details in different works and note their variations.

In making comparisons, the reader must first establish connections of similarity—some common tie or link between the materials. These connections can be made at any of the levels of generality in the story, but they must be made between the same levels in both. That is, one can establish a similarity in the broad subject covered—marriage, for example—or in a more limited subject—the pressures on the husband in a marriage. Or a reader can establish a connection on the basis of a similar character or a similar relationship between characters, on a similar plot situation or climactic action, on a similar (or even meaningfully contrasting) style, on point of view, or on use of setting. But one should be most wary of comparing, say, the function of a character in one story with the function of setting in another, or even a main character or action in one with a peripheral, minor character or action in another. The points of comparison must be on an equal scale and relevant to each other.

But the similarity is not enough. As in the work itself, unity must be complemented by complexity. No two works—even by the same writer—will be exactly the same or reveal exactly the same insights. The reader, and critic, must then complete his job of work by discriminating between the distinctions and differences that are necessary for the fullest understanding of the unifying point of similarity. In this, the study of literature is like literature itself. Both seek to order their materials into a meaningful unity, while maintaining, as much as is possible, the complexity of human life itself or of the works of art that seek to give that life meaning.

# PART TWO

*Stories—Eleven Pairs*

PART TWO

---

# MY KINSMAN, MAJOR MOLINEUX
## *Nathaniel Hawthorne*

After the kings of Great Britain had assumed the right of appointing the colonial governors, the measures of the latter seldom met with the ready and general approbation which had been paid to those of their predecessors, under the original charters. The people looked with most jealous scrutiny to the exercise of power which did not emanate from themselves, and they usually rewarded their rulers with slender gratitude for the compliances by which, in softening their instructions from beyond the sea, they had incurred the reprehension of those who gave them. The annals of Massachusetts Bay will inform us, that of six governors in the space of about forty years from the surrender of the old charter, under James II, two were imprisoned by a popular insurrection; a third, as Hutchinson inclines to believe, was driven from the province by the whizzing of a musket-ball; a fourth, in the opinion of the same historian, was hastened to his grave by continual bickerings with the House of Representatives; and the remaining two, as well as their successors, till the Revolution, were favored with few and brief intervals of peaceful sway. The inferior members of the court party, in times of high political excitement, led scarcely a more desirable life. These remarks may serve as a preface to the following adventures, which chanced upon a summer night, not far from a hundred years ago. The reader, in order to avoid a long and dry detail of colonial affairs, is requested to dispense with an account of the train of circumstances that had caused much temporary inflammation of the popular mind.

It was near nine o'clock of a moonlight evening, when a boat crossed the ferry with a single passenger, who had obtained his conveyance at that unusual hour by the promise of an extra fare. While he stood on the landing-place, searching in either pocket for the means of fulfilling his agreement, the ferryman lifted a lantern, by the aid of which, and the newly risen moon, he took a very accurate survey of the stranger's figure. He was a youth of barely eighteen years, evidently country-bred, and now, as it should seem, upon his first visit to town. He was clad in a coarse gray coat, well worn, but in excellent repair; his under garments were durably constructed of leather, and fitted tight to a pair of serviceable and well-shaped limbs; his stockings of blue yarn were the incontrovertible work of a mother or a sister; and on his head was a three-cornered hat, which in its better days had perhaps sheltered the graver brow of the lad's father. Under his left arm was a heavy cudgel, formed of an oak sapling, and retaining a part of the hardened root; and his equipment was completed by a wallet, not so abundantly stocked as to incommode the vigorous shoulders on which it hung. Brown, curly hair, well-shaped features, and bright, cheerful eyes were nature's gifts, and worth all that art could have done for his adornment.

The youth, one of whose names was Robin, finally drew from his pocket the half of a little province bill of five shillings, which, in the depreciation of that sort of currency, did not satisfy the ferryman's demand, with the surplus of a sexangular piece of parchment, valued at three pence. He then walked forward into the town, with as light a step as if his day's journey had not already exceeded thirty miles, and with as eager an eye as if he were entering London city, instead of the little metropolis of a New England colony. Before Robin had proceeded far, however, it occurred to him that he knew not whither to direct his steps; so he paused, and looked up and down the narrow street, scrutinizing the small and mean wooden buildings that were scattered on either side.

"This low hovel cannot be my kinsman's dwelling," thought he, "nor yonder old house, where the moonlight enters at the broken casement; and truly I see none hereabouts that might be worthy of him. It would have been wise to inquire my way of the ferryman, and doubtless he would have gone with me, and earned a shilling from the Major for his pains. But the next man I meet will do as well."

He resumed his walk, and was glad to perceive that the street now became wider, and the houses more respectable in their appearance. He soon discerned a figure moving on moderately in advance, and hastened his steps to overtake it. As Robin drew nigh, he saw that the passenger was a man in years, with a full periwig of gray hair, a wide-skirted coat of dark cloth, and silk stockings rolled above his knees. He carried a long and polished cane, which he struck down perpendicularly before him, at every step; and at regular intervals he uttered two successive hems, of a peculiarly solemn and sepulchral intonation. Having made these observations, Robin laid hold of the skirt of the old man's coat, just when the light from the open door and windows of a barber's shop fell upon both their figures.

"Good evening to you, honored sir," said he, making a low bow, and still retaining his hold of the skirt. "I pray you tell me whereabouts is the dwelling of my kinsman, Major Molineux."

The youth's question was uttered very loudly; and one of the barbers, whose razor was descending on a well-soaped chin, and another who was dressing a Ramillies wig, left their occupations, and came to the door. The citizen, in the mean time, turned a long-favored countenance upon Robin, and answered him in a tone of excessive anger and annoyance. His two sepulchral hems, however, broke into the very centre of his rebuke, with most singular effect, like a thought of the cold grave obtruding among wrathful passions.

"Let go my garment, fellow! I tell you, I know not the man you speak of. What! I have authority, I have—hem, hem—authority; and if this be the respect you show for your betters, your feet shall be brought acquainted with stocks by daylight, tomorrow morning!"

Robin released the old man's skirt, and hastened away, pursued by an ill-mannered roar of laughter from the barber's shop. He was at first considerably surprised by the result of his question, but, being a shrewd youth, soon thought himself able to account for the mystery.

"This is some country representative," was his conclusion, "who has never seen the inside of my kinsman's door, and lacks the breeding to answer a stranger civilly. The man is old, or verily—I might be tempted to turn back and smite him on the nose. Ah, Robin, Robin! even the barber's boys laugh at you for choosing such a guide! You will be wiser in time, friend Robin."

He now became entangled in a succession of crooked and narrow streets, which crossed each other, and meandered at no great distance from the water-side. The smell of tar was obvious to his nostrils, the masts of vessels pierced the moonlight above the tops of the buildings, and the numerous signs, which Robin paused to read, informed him that he was near the centre of business. But the streets were empty, the shops were closed, and lights were visible only in the second stories of a few dwelling-houses. At length, on the corner of a narrow lane, through which he was passing, he beheld the broad countenance of a British hero swinging before the door of an inn, whence proceeded the voices of many guests. The casement of one of the lower windows was thrown back, and a very thin curtain permitted Robin to distinguish a party at supper, round a well-furnished table. The fragrance of the good cheer steamed forth into the outer air, and the youth could not fail to recollect that the last remnant of his traveling stock of provision had yielded to his morning appetite, and that noon had found and left him dinnerless.

"Oh, that a parchment three-penny might give me a right to sit down at yonder table!" said Robin, with a sigh. "But the Major will make me welcome to the best of his victuals; so I will even step boldly in, and inquire my way to his dwelling."

He entered the tavern, and was guided by the murmur of voices and the fumes of tobacco to the public-room. It was a long and low apartment, with oaken walls, grown dark in the continual smoke, and a floor which was thickly sanded, but of no immaculate purity. A number of persons—the larger part of whom appeared to be mariners, or in some way connected with the sea—occupied the wooden benches, or leather-bottomed chairs, conversing on various matters, and occasionally lending their attention to some topic of general interest. Three or four little groups were draining as many bowls of punch, which the West India trade had long since made a familiar drink in the colony. Others, who had the appearance of men who lived by regular and laborious handicraft, preferred the insulated bliss of an unshared potation, and became more taciturn under its influence. Nearly all, in short, evinced a predilection for the Good Creature in some of its various shapes, for this is a vice to which, as Fast Day sermons of a hundred years ago will testify, we have a long hereditary claim. The only guests to whom Robin's sympathies inclined him were two or three sheepish countrymen, who were using the inn somewhat after the fashion of a Turkish caravansary; they had gotten themselves into the darkest corner of the room, and heedless of the Nicotian atmosphere, were supping on the bread of their own ovens, and the bacon cured in their own chimney-smoke. But though Robin felt a sort of brotherhood with these strangers, his eyes were attracted from them to a person who stood near the door, holding whispered conversation with a group of ill-dressed associates. His features were separately striking almost to grotesqueness, and the whole face left a deep impression on the memory. The forehead bulged out into a double prominence, with a vale between; the nose came boldly forth in an irregular curve, and its bridge was of more than a finger's breadth; the eyebrows were deep and shaggy, and the eyes glowed beneath them like a fire in a cave.

While Robin deliberated of whom to inquire respecting his kinsman's dwelling, he was accosted by the innkeeper, a little man in a stained white apron, who had come to pay his professional welcome to the stranger. Being in the second generation from a French Protestant, he seemed to have inherited the courtesy of his parent nation; but no variety of circumstances was ever known to change his voice from the one shrill note in which he now addressed Robin.

"From the country, I presume, sir?" said he, with a profound bow. "Beg leave to congratulate you on your arrival, and trust you intend a long stay with us. Fine town here, sir, beautiful buildings, and much that may interest a stranger. May I hope for the honor of your commands in respect to supper?"

"The man sees a family likeness! the rogue has guessed that I am related to the Major!" thought Robin, who had hitherto experienced little superfluous civility.

All eyes were now turned on the country lad, standing at the door, in his worn three-cornered hat, gray coat, leather breeches, and blue yarn stockings, leaning on an oaken cudgel, and bearing a wallet on his back.

Robin replied to the courteous innkeeper, with such an assumption of confidence as befitted the Major's relative. "My honest friend," he said, "I shall make it a point to patronize your house on some occasion, when"—here he could not help lowering his voice—"when I may have more than a parchment three-pence in my pocket. My present business," continued he, speaking with lofty confidence, "is merely to inquire my way to the dwelling of my kinsman, Major Molineux."

There was a sudden and general movement in the room, which Robin interpreted as expressing the eagerness of each individual to become his guide. But the innkeeper turned his eyes to a written paper on the wall, which he read, or seemed to read, with occasional recurrences to the young man's figure.

"What have we here?" he said, breaking his speech into little dry fragments. " 'Left the house of the subscriber, bounden servant, Hezekiah Mudge,—had on, when he went away, gray coat, leather breeches, master's third-best hat. One pound currency reward to whosoever shall lodge him in any jail of the province.' Better trudge, boy; better trudge."

Robin had begun to draw his hand towards the lighter end of the oak cudgel, but a strange hostility in every countenance induced him to relinquish his purpose of breaking the courteous innkeeper's head. As he turned to leave the room, he encountered a sneering glance from the bold-featured personage whom he had before noticed; and no sooner was he beyond the door, than he heard a general laugh, in which the innkeeper's voice might be distinguished, like the dropping of small stones into a kettle.

"Now, is it not strange," thought Robin, with his usual shrewdness,—"is it not strange that the confession of an empty pocket should outweigh the name of my kinsman, Major Molineux? Oh, if I had one of those grinning rascals in the woods, where I and my oak sapling grew up together, I would teach him that my arm is heavy though my purse be light!"

On turning the corner of the narrow lane, Robin found himself in a spacious street, with an unbroken line of lofty houses on each side, and a steepled building at the upper end, whence the ringing of a bell announced the hour of nine. The light of the moon, and the lamps from the numerous shop-windows, discovered people promenading on the pavement, and amongst them Robin hoped to recognize his hitherto inscrutable relative. The result of his former inquiries made him unwilling to hazard another, in a scene of such publicity, and he determined to walk slowly and silently up the street, thrusting his face close to that of every elderly gentleman, in search of the Major's lineaments. In his progress, Robin encountered many gay and gallant figures. Embroidered garments of showy colors, enormous periwigs, gold-laced hats, and silver-hilted swords glided past him and dazzled his optics. Travelled youths, imitators of the European fine gentlemen of the period, trod jauntily along, half dancing to the fashionable tunes which they hummed, and making poor Robin ashamed of his quiet and natural gait. At length, after many pauses to examine the gorgeous display of goods in the shop-windows, and after suffering some rebukes for the impertinance of his scrutiny into people's faces, the Major's kinsman found himself near the steepled building, still unsuccessful in his search. As yet, however, he had seen only one side of the thronged street; so Robin crossed, and continued the same sort of inquisition down the opposite pavement, with stronger hopes than the philosopher seeking an honest man, but with no better fortune. He had arrived about midway towards the lower end, from which his course began, when he overheard the approach of some one who struck down a cane on the flag-stones at every step, uttering, at regular intervals, two sepulchral hems.

"Mercy on us!" quoth Robin, recognizing the sound.

Turning a corner, which chanced to be close at his right hand, he hastened to pursue his research in some other part of the town. His patience now was wearing low, and he seemed to feel more fatigue from his rambles since he crossed the ferry, than from his journey of several days on the other side. Hunger also pleaded loudly within him, and Robin began to balance the propriety of demanding, violently, and with lifted cudgel, the necessary guidance from the first solitary passenger whom he should meet. While a resolution to this effect was gaining strength, he entered a street of mean appearance, on either side of which a row of ill-built houses was straggling towards the harbor. The moonlight fell upon no passenger along the whole extent, but in the third domicile which Robin passed there was a half-opened door, and his keen glance detected a woman's garment within.

"My luck may be better here," said he to himself.

Accordingly, he approached the door, and beheld it shut closer as he did so; yet an open space remained, sufficing for the fair occupant to observe the stranger, without a corresponding display on her part. All that Robin could discern was a strip of scarlet petticoat, and the occasional sparkle of an eye, as if the moonbeams were trembling on some bright thing.

"Pretty mistress," for I may call her so with a good conscience, thought the shrewd youth, since I know nothing to the contrary,— "my sweet pretty mistress, will you be kind enough to tell me whereabouts I must seek the dwelling of my kinsman, Major Molineux?"

Robin's voice was plaintive and winning, and the female, seeing nothing to be shunned in the handsome country youth, thrust open the door, and came forth into the moonlight. She was a dainty little figure, with a white neck, round arms, and a slender waist, at the extremity of which her scarlet petticoat jutted out over a hoop, as if she were standing in a balloon. Moreover, her face was oval and pretty, her hair dark beneath the little cap, and her bright eyes possessed a sly freedom, which triumphed over those of Robin.

"Major Molineux dwells here," said this fair woman.

Now, her voice was the sweetest Robin had heard that night, the airy counterpart of a stream of melted silver; yet he could not help doubting whether that sweet voice spoke Gospel truth. He looked up and down the mean street, and then surveyed the house before which they stood. It was a small, dark edifice of two stories, the second of which projected over the lower floor; and the front apartment had the aspect of a shop for petty commodities.

"Now, truly, I am in luck," replied Robin cunningly, "and so indeed is my kinsman, the Major, in having so pretty a housekeeper. But I prithee trouble him to step to the door; I will deliver him a message from his friends in the country, and then go back to my lodgings at the inn."

"Nay, the Major has been abed this hour or more," said the lady of the scarlet petticoat, "and it would be to little purpose to disturb him tonight, seeing his evening draught was of the strongest. But he is a kindhearted man, and it would be as much as my life's worth to let a kinsman of his turn away from the door. You are the good old gentleman's very picture, and I could swear that was his rainy-weather hat. Also he has garments very much resembling those leather small-clothes. But come in, I pray, for I bid you hearty welcome in his name."

So saying, the fair and hospitable dame took our hero by the hand; and the touch was light, and the force was gentleness, and though Robin read in her eyes what he did not hear in her words, yet the slenderwaisted woman in the scarlet petticoat proved stronger than the athletic country youth. She had drawn his half-willing footsteps nearly to the threshold, when the opening of a door in the neighborhood startled the Major's housekeeper, and, leaving the Major's kinsman, she vanished speedily into her own domicile. A heavy yawn preceded the appearance of a man, who, like the Moonshine of Pyramus and Thisbe, carried a lantern, needlessly aiding his sister luminary in the heavens. As he walked sleepily up the street, he turned his broad, dull face on Robin, and displayed a long staff, spiked at the end.

"Home, vagabond, home!" said the watchman, in accents that seemed to fall asleep as soon as they were uttered. "Home, or we'll set you in the stocks, by peep of day!"

"This is the second hint of the kind," thought Robin. "I wish they would end my difficulties, by setting me there to-night."

Nevertheless, the youth felt an instinctive antipathy towards the guardian of midnight order, which at first prevented him from asking his usual question. But just when the man was about to vanish behind the corner, Robin resolved not to lose the opportunity, and shouted lustily after him,—

"I say, friend! will you guide me to the house of my kinsman, Major Molineux?"

The watchman made no reply, but turned the corner and was gone; yet Robin seemed to hear the sound of drowsy laughter stealing along the solitary street. At that moment, also, a pleasant titter saluted him from the open window above his head; he looked up, and caught the sparkle of a saucy eye; a round arm beckoned to him, and next he heard light footsteps descending the staircase within. But Robin, being of the household of a New England clergyman, was a good youth, as well as a shrewd one; so he resisted temptation, and fled away.

He now roamed desperately, and at random, through the town, almost ready to believe that a spell was on him, like that by which a wizard of his country had once kept three pursuers wandering, a whole winter night, within twenty paces of the cottage which they sought. The streets lay before him, strange and desolate, and the lights were extinguished in almost every house. Twice, however, little parties of men, among whom Robin distinguished individuals in outlandish attire, came hurrying along; but though on both occasions they paused to address him, such intercourse did not at all enlighten his perplexity. They did but utter a few words in some language of which Robin knew nothing, and perceiving his inability to answer, bestowed a curse upon him in plain English, and hastened away. Finally, the lad determined to knock at the door of every mansion that might appear worthy to be occupied by his kinsman, trusting that perseverance would overcome the fatality that had hitherto thwarted him. Firm in this resolve, he was passing beneath the walls of a church, which formed the corner of two streets, when, as he turned into the shade of its steeple, he encountered a bulky stranger, muffled in a cloak. The man was proceeding with the speed of earnest business, but Robin planted himself full before him, holding the oak cudgel with both hands across his body as a bar to further passage.

"Halt, honest man, and answer me a question," said he, very resolutely. "Tell me, this instant, whereabouts is the dwelling of my kinsman, Major Molineux!"

"Keep your tongue between your teeth, fool, and let me pass!" said a deep, gruff voice, which Robin partly remembered. "Let me pass, I say, or I'll strike you to the earth!"

"No, no, neighbor!" cried Robin, flourishing his cudgel, and then thrusting its larger end close to the man's muffled face. "No, no, I'm not the fool you take me for, nor do you pass till I have an answer to my question. Whereabouts is the dwelling of my kinsman, Major Molineux?"

The stranger, instead of attempting to force his passage, stepped back into the moonlight, unmuffled his face, and stared full into that of Robin.

"Watch here an hour, and Major Molineux will pass by," said he.

Robin gazed with dismay and astonishment on the unprecedented physiognomy of the speaker. The forehead with its double prominence, the broad hooked nose, the shaggy eyebrows, and fiery eyes were those which he had noticed at the inn, but the man's complexion had undergone a singular, or, more properly, a twofold change. One side of the face blazed an intense red, while the other was black as midnight, the division line being in the broad bridge of the nose; and a mouth which seemed to extend from ear to ear was black or red, in contrast to the color of the cheek. The effect was as if two individual devils, a fiend of fire and a fiend of darkness, had united themselves to form this infernal visage. The stranger grinned in Robin's face, muffled his particolored features, and was out of sight in a moment.

"Strange things we travellers see!" ejaculated Robin.

He seated himself, however, upon the steps of the church-door, resolving to wait the appointed time for his kinsman. A few moments were consumed in philosophical speculations upon the species of man who had just left him; but having settled this point shrewdly, rationally, and satisfactorily, he was compelled to look elsewhere for his amusement. And first he threw his eyes along the street. It was of more respectable appearance than most of those into which he had wandered, and the moon, creating, like the imaginative power, a beautiful strangeness in familiar objects, gave something of romance to a scene that might not have possessed it in the light of day. The irregular and often quaint architecture of the houses, some of whose roofs were broken into numerous little peaks, while others ascended, steep and narrow, into a single point, and others again were square; the pure snow-white of some of their complexions, the aged darkness of others, and the thousand sparklings, reflected from bright substances in the walls of many; these matters engaged Robin's attention for a while, and then began to grow wearisome. Next he endeavored to define the forms of distant objects, starting away, with almost ghostly indistinctness, just as his eye appeared to grasp them; and finally he took a minute survey of an edifice which stood on the opposite side of the street, directly in front of the church-door, where he was stationed. It was a large, square mansion, distinguished from its neighbors by a balcony, which rested on tall pillars, and by an elaborate Gothic window, communicating therewith.

"Perhaps this is the very house I have been seeking," thought Robin.

Then he strove to speed away the time, by listening to a murmur which swept continually along the street, yet was scarcely audible, except to an unaccustomed ear like his; it was a low, dull, dreamy sound, compounded of many noises, each of which was at too great a distance to be separately heard. Robin marvelled at this snore of a sleeping town, and marvelled more whenever its continuity was broken by now and then a distant shout, apparently loud where it originated. But altogether it was a sleep-inspiring sound, and, to shake off its drowsy influence, Robin arose, and climbed a window-frame, that he might view the interior of the church. There the moonbeams came trembling in, and fell down upon the deserted pews, and extended along the quiet aisles. A fainter yet more awful radiance was hovering around the pulpit, and one solitary ray had dared to rest upon the open page of the great Bible. Had nature, in that deep hour, become a worshipper in the house which man had builded? Or was that heavenly light the visible sanctity of the place,—visible because no earthly and impure feet were within the walls? The scene made Robin's heart shiver with a sensation of loneliness stronger than he had ever felt in the remotest depths of his native woods; so he turned away and sat down again before the door. There were graves around the church, and now an uneasy thought obtruded into Robin's breast. What if the object of his search, which had been so often and so strangely thwarted, were all the time mouldering in his shroud? What if his kinsman should glide through yonder gate, and nod and smile to him in dimly passing by?

"Oh that any breathing thing were here with me!" said Robin.

Recalling his thoughts from this uncomfortable tract, he sent them over forest, hill, and stream, and attempted to imagine how that evening of ambiguity and weariness had been spent by his father's household. He pictured them assembled at the door, beneath the tree, the great old tree, which had been spared for its huge twisted trunk and venerable shade, when a thousand leafy brethren fell. There, at the going down of the summer sun, it was his father's custom to perform domestic worship, that the neighbors might come and join with him like brothers of the family, and that the wayfaring man might pause to drink at that fountain, and keep his heart pure by freshening the memory of home. Robin distinguished the seat of every individual of the little audience; he saw the good man in the midst, holding the Scriptures in the golden light that fell from the western clouds; he beheld him close the book and all rise up to pray. He heard the old thanksgivings for daily mercies, the old supplications for their continuance, to which he had so often listened in weariness, but which were now among his dear remembrances. He perceived the slight inequality of his father's voice when he came to speak of the absent one; he noted how his mother turned her face to the broad and knotted trunk; how his elder brother scorned, because the beard was rough upon his upper lip, to permit his features to be moved; how the younger sister drew down a low hanging branch before her eyes; and how the little one of all, whose sports had hitherto broken the decorum of the scene, understood the prayer for her playmate, and burst into clamorous grief. Then he saw them go in at the door; and when Robin would have entered also, the latch tinkled into its place, and he was excluded from his home.

"Am I here, or there?" cried Robin, starting; for all at once, when his thoughts had become visible and audible in a dream, the long, wide solitary street shone out before him.

He aroused himself, and endeavored to fix his attention steadily upon the large edifice which he had surveyed before. But still his mind kept vibrating between fancy and reality; by turns, the pillars of the balcony lengthened into the tall, bare stems of pines, dwindled down to human figures, settled again into their true shape and size, and then commenced a new succession of changes. For a single moment, when he deemed himself awake, he could have sworn that a visage—one which he seemed to remember, yet could not absolutely name as his kinsman's—was looking towards him from the Gothic window. A deeper sleep wrestled with and nearly overcame him, but fled at the sound of footsteps along the opposite pavement. Robin rubbed his eyes, discerned a man passing at the foot of the balcony, and addressed him in a loud, peevish, and lamentable cry.

"Hallo, friend! must I wait here all night for my kinsman, Major Molineux?"

The sleeping echoes awoke, and answered the voice; and the passenger, barely able to discern a figure sitting in the oblique shade of the steeple, traversed the street to obtain a nearer view. He was himself a gentleman in his prime, of open, intelligent, cheerful, and altogether prepossessing countenance. Perceiving a country youth, apparently homeless and without friends, he accosted him in a tone of real kindness, which had become strange to Robin's ears.

"Well, my good lad, why are you sitting here?" inquired he. "Can I be of service to you in any way?"

"I am afraid not, sir," replied Robin despondingly; "yet I shall take it kindly, if you'll answer me a single question. I've been searching, half the night, for one Major Molineux; now, sir, is there really such a person in these parts, or am I dreaming?"

"Major Molineux! The name is not altogether strange to me," said the gentleman, smiling. "Have you any objection to telling me the nature of your business with him?"

Then Robin briefly related that his father was a clergyman, settled on a small salary, at a long distance back in the country, and that he and Major Molineux were brothers' children. The Major, having inherited riches, and acquired civil and military rank, had visited his cousin, in great pomp, a year or two before; had manifested much interest in Robin and an elder brother, and, being childless himself, had thrown out hints respecting the future establishment of one of them in life. The elder brother was destined to succeed to the farm which his father cultivated in the interval of sacred duties; it was therefore determined that Robin should profit by his kinsman's generous intentions, especially as he seemed to be rather the favorite, and was thought to possess other necessary endowments.

"For I have the name of being a shrewd youth," observed Robin, in this part of his story.

"I doubt not you deserve it," replied his new friend, good-naturedly; "but pray proceed."

"Well, sir, being nearly eighteen years old, and well grown, as you see," continued Robin, drawing himself up to his full height, "I thought it high time to begin the world. So my mother and sister put me in handsome trim, and my father gave me half the remnant of his last year's salary, and five days ago I started for this place, to pay the Major a visit. But, would you believe it, sir! I crossed the ferry a little after dark, and have yet found nobody that would show me the way to his dwelling; only, an hour or two since, I was told to wait here, and Major Molineux would pass by."

"Can you describe the man who told you this?" inquired the gentleman.

"Oh, he was a very ill-favored fellow, sir," replied Robin, "with two great bumps on his forehead, a hook nose, fiery eyes; and, what struck me as the strangest, his face was of two different colors. Do you happen to know such a man, Sir?"

"Not intimately," answered the stranger, "but I chanced to meet him a little time previous to your stopping me. I believe you may trust his word, and that the Major will very shortly pass through this street. In the meantime, as I have a singular curiosity to witness your meeting, I will sit down here upon the steps, and bear you company."

He seated himself accordingly, and soon engaged his companion in animated discourse. It was but of brief continuance, however, for a noise of shouting, which had long been remotely audible, drew so much nearer that Robin inquired its cause.

"What may be the meaning of this uproar?" asked he. "Truly, if your town be always as noisy, I shall find little sleep, while I am an inhabitant."

"Why, indeed, friend Robin, there do appear to be three or four riotous fellows abroad to-night," replied the gentleman. "You must not expect all the stillness of your native woods, here in our streets. But the watch will shortly be at the heels of these lads, and—"

"Ay, and set them in the stocks by peep of day," interrupted Robin, recollecting his own encounter with the drowsy lantern-bearer. "But, dear sir, if I may trust my ears, an army of watchmen would never make head against such a multitude of rioters. There were at least a thousand voices went up to make that one shout."

"May not a man have several voices, Robin, as well as two complexions?" said his friend.

"Perhaps a man may; but Heaven forbid that a woman should!" responded the shrewd youth, thinking of the seductive tones of the Major's housekeeper.

The sounds of a trumpet in some neighboring street now became so evident and continual, that Robin's curiosity was strongly excited. In addition to the shouts, he heard frequent bursts from many instruments of discord and a wild and confused laughter filled up the intervals. Robin rose from the steps, and looked wistfully towards a point whither several people seemed to be hastening.

"Surely some prodigious merry-making is going on," exclaimed he. "I have laughed very little since I left home, sir, and should be sorry to lose an opportunity. Shall we step round the corner by that darkish house, and take our share of the fun?"

"Sit down again, sit down, good Robin," replied the gentleman, laying his hand on the skirt of the gray coat. "You forget that we must wait here for your kinsman; and there is reason to believe that he will pass by, in the course of a very few moments."

The near approach of the uproar had now disturbed the neighborhood; windows flew open on all sides; and many heads, in the attire of the pillow, and confused by sleep suddenly broken, were protruded to the gaze of whoever had leisure to observe them. Eager voices hailed each other from house to house, all demanding the explanation, which not a soul could give. Half-dressed men hurried towards the unknown commotion, stumbling as they went over the stone steps that thrust themselves into the narrow foot-walk. The shouts, the laughter, and the tuneless bray, the antipodes of music, came onwards with increasing din, till scattered individuals, and then denser bodies, began to appear round a corner at the distance of a hundred yards.

"Will you recognize your kinsman, if he passes in this crowd?" inquired the gentleman.

"Indeed, I can't warrant it, sir; but I'll take my stand here, and keep a bright lookout," answered Robin, descending to the outer edge of the pavement.

A mighty stream of people now emptied into the street, and came rolling slowly towards the church. A single horseman wheeled the corner in the midst of them, and close behind him came a band of fearful wind-instruments, sending forth a fresher discord now that no intervening buildings kept it from the ear. Then a redder light disturbed the moonbeams, and a dense multitude of torches shone along the street, concealing, by their glare, whatever object they illuminated. The single horseman, clad in a military dress, and bearing a drawn sword, rode onward as the leader, and, by his fierce and variegated countenance, appeared like war personified; the red of one cheek was an emblem of fire and sword; the blackness of the other betokened the mourning that attends them. In his train were wild figures in the Indian dress, and many fantastic shapes without a model, giving the whole march a visionary air, as if a dream had broken forth from some feverish brain, and were sweeping visibly through the midnight streets. A mass of people, inactive, except as applauding spectators, hemmed the procession in; and several women ran along the sidewalk, piercing the confusion of heavier sounds with their shrill voices of mirth or terror.

"The double-faced fellow has his eye upon me," muttered Robin, with an indefinite but an uncomfortable idea that he was himself to bear a part in the pageantry.

The leader turned himself in the saddle, and fixed his glance full upon the country youth, as the steed went slowly by. When Robin had freed his eyes from those fiery ones, the musicians were passing before him, and the torches were close at hand; but the unsteady brightness of the latter formed a veil which he could not penetrate. The rattling of wheels over the stones sometimes found its way to his ear, and confused traces of a human form appeared at intervals, and then melted into the vivid light. A moment more, and the leader thundered a command to halt: the trumpets vomited a horrid breath, and then held their peace; the shouts and laughter of the people died away, and there remained only a universal hum, allied to silence. Right before Robin's eyes was an uncovered cart. There the torches blazed the brightest, there the moon shone out like day, and there, in tar-and-feathery dignity, sat his kinsman, Major Molineux!

He was an elderly man, of large and majestic person, and strong, square features, betokening a steady soul; but steady as it was, his enemies had found means to shake it. His face was pale as death, and far more ghastly; the broad forehead was contracted in his agony, so that his eyebrows formed one grizzled line; his eyes were red and wild, and the foam hung white upon his quivering lip. His whole frame was agitated by a quick and continual tremor, which his pride strove to quell, even in those circumstances of overwhelming humiliation. But perhaps the bitterest pang of all was when his eyes met those of Robin; for he evidently knew him on the instant, as the youth stood witnessing the foul disgrace of a head grown gray in honor. They stared at each other in silence, and Robin's knees shook, and his hair bristled, with a mixture of pity and terror. Soon, however, a bewildering excitement began to seize upon his mind; the preceding adventures of the night, the unexpected appearance of the crowd, the torches, the confused din and the hush that followed, the spectre of his kinsman reviled by that great multitude,—all this, and, more than all, a perception of tremendous ridicule in the whole scene, affected him with a sort of mental inebriety. At that moment a voice of sluggish merriment saluted Robin's ears; he turned instinctively, and just behind the corner of the church stood the lantern-bearer, rubbing his eyes, and drowsily enjoying the lad's amazement. Then he heard a peal of laughter like the ringing of silvery bells; a woman twitched his arm, a saucy eye met his, and he saw the lady of the scarlet petticoat. A sharp, dry cachinnation appealed to his memory, and, standing on tiptoe in the crowd, with his white apron over his head, he beheld the courteous little innkeeper. And lastly, there sailed over the heads of the multitude a great, broad laugh, broken in the midst by two sepulchral hems; thus, "Haw, haw, haw,—hem, hem,—haw, haw, haw, haw!"

The sound proceeded from the balcony of the opposite edifice, and thither Robin turned his eyes. In front of the Gothic window stood the old citizen, wrapped in a wide gown, his gray periwig exchanged for a nightcap, which was thrust back from his forehead, and his silk stockings hanging about his legs. He supported himself on his polished cane in a fit of convulsive merriment, which manifested itself on his solemn old features like a funny inscription on a tombstone. Then Robin seemed to hear the voices of the barbers, of the guests of the inn, and of all who had made sport of him that night. The contagion was spreading among the multitude, when, all at once, it seized upon Robin, and he sent forth a shout of laughter that echoed through the street;—every man shook his sides, every man emptied his lungs, but Robin's shout was the loudest there. The cloud-spirits peeped from their silvery islands, as the congregated mirth went roaring up the sky! The Man in the Moon heard the far bellow. "Oho," quoth he, "the old earth is frolicsome tonight!"

When there was a momentary calm in that tempestuous sea of sound, the leader gave the sign, the procession resumed its march. On they went, like fiends that throng in mockery around some dead potentate, mighty no more, but majestic still in his agony. On they went, in counterfeited pomp, in senseless uproar, in frenzied merriment, trampling all on an old man's heart. On swept the tumult, and left a silent street behind.

"Well, Robin, are you dreaming?" inquired the gentleman, laying his hand on the youth's shoulder.

Robin started, and withdrew his arm from the stone post to which he had instinctively clung, as the living stream rolled by him. His cheek was somewhat pale, and his eye not quite as lively as in the earlier part of the evening.

"Will you be kind enough to show me the way to the ferry?" said he, after a moment's pause.

"You have, then, adopted a new subject of inquiry?" observed his companion, with a smile.

"Why, yes, sir," replied Robin, rather dryly. "Thanks to you, and to my other friends, I have at last met my kinsman, and he will scarce desire to see my face again. I begin to grow weary of a town life, sir. Will you show me the way to the ferry?"

"No, my good friend Robin,—not to-night, at least," said the gentleman. "Some few days hence, if you wish it, I will speed you on your journey. Or, if you prefer to remain with us, perhaps, as you are a shrewd youth, you may rise in the world without the help of your kinsman, Major Molineux."

---

# A TREE OF NIGHT
## *Truman Capote*

It was winter. A string of naked light bulbs, from which it seemed all warmth had been drained, illuminated the little depot's cold, windy platform. Earlier in the evening it had rained, and now icicles hung along the station-house eaves like some crystal monster's vicious teeth. Except for a girl, young and rather tall, the platform was deserted. The girl wore a gray flannel suit, a raincoat, and a plaid scarf. Her hair, parted in the middle and rolled up neatly on the sides, was rich blond-ish-brown; and, while her face tended to be too thin and narrow, she was, though not extraordinarily so, attractive. In addition to an assort-ment of magazines and a gray suede purse on which elaborate brass letters spelled Kay, she carried conspicuously a green Western guitar.

When the train, spouting steam and glaring with light, came out of the darkness and rumbled to a halt, Kay assembled her paraphernalia and climbed up into the last coach.

The coach was a relic with a decaying interior of ancient red-plush seats, bald in spots, and peeling iodine-colored woodwork. An old-time copper lamp, attached to the ceiling, looked romantic and out of place. Gloomy dead smoke sailed the air; and the car's heated closeness accentuated the stale odor of discarded sandwiches, apple cores, and orange hulls: this garbage, including Lily cups, soda-pop bottles, and mangled newspapers, littered the long aisle. From a water cooler, embedded in the wall, a steady stream trickled to the floor. The passengers, who glanced up wearily when Kay entered, were not, it seemed, at all conscious of any discomfort.

Kay resisted a temptation to hold her nose and threaded her way carefully down the aisle, tripping once, without disaster, over a dozing fat man's protruding leg. Two nondescript men turned an interested eye as she passed; and a kid stood up in his seat, squalling, "Hey, Mama, look at de banjo! Hey, lady, lemme play ya banjo!" till a slap from Mama quelled him.

There was only one empty place. She found it at the end of the car in an isolated alcove occupied already by a man and woman who were sitting with their feet settled lazily on the vacant seat opposite. Kay hesitated a second then said, "Would you mind if I sat here?"

The woman's head snapped up as if she had not been asked a simple question, but stabbed with a needle, too. Nevertheless, she managed a smile. "Can't say as I see what's to stop you, honey," she said, taking her feet down and also, with a curious impersonality, removing the feet of the man who was staring out the window, paying no attention whatsoever.

Thanking the woman, Kay took off her coat, sat down, and arranged herself with purse and guitar at her side, magazines in her lap: comfortable enough, though she wished she had a pillow for her back.

The train lurched; a ghost of steam hissed against the window; slowly the dingy lights of the lonesome depot faded past.

"Boy, what a jerkwater dump," said the woman. "No town, no nothin'."

Kay said, "The town's a few miles away."

"That so? Live there?"

No. Kay explained she had been at the funeral of an uncle. An uncle who, though she did not of course mention it, had left her nothing in his will but the green guitar. Where was she going? Oh, back to college.

After mulling this over, the woman concluded, "What'll you ever learn in a place like that? Let me tell you, honey, I'm plenty educated and I never saw the inside of no college."

"You didn't?" murmured Kay politely and dismissed the matter by opening one of her magazines. The light was dim for reading and none of the stories looked in the least compelling. However, not wanting to become involved in a conversational marathon, she continued gazing at it stupidly till she felt a furtive tap on her knee.

"Don't read," said the woman. "I need somebody to talk to. Naturally, it's no fun talking to *him*." She jerked a thumb toward the silent man. "He's afflicted: deaf and dumb, know what I mean?"

Kay closed the magazine and looked at her more or less for the first time. She was short; her feet barely scraped the floor. And like many undersized people she had a freak of structure, in her case an enormous, really huge head. Rouge so brightened her sagging, fleshy-featured face it was difficult even to guess at her age: perhaps fifty, fifty-five. Her big sheep eyes squinted, as if distrustful of what they saw. Her hair was an obviously dyed red, and twisted into parched, fat corkscrew curls. A once-elegant lavender hat of impressive size flopped crazily on the side of her head, and she was kept busy brushing back a drooping cluster of celluloid cherries sewed to the brim. She wore a plain, somewhat shabby blue dress. Her breath had a vividly sweetish gin smell.

"You do wanna talk to me, don't you, honey?"

"Sure," said Kay, moderately amused.

"Course you do. You bet you do. That's what I like about a train. Bus people are a close-mouthed buncha dopes. But a train's the place for putting your cards on the table, that's what I always say." Her voice was cheerful and booming, husky as a man's. "But on accounta *him,* I always try to get us this here seat; it's more private, like a swell compartment, see?"

"It's very pleasant," Kay agreed. "Thanks for letting me join you."

"Only too glad to. We don't have much company; it makes some folks nervous to be around him."

As if to deny it, the man made a queer, furry sound deep in his throat and plucked the woman's sleeve. "Leave me alone, dear-heart," she said, as if she were talking to an inattentive child. "I'm O.K. We're just having us a nice little ol' talk. Now behave yourself or this pretty girl will go away. She's very rich; she goes to college." And winking, she added, "He thinks I'm drunk."

The man slumped in the seat, swung his head sideways, and studied Kay intently from the corners of his eyes. These eyes, like a pair of clouded milky-blue marbles, were thickly lashed and oddly beautiful. Now, except for a certain remoteness, his wide, hairless face had no real expression. It was as if he were incapable of experiencing or reflecting the slightest emotion. His gray hair was clipped close and combed forward into uneven bangs. He looked like a child aged abruptly by some uncanny method. He wore a frayed blue serge suit, and he had anointed himself with a cheap, vile perfume. Around his wrist was strapped a Mickey Mouse watch.

"He thinks I'm drunk," the woman repeated. "And the real funny part is, I am. Oh, shoot—you gotta do something, ain't that right?" she bent closer. "Say, ain't it?"

Kay was still gawking at the man; the way he was looking at her made her squeamish, but she could not take her eyes off him. "I guess so," she said.

"Then let's have us a drink," suggested the woman. She plunged her hand into an oilcloth satchel and pulled out a partially filled gin bottle. She began to unscrew the cap but, seeming to think better of this, handed the bottle to Kay. "Gee, I forgot about you being company," she said. "I'll go get us some nice paper cups."

So, before Kay could protest that she did not want a drink, the woman had risen and started none too steadily down the aisle toward the water cooler.

Kay yawned and rested her forehead against the windowpane, her fingers idly strumming the guitar: the strings sang a hollow, lulling tune, as monotonously soothing as the Southern landscape, smudged in darkness, flowing past the window. An icy winter moon rolled above the train across the night sky like a thin white wheel.

And then, without warning, a strange thing happened: the man reached out and gently stroked Kay's cheek. Despite the breathtaking delicacy of this movement, it was such a bold gesture Kay was at first too startled to know what to make of it: her thoughts shot in three or four fantastic directions. He leaned forward till his queer eyes were very near her own; the reek of his perfume was sickening. The guitar was silent while they exchanged a searching gaze. Suddenly, from some spring of compassion, she felt for him a keen sense of pity; but also, and this she could not suppress, an overpowering disgust, an absolute loathing: something about him, an elusive quality she could not quite put a finger on, reminded her of—of what?

After a little, he lowered his hand solemnly and sank back in his seat, an asinine grin transfiguring his face, as if he had performed a clever stunt for which he wished applause.

"Giddyup! Giddyup! my little bucker-ROOS . . ." shouted the woman. And she sat down, loudly proclaiming to be, "Dizzy as a witch! Dog tired! Whew!" From a handful of Lily cups she separated two and casually thrust the rest down her blouse. "Keep 'em safe and dry, ha ha ha. . . ." A coughing spasm seized her, but when it was over she appeared calmer. "Has my boy friend been entertaining?" she asked, patting her bosom reverently. "Ah, he's so sweet." She looked as if she might pass out. Kay rather wished she would.

"I don't want a drink," Kay said, returning the bottle. "I never drink: I hate the taste."

"Mustn't be a kill-joy," said the woman firmly. "Here now, hold your cup like a good girl."

"No, please . . ."

"Formercysake, hold it still. Imagine, nerves at your age! Me, I can shake like a leaf, I've got reasons. Oh, Lordy, have I got 'em."

"But . . ."

A dangerous smile tipped the woman's face hideously awry. "What's the matter? Don't you think I'm good enough to drink with?"

"Please, don't misunderstand," said Kay, a tremor in her voice. "It's just that I don't like being forced to do something I don't want to. So look, couldn't I give this to the gentleman?"

"Him? No sirree: he needs what little sense he's got. Come on, honey, down the hatch."

Kay, seeing it was useless, decided to succumb and avoid a possible scene. She sipped and shuddered. It was terrible gin. It burned her throat till her eyes watered. Quickly, when the woman was not watching, she emptied the cup out into the sound hole of the guitar. It happened, however, that the man saw; and Kay, realizing it, recklessly signaled to him with her eyes a plea not to give her away. But she could not tell from his clear-blank expression how much he understood.

"Where you from, kid?" resumed the woman presently.

For a bewildered moment, Kay was unable to provide an answer. The names of several cities came to her all at once. Finally, from this confusion, she extracted: "New Orleans. My home is in New Orleans."

The woman beamed. "N.O.'s where I wanna go when I kick off. One time, oh, say 1923, I ran me a sweet little fortune-telling parlor there. Let's see, that was on St. Peter Street." Pausing, she stooped and set the empty gin bottle on the floor. It rolled into the aisle and rocked back and forth with a drowsy sound. "I was raised in Texas—on a big ranch—my papa was rich. Us kids always had the best; even Paris, France, clothes. I'll bet you've got a big swell house, too. Do you have a garden? Do you grow flowers?"

"Just lilacs."

A conductor entered the coach, preceded by a cold gust of wind that rattled the trash in the aisle and briefly livened the dull air. He lumbered along, stopping now and then to punch a ticket or talk with a passenger. It was after midnight. Someone was expertly playing a harmonica. Someone else was arguing the merits of a certain politician. A child cried out in his sleep.

"Maybe you wouldn't be so snotty if you knew who we was," said the woman, bobbing her tremendous head. "We ain't hobodies, not by a long shot."

Embarrassed, Kay nervously opened a pack of cigarettes and lighted one. She wondered if there might not be a seat in a car up ahead. She could not bear the woman, or, for that matter, the man, another minute. But she had never before been in a remotely comparable situation. "If you'll excuse me now," she said, "I have to be leaving. It's been very pleasant, but I promised to meet a friend on the train. . . ."

With almost invisible swiftness the woman grasped the girl's wrist.

"Didn't your mama ever tell you it was sinful to lie?" she stage-whispered. The lavender hat tumbled off her head but she made no effort to retrieve it. Her tongue flicked out and wetted her lips. And, as Kay stood up, she increased the pressure of her grip. "Sit down, dear . . . there ain't any friend . . . Why, we're your only friends and we wouldn't have you leave us for the world."

"Honestly, I wouldn't lie."

"Sit down, dear."

Kay dropped her cigarette and the man picked it up. He slouched in the corner and became absorbed in blowing a chain of lush smoke rings that mounted upward like hollow eyes and expanded into nothing.

"Why, you wouldn't want to hurt his feelings by leaving us, now, would you, dear?" crooned the woman softly. "Sit down—down— now, that's a good girl. My, what a pretty guitar. What a pretty, pretty guitar . . ." Her voice faded before the sudden whooshing, static noise of a second train. And for an instant the lights in the coach went off; in the darkness the passing train's golden windows winked black-yellow-black-yellow-black-yellow. The man's cigarette pulsed like the glow of a firefly, and his smoke rings continued rising tranquilly. Outside, a bell pealed wildly.

When the lights came on again, Kay was massaging her wrist where the woman's strong fingers had left a painful bracelet mark. She was more puzzled than angry. She determined to ask the conductor if he would find her a different seat. But when he arrived to take her ticket, the request stuttered on her lips incoherently.

"Yes, miss?"

"Nothing," she said.

And he was gone.

The trio in the alcove regarded one another in mysterious silence till the woman said, "I've got something here I wanna show you, honey." She rummaged once more in the oilcloth satchel. "You won't be so snotty after you get a gander at this."

What she passed to Kay was a handbill, published on such yellowed, antique paper it looked as if it must be centuries old. In fragile, overly fancy lettering, it read:

## LAZARUS

### The Man Who Is Buried Alive

### A MIRACLE

#### SEE FOR YOURSELF

*Adults, 25¢—Children, 10¢*

"I always sing a hymn and read a sermon," said the woman. "It's awful sad: some folks cry, especially the old ones. And I've got me a perfectly elegant costume: a black veil and a black dress, oh, very becoming. *He* wears a gorgeous made-to-order bridegroom suit and a turban and lotsa talcum on his face. See, we try to make it as much like a bonafide funeral as we can. But shoot, nowadays you're likely to get just a buncha smart alecks come for laughs—so sometimes I'm real glad he's afflicted like he is accounta otherwise his feelings would be hurt, maybe."

Kay said, "You mean you're with a circus or a sideshow or something like that?"

"Nope, us alone," said the woman as she reclaimed the fallen hat. "We've been doing it for years and years—played every tank town in the South: Singasong, Mississippi—Spunky, Louisiana—Eureka, Alabama . . ."—these and other names rolled off her tongue musically, running together like rain. "After the hymn, after the sermon, we bury him."

"In a coffin?"

"Sort of. It's gorgeous, it's got silver stars painted all over the lid."

"I should think he would suffocate," said Kay, amazed. "How long does he stay buried?"

"All told it takes maybe an hour—course that's not counting the lure."

"The lure?"

"Uh huh. It's what we do the night before a show. See, we hunt up a store, any ol' store with a big glass window'll do, and get the owner to let *him* sit inside this window, and, well, hypnotize himself. Stays there all night stiff as a poker and people come and look: scares the livin' hell out of 'em. . . ." While she talked she jiggled a finger in her ear, withdrawing it occasionally to examine her find. "And one time this ol' bindlestiff Mississippi sheriff tried to . . ."

The tale that followed was baffling and pointless: Kay did not bother to listen. Nevertheless, what she had heard already inspired a reverie, a vague recapitulation of her uncle's funeral; an event which, to tell the truth, had not much affected her since she had scarcely known him. And so, while gazing abstractedly at the man, an image of her uncle's face, white next the pale silk casket pillow, appeared in her mind's eye. Observing their faces simultaneously, both the man's and uncle's, as it were, she thought she recognized an odd parallel: there was about the man's face the same kind of shocking, embalmed, secret stillness, as though, in a sense, he were truly an exhibit in a glass cage, complacent to be seen, uninterested in seeing.

"I'm sorry, what did you say?"

"I said: I sure wish they'd lend us the use of a regular cemetery. Like it is now we have to put on the show wherever we can . . . mostly in empty lots that are nine times outa ten smack up against some smelly fillin' station, which ain't exactly a big help. But like I say, we got us a swell act, the best. You oughta come see it if you get a chance."

"Oh, I should love to," Kay said, absently.

"Oh, I should love to," mimicked the woman. "Well, who ask you? Anybody ask you?" She hoisted up her skirt and enthusiastically blew her nose on the ragged hem of a petticoat. "Bu-leeve me, it's a hard way to turn a dollar. Know what our take was last month? Fifty-three bucks! Honey, you try living on that sometime." She sniffed and re-arranged her skirt with considerable primness. "Well, one of these days my sweet boy's sure enough going to die down there; and even then somebody'll say it was a gyp."

At this point the man took from his pocket what seemed to be a finely shellacked peach seed and balanced it on the palm of his hand. He looked across at Kay and, certain of her attention, opened his eye-lids wide and began to squeeze and caress the seed in an undefinably obscene manner.

Kay frowned. "What does he want?"

"He wants you to buy it?"

"But what is it?"

"A charm," said the woman. "A love charm."

Whoever was playing the harmonica stopped. Other sounds, less unique, became at once prominent: someone snoring, the gin bottle seesaw rolling, voices in sleepy argument, the train wheels' distant hum.

"Where could get you love cheaper, honey?"

"It's nice. I mean it's cute . . ." Kay said, stalling for time. The man rubbed and polished the seed on his trouser leg. His head was lowered at a supplicating, mournful angle, and presently he stuck the seed between his teeth and bit it, as if it were a suspicious piece of silver. "Charms always bring me bad luck. And besides . . . please, can't you make him stop acting that way?"

"Don't look so scared," said the woman, more flat-voiced than ever. "He ain't gonna hurt you."

"Make him stop, damn it!"

"What can I do?" asked the woman, shrugging her shoulders. "You're the one that's got money. You're rich. All he wants is a dollar, one dollar."

Kay tucked her purse under her arm. "I have just enough to get back to school," she lied, quickly rising and stepping out into the aisle. She stood there a moment, expecting trouble. But nothing happened.

The woman, with rather deliberate indifference, heaved a sigh and closed her eyes; gradually the man subsided and stuck the charm back in his pocket. Then his hand crawled across the seat to join the woman's in a lax embrace.

Kay shut the door and moved to the front of the observation platform. It was bitterly cold in the open air, and she had left her raincoat in the alcove. She loosened her scarf and draped it over her head.

Although she had never made this trip before, the train was traveling through an area strangely familiar: tall trees, misty, painted pale by malicious moonshine, towered steep on either side without a break or clearing. Above, the sky was a stark, unexplorable blue thronged with stars that faded here and there. She could see streamers of smoke trailing from the train's engine like long clouds of ectoplasm. In one corner of the platform a red kerosene lantern cast a colorful shadow.

She found a cigarette and tried to light it: the wind snuffed match after match till only one was left. She walked to the corner where the lantern burned and cupped her hands to protect the last match: the flame caught, sputtered, died. Angrily she tossed away the cigarette and empty folder; all the tension in her tightened to an exasperating pitch and she slammed the wall with her fist and began to whimper softly, like an irritable child.

The intense cold made her head ache, and she longed to go back inside the warm coach and fall asleep. But she couldn't, at least not yet; and there was no sense in wondering why, for she knew the answer very well. Aloud, partly to keep her teeth from chattering and partly because she needed the reassurance of her own voice, she said: "We're in Alabama now, I think, and tomorrow we'll be in Atlanta and I'm nineteen and I'll be twenty in August and I'm a sophomore. . . ." She glanced around at the darkness, hoping to see a sign of dawn, and finding the same endless wall of trees, the same frosty moon. "I hate him, he's horrible and I hate him. . . ." She stopped, ashamed of her foolishness and too tired to evade the truth: she was afraid.

Suddenly she felt an eerie compulsion to kneel down and touch the lantern. Its graceful glass funnel was warm, and the red glow seeped through her hands, making them luminous. The heat thawed her fingers and tingled along her arms.

She was so preoccupied she did not hear the door open. The train wheels roaring clickety-clack-clackety-click hushed the sound of the man's footsteps.

It was a subtle zero sensation that warned her finally, but some seconds passed before she dared look behind.

He was standing there with a mute detachment, his head tilted, his arms dangling at his sides. Staring up into his harmless, vapid face, flushed brilliant by the lantern light, Kay knew of what she was afraid: it was a memory, a childish memory of terrors that once, long ago, had hovered above her like haunted limbs on a tree of night. Aunts, cooks, strangers—each eager to spin a tale or teach a rhyme of spooks and death, omens, spirits, demons. And always there had been the unfailing threat of the wizard man: stay close to the house, child, else a wizard man'll snatch and eat you alive! He lived everywhere, the wizard man, and everywhere was danger. At night, in bed, hear him tapping at the window? Listen!

Holding onto the railing, she inched upward till she was standing erect. The man nodded and waved his hand toward the door. Kay took a deep breath and stepped forward. Together they went inside.

The air in the coach was numb with sleep: a solitary light now illuminated the car, creating a kind of artificial dusk. There was no motion but the train's sluggish sway, and the stealthy rattle of discarded newspapers.

The woman alone was wide awake. You could see she was greatly excited: she fidgeted with her curls and celluloid cherries, and her plump little legs, crossed at the ankles, swung agitatedly back and forth. She paid no attention when Kay sat down. The man settled in the seat with one leg tucked beneath him and his arms folded across his chest.

In an effort to be casual, Kay picked up a magazine. She realized the man was watching her, not removing his gaze an instant: she knew this though she was afraid to confirm it, and she wanted to cry out and waken everyone in the coach. But suppose they did not hear? What if they were not really *asleep?* Tears started in her eyes, magnifying and distorting the print on a page till it became a hazy blur. She shut the magazine with fierce abruptness and looked at the woman.

"I'll buy it," she said. "The charm, I mean. I'll buy it, if that's all—just all you want."

The woman made no response. She smiled apathetically as she turned toward the man.

As Kay watched, the man's face seemed to change form and recede before her like a moon-shaped rock sliding downward under a surface of water. A warm laziness relaxed her. She was dimly conscious of it when the woman took away her purse, and when she gently pulled the raincoat like a shroud above her head.

## Study Aids: Hawthorne

1. What kind of person is Robin and what general type does he represent? Where has he come from, what is he seeking, how does he hope to get it? What are the things he thinks he can count on? Does he find what he expects to find?

2. The characteristics of the town and of the encounters Robin has with the townspeople suggest what about the symbolic nature of his journey and search?

3. What does the man with the "parti-colored face" of red and black represent in the process of Robin's discovery? What is Robin learning?

4. What does Robin's kinsman, Major Molineux, represent? Why is the particular nature of his fate central in the process of Robin's discovery?

5. How does Robin react to his discovery? Why does he emit a wild "shout of laughter"? What is his final position?

## Study Aids: Capote

1. What type of person is Kay? How do the characteristics of her way of life and her way of responding to the death and funeral of her uncle help to define her?
2. The details of the setting of the railroad car provide what kind of context for the discovery Kay makes? What aspects of life do they suggest?
3. Why is the face of the man opposite her related to the face of her dead uncle and the wizard man? What is the significance of the man's particular carnival act, his deaf muteness, his face without "real expression"?
4. What does Kay discover as a result of her encounter with the man and the woman?
5. What is her response to this discovery? Why is the phrase "like a shroud" used in the last sentence?

# THE CHRYSANTHEMUMS
## *John Steinbeck*

The high grey-flannel fog of winter closed off the Salinas Valley from the sky and from all the rest of the world. On every side it sat like a lid on the mountains and made of the great valley a closed pot. On the broad, level land floor the gang plows bit deep and left the black earth shining like metal where the shares had cut. On the foothill ranches across the Salinas River, the yellow stubble fields seemed to be bathed in pale cold sunshine, but there was no sunshine in the valley now in December. The thick willow scrub along the river flamed with sharp and positive yellow leaves.

It was a time of quiet and of waiting. The air was cold and tender. A light wind blew up from the southwest so that the farmers were mildly hopeful of a good rain before long; but fog and rain do not go together.

Across the river, on Henry Allen's foothill ranch there was little work to be done, for the hay was cut and stored and the orchards were plowed up to receive the rain deeply when it should come. The cattle on the higher slopes were becoming shaggy and rough-coated.

Elisa Allen, working in her flower garden, looked down across the yard and saw Henry, her husband, talking to two men in business suits. The three of them stood by the tractor shed, each man with one foot on the side of the little Fordson. They smoked cigarettes and studied the machine as they talked.

Elisa watched them for a moment and then went back to her work. She was thirty-five. Her face was lean and strong and her eyes were as clear as water. Her figure looked blocked and heavy in her gardening costume, a man's black hat pulled low down over her eyes, clodhopper shoes, a figured print dress almost completely covered by a big corduroy apron with four big pockets to hold the snips, the trowel and scratcher, the seeds and the knife she worked with. She wore heavy leather gloves to protect her hands while she worked.

She was cutting down the old year's chrysanthemum stalks with a pair of short and powerful scissors. She looked down toward the men by the tractor shed now and then. Her face was eager and mature and handsome; even her work with the scissors was over-eager, over-powerful. The chrysanthemum stems seemed too small and easy for her energy.

She brushed a cloud of hair out of her eyes with the back of her glove, and left a smudge of earth on the cheek in doing it. Behind her stood the neat white farm house with red geraniums close-banked around it as high as the windows. It was a hard-swept looking little house, with hard-polished windows, and a clean mud-mat on the front steps.

Elisa cast another glance toward the tractor shed. The strangers were getting into their Ford coupe. She took off a glove and put her strong fingers down into the forest of new green chrysanthemum sprouts that were growing around the old roots. She spread the leaves and looked down among the close-growing stems. No aphids were there, no sowbugs or snails or cutworms. Her terrier fingers destroyed such pests before they could get started.

Elisa started at the sound of her husband's voice. He had come near quietly, and he leaned over the wire fence that protected her flower garden from cattle and dogs and chickens.

"At it again," he said. "You've got a strong new crop coming."

Elisa straightened her back and pulled on the gardening glove again. "Yes. They'll be strong this coming year." In her tone and on her face there was a little smugness.

"You've got a gift with things," Henry observed. "Some of those yellow chrysanthemums you had this year were ten inches across. I wish you'd work out in the orchard and raise some apples that big."

Her eyes sharpened. "Maybe I could do it, too. I've a gift with things, all right. My mother had it. She could stick anything in the ground and make it grow. She said it was having planters' hands that knew how to do it."

"Well, it sure works with flowers," he said.

"Henry, who were those men you were talking to?"

"Why, sure, that's what I came to tell you. They were from the Western Meat Company. I sold those thirty head of three-year-old steers. Got nearly my own price, too."

"Good," she said. "Good for you."

"And I thought," he continued, "I thought how it's Saturday afternoon, and we might go to Salinas for dinner at a restaurant, and then to a picture show—to celebrate, you see."

"Good," she repeated. "Oh, yes. That will be good."

Henry put on his joking tone. "There's fights tonight. How'd you like to go to the fights?"

"Oh, no," she said breathlessly. "No, I wouldn't like fights."

"Just fooling, Elisa. We'll go to a movie. Let's see. It's two now. I'm going to take Scotty and bring down those steers from the hill. It'll take us maybe two hours. We'll go in town about five and have dinner at the Cominos Hotel. Like that?"

"Of course I'll like it. It's good to eat away from home."

"All right, then. I'll go get up a couple of horses."

She said, "I'll have plenty of time to transplant some of these sets, I guess."

She heard her husband calling Scotty down by the barn. And a little later she saw the two men ride up the pale yellow hillside in search of the steers.

There was a little square sandy bed kept for rooting the chrysanthemums. With her trowel she turned the soil over and over, and smoothed it and patted it firm. Then she dug ten parallel trenches to receive the sets. Back at the chrysanthemum bed she pulled out the little crisp shoots, trimmed off the leaves of each one with her scissors and laid it on a small orderly pile.

A squeak of wheels and plod of hoofs came from the road. Elisa looked up. The country road ran along the dense bank of willows and cottonwoods that bordered the river, and up this road came a curious vehicle, curiously drawn. It was an old spring-wagon, with a round canvas top on it like the cover of a prairie schooner. It was drawn by an old bay horse and a little grey-and-white burro. A big stubble-bearded man sat between the cover flaps and drove the crawling team. Underneath the wagon, between the hind wheels, a lean and rangy mongrel dog walked sedately. Words were painted on the canvas in clumsy, crooked letters. "Pots, pans, knives, sisors, lawn mores. Fixed." Two rows of articles and the triumphantly definitive "Fixed" below. The black paint had run down in little sharp points beneath each letter.

Elisa, squatting on the ground, watched to see the crazy, loose-jointed wagon pass by. But it didn't pass. It turned into the farm road in front of her house, crooked old wheels skirling and squeaking. The rangy dog darted from between the wheels and ran ahead. Instantly the two ranch shepherds flew out at him. Then all three stopped, and with stiff and quivering tails, with taut straight legs, with ambassadorial dignity, they slowly circled, sniffing daintily. The caravan pulled up to Elisa's wire fence and stopped. Now the newcomer dog, feeling outnumbered, lowered his tail and retired under the wagon with raised hackles and bared teeth.

The man on the wagon seat called out. "That's a bad dog in a fight when he gets started."

Elisa laughed. "I see he is. How soon does he generally get started?"

The man caught up her laughter and echoed it heartily. "Sometimes not for weeks and weeks," he said. He climbed stiffly down, over the wheel. The horse and the donkey drooped like unwatered flowers.

Elisa saw that he was a very big man. Although his hair and beard were greying, he did not look old. His worn black suit was wrinkled and spotted with grease. The laughter had disappeared from his face and eyes the moment his laughing voice ceased. His eyes were dark and they were full of the brooding that gets in the eyes of teamsters and of sailors. The calloused hands he rested on the wire fence were cracked, and every crack was a black line. He took off his battered hat.

"I'm off my general road, ma'am," he said. "Does this dirt road cut over across the river to the Los Angeles highway?"

Elisa stood up and shoved the thick scissors in her apron pocket. "Well, yes, it does, but it winds around and then fords the river. I don't think your team could pull through the sand."

He replied with some asperity, "It might surprise you what them beasts can pull through."

"When they get started?" she asked.

He smiled for a second. "Yes. When they get started."

"Well," said Elisa, "I think you'll save time if you go back to the Salinas road and pick up the highway there."

He drew a big finger down the chicken wire and made it sing. "I ain't in any hurry, ma'am. I go from Seattle to San Diego and back every year. Takes all my time. About six months each way. I aim to follow nice weather."

Elisa took off her gloves and stuffed them in the apron pocket with the scissors. She touched the under edge of her man's hat, searching for fugitive hairs. "That sounds like a nice kind of a way to live," she said.

He leaned confidentially over the fence. "Maybe you noticed the writing on my wagon. I mend pots and sharpen knives and scissors. You got any of them things to do?"

"Oh, no," she said quickly. "Nothing like that." Her eyes hardened with resistance.

"Scissors is the worst thing," he explained. "Most people just ruin scissors trying to sharpen 'em, but I know how. I got a special tool. It's a little bobbit kind of thing, and patented. But it sure does the trick."

"No. My scissors are all sharp."

"All right, then. Take a pot," he continued earnestly, "a bent pot, or a pot with a hole. I can make it like new so you don't have to buy no new ones. That's a saving for you."

"No," she said shortly. "I tell you I have nothing like that for you to do."

His face fell to an exaggerated sadness. His voice took on a whining undertone. "I ain't had a thing to do today. Maybe I won't have no supper tonight. You see I'm off my regular road. I know folks on the highway clear from Seattle to San Diego. They save their things for me to sharpen up because they know I do it so good and save them money."

"I'm sorry," Elisa said irritably. "I haven't anything for you to do."

His eyes left her face and fell to searching the ground. They roamed about until they came to the chrysanthemum bed where she had been working. "What's them plants, ma'am?"

The irritation and resistance melted from Elisa's face. "Oh, those are chrysanthemums, giant whites and yellows. I raise them every year, bigger than anybody around here."

"Kind of a long-stemmed flower? Looks like a quick puff of colored smoke?" he asked.

"That's it. What a nice way to describe them."

"They smell kind of nasty till you get used to them," he said.

"It's a good bitter smell," she retorted, "not nasty at all."

He changed his tone quickly. "I like the smell myself."

"I had ten-inch blooms this year," she said.

The man leaned farther over the fence. "Look. I know a lady down the road a piece, has got the nicest garden you ever seen. Got nearly every kind of flower but no chrysanthemums. Last time I was mending a copper-bottom washtub for her (that's a hard job but I do it good), she said to me, 'If you ever run acrost some nice chrysanthemums I wish you'd try to get me a few seeds.' That's what she told me."

Elisa's eyes grew alert and eager. "She couldn't have known much about chrysanthemums. You can raise them from seed, but it's much easier to root the little sprouts you see there."

"Oh," he said. "I s'pose I can't take none to her, then."

"Why yes you can," Elisa cried. "I can put some in damp sand, and you can carry them right along with you. They'll take root in the pot if you keep them damp. And then she can transplant them."

"She'd sure like to have some, ma'am. You say they're nice ones?"

"Beautiful," she said. "Oh, beautiful." Her eyes shone. She tore off the battered hat and shook out her dark pretty hair. "I'll put them in a flower pot, and you can take them right with you. Come into the yard."

While the man came through the picket gate Elisa ran excitedly along the geranium-bordered path to the back of the house. And she returned carrying a big red flower pot. The gloves were forgotten now. She kneeled on the ground by the starting bed and dug up the sandy soil with her fingers and scooped it into the bright new flower pot. Then she picked up the little pile of shoots she had prepared. With her strong fingers she pressed them into the sand and tamped around them with her knuckles. The man stood over her. "I'll tell you what to do," she said. "You remember so you can tell the lady."

"Yes, I'll try to remember."

"Well, look. These will take root in about a month. Then she must set them out, about a foot apart in good rich earth like this, see?" She lifted a handful of dark soil for him to look at. "They'll grow fast and tall. Now remember this. In July tell her to cut them down, about eight inches from the ground."

"Before they bloom?" he asked.

"Yes, before they bloom." Her face was tight with eagerness. "They'll grow right up again. About the last of September the buds will start."

She stopped and seemed perplexed. "It's the budding that takes the most care," she said hesitantly. "I don't know how to tell you." She looked deep into his eyes, searchingly. Her mouth opened a little, and she seemed to be listening. "I'll try to tell you," she said. "Did you ever hear of planting hands?"

"Can't say I have, ma'am."

"Well, I can only tell you what it feels like. It's when you're picking off the buds you don't want. Everything goes right down into your fingertips. You watch your fingers work. They do it themselves. You can feel how it is. They pick and pick the buds. They never make a mistake. They're with the plant. Do you see? Your fingers and the plant. You can feel that, right up your arm. They know. They never make a mistake. You can feel it. When you're like that you can't do anything wrong. Do you see that? Can you understand that?"

She was kneeling on the ground looking up at him. Her breast swelled passionately.

The man's eyes narrowed. He looked away self-consciously. "Maybe I know," he said. "Sometimes in the night in the wagon there——"

Elisa's voice grew husky. She broke in on him. "I've never lived as you do, but I know what you mean. When the night is dark—why, the stars are sharp-pointed, and there's quiet. Why, you rise up and up! Every pointed star gets driven into your body. It's like that. Hot and sharp and—lovely."

Kneeling there, her hand went out toward his legs in the greasy black trousers. Her hesitant fingers almost touched the cloth. Then her hand dropped to the ground. She crouched low like a fawning dog.

He said, "It's nice, just like you say. Only when you don't have no dinner, it ain't."

She stood up then, very straight, and her face was ashamed. She held the flower pot out to him and placed it gently in his arms. "Here. Put it in your wagon, on the seat, where you can watch it. Maybe I can find something for you to do."

At the back of the house she dug in the can pile and found two old and battered aluminum saucepans. She carried them back and gave them to him. "Here, maybe you can fix these."

His manner changed. He became professional. "Good as new I can fix them." At the back of his wagon he set a little anvil, and out of an oily tool box dug a small machine hammer. Elisa came through the gate to watch him while he pounded out the dents in the kettles. His mouth grew sure and knowing. At a difficult part of the work he sucked his under-lip.

"You sleep right in the wagon?" Elisa asked.

"Right in the wagon, ma'am. Rain or shine I'm dry as a cow in there."

"It must be nice," she said. "It must be very nice. I wish women could do such things."

"It ain't the right kind of a life for a woman."

Her upper lip raised a little, showing her teeth. "How do you know? How can you tell?" she said.

"I don't know ma'am," he protested. "Of course I don't know. Now here's your kettles, done. You don't have to buy no new ones."

"How much?"

"Oh, fifty cents'll do. I keep my prices down and my work good. That's why I have all them satisfied customers up and down the highway."

Elisa brought him a fifty-cent piece from the house and dropped it in his hand. "You might be surprised to have a rival some time. I can sharpen scissors, too. And I can beat the dents out of little pots. I could show you what a woman might do."

He put his hammer back in the oily box and shoved the little anvil out of sight. "It would be a lonely life for a woman, ma'am, and a scarey life, too, with animals creeping under the wagon all night." He climbed over the single-tree, steadying himself with a hand on the burro's white rump. He settled himself in the seat, picked up the lines. "Thank you kindly, ma'am," he said. "I'll do like you told me; I'll go back and catch the Salinas road."

"Mind," she called, "if you're long in getting there, keep the sand damp."

"Sand, ma'am? . . . Sand? Oh, sure. You mean round the chrysanthemums. Sure I will." He clucked his tongue. The beasts leaned luxuriously into their collars. The mongrel dog took his place between the back wheels. The wagon turned and crawled out the entrance road and back the way it had come, along the river.

Elisa stood in front of her wire fence watching the slow progress of the caravan. Her shoulders were straight, her head thrown back, her eyes half-closed, so that the scene came vaguely into them. Her lips moved silently, forming the words "Good-bye—good-bye." Then she whispered, "That's a bright direction. There's a glowing there." The sound of her whisper startled her. She shook herself free and looked about to see whether anyone had been listening. Only the dogs had heard. They lifted their heads toward her from their sleeping in the dust, and then stretched out their chins and settled asleep again. Elisa turned and ran hurriedly into the house.

In the kitchen she reached behind the stove and felt the water tank. It was full of hot water from the noonday cooking. In the bathroom she tore off her soiled clothes and flung them into the corner. And then she scrubbed herself with a little block of pumice, legs and thighs, loins and chest and arms, until her skin was scratched and red. When she had dried herself she stood in front of a mirror in her bedroom and looked at her body. She tightened her stomach and threw out her chest. She turned and looked over her shoulder at her back.

After a while she began to dress, slowly. She put on her newest under-clothing and her nicest stockings and the dress which was the symbol of her prettiness. She worked carefully on her hair, pencilled her eyebrows and rouged her lips.

Before she was finished she heard the little thunder of hoofs and the shouts of Henry and his helper as they drove the red steers into the corral. She heard the gate bang shut and set herself for Henry's arrival.

His step sounded on the porch. He entered the house calling "Elisa, where are you?"

"In my room, dressing. I'm not ready. There's hot water for your bath. Hurry up. It's getting late."

When she heard him splashing in the tub, Elisa laid his dark suit on the bed, and shirt and socks and tie beside it. She stood his polished shoes on the floor beside the bed. Then she went to the porch and sat primly and stiffly down. She looked toward the river road where the willow-line was still yellow with frosted leaves so that under the high grey fog they seemed a thin band of sunshine. This was the only color in the grey afternoon. She sat unmoving for a long time. Her eyes blinked rarely.

Henry came banging out of the door, shoving his tie inside his vest as he came. Elisa stiffened and her face grew tight. Henry stopped short and looked at her. "Why—why, Elisa. You look so nice!"

"Nice? You think I look nice? What do you mean by 'nice?' "

Henry blundered on. "I don't know. I mean you look different, strong and happy."

"I am strong? Yes, strong. What do you mean 'strong?' "

He looked bewildered. "You're playing some kind of a game," he said helplessly. "It's a kind of a play. You look strong enough to break a calf over your knee, happy enough to eat it like watermelon."

For a second she lost her rigidity. "Henry! Don't talk like that. You didn't know what you said." She grew complete again. "I'm strong," she boasted. "I never knew before how strong."

Henry looked down toward the tractor shed, and when he brought his eyes back to her, they were his own again. "I'll get out the car. You can put on your coat while I'm starting."

Elisa went into the house. She heard him drive to the gate and idle down his motor, and then she took a long time to put on her hat. She pulled it here and pressed it there. When Henry turned the motor off she slipped into her coat and went out.

The little roadster bounced along on the dirt road by the river, raising the birds and driving the rabbits into the brush. Two cranes flapped heavily over the willow-line and dropped into the river-bed.

Far ahead on the road Elisa saw a dark speck. She knew.

She tried not to look as they passed it, but her eyes would not obey. She whispered to herself sadly. "He might have thrown them off the road. That wouldn't have been much trouble, not very much. But he kept the pot," she explained. "He had to keep the pot. That's why he couldn't get them off the road."

The roadster turned a bend and she saw the caravan ahead. She swung full around toward her husband so she could not see the little covered wagon and the mismatched team as the car passed them.

In a moment it was over. The thing was done. She did not look back. She said loudly, to be heard above the motor, "It will be good, tonight, a good dinner."

"Now you're changed again," Henry complained. He took one hand from the wheel and patted her knee. "I ought to take you in to dinner oftener. It would be good for both of us. We get so heavy out on the ranch."

"Henry," she asked, "could we have wine at dinner?"

"Sure we could. Say! That will be fine."

She was silent for a little while; then she said, "Henry, at those prize fights, do the men hurt each other very much?"

"Sometimes a little, not often. Why?"

"Well, I've read how they break noses, and blood runs down their chests. I've read how the fighting gloves get heavy and soggy with blood."

He looked around at her. "What's the matter, Elisa? I didn't know you read things like that." He brought the car to a stop, then turned to the right over the Salinas River bridge.

"Do any women ever go to the fights?" she asked.

"Oh, sure, some. What's the matter, Elisa? Do you want to go? I don't think you'd like it, but I'll take you if you really want to go."

She relaxed limply in the seat. "Oh, no. No. I don't want to go. I'm sure I don't." Her face was turned away from him. "It will be enough if we can have wine. It will be plenty." She turned up her coat collar so he could not see that she was crying weakly—like an old woman.

# THE COUNTRY HUSBAND
*John Cheever*

To begin at the beginning, the airplane from Minneapolis in which Francis Weed was travelling East ran into heavy weather. The sky had been a hazy blue, with the clouds below the plane lying so close together that nothing could be seen of the earth. Then mist began to form outside the windows, and they flew into a white cloud of such density that it reflected the exhaust fires. The color of the cloud darkened to gray, and the plane began to rock. Francis had been in heavy weather before, but he had never been shaken up so much. The man in the seat beside him pulled a flask out of his pocket and took a drink. Francis smiled at his neighbor, but the man looked away; he wasn't sharing his painkiller with anyone. The plane had begun to drop and flounder wildly. A child was crying. The air in the cabin was overheated and stale, and Francis' left foot went to sleep. He read a little from a paper book that he had bought at the airport, but the violence of the storm divided his attention. It was black outside the ports. The exhaust fires blazed and shed sparks in the dark, and, inside, the shaded lights, the stuffiness, and the window curtains gave the cabin an atmosphere of intense and misplaced domesticity. Then the lights flickered and went out. "You know what I've always wanted to do?" the man beside Francis said suddenly. "I've always wanted to buy a farm in New Hampshire and raise beef cattle." The stewardess announced that they were going to make an emergency landing. All but the child saw in their minds the spreading wings of the Angel of Death. The pilot could be heard singing faintly, "I've got sixpence, jolly, jolly sixpence. I've got sixpence to last me all my life . . ." There was no other sound.

The loud groaning of the hydraulic valves swallowed up the pilot's song, and there was a shrieking high in the air, like automobile brakes, and the plane hit flat on its belly in a cornfield and shook them so violently that an old man up forward howled, "Me kidneys! Me kidneys!" The stewardess flung open the door, and someone opened an emergency door at the back, letting in the sweet noise of their continuing mortality—the idle splash and smell of a heavy rain. Anxious for their lives, they filed out of the doors and scattered over the cornfield in all directions, praying that the thread would hold. It did. Nothing happened. When it was clear that the plane would not burn or explode, the crew and the stewardess gathered the passengers together and led them to the shelter of a barn. They were not far from Philadelphia, and in a little while a string of taxis took them into the city. "It's just like the Marne," someone said, but there was surprisingly

little relaxation of that suspiciousness with which many Americans regard their fellow-travellers.

In Philadelphia, Francis Weed got a train to New York. At the end
of that journey, he crossed the city and caught, just as it was about to
pull out, the commuting train that he took five nights a week to his
home in Shady Hill.

He sat with Trace Bearden. "You know, I was in that plane that
just crashed outside Philadelphia," he said. "We came down in a
field . . ." He had travelled faster than the newspapers or the rain, and
the weather in New York was sunny and mild. It was a day in late
September, as fragrant and shapely as an apple. Trace listened to the
story, but how could he get excited? Francis had no powers that would
let him recreate a brush with death—particularly in the atmosphere
of a commuting train, journeying through a sunny countryside where
already, in the slum gardens, there were signs of harvest. Trace picked
up his newspaper, and Francis was left alone with his thoughts. He
said good night to Trace on the platform at Shady Hill and drove in
his second-hand Volkswagen up to the Blenhollow neighborhood,
where he lived.

The Weeds' Dutch Colonial house was larger than it appeared to be
from the driveway. The living room was spacious and divided like Gaul
into three parts. Around an ell to the left as one entered from the
vestibule was the long table, laid for six, with candles and a bowl of
fruit in the center. The sounds and smells that came from the open
kitchen door were appetizing, for Julia Weed was a good cook. The
largest part of the living room centered around a fireplace. On the
right were some bookshelves and a piano. The room was polished and
tranquil, and from the windows that opened to the west there was
some late-summer sunlight, brilliant and as clear as water. Nothing
here was neglected; nothing had not been burnished. It was not the
kind of household where, after prying open a stuck cigarette box, you
would find an old shirt button and a tarnished nickel. The hearth was
swept, the roses on the piano were reflected in the polish of the broad
top, and there was an album of Schubert waltzes on the rack. Louisa
Weed, a pretty girl of nine, was looking out the western windows. Her
younger brother Henry was standing beside her. Her still younger
brother, Toby, was studying the figures of some tonsured monks drinking beer on the polished brass of the wood box. Francis, taking off his
hat and putting down his paper, was not consciously pleased with the
scene; he was not that reflective. It was his element, his creation, and
he returned to it with that sense of lightness and strength with which
any creature returns to its home. "Hi, everybody," he said. "The plane
from Minneapolis . . ."

Nine times out of ten, Francis would be greeted with affection, but tonight the children are absorbed in their own antagonisms. Francis has not finished his sentence about the plane crash before Henry plants a kick in Louisa's behind. Louisa swings around, saying *"Damn you!"* Francis makes the mistake of scolding Louisa for bad language before he punishes Henry. Now Louisa turns on her father and accuses him of favoritism. Henry is always right; she is persecuted and lonely; her lot is hopeless. Francis turns to his son, but the boy has justification for the kick—she hit him first; she hit him on the ear, which is dangerous. Louisa agrees with this passionately. She hit him on the ear, and she *meant* to hit him on the ear, because he messed up her china collection. Henry says that this is a lie. Little Toby turns away from the wood box to throw in some evidence for Louisa. Henry claps his hand over little Toby's mouth. Francis separates the two boys but accidentally pushes Toby into the wood box. Toby begins to cry. Louisa is already crying. Just then, Julia Weed comes into that part of the room where the table is laid. She is a pretty, intelligent woman, and the white in her hair is premature. She does not seem to notice the fracas. "Hello, darling," she says serenely to Francis. "Wash your hands, everyone. Dinner is ready." She strikes a match and lights the six candles in this vale of tears.

This simple announcement, like the war cries of the Scottish chieftains, only refreshes the ferocity of the combatants. Louisa gives Henry a blow on the shoulder. Henry, although he seldom cries, has pitched nine innings and is tired. He bursts into tears. Little Toby discovers a splinter in his hand and begins to howl. Francis says loudly that he has been in a plane crash and that he is tired. Julia appears again, from the kitchen, and, still ignoring the chaos, asks Francis to go upstairs and tell Helen that everything is ready. Francis is happy to go; it is like getting back to headquarters company. He is planning to tell his oldest daughter about the airplane crash, but Helen is lying on her bed reading a *True Romance* magazine, and the first thing Francis does is to take the magazine from her hand and remind Helen that he has forbidden her to buy it. She did not buy it, Helen replies. It was given to her by her best friend, Bessie Black. Everybody reads *True Romance*. Bessie Black's father reads *True Romance*. There isn't a girl in Helen's class who doesn't read *True Romance*. Francis expresses his detestation of the magazine and then tells her that dinner's ready—although from the sounds downstairs it doesn't seem so. Helen follows him down the stairs. Julia has seated herself in the candlelight and spread a napkin over her lap. Neither Louia nor Henry has come to the table. Little Toby is still howling, lying face down on the floor. Francis speaks to him gently: "Daddy was in a plane crash this afternoon, Toby. Don't you want to hear about it?" Toby goes on crying. "If you don't come to the table now, Toby," Francis says, "I'll have to send you to bed without any supper." The little boy rises, gives him a cutting look, flies up the stairs to his bedroom, and slams the door.

"Oh dear," Julia says, and starts to go after him. Francis says that she will spoil him. Julia says that Toby is ten pounds underweight and has to be encouraged to eat. Winter is coming, and he will spend the cold months in bed unless he has his dinner. Julia goes upstairs. Francis sits down at the table with Helen. Helen is suffering from the dismal feeling of having read too intently on a fine day and she gives her father and the room a jaded look. She doesn't understand about the plane crash, because there wasn't a drop of rain in Shady Hill.

Julia returns with Toby, and they all sit down and are served. "Do I have to look at that big, fat slob?" Henry says, of Louisa. Everybody but Toby enters into this skirmish, and it rages up and down the table for five minutes. Toward the end, Henry puts his napkin over his head and, trying to eat that way, spills spinach all over his shirt. Francis asks Julia if the children couldn't have their dinner earlier. Julia's guns are loaded for this. She can't cook two dinners and lay two tables. She paints with lightning strokes that panorama of drudgery in which her youth, her beauty, and her wit have been lost. Francis says that he must be understood; he was nearly killed in an airplane crash, and he doesn't like to come home every night to a battlefield. Now Julia is deeply committed. Her voice trembles. He doesn't come home every night to a battlefield. The accusation is stupid and mean. Everything was tranquil until he arrived. She stops speaking, puts down her knife and fork, and looks into her plate as if it is a gulf. She begins to cry. "Poor Mummy!" Toby says, and when Julia gets up from the table, drying her tears with a napkin, Toby goes to her side. "Poor Mummy," he says. "Poor Mummy!" And they climb the stairs together. The other children drift away from the battlefield, and Francis goes into the back garden for a cigarette and some air.

It was a pleasant garden, with walks and flower beds and places to sit. The sunset had nearly burned out, but there was still plenty of light. Put into a thoughtful mood by the crash and the battle, Francis listened to the evening sounds of Shady Hill. "Varmints! Rascals!" old Mr. Nixon shouted to the squirrels in his bird-feeding station. "Avaunt and quit my sight!" A door slammed. Someone was playing tennis on the Babcocks' court; someone was cutting grass. Then Donald Goslin, who lived at the corner, began to play the "Moonlight Sonata." He did this nearly every night. He threw the tempo out the window and played it *rubato* from beginning to end, like an outpouring of tearful petulance, lonesomeness, and self-pity—of everything it was Beethoven's greatness not to know. The music rang up and down the street beneath the trees like an appeal for love, for tenderness, aimed at some lonely housemaid—some fresh-faced, homesick girl from Galway, looking at old snapshots in her third-floor room. "Here, Jupiter, here, Jupiter," Francis called to the Mercers' retriever. Jupiter crashed through the tomato vines with the remains of a felt hat in his mouth.

Jupiter was an anomaly. His retrieving instincts and his high spirits were out of place in Shady Hill. He was as black as coal, with a long, alert, intelligent, rakehell face. His eyes gleamed with mischief, and he held his head high. It was the fierce, heavily collared dog's head that appears in heraldry, in tapestry, and that used to appear on umbrella handles and walking sticks. Jupiter went where he pleased, ransacking wastebaskets, clotheslines, garbage pails, and shoe bags. He broke up garden parties and tennis matches, and got mixed up in the processional at Christ's Church on Sunday, barking at the men in red dresses. He crashed through old Mr. Nixon's rose garden two or three times a day, cutting a wide swath through the Condesa de Sastagos, and as soon as Donald Goslin lighted his barbecue fire on Thursday nights, Jupiter would get the scent. Nothing the Goslins did could drive him away. Sticks and stones and rude commands only moved him to the edge of the terrace, where he remained, with his gallant and heraldic muzzle, waiting for Donald Goslin to turn his back and reach for the salt. Then he would spring onto the terrace, lift the steak lightly off the fire, and run away with the Goslins' dinner. Jupiter's days were numbered. The Wrightsons' German gardener or the Farquarsons' cook would soon poison him. Even old Mr. Nixon might put some arsenic in the garbage that Jupiter loved. "Here, Jupiter, Jupiter!" Francis called, but the dog pranced off, shaking the hat in his white teeth. Looking in at the windows of his house, Francis saw that Julia had come down and was blowing out the candles.

Julia and Francis Weed went out a great deal. Julia was well liked and gregarious, and her love of parties sprang from a most natural dread of chaos and loneliness. She went through her morning mail with real anxiety, looking for invitations, and she usually found some, but she was insatiable, and if she had gone out seven nights a week, it would not have cured her of a reflective look—the look of someone who hears distant music—for she would suppose that there was a more brilliant party somewhere else. Francis limited her to two weeknight parties, putting a flexible interpretation on Friday, and rode through the weekend like a dory in a gale. The day after the airplane crash, the Weeds were to have dinner with the Farquarsons.

Francis got home late from town, and Julia got the sitter while he dressed, and then hurried him out of the house. The party was small and pleasant, and Francis settled down to enjoy himself. A new maid passed the drinks. He hair was dark, and her face was round and pale and seemed familiar to Francis. He had not developed his memory as a sentimental faculty. Wood smoke lilac, and other such perfumes did not stir him, and his memory was something like his appendix—a vestigial repository. It was not his limitation at all to be unable to escape the past; it was perhaps his limitation that he had escaped it so successfully. He might have seen the maid at other parties, he might have seen her taking a walk on Sunday afternoons, but in either case he would not be searching his memory now. Her face was, in a wonderful way, a moon face—Norman or Irish—but it was not beautiful enough to account for his feeling that he had seen her before, in circumstances that he ought to be able to remember. He asked Nellie Farquarson who she was. Nellie said that the maid had come through an agency, and that her home was Trenon, in Normandy—a small place with a church and a restaurant that Nellie had once visited. While Nellie talked on about her travels abroad, Francis realized where he had seen the woman before. It had been at the end of the war. He had left a replacement depot with some other men and taken a three-day pass in Trenon. On their second day, they had walked out to a crossroads to see the public chastisement of a young woman who had lived with the Germany commandant during the Occupation.

It was a cool morning in the fall. The sky was overcast, and poured down onto the dirt crossroads a very discouraging light. They were on high land and could see how like one another the shapes of the clouds and the hills were as they stretched off toward the sea. The prisoner arrived sitting on a three-legged stool in a farm cart. She stood by the cart while the mayor read the accusation and the sentence. Her head was bent and her face was set in that empty half smile behind which the whipped soul is suspended. When the mayor was finished, she undid her hair and let it fall across her back. A little man with a gray mustache cut off her hair with shears and dropped it on the ground. Then, with a bowl of soapy water and a straight razor, he shaved her skull clean. A woman approached and began to undo the fastenings of her clothes, but the prisoner pushed her aside and undressed herself. When she pulled her chemise over her head and threw it on the ground, she was naked. The woman jeered; the men were still. There was no change in the falseness or the plaintiveness of the prisoner's smile. The cold wind made her white skin rough and hardened the nipples of her breasts. The jeering ended gradually, put down by the recognition of their common humanity. One woman spat on her, but some inviolable grandeur in her nakedness lasted through the ordeal. When the crowd was quiet, she turned—she had begun to cry—and, with nothing on but a pair of worn black shoes and stockings, walked down the dirt road alone away from the village. The round white face had aged a little, but there was no question but that the maid who passed his cocktails and later served Francis his dinner was the woman who had been punished at the crossroads.

The war seemed now so distant and that world where the cost of partisanship had been death or torture so long ago. Francis had lost track of the men who had been with him in Vesey. He could not count on Julia's discretion. He could not tell anyone. And if he had told the story now, at the dinner table, it would have been a social as well as a human error. The people in the Farquarsons' living room seemed united in their tacit claim that there had been no past, no war—that there was no danger or trouble in the world. In the recorded history of human arrangements, this extraordinary meeting would have fallen into place, but the atmosphere of Shady Hill made the memory unseemly and impolite. The prisoner withdrew after passing the coffee, but the encounter left Francis feeling languid; it had opened his memory and his senses, and left them dilated. He and Julia drove home when the party ended, and Julia went into the house. Francis stayed in the car to take the sitter home.

Expecting to see Mrs. Henlein, the old lady who usually stayed with the children, he was surprised when a young girl opened the door and came out onto the lighted stoop. She stayed in the light to count her textbooks. She was frowning and beautiful. Now, the world is full of beautiful young girls, but Francis saw here the difference between beauty and perfection. All those endearing flaws, moles, birthmarks, and healed wounds were missing, and he experienced in his consciousness that moment when music breaks glass, and felt a pang of recognition as strange, deep, and wonderful as anything in his life. It hung from her frown, from an impalpable darkness in her face—a look that impressed him as a direct appeal for love. When she had counted her books, she came down the steps and opened the car door. In the light, he saw that her cheeks were wet. She got in and shut the door.

"You're new," Francis said.

"Yes. Mrs. Henlein is sick. I'm Anne Murchison."

"Did the children give you any trouble?"

"Oh, no, no." She turned and smiled at him unhappily in the dim dashboard light. Her light hair caught on the collar of her jacket, and she shook her head to set it loose.

"You've been crying."

"Yes."

"I hope it was nothing that happened in our house."

"No, no, it was nothing that happened in your house." Her voice was bleak. "It's no secret. Everybody in the village knows. Daddy's an alcoholic, and he just called me from some saloon and gave me a piece of his mind. He thinks I'm immoral. He called just before Mrs. Weed came back."

"I'm sorry."

"Oh, *Lord!*" She gasped and began to cry. She turned toward Francis, and he took her in his arms and let her cry on his shoulder. She shook in his embrace, and this movement accentuated his sense of the fineness of her flesh and bone. The layers of their clothing felt thin, and when her shuddering began to diminish, it was so much like a paroxysm of love that Francis lost his head and pulled her roughly against him. She drew away. "I live on Belleview Avenue," she said. "You go down Lansing Street to the railroad bridge."

"All right." He started the car.

"You turn left at that traffic light. . . . Now you turn right here and go straight on toward the tracks."

The road Francis took brought him out of his own neighborhood, across the tracks, and toward the river, to a street where the near-poor lived, in houses whose peaked gables and trimmings of wooden lace conveyed the purest feelings of pride and romance, although the houses themselves could not have offered much privacy or comfort, they were all so small. The street was dark, and, stirred by the grace and beauty of the troubled girl, he seemed, in turning in to it, to have come into the deepest part of some submerged memory. In the distance, he saw a porch light burning. It was the only one, and she said that the house with the light was where she lived. When he stopped the car, he could see beyond the porch light into a dimly-lighted hallway with an old-fashioned clothes tree. "Well, here we are," he said, conscious that a young man would have said something different.

She did not move her hands from the books, where they were folded, and she turned and faced him. There were tears of lust in his eyes. Determinedly—not sadly—he opened the door on his side and walked around to open hers. He took her free hand, letting his fingers in between hers, climbed at her side the two concrete steps, and went up a narrow walk through a front garden where dahlias, marigolds, and roses—things that had withstood the light frosts—still bloomed, and made a bittersweet smell in the night air. At the steps, she freed her hand and then turned and kissed him swiftly. Then she crossed the porch and shut the door. The porch light went out, then the light in the hall. A second later, a light went on upstairs at the side of the house, shining into a tree that was still covered with leaves. It took her only a few minutes to undress and get into bed, and then the house was dark.

Julia was asleep when Francis got home. He opened a second window and got into bed to shut his eyes on that night, but as soon as they were shut—as soon as he had dropped off to sleep—the girl entered his mind, moving with perfect freedom through its shut doors and filling chamber after chamber with her light, her perfume, and the music of her voice. He was crossing the Atlantic with her on the old Mauretania and, later, living with her in Paris. When he woke from this dream, he got up and smoked a cigarette at the open window. Getting back into bed, he cast around in his mind for something he desired to do that would injure no one, and he thought of skiing. Up through the dimness in his mind rose the image of a mountain deep in snow. It was late in the day. Wherever his eyes looked, he saw broad and heartening things. Over his shoulder, there was a snow-filled valley, rising into wooded hills where the trees dimmed the whiteness like a sparse coat of hair. The cold deadened all sound but the loud, iron clanking of the lift machinery. The light on the trails was blue, and it was harder than it had been a minute or two earlier to pick the turns, harder to judge—now that the snow was all deep blue—the crust, the ice, the bare spots, and the deep piles of dry powder. Down the mountain he swung, matching his speed against the contours of a slope that had been formed in the first ice age, seeking with ardor some simplicity of feeling and circumstance. Night fell then, and he drank a Martini with some old friend in a dirty country bar.

In the morning, Francis's snow-covered mountain was gone, and he was left with his vivid memories of Paris and the Mauretania. He had been bitten gravely. He washed his body, shaved his jaws, drank his coffee, and missed the seven-thirty-one. The train pulled out just as he brought his car to the station, and the longing he felt for the coaches as they drew stubbornly away from him reminded him of the humors of love. He waited for the eight-two, on what was now an empty platform. It was a clear morning; the morning seemed thrown like a gleaming bridge of light over his mixed affairs. His spirits were feverish and high. The image of the girl seemed to put him into a relationship to the world that was mysterious and enthralling. Cars were beginning to fill up the parking lot, and he noticed that those that had driven down from the high land above Shady Hill were white with hoarfrost. This first clear sign of autumn thrilled him. An express train—a night train from Buffalo or Albany—came down the tracks between the platforms, and he saw that the roofs of the foremost cars were covered with a skin of ice. Struck by the miraculous physicalness of everything, he smiled at the passengers in the dining car, who could be seen eating eggs and wiping their mouths with napkins as they travelled. The sleeping-car compartments, with their soiled bed linen, trailed through the fresh morning like a string of rooming-house windows. Then he saw an extraordinary thing: at one of the bedroom windows sat an unclothed woman of exceptional beauty, combing her golden hair. She passed like an apparition through Shady Hill, combing and combing her hair, and Francis followed her with his eyes until she was out of sight. Then old Mrs. Wrightson joined him on the platform and began to talk.

"Well, I guess you must be surprised to see me here the third morning in a row," she said, "but because of my window curtains I'm becoming a regular commuter. The curtains I bought on Monday I returned on Tuesday, and the curtains I bought Tuesday I'm returning today. On Monday, I got exactly what I wanted—it's a wool tapestry with roses and birds—but when I got them home, I found they were the wrong length. Well, I exchanged them yesterday, and when I got them home, I found they were still the wrong length. Now I'm praying to high Heaven that the decorator will have them in the right length, because you know my house, you *know* my living-room windows, and you can imagine what a problem they present. I don't know what to do with them."

"I know what to do with them," Francis said.

"What?"

"Paint them black on the inside, and shut up."

There was a gasp from Mrs. Wrightson, and Francis looked down at her to be sure that she knew he meant to be rude. She turned and walked away from him, so damaged in spirit that she limped. A wonderful feeling enveloped him, as if light were being shaken about him, and he thought again of Venus combing and combing her hair as she drifted through the Bronx. The realization of how many years had passed since he had enjoyed being deliberately impolite sobered him. Among his friends and neighbors, there were brilliant and gifted people—he saw that—but many of them, also, were bores and fools, and he had made the mistake of listening to them all with equal attention. He had confused a lack of discrimination with Christian love, and the confusion seemed general and destructive. He was grateful to the girl for this bracing sensation of independence. Birds were singing—cardinals and the last of the robins. The sky shone like enamel. Even the smell of ink from his morning paper honed his appetite for life, and the world that was spread out around him was plainly a paradise.

If Francis had believed in some hierarchy of love—in spirits armed with hunting bows, in the capriciousness of Venus and Eros—or even in magical potions, philtres, and stews, in scapulae and quarters of the moon, it might have explained his susceptibility and his feverish high spirits. The autumnal loves of middle age are well publicized, and he guessed that he was face to face with one of these, but there was not a trace of autumn in what he felt. He wanted to sport in the green woods, scratch where he itched, and drink from the same cup.

His secretary, Miss Rainery, was late that morning—she went to a psychiatrist three mornings a week—and when she came in, Francis wondered what advice a psychiatrist would have for him. But the girl promised to bring back into his life something like the sound of music. The realization that this music might lead him straight to a trial for statutory rape at the county courthouse collapsed his happiness. The photograph of his four children laughing into the camera on the beach at Gay Head reproached him. On the letterhead of his firm there was a drawing of the Laocoon, and the figure of the priest and his sons in the coils of the snake appeared to him to have the deepest meaning.

He had lunch with Pinky Trabert, who told him a couple of dirty stories. At a conversational level, the mores of his friends were robust and elastic, but he knew that the moral card house would come down on them all—on Julia and the children as well—if he got caught taking advantage of a babysitter. Looking back over the recent history of Shady Hill for some precedent, he found there was none. There was no turpitude; there had not been a divorce since he lived there; there had not even been a breath of scandal. Things seemed arranged with more propriety even than in the Kingdom of Heaven. After leaving Pinky, Francis went to a jeweller's and bought the girl a bracelet. How happy this clandestine purchase made him, how stuffy and comical the jeweller's clerks seemed, how sweet the woman who passed at his back smelled! On Fifth Avenue, passing Atlas with his shoulders bent under the weight of the world, Francis thought of the strenuousness of containing his physicalness within the patterns he had chosen.

He did not know when he would see the girl next. He had the bracelet in his inside pocket when he got home. Opening the door of his house, he found her in the hall. Her back was to him, and she turned when she heard the door close. Her smile was open and loving. Her perfection stunned him like a fine day—a day after a thunderstorm. He seized her and covered her lips with his, and she struggled but she did not have to struggle for long, because just then little Gertrude Flannery appeared from somewhere and said, "Oh, Mr. Weed . . ."

Gertrude was a stray. She had been born with a taste for exploration, and she did not have it in her to center her life with her affectionate parents. People who did not know the Flannerys concluded from Gertrude's behavior that she was the child of a bitterly divided family, where drunken quarrels were the rule. This was not true. The fact that little Gertrude's clothing was ragged and thin was her own triumph over her mother's struggle to dress her warmly and neatly. Garrulous, skinny, and unwashed, she drifted from house to house around the Blenhollow neighborhood, forming and breaking alliances based on an attachment to babies, animals, children her own age, adolescents, and sometimes adults. Opening your front door in the morning, you would find Gertrude sitting on your stoop. Going into the bathroom to shave, you would find Gertrude using the toilet. Looking into your son's crib, you would find it empty, and, looking further, you would find that Gertrude had pushed him in his baby carriage into the next village. She was helpful, pervasive, honest, hungry, and loyal. She never went home of her own choice. When the time to go arrived, she was indifferent to all its signs. "Go home, Gertrude," people could be heard saying in one house or another, night after night. "Go home, Gertrude." "It's time for you to go home now, Gertrude." "You had better go home and get your supper, Gertrude." "I told you to go home twenty minutes ago, Gertrude." "Your mother will be worrying about you, Gertrude." "Go home, Gertrude, go home."

There are times when the lines around the human eye seem like shelves of eroded stone and when the staring eye itself strikes us with such a wilderness of animal feeling that we are at a loss. The look Francis gave the little girl was ugly and queer, and it frightened her. He reached into his pocket—his hands were shaking—and took out a quarter. "Go home, Gertrude, go home, and don't tell anyone, Gertrude. Don't—" He choked and ran into the living room as Julia called down to him from upstairs to hurry and dress.

The thought that he would drive Anne Murchison home later that night ran like a golden thread through the events of the party that Francis and Julia went to, and he laughed uproariously at dull jokes, dried a tear when Mabel Mercer told him about the death of her kitten, and stretched, yawned, sighed, and grunted like any other man with a rendezvous at the back of his mind. The bracelet was in his pocket. As he sat talking, the smell of grass was in his nose, and he was wondering where he would park the car. Nobody lived in the old Parker mansion, and the driveway was used as a lovers' lane. Townsend Street was a dead end, and he could park there, beyond the last house. The old lane that used to connect Elm Street to the riverbanks was overgrown, but he had walked there with his children, and he could drive his car deep enough into the brushwoods to be concealed.

The Weeds were the last to leave the party, and their host and hostess spoke of their own married happiness while they all four stood in the hallway saying good night. "She's my girl," their host said, squeezing his wife. "She's my blue sky. After sixteen years, I still bite her shoulders. She makes me feel like Hannibal crossing the Alps."

The Weeds drove home in silence. Francis brought the car up the driveway and sat still, with the motor running. "You can put the car in the garage," Julia said as she got out. "I told the Murchison girl she could leave at eleven. Someone drove her home." She shut the door, and Francis sat in the dark. He would be spared nothing then, it seemed, that a fool was not spared: ravening lewdness, jealousy, this hurt to his feelings that put tears in his eyes, even scorn—for he could see clearly the image he now presented, his arms spread over the steering wheel and his head buried in them for love.

Francis had been a dedicated Boy Scout when he was young, and, remembering the precepts of his youth, he left his office early the next afternoon and played some round-robin squash, but, with his body toned up by exercise and a shower, he realized that he might better have stayed at his desk. It was a frosty night when he got home. The air smelled sharply of change. When he stepped into the house, he sensed an unusual stir. The children were in their best clothes, and when Julia came down, she was wearing a lavender dress and her diamond sunburst. She explained the stir: Mr. Hubber was coming at seven to take their photograph for the Christmas card. She had put out Francis' blue suit and a tie with some color in it, because the picture was going to be in color this year. Julia was lighthearted at the thought of being photographed for Christmas. It was the kind of ceremony she enjoyed.

Francis went upstairs to change his clothes. He was tired from the day's work and tired with longing, and sitting on the edge of the bed had the effect of deepening his weariness. He thought of Anne Murchison, and the physical need to express himself, instead of being restrained by the pink lamps on Julia's dressing table, engulfed him. He went to Julia's desk, took a piece of writing paper, and began to write on it. "Dear Anne, I love you, I love you, I love you . . ." No one would see the letter, and he used no restraint. He used phrases like "heavenly bliss," and "love nest." He salivated, sighed, and trembled. When Julia called him to come down, the abyss between his fantasy and the practical world opened so wide that he felt it affect the muscles of his heart.

Julia and the children were on the stoop, and the photographer and his assistant had set up a double battery of floodlights to show the family and the architectural beauty of the entrance to their house. People who had come home on a late train slowed their cars to see the Weeds being photographed for their Christmas card. A few waved and called to the family. It took half an hour of smiling and wetting their lips before Mr. Hubber was satisfied. The heat of the lights made an unfresh smell in the frosty air, and when they were turned off, they lingered on the retina of Francis' eyes.

Later that night, while Francis and Julia were drinking their coffee in the living room, the doorbell rang. Julia answered the door and let in Clayton Thomas. He had come to pay her for some theatre tickets that she had given his mother some time ago, and that Helen Thomas had scrupulously insisted on paying for, though Julia had asked her not to. Julia invited him in to have a cup of coffee. "I won't have any coffee," Clayton said, "but I will come in for a minute." He followed her into the living room, said good evening to Francis, and sat awkwardly in a chair.

Clayton's father had been killed in the war, and the young man's fatherlessness surrounded him like an element. This may have been conspicuous in Shady Hill because the Thomases were the only family that lacked a piece; all the other marriages were intact and productive. Clayton was in his second or third year of college, and he and his mother lived alone in a large house, which she hoped to sell. Clayton had once made some trouble. Years ago, he had stolen some money and run away; he had got to California before they caught up with him. He was tall and homely, wore horn-rimmed glasses, and spoke in a deep voice.

"When do you go back to college, Clayton?" Francis asked.

"I'm not going back," Clayton said. "Mother doesn't have the money, and there's no sense in all this pretense. I'm going to get a job, and if we sell the house, we'll take an apartment in New York."

"Won't you miss Shady Hill?" Julia asked.

"No," Clayton said. "I don't like it."

"Why not?" Francis asked.

"Well, there's a lot here I don't approve of," Clayton said gravely. "Things like the club dances. Last Saturday night, I looked in toward the end and saw Mr. Granner trying to put Mrs. Minot into the trophy case. They were both drunk. I disapprove of so much drinking."

"It was Saturday night," Francis said.

"And all the dovecotes are phony," Clayton said. "And the way people clutter up their lives. I've thought about it a lot, and what seems to me to be really wrong with Shady Hill is that it doesn't have any future. So much energy is spent in perpetuating the place—in keeping out undesirables, and so forth—that the only idea of the future anyone has is just more and more commuting trains and more parties. I don't think that's healthy. I think people ought to be able to dream big dreams about the future. I think people ought to be able to dream great dreams."

"It's too bad you couldn't continue with college," Julia said.

"I wanted to go to divinity school," Clayton said.

"What's your church?" Francis asked.

"Unitarian, Theosophist, Transcendentalist, Humanist," Clayton said.

"Wasn't Emerson a transcendentalist?" Julia asked.

"I mean the English transcendentalists," Clayton said. "All the American transcendentalists were goops."

"What kind of a job do you expect to get?" Francis asked.

"Well, I'd like to work for a publisher," Clayton said, "but everyone tells me there is nothing doing. But it's the kind of thing I'm interested in. I'm writing a long verse play about good and evil. Uncle Charlie might get me into a bank, and that would be good for me. I need the discipline. I have a long way to go in forming my character. I have some terrible habits. I talk too much. I think I ought to take vows of silence. I ought to try not to speak for a week, and discipline myself. I've thought of making a retreat at one of the Episcopalian monasteries, but I don't like Trinitarianism."

"Do you have any girl friends?" Francis asked.

"I'm engaged to be married," Clayton said. "Of course, I'm not old enough or rich enough to have my engagement observed or respected or anything, but I bought a simulated emerald for Anne Murchison with the money I made cutting lawns this summer. We're going to be married as soon as she finishes school."

Francis recoiled at the mention of the girl's name. Then a dingy light seemed to emanate from his spirit, showing everything—Julia, the boy, the chairs—in their true colorlessness. It was like a bitter turn of the weather.

"We're going to have a large family," Clayton said. "Her father's a terrible rummy, and I've had my hard times, and we want to have lots of children. Oh, she's wonderful, Mr. and Mrs. Weed, and we have so much in common. We like all the same things. We sent out the same Christmas card last year without planning it, and we both have an allergy to tomatoes, and our eyebrows grow together in the middle. Well, good night."

Julia went to the door with him. When she returned, Francis said that Clayton was lazy, irresponsible, affected, and smelly. Julia said that Francis seemed to be getting intolerant; the Thomas boy was young and should be given a chance. Julia had noticed other cases where Francis had been short-tempered. "Mrs. Wrightson has asked everyone in Shady Hill to her anniversary party but us," she said.

"I'm sorry, Julia."

"Do you know why they didn't ask us?"

"Why?"

"Because you insulted Mrs. Wrightson."

"Then you know about it?"

"June Masterson told me. She was standing behind you."

Julia walked in front of the sofa with a small step that expressed, Francis knew, a feeling of anger.

"I did insult Mrs. Wrightson, Julia, and I meant to. I've never liked her parties, and I'm glad she's dropped us."

"What about Helen?"

"How does Helen come into this?"

"Mrs. Wrightson's the one who decides who goes to the assemblies."

"You mean she can keep Helen from going to the dances?"

"Yes."

"I hadn't thought of that."

"Oh, I knew you hadn't thought of it," Julia cried, thrusting hilt-deep into this chink of his armor. "And it makes me furious to see this kind of stupid thoughtlessness wreck everyone's happiness."

"I don't think I've wrecked anyone's happiness."

"Mrs. Wrightson runs Shady Hill and has run it for the last forty years. I don't know what makes you think that in a community like this you can indulge every impulse you have to be insulting, vulgar, and offensive."

"I have very good manners," Francis said, trying to give the evening a turn toward the light.

"Damn you, Francis Weed!" Julia cried, and the spit of her words struck him in the face. "I've worked hard for the social position we enjoy in this place, and I won't stand by and see you wreck it! You must have understood when you settled here that you couldn't expect to live like a bear in a cave."

"I've got to express my likes and dislikes."

"You can conceal your dislikes. You don't have to meet everything head-on, like a child. Unless you're anxious to be a social leper. It's no accident that we get asked out a great deal. It's no accident that Helen has so many friends. How would you like to spend your Saturday nights at the movies? How would you like to spend your Sundays raking up dead leaves? How would you like it if your daughter spent the assembly nights sitting at her window, listening to the music from the club? How would you like it—" He did something then that was, after all, not so unaccountable, since her words seemed to raise up between them a wall so deadening that he gagged: He struck her full in the face. She staggered and then, a moment later, seemed composed. She went up the stairs to their room. She didn't slam the door. When Francis followed, a few minutes later, he found her packing a suitcase.

"Julia, I'm very sorry."

"It doesn't matter," she said. She was crying.

"Where do you think you're going?"

"I don't know. I just looked at a timetable. There's an eleven-sixteen into New York. I'll take that."

"You can't go, Julia."

"I can't stay. I know that."

"I'm sorry about Mrs. Wrightson, Julia, and I'm—"

"It doesn't matter about Mrs. Wrightson. That isn't the trouble."

"What is the trouble?"

"You don't love me."

"I do love you, Julia."

"No, you don't."

"Julia, I do love you, and I would like to be as we were—sweet and bawdy and dark—but now there are so many people."

"You hate me."

"I don't hate you, Julia."

"You have no idea of how much you hate me. I think it's subconscious. You don't realize the cruel things you've done."

"What cruel things, Julia?"

"The cruel acts your subconscious drives you to in order to express your hatred of me."

"What, Julia?"

"I've never complained."

"Tell me."

"You don't know what you're doing."

"Tell me."

"Your clothes."

"What do you mean?"

"I mean the way you leave your dirty clothes around in order to express your subconscious hatred of me."

"I don't understand."

"I mean your dirty socks and your dirty pajamas and your dirty underwear and your dirty shirts!" She rose from kneeling by the suitcase and faced him, her eyes blazing and her voice ringing with emotion. "I'm talking about the fact that you've never learned to hang up anything. You just leave your clothes all over the floor where they drop, in order to humiliate me. You do it on purpose!" She fell on the bed, sobbing.

"Julia, darling!" he said, but when she felt his hand on her shoulder she got up.

"Leave me alone," she said. "I have to go." She brushed past him to the closet and came back with a dress. "I'm not taking any of the things you've given me," she said. "I'm leaving my pearls and the fur jacket."

"Oh, Julia!" Her figure, so helpless in its self-deceptions, bent over the suitcase made him nearly sick with pity. She did not understand how desolate her life would be without him. She didn't understand the hours that working women have to keep. She didn't understand that most of her friendships existed within the framework of their marriage, and that without this she would find herself alone. She didn't understand about travel, about hotels, about money. "Julia, I can't let you go! What you don't understand, Julia, is that you've come to be dependent on me."

She tossed her head back and covered her face with her hands. "Did you say that *I* was dependent on *you?*" she asked. "Is that what you said? And who is it that tells you what time to get up in the morning and when to go to bed at night? Who is it that prepares your meals and picks up your dirty closet and invites your friends to dinner? If it weren't for me, your neckties would be greasy and your clothing would be full of moth holes. You were alone when I met you, Francis Weed, and you'll be alone when I leave. When Mother asked you for a list to send out invitations to our wedding, how many names did you have to give her? Fourteen!"

"Cleveland wasn't my home, Julia."

"And how many of your friends came to the church? Two!"

"Cleveland wasn't my home, Julia."

"Since I'm not taking the fur jacket," she said quietly, "you'd better put it back into storage. There's an insurance policy on the pearls that comes due in January. The name of the laundry and the maid's telephone number—all those things are in my desk. I hope you won't drink too much, Francis. I hope that nothing bad will happen to you. If you do get into serious trouble, you can call me."

"Oh, my darling, I can't let you go!" Francis said. "I can't let you go, Julia!" He took her in his arms.

"I guess I'd better stay and take care of you for a little while longer," she said.

Riding to work in the morning, Francis saw the girl walk down the aisle of the coach. He was surprised; he hadn't realized that the school she went to was in the city, but she was carrying books, she seemed to be going to school. His surprise delayed his reaction, but then he got up clumsily and stepped into the aisle. Several people had come between them, but he could see her ahead of him, waiting for someone to open the car door, and then, as the train swerved, putting out her hand to support herself as she crossed the platform into the next car. He followed her through that car and halfway through another before calling her name—"Anne! Anne!"—but she didn't turn. He followed her into still another car, and she sat down in an aisle seat. Coming up to her, all his feelings warm and bent in her direction, he put his hand on the back of her seat—even this touch warmed him—and, leaning down to speak to her, he saw that it was not Anne. It was an older woman wearing glasses. He went on deliberately into another car, his face red with embarrassment and the much deeper feeling of having his good sense challenged; for if he couldn't tell one person from another, what evidence was there that his life with Julia and the children had as much reality as his dreams of iniquity in Paris or the litter, the grass smell, and the cave-shaped trees in Lovers' Lane.

Late that afternoon, Julia called to remind Francis that they were going out for dinner. A few minutes later, Trace Bearden called. "Look, fellar," Trace said. "I'm calling for Mrs. Thomas. You know? Clayton, that boy of hers, doesn't seem able to get a job, and I wondered if you could help. If you'd call Charlie Bell—I know he's indebted to you—and say a good word for the kid, I think Charlie would—"

"Trace, I hate to say this," Francis said, "but I don't feel that I can do anything for that boy. The kid's worthless. I know it's a harsh thing to say, but it's a fact. Any kindness done for him would backfire in everybody's face. He's just a worthless kid, Trace, and there's nothing to be done about it. Even if we got him a job, he wouldn't be able to keep it for a week. I know that to be a fact. It's an awful thing, Trace, and I know it is, but instead of recommending that kid, I'd feel obliged to warn people against him—people who knew his father and would naturally want to step in and do something. I'd feel obliged to warn them. He's a thief . . ."

The moment this conversation was finished, Miss Rainey came in and stood by his desk. "I'm not going to be able to work for you any more, Mr. Weed," she said. "I can stay until the seventeenth if you need me, but I've been offered a whirlwind of a job, and I'd like to leave as soon as possible."

She went out, leaving him to face alone the wickedness of what he had done to the Thomas boy. His children in their photograph laughed and laughed, glazed with all the bright colors of summer, and he remembered that they had met a bagpiper on the beach that day and he had paid the piper a dollar to play them a battle song of the Black Watch. The girl would be at the house when he got home. He would spend another evening among his kind neighbors, picking and choosing dead-end streets, cart tracks, and the driveways of abandoned houses. There was nothing to mitigate his feeling—nothing that laughter or a game of softball with the children would change—and, thinking back over the plane crash, the Farquarsons' new maid, and Anne Murchison's difficulties with her drunken father, he wondered how he could have avoided arriving at just where he was. He was in trouble. He had been lost once in his life, coming back from a trout stream in the north woods, and he had now the same bleak realization that no amount of cheerfulness or hopefulness or valor or perseverance could help him find, in the gathering dark, the path that he'd lost. He smelled the forest. The feeling of bleakness was intolerable, and he saw clearly that he had reached the point where he would have to make a choice.

He could go to a psychiatrist, like Miss Rainey; he could go to church and confess his lusts; he could go to a Danish massage parlor in the West Seventies that had been recommended by a salesman; he could rape the girl or trust that he would somehow be prevented from doing this; or he could get drunk. It was his life, his boat, and, like every other man, he was made to be the father of thousands, and what harm could there by in a tryst that would make them both feel more kindly toward the world? This was the wrong train of thought, and he came back to the first, the psychiatrist. He had the telephone number of Miss Rainey's doctor, and he called and asked for an immediate appointment. He was insistent with the doctor's secretary—it was his manner in business—and when she said that the doctor's schedule was full for the next few weeks, Francis demanded an appointment that day and was told to come at five.

The psychiatrist's office was in a building that was used mostly by doctors and dentists, and the hallways were filled with the candy smell of mouthwash and memories of pain. Francis' character had been formed upon a series of private resolves—resolves about cleanliness, about going off the high diving board or repeating any other feat that challenged his courage, about punctuality, honesty, and virtue. To abdicate the perfect loneliness in which he had made his most vital decisions shattered his concept of character and left him now in a condition that felt like shock. He was stupefied. The scene for his *miserere mei Deus* was, like the waiting room of so many doctors' offices, a crude token gesture toward the sweets of domestic bliss: a place arranged with antiques, coffee tables, potted plants, and etchings of snow-covered bridges and geese in flight, although there were no children, no marriage bed, no stove, even, in this travesty of a house, where no one had ever spent the night and where the curtained windows looked straight onto a dark air shaft. Francis gave his name and address to a secretary and then saw, at the side of the room, a policeman moving toward him. "Hold it, hold it," the policeman said. "Don't move. Keep your hands where they are."

"I think it's all right, Officer," the secretary began. "I think it will be—"

"Let's make sure," the policeman said, and he began to slap Francis' clothes, looking for what—pistols, knives, an icepick? Finding nothing, he went off, and the secretary began a nervous apology: "When you called on the telephone, Mr. Weed, you seemed very excited, and one of the doctor's patients has been threatening his life, and we have to be careful. If you want to go in now?" Francis pushed open a door connected to an electrical chime, and in the doctor's lair sat down heavily, blew his nose into a handkerchief, searched in his pockets for cigarettes, for matches, for something, and said hoarsely, with tears in his eyes, "I'm in love, Dr. Herzog."

It is a week or ten days later in Shady Hill. The seven-fourteen has come and gone, and here and there dinner is finished and the dishes are in the dishwashing machine. The village hangs, morally and economically, from a thread but it hangs by its thread in the evening light. Donald Goslin has begun to worry the "Moonlight Sonata" again. *Marcato ma sempre pianissimo!* He seems to be wringing out a wet bath towel, but the housemaid does not heed him. She is writing a letter to Arthur Godfrey. In the cellar of his house, Francis Weed is building a coffee table. Dr. Herzog recommended woodwork as a therapy, and Francis finds some true consolation in the simple arithmetic involved and in the holy smell of new wood. Francis is happy. Upstairs, little Toby is crying, because he is tired. He puts off his cowboy hat, gloves, and fringed jacket, unbuckles the belt studded with gold and rubies, the silver bullets and holsters, slips off his suspenders, his checked shirt, and Levis, and sits on the edge of his bed to pull off his high boots. Leaving this equipment in a heap, he goes to the closet and takes his space suit off a nail. It is a struggle for him to get into the long tights, but he succeeds. He loops the magic cape over his shoulders and, climbing onto the footboard of his bed, he spreads his arms and flies the short distance to the floor, landing with a thump that is audible to everyone in the house but himself.

"Go home, Gertrude, go home," Mrs. Masterson says. "I told you to go home an hour ago, Gertrude. It's way past your suppertime, and your mother will be worried. Go home!" A door on the Babcocks' terrace flies open, and out comes Mrs. Babcock without any clothes on, pursued by her naked husband. (Their children are away at boarding school, and their terrace is screened by a hedge.) Over the terrace they go and in at the kitchen door, as passionate and handsome a nymph and satyr as you will find on any wall in Venice. Cutting the last of the roses in her garden, Julia hears old Mr. Nixon shouting at the squirrels in his bird-feeding station. "Rapscallions! Varmits! Avaunt and quit my sight!" A miserable cat wanders into the garden, sunk in spiritual and physical discomfort. Tied to its head is a small straw hat—a doll's hat—and it is securely buttoned into a doll's dress, from the skirts of which protrudes its long, hairy tail. As it walks, it shakes its feet, as if it had fallen into water.

"Here, pussy, pussy, pussy!" Julia calls.

"Here, pussy, here, poor pussy!" But the cat gives her a skeptical look and stumbles away in its skirts. The last to come is Jupiter. He prances through the tomato vines, holding in his generous mouth the remains of an evening slipper. Then it is dark; it is a night where kings in golden suits ride elephants over the mountains.

## Study Aids: Steinbeck

1. What is the pattern of Eliza's life, and what does her attitude toward it seem to be as the story opens? How are these conditions suggested and dramatized by the opening descriptions of the setting and of Eliza herself? What are the positive and negative aspects of our first glimpse of her?

2. What is it about the traveling man that produces a response in Eliza? What is her response? How is that response dramatized by the physical images in her outburst to the man and by the descriptions of her in relation to him?

3. Compare Eliza's actions and her attitude toward her body after the man leaves with the opening descriptions of her. What is suggested by this comparison?

4. What does the gift of the chrysanthemums mean to her? And the eventual treatment of that gift by the traveling man?

5. Eliza's possibilities for change, however, are not affected only by the traveling man's treatment of her gift. How do the specific details of the scene in which her husband returns to the house depict what is happening to these possibilities? At the close of the story, why does she talk about the fights?

## Study Aids: Cheever

1. Something about the pattern of his life ("the patterns he had chosen") is troubling Francis Weed. What statements and situations in the story help to define what this something consists of?

2. What events bring this dissatisfaction to the surface and impel him to break the pattern? Why these particular events? What are their characteristics and significance?

3. What does the sitter represent? What are the implications of her situation with her father, her age, her engagement to Clayton?
4. What causes Francis to realize he must make a choice? What is his choice? What is the author's attitude toward that choice? Why, for example, the do-it-yourself workshop, why the coffee table?
5. What is the significance of Jupiter, the dog, and especially the final description of him in the last paragraph?

# THE FACE WITHIN THE FACE
## *Mark Schorer*

"Don't!" Laura Newman said, too sharply for the occasion, and Robert, her husband, who had just begun to trace a light imaginary line along her smooth brown thigh, pulled his hand away and fell back on the sand. Laura did not move. In a white swimming suit, she lay stretched out on a white towel, as arranged and quiet as a statue, hair flowing back, eyes closed, lips a little parted, face and body gleaming, offering herself to the sun as supine marble figures on monuments coldly offer themselves to God.

On the sand beyond his father, staring out at the sea, sat David, their thirteen-year-old son, who looked over toward his mother speculatively now and asked, "Don't what?"

"She was talking to me," Robert said. He stretched out and, leaning on his elbow, looked gloomily down at his wife's ear—an object strange and perfect, as if wrought, like an artifact, by cautious, astonishing skill. He turned away, toward the boy. "Let's swim," he said.

Laura did not speak or move. *Burn, burn,* she was thinking, *burn, burn burn,* in the rhythm of the small, lapping waves that endlessly, warmly buffeted the yellow shore. The perfect, paradoxical, immaculate pleasure as the hot sun burns and burns on the skin! The accumulated and clinging irritations and frustrations and dismal intensities of four wet and cold winter months seemed to dry upon her and fall away like scales, and she could almost feel herself emerging, with this hot balm, new and absolutely pure, and in her mind she likened the images, from a forgotten school poem, of fire and ice.

She could hear, high above her or far out over the blue cove, the distant, whimpering cry of gulls—shrill whispers—and behind her closed lids she pictured them wheeling in silvery arcs against the cool blue of the sky. Nearer, travelling along the sand to her ear, she heard the swishing sound of feet as Robert and David went down to the water. Then she heard them splashing. Then she thought, *Puberty,* and at once, with the thought, she shuddered, and her warm skin was chilled, as if the sun had gone under a cloud and a cold wind abruptly blew.

"You should take him South with you if you can manage," Mr. Lowell, the headmaster, had written. "He is well along toward puberty now, you know, growing a little too fast, and he needs some sun, needs to be built up. He's not a rugged boy by nature. Of course, we would be glad to keep him here at the school during the spring holiday—he's a most likable and tractable lad, and I'm confident that the arrangements could be made—but in his own interest we all feel that you should consider taking him with you." And so on, and, of course, there had been no question but that the headmaster was right, only there had been the somewhat irritating question of revising their plans, of cutting their three weeks to a little less than two. Yet here they were, their sixth gorgeous day, and she expressed her gratitude to the sun in a luxurious arching of her back and stretching of her toes, until her body was taut with pleasure. Into this momentary intense delight, voices broke. She relaxed and slowly turned, and raised her head and shoulders with her elbows under her.

Robert and David were still in the water, Robert swimming briskly out, David standing still, water to his knees, a bony little figure in the forefront of the vast expanse of empty sea. Turning her head, she saw that other people had come and were settling themselves on the sand at a barely reasonable distance behind her—a man and woman and two girls and a boy.

Laura swore softly. On their first day, the Newmans had wandered away from the big stretch of beach in front of their hotel and had found this quiet cove, where the surf broke far out and where almost no one ever came. They had enjoyed the empty sea from the small empty beach fringed with barren dunes, where there was no intrusion of strident voices, no gross intimacy with other bodies. Then who were these people disposing themselves now on the sand just behind her, already shouting and calling and shrilling, the mother to her scattering children, the husband to the wife? Not, Laura thought, guests of the hotel.

She stared at them. The man wore droopy flowered trunks. He had a long, skinny white body, with a scrawny patch of black hair on his white chest, and black forearms and legs, and a narrow head with too much black hair above his ears, and the white scalp showing through the thin hair on top. The wife was short and round, with a round head and, again, too much black, untidy hair. The children were like their mother—short and round, with round heads and faces, the girls with fuzzy black pigtails, the boy with a black shock that stood up in ragged thrusts. The man was pulling towels from a basket and spreading them on the sand, and when the wife had seated herself on one, she reached into the basket and brought out a tube, and Laura watched her spread a thick layer of white salve over her nose, under her eyes, and on her cheekbones, so that she suddenly gave the fantastic impression of wearing a white domino that had been cut in half. Then Laura saw that something was wrong with her right arm; it seemed, somehow, crippled, the fingers that applied the ointment knotted in a queer way and the elbow not quite free. And when, suddenly, she shouted to her children, who had run down to the water, her face, too, or the right side of it, showed some similar defect—a partial paralysis, which made her seem to leer. When she stopped shouting, her face settled into what was apparently its perpetual expression—a horrid, rigid simper.

Laura shuddered with distaste, turned around and sat up, and determinedly faced the sea. Two things she passionately claimed as belonging to her life, and she wanted them in no less than large ways. They were privacy and self-possession. At this moment, in a small way, this family had snatched the second with the first. As she watched Robert helping David with his crawl in the quiet water of the cove, she wondered irritably how people such as these could disturb her composure, until, in a sudden misery of recollection, she knew that it was because of their disgusting domesticity; somehow they gave the impression of having brought their entire household onto the immaculate beach, spilled out on the sand the whole steamy clutter of their lives, so that Laura thought of a cantankerous parrot in a parlor cage, some potted ferns before stiff lace curtains, a kitchen sink full of greasy dishes, and soiled bed linen, gray.

Laura sat stiffly on the sand in the abrupt and heavy grip of a life long since dead—of a sordid beach town in New Jersey, of a cheap, flimsily built cottage, a girl lying at night with her head under her pillow to shut out the sounds that came through the walls from the bedroom next to hers, and the girl in the day, seeking out some lonely place on the beach where she could lie in the sun for hours, unmolested, to purge herself. The people behind her, by their presence alone, had destroyed her careful peace, and through closed teeth she swore in anger, because now the sun was helpless.

The woman was screaming at the boy, who had walked down to the water and was watching Robert and David. "Lou-ee! Lou-ee!" she shrilled, and then some word that came to Laura as "Ny-ah! Ny-ah!" —like an abstraction from all negatives. Laura glanced over her shoulder at the distorted mouth under the white mask, and the stiff arm gesticulating, and then, turning back, lowered her head into her cupped hands, so that she sat with her fingers pressed over her ears. Yet she could hear the father, calling more gently, "Lou-ee, come!" The boy stared at his parents and, at last, laggingly, came back to where they sat. Laura heard his grunt as he flung himself on the sand behind her, saying, "What's the fun? What'd we come for?" The mother said, "Just wait," and the father said, "We'll go in soon."

Dripping, gleaming in the sun, Robert and David came out of the water, up the sand. "We have company," Laura said quietly when they stood before her. With identical indifferences in their eyes, they looked at the group behind her. "What's wrong with the woman's face and arm, Robert?" she asked with whispered irritation.

"I don't know," Robert said. He dropped to the sand and sat cross-legged beside her towel, at her feet. David duplicated the position on her other side.

"Ny-ah, Ny-ah!" the woman called out to one of her little girls, who was digging in the sand and scattering it. Involuntarily, Laura glanced at her again.

"Some slight paralysis," Robert said, his face turned away, and Laura, watching the stiff arm stuck out with its twisted fingers, said "Ugh!" and turned away, too.

Briskly, Robert said, "Well, David's getting good," but even when he leaned over and slapped the boy lightly on the shoulder in congratulation, David continued to stare at the woman and then let his eyes move to the white-faced boy who sat near her, sifting sand through his fingers.

"Aren't you, David?" Robert said loudly.

"What?" the boy asked vaguely, blinking suddenly as he looked at his father.

"Your crawl. It's good."

"Oh."

The blank indifference in David's voice made Laura shift her gaze from the glinting sea to the boy's impassive face. Once more he was staring at the people behind her while his hands, too, idly sifted sand. Then, as she looked at him, she saw that some subtle difference had overtaken his features since she had last really studied them. He was on the way to becoming a different boy. Since his last holiday, she thought, his neck had visibly lengthened, and all the bones of his face had coarsened—the jaw longer, the cheekbones more prominent, the forehead higher. And yet he was still a little boy. It was almost as if, within the hairless, child's face, another face was pushing through. That was a man's face. It was—she glanced at her husband—it was, indeed, Robert's face. *Puberty*, she thought, staring at the boy with a kind of horror. She saw him lengthening out and broadening, the chest swelling, the arms swelling, nails thickening, hair—and her legs and arms were suddenly covered with goose-flesh, shivering prickles sweeping her skin as, for the first time, she recognized in him the gross, inevitable thrust into manhood.

Then, behind her, the woman began noisily to scold, and Laura, who was clutching her arms to her sides, as if she were cold, lay back and tried to relax, closed her eyes once more, and sought to regain her private exchange with the sun, her perfect isolation in light. But she was too aware of everything around her to capture that pure sensation of complete and separate being. Even as her body warmed and her skin began to burn, she heard the people behind her moving about, preparing at last to go down to the water, and the sounds of running, sliding in the sand and their shifting cries told her when they went. Robert and David were talking together in low voices, and then she was aware of David's moving off a bit and beginning to dig in the sand. She heard the distant sound of splashing water, of voices laughing and shouting, of David's hands digging, slapping wet sand, scraping, and she felt Robert's eyes on her as he still sat at her feet.

Then he spoke. "What do you think of David?" he asked.

She lay completely quiet. "Think of him?"

"We haven't talked about him. How do you think he is?"

"I think he's fine. Don't you?"

"No. I think we should bring him home."

She sat up abruptly. "What did you say, Robert?" The sun seemed to blind her as she tried to see his face.

"The end of this term would be a good time to break. Bring him back to a school in the city."

"But why *break* from a good school to a less good one? There's no city school that—"

"The schooling isn't all that matters. He needs us. He needs a home."

"David? He's thirteen! He's been away for three years. What does he need with us now? I've just thought—he's—why, he's nearly a man. . . ."

"He's lonely."

"Lonely? David?"

"Lonely. Yes. It hurts me."

She looked at him with blind eyes, staring, and he said, "A man? He's nearly a *man?*"

With this question, the mad shimmering of the sun suddenly died, and she saw him clearly. He was *there,* thin and clear and brown and tractable. She said, "Yes. After all, only four or five more years . . . just now, I could see you in him, emerging. He's a big boy. He *needs* to be away from home. He shouldn't have to depend on us now. What can we do for him?"

"Everything we've never done," Robert said.

"I don't know what you're talking about."

"He doesn't seem to have any anchorage. Least of all in us. He's adrift—lost in himself some way."

She said curtly, "Nonsense."

He looked at her steadily before he spoke. "You're so beautiful," he said at last, almost as if he were meditating upon a theory, and then he went on quietly, "But something's wrong with our life. I don't know what it is, but. . . ."

"But?" she asked.

"But. . . ."

"Yes?"

He began to run his hands through the sand aimlessly, letting the grains sift slowly between his fingers. She watched him, and at last she said, "Well, that's gratitude!" She looked away from him to the running figures on the shore—the man and his wife and the three children, in and out of the water at the shallow edge of beach, shouting and ridiculously running. "I thought that we lived the way you wanted. I thought we had a—"

"We have," he said for her. "It's a beautiful, smooth, perfectly organized life. But what's missing?"

"Is anything?"

"Well, for example, whatever it is that David ought to feel about you."

"I don't know what you're talking about."

"Do you think you know him?"

"Of course."

"Look," Robert said. "Does he ever *talk* to you? Do you know what he's thinking about? Do you know what he's *like?*"

Laura looked at him. "It's you—I don't know what *you're* like," she said.

"Ahh!" he said, a long, disparaging denial, and turned away from her.

She lay back and began to cry. With a certain luxury, she felt the tears push up through her locked lids and run down and over her cheeks. They must be dropping on her towel! She said, "At last. I knew it would come sometime—it had to—and now it has. You—always so reservedly kind and unclaiming. Now, at last, you're using your position that until now you've hardly ever admitted. Now you tell me that I've failed—from *my* position!"

"Position?" he cried. "Oh, my God!"

She felt her tears burning on her skin, and, eyes still closed, she said, "Don't exclaim. I know it's true. I've always waited. I knew it would come someday. *My* inadequacy. So now it's come." Then, roughly brushing her cheeks with her fingers, she sat up. She tossed her hair back and cried, "But why today? Why, on the day that...." She looked to the water's edge, where the other family, gathered in a group, was starting back up the beach. "Why today, with those people here?"

He glanced at them. "What of them? What have they got to do with anything?" And, looking back at her, he cried, "Oh, look, don't be a fool!" Then he came through the sand on his knees and seized her hands. He held them and rubbed them and looked at her blurred brown eyes. "Laura, don't be a fool," he said, and hearing the protestation of love in these unlikely words, she looked away from him and down at the sand. She detached her hands. She felt the sun blessedly burn away the dampness around her eyelids. She looked out to the sea —the miles of blue, endless blue, nothing but blue, and over it the interminable reaches of cool blue sky—and she looked back at Robert, anxious beside her, and said with slow ease, "I'm sorry."

"I am, too."

"But you agree, don't you, that David shouldn't be taken from his school?"

Robert looked past her face and said, "David's heard. Perhaps all of it," and when Laura turned, she saw that, yes, there he was, only twelve or fifteen feet away from them, his hands deep in the bowels of a sand castle, stopped there for Lord knew how long, and his face turned toward them, his eyes wide and watchful. She could think of nothing to say except "They're coming back."

The others were just passing David. They had walked in a group from the shore, the mother in the lead, her foolish round face, encumbered with its unintended grin and its ridiculous swath of white ointment, lifted as she led her throng, her tribe. Behind her was the skinny, hairy, fish-white husband, behind him the homely little girls and, lagging now at David's castle, the boy. He stopped there and watched while the others went on, until David made some gesture of invitation, and then he dropped to his knees and both began silently to dig. The rest of the family settled itself again in its place, and when the little girls began a tentative movement towards the boys, the mother said sharply, "Ny-ah! Esther! Mir!" Reluctantly, they turned back and sat on the sand beside her.

Laura looked away from her. "What mad possessiveness!" she said.

The two boys were standing over the castle now, facing the sea, and the strange boy asked David a question, which he answered by ducking his head, hunching his shoulders, and moving his arms in the motion of a crawl. The other boy imitated them. Then, talking, they moved down to the water, and both ran in. David swam and the other boy watched, but only for a moment. Then the boy's mother was on her feet and screaming again, "Ny-ah! Ny-ah! Lou-ee! Come!" Her right cheek was distorted in her excitement, and her injured arm flailed grotesquely at the air.

The boy turned slowly and looked at her. Now, at last, he was outraged. Over the bright distance, Laura could see the fury in his tense, white face. He did not look back at David but came walking with slow deliberation up the beach, past the Newmans, whose heads turned as he walked, to his mother, who was still shaking her hand at him. Then, standing perhaps six feet before her, his arms flailing, too, but in a rage, he yelled at her, "Ny-ah! Ny-ah! Ny-ah!"

She looked at him in amazement for a moment and then seemed to wilt. All the perky animation left her round body as she turned slowly and settled saggingly on her towel and, at last, sinking prone, with her face pressed into its folds, wept. Her husband hurried to her, and Laura looked back to the sea. She saw David standing in the shallow water, watching intently, and then, glancing at his lifted hand, move his fingers experimentally. Then he started back to them.

The husband, kneeling beside his wife with his arm over her shoulders, murmured consolingly to her, and her sobs began to subside. The boy, quiet now, with a kind of shamed determination on his face, stood stiffly on the spot where he had faced her. Then the father summoned him with an uncompromising gesture, until the boy moved reluctantly to her. There were words that the Newmans could not hear, but the boy presently knelt beside his mother, where his father had been, and spoke softly to her. Then the mother swiftly twisted to a sitting position, her contorted face red, and, seizing the boy in her arms, she broke again into sobs as she embraced him in a convulsion of love.

"My God! Let's go," Laura said, and leaped up. Hastily, Robert helped her put their belongings in their beach basket and, without looking at the other family again, they walked away as rapidly as the loose sand allowed. Only David, lagging behind his parents, kept looking back, until the dunes cut off his view.

On the way to the hotel, the Newmans did not talk much, and they did not mention the other family, but a few hours later, when Laura was brushing her hair before a tall triple mirror in the dressing-room alcove off her bedroom, she suddenly exclaimed, "I can't get them out of my mind!"

Robert was sitting on the edge of her bed, leafing through a magazine, and he looked up and asked, "Who?"

"That awful family—that woman."

"Oh."

David, who was lying on his back on a chaise lounge, his legs flung out in masculine abandon, was doing something with his hands, which he held close before his face. Apparently preoccupied with his fingers and oblivious of his parents, he nevertheless now said quietly, "They weren't bad."

"That man's—*drawers!* That's all you can call them."

Robert laughed, but David asked in an innocent tone, "Just ordinary trunks, weren't they?" He rolled over on his stomach, as if to study his hands more closely.

Laura said, "You could hardly blame the boy for screaming back at her."

David said, "The boy was O.K. I like him."

Laura watched him in the glass. "What are you doing, David?"

He stood up lazily. "Nothing," he said. He walked to a window and leaned against the frame, and then he was fooling with his fingers again.

Suddenly, Laura saw what he was doing. "Stop it, David!" she said sharply.

Robert looked up again. "What's the matter?"

She watched David closely. He was standing by the window in such a way that the late-afternoon sunlight made a nimbus of the down on one cheek and along his chin. She thought of that down as a precursor to coarse stubble, and she said, "David, get out of here, will you? You make me nervous. Go wash your face."

"It's clean," he said as he started toward the door. He watched her with empty eyes as he sidled away.

Robert moved, and presently he was standing behind her. She looked up in the central mirror and met his sad, inquiring, forgiving eyes. "What was he doing?" Robert asked.

"I think he was trying to make his fingers look paralyzed, like that grotesque woman's."

Robert laughed uneasily. "Curiosity, probably. You know boys— they're interested in oddity. Probably not at all grotesque to him. Perhaps the contrary. Rather fascinating."

Laura brushed her hair with renewed vigor, until she had counted ten, twenty, thirty strokes. "He practically said he liked them."

"Well," Robert allowed, "perhaps he did."

Her brush paused in her hair. "Is it time for a drink?"

"I'll get you one." But he did not go. He put his hands on her shoulders and stroked her upper arms. "You are beautiful," he said.

For a moment or two, she sat immobile, unprotesting, under his hand. Then she said, "What about that drink?" She watched his reflection move away, and when he was out of the room, she leaned toward the mirror, toward her reflection. Her face cleared, as if shadows were passing from it, as if shadows had vanished from the shadows of her mind, and she smiled.

She opened a drawer of the dressing table and took out two gold bracelets—one with square chunks of jewels held in heavy links, and one with coins the size of half dollars—and put one on each wrist. Late sunlight shone upon her and flashed off the chains and the jewels in darting angles on the glass surfaces around her. Then, in the triple mirror, she caught sight of a figure moving. It was David again—moving, stopping. She watched his reflection. He was looking not at her but at his right hand, as he held it before him and forced his fingers into an imitation of gnarled paralysis.

"David," she said quietly, "please don't do that. Why do you keep doing that?"

He looked up and met her eyes in the mirror. "I just want to know how it feels," he said. "That woman—how she feels."

"If her hand is paralyzed, she probably doesn't feel anything. And why should you want to know how *she* feels?"

"I kind of liked her." He looked at Laura blandly.

"She was so loud—screaming all the time."

"They just weren't used to a beach, that was all. She was worried."

Laura lifted her hands to fasten a gold barrette in her brushed hair so that one ear would show, but she still watched David manipulating his fingers.

Suddenly, his face brightened. At last, he had duplicated the crippled arm. "This is the way it feels!"

Her eyes searched the mirror until his glance met hers. Then she grimaced in disgust and said with sharp finality. "Don't be perverse! She was—ugly!"

David was standing rigid behind her. His arm rose until it pointed out at her with a stiff, accusing crook at the elbow and in the clumsy-knuckled fingers. His drawn face was stiff with revulsion, only his eyes alive, glimmering upon her. "Says who?" he asked in a dead voice, and as his wild, unhappy eyes held and held hers, her bracelets clanked down on the mirrored top of the dressing table with a metallic chorus, and the mirrors flashed.

---

# SUICIDES
## *Cesare Pavese*

There are days when everything in the city I live in—the people in the streets, the traffic, trees—awakens in the morning with a strange aspect, the same as always yet unrecognizable, like the times when you look into the mirror and ask: "who's that?" These for me are the loveliest days of the year.

On such mornings, whenever I can, I leave the office a little earlier and go into the streets, mingling with the crowd, and I don't mind staring at all who pass in the very way, I suspect, that some of them look at me, for in truth at these moments I have a feeling of assurance that makes me another man.

I am convinced that I shall obtain from life nothing more precious perhaps than the revelation of how I may stimulate these moments at will. One way of making them longer which I have sometimes found successful is to sit in a new cafe, glassed-in and bright, and absorb the noise of all the hurry-scurry and the street, the flare of colors and of voices, and the peaceful interior moderating all the tumult.

In only a few years I have suffered keen stabs of disappointment and regret; still, I may say that my most heartfelt prayer is for this peace, this tranquillity alone. I am not cut out for storms and struggle: even though there are mornings when I go forth to walk the streets vibrant with my life and my stride may be taken for a challenge, I repeat, I ask of life no more than that she let herself be observed.

And yet even this modest pleasure sometimes leaves me with a bitterness which is precisely that of a vice. It wasn't only yesterday that I realized that in order to live one had to exercise cunning with oneself, and only then with others. I envy the people—they are women mostly —who are able to commit a misdeed or an injustice, or merely to indulge a whim, having contrived beforehand a chain of circumstances so as to give their conduct, in their own eyes, the appearance of being altogether proper. I do not have serious vices—provided this withdrawal from the struggle from lack of confidence, in search of lonely serenity, is not the most serious vice of all—but I do not even know how to handle myself wisely and to hold myself in check when enjoying the little that comes my way.

It sometimes happens, in fact, that I stop in my tracks, glancing about, and ask myself whether I have any right to enjoy my assurance. This occurs especially when my moments out have been rather frequent. Not that I take time off from my work: I provide decently for myself, and support in boarding school an orphaned niece whom the old lady who calls herself my mother doesn't want around the house. But the thing I ask myself is whether—on these ecstatic strolls of mine —I am not ludicrous, ludicrous and disgusting; for I think sometimes that I am not really due my ecstasy.

Or else, as happened the other morning, I need only to assist offhand at some singular scene in a cafe, which intrigues me from the outset by the normalness of its participants, in order to fall a prey to a guilt-ridden sense of loneliness and to so many bleak memories that the farther they recede the more they reveal to me, in their immutable natures, twisted and terrible meanings.

It was five minutes of play between the young cashier and a customer in a light-colored topcoat, accompanied by a friend. The young man was shouting that the cashier owed him change from a hundred-lira note and was slamming his fist on the desk top as he pretended to check through her handbag and pockets.

"Young lady, that's certainly no way to treat customers," he said, winking at his friend, who stood by looking ill at ease. The cashier laughed. The young man then concocted some story about a ride they would take in the elevator of a public bath. Between controlled bursts of laughter they finally decided that they would deposit the money in a bank—once they had it.

"Good-by, young lady," he shouted back as he left at last. "Think of me tonight."

The cashier, exhilarated and laughing, turned to the waiter: "What a character!"

I had noticed her on other mornings, and sometimes smiled without looking at her, in moments of abstraction. But my peace is too flimsy, a tissue of nothing. The usual stab of remorse returns.

"We are all sordid, but there's a good-natured sordidness, with a smile, that provokes a smile from others, and there's another sordidness that is lonely and holds people off. The sillier, after all, is not the former."

It is on such mornings that I am surprised, each time anew, by the thought that what is truly sinful in my life is only silliness. Others may achieve out-and-out evil by design, sure of themselves, taking an interest in their victims and in the sport—and I suspect that a life so spent may afford many satisfactions—but as for myself, I have never done anything but suffer from great bumbling uncertainty, and writhe, when brought into contact with others, in my own stupid cruelty. Because—and there's no solution—it's enough that I give in to that remorse of my loneliness for an instant or so and I think again of Carlotta.

She has been dead for more than a year, and now I know all the routes that my memory of her may take to surprise me. I can, so wishing, even recognize the initial state of mind that announces her appearance, abruptly diverting my thoughts. But I do not always wish it; and even now my remorse provides me with dark corners, new points, that I study with the trepidation of a year ago. I was so tortuously true with her that each of those far-off days stands in my memory not as a fixed thing, but as an elusive face possessing for me the same reality of today.

Not that Carlotta was a mystery. She was, rather, one of those transparently simple souls—pitiful women—who become irritating if they cease for only an instant being themselves and attempt subterfuge or flirtation. But so long as they are simple no one notices them. I have never understood how she could bear to earn her living as a cashier. She had the makings of an ideal sister.

What I have not fathomed, even yet, are my feelings and my behavior then. What, for instance, should I say of the evening in Carlotta's two-room lodgings when she had put on a velvet dress—an old dress— to receive me, and I told her that I should have preferred her in a bathing suit? It was one of my first visits and I had not even kissed her.

Well, making a shy grimace, Carlotta withdrew into the anteroom and—of all things—actually reappeared in a bathing suit! That evening I took her into my arms and forced her down onto the davenport; but then—the moment it was over—I told her I liked being alone and left, and I did not return for three days; and when I did I addressed her formally.

Thereupon another ridiculous courtship began, consisting of timid confidences on her part and few words on my own. Suddenly I addressed her familiarly, but she resisted. Then I asked her if she had reconciled with her husband. Carlotta began to whimper. "He never treated me the way you do," she said.

It was easy to press her head to my chest and caress her and to tell her I loved her; after all, being so alone, couldn't I love a grass widow? And Carlotta let herself go; softly, she confessed that she had loved me from the very beginning, that I struck her as being an extraordinary man, but already, in the short time we had known each other, I had caused her to suffer miserably, and she—she didn't know why—all men treated her the same.

"Blowing hot and cold," I smiled into her hair: "that's how you keep love alive."

Carlotta was sallow, with enormous eyes a little worn with fatigue, and her body was pale too. In the shadows of her bedroom that night, I asked myself if it was because I didn't like her body that I had hurried off the time before.

But even this time I didn't have pity on her: in the middle of the night I dressed and, making no excuses, announced that I had to be going, and went. Carlotta wanted to come along.

"No, I like being alone."

And, giving her a kiss, I left.

When I met Carlotta I was just emerging from a tempest that had nearly cost me my life; and now, returning to the empty streets, retreating from a woman who loved me, I was possessed by a wry mirth. For quite some time I had had to spend days and nights browbeaten and in a fury on account of a woman's whims.

I am convinced now that no passion is so strong as to alter the nature of one who endures it. One may die of it, but that doesn't change a thing. When the frenzy has passed, one returns to being the decent man or the rogue, the family man or the boy, whatever one was, and proceeds with one's life. Or more precisely: from the ordeal our true nature comes out, and it horrifies us; normality disgusts us; and we would wish even to be dead, the insult is so unspeakable, but we have no one to blame but ourselves. I owe it to that woman if I am reduced to this singular life I lead, from day to day, aimlessly, incapable of securing ties with the world, estranged from my fellows—estranged even from my mother whom I only just tolerate, and from my niece whom I don't love—I owe it all to her; but might I not have fared better in the end with another woman? With a woman, I mean, capable of humbling me as my nature required?

Nonetheless, at the time, the thought that I had been wronged, that my mistress could be called treacherous, did afford me a measure of comfort. There is a point in suffering when it is inevitable—it is a natural anesthetic—that one should believe oneself to be suffering unjustly: this brings into force again, according to our most coveted desires, fascination for life; it restores a sense of our worth in the face of things; it is flattering. I had found, and I should have liked, injustice, ingratitude, to be even more unspeakable. I recall—during those interminable days and those evenings of anguish—being aware of a pervasive and secret feeling, like an atmosphere or an irradiance: wonderment that it all happened—that the woman was indeed the woman, that the periods of delirium and stabbing pains were quite what they were, that the sighs, the words, the deeds, that I myself—that it all happened just as it did.

And now here I was, having suffered injustice, repaying, as inevitably happens, not the guilty one, but another.

I would leave Carlotta's little apartment at night satisfied and absent of mind, delighted to be walking alone, retreating from all solicitude, freely enjoying the long avenue, in vague pursuit of the sensations and thoughts of early youth. The simplicity of the night—darkness and street lamps—has always welcomed me with tenderness, and made for the wildest and most precious fantasies, heightening them with its contrasts and magnifying them. There, even the blind rancor I showed toward Carlotta for her eager humility had full rein, freed of a kind of awkwardness which pitying her made me feel when we were together.

But I was not young any longer. And the better to disengage myself from Carlotta, I reconsidered and anatomized her body and her caresses. Crudely, I considered that separated from her husband as she was, still young and without children, she was simply jumping at the chance for whatever outlet she could find in me. But—poor Carlotta —she was too simple a mistress, and it may have been precisely for this that her husband betrayed her.

I remember returning arm in arm with her from the cinema one evening, wandering through the semilit streets, when she said to me: "I'm happy. It's nice going to the movies with you."

"Did you ever go with your husband?"

Carlotta smiled at me. "Are you jealous?"

I shrugged. "In any case, it doesn't change anything."

"I'm tired," Carlotta would say, pressing against my arm; "this good-for-nothing chain that holds us is ruining both his life and mine, and making me respect a name that has brought me nothing but suffering. Divorce ought to be possible, at least when there aren't children."

I was lulled that evening by my long, warm contact with her, and by desire. "You have scruples, in other words?"

"Oh, darling," Carlotte said, "why aren't you good all the time, like you are this evening? Think, if only I could have a divorce."

I didn't say anything. Once before when she had mentioned divorce I had burst out: "Now just look here, can anyone be better off than you? You do whatever you please—and I'll wager he still slips you a little, if it's true it was he who betrayed you."

"I have never accepted a thing," Carlotte had replied. "I've worked from that day on"—and she had looked at me. "Now that I have you I'd feel as if I were betraying you."

The evening we went to the movies I shut her up with a kiss. Then I took her to the station cafe where I bought her a couple of glasses of liquor.

We sat like a pair of lovers in the steamy light of the glass panes. I downed quite a few jiggers myself. Presently, in a loud voice, I said to her: "Carlotta, shall we make a baby tonight?"

Some of the people looked at us because Carlotta, radiant and flushed, closed my mouth with her hand.

I talked and talked. Carlotta talked about the film, making silly remarks—passionately—finding comparisons between us and the characters in it. And I—aware that only by drinking could I love her—I drank.

Outside, the cold was invigorating and we hurried home. I spent the night with her, and waking in the morning I felt her by my side, disheveled and full of sleep, fumbling to hug me. I did not repulse her; but when I got up my head was aching and Carlotta's repressed joy as she got my coffee, humming to herself, grated on my nerves. Then we had to leave together, but remembering the concierge, Carlotta sent me out first, not without a wifely hug and a kiss behind the door.

My keenest memory of waking that morning is of the boughs of the trees bordering the walk, stark and dripping in the fog, visible through the curtains in the room. The warmth and solicitude inside, and the raw morning air awaiting me, charged my blood; however, I should have liked to be alone, thinking and smoking by myself, imagining an altogether different waking and another mate.

The tenderness that Carlotta extracted from me at such moments was something I reproached myself for the instant I was alone. I underwent moments of fury, scouring my soul to be rid of the slightest memory of her; I made up my mind to be hard and then was even too hard. It must have been apparent that we loved each other out of indolence, out of some vice—for all the reasons except the very one she sought to delude herself about. The memory of her grave, blissful look after the embrace irritated me, noticing it on her face angered me; whereas the only woman on whom I had wanted to see it had never given me that satisfaction.

"If you accept me as I am, fine," I told her once; "but get it out of your head that you can ever mean anything to me."

"Don't you love me?" Carlotta stammered.

"The little bit of love I was capable of I burned out in my youth."

But there were also times when I lost my temper, having admitted, out of shame or desire, that I did love her a little.

Carlotta would force a smile. "We're good friends at least, aren't we?"

"Listen," I told her seriously, "all this nonsense repels me; we're a man and a woman who are bored; we get on in bed—"

"Oh, yes, that we do!" she said; she clutched my arm, hiding her face. "I like you, I do like you—"

"—period."

It was enough to have just one of these exchanges, in which I struck myself as spineless, for me to avoid her for weeks on end; and if she rang me up at the office from her cafe I told her I was busy. The first time Carlotta tried being angry, I let her spend the evening in torment, while I sat frigid on the davenport—the lampshade cast a white light on her knees—and in the half-light I could sense the contained spasms of her glances. It was I, in the unbearable tension, who finally said: "Thank me, Signora: you're likely to remember this session more than many others."

Carlotta didn't stir.

"Why don't you kill me, Signora? If you think you can play the woman with me, you're wasting your time. The flighty one I'll play myself."

She was breathing heavily.

"Not even your bathing suit," I said to her, "will help you this evening. . . ."

Suddenly Carlotta bounded at me. I saw her blackhaired head go through the white light like some hurled object. I thrust out my hands. But Carlotta collapsed at my knees in tears. I laid a hand on her head two or three times. Then I rose.

"I ought to be crying too, Carlotta. But I know that tears are no use. All this you're going through I've been through myself. I've been on the point of killing myself, and then my nerve failed me. This is the rub: a person so weak as to think of suicide is also too weak to commit it. . . . Come now, Carlotta, be good."

"Don't treat me like that . . ." she stammered.

"I'm not treating you like anything. But you know I like being alone. If you let me be alone, I'll come back; if not, we'll never see each other again. Look, would you like me to love you?"

Beneath my hand, Carlotta looked up with her swollen face.

"Well, then, you must stop loving me. There's no other way. The hare's the hunter."

Scenes of this sort shook Carlotta too deeply for her to consider giving me up. But didn't they also denote a fundamental similarity in temperament? At bottom, Carlotta was a simple soul—too simple—and incapable of clearly recognizing it; but certainly she sensed it. She tried—poor creature—to hold me by being lighthearted, and would sometimes say things like "Such is life!" and "Poor little me!"

I believe that if at that time she had firmly repulsed me I should have suffered a little. But it wasn't in her power. If I remained away for two evenings running, I found her with sunken eyes. And whenever, on occasion, I took pity on her or was kind, and stopped by her cafe and asked her to come out with me, she got up flushed and flustered, even more beautiful.

My rancor was not directed at her; rather, at all the restrictions and the enslavement our liaison seemed likely to produce. Since I didn't love her, her smallest claim on me struck me as an outrage. There were days when addressing her in the *tu*-form disgusted and degraded me. Who was this woman clamped onto my arm?

In return, I seemed to experience a rebirth, certain half days, certain hours when, after hurrying through my work, I was able to go out into the cool sun and walk the sunlit streets, unencumbered by her, by anything, feeling satisfied of body, my old sorrow soothed: eager to see, to smell, to feel as I had when I was young. That Carlotta might suffer on my account alleviated my past griefs and made them paltry, and estranged them from me a little, as from a laughable world; and far removed from her, I found myself whole again, more adept. She was the sponge I used to cleanse myself. I thought this often of her.

Some evenings when I talked and talked, engrossed in the game, I was a youngster again and I put my rancor behind me.

"Carlotta," I would say, "what is it like to be a lover? It's so long since I was one. All told, it must be a fine thing, I imagine. When all goes well, you enjoy it; when it doesn't, you hope. You live from day to day, they say. What is it like, Carlotta?"

Carlotta would shake her head, smiling.

"Another thing, you have so many wonderful thoughts, Carlotta. Whoever takes love lightly will never be happy like the lover. Unless," I smiled, "he sleeps with another woman and then makes game of the lover."

Carlotta knitted her brows.

"Love is a fine thing," I concluded. "And no one escapes it."

Carlotta served as my public. I was talking to myself, those evenings. It's the pleasantest of talks.

"There is love and there is betrayal. In order really to enjoy love there's also got to be betrayal. This is the thing young boys don't realize. You women learn it earlier. Did you betray your husband?"

Carlotta essayed a cunning smile, going red.

"We boys were stupider. Scrupulously, we fell in love with an actress or schoolmate and offered her our finest thoughts. Except that we never got around to telling them. To my knowledge there wasn't a girl our age who didn't realize that love is a matter of craft. It doesn't seem possible, but boys go to brothels and conclude that the women outside are different. What were you up to at sixteen, Carlotta?"

But Carlotta's thoughts were elsewhere. With her eyes, before answering, she told me that I was hers, and I hated the hardness of the solicitude her glance gave off.

"What were you doing at sixteen?" I asked her again, staring down at the floor.

"Nothing," she replied gravely. I knew what she was thinking.

Then she asked me to forgive her—she was acting the poor forlorn creature and she knew she hadn't the right—but her glance was enough. "Do you know you're stupid? For all I care, your husband could take you back!" And off I went with a feeling of relief.

Next day in the office I received a timid telephone call, to which I replied dryly. That evening I saw her again.

Carlotta was amused whenever I talked about my niece who was away at boarding school, and she shook her head with disbelief when I told her that I would rather have shut my mother up in school and lived with the child. She pictured us as two quite different beings, playing at being uncle and niece, but actually having a whole world of secrets and petty grievances to delight and occupy us. She asked me, put out, if the girl was not my daughter.

"Of course. Born when I was sixteen. She decided to be blond just to spite me. How can one be born blond? Blonds for me are creatures like monkeys or lions. It must be like always being in the sun, I should imagine."

Carlotta said: "I was blond when I was little."

"I was bald myself."

My interest in Carlotta's past, during that final period, was a bored curiosity which from time to time allowed me to forget all she had previously told me. I scanned her as one scans the page of local news in the paper. I delighted in puzzling her with whimsical sallies, I put cruel questions to her and then supplied the answers. I was actually listening to no one but myself.

But Carlotta had seen through me. "Tell me about yourself," she would say some evenings, pressing my arm. She knew that only by getting me to talk about myself could she make a friend of me.

"Carlotta, did I ever tell you that a man once killed himself because of me?" I asked her one evening.

She looked at me radiant and half amazed.

"It's nothing to laugh at," I went on. "We killed ourselves together —but he actually died. Youthful shenanigans." Wasn't it curious, I thought suddenly, I had never told a soul, and of all people Carlotta would be the first. "He was a friend of mine, a fine-looking blond boy. And he really did look a lion. You girls, you don't make friendships like that. At that age you're already too jealous. We were schoolmates, but we always met afterward, in the evening. We talked in the dirty ways boys will, but we were in love with a woman. She must still be living. She was our first love, Carlotta. We spent our evenings talking about love and death. No one in love has ever been more certain of being understood by his best friend than we were of each other. Jean —his name was Jean—had a bold sadness that used to put me to shame. All by himself he created the melancholy of those evenings we spent walking together through the fog. We didn't believe one could suffer so much—"

"You were in love, too?"

"I suffered for being less melancholy than Jean. Finally I discovered that we might kill ourselves, and I told him. Jean took to the idea slowly, he who was normally so imaginative. We had a revolver between us. We went out to the hills to test it, in case it should explode. It was Jean who fired. He had always been foolhardy, and I think that if he had stopped loving the woman I should have stopped too. After the test—we were on a barren footpath, halfway up; it was winter—I was still thinking about the force of the shot when Jean put the barrel into his mouth and said: 'Some guys do it this way . . .' And the gun went off and killed him."

Carlotta stared at me horrified.

"I didn't know what to do and ran away."

Later that evening Carlotta said to me: "And you really loved that woman?"

"What woman? I loved Jean; I told you."

"And did you want to kill yourself too?"

"Naturally. It would have been foolish, though. But not doing it was rank cowardice. I'm sorry I didn't."

Carlotta often returned to the story, and spoke to me of Jean as though she had known him. She had me describe him and asked me what I myself was like then. She wanted to know if I had kept the revolver.

"Don't go killing yourself now. Have you never thought of killing yourself?" So saying, she rested her eyes on me.

"Every time you fall in love you think of it."

Carlotta didn't even smile. "Do you think of it still?"

"I think of Jean sometimes."

At noon, the thought of Carlotta distressed me terribly when, after I had left the office, I passed her cafe window, hurrying by so as not to have to look in and kid with her a little. I did not go home at noon. I especially liked seating myself alone in an eating house and whiling away that part of an hour I had, with my eyes barely open, smoking. Carlotta, in her chair, would be ringing up change automatically, tilting and nodding her head, smiling and frowning, at times with a customer joking with her.

She was there, in her blue dress, from seven in the morning till four in the afternoon. They paid her four hundred and eighty lire a month. Carlotta liked rushing through the day in a single sitting, and would take lunch, with a big cup of milk, without rising from her place. It would have been an easy job, she told me, except for the way the door banged with all the coming and going. There were times when she felt it like punches on the raw surface of her brain.

Ever since, on entering cafes, I have closed the doors carefully. With me, Carlotta tried to describe the little scenes with the customers, but she could never bring off my way of talking, just as she was never able to get a rise out of me with her sly allusions to the proposals some old goat was making to her.

"Go right ahead," I told her; "just don't let me see him. Receive him on odd days. And take care you don't pick up any diseases."

Carlotta made a wry mouth.

For some days a thought had been gnawing at her. "Are we in love again, Carlotta?" I said to her one evening.

Carlotta looked at me like a whipped dog. And I lost patience with her again. Those shining glances of hers, that evening, in the half-light of the little room, her squeezing my hand—it all infuriated me. With Carlotta I was forever afraid of being tied down. I hated the very thought of it.

I grew sullen again; surly. But Carlotta had stopped taking my outbursts with her former injured paroxysms. She simply looked at me, without moving, and sometimes when, to comfort her, I reached out to caress her, she would draw back in an affectionate motion.

Which was something I liked even less. Being compelled to court her in order to have her was repugnant to me. But it would not begin without a prelude. Carlotta would start: "I have a headache ... oh, that door! Let's be good this evening. Talk to me."

The moment I realized she was really serious, regarding herself as a poor unfortunate, dredging up regrets, my outbursts would end: I simply betrayed her. I relived one of those colorless evenings of the past when, returning from a brothel, I had sat in any wretched, cheap cafe to rest, neither happy nor sad, muzzy. It seemed only just: one either accepted love with all its hazards or nothing remained but prostitution.

I believed Carlotta's jealousy to be an act, and it amused me. She suffered. But she was too simple a soul to turn it to her gain. Rather, as happens to those who really suffer, it made her ugly. I was sorry, but I would have to have done with her, I felt.

Carlotta saw the blow coming. One evening when we were in bed together, while I was instinctively avoiding conversation, she suddenly thrust me away and curled up toward the wall.

"What's eating you?" I demanded, annoyed.

"If I were to disappear tomorrow," she said, suddenly turning back, "would it make any difference to you?"

"I don't know," I stammered.

"And if I betrayed you?"

"Life itself is a betrayal."

"And if I returned to my husband?"

She was serious. I shrugged.

"I'm only a poor woman," Carlotta continued. "And I'm not able to betray you . . . I've seen my husband."

"What?"

"He came to the cafe."

"But didn't he go to America?"

"I don't know," Carlotta said. "I saw him at the cafe."

She may not have meant to tell me, but it came out that her husband had also come with a woman in a fur coat.

"In that case, you weren't able to talk?"

Carlotta hesitated. "He came back the next day. He talked to me then, and afterward saw me home."

I must confess that I felt uncomfortable. I said softly: "Here?"

Carlotta clung to me with all her body. "But I love you," she whispered. "You mustn't think—"

"Here?"

"It was nothing, darling. He simply talked about his business. Only, seeing him again I realized how much I love you. He can beg and I won't go back to him."

"Then he begged you?"

"No. He just said that if he were to marry again he would still marry me."

"Have you seen him since?"

"He came to the cafe again, with that woman . . ."

That was the last time I spent the night with Carlotta. Without taking leave of her body, without regrets, I stopped ringing her up and stopped visiting her at her flat. I let her telephone me and then wait to meet me in cafes—nor was it every evening: only now and then. Carlotta would come each time and devour me with her eyes, and when we were about to leave her voice would quaver.

"I haven't seen him again," she whispered one evening.

"You're making a mistake," I answered; "you ought to try to get him back."

It annoyed me that Carlotta missed her husband—as she unquestionably did—and that with such talk she hoped to entice me. That unconsummated love of hers was worth neither her regrets nor my own risks.

One evening I told her over the telephone that I'd call on her. She let me in with a look of disbelief and anxiety. I glanced around the entry hall, a little apprehensive. Carlotta was wearing velvet. And I recall that she had a cold and kept squeezing her handkerchief and pressing it to her red nose.

At once, I saw that she understood. She was quiet and meek, and she answered me with pitiful looks. She let me do all the talking, while she cast furtive glances over the top of her handkerchief. Then she rose and came to me, leaning her body against my face, and I had to place an arm around her.

Softly, in the same tone, she said: "Won't you come to bed?"

We went to bed, and through all of it I disliked her damp face, inflamed by her cold. At midnight I jumped out of bed and began dressing. Carlotta turned on the light, looking at me for an instant. Then she turned it off and said: "Yes, go if you wish." Embarrassed, I stumbled out.

In the days that followed I feared a telephone call, but nothing disturbed me, and I was able to work in peace for weeks on end. And then, one evening, desire for Carlotta took hold of me again, but shame helped me to overcome it. Even so, I knew that if I had rung at that door I would have brought happiness. This certainty I have always had.

I didn't yield; but, the day after, I went by her cafe. There was a blond at the cash register. They must have changed hours. But she wasn't there in the evening, either. I thought that perhaps she was ill or that her husband had taken her back. This was not an appealing idea.

But my legs shook when the concierge, with extreme ill grace, fixing me with a hard beady gaze, told me that they had found her in bed a month before, dead, with the gas jets on.

## Study Aids: Schorer

1. In what ways do the first word, the action, and the final comparison of the opening paragraph foreshadow the conflict, the character insights, and the themes of the story?

2. "Some slight paralysis," Robert says of the condition of the other mother. What are the ironic uses and implications of the word paralysis in the story?

3. Notice the numerous and important contrasts between the two families. What are the first impressions left by the descriptions of the appearance and actions of "That awful family," as Laura calls them? Are these the final impressions? How does the brief glimpse of the life of the other people indirectly reveal what is wrong with the life of Robert, Laura and David? How does it directly affect them? Why does Laura say, "My God! Let's go," immediately after the other mother embraces her son "in a convulsion of love"?

4. What is the significance of David's imitation of the other woman's paralyzed hand? What is Laura doing when this occurs? Why the emphasis on the bracelet and mirror at the story's close?

5. How is Laura's response to "Puberty" revealing of the relationship between her and her son? What shift has occurred in their relationship by the end of the story?

## Study Aids: Pavese

1. There are two literal deaths in the story, but what other kind of death and self-destruction might the title also be suggesting? What would be the relationship between the two kinds of "death"?

2. Much of the impact and point of the story is carried by the narrative point of view. What does the narrator reveal about himself with such statements as "the old lady who calls herself my mother," "The evening we went to the movies I shut her up with a kiss," "looked at me like a whipped dog"? How are such statements related to the destructiveness of his relationships?

3. The narrator's statements are, of course, related to his attitudes and interpretations. Whom does he feel is the victim of the events and for what reasons? Does the author agree?

4. What is the narrator's response to Carlotta's suffering? What does he have to say about *guilt?* Why does he stop seeing her?

5. What are the purpose and effect of not having the narrator comment on her death at the end of the story? What can be conjectured about his final attitude?

# FOUR SUMMERS
*Joyce Carol Oates*

### I

It is some kind of special day. "Where's Sissie?" Ma says. Her face gets sharp, she is frightened. When I run around her chair she laughs and hugs me. She is pretty when she laughs. Her hair is long and pretty.

We are sitting at the best table of all, out near the water. The sun is warm and the air smells nice. Daddy is coming back from the building with some glasses of beer, held in his arms. He makes a grunting noise when he sits down.

"Is the lake deep?" I ask them.

They don't hear me, they're talking. A woman and a man are sitting with us. The man marched in the parade we saw just awhile ago; he is a volunteer fireman and is wearing a uniform. Now his shirt is pulled open because it is hot. I can see the dark curly hair way up by his throat; it looks hot and prickly.

A man in a soldier's uniform comes over to us. They are all friends, but I can't remember him. We used to live around here, Ma told me, and then we moved away. The men are laughing. The man in the uniform leans back against the railing, laughing, and I am afraid it will break and he will fall into the water.

"Can we go out in a boat, Dad?" says Jerry.

He and Frank keep running back and forth. I don't want to go with them. I want to stay by Ma. She smells nice. Frank's face is dirty with sweat. "Dad," he says, whining, "can't we go out in a boat? Them kids are going out."

A big lake is behind the building and the open part where we are sitting. Some people are rowing on it. This tavern is noisy and everyone is laughing; it is too noisy for Dad to think about what Frank said.

"Harry," says Ma, "the kids want a boat ride. Why don't you leave off drinking and take them?"

"What?" says Dad.

He looks up from laughing with the men. His face is damp with sweat and he is happy. "Yeah, sure, in a few minutes. Go over there and play and I'll take you out in a few minutes."

The boys run out back by the rowboats, and I run after them. I have a bag of potato chips.

An old man with a white hat pulled down over his forehead is sitting by the boats, smoking. "You kids be careful," he says.

Frank is leaning over and looking at one of the boats. "This here is the best one," he says.

"Why's this one got water in it?" says Jerry.

"You kids watch out. Where's your father?" the man says.

"He's gonna take us for a ride," says Frank.

"Where is he?"

The boys run along, looking at the boats that are tied up. They don't bother with me. The boats are all painted dark green, but the paint is peeling off some of them in little pieces. There is water inside some of them. We watch two people come in, a man and a woman. The woman is giggling. She has on a pink dress and she leans over to trail one finger in the water. "What's all this filthy stuff by the shore?" she says. There is some scum in the water. It is colored a light brown, and there are little seeds and twigs and leaves in it.

The man helps the woman out of the boat. They laugh together. Around their rowboat little waves are still moving: they make a churning noise that I like.

"Where's Dad?" Frank says.

"He ain't coming," says Jerry.

They are tossing pebbles out into the water. Frank throws his sideways, twisting his body. He is ten and very big. "I bet he ain't coming," Jerry says, wiping his nose with the back of his hand.

After awhile we go back to the table. Behind the table is the white railing, and then the water, and then the bank curves out so that the weeping willow trees droop over the water. More men in uniforms, from the parade, are walking by.

"Dad," says Frank, "can't we go out? Can't we? There's a real nice boat there—"

"For Christ's sake, get them off me," Dad says. He is angry with Ma. "Why don't you take them out?"

"Honey, I can't row."

"Should we take out a boat, us two?" the other woman says. She has very short, wet-looking hair. It is curled in tiny little curls close to her head and is very bright. "We'll show them, Lenore. Come on, let's give your kids a ride. Show these guys how strong we are."

"That's all you need, to sink a boat," her husband says.

They all laugh.

The table is filled with brown beer bottles and wrappers of things. I can feel how happy they all are together, drawn together by the round table. I lean against Ma's warm leg and she pats me without looking down. She lunges forward and I can tell even before she says something that she is going to be loud.

"You guys're just jealous! Afraid we'll meet some soldiers!" she says.

"Can't we go out, Dad? Please?" Frank says. "We won't fight. . . ."

"Go and play over there. What're those kids doing—over there?" Dad says, frowning. His face is damp and loose, the way it is sometimes when he drinks. "In a little while, okay? Ask your mother."

"She can't do it," Frank says.

"They're just jealous," Ma says to the other woman, giggling. "They're afraid we might meet somebody somewhere."

"Just who's gonna meet this one here?" the other man says, nodding with his head at his wife.

Frank and Jerry walk away. I stay by Ma. My eyes burn and I want to sleep, but they won't be leaving for a long time. It is still daylight. When we go home from places like this it is always dark and getting chilly and the grass by our house is wet.

"Duane Dorsey's in jail," Dad says. "You guys heard about that?"

"Duane? Yeah, really?"

"It was in the newspaper. His mother-in-law or somebody called the police, he was breaking windows in her house."

"That Duane was always a nut!"

"Is he out now, or what?"

"I don't know. I don't see him these days. We had a fight," Dad says.

The woman with the short hair looks at me. "She's a real cute little thing," she says, stretching her mouth. "She drink beer, Lenore?"

"I don't know."

"Want some of mine?"

She leans toward me and holds the glass by my mouth. I can smell the beer and the warm stale smell of perfume. There are pink lipstick smudges on the glass.

"Hey, what the hell are you doing?" her husband says.

When he talks rough like that I remember him: we were with him once before.

"Are you swearing at me?" the woman says.

"Leave off the kid, you want to make her a drunk like yourself?"

"It don't hurt, one little sip. . . ."

"It's okay," Ma says. She puts her arm around my shoulders and pulls me closer to the table.

"Let's play cards. Who wants to?" Dad says.

"Sissie wants a little sip, don't you?" the woman says. She is smiling at me and I can see that her teeth are darkish, not nice like Ma's.

"Sure, go ahead," says Ma.

"I said leave off that, Sue, for Christ's sake," the man says. He jerks the table. He is a big man with a thick neck; he is bigger than Dad. His eyebrows are blond, lighter than his hair, and are thick and tufted. Dad is staring at something out on the lake without seeing it. "Harry, look, my goddam wife is trying to make your kid drink beer."

"Who's getting hurt?" Ma says angrily.

Pa looks at me all at once and smiles. "Do you want it, baby?"

I have to say yes. The woman grins and holds the glass down to me, and it clicks against my teeth. They laugh. I stop swallowing right away because it is ugly, and some of the beer drips down on me. "Honey, you're so clumsy," Ma says, wiping me with a napkin.

"She's a real cute girl," the woman says, sitting back in her chair. "I wish I had a nice little girl like that."

"Lay off of that," says her husband.

"Hey, did you bring any cards?" Dad says to the soldier.

"They got some inside."

"Look, I'm sick of cards," Ma says.

"Yeah, why don't we all go for a boat ride?" says the woman. "Be real nice, something new. Every time we get together we play cards. How's about a boat ride?"

"It better be a big boat, with you in it," her husband says. He is pleased when everyone laughs, even the woman. The soldier lights a cigarette and laughs. "How come your cousin here's so skinny and you're so fat?"

"She isn't fat," says Ma. "What the hell do you want? Look at yourself."

"Yes, the best days of my life are behind me," the man says. He wipes his face and then presses a beer bottle against it. "Harry, you're lucky you moved out. It's all going downhill, back in the neighborhood."

"You should talk, you let our house look like hell," the woman says. Her face is blotched now, some parts pale and some red. "Harry don't sit out in his back yard all weekend drinking. He gets something done."

"Harry's younger than me."

Ma reaches over and touches Dad's arm. "Harry, why don't you take the kids out? Before it gets dark."

Dad lifts his glass and finishes his beer. "Who else wants more?" he says.

"I'll get them, you went last time," the soldier says.

"Get a chair for yourself," says Dad. "We can play poker."

"I don't want to play poker, I want to play rummy," the woman says.

"At church this morning Father Reilly was real mad," says Ma. "He said some kids or somebody was out in the cemetery and left some beer bottles. Isn't that awful?"

"Duane Dorsey used to do worse than that," the man says, winking.

"Hey, who's that over there?"

"You mean that fat guy?"

"Isn't that the guy at the lumberyard that owes all that money?"

Dad turns around. His chair wobbles and he almost falls; he is angry. "This goddamn place is too crowded," he says.

"This is a real nice place," the woman says. She is taking something out of her purse. "I always liked it, didn't you, Lenore?"

"Sue and me used to come here a lot," says Ma. "And not just with you two, either."

"Yeah, we're real jealous," the man says.

"You should be," says the woman.

The soldier comes back. Now I can see that he is really a boy. He runs to the table with the beer before he drops anything. He laughs.

"Jimmy, your ma wouldn't like to see you drinking!" the woman says happily.

"Well, she ain't here."

"Are they still living out in the country?" Ma says to the woman.

"Sure. No electricity, no running water, no bathroom—same old thing. What can you do with people like that?"

"She always talks about going back to the Old Country," the soldier says. "Thinks she can save up money and go back."

"Poor old bastards don't know there was a war," Dad says. He looks as if something tasted bad in his mouth. "My old man died thinking he could go back in a year or two. Stupid bastards!"

"Your father was real nice. . . ." Ma says.

"Yeah, real nice," says Dad. "Better off dead."

Everybody is quiet.

"June Dieter's mother's got the same thing," the woman says in a low voice to Ma. "She's had it a year now and don't weigh a hundred pounds—you remember how big she used to be."

"She was big, all right," Ma says.

"Remember how she ran after June and slapped her? We were there—some guys were driving us home."

"Yeah. So she's got it too."

"Hey," says Dad, "why don't you get a chair, Jimmy? Sit down here."

The soldier looks around. His face is raw in spots, broken out. But his eyes are nice. He never looks at me.

"Get a chair from that table," Dad says.

"Those people might want it."

"Hell, just take it. Nobody's sitting on it."

"They might—"

Dad reaches around and yanks the chair over. The people look at him but don't say anything. Dad is breathing hard. "Here, sit here," he says. The soldier sits down.

Frank and Jerry come back. They stand by Dad, watching him. "Can we go out now?" Frank says.

"What?"

"Out for a boat ride."

"What? No, next week. Do it next week. We're going to play cards."

"You said—"

"Shut up, we'll do it next week." Dad looks up and shades his eyes. "The lake don't look right anyway."

"Lots of people are out there—"

"I said shut up."

"Honey," Ma whispers, "let him alone. Go and play by yourselves."

"Can we sit in the car?"

"Okay, but don't honk the horn."

"Ma, can't we go for a ride?"

"Go and play by yourselves, stop bothering us," she says. "Hey, will you take Sissie?"

They look at me. They don't like me, I can see it, but they take me with them. We run through the crowd and somebody spills a drink— he yells at us. "Oops, got to watch it!" Frank giggles.

We run along the walk by the boat. A woman in a yellow dress is carrying a baby. She looks at us like she doesn't like us.

Down at the far end some kids are standing together.

"Hey, lookit that," Frank says.

A blackbird is caught in the scum, by one of the boats. It can't fly up. One of the kids, a long-legged girl in a dirty dress, is poking at it with a stick.

The bird's wings keep fluttering but it can't get out. If it could get free it would fly and be safe, but the scum holds it down.

One of the kids throws a stone at it. "Stupid old goddamn bird," somebody says. Frank throws a stone. They are all throwing stones. The bird doesn't know enough to turn away. Its feathers are all wet and dirty. One of the stones hits the bird's head.

"Take that!" Frank says, throwing a rock. The water splashes up and some of the girls scream.

I watch them throwing stones. I am standing at the side. If the bird dies, then everything can die, I think. Inside the tavern there is music from the jukebox.

## II

We are at the boathouse tavern again. It is a mild day, a Sunday afternoon. Dad is talking with some men; Jerry and I are waiting by the boats. Mommy is at home with the new baby. Frank has gone off with some friends of his, to a stock-car race. There are some people here, sitting out at the tables, but they don't notice us.

"Why doesn't he hurry up?" Jerry says.

Jerry is twelve now. He has pimples on his forehead and chin.

He pushes one of the rowboats with his foot. He is wearing sneakers that are dirty. I wish I could get in that boat and sit down, but I am afraid. A boy not much older than Jerry is squatting on the boardwalk, smoking. You can tell he is in charge of the boats.

"Daddy, come on. Come on," Jerry says, whining. Daddy can't hear him.

I have mosquito bites on my arms and legs. There are mosquitoes and flies around here; the flies crawl around the sticky mess left on tables. A car over in the parking lot has its radio on loud. You can hear the music all this way. "He's coming," I tell Jerry so he won't be mad. Jerry is like Dad, the way his eyes look.

"Oh, that fat guy keeps talking to him," Jerry says.

The fat man is one of the bartenders; he has on a dirty white apron. All these men are familiar. We have been seeing them for years. He punches Dad's arm, up by the shoulder, and Dad pushes him. They are laughing, though. Nobody is mad.

"I'd sooner let a nigger—" the bartender says. We can't hear anything more, but the men laugh again.

"All he does is drink," Jerry says. "I hate him."

At school, up on the sixth-grade floor, Jerry got in trouble last month. The principal slapped him. I am afraid to look at Jerry when he's mad.

"I hate him, I wish he'd die," Jerry says.

Dad is trying to come to us, but every time he takes a step backward and gets ready to turn, one of the men says something. There are three men beside him. Their stomachs are big, but Dad's isn't. He is wearing dark pants and a white shirt; his tie is in the car. He wears a tie to church, then takes it off. He has his shirt sleeves rolled up and you can see how strong his arms must be.

Two women cross over from the parking lot. They are wearing high-heeled shoes and hats and bright dresses—orange and yellow—and when they walk past the men look at them. They go into the tavern. The men laugh about something. The way they laugh makes my eyes focus on something away from them—a bird flying in the sky—and it is hard for me to look anywhere else. I feel as if I'm falling asleep.

"Here he comes!" Jerry says.

Dad walks over to us, with his big steps. He is smiling and carrying a bottle of beer. "Hey, kid," he says to the boy squatting on the walk, "how's about a boat?"

"This one is the best," Jerry says.

"The best, huh? Great." Dad grins at us. "Okay, Sissie, let's get you in. Be careful now." He picks me up even though I am too heavy for it, and sets me in the boat. It hurts a little where he held me, under the arms, but I don't care.

Jerry climbs in. Dad steps and something happens—he almost slips, but he catches himself. With the wet oar he pushes us off from the boardwalk.

Dad can row fast. The sunlight is gleaming on the water. I sit very still, facing him, afraid to move. The boat goes fast, and Dad is leaning back and forth and pulling on the oars, breathing hard, doing everything fast like he always does. He is always in a hurry to get things done. He has set the bottle of beer down by his leg, pressed against the side of the boat so it won't fall.

"There's the guys we saw go out before," Jerry says. Coming around the island is a boat with three boys in it, older than Jerry. "They went on the island. Can we go there too?"

"Sure," says Dad. His eyes squint in the sun. He is sun-tanned, and there are freckles on his forehead. I am sitting close to him, facing him, and it surprises me what he looks like—he is like a stranger, with his eyes narrowed. The water beneath the boat makes me feel funny. It keeps us up now, but if I fell over the side I would sink and drown.

"Nice out here, huh?" Dad says. He is breathing hard.

"We should go over that way to get on the island," Jerry says.

"This goddamn oar has splinters in it," Dad says. He hooks the oar up and lets us glide. He reaches down to get the bottle of beer. Though the lake and some trees and the buildings back on shore are in front of me, what makes me look at it is my father's throat, the way it bobs when he swallows. He wipes his forehead. "Want to row, Sissie?" he says.

"Can I?"

"Let me do it," says Jerry.

"Naw, I was just kidding," Dad says.

"I can do it. It ain't hard."

"Stay where you are," Dad says.

He starts rowing again, faster. Why does he go so fast? His face is getting red, the way it does at home when he has trouble with Frank. He clears his throat and spits over the side; I don't like to see that but I can't help but watch. The other boat glides past us, heading for shore. The boys don't look over at us.

Jerry and I look to see if anyone else is on the island, but no one is. The island is very small. You can see around it.

"Are you going to land on it, Dad?" Jerry says.

"Sure, okay." Dad's face is flushed and looks angry.

The boat scrapes bottom and bumps. "Jump out and pull it in," Dad says. Jerry jumps out. His shoes and socks are wet now, but Dad doesn't notice. The boat bumps; it hurts me. I am afraid. But then we're up on the land and Dad is out and lifting me. "Nice ride, sugar?" he says.

Jerry and I run around the island. It is different from what we thought, but we don't know why. There are some trees on it, some wild grass, and then bare caked mud that goes down to the water. The water looks dark and deep on the other side, but when we get there it's shallow. Lily pads grow there; everything is thick and tangled. Jerry wades in the water and gets his pants legs wet. "There might be money in the water," he says.

Some napkins and beer cans are nearby. There is part of a hotdog bun, with flies buzzing around it.

When we go back by Dad, we see him squatting over the water doing something. His back jerks. Then I see that he is being sick. He is throwing up in the water and making a noise like coughing.

Jerry turns around right away and runs back. I follow him, afraid. On the other side we can look back at the boathouse and wish we were there.

## III

Marian and Betty went to the show, but I couldn't. She made me come along here with them. "And cut out that snippy face," Ma said, to let me know she's watching. I have to help her take care of Linda— poor fat Linda, with her runny nose! So here we are inside the tavern. There's too much smoke, I hate smoke. Dad is smoking a cigar. I won't drink any more root beer, it's flat, and I'm sick of potato chips. Inside me there is something that wants to run away, that hates them. How loud they are, my parents! My mother spilled something on the front of her dress, but does she notice? And my aunt Lucy and uncle Joe, they're here. Try to avoid them. Lucy has false teeth that make everyone stare at her. I know that everyone is staring at us. I could hide my head in my arms and turn away, I'm so tired and my legs hurt from sunburn and I can't stand them any more.

"So did you ever hear from them? That letter you wrote?" Ma says to Lucy.

"I'm still waiting. Somebody said you got to have connections to get on the show. But I don't believe it. That Howie Masterson that's the emcee, he's a real nice guy. I can tell."

"It's all crap," Dad says. "You women believe anything."

"I don't believe it," I say.

"Phony as hell," says my uncle.

"You do too believe it, Sissie," says my mother. "Sissie thinks he's cute. I know she does."

"I hate that guy!" I tell her, but she and my aunt are laughing. "I said I hate him! He's greasy."

"All that stuff is phony as hell," says my Uncle Joe. He is tired all the time, and right now he sits with his head bowed. I hate his bald head with the little fringe of gray hair on it. At least my father is still handsome. His jaws sag and there are lines in his neck—edged with dirt. I can see, embarrassed—and his stomach is bulging a little against the table, but still he is a handsome man. In a place like this women look at him. What's he see in *her?* they think. My mother had her hair cut too short last time; she looks queer. There is a photograph taken of her when she was young, standing by someone's motorcycle, with her hair long. In the photograph she was pretty, almost beautiful, but I don't believe it. Not really. I can't believe it, and I hate her. Her forehead gathers itself up in little wrinkles whenever she glances down at Linda, as if she can't remember who Linda is.

"Well, nobody wanted you, kid," she once said to Linda. Linda was a baby then, one year old. Ma was furious, standing in the kitchen where she was washing the floor, screaming: "Nobody wanted you, it was a goddamn accident! An accident!" That surprised me so I didn't know what to think, and I didn't know if I hated Ma or not; but I kept it all a secret . . . only my girl friends know, and I won't tell the priest either. Nobody can make me tell. I narrow my eyes and watch my mother leaning forward to say something—it's like she's going to toss something out on the table—and think that maybe she isn't my mother after all, and she isn't that pretty girl in the photograph, but someone else.

"A woman was on the show last night that lost two kids in a fire. Her house burned down," my aunt says loudly. "And she answered the questions right off and got a lot of money and the audience went wild. You could see she was a real lady. I love that guy, Howie Masterson. He's real sweet."

"He's a bastard," Dad says.

"Harry, what the hell? You never even seen him," Ma says.

"I sure as hell never did. Got better things to do at night." Dad turns to my uncle and his voice changes. "I'm on the night shift, now."

"Yeah, I hate that, I—"

"I can sleep during the day. What's the difference?"

"I hate those night shifts."

"What's there to do during the day?" Dad says flatly. His eyes scan us at the table as if he doesn't see anything, then they seem to fall off me and go behind me, looking at nothing.

"Not much," says my uncle, and I can see his white scalp beneath his hair. Both men are silent.

Dad pours beer into his glass and spills some of it. I wish I could look away. I love him, I think, but I hate to be here. Where would I rather be? With Marian and Betty at the movies, or in my room, lying on the bed and staring at the photographs of movie stars on my walls

—those beautiful people that never say anything—while out in the kitchen my mother is waiting for my father to come home so they can continue their quarrel. It never stops, that quarrel. Sometimes they laugh together, kid around, they kiss. Then the quarrel starts up again in a few minutes.

"Ma, can I go outside and wait in the car?" I say. "Linda's asleep."

"What's so hot about the car?" she says, looking at me.

"I'm tired. My sunburn hurts."

Linda is sleeping in Ma's lap, with her mouth open and drooling on the front of her dress. "Okay, go on," Ma says. "But we're not going to hurry just for you." When she has drunk too much there is a struggle in her between being angry and being affectionate; she fights both of them, as if standing with her legs apart and her hands on her hips, bracing a strong wind.

When I cross through the crowded tavern I'm conscious of people looking at me. My hair lost its curl because it was so humid today, my legs are too thin, my figure is flat and not nice like Marian's—I want to hide somewhere, hide my face from them. I hate this noisy place and these people. Even the music is ugly because it belongs to them. Then, when I'm outside, the music gets faint right away and it doesn't sound so bad. It's cooler out here. No one is around. Out back, the old rowboats are tied up. Nobody's on the lake. There's no moon, the sky is overcast, it was raining earlier.

When I turn around, a man is standing by the door watching me.

"What're you doing?" he says.

"Nothing."

He has dark hair and a tanned face, I think, but everything is confused because the light from the door is pinkish—there's a neon sign there. My heart starts to pound. The man leans forward to stare at me. "Oh, I thought you were somebody else," he says.

I want to show him I'm not afraid. "Yeah, really? Who did you think I was?" When we ride on the school bus we smile out the windows at strange men, just for fun. We do that all the time. I'm not afraid of any of them.

"You're not her," he says.

Some people come out the door and he has to step out of their way. I say to him, "Maybe you seen me around here before. We come here pretty often."

"Who do you come with?" He is smiling as if he thinks I'm funny. "Anybody I know?"

"That's my business."

It's a game. I'm not afraid. When I think of my mother and father inside, something makes me want to step closer to this man—why should I be afraid? I could be wild like some of the other girls. Nothing surprises me.

We keep on talking. At first I can tell he wants me to come inside the tavern with him, but then he forgets about it; he keeps talking. I don't know what we say, but we talk in drawling voices, smiling at each other but in a secret, knowing way, as if each one of us knew more than the other. My cheeks start to burn. I could be wild like Betty is sometimes—like some of the other girls. Why not? Once before I talked with a man like this, on the bus. We were both sitting in the back. I wasn't afraid. This man and I keep talking and we talk about nothing, he wants to know how old I am, but it makes my heart pound so hard that I want to touch my chest to calm it. We are walking along the old boardwalk and I say: "Somebody took me out rowing once here."

"Is that so?" he says. "You want me to take you out?"

He has a hard, handsome face. I like that face. Why is he alone? When he smiles I know he's laughing at me, and this makes me stand taller, walk with my shoulders raised.

"Hey, are you with somebody inside there?" he says.

"I left them."

"Have a fight."

"A fight, yes."

He looks at me quickly. "How old are you anyway?"

"That's none of your business."

"Girls your age are all alike."

"We're not all alike!" I arch my back and look at him in a way I must have learned somewhere—where?—with my lips not smiling but ready to smile, and my eyes narrowed. One leg is turned as if I'm ready to jump away from him. He sees all this. He smiles.

"Say, you're real cute."

We're walking over by the parking lot now. He touches my arm. Right away my heart trips, but I say nothing. I keep walking. High above us the tree branches are moving in the wind. It's cold for June. It's late—after eleven. The man is wearing a jacket, but I have on a sleeveless dress and there are goose-pimples on my arms.

"Cold, huh?" he says.

He takes hold of my shoulders and leans toward me. This is to show me he's no kid, he's grown-up, this is how they do things; when he kisses me his grip on my shoulders gets tighter. "I better go back," I say to him. My voice is queer.

"What?" he says.

I am wearing a face like one of those faces pinned up in my room, and what if I lose it? This is not my face. I try to turn away from him.

He kisses me again. His breath smells like beer, maybe, it's like my father's breath, and my mind is empty; I can't think what to do. Why am I here? My legs feel numb, my fingers are cold. The man rubs my arms and says, "You should have a sweater or something...."

He is waiting for me to say something, to keep on the way I was before. But I have forgotten how to do it. Before, I was Marian or one of the older girls; now I am just myself. I am fourteen. I think of Linda sleeping in my mother's lap, and something frightens me.

"Hey, what's wrong?" the man says.

He sees I'm afraid but pretends he doesn't. He comes to me again and embraces me, his mouth presses against my neck and shoulder, I feel as if I'm suffocating. "My car's over here," he says, trying to catch his breath. I can't move. Something dazzling and icy rises up in me, an awful fear, but I can't move and can't say anything. He is touching me with his hands. His mouth is soft but wants too much from me. I think, What is he doing? Do they all do this? Do I have to have it done to me too?

"You cut that out," I tell him.

He steps away. His chest is heaving and his eyes look like a dog's eyes, surprised and betrayed. The last thing I see of him is those eyes, before I turn and run back to the tavern.

## IV

Jesse says, "Let's stop at this place. I been here a few times before."

It's the Lakeside Bar. That big old building with the grubby siding, and a big pink neon sign in front, and the cinder driveway that's so bumpy. Yes, everything the same. But different too—smaller, dirtier. There is a custard stand nearby with a glaring orange roof, and people are crowded around it. That's new. I haven't been here for years.

"I feel like a beer," he says.

He smiles at me and caresses my arm. He treats me as if I were something that might break; in my cheap linen maternity dress I feel ugly and heavy. My flesh is so soft and thick that nothing could hurt it.

"Sure, honey. Pa used to stop in here too."

We cross through the parking lot to the tavern. Wild grass grows along the sidewalk and in the cracks of the sidewalk. Why is this place so ugly to me? I feel as if a hand were pressing against my chest, shutting off my breath. Is there some secret here? Why am I afraid?

I catch sight of myself in a dusty window as we pass. My hair is long, down to my shoulders. I am pretty, but my secret is that I am pretty like everybody is. My husband loves me for this but doesn't know it. I have a pink mouth and plucked darkened eyebrows and soft bangs over my forehead; I know everything, I have no need to learn from anyone else now. I am one of those girls younger girls study closely, to learn from. On buses, in five-and-tens, thirteen-year-old girls must look at me solemnly, learning, memorizing.

"Pretty Sissie!" my mother likes to say when we visit, though I told her how I hate that name. She is proud of me for being pretty, but thinks I'm too thin. "You'll fill out nice, after the baby," she says. Herself, she is fat and veins have begun to darken on her legs; she scuffs around the house in bedroom slippers. Who is my mother? When I think of her I can't think of anything—do I love her or hate her, or is there nothing there?

Jesse forgets and walks ahead of me, I have to walk fast to catch up. I'm wearing pastel-blue high heels—that must be because I am proud of my legs. I have little else. Then he remembers and turns to put out his hand for me, smiling to show he is sorry. Jesse is the kind of young man thirteen-year-old girls stare at secretly; he is not a man, not old enough, but not a boy either. He is a year older than I am, twenty. When I met him he was wearing a navy uniform and he was with a girl friend of mine.

Just a few people sitting outside at the tables. They're afraid of rain —the sky doesn't look good. And how bumpy the ground is here, bare spots and little holes and patches of crab grass, and everywhere napkins and junk. Too many flies outside. Has this place changed hands? The screens at the windows don't fit right; you can see why flies get inside. Jesse opens the door for me and I go in. All bars smell alike. There is a damp, dark odor of beer and something indefinable—spilled soft drinks, pretzels getting stale? This bar is just like any other. Before we were married we went to places like this, Jesse and me and other couples. We had to spend a certain amount of time doing things like that—and going to movies, playing miniature golf, bowling, dancing, swimming—then we got married, now we're going to have a baby. I think of the baby all the time, because my life will be changed then; everything will be different. Four months from now. I should be frightened, but a calm laziness has come over me. It was so easy for my mother.... But it will be different with me because my life will be changed by it, and nothing ever changed my mother. You couldn't change her! Why should I think? Why should I be afraid? My body is filled with love for this baby, and I will never be the same again.

We sit down at a table near the bar. Jesse is in a good mood. My father would have liked him, I think; when he laughs Jesse reminds me of him. Why is a certain kind of simple, healthy, honest man always destined to lose everything? Their souls are as clean and smooth as the muscular line of their arms. At night I hold Jesse, thinking of my father and what happened to him—all that drinking, then the accident at the factory—and I pray that Jesse will be different. I hope that his quick, open, loud way of talking is just a disguise, that really he is someone else—slower and calculating. That kind of man grows old without jerks and spasms. Why did I marry Jesse?

Someone at the bar turns around, and it's a man I think I know—I have known. Yes. That man outside, the man I met outside. I stare at him, my heart pounding, and he doesn't see me. He is dark, his hair is neatly combed but is thinner than before; he is wearing a cheap gray suit. But is it the same man? He is standing with a friend and looking around, as if he doesn't like what he sees. He is tired too. He has grown years older.

Our eyes meet. He glances away. He doesn't remember—that frightened girl he held in his arms.

I am tempted to put my hand on Jesse's arm and tell him about that man, but how can I? Jesse is talking about trading in our car for a new one. . . . I can't move, my mind seems to be coming to a stop. Is that the man I kissed, or someone else? A feeling of angry loss comes over me. Why should I lose everything? Everything? Is it the same man, and would he remember? My heart bothers me, it's stupid to be like this: here I sit, powdered and sweet, a girl safely married, pregnant and secured to the earth, with my husband beside me. He still loves me. Our love keeps on. Like my parents' love, it will subside someday, but nothing surprises me because I have learned everything.

The man turns away, talking to his friend. They are weary, tired of something. He isn't married yet, I think, and that pleases me. Good. But why are these men always tired? Is it the jobs they hold, the kind of men who stop in at this tavern? Why do they flash their teeth when they smile, but stop smiling so quickly? Why do their children cringe from them sometimes—an innocent upraised arm a frightening thing? Why do they grow old so quickly, sitting at kitchen tables with bottles of beer? They are everywhere, in every house. All the houses in this neighborhood and all neighborhoods around here. Jesse is young, but the outline of what he will be is already in his face; do you think I can't see it? Their lives are like hands dealt out to them in their innumerable card games. You pick up the sticky cards, and there it is: there it is. Can't change anything, all you can do is switch some cards around, stick one in here, one over here . . . pretend there is some sense, a secret scheme.

The man at the bar tosses some coins down and turns to go. I want to cry out to him, "Wait, wait!" But I cannot. I sit helplessly and watch him leave. Is it the same man? If he leaves I will be caught here, what can I do? I can almost hear my mother's shrill laughter coming in from outside, and some drawling remark of my father's—lifting for a moment above the music. Those little explosions of laughter, the slap of someone's hand on the damp table in anger, the clink of bottles accidentally touching—and there, there, my drunken aunt's voice, what is she saying? I am terrified at being left with them. I watch the man at the door and think that I could have loved him. I know it.

He has left, he and his friend. He is nothing to me, but suddenly I feel tears in my eyes. What's wrong with me? I hate everything that springs upon me and seems to draw itself down and oppress me in a way I could never explain to anyone. . . . I am crying because I am pregnant, but not with that man's child. It could have been his child,

I could have gone with him to his car, but I did nothing, I ran away, I was afraid, and now I'm sitting here with Jesse, who is picking the label off his beer bottle with his thick squarish fingernails. I did nothing. I was afraid. Now he has left me here and what can I do?

I let my hand fall onto my stomach to remind myself that I am in love: with this baby, with Jesse, with everything. I am in love with our house and our life and the future and even this moment—right now —that I am struggling to live through.

---

# IN SEARCH OF A MISSING IUD
## *Anne Higgins*

Dear Dr. Lunt,

You remember the other day when you had me trussed up on the examining table like a chicken and told me for my own reassurance, peace of mind I think you said, that I should have an abdominal X ray made; that you would write the instruction on a slip of paper: "For the presence of a missing IUD," to be handed to the X-ray man . . . ? It struck me then, as now, as a comic line. I wonder that you didn't see the humor of it. I suppose in your line of work these little physical ironies cease to be funny. Or maybe you simply deem it more politic not to snicker at your patients' dilemmas, at least not in front of them.

To sidetrack a little bit, because I've never had the courage to ask directly, what makes a man decide on an Ob-Gyn specialty? I can't help but think that as a day-by-day way of making one's living it must be a bore. To peer at nothing but the hind quarters of trussed-up women. *Chacun à son goût,* I suppose. Still. My apologies for getting personal, but remember that you asked a great many personal questions of me and on the strength of my answers made a great many personal comments and judgments. I must confess that I was rather offended by the whole interview, however professionally motivated your questions and well intended your advice. I suppose it's nothing more than a matter of pride—I have an MA in English and a PhD in Comparative Literature—and I do hate to be talked down to. (You wouldn't have expected a PhD in Comp Lit to have ended a sentence with a preposition, would you. To down hate to be talked?) Frankly you sounded like the Doctor's Advice column out of *Redbook* magazine. And I must say that your hands are unusually small. I'm not being indelicate and I'm sure that you know what you're doing, but analogously speaking, would you expect an extremely short-fingered man to go into concert-piano work? What I'm trying to say is, is it possible that you're hampered professionally by your small hands? Personally speaking, is it possible that you missed something you would otherwise have found had you been more generously endowed? Manually, that is. Look, the fact of the matter is, bluntly, this: you thought, via your probe instruments and look-see devices that the IUD was still there but you couldn't find the nylon strings that would indicate its presence to you. Now: if you think the IUD is still there then where could the nylon strings have gone? Surely they're not wafting around up there in sub-uterine breezes. All right, I'll have the X ray made to make sure of what's where. But the reason I went to you in the first place was to avoid just such an ambiguous mess as this. I have no professional quarrel with you, but at this point I do wonder about the possible professional handicap of your hands.

Dear Father Zimmel,

Just a quick note from a former student of yours. You may remember that I took your adult theology courses off and on for five years. I was that striving, conscientious woman in the back of the room who beleaguered your life for so many years. Your eyes would shine with Holy Spirited light as you put the one of little faith in her proper place: i.e., down. Oh I know you, Father, you can't deny your venomous delight, your wicked pride in your debating skills. (Was it a subject for confession, this theological hubris?) But I know myself too, a pseudo-student of Voltaire and Diderot, a one-time admirer of Plato's Philosopher-King, a long-time disciple of Marx the Idealist, a camp follower of Dorothy Day, an early devotee of Teilhard de Chardin (did *you* ever get through him? Ah, gotcha!), an enthusiast at the same time of Catherine the Great, Hamilton, Jefferson, Walt Whitman, Ezra Pound, Henry Miller, Thérèse the Little Flower, Genet, Bertrand Russell, Dietrich Bonhoeffer, *yes* to Meister Eckhart, Phyllis McGinley, and Betty Friedan. Paradoxes, paradoxes. And guilty of rationalizations, neuroses. I never got anywhere with any of them; unlike John the Baptist I was a reed shaken by every wind, swayed from right to left depending on the suasiveness of the breeze. How I used to pore over those books and pamphlets on the Church as Magister, the pronouncements on authority and obedience, the summonses to the logic and truth of Natural Law. In spite of them and your eloquence I remained unconvinced. Married to a Catholic, I practiced the precepts of the Church. (I'm sure you remember me now: I was that lady who was *always* pregnant.) On my own I decided to summon a different natural law into account: the one concerned with the point of diminishing returns. You would consider yourself justified in a good theologically sneering belly laugh. God is not mocked, His Law will not be abrogated by the libertine advances of twentieth-century science. Madam, I can hear you thunder, do you understand now that the Hound of Heaven will pursue you into every wickedly free-thinking gynecologist's office that you enter?

Well, Father, what is at stake? The Pascalian Wager? What it boils down to is this: candy is dandy but nothing at all would be safer. Galilean, thou hast conquered.

Dear Sister Seraphim,

I've been meaning to write for months, to tell you how much I enjoyed seeing you again; and really how impressed I am at the changes that have taken place in the last fifteen years. Nuns certainly have become swingers, haven't they? No more of those ridiculous social censures (you probably don't remember, but I do, that I spent my whole last senior semester campused as a punitive result of my contempt of those censures); full-fledged departments now in soc., psych., and poli sci.; a mixed drama department, taking advantage of nearby men's colleges (didn't you—honestly now—want to writhe at the sight of girls playing Lear and Othello?); Saul Alinsky and Paul Goodman invited to speak on campus. No administrative pronouncements on the proper length of skirts ... Talk about progress!

Could I interject here that nineteen years ago, when I was in your freshman philosophy class, you gave one of the most brilliant lectures I've ever heard, on Augustine's concept of time. All these years and I've never told you. Ah, sins of omission.

One jarring note: it disturbed me—it bugged me, if you want to know the truth—that you referred to Alinsky as "a smart Jew." Really, I felt that was beneath you; certainly it was hitting below the ecumenical belt. I've often wondered since whether it slipped out as a remnant of pre-ecumenical indoctrination or whether you cast it out as a barb to me. At any rate I didn't challenge it, I let it pass. I should have said something. But a first meeting in fifteen years ... one tends to be polite, one is awed by the passage of time. And plain old nostalgia. Anyway, for the record, I object to stereotypes. Particularly, you middle-class-lace-curtain-Irish nun you, ones that refer to Jews.

One more thing for the record: if it appears in the Alumnae News that Mrs. Michael Callahan, nee Leslie Goldman, wife of the successful Omaha attorney and busy mother of eight visited St. Rose's over the holidays and had a nice long chat with Sr. Seraphim ... boom! There goes my annual contribution. I can see it now: "Leslie Callahan, who incidentally holds a graduate degree, is a shining example of the Educated Catholic (sic) Woman we try to turn out here at St. Rose's. Welcoming each new bundle of joy as they appear in annual succession, Leslie realizes the tremendous advantages of her educational background as a guide for teaching and nourishing these tender souls entrusted by God to her care. As she told Sr. Seraphim ..."

Well, I won't have it. I was long gone from St. Rose's, and immersed in (and rather exhausted by) and arduous process of "finding myself" at Columbia . . . when along came Mike Callahan, that handsome Irish charmer with glittering teeth and eyes burning blue pockets of salvation and ambition. Save me from myself, would Mike Callahan. Redeem the Left-wing Jewess. Impose order on anarchy, true-love on falsesex. What could be more seductive? I fell hard and fast, swept off my feet by the passion of chaste kisses. Who needed a career, a sterile PhD, when Love beckoned in the marriage bed behind the altar? I took all the pre-Cana courses, signed everything, all the dotted lines everywhere. Sewed up everything tight. Including myself. And little heaven-sent Callahans appeared with the regularity that other women get their periods. Of course I love my children, and Mike is generous about providing a weekly cleaning woman, a personal allowance, and so on. That point is: what's the point? What's the point of enshrining a fertile woman? Fertility, like rain in season, is easy to come by. One prays against droughts but against floods too. If one prays at all and/or has any common sense. At any rate the Callahans —Successful Corporation Lawyer Michael Callahan and His Lovely Family—appear regularly in the Omaha press. Mrs. Callahan is expecting her third child, her fifth, her seventh, her eighth. The fantastic Mrs. Callahan has just given birth to her thirty-fourth child. Mrs. Callahan, in spite of her busy schedule, finds time for community work, is active in many charitable and social organizations, and is on the board of the Omaha Arts and Culture Program. Mr. Callahan is an outstanding Catholic layman, well known in the business community, leader of the Anti-Smut Campaign, "a dabbler," he laughs modestly, "in politics," and twice voted Mr. Omaha by the Omaha Chamber of Commerce.

Dear Sister Seraphim, do you realize that some of the priests we have over for dinner are still disgruntled over the introduction of lay participation in the Mass? That Mike and I didn't speak to each other for three months before the last election? That Mike Callahan, that outstanding Catholic layman-lawyer—and *here's* a choice bit of *sub rosa* gossip for you—contributed fifteen hundred dollars toward the purchase of a neighboring house, in a nonexistent family's name, in order that it wouldn't be purchased by "undesirable elements" (read: a Negro dentist and his family).

Well. Greetings from Omaha. I didn't intend this to be so personal. I understand there are great changes going on which have not yet hit this acreage of the universe. Blessings on you and forge ahead! It was nice to be East again and to see you after so long, even under the circumstances. P.S. My late father used to ponder—with sly humor— why so many nuns took the names of male saints: Sr. Mary Michael, Sr. Francis, Sr. Paul, Sr. William Marie, etc. Frankly, if you want to know my honest opinion, I can't see names like Sr. Celestine, Sr. Il-

luminata, Sr. Immaculata, or Sr. Seraphim either. P.P.S. I'm sure
Father, wherever he is, thanks you for your prayers. He was a secularist
most of his life but he was a *good* man.

Dear Mr. Herzog,
I'll get right to the point: *don't* settle for Ramona. I know you have
your needs, your faults, your weaknesses like everybody else, but the
more I think about the possibility of that liaison, the more I think it
would be a bad mistake. A really bad mistake. You know what would
happen, she'd sap your creativity in a wink. No, no, that's wrong.
Gradually. You wouldn't even realize it was happening until you
found yourself so thoroughly attuned to Food, to Culture, to Ramona's
Orphic rites that you would never even have the desire to take up
your pen again, never mind the strength. You would complain, only
once, and only of a very slight headache, and there would be Ramona:
"Oh no, Moses darling, don't tire yourself. Rest now." Perhaps she
would put on Egyptian music to soothe you—though I have more
than the suspicion that after a while the Egyptian stuff would go,
you'd be getting Mantovani, don't kid yourself. Remember that Ramona is in her late thirties and that these exotic binges become tiresome, they're *wearing* on a woman that age. Ramona too will be getting headaches, but not slight ones. Huge ones. And then there will be
lowered blinds and vinegar cloths for her forehead; no music at all,
not even Mantovani. But for the present Ramona will soothe you,
comfort you, build up your still undernourished ego. Ramona understands everything, anticipates your every desire. After a while you will
want to put your *own* sugar in your coffee. You think you will scream
if you hear the sympathetic assent of "poor Moses" one more time.
(And you will feel guilty about that precisely because Ramona *is* a
dear, good woman and undoubtedly she *does* love you and want your
happiness.) But for right now, Ramona will put on her clanging
Egyptian music—oh yes, I've heard those sensuous wails—and dance
tenderly naked for you, clad only in Vita Dew Youth Emulsion,
jingling jangling gold bracelets and her black lace underpants.
(Panties to women like Ramona.) Oh God, and the high heels of
course.
Moses, that's the crux: don't marry a woman who Prepares herself.
At thirty-seven or so she's a looker still with superb shoulders and good
breasts—and by your own admission the shape of a woman's breasts is
important to you (as appalling a weakness as I find that to be in you,
still it's honest, it's an honest weakness)—but think, Moses, think that
when Ramona is forty-seven and her whole life is a dedicated, con-
suming passion to keeping those shoulders soft, that bosom high and
firm, those Orphic elements trim. Hours, whole days will be spent
Preparing herself. At sixty, after a month of grim, self-disciplined

Preparation, she will still be standing coyly in the bedroom door (the bedroom lighting will have been rearranged to forbid harshness at any hour) and asking, "Moses darling, do I please you?" *That* is what will become of your life, you a domesticated poodle leafing through Ramona's magazines, waiting for the mistress to appear, in order to give a few appreciative barks (quacks, the old quack-quack phenomenon, as you so well described it) and be led, sniffing tamely and with an increasing exhaustion, through the hoops of the Orphic rituals.

I sound shrill. Perhaps I am simply jealous of Ramona. Ramona, after all, is a woman of the world, perfumed, a cooker of fancy shrimp and arbiter of dry wines. She has the good sense to serve chilled grapes for dessert and not strawberry shortcake; she attends lectures and is sexually mature. (I suppose I hate her because she's a realist at heart as well as a narcissist.) Certainly Ramona regards Precautions as a necessary part of Preparations. Ramona knew that when she was six-teen. How do some women know all about these things and manage them successfully? I assure you that other women are not so fortunate in these affairs.

At any rate, I beg you not to marry Ramona. I feel no immodesty about proposing myself; on the other hand, no shame, only a little sadness knowing you wouldn't have me. I used to be one of those dungareed, flat-chested, hawk-nosed beauties that are prone to prowl around Eastern universities talking literature and art in coffee houses and crummy pubs. After eight children I am still flat-chested and hawk-nosed but I have acquired a mid-aged, mid-west spread. They like wide-hipped women out here; their greatest compliment is to ask if you are a local girl. Wealthy Nebraskan businessmen would overlook (forgive!) my Semitic nose for the pleasure of my heavy thighs. Faagh, I look down my fine curved beak at them. Go eat corn, man, you and I could make no good music together. On the other hand, I see myself clearly on the Ludeyville wavelength, attuned to your marvelous old place up there, running green through the summers, crouching low by fires in winter. The acreage, the solitude, the physical work in-volved in keeping up a place like that: bliss. Just that. Real work pleasures, like driving nails into hard wood and bringing an aban-doned garden to ordered life. My husband calls the carpenter, the plumber, the electrician. Appliances whir softly, constantly. Things that go whir in the night. How blissful the silence of the Berkshires. How divine a stove that didn't blind you with chrome! I could be happy in Ludeyville. I repeat without shame, I could make you happy. No go, eh? Moses in the fullness of his Jewish heart may love children, but not eight little Callahans and their wide-hipped Omaha ma. I don't blame you for a minute, it's a preposterous idea.

I didn't start out intending this proposal at all. I started out giving you a little piece of well-meant advice on Ramona, which I will now (tiresomely) repeat and for the last time: don't do it. The temptation is great. But dear Moses Herzog, you are too close to sainthood to give it up now for a few years of mortal happiness. The end. And anyway you probably wouldn't even be that happy.

Dear Gypsy,

Remember that time you and Jon were living in Lima and you got stored on pisco sours one afternoon and the Terrible Thing happened? After four years I still giggle thinking about it. There you were, smashed as could be, and in desperation hanging your head over the toilet when Jon comes staggering in, cross-eyed drunk, and says, "Gypsy darling, let me help you" and *drops the toilet seat on your nose*. I'm laughing now, just at the thought of that letter. You thought for sure your nose was broken, the poor bridge was bent all out of shape and it swelled immediately and turned seven shades of green and purple and you had dinner guests that night. And you couldn't say a word. As I remember, you made some feeble excuse about bumping into a doorway in the middle of the night, and everyone thought Jon had beaten you up and exchanged raised eyebrows over the dinner candles. You couldn't even write to anyone about it, except me. That always struck me as the funniest part, not being able to explain it. How can you say: my throbbing nose is big as a potato because my husband dropped the toilet seat on it. It's like suffering from hemorrhoids. You can complain in company about a migraine headache, about having cancer, ulcers, sinusitis, arthritis, neuralgia, neuritis. But you *can't* writhe on the edge of your chair and moan Oh my aching ass!

Which brings me to the point of this letter. To whom else could I write about this comedy of the absurd? Remember at Father's funeral when you advised me that if I didn't want to go on proliferating like a rabbit I Should Do Something About It? Well, I did. I went to the most discreet gynecologist in town and got one of those squiggly loop-de-loops. And you know what's happened to it? I don't either. Neither does the Gyn. Maybe it's there, maybe it's not. I'm supposed to go get an X ray to find out. What's Mike going to say when he gets a bill for one flat abdominal X-ray plate? I can always pay cash, that's not the real problem. It's simply the psychological effect it has on me. Frankly, at this point I feel like a damned sneak. I don't agree with Mike, I think he's all wrong on a lot of issues, but there's a certain basic honesty and integrity that must be preserved in a marriage if it's going to work at all. It was bad enough having to sneak to the Gyn, but now this sneaking off to the X-ray man . . . where did I read once that guilty people get caught because they have a subconscious *need* to get caught? I feel like the unholy alliance of Freud and the

Catholic church has teamed up, in a spurt of black humor, to get me. (Good grief, not only guilt but paranoia. What next?) Mike is simply intransigent on the whole issue. He was furious with me even for talking to the priest to get "permission" to use the Pill (if I never read another article or listen to another discussion on Morality and the Pill I'll die happy). His final words (cold, but concessive) (for him) were that if I wanted to take The Pill (why do they always capitalize it, like some divinity or higher institution) he wouldn't object, though he certainly didn't approve of "thwarting Nature" like that. (When he had that kidney operation last year he darn well had an anesthetic and I didn't hear any objections *then* about "thwarting Nature.") Anyway, it was at that point I decided *I* didn't want to take the Pill. Talk about interfering with Nature! Why should I let my body chemistry and whole hormone system get thrown out of whack. So off I sneaked to the loop-de-loop man and only to have the Final Solution turn out like this.

What's really funny about it is that the whole thing is right out of a best-seller. Some Mary McCarthy character would get herself in a situation like this. The girl goes to the clinic and gets her device. Three months later she goes back for the routine checkup and they can't find it. Trauma. She comes home, expecting her boyfriend to take her in his arms and say something consoling like, "Never mind, love, we'll find another one." Instead, bored by her hysterics and uninterested in the femaleness of the problem anyway, he is crass, callow. He finally says something really boorish, like, "What do you expect me to do? Send up a search party?" The girl sobs, rages. She accuses him of not loving her and by then she is right, he doesn't, he couldn't care less. He takes up painting and hashish again, and she goes home to Mother. There's even material here for a television script, one of those deadly family situation comedies. Outline: everyone loses something and finds it again. Junior's lost dog finds its way home (accompanied, of course, by a litter of pups—cute!), Sister discovers the lost Atlantis (in the encyclopedia—educational!), Pop finds his misplaced pipe on the roof (hilarious!—American Pops are such sweet, inept bunglers), Mom discovers her missing IUD (in the garden? *in the asparagus patch?* We just lost the sponsor), and Grandma finds the lost chord. Sound of a great Amen as the camera pans to a long shot of the mountains.

Dear oh dear, Gypsy, how did identical twins ever turn out so different as we? You still barren after three marriages and I caught up on the proverbial horns over this idiotic birth-control business. I know your childlessness is a source of great sorrow to you but truly, Gypsy, I couldn't hand over even one of my children, not even to you who I know would love it dearly and spoil it rotten. (I'm still not sure whether when I saw you at the funeral you were serious or facetious about that proposal.) I'm a neurotic and at times a crappy mother but I have this *thing* about my kids. On the other hand, I often envy (read: turn pea-green with frustrated jealousy) your freedom to travel, to indulge your artistic and intellectual caprices, to meet the Beautiful *and* the Interesting People! (*We* are on a *tu-toi* basis with the chairman of the State Republican Club. Oh, we are *Important* People!) I could even get interested in politics—if politics were the subject at hand and not wheeler-dealer political games. These disgusting exhibitions of avarice and cynicism which we entertain in our living room are what are known as grass-roots politics. Hear my cries of disavowal... And yet what am *I* contributing to the Betterment of Mankind? Well. More later.

Dear Father,

I've just been writing to Gypsy and wondering how the two of us, she and I, managed to turn out so unalike. But now I am thinking, No, we're not really that much different. The real mystery here is how you managed to turn out two who are so different from *you*. Also, I was writing to Sr. Seraphim and ended up with some inane postscript defending you as a "good man." I don't know why. I suppose it has something to do with the old De Mortuis etc. theme. And in the conversation I had with Sr. S. when I went to see her after the funeral, I laid it on quite a bit thicker than merely a good man. I made you out to be one of those heart-of-gold humanists; Father, forgive me, I had you embracing Orthodoxy at the very end, and not only buried with your *tallis* in the casket but facing toward Zion with a little sack of Israeli soil under your head. I don't know what got into me. I suppose maybe I just wanted to one-up her with religion. I can hear you rattling your coffin with laughter. Even worse, and this will really tickle you, she fell for it. The only thing that would have impressed her more would have geen a deathbed conversion to Catholicism. However, the Orthodoxy bit was quite dramatically correct. I conjured pictures of Yahrzeit lights and keening relatives rending their garments... I'm not proud of myself. I suppose deep down I always wanted you to be exactly that sort of man who would have a funeral like that.

When I was growing up—and Gypsy too—we craved the identity that other kids had. They rebelled against their immigrant parents or grandparents, when they went to college they had nose jobs done and pretended not to understand Yiddish, but Father, we were steeped in European readings, how we wanted you to grow a long patriarchal beard, to strap on phylacteries and sit swaying and wailing and muttering ancient prayers and incantations. How we used to hope that one of your silvery-laughed lady friends would turn out to be a Jewish mama and light the candles on Friday nights. Your funeral, by the way, was filled with these ladies, aging now but heavily mascaraed, all with lacquered hair, both young and old—both men and women too, yes, Father, they all turned out—all trilling in their thrilling theatrical voices, a regular chapelful of preening peacocks. I think half of them came to meet their agents. If it's any comfort to you it was a grand affair. The embarrassed rabbi, worldly fellow though he was, broke out in a bad case of hives. He was assisted by a nondenominational minister whose chief claim to fame is that he once officiated at the marriage of a homosexual pair in an East Village apartment; his homily on tolerance is still widely remembered. The funeral cortege was a status admixture of limousines and roaring Hondas: who could be farther In or farther Out. At the final chapel service several ladies fainted from the heat, and Gypsy's purse got snatched. Wild. It was right up your alley.

Gypsy and I didn't think it was very funny. Gypsy, in fact, became so enraged at the oleaginous minister that she threatened to report him to the Better Business Bureau. (That *did* strike me as funny but she wouldn't laugh about it even later.)

I'm thinking that the reason "good man" sticks in my craw was not anything to do with your succession of ladies—though by what quirk of paternal tenderness did you keep them hidden from Gypsy and me for so long?—but with your diabolical refusal to make any judgments except as they concerned pleasure. You didn't mix the sacred and the profane, you refused to acknowledge any distinction. Thus you were not a bad man or a good man but a neuter neutral laughing man. I'm convinced that the only reason you honored that absurd deathbed wish of Mother's to send one of us to a Baptist and the other to a Catholic college was because you found it so outrageously funny. Ethical Culture Mother's half-Jewish daughters separated and sent off at age seventeen to cope with the formal rigors of Christian theology. And you waving a debonair handkerchief at the train station and laughing like a madman up your agnostic sleeve. Good God, what a joke. I must hand it to you, you preceded the black humorists by forty years. You were op/pop art fleshed out. Really Father, you would have enjoyed your funeral. You knew all along you were going to die. It was your best joke, your lifetime *coup,* and with unerring sense of theater you saved it for last.

The only good thing about your funeral, really the only decent thing that happened during that whole fluttering travesty of death and burial, was a meeting I had with the Anderssons. You may not even remember them; they were Ethical Culture people, friends of Mother's. I remember meeting them several times as a child, and they were old then. Gypsy and I found them fascinating because they "talked funny." They're Scandinavian, Swedes I think. Anyway, there they were at your funeral. They had kept up with your career all these years and had come to "pay their respects." In that milling mob of self-seekers these two old humble eccentrics were like a whiff of strong ozone. Gypsy and I took them out for dinner, and here comes the story: they had no children and in their later years took to breeding and raising chihuahuas. One day, close to the lying-in time of one of the females, they spent the whole afternoon and evening away from home. Came home after midnight completely exhausted, only to find carnage all over the apartment. The female had started to whelp and was whimpering and making a mess of the living room rug; in the meantime the other dogs had gotten hold of a feather pillow from the bedroom, ripped it apart, and scattered it from one end of the apartment to the other. Feathers, mounds and heaps of feathers, wet, dry, sticky, floating, clinging feathers every place they looked, and in the midst of this the mother having pups in the middle of the living room rug. Poor weary old Anderssons, to be faced with this! Mrs. A. got a cardboard box and started assisting the mother while Mr. A. began the cleanup job. He had gathered several armloads of feathers and stuffed them in a paper bag in the kitchen when he heard a squeak. He rocked back and forth thinking he had never heard that particular floorboard squeak before. And then he realized it was coming from the paper bag and he went over and began digging through the feathers and *found* it, down in the bottom of the bag, a puppy, half smothered, still wet, and completely covered by feathers. Gently he fished it out and took it to Mrs. A. who licked it clean.

Mr. A. went on with the story but I'm stopping here. Father, *she licked it clean!* That's the point. There was nothing else to be done—such a fragile newborn couldn't be exposed to the shock of water—and without thinking twice about it she did what its mother would do. Father, I was so excited by that small incident I nearly jumped up in the restaurant and cheered. (When I told the story to Mike he was so repelled he walked out of the room.) I'm sure you never read it, but in *Kristin Lavransdatter* there was one sentence which stated simply that one of Kristin's sons had trouble with his eyes and that Kristin would clear them of matter with her tongue. Father, you understand the importance of these things, don't you? In spite of, beneath your devilish laughter you understood what it meant to be human, didn't you? To perform a human act, one of service, and in loving humility? A *Chesed shel emet?*

If you don't understand these things now I suppose you never will; not that it makes any difference. Although I must admit I would like it to make a difference.

That's about all I have to tell you right now. I'm tiring; these graphomania sieges take their toll. We're all well here, we push on from day to day. Who knows, maybe in the long run we'll find all the things we've been looking for, including our souls.

MEMO: Call Dr. Lunt's office, make an appointment. Proceed directly to the drugstore, do not pass Go, do not collect two hundred dollars. Buy arsenic. Skip Lunt, just go to the drugstore. I know the symptoms, there's no sense having Lunt confirm them. And I might end up crying in his office and then he'd have to go through his male doctor comforts his female patient routine. The old pat on the shoulder, there there buck up. Followed by the slightly impatient, "Can't you gals learn to take care of yourselves we're not in the Stone Age you know." Maybe I should just wait till the last minute and then pop over to the hospital—"There's something in my stomach, I can't imagine, do you suppose it's a gall stone?" "No, lady, it's a Mound's chocolate bar, it's a Peter Paul Almond Joy." Oh Doctor, you wit, fancy that, another bundle of almond joy.

No, I've got to see Lunt. For one thing, I've got to ask him how the baby is going to turn out. It's stupid, but I can't get over the idea that the fetus is going to form itself around the loop—sort of the way an oyster forms a pearl. Imagine a baby being born in the shape of a Lippy's loop! Or being born clutching the loop in one hand. "Nurse, do me a favor, check the kid's fists before you show him to my husband."

I'm worn out with exhaustion and chronic queasiness. I wake in the middle of the night and feel hysteria all around me—not lurking, not ready to pounce, but seeping through the room like gas. I press myself into Mike's flannel-clad back and fight the urge to bite clean through his backbone. I haven't told him yet. I think about abortion but I know I couldn't go through with it—even if I could find someone who wasn't a butcher, even if I started hanging around poolrooms and downtown bars to find out a name, a referral, even if I told Mike I wanted a week's vacation in Puerto Rico by myself and he agreed to stay home with the children ha ha ha ha ha. . . . But I couldn't. The idea is too grisly. Not the idea, the reality. To rip out a life like that, to rip it out of me and rinse it down some stainless-steel drain. But suppose I were desperate enough, would I do it? Probably. I guess that's my biggest problem. I despair, but I'm not desperate. In frustration I watch my own life go down the drain but I know I can cope with that. I'll survive. I'm strong, and even now, feeling sick all the time, I get goose-pimply with the anticipation of birth. I labor easily, though under delusion. I'm a lucky woman.

Goddamn him. I'll get a full-time housekeeper out of this one. I'll fix him. Let him see if he has any extra fifteen hundred dollars from now on to keep the niggers out of the neighborhood. Or to contribute to this or that one's campaign. Or to entertain on. I'll put laxatives in the pâté and Spanish Fly in the roe. Oh he's so cool, he has everything so neatly under control. He won't even divorce me, he says children need a mother, and then he keeps giving me more children to prove it. Irrefutable logic. He and Father Zimmel, incestuous twins! Why won't rhythm work for me? I've licked the glass off a dozen thermometers—I should have swallowed the mercury—and each time I have either a boy or a girl for my bother. Suppose I called in the carpenters and had an extra wing built onto the house. Put up a sign: No Admittance Except With Prophylactic In Hand. But he'd see me locked away in a home for the unfit, he'd have me committed to an institution before he'd walk in that door.

And me? I? What options do I have? I'm that sexually sloppy Jewess his mother warned him about. "Jews are sexually sloppy," she told him, and she pursed her lips in scorn and fear; an Irish parody of a Jewish mother. And what of it, I gloried at the time, I'm rich with the juices of honey and pressed olives. Or was . . . But that's *it,* that's what I have to guard against. Not the frustration, not even the encroaching hysteria, but the wine turning to vinegar. The slow corrosion, the final bankruptcy. Of all defeats that's the most insidious. Its tentacles are silent, it sidles up and grabs you over coffee, and you're caught. Bitterness and anger—you can hear your own death rattles.

He won't divorce me, that's sure as the night, the day. Just let me even see a lawyer, he said, and I'd rue the day forever. The children would be caught like butterflies in a net; he'd see to it that he was left with the net. The depth and breadth of his arrogance never stop surprising me. I live in the wrong century. In another time I could have hired a band of thugs to waylay him on a dark night and do their swift razor work. Poor denuded Abelard, singing mournfully to himself, No no, they can't take that away from me. Mike impotent, the loveliest of lovers. I won't hire anyone, I'll do the dire deed myself, and I won't use a razor, not even a rusty one; I'll use the goddamned pruning shears.

Maybe when I tell Mike he'll give me another diamond sunburst. Diamonds are a girl's best friend—I'll pin it between my legs. Won't he be surprised! He thinks I care about the jewelry, the furs, he honestly thinks they should make a woman happy. I could be happy in Ludeyville with Moses Herzog, that's how I could be happy. Well, it's no use. My sagging breasts wouldn't please him, neither would my reluctance to nourish his ego. My own inner house needs refurbishing; I couldn't take on the care and feeding of his. Let that fantasy go. I'll survive this baby, I'll name it Omega—just the way I named the last five. Those Greeks, they just didn't know where to end their alphabet. Should I have an abortion or a frontal lobotomy. I'm being funny again, I can't even despair properly. The odd thing is, I don't feel suicidal. I feel used, angry, vindictive—and this *will* be the last baby, I swear that—but not suicidal. Please God in my next reincarnation I'll come back as other than a cow or a dancing bear. A fish, a Clown Loach—that would suit me. An electric stargazer: I shoot out my tongue to trap my victims and emit fifty-volt charges. (Though that sounds more like Mike.) I'll be a Moray eel, ferocious; powerful jaws, strong teeth, a savage bite. I'll be a Porcupine Globefish, inflating myself when in danger, with erected spines—why hasn't anyone thought of that before as a birth-control measure? A Brown-headed Cowbird who lays her eggs in other birds' nests; nasty wily lady, she then takes off and someone else has to brood and rear her young. I'd like to be a wild horse, even a deer—but then there's hunting season and I don't want any strain on me, any tension. Not the next time around.

Once in the Baltimore zoo I saw a guanaco. Standing so close to the fence that I could have reached in and touched her eyelashes, still she didn't move and neither did I. Her eyes were extraordinarily beautiful. Deep brown, lambent. Lashes a full inch long, thick as a painter's brush. Straight. Her fur a rich red brown, whitish underneath; black forehead and head patches. For all I know guanacos are as stupid as mules, but I know this one was not. She stood poised in perfection and it didn't matter that she was behind a Baltimore fence and not roaming the Patagonian uplands and valleys. I wanted to climb inside her skin and look out at me on the other side of the fence. I ached to reach in and stroke her, but for the world I wouldn't have demeaned her with a pat. When a kid came by and threw a handful of popcorn at her she didn't move a foreleg. Not even a glance. Keep your lousy popcorn, we guanacos are an ancient race. We may not fly, or arrow through the oceans, we may not terrorize the jungle, but we copulate with gusto, we rear our young with affection, and then free them to early independence, we're agile, curious, gentle, loyal. We have our own vision. So take your popcorn and stuff it.

She wouldn't have said that: take your popcorn and stuff it. She wasn't vulgar. But I must stop this. I'm way behind on mending, on reading. I'll come back to you, guanaco, another time.

## Study Aids: Oates

1. What is the parallel established among all of the four summers at the lake? What does this parallel show about the life situation that is developing for the narrator?
2. Through the passage of time, what cycles of repetition are established? What is the relationship of Sissie and her mother? She insists she is different; is she? What is implied by her pregnancy in the fourth section? What is the relationship of Jessie and her father?
3. In section one, what is established when she asks, "Is the lake deep?" How is this scene related to other events in the section? To the promised boat ride? To the stoning of the bird? To her life with Jessie in section four?
4. What happens when the boat ride is taken in section two? What is the father's role in this? What does it show about the pattern of Sissie's life?
5. What meaning does she give to the man whom she sees again in section

four? Is her interpretation of him in agreement with the reality of her encounter with him in section three? What does he now mean to her, and what does this show about her state of awareness at the close of the story?

## Study Aids: Higgins

1. An IUD is an interuterine device used as a contraceptive. Why is it symbolic of the letter-writing narrator's life that it has been lost, having been placed by a male gynecologist? How is this loss related to her father, her becoming a Catholic, her marriage, her husband?
2. What is achieved by the device of telling the story in letters that obviously are not really going to be mailed?
3. The two sides of her paradoxical feelings about constant motherhood are especially revealed in her letter to Sister Seraphim and in her story about Mrs. Andersson's licking of the newborn pup. What are these two sides?
4. Moses Herzog is the title character in a novel by Saul Bellow; he, too, wrote letters that were never mailed. From the evidence of her letter to him, what did Herzog see as the solution for his troubled life? What is her opinion of that solution?
5. Why does she end her narrative with the image of the guanaco?

# SON IN THE AFTERNOON
*John A. Williams*

It was hot. I tend to be a bitch when it's hot. I goosed the little Ford over Sepulveda Boulevard toward Santa Monica until I got stuck in the traffic that pours from L.A. into the surrounding towns. I'd had a very lousy day at the studio.

I was—still am—a writer and this studio had hired me to check scripts and films with Negroes in them to make sure the Negro moviegoer wouldn't be offended. The signs were already clear one day the whole of American industry would be racing pell-mell to get a Negro, showcase a spade. I was kind of a pioneer. I'm a *Negro* writer, you see. The day had been tough because of a couple of verbs—slink and walk. One of those Hollywood hippies had done a script calling for a Negro waiter to slink away from the table where a dinner party was glaring at him. I said the waiter should walk, not slink, because later on he becomes a hero. The Hollywood hippie, who understood it all because he had some colored friends, said that it was essential to the plot that the waiter slink. I said you don't slink one minute and become a hero the next; there has to be some consistency. The Negro actor I was standing up for said nothing either way. He had played Uncle Tom roles so long that he had become Uncle Tom. But the director agreed with me.

Anyway . . . hear me out now. I was on my way to Santa Monica to pick up my mother, Nora. It was a long haul for such a hot day. I had planned a quiet evening. a nice shower, fresh clothes, and then I would have dinner at the Watkins and talk with some of the musicians on the scene for a quick taste before they cut to their gigs. After, I was going to the Pigalle down on Figueroa and catch Earl Grant at the organ, and still later, if nothing exciting happened, I'd pick up Scottie and make it to the Lighthouse on the Beach or to the Strollers and listen to some of the white boys play. I liked the long drive, especially while listening to Sleepy Stein's show on the radio. Later, much later of course, it would be home, back to Watts.

So you see, this picking up Nora was a little inconvenient. My mother was a maid for the Couchmans. Ronald Couchman was an architect, a good one I understood from Nora who has a fine sense for this sort of thing; you don't work in some hundred-odd houses during your life without getting some idea of the way a house should be laid out. Couchman's wife, Kay, was a playgirl who drove a white Jaguar from one party to another. My mother didn't like her too much; she didn't seem to care much for her son, Ronald, junior. There's something wrong with a parent who can't really love her own child, Nora thought. The Couchmans lived in a real fine residential section, of course. A number of actors lived nearby, character actors, not really big stars.

Somehow it is very funny. I mean that the maids and butlers knew everything about these people, and these people knew nothing at all about the help. Through Nora and her friends I knew who was laying whose wife; who had money and who *really* had money; I knew about the wild parties hours before the police, and who smoked marijuana, when, and where they got it.

To get to Couchman's driveway I had to go three blocks up one side of a palm-planted center strip and back down the other. The driveway bent gently, then swept back out of sight of the main road. The house, sheltered by slim palms, looked like a transplanted New England Colonial. I parked and walked to the kitchen door, skirting the growling Great Dane who was tied to a tree. That was the route to the kitchen door.

I don't like kitchen doors. Entering people's houses by them, I mean. I'd done this thing most of my life when I called at places where Nora worked to pick up the patched or worn sheets or the half-eaten roasts, the battered, tarnished silver—the fringe benefits of a housemaid. As a teen-ager I'd told Nora I was through with that crap; I was not going through anyone's kitchen door. She only laughed and said I'd learn. One day soon after, I called for her and without knocking walked right through the front door of this house and right on through the living room. I was almost out of the room when I saw feet behind the couch. I leaned over and there was Mr. Jorgensen and his wife making out like crazy. I guess they thought Nora had gone and it must have hit them sort of suddenly and they went at it like the hell-bomb was due to drop any minute. I've been that way too, mostly in the spring. Of course, when Mr. Jorgensen looked over his shoulder and saw me, you know what happened. I was thrown out and Nora right behind me. It was the middle of winter, the old man was sick and the coal bill three months overdue. Nora was right about those kitchen doors: I learned.

My mother saw me before I could ring the bell. She opened the door. "Hello," she said. She was breathing hard, like she'd been running or something. "Come in and sit down. I don't know *where* that Kay is. Little Ronald is sick and she's probably out gettin' drunk again." She left me then and trotted back through the house, I guess to be with Ronnie. I hated the combination of her white nylon uniform, her dark brown face and the wide streaks of gray in her hair. Nova had married this guy from Texas a few years after the old man had died. He was all right. He made out okay. Nora didn't have to work, but she just couldn't be still; she always had to be doing something. I suggested she quit work, but I had as much luck as her husband. I used to tease her about liking to be around those white folks. It would have been good for her to take an extended trip around the country visiting my brothers and sisters. Once she got to Philadelphia, she could go right out to the cemetery and sit awhile with the old man.

I walked through the Couchman home. I liked the library. I thought if I knew Couchman I'd like him. The room made me feel like that. I left it and went into the big living room. You could tell that Couchman had let his wife do that. Everything in it was fast, dart-like, with no sense of ease. But on the walls were several of Couchman's conceptions of buildings and homes. I guess he was a disciple of Wright. My mother walked rapidly through the room without looking at me and said, "Just be patient, Wendell. She should be here real soon."

"Yeah," I said, "with a snootful." I had turned back to the drawings when Ronnie scampered into the room, his face twisted with rage.

"Nora!" he tried to roar, perhaps the way he'd seen the parents of some of his friends roar at their maids. I'm quite sure Kay didn't shout at Nora, and I don't think Couchman would. But then no one shouts Nora was supposed to come to roost. I have a nasty temper. Some- at Nora. "Nora, you come right back here this minute!" the little bas- tard shouted and stamped and pointed to a spot on the floor where times it lies dormant for ages and at other times, like when the weather is hot and nothing seems to be going right, it's bubbling and ready to explode. "Don't talk to *my* mother like that, you little —!" I said sharply, breaking off just before I cursed. I wanted him to be large enough for me to strike. "How'd you like for me to talk to *your* mother like that?"

The nine-year-old looked up at me in surprise and confusion. He hadn't expected me to say anything. I was just another piece of furniture. Tears rose in his eyes and spilled out onto his pale cheeks. He put his hands behind him, twisted them. He moved backwards, away from me. He looked at my mother with a "Nora, come help me" look. And sure enough, there was Nora, speeding back across the room, gathering the kid in her arms, tucking his robe together. I was too angry to feel hatred for myself.

Ronnie was the Couchman's only kid. Nora loved him. I suppose that was the trouble. Couchman was gone ten, twelve hours a day. Kay didn't stay around the house any longer than she had to. So Ronnie had only my mother. I think kids should have someone to love, and Nora wasn't a bad sort. But somehow when the six of us, her own children, were growing up we never had her. She was gone, out scuffling to get those crumbs to put into our mouths and shoes for our feet and praying for something to happen so that all the space in between would be taken care of. Nora's affection for us took the form of rushing out into the morning's five o'clock blackness to wake some silly bitch and get her coffee; took form in her trudging five miles home every night instead of taking the streetcar to save money to buy tablets for us, to use at school, we said. But the truth was that all of us liked to draw and we went through a writing tablet in a couple of hours every day. Can you imagine? There's not a goddamn artist among us. We never had the physical affection, the pat on the head, the quick, smiling kiss, the "gimmee a hug" routine. All of this Ronnie was getting.

Now he buried his little blond head in Nora's breast and sobbed. "There, there now," Nora said. "Don't you cry, Ronnie. Ol' Wendell is just jealous, and he hasn't much sense either. He didn't mean nuthin'."

I left the room. Nora had hit it of course, hit it and passed on. I looked back. It didn't look so incongruous, the white and black together, I mean. Ronnie was still sobbing. His head bobbed gently on Nora's shoulder. The only time I ever got that close to her was when she trapped me with a bearhug so she could whale the daylights out of me after I put a snowball through Mrs. Grant's window. I walked outside and lit a cigarette. When Ronnie was in the hospital the month before, Nora got me to run her way over to Hollywood every night to see him. I didn't like that worth a damn. All right, I'll admit it: it did upset me. All that affection I didn't get nor my brothers and sisters going to that little white boy who, without a doubt, when away from her called her the names he'd learned from adults. Can you imagine a nine-year-old kid calling Nora a "girl," "our girl?" I spat at the Great Dane. He snarled and then I bounced a rock off his fanny. "Lay down, you bastard," I muttered. It was a good thing he was tied up.

I heard the low cough of the Jaguar slapping against the road. The car was throttled down, and with a muted roar it swung into the driveway. The woman aimed it for me. I was evil enough not to move. I was tired of playing with these people. At the last moment, grinning, she swung the wheel over and braked. She bounded out of the car like a tennis player vaulting over a net.

"Hi," she said, tugging at her shorts.

"Hello."

"You're Nora's boy?"

"I'm Nora's son." Hell, I was as old as she was; besides, I can't stand "boy."

"Nora tells us you're working in Hollywood. Like it?"

"It's all right."

"You must be pretty talented."

We stood looking at each other while the dog whined for her attention. Kay had a nice body and it was well tanned. She was high, boy, was she high. Looking at her, I could feel myself going into my sexy bastard routine; sometimes I can swing it great. Maybe it all had to do with the business inside. Kay took off her sunglasses and took a good look at me. "Do you have a cigarette?"

I gave her one and lit it. "Nice tan," I said. Most white people I know think it's a great big deal if a Negro compliments them on their tans. It's a large laugh. You have all this volleyball about color and come summer you can't hold the white folks back from the beaches, anyplace where they can get some sun. And of course the blacker they get, the more pleased they are. Crazy. If there is ever a Negro revolt, it will come during the summer and Negroes will descend upon the beaches around the nation and paralyze the country. You can't conceal cattle prods and bombs and pistols and police dogs when you're showing your birthday suit to the sun.

"You like it?" she asked. She was pleased. She placed her arm next to mine. "Almost the same color," she said.

"Ronnie isn't feeling well," I said.

"Oh, the poor kid. I'm so glad we have Nora. She's such a charm. I'll run right in and look at him. Do have a drink in the bar. Fix me one too, will you?" Kay skipped inside and I went to the bar and poured out two strong drinks. I made hers stronger than mine. She was back soon. "Nora was trying to put him to sleep and she made me stay out." She giggled. She quickly tossed off her drink. "Another, please?" While I was fixing her drink she was saying how amazing it was for Nora to have such a talented son. What she was really saying was that it was amazing for a servant to have a son who was not also a servant. "Anything can happen in a democracy," I said. "Servants' sons drink with madames and so on."

"Oh, Nora isn't a servant," Kay said. "She's part of the family."

Yeah, I thought. Where and how many times had I heard *that* before?

In the ensuing silence, she started to admire her tan again. "You think it's pretty good, do you? You don't know how hard I worked to get it." I moved close to her and held her arm. I placed my other arm around her. She pretended not to see or feel it, but she wasn't trying to get away either. In fact she was pressing closer and the register in my brain that tells me at the precise moment when I'm in, went off.

Kay was very high. I put both arms around her and she put both hers around me. When I kisssed her, she responded completely.

"Mom!"

"Ronnie, come back to bed," I heard Nora shout from the other room. We could hear Ronnie running over the rug in the outer room. Kay tried to get away from me, push me to one side, because we could tell that Ronnie knew where to look for his Mom: he was running right for the bar, where we were. "Oh, please," she said, "don't let him see us." I wouldn't let her push me away. "Stop!" she hissed. "He'll *see* us!" We stopped struggling just for an instant, and we listened to the echoes of the word *see*. She gritted her teeth and renewed her efforts to get away.

Me? I had the scene laid right out. The kid breaks into the room, see, and sees his mother in this real wriggly clinch with this colored guy who's just shouted at him, see, and no matter how his mother explains it away, the kid has the image—the colored guy and his mother—for the rest of his life, see?

That's the way it happened. The kid's mother hissed under her breath, *"You're crazy!"* and she looked at me as though she were seeing me or something about me for the very first time. I'd released her as soon as Ronnie, romping into the bar, saw us and came to a full, open-mouthed halt. Kay went to him. He looked first at me, then at his mother. Kay turned to me, but she couldn't speak.

Outside in the living room my mother called, "Wendell, where are you? We can go now."

I started to move past Kay and Ronnie. I felt many things, but I made myself think mostly, *There you little bastard, there.*

My mother thrust her face inside the door and said, "Good-bye, Mrs. Couchman. See you tomorrow. 'Bye, Ronnie."

"Yes," Kay said, sort of stunned. "Tomorrow." She was reaching for Ronnie's hand as we left, but the kid was slapping her hand away. I hurried quickly after Nora, hating the long drive back to Watts.

---

# GOLD COAST
*James Alan McPherson*

That spring, when I had a great deal of potential and no money at all, I took a job as a janitor. That was when I was still very young and spent money very freely, and when, almost every night, I drifted off to sleep lulled by sweet anticipation of that time when my potential would suddenly be realized and there would be capsule biographies of my life on dust jackets of many books, all proclaiming: "... He knew life on many levels. From shoeshine boy, free-lance writer, 3rd cook, janitor, he rose to . . ." I had never been a janitor before, and I did not really have to be one, and that is why I did it. But now, much later, I think it might have been because it is possible to be a janitor without becoming one, and at parties or at mixers, when asked what it was I did for a living, it was pretty good to hook my thumbs in my vest pockets and say comfortably: "Why, I am an apprentice janitor." The hippies would think it degenerate and really dig me and people in Philosophy and Law and Business would feel uncomfortable trying to make me feel better about my station while wondering how the hell I had managed to crash the party.

"What's an apprentice janitor?" they would ask.

"I haven't got my card yet," I would reply. "Right now I'm just taking lessons. There's lots of complicated stuff you have to learn before you get your own card and your own building."

"What kind of stuff?"

"Human nature, for one thing. *Race* nature, for another."

"Why race?"

"Because," I would say in a low voice, looking around lest someone else should overhear, "you have to be able to spot Jews and Negroes who are passing."

"That's terrible," would surely be said then with a hint of indignation.

"It's an art," I would add masterfully.

After a good pause I would invariably be asked: "But you're a Negro yourself, how can you keep your own people out?"

At which point I would look terribly disappointed and say: "*I* don't keep them out. But if they get in it's my job to make their stay just as miserable as possible. Things are changing."

Now the speaker would just look at me in disbelief.

"It's Janitorial Objectivity," I would say to finish the thing as the speaker began to edge away. "Don't hate me," I would call after him to his considerable embarrassment. "Somebody has to do it."

It was an old building near Harvard Square. Conrad Aiken had once lived there, and in the days of the Gold Coast, before Harvard built its great houses, it had been a very fine haven for the rich; but that was a world ago, and this building was one of the few monuments of that era which have survived. The lobby had a high ceiling with thick redwood beams, and it was replete with marble floor, fancy ironwork, and an old-fashioned house telephone which no longer worked. Each apartment had a small fireplace, and even the large bathtubs and chain toilets, when I was having my touch of nature, made me wonder what prominent personage of the past had worn away all the newness. And, being there, I felt a certain affinity toward the rich.

It was a funny building, because the people who lived there made it old. Conveniently placed as it was between the Houses and Harvard Yard, I expected to find it occupied by a company of hippies, hopeful working girls, and assorted graduate students. Instead, there was a majority of old maids, dowagers, asexual middle-aged men, homosexual young men, a few married couples, and a teacher. No one was shacking up there, and walking through the quiet halls in the early evening, I sometimes had the urge to knock on a door and expose myself just to hear someone breathe hard for once.

It was a Cambridge spring: down by the Charles happy students were making love while sad-eyed middle-aged men watched them from the bridge. It was a time of activity: Law students were busy sublimating, Business School people were making records of the money they would make, the Harvard Houses were clearing out, and in the Square bearded pot-pushers were setting up their restaurant tables in anticipation of the Summer School faithfuls. There was a change of season in the air, and to comply with its urgings, James Sullivan, the old superintendent, passed his three beaten garbage cans on to me with the charge that I should take up his daily rounds of the six floors, and with unflinching humility, gather whatever scraps the old-maid tenants had refused to husband.

I then became very rich, with my own apartment, a sensitive girl, a stereo, two speakers, one tattered chair, one fork, a job, and the urge to acquire. Having all this and youth besides made me pity Sullivan: he had been in that building thirty years and had its whole history recorded in the little folds of his mind, as his own life was recorded in the wrinkles of his face. All he had to show for his time there was a berserk dog, a wife almost as mad as the dog, three cats, bursitis, acute myopia, and a drinking problem. He was well over seventy and could hardly walk, and his weekly check of twenty-two dollars from the company that managed the building would not support anything. So, out of compromise, he was retired to superintendent of my labor.

My first day as janitor, while I skillfully lugged my three over-flowing cans of garbage out of the building, he sat on his bench in the lobby, faded and old and smoking, in patched, loose blue pants. He watched me. He was a chain smoker, and I noticed right away that he very carefully dropped all of the ashes and butts on the floor and crushed them under his feet until there was a yellow and gray smear. Then he laboriously pushed the mess under the bench with his shoe, all the while eyeing me like a cat in silence as I hauled the many cans of muck out to the big disposal unit next to the building. When I had finished, he gave me two old plates to help stock my kitchen and his first piece of advice.

"Sit down, for Chrisake, and take a load off your feet," he told me.

I sat on the red bench next to him and accepted the wilted cigarette he offered me from the crushed package he kept in his sweater pocket.

"Now, I'll tell you something to help you get along in the building," he said.

I listened attentively.

"If any of these sons of bitches ever ask you to do something extra, be sure to charge them for it."

I assured him that I absolutely would.

"If they can afford to live here, they can afford to pay. The bastards."

"Undoubtedly," I assured him again.

"And another thing," he added, "Don't let any of these girls shove any cat shit under your nose. That ain't your job. You tell them to put it in a bag and take it out themselves."

I reminded him that I knew very well my station in life, and that I was not about to haul cat shit or anything of that nature. He looked at me through his thick-lensed glasses for a long time. He looked like a cat himself. "That's right," he said at last. "And if they still try to sneak it in the trash be sure to make the bastards pay. They can afford it." He crushed his seventh butt on the floor and scattered the mess some more while he lit up another. "I never hauled out no cat shit in the thirty years I been here, and you don't do it either."

"I'm going up to wash my hands," I said.

"Remember," he called after me, "don't take no shit from any of them."

I protested once more that, upon my life, I would never, never do it, not even for the prettiest girl in the building. Going up in the elevator, I felt comfortably resolved that I would never do it. There were no pretty girls in the building.

I never found out what he had done before he came there, but I do know that being a janitor in that building was as high as he ever got in life. He had watched two generations of the rich pass the buildings on their way to the Yard, and he had seen many governors ride white horses into that same Yard to send sons and daughters of the rich out into life to produce, to acquire, to procreate, and to send back sons and daughters so that the cycle would continue. He had watched the cycle from when he had been able to haul the cans out for himself, and now he could not, and he was bitter.

He was Irish, of course, and he took pride in Irish accomplishments when he could have none of his own. He had known Frank O'Connor when that writer had been at Harvard. He told me on many occasions how O'Connor had stopped to talk every day on his way to the Yard. He had also known James Michael Curley, and his most colorful memory of the man was a long-ago day when he and James Curley sat in a Boston bar and one of Curley's runners had come in and said: "Hey, Jim, Sol Bernstein the Jew wants to see you." And Curley, in his deep, memorial voice, had said to James Sullivan: "Let us go forth and meet this Israelite Prince." These were his memories, and I would obediently put aside my garbage cans and laugh with him over the hundred or so colorful, insignificant little details which made up a whole lifetime of living in the basement of Harvard. And although they were of little value to me then, I knew that they were the reflections of a lifetime and the happiest moments he would ever have, being sold to me cheap, as youthful time is cheap, for as little time and interest as I wanted to spend. It was a buyer's market.

In those days I believed myself gifted with a boundless perception and attacked my daily garbage route with a gusto superenforced by the happy knowledge that behind each of the fifty or so doors in our building lived a story which could, if I chose to grace it with the magic of my pen, become immortal. I watched my tenants fanatically, noting their perversions, their visitors, and their eating habits. So intense was my search for material that I had to restrain myself from going through their refuse scrap by scrap; but at the topmost layers of muck, without too much hand soiling in the process, I set my perception to work. By late June, however, I had discovered only enough to put together a skimpy, rather naive Henry Miller novel, the most colorful discoveries being:

1. The lady in #24 was an alumnus of Paducah College
2. The couple in #55 made love at least 500 times a week, and the wife had not yet discovered the pill
3. The old lady in #36 was still having monthly inconvenience
4. The two fatsos in #56 consumed nightly an extraordinary amount of chili
5. The fat man in #54 had two dogs that were married to each other, but he was not married to anyone at all
6. The middle-aged single man in #63 threw out an awful lot of flowers

Disturbed by the snail's progress I was making, I confessed my futility to James one day as he sat on his bench chain-smoking and smearing butts on my newly waxed lobby floor. "So you want to know about the tenants?" he said, his cat's eyes flickering over me.

I nodded.

"Well, the first thing to notice is how many Jews there are."

"I haven't noticed any Jews," I said.

He eyed me in amazement.

"Well, a few," I said quickly to prevent my treasured perception from being dulled any further.

"A few, hell," he said. "There's more Jews here than anybody."

"How can you tell?"

He gave me that undecided look again. "Where do you think all that garbage comes from?" He nodded feebly toward my bulging cans. I looked just in time to prevent a stray noodle from slipping over the brim. "That's right," he continued. "Jews are the biggest eaters in the world. They eat the best too."

I confessed then that I was of the chicken-soup generation and believed that Jews ate only enough to muster strength for their daily trips to the bank.

"Not so!" he replied emphatically. "You never heard the expression: 'Let's get to the restaurant before the Jews get there'?"

I shook my head sadly.

"You don't know that in certain restaurants they take the free onions and pickles off the tables when they see Jews coming?"

I held my head down in shame over the bounteous heap.

He trudged over to my can and began to turn back the leaves of noodles and crumpled tissues from #47 with his hand. After a few seconds of digging, he unmucked an empty pâté can. "Look at that," he said triumphantly. "Gourmet stuff, no less."

"That's from #44," I said.

"What else?" he said, all-knowingly. "In 1946 a Swedish girl moved in up there and took a Jewish girl for her roommate. Then the Swedish girl moved out and there's been a Jewish Dynasty up there ever since."

I recalled that #44 was occupied by a couple that threw out a good number of S. S. Pierce cans, Chivas Regal bottles, assorted broken records, and back issues of *Evergreen* and the *Realist*.

"You're right," I said.

"Of course," he replied, as if there were never any doubt. "I can spot them anywhere, even when they think they're passing." He leaned closer and said in a you-and-me voice: "But don't ever say anything bad about them in public. The Anti-Defamation League will get you."

Just then his wife screamed for him from the second floor, and the dog joined her and beat against the door. He got into the elevator painfully and said: "Don't ever talk about them in public. You don't know who they are, and that Defamation League will take everything you got."

Sullivan did not really dislike Jews. He was just bitter toward anyone better off than himself. He lived with his wife on the second floor and his apartment was very dirty because both of them were sick and old, and neither could move very well. His wife swept dirt out into the hall, and two hours after I had mopped and waxed their section of the floor, there was sure to be a layer of dirt, grease, and crushed-scattered tobacco from their door to the end of the hall. There was a smell of dogs and cats and age and death about their door, and I did not ever want to have to go in there for any reason because I feared something about it I cannot name.

Mrs. Sullivan, I found out, was from South Africa. She loved animals much more than people, and there was a great deal of pain in her face. She kept little cans of meat posted at strategic points about the building, and I often came across her in the early morning or late at night throwing scraps out of the second-floor window to stray cats. Once, when James was about to throttle a stray mouse in their apartment, she had screamed at him to give the mouse a sporting chance. Whenever she attempted to walk she had to balance herself against a wall or a rail, and she hated the building because it confined her. She also hated James and most of the tenants. On the other hand, she loved the "Johnny Carson Show," she loved to sit outside on the front steps (because she could go no further unassisted), and she loved to talk to anyone who would stop to listen. She never spoke coherently except when she was cursing James, and then she had a vocabulary like a drunken sailor. She had great, shrill lungs, and her screams, accompanied by the rabid barks of the dog, could be heard all over the building. She was never really clean, her teeth were bad, and the first most pathetic thing in the world was to see her sitting on the steps in the morning watching the world pass, in a stained smock and a fresh summer blue hat she kept just to wear downstairs, with no place in the world to go. James told me, on the many occasions of her screaming, that she was mentally disturbed and could not help herself. The admirable thing about him was that he never lost his temper with her, no matter how rough her curses became and no matter who heard them. And the second most pathetic thing in the world was to see them slowly making their way in Harvard Square, he supporting her, through the hurrying crowds of miniskirted summer girls, J-Pressed Ivy Leaguers, beatniks, and bused Japanese tourists, decked in cameras, who would take pictures of every inch of Harvard Square except them. Once a hippy had brushed past them and called back over his shoulder: "Don't break any track records, Mr. and Mrs. Speedy Molasses."

Also on the second floor lived Miss O'Hara, a spinster who hated Sullivan as only an old maid can hate an old man. Across from her lived a very nice, gentle celibate named Murphy, who had once served with Montgomery in North Africa and who was now spending the rest of his life cleaning his little apartment and gossiping with Miss O'Hara. It was an Irish floor.

I never found out just why Miss O'Hara hated the Sullivans with such a passion. Perhaps it was because they were so unkempt and she was so superciliously clean. Perhaps it was because Miss O'Hara had a great deal of Irish pride, and they were stereotyped Irish. Perhaps it was because she merely had no reason to like them. She was a fanatic about cleanliness and put out her little bit of garbage wrapped very neatly in yesterday's *Christian Science Monitor* and tied in a bow with a fresh piece of string. Collecting all those little neat packages, I would wonder where she got the string and imagined her at night breaking meat market locks with a hairpin and hobbling off with yards and yards of white cord concealed under the gray sweater she always wore. I could even imagine her back in her little apartment chuckling and rolling the cord into a great white ball by candlelight. Then she would stash it away in her bread box. Miss O'Hara kept her door slightly open until late at night, and I suspected that she heard everything that went on in the building. I had the feeling that I should never dare to make love with gusto for fear that she would overhear and write down all my happy-time phrases, to be maliciously recounted to me if she were ever provoked.

She had been in the building longer than Sullivan, and I suppose that her greatest ambition in life was to outlive him and then attend his wake with a knitting ball and needle. She had been trying to get him fired for twenty-five years or so, and did not know when to quit. On summer nights when I painfully mopped the second floor, she would offer me root beer, apples, or cupcakes while trying to pump me for evidence against him.

"He's just a filthy old man, Robert," she would declare in a little-old-lady whisper. "And don't think you have to clean up those dirty old butts of his. Just report him to the Company."

"Oh, I don't mind," I would tell her, gulping the root beer as fast as possible.

"Well, they're both a couple of lushes, if you ask me. They haven't been sober a day in twenty-five years."

"Well, she's sick too, you know."

"Ha!" She would throw up her hands in disgust. "She's only sick when he doesn't give her the booze."

I fought to keep down a burp. "How long have *you* been here?"

She motioned for me to step out of the hall and into her dark apartment. "Don't tell him"—she nodded toward Sullivan's door—"but I've been here thirty-four years." She waited for me to be taken aback. Then she added: "And it was a better building before those two lushes came."

She then offered me an apple, asked five times if the dog's barking bothered me, forced me to take a fudge brownie, said that the cats had wet the floor again last night, got me to dust the top of a large chest too high for her to reach, had me pick up the minute specks of dust which fell from my dustcloth, pressed another root beer on me, and then showed me her family album. As an afterthought, she had me take down a big old picture of her great-grandfather, also too high for her to reach, so that I could dust that too. Then together we picked up the dust from it which might have fallen to the floor. "He's really a filthy old man, Robert," she said in closing, "and don't be afraid to report him to the Property Manager anytime you want."

I assured her that I would do it at the slightest provocation from Sullivan, finally accepted an apple but refused the money she offered, and escaped back to my mopping. Even then she watched me, smiling, from her half-opened door.

"Why does Miss O'Hara hate you?" I asked James once.

He lifted his cigaretted hand and let the long ash fall elegantly to the floor. "That old bitch has been an albatross around my neck ever since I got here," he said. "Don't trust her, Robert. It was her kind that sat around singing hymns and watching them burn saints in this state."

In those days I had forgotten that I was first of all a black and I had a very lovely girl who was not first of all a black. It is quite possible that my ancestors rowed her ancestors across on the *Mayflower,* and she was very rich in that alone. We were both very young and optimistic then, and she believed with me in my potential and liked me partly because of it; and I was happy because she belonged to me and not to the race, which made her special. It made me special too because I did not have to wear a beard or hate or be especially hip or ultra Ivy Leagueish. I did not have to smoke pot or supply her with it, or be for any cause at all except myself. I only had to be myself, which pleased me; and I only had to produce, which pleased both of us. Like many of the artistically inclined rich, she wanted to own in someone else what she could not own in herself. But this I did not mind, and I forgave her for it because she forgave me moods and the constant smell of garbage and a great deal of latent hostility. She only minded James Sullivan, and all the valuable time I was wasting listening to him rattle on and on. His conversations, she thought, were useless, repetitious, and promised nothing of value to me. She was accustomed to the old-rich, whose conversations meandered around a leitmotiv of how well off they were and how much they would leave behind very soon. She was not at all cold, but she had been taught how to tolerate the old-poor and perhaps toss them a greeting in passing. But nothing more.

Sullivan did not like her when I first introduced them because he saw that she was not a beatnik and could not be dismissed. It is in the nature of things that liberal people will tolerate two interracial beatniks more than they will an intelligent, serious-minded mixed couple. The former liaison is easy to dismiss as the dregs of both races, deserving of each other and the contempt of both races; but the latter poses a threat because there is no immediacy of overpowering sensuality or "you-pick-my-fleas-I'll-pick-yours" apparent on the surface of things, and people, even the most publicly liberal, cannot dismiss it so easily.

"That girl is Irish, isn't she?" he had asked one day in my apartment soon after I had introduced them.

"No," I said definitely.

"What's her name?"

"Judy Smith," I said, which was not her name at all.

"Well, I can spot it," he said. "She's got Irish blood all right."

"Everybody's got a little Irish blood," I told him.

He looked at me cattily and craftily from behind his thick lenses. "Well, she's from a good family, I suppose."

"I suppose," I said.

He paused to let some ashes fall to the rug. "They say the Colonel's Lady and Nelly O'Grady are sisters under the skin." Then he added: "Rudyard Kipling."

"That's true," I said with equal innuendo, "that's why you have to maintain a distinction by marrying the Colonel's Lady."

An understanding passed between us then, and we never spoke more on the subject.

Almost every night the cats wet the second floor while Meg Sullivan watched the "Johnny Carson Show" and the dog howled and clawed the door. During commercials Meg would curse James to get out and stop dropping ashes on the floor or to take the dog out or something else, totally unintelligible to those of us on the fourth, fifth, and sixth floors. Even after the Carson show she would still curse him to get out, until finally he would go down to the basement and put away a bottle or two of wine. There was a steady stench of cat functions in the basement, and with all the grease and dirt, discarded trunks, beer bottles, chair, old tools, and the filthy sofa on which he sometimes slept, seeing him there made me want to cry. He drank the cheapest sherry, the wino kind, straight from the bottle: and on many nights that summer at 2:00 A.M. my phone would ring me out of bed.

"Rob? Jimmy Sullivan here. What are you doing?"

There was nothing suitable to say.

"Come on down to the basement for a drink."

"I have to be at work at 8:30," I would protest.

"Can't you have just one drink?" he would say pathetically.

I would carry down my own glass so that I would not have to drink out of the bottle. Looking at him on the sofa, I could not be mad because now I had many records for my stereo, a story that was going well, a girl who believed in me and who belonged to me and not to the race, a new set of dishes, and a tomorrow morning with younger people.

"I don't want to burden you unduly," he would always preface.

I would force myself not to look at my watch and say: "Of course not."

"My Meg is not in the best health, you know," he would say, handing the bottle to me.

"She's just old."

"The doctors say she should be in an institution."

"That's no place to be."

"I'm a sick man myself, Rob. I can't take much more. She's crazy."

"Anybody who loves animals can't be crazy."

He took another long draw from the bottle. "I won't live another year. I'll be dead in a year."

"You don't know that."

He looked at me closely, without his glasses, so that I could see the desperation in his eyes. "I just hope Meg goes before I do. I don't want them to put her in an institution after I'm gone."

At 2:00 A.M., with the cat stench in my nose and a glass of bad sherry standing still in my hand because I refuse in my mind to touch it, and all my dreams of greatness are above him and the basement and the building itself, I did not know what to say. The only way I could keep from hating myself was to start him talking about the AMA or the Medicare program or beatniks. He was pure hell on all three. To him, the Medical Profession was "morally bankrupt," Medicare was a great farce which deprived oldsters like himself of their "rainy-day dollars," and beatniks were "dropouts from the human race." He could rage on and on in perfect phrases about all three of his major dislikes, and I had the feeling that because the sentences were so well constructed and well turned, he might have memorized them from something he had read. But then he was extremely well read, and it did not matter if he had borrowed a phrase or two from someone else. The ideas were still his own.

It would be 3:00 A.M. before I knew it, and then 3:30, and still he would go on. He hated politicians in general and liked to recount, at these times, his private catalog of political observations. By the time he got around to Civil Rights it would be 4:00 A.M., and I could not feel responsible for him at that hour. I would begin to yawn, and at first he would just ignore it. Then I would start to edge toward the door, and he would see that he could hold me no longer, not even by declaring that he wanted to be an honorary Negro because he loved the race so much.

"I hope I haven't burdened you unduly," he would say again.

"Of course not," I would say, because it was over then, and I could leave him and the smell of the cats there, and sometimes I would go out in the cool night and walk around the Yard and be thankful that I was only an assistant janitor, and an transient one at that. Walking in the early dawn and seeing the Summer School fellows sneak out of the girls' dormitories in the Yard gave me a good feeling, and I thought that tomorrow night it would be good to make love myself so that I could be busy when he called.

"Why don't you tell that old man your job doesn't include babysitting with him," Jean told me many times when she came over to visit during the day and found me sleeping.

I would look at her and think to myself about social forces and the pressures massing and poised, waiting to attack us. It was still July then. It was hot, and I was working good.

"He's just an old man," I said. "Who else would listen to him."

"You're too soft. As long as you do your work you don't have to be bothered with him."

"He could be a story if I listened long enough."

"There are too many stories about old people."

"No," I said, thinking about us again, "there are just too many people who have no stories."

Sometimes he would come up and she would be there, but I would let him come in anyway, and he would stand there looking dirty and uncomfortable, offering some invented reason for having intruded. At these times something silent would pass between them, something I cannot name, which would reduce him to exactly what he was: an old man, come out of his basement to intrude where he was not wanted. But all the time this was being communicated, there would be a surface, friendly conversation between them. And after five minutes or so of being unwelcome, he would apologize for having come, drop a few ashes on the rug, and back out the door. Downstairs we could hear this wife screaming.

We endured the aged and August was almost over. Inside the building the cats were still wetting, Meg was still screaming, the dog was getting madder, and Sullivan began to drink during the day. Outside it was hot and lush and green, and the Summer girls were wearing shorter miniskirts and no panties and the middle-aged men down by the Charles were going wild on their bridge. Everyone was restless for change, for August is the month when undone summer things must be finished or regretted all through the winter.

Being imaginative people, Jean and I played a number of original games. One of them we called "Social Forces," the object of which was to see which side could break us first. We played it with the unknown night riders who screamed obscenities from passing cars. And because that was her side I would look at her expectantly, but she would laugh and say: "No." We played it at parties with unaware blacks who attempted to enchant her with skillful dances and hip vocabularies, believing her to be community property. She would be polite and aloof, and much later, it then being my turn, she would look at me expectantly. And I would force a smile and say: "No." The last round was played while taking her home in a subway car, on a hot August night, when one side of the car was black and tense and hating and the other side was white and of the same mind. There was not enough room on either side for the two of us to sit and we would not separate; so we stood, holding on to a steel post through all the stops, feeling all of the eyes, between the two sides of the car and the two sides of the world. We aged. And getting off finally at the stop which was no longer ours, we looked at each other, again expectantly, and there was nothing left to say.

I began to avoid the old man, would not answer the door when I knew it was he who was knocking, and waited until very late at night, when he could not possibly be awake, to haul the trash down. I hated the building then; and I was really a janitor for the first time. I slept a lot and wrote very little. And I did not give a damn about Medicare, the AMA, the building, Meg, or the crazy dog. I began to consider moving out.

In that same week, Miss O'Hara finally succeeded in badgering Murphy, the celibate Irishman, and a few other tenants into signing a complaint about the dog. No doubt Murphy signed because he was a nice fellow and women like Miss O'Hara had always dominated him. He did not really mind the dog: he did not really mind anything. She called him "Frank Dear," and I had the feeling that when he came to that place, fresh from Montgomery's Campaign, he must have had a will of his own; but she had drained it all away, year by year, so that now he would do anything just to be agreeable.

One day soon after the complaint, the little chubby Property Manager came around to tell Sullivan that the dog had to be taken away. Miss O'Hara told me the good news later, when she finally got around to my door.

"Well, that crazy dog is gone now, Robert. Those two are enough."

"Where is the dog?" I asked.

"I don't know, but Albert Rustin made them get him out. You should have seen the old drunk's face," she said. "That dirty old useless man."

"You should be at peace now," I said.

"Almost," was her reply. "The best thing is to get rid of those two old boozers along with the dog."

I congratulated Miss O'Hara and went out. I knew that the old man would be drinking and would want to talk. But very late that evening he called on the telephone and caught me in.

"Rob?" he said. "James Sullivan here. Would you come down to my apartment like a good fellow? I want to ask you something important."

I had never been in his apartment before and did not want to go then. But I went anyway.

They had three rooms, all grimy from corner to corner. There was a peculiar odor in that place I did not ever want to smell again, and his wife was dragging herself around the room talking in mumbles. When she saw me come in the door, she said: "I can't clean it up. I just can't. Look at that window. I can't reach it. I can't keep it clean." She threw up both her hands and held her head down and to the side. "The whole place is dirty, and I can't clean it up."

"What do you want?" I said to Sullivan.

"Sit down." He motioned me to a kitchen chair. "Have you changed that bulb on the fifth floor?"

"It's done."

He was silent for a while, drinking from a bottle of sherry, and he gave me some and a dirty glass. "You're the first person who's been here in years," he said. "We couldn't have company because of the dog."

Somewhere in my mind was a note that I should never go into his apartment. But the dog had never been the reason. "Well, he's gone now," I said, fingering the dirty glass of sherry.

He began to cry. "They took my dog away," he said. "It was all I had. How can they take a man's dog away from him?"

There was nothing I could say.

"I couldn't do nothing," he continued. After a while he added: "But I know who it was. It was that old bitch O'Hara. Don't ever trust her, Rob. She smiles in your face, but it was her kind that laughed when they burned Joan of Arc in this state."

Seeing him there, crying and making me feel unmanly because I wanted to touch him or say something warm, also made me eager to be far away and running hard.

"Everybody's got problems," I said. "I don't have a girl now."

He brightened immediately, and for a while he looked almost happy in his old cat's eyes. Then he staggered over to my chair and held out his hand. I did not touch it, and he finally pulled it back. "I know how you feel," he said. "I know just how you feel."

"Sure," I said.

"But you're a young man, you have a future. But not me. I'll be dead inside of a year."

Just then his wife dragged herself in to offer me a cigar. They were being hospitable, and I forced myself to drink a little of the sherry.

"They took my dog away today," she mumbled. "That's all I had in the world, my dog."

I looked at the old man. He was drinking from the bottle.

During the first week of September one of the middle-aged men down by the Charles got tired of looking and tried to take a necking girl away from her boyfriend. The police hauled him off to jail, and the girl pulled down her dress tearfully. A few days later another man exposed himself near the same spot. And that same week a dead body was found on the banks of the Charles.

The miniskirted brigade had moved out of the Yard, and it was quiet and green and peaceful there. In our building another Jewish couple moved into #44. They did not eat gourmet stuff, and on occasion, threw out pork-and-beans cans. But I had lost interest in perception. I now had many records for my stereo, loads of S. S. Pierce stuff, and a small bottle of Chivas Regal which I never opened. I was working good again, and I did not miss other things as much; or at least I told myself that.

The old man was coming up steadily now, at least three times a day, and I had resigned myself to it. If I refused to let him in, he would always come back later with a missing bulb on the fifth floor. We had taken to buying cases of beer together, and when he had finished his half, which was very frequently, he would come up to polish off mine. I began to enjoy talking politics, the AMA, Medicare, beatniks, and listening to him recite from books he had read. I discovered that he was very well read in history, philosophy, literature, and law. He was extraordinarily fond of saying: "I am really a cut above being a building superintendent. Circumstances made me what I am." And even though he was drunk and dirty and it was very late at night, I believed him and liked him anyway because having him there was much better than being alone. After he had gone I could sleep, and I was not lonely in sleep; and it did not really matter how late I was at work the next morning because when I thought about it all, I discovered that nothing really matters except not being old and being alive and having potential to dream about, and not being alone.

## Study Aids: Williams

1. What is the narrator's attitude toward his situation? How is this revealed, directly or indirectly, in the tone and manner of his narration?
2. How does his job reflect his situation? How is it related to his mother's job?
3. What mixture of feelings is involved in his relationship to his mother?
4. What emphasized aspects of the conversations at the Couchman's home bring his feelings into angry focus?
5. Why does he kiss Mrs. Couchman? What is his main target? Why? How does his "victory" make him feel?

## Study Aids: McPherson

1. What attitude toward his situation does the narrator try to maintain throughout the story? What is his tone? Why does he not describe in any

detail what happened to Jean and himself? Does it not mean anything to him?

2. What is suggested by the game of "Social Forces" that he and Jean play? What is the irony involved in what happens to them while they are playing?

3. A number of meaningful ironic parallels are developed through the course of the story. What is the relationship of Sullivan's discussions of Jews and Miss O'Hara's attitude toward Sullivan and Jean's attitude toward Sullivan? How are these related to what happens to Jean and the narrator?

4. What does the narrator finally see about Sullivan and himself when he finally visits Sullivan's apartment? How does what happens to Sullivan's dog relate to what has happened to the narrator and to what he now understands?

5. What are the implications of the last phrase—"not being alone"? How does this tie together many of the people and events of the story? How is it related to the "social forces"?

---

# CUTTING EDGE
## *James Purdy*

Mrs. Zeller opposed her son's beard. She was in her house in Florida when she saw him wearing it for the first time. It was as though her mind had come to a full stop. This large full-bearded man entered the room and she remembered always later how ugly he had looked and how frightened she felt seeing him in the house; then the realization it was someone she knew, and finally the terror of recognition.

He had kissed her, which he didn't often do, and she recognized in this his attempt to make her discomfort the more painful. He held the beard to her face for a long time, then he released her as though she had suddenly disgusted him.

"Why did you do it?" she asked. She was, he saw, almost broken by the recognition.

"I didn't dare tell you and come."

"That's of course true," Mrs. Zeller said. "It would have been worse. You'll have to shave it off, of course. Nobody must see you. Your father of course didn't have the courage to warn me, but I knew something was wrong the minute he entered the house ahead of you. I suppose he's upstairs laughing now. But it's not a laughing matter."

Mrs. Zeller's anger turned against her absent husband as though all error began and ended with him. "I suppose he likes it." Her dislike of Mr. Zeller struck her son as staggeringly great at that moment.

He looked at his mother and was surprised to see how young she was. She did not look much older than he did. Perhaps she looked younger now that he had his beard.

"I had no idea a son of mine would do such a thing," she said. "But why a beard, for heaven's sake," she cried, as though he had chosen something permanent and irreparable which would destroy all that they were.

"Is it because you are an artist? No, don't answer me," she commanded. "I can't stand to hear any explanation from you. . . ."

"I have always wanted to wear a beard," her son said. "I remember wanting one as a child."

"I don't remember that at all," Mrs. Zeller said.

"I remember it quite well. I was in the summer house near that old broken-down wall and I told Ellen Whitelaw I wanted to have a beard when I grew up."

"Ellen Whitelaw, that big fat stupid thing. I haven't thought of her in years."

Mrs. Zeller was almost as much agitated by the memory of Ellen Whitelaw as by her son's beard.

"You didn't like Ellen Whitelaw," her son told her, trying to remember how they had acted when they were together.

"She was a common and inefficient servant," Mrs. Zeller said, more quietly now, masking her feelings from her son.

"I suppose *he* liked her," the son pretended surprise, the cool cynical tone coming into his voice.

"Oh, your father," Mrs. Zeller said.

"Did he then?" the son asked.

"Didn't he like all of them?" she asked. The beard had changed this much already between them, she talked to him now about his father's character, while the old man stayed up in the bedroom fearing a scene.

"Didn't he always," she repeated, as though appealing to this new hirsute man.

"So," the son said, accepting what he already knew.

"Ellen Whitelaw, for God's sake," Mrs. Zeller said. The name of the servant girl brought back many other faces and rooms which she did not know were in her memory. These faces and rooms served to make the bearded man who stared at her less and less the boy she remembered in the days of Ellen Whitelaw.

"You must shave it off," Mrs. Zeller said.

"What makes you think I would do that?" the boy wondered.

"You heard me. Do you want to drive me out of my mind?"

"But I'm not going to. Or rather it's not going to."

"I will appeal to him, though a lot of good it will do," Mrs. Zeller said. "He ought to do something once in twenty years at least."

"You mean," the son said laughing, "he hasn't done anything in that long."

"Nothing I can really remember," Mrs. Zeller told him.

"It will be interesting to hear you appeal to him," the boy said. "I haven't heard you do that in such a long time."

"I don't think you ever heard me."

"I did, though," he told her. "It was in the days of Ellen Whitelaw again, in fact."

"In *those* days," Mrs. Zeller wondered. "I don't see how that could be."

"Well, it was. I can remember that much."

"You couldn't have been more than four years old. How could **you** remember then?"

"I heard you say to him, *You have to ask her to go.*"

Mrs. Zeller did not say anything. She really could not remember the words, but she supposed that the scene was true and that he actually remembered.

"Please shave off that terrible beard. If you only knew how awful it looks on you. You can't see anything else but it."

"Everyone in New York thought it was particularly fine."

"Particularly fine," she paused over his phrase as though its meaning eluded her.

"It's nauseating," she was firm again in her judgment.

"I'm not going to do away with it," he said, just as firm.

She did not recognize his firmness, but she saw everything changing a little, including perhaps the old man upstairs.

"Are you going to 'appeal' to him?" The son laughed again when he saw she could say no more.

"Don't mock me," the mother said. "I will speak to your father." She pretended decorum. "You can't go anywhere with us, you know."

He looked unmoved.

"I don't want any of my friends to see you. You'll have to stay in the house or go to your own places. You can't go out with us to our places and see our friends. I hope none of the neighbors see you. If they ask who you are, I won't tell them."

"I'll tell them then."

They were not angry, they talked it out like that, while the old man was upstairs.

"Do you suppose he is drinking or asleep?" she said finally.

"I thought he looked good in it, Fern," Mr. Zeller said.

"What about it makes him look good?" she said.

"It fills out his face," Mr. Zeller said, looking at the wallpaper and surprised he had never noticed what a pattern it had before; it showed the sacrifice of some sort of animal by a youth.

He almost asked his wife how she had come to pick out this pattern, but her growing fury checked him.

He saw her mouth and throat moving with unspoken words.

"Where is he now?" Mr. Zeller wondered.

"What does that matter where he is?" she said. "He has to be some-where while he's home, but he can't go out with us."

"How idiotic," Mr. Zeller said, and he looked at his wife straight in the face for a second."

"Why did you say that?" She tried to quiet herself down.

"The way you go on about nothing, Fern." For a moment a kind of revolt announced itself in his manner, but then his eyes went back to the wallpaper, and she resumed her tone of victor.

"I've told him he must either cut it off or go back to New York."

"Why is it a beard upsets you so?" he wondered, almost to himself.

"It's not the beard so much. It's the way he is now too. And it disfigures him so. I don't recognize him at all now when he wears it."

"So, he's never done anything of his own before," Mr. Zeller protested suddenly.

"Never done anything!" He could feel her anger covering him and glancing off like hot sun onto the wallpaper.

"That's right," he repeated. "He's never done anything. I say let him keep the beard and I'm not going to talk to him about it." His gaze lifted toward her but rested finally only on her hands and skirt.

"This is still my house," she said, "and I have to live in this town."

"When they had the centennial in Collins, everybody wore beards."

"I have to live in this town," she repeated.

"I won't talk to him about it," Mr. Zeller said.

It was as though the voice of Ellen Whitelaw reached her saying, *So that was how you appealed to him.*

She sat on the deck chair on the porch and smoked five cigarettes. The two men were somewhere in the house and she had the feeling now that she only roomed here. She wished more than that the beard was gone that her son had never mentioned Ellen Whitelaw. She found herself thinking only about her. Then she thought that now twenty years later she could not have afforded a servant, not even her.

She supposed the girl was dead. She did not know why, but she was sure she was.

She thought also that she should have mentioned her name to Mr. Zeller. It might have broken him down about the beard, but she supposed not. He had been just as adamant and unfeeling with her about the girl as he was now about her son.

Her son came through the house in front of her without speaking, dressed only in his shorts and, when he had got safely beyond her in the garden, he took off those so that he was completely naked with his back to her, and lay down in the sun.

She held the cigarette in her hand until it began to burn her finger. She felt she should not move from the place where she was and yet she did not know where to go inside the house and she did not know what pretext to use for going inside.

In the brilliant sun his body, already tanned, matched his shining black beard.

She wanted to appeal to her husband again and she knew then she could never again. She wanted to call a friend and tell her but she had no friend to whom she could tell this.

The events of the day, like a curtain of extreme bulk, cut her off from her son and husband. She had always ruled the house and them even during the awful Ellen Whitelaw days and now as though they did not even recognize her, they had taken over. She was not even here. Her son could walk naked with a beard in front of her as though she did not exist. She had nothing to fight them with, nothing to make them see with. They ignored her as Mr. Zeller had when he looked at the wallpaper and refused to discuss their son.

"You can grow it back when you're in New York," Mr. Zeller told his son.

He did not say anything about his son lying naked before him in the garden but he felt insulted almost as much as his mother had, yet he needed his son's permission and consent now and perhaps that was why he did not mention the insult of his nakedness.

"I don't know why I have to act like a little boy all the time with you both."

"If you were here alone with me you could do anything you wanted. You know I never asked anything of you. . . ."

When his son did not answer, Mr. Zeller said, "Did I?"

"That was the trouble," the son said.

"What?" the father wondered.

"You never wanted anything from me and you never wanted to give me anything. I didn't matter to you."

"Well, I'm sorry," the father said doggedly.

"Those were the days of Ellen Whitelaw," the son said in tones like the mother.

"For God's sake," the father said and he put a piece of grass between his teeth.

He was a man who kept everything down inside of him, everything had been tied and fastened so long there was no part of him any more that could struggle against the stricture of his life.

There were no words between them for some time; then Mr. Zeller could hear himself bringing the question out: "Did she mention that girl?"

"Who?" the son pretended blankness.

"Our servant."

The son wanted to pretend again blankness but it was too much work. He answered: "No, I mentioned it. To her surprise."

"Don't you see how it is?" the father went on to the present. "She doesn't speak to either of us now and if you're still wearing the beard when you leave it's me she will be punishing six months from now."

"And you want me to save you from your wife."

"Bobby," the father said, using the childhood tone and inflection. "I wish you would put some clothes on too when you're in the garden. With me it doesn't matter, you could do anything. I never asked you anything. But with her . . ."

"God damn *her*," the boy said.

The father could not protest. He pleaded with his eyes at his son.

The son looked at his father and he could see suddenly also the youth hidden in his father's face. He was young like his mother. They were both young people who had learned nothing from life, were stopped and drifting where they were twenty years before with Ellen Whitelaw. Only *she*, the son thought, must have learned from life, must have gone on to some development in her character, while they had been tied to the shore where she had left them.

"Imagine living with someone for six months and not speaking," the father said as if to himself. "That happened once before, you know, when you were a little boy."

"I don't remember that," the son said, some concession in his voice.

"You were only four," the father told him.

"I believe this is the only thing I ever asked of you," the father said. "Isn't that odd, I can't remember ever asking you anything else. Can you?"

The son looked coldly away at the sky and then answered, contempt and pity struggling together, "No, I can't."

"Thank you, Bobby," the father said.

"Only don't *plead* any more, for Christ's sake." The son turned from him.

"You've only two more days with us, and if you shaved it off and put on just a few clothes, it would help me through the year with her."

He spoke as though it would be his last year.

"Why don't you beat some sense into her?" The son turned to him again.

The father's gaze fell for the first time complete on his son's nakedness.

Bobby had said he would be painting in the storeroom and she could send up a sandwich from time to time, and Mr. and Mrs. Zeller were left downstairs together. She refused to allow her husband to answer the phone.

In the evening Bobby came down dressed carefully and his beard combed immaculately and looking, they both thought, curled.

They talked about things like horse racing, in which they were all somehow passionately interested, but which they now discussed irritably as though it too were a menace to their lives. They talked about the uselessness of art and why people went into it with a detachment that would have made an outsider think that Bobby was as unconnected with it as a jockey or oil magnate. They condemned nearly everything and then the son went upstairs and they saw one another again briefly at bedtime.

The night before he was to leave they heard him up all hours, the water running, and the dropping of things made of metal.

Both parents were afraid to get up and ask him if he was all right. He was like a wealthy relative who had commanded them never to question him or interfere with his movements even if he was dying.

He was waiting for them at breakfast, dressed only in his shorts but he looked more naked than he ever had in the garden because his beard was gone. Over his chin lay savage and profound scratches as though he had removed the hair with a hunting knife and pincers.

Mrs. Zeller held her breast and turned to the coffee and Mr. Zeller said only his son's name and sat down with last night's newspaper.

"What time does your plane go?" Mrs. Zeller said in a dead, muffled voice.

The son began putting a white paste on the scratches of his face and did not answer.

"I believe your mother asked you a question," Mr. Zeller said, pale and shaking.

"Ten-forty," the son replied.

The son and the mother exchanged glances and he could see at once that his sacrifice had been in vain: she would also see the beard there again under the scratches and the gashes he had inflicted on himself, and he would never really be her son again. Even for his father it must be much the same. He had come home as a stranger who despised them and he had shown his nakedness to both of them. All three longed for separation and release.

But Bobby could not control the anger coming up in him, and his rage took an old form. He poured the coffee into his saucer because Mr. Zeller's mother had always done this and it had infuriated Mrs. Zeller because of its low-class implications.

He drank viciously from the saucer, blowing loudly.

Both parents watched him helplessly like insects suddenly swept against the screen.

"It's not too long till Christmas," Mr. Zeller brought out. "We hope you'll come back for the whole vacation."

"We do," Mrs. Zeller said in a voice completely unlike her own.

"So," Bobby began, but the torrent of anger would not let him say the thousand fierce things he had ready.

Instead, he blew savagely from the saucer and spilled some onto the chaste white summer rug below him. Mrs. Zeller did not move.

"I would invite you to New York," Bobby said quietly now, "but of course I will have the beard there and it wouldn't work for you."

"Yes," Mr. Zeller said, incoherent.

"I do hope you don't think I've been. . . ." Mrs. Zeller cried suddenly and they both waited to hear whether she was going to weep or not, but she stopped herself perhaps by the realization that she had no tears and that the feelings which had come over her about Bobby were likewise spent.

"I can't think of any more I can do for you," Bobby said suddenly.

They both stared at each other as though he had actually left and they were alone at last.

"Is there anything more you want me to do?" he said, coldly vicious.

They did not answer.

"I hate and despise what both of you have done to yourselves, but the thought that you would be sitting here in your middle-class crap not speaking to one another is too much even for me. That's why I did it, I guess, and not out of any love. I didn't want you to think that."

He sloshed in the saucer.

"Bobby," Mr. Zeller said.

The son brought out his *What?* with such finished beauty of coolness that he paused to admire his own control and mastery.

"Please, Bobby," Mr. Zeller said.

They could all three of them hear a thousand speeches. The agony of awkwardness was made unendurable by the iciness of the son, and all three paused over this glacial control which had come to him out of art and New York, as though it was the fruit of their lives and the culmination of their twenty years.

---

# THE RAPIDS
*Walter Van Tilburg Clark*

Where the unpaved road curved over the top of the hill and descended to the river, a man appeared, walking by himself. He was thin, and wore spectacles, and his legs, when they showed through the flapping wings of his red and blue dressing gown, were very white. He carried a towel in one hand. Walking carefully, for his slippers were thin, he came down between the fir trees, then between the alders and the willows, and stood at the edge of the river.

Four terraces of red rock lay diagonally across the river at this point, but they were tilted away from him, so that the heavy water gushed all on the farther side, and narrowed until, from the lowest edge, it jetted forth in a single head, making a big, back-bellying bubble rimmed with foam in the pool below. Closer to him, eddies from the main stream came over the terraces at intervals, making thin, transparent falls a foot or two high. Swarms of midget flies danced against these falls, keeping just free of the almost invisible mist which blew from them.

Climbing cautiously from the bank to the rocks, the man walked out onto the second terrace, which was the broadest, and had a gentle incline. He bent over and felt of the rock. It was warm with sun. He took off his dressing gown and sat down. Then he fished in the pocket of the gown, drew out a piece of soap, and put it beside the towel. Finally he pulled off his slippers and placed them on the edge of the towel, to hold it down if the wind blew. After this preparation, he sat with his arms around his knees and stared at the running water.

The sun felt good on his back. He wondered if he dared to remove his shorts, but the bridge from his road lay across the river close above him, so he decided not to. Also there was a building on the opposite bank at the point where the river jumped out into the pool. There were only two and a half walls of the building standing, and the windows had been out of those for a long time. Vines grew over the gray-tan stones and into the windows, and nothing was left of the roof. Still, it was a building, four stories high. So he kept on his shorts and sat in the sun and looked at the building, remembering the bit of its history he had heard. It had been a mill, way back toward the days of the Revolution. Since then this part of the country had failed. There were only small, poor farms in it now, and the remnants of villages. It gave him a queer feeling to look through the empty windows and see trees growing inside, and the steep, green bank behind them. The ruin was old for America. He was used to seeing empty mills that weren't ten years old. This one went a long way back.

After a time the draft in the river canyon felt chilly in spite of the sun. The man removed his spectacles with both hands, placed them on his dressing gown, picked up the cake of soap, and approached the nearest of the little falls. Standing beside it, with his feet in the shallow basin of turning water, he shivered before the breath of the river. Timidly he began to wash, laving his forearms and the back of his neck, determinedly splashing a palmful of water over his white chest and belly. Encouraged, he wet himself all over and rubbed on the soap vigorously, ducking his head into the fall and then working up a great lather on it, like a shining white wig. When he was well soaped, he couldn't open his eyes. Feeling for the rim of the fall, he moved gingerly, for the basin was slimy. Having come close enough, he squatted under the fall and let it drive the soap down from him until he could open his eyes and see the iridescent trail of the soap, like an oil mark, draining away from him down the gutter of rock. All of this time he moved his arms as much as he dared, because the water was cold.

Back out in the sun, he realized that he would have to do more. He had been too cramped in the basin, and much of his body was still greasy with soap. He walked carefully down the terrace toward the pool, gripping the stone with his toes, for his wet feet were uncertain. They left a train of increasingly perfect tracks from the small puddle where he had stood beside his dressing gown to the last print at the edge of the terrace, which showed each toe faintly but distinctly, and the ball, the arch, and the heel—clearly a man's foot.

After hesitating, he let himself down over the edge until the cool water was about his shins. Then he stood on slimy stone like that in the basin. On all fours, he moved slowly, crabwise, along this submerged ledge, and slid off into deeper water. This was at the center of the pool, and the water was quiet, moved only by a side flow circling the pool from the falls, and occasionally by a light wind-ripple along the surface. Awkwardly, and with some splashing, he rubbed himself under water until the last slickness of soap was gone and his hands adhered to his thighs. Then he paddled aimlessly in the pool for a few minutes, treading water and observing himself below. His arms and legs appeared dwarfed and misshapen, his hands and feet immense and square. All of him that was under water looked yellow, and was hairy with particles of the slime he had stirred getting in. Altogether, he was a much more powerful and formidable man, seen through the glass of the pool. He began to feel adventurous.

He noticed that the green darkness of the pool paled on the side across from the ledges. A sub-aqueous, changeable gold was visible there under the black surface reflection of the forest on the hill. He paddled toward it, keeping his head above water and feeling before him with his hands. When he came to rest, balanced on his hands, he was on a sunken sand-bar—the dam which made the pool. The sand was coarse and white, and felt clean to his touch after the scum in the basin and on the ledge. Letting his feet down, he planted them firmly and walked up the incline of the sand-bar, feeling himself emerge into gusty air. At last he was on top, the water ankle-deep. Looking down from this eminence, he saw a boat farther along the ridge of the bar. It lay bottom up, and was so water-logged that it had ground into the sand until no part of it but the very center of the bottom was above water. Now and then a wind-ripple passed over even that.

The man was excited by the discovery. He waded to the boat and attempted to turn it right side up. The vacuum under it, or simply its weight, held it solidly. He was angered, and put forth all his thin might in repeated efforts, standing upright between tries, to breathe deeply and let the blood subside from his head. To the best of his efforts the boat rocked, and straining, he raised the gunwale as far as his knee. This encouraged him, but when he lifted again, the boat came no higher, and then remained passively immovable. He had to let it fall back into the water, where it rolled lightly, splashing around its shape like a stubborn life thing, run aground, but insisting upon its element.

The man's feet had been driven down into the sand until he could not lift well from his position. Freeing himself, he climbed onto the crest of the bar again and stood with his legs apart, glaring at the boat. He considered leaving it and relinquishing himself to placid floating in the pool, whence he could eye the useless boat disdainfully. But when the blood in his temples ceased pounding, he had a cunning thought. Moving down into the water until he was on the outer side of the boat, he slid it backwards off the bar. Once it floated free, he could get his shoulder under it. This stratagem succeeded. The boat rolled bulkily over, sending out a wave which broke on the sand-bar.

"That fixes you," the man said aloud.

However, the water in the boat was level with the water in the pool. Only a portion of the prow and of the square stern protruded. The man found that tilting the boat let in as much water as it let out. He laid hold of a chain at the prow and drew the boat onto the crest of the bar. It followed him with lumbering unwillingness. On the bar, a great deal more of it stood above water, and by teetering it fore and aft, he drove several belches of water out over the stern. Still the boat would not rise. The man climbed into it and began to scoop with both hands. The water flew in silver sheets, spread into silver drops, and splattered on the pool, but more of it fell through his hands than went overboard. He stood up and looked around. On a flat rock at the west edge of the pool, there sat a shining two-quart tin can. He clambered out of the boat, went down into the water, paddled industriously across, hoisted himself up the irregular rock steps, and procured the can.

Shortly he had all but an inch or two of water out of the boat. That persisted because of three little leaks, through which he could see minute streams gliding steadily in. He pushed the boat, with the can in it, off the sand-bar, and kicking noisily, propelled it to shore. Here he pulled grass and made small wads of it, with the heads standing up in tufts. These plugged the leaks quite effectively, and the man began to hum to himself while he bailed out the last water.

The boat, clumsy and flat-bottomed, with two bowed planks forming each side, had been battered down-stream in the flood of the spring rains. Much of the orange paint had been beaten from it, and the single thwart had been torn out, leaving four rusty nails projecting from each scar. The man searched out a squarish stone and hammered the nails down, humming more loudly. He was formulating a daring plan. He would work the boat around in front of the falls, where the big bubble bellied, and see how far he could go down the stony rapids below the pool. A man taking a risk like that couldn't have nails sticking out where they'd rake his legs if he had to move quickly.

At last he drifted on the pool, keeping the can with him. "Quite a boat," he maintained in a clear voice, and then, argumentatively, but with satisfaction, "I say it's quite a boat."

The boat, dull with the water it had soaked up, rode low and heavily. It refused to be coerced by hand paddling, and cruised, half sidewards, out into the middle of the pool, where it spun slowly three times in the circular current and then headed—or rather tailed—for the stagnant backwash between the shore boulders and the terrace of red rock. The man ceased humming and paddled frantically with his hands, first on one side and then on the other, for the boat was too wide for him to reach water on both sides at once. The boat turned completely around once more, and continued to back toward the extremely green scum in the crevice. The man abandoned himself, held onto the sides, and rode in backwards, muttering. The boat bumped gently, grated along the stone, stirred sinuously, and succeeded in wedging itself. The man sat and observed the pond scum with aversion.

Then he saw a long bamboo pole caught under a ledge. His spirits rose. The pole was within reach, and by bruising his knees a little, slithering on the wet mossiness of the boat, he grasped it. It was heavy, and rotten from enduring the river and from its long hiding in the pool, but having it, he felt confident again. "You'll do," he told the pole. He stood erect, and brandished it in both hands, like a cudgel. "Swell pole." He pressed it firmly against the holding rock, and leaned on it. The boat gave way and swam sluggishly out through the scum. The man, still standing, was immensely elated. "And now, Mr. Boat," he cried.

Maintaining his heroic erectness, he jabbed at rocks along the side and bottom, and brought the boat circuitously toward the back-rolling bubble. As he poled, he hummed grandly, even venturing some open-mouthed tra-las. Approaching the bubble more closely, he became quiet and knelt, preparatory to sitting. In this position, he watched the waterfall steadily. Coming very close, he was suddenly alarmed by the rapid streaming-away of the foam towards the rocks where the water jumped at a hundred points and turned white, like a miniature surf in a cross-rip. He made a spasmodic thrust with the pole. The boat swung sedately around, slid its stern directly under the fall, lifted its snout, and sank backwards. The man clung amazed until the water was under his chin, and then, with a shout, let go and struck out wildly to avoid the rise of the boat.

He continued to swim, growing calmer, until he bumped on the sand-bar and could stand up in the water. Thence he saw his boat lodged against a rock below the bar, the waters protesting around it. The sight enraged him. He remained angry until he had secured the boat, bailed it out, recovered his pole, and returned round the edge of the pool to the fall. Then he swore at the fall to keep his temper up, and this time managed to enter the current just below the bubble. He sat down quickly, nervous because of the speed he expected, believing all at once that his pole was useless. But the boat was too water-logged. Slow and stately it turned upon the stream, let the anxious waters divide about it, coasted past the sand-bar, knocked gently from one rock to another at the head of the shallow rapids, and came to rest between two of them. The man relaxed and took his hands from the sides. "Well," he said, "Well, well."

Thereafter he became pink over his whole body from the exertion of dragging his boat back to the pool. He scraped his feet among the stones of the river bed and never noticed. He took three more rides, going a little farther each time, as he became acquainted with the most prominent rocks. He was so confident on the fifth ride that during the burdensome start he sat with his pole in his hands and regarded the world before him.

In the canyon below the rapids, where the rocky shores grew into cliffs with dense cedar and spruce forests above them, was a splendid curve which hid the lower river. Over the cliff and the forest, a great rounded thunderhead swelled voluminously out of the west and darkened the trees. It appeared to fill the sky, and its upper bosses were bright with sun. The man felt this cloud to be a recognition of the dimension of his undertaking, and gazed at it with stern exultation.

In the late afternoon a woman came over the hill on the road. When she first appeared, irritation was in her walk. The clouds had spread far east and were no longer gilded. The wind kept blowing her hair.

Part way down, she stopped, and stood with her hands on her hips. "For goodness sake," she exclaimed. "For goodness sake, what does that man think he's doing?" She stared. "And yelling his head off like a lunatic," she exclaimed.

The man was just launching out from the jade-colored, white-streaked, back-bellying bubble. He was standing upright in the orange boat, the bamboo pole held aloft like a spear. As he gravitated toward the rapids, his mouth could be seen to open tremendously and repeatedly. He waved his left arm in accompaniment. Faintly, even over the wind and the rush of the falls, the woman could hear the words. "Sailing, sailing," roared the man in the boat. He shook his spear. "Sailing, sailing," he roared, until the boat stumbled and knocked him to his knees. Even then his mouth opened and closed in the same way. Only when the boat stalled, with a white fan of water behind it, did he close his mouth. Then he scrambled out, grabbed the chain on the prow, and dragged, tugged and jerked the boat up the slope of rock and froth.

When the boat was in the pool again, he commenced at once to climb into it and to work his mouth. "Sailing, sailing," he bellowed.

The woman said, "Gracious heavens, he's absolutely crazy," and recovered herself. She advanced to the edge of the rock and yelled at the man. He was then half-way over the stern and kicking valiantly. The woman yelled, "John!" She leaned forward and stuck her chin out when she yelled. The man lay perfectly still for an instant, half-way over the stern. Then he slid back into the water and held onto the stern with one hand. He looked across at the woman. "Yes?" he said.

The woman could see his mouth move. She looked angry but relieved, and eased her voice a little. "D. L. called you," she cried. "He wants you back in town."

"Bother D. L.," the man said to himself.

"What's that you said?" cried the woman.

"I said all right," the man yelled suddenly.

The woman put one hand on her hip. "He called hours ago. He'll be wild."

The man let go of the boat reluctantly and paddled across to the terrace. The woman stood where she was, waiting. The man drew himself out of the water slowly, with great care for his battered toes. Crabwise he ascended the slimy, submerged rock and crawled up onto the red rock in the wind. Cautiously he walked across the red rock to the spot where he had left his things. His tracks grew more distinct as he went.

"For goodness sake, get a move on," the woman called up at him.

His thin, unmuscular body was turning blue in the wind. Bending stiffly, he removed his slippers from the towel, straightened up, and began to wipe himself. He sat down to wipe his feet, and was tender of his toes. He put his spectacles on, using both hands. Then he stood up and donned the red and blue dressing gown and the leather slippers. He wobbled on one leg at a time while putting on his slippers, and screwed his face up while each rubbed over his toes. He searched a moment for the cake of soap. When he found it, he put it in his pocket and, carrying his towel in one hand, descended carefully to where the woman was waiting.

"What on earth were you doing out there?" she asked. But having seen what he was doing, she went on. "D. L. called up hours ago. How on earth did I know I'd have to come way down here after you? How could I know you'd be . . ."

They went on up the road.

"Well, I'm sure I don't know what you were doing," said the woman. "You're so cold your teeth are chattering."

The man was avoiding sharp pebbles in the road, and said nothing. His peeled knees worked in and out of the opening of the dressing gown, which occasionally fled out behind him on the wind.

"How would I know you'd take all afternoon?" asked the woman sharply. "D. L. will be wild. And all because—well, what on earth were you doing out there?"

"Oh, I don't know," said the man. "I found an old boat."

The woman was unpleasantly silent.

"I was just fooling around with an old boat," the man explained, and again, "That's all I was doing, just fooling around with an old boat I found."

The wind on top of the hill was unexpectedly sustained. The woman, holding down her hair with both hands, made no reply. The man had to clutch at his dressing gown tightly, to keep it from streaming out and leaving him uncovered.

## Study Aids: Purdy

1. The incident over the beard dramatizes what conflicting needs of the son, on the one side, and the parents, on the other? What two ways of approaching life are contrasted?
2. The father's response shifts. Why? What does it show about the choices he has made in his life? What does he need to accept?
3. Why is the mother so insistent? Why does the beard frighten her so? What things is she afraid of?
4. What is the relationship between the Ellen Whitelaw episode in the past and the present incident of the beard? What similarities and what differences are involved?
5. What are the son's motives in shaving the beard? What emotions are involved, besides the reasons he mentions in his speech to his parents?

## Study Aids: Clark

1. The contrast on which the story is based is introduced by the descriptions of the man in the first paragraph and a part of the rapids in the second. What are the characteristics of each? What do they represent? How is their connection in the story further clarified, in paragraph four, by the man's decision to keep his shorts on?
2. What is the significance of the statment on Page 177 in paragraph two, "Altogether, he was a much more powerful and formidable man, seen through the glass of the pool"? What transition does this statement mark?
3. What is the sequence of the man's responses to the problems set by the boat? How does he change, and what does he retain? Why does he take the boat over the rapids again and again?
4. What has he achieved—in several ways—when his wife comes upon him? What is her response? Why?
5. What is the significance of his reason for leaving? What happens to him when he comes out of the water? What is implied by the last sentence of the story? Which world has won?

# A WORN PATH
## *Eudora Welty*

It was December—a bright frozen day in the early morning. Far out in the country there was an old Negro woman with her head tied in a red rag, coming along a path through the pinewoods. Her name was Phoenix Jackson. She was very old and small and she walked slowly in the dark pine shadows, moving a little from side to side in her steps, with the balanced heaviness and lightness of a pendulum in a grandfather clock. She carried a thin, small cane made from an umbrella, and with this she kept tapping the frozen earth in front of her. This made a grave and persistent noise in the still air, that seemed meditative, like the chirping of a solitary little bird.

She wore a dark striped dress reaching down to her shoetops, and an equally long apron of bleached sugar sacks, with a full pocket; all neat and tidy, but every time she took a step she might have fallen over her shoe-laces, which dragged from her unlaced shoes. She looked straight ahead. Her eyes were blue with age. Her skin had a pattern all its own of numberless branching wrinkles and as though a whole little tree stood in the middle of her forehead, but a golden color ran underneath, and the two knobs of her cheeks were illuminated by a yellow burning under the dark. Under the red rag her hair came down on her neck in the frailest of ringlets, still black, and with an odor like copper.

Now and then there was a quivering in the thicket. Old Phoenix said, "Out of my way, all you foxes, owls, beetles, jack rabbits, coons, and wild animals! . . . Keep out from under these feet, little bobwhites. . . . Keep the big wild hogs out of my path. Don't let none of those come running my direction. I got a long way." Under her small black-freckled hand her cane, limber as a buggy whip, would switch at the brush as if to rouse up any hiding things.

On she went. The woods were deep and still. The sun made the pine needles almost too bright to look at, up where the wind rocked. The cones dropped as light as feathers. Down in the hollow was the mourning dove—it was not too late for him.

The path ran up a hill. "Seems like there is chains about my feet, time I get this far," she said, in the voice of argument old people keep to use with themselves. "Something always take a hold on his hill— pleads I should stay."

After she got to the top she turned and gave a full, severe look behind her where she had come. "Up through pines," she said at length. "Now down through oaks."

Her eyes opened their widest and she started down gently. But before she got to the bottom of the hill a bush caught her dress.

Her fingers were busy and intent, but her skirts were full and long, so that before she could pull them free in one place they were caught in another. It was not possible to allow the dress to tear. "I in the thorny bush," she said. "Thorns, you doing your appointed work. Never want to let folks pass—no sir. Old eyes thought you was a pretty little green bush."

Finally, trembling all over, she stood free, and after a moment dared to stoop for her cane.

"Sun so high!" she cried, leaning back and looking, while the thick tears went over her eyes. "The time getting all gone here."

At the foot of this hill was a place where a log was laid across the creek.

"Now comes the trial," said Phoenix.

Putting her right foot out, she mounted the log and shut her eyes. Lifting her skirt, levelling her cane fiercely before her, like a festival figure in some parade, she began to march across. Then she opened her eyes and she was safe on the other side.

"I wasn't as old as I thought," she said.

But she sat down to rest. She spread her skirts on the bank around her and folded her hands over her knees. Up above her was a tree in a pearly cloud of mistletoe. She did not dare to close her eyes, and when a little boy brought her a little plate with a slice of marble-cake on it she spoke to him. "That would be acceptable," she said. But when she went to take it there was just her own hand in the air.

So she left that tree, and had to go through a barbed-wire fence. There she had to creep and crawl, spreading her knees and stretching her fingers like a baby trying to climb the steps. But she talked loudly to herself: she could not let her dress be torn now, so late in the day, and she could not pay for having her arm or her leg sawed off if she got caught fast where she was.

At last she was safe through the fence and risen up out in the clearing. Big dead trees, like black men with one arm, were standing in the purple stalks of the withered cotton field. There sat a buzzard.

"Who you watching?"

In the burrow she made her way along.

"Glad this not the season for bulls," she said, looking sideways, "and the good Lord made his snakes to curl up and sleep in the winter. A pleasure I don't see no two-headed snake coming around that tree, where it come once. It took a while to get by him, back in the summer."

She passed through the old cotton and went into a field of dead corn. It whispered and shook, and was taller than her head. "Through the maze now," she said, for there was no path.

Then there was something tall, black, and skinny there, moving before her.

At first she took it for a man. It could have been a man dancing in the field. But she stood still and listened, and it did not make a sound. It was as silent as a ghost.

"Ghost," she said sharply, "who be you the ghost of? For I have heard of nary death close by."

But there was no answer, only the ragged dancing in the wind.

She shut her eyes, reached out her hand, and touched a sleeve. She found a coat and inside that an emptiness, cold as ice.

"You scarecrow," she said. Her face lighted. "I ought to be shut up for good," she said with laughter. "My senses is gone. I too old. I the oldest people I ever know. Dance, old scarecrow," she said, "while I dancing with you."

She kicked her foot over the furrow, and with mouth drawn down shook her head once or twice in a little strutting way. Some husks blew down and whirled in streamers about her skirts.

Then she went on, parting her way from side to side with the cane, through the whispering field. At last she came to the end, to a wagon track, where the silver grass blew between the red ruts. The quail were walking around like pullets, seeming all dainty and unseen.

"Walk pretty," she said. "This the easy place. This the easy going."

She followed the track, swaying through the quiet bare fields, through the little strings of trees silver in their dead leaves, past cabins silver from weather, with the doors and windows boarded shut, all like old women under a spell sitting there. "I walking in their sleep," she said, nodding her head vigorously.

In a ravine she went where a spring was silently flowing through a hollow log. Old Phoenix bent and drank. "Sweetgum makes the water sweet," she said, and drank more. "Nobody knows who made this well, for it was here when I was born."

The track crossed a swampy part where the moss hung as white as lace from every limb. "Sleep on, alligators, and blow your bubbles." Then the track went into the road.

Deep, deep the road went down between the high green-colored banks. Overhead the live-oaks met, and it was as dark as a cave.

A black dog with a lolling tongue came up out of the weeds by the ditch. She was meditating, and not ready, and when he came at her she only hit him a little with her cane. Over she went in the ditch, like a little puff of milk-weed.

Down there, her senses drifted away. A dream visited her, and she reached her hand up, but nothing reached down and gave her a pull. So she lay there and presently went to talking. "Old woman," she said to herself, "that black dog came up out of the weeds to stall you off, and now there he sitting on his fine tail, smiling at you."

A white man finally came along and found her—a hunter, a young man, with his dog on a chain.

"Well, Granny!" he laughed. "What are you doing there?"

"Lying on my back like a June-bug waiting to be turned over, mister," she said, reaching up her hand.

He lifted her up, gave her a swing in the air, and set her down, "Anything broken, Granny?"

"No sir, them old dead weeds is springy enough," said Phoenix, when she had got her breath. "I thank you for your trouble."

"Where do you live, Granny?" he asked, while the two dogs were growling at each other.

"Away back yonder, sir, behind the ridge. You can't even see it from here."

"On your way home?"

"No, sir, I going to town."

"Why, that's too far! That's as far as I walk when I come out myself, and I get something for my trouble." He patted the stuffed bag he carried, and there hung down a little closed claw. It was one of the bobwhites, with its beak hooked bitterly to show it was dead. "Now you go on home, Granny!"

"I bound to go to town, mister," said Phoenix. "The time come around."

He gave another laugh, filling the whole landscape. "I know you colored people! Wouldn't miss going to town to see Santa Claus!"

But something held Old Phoenix very still. The deep lines in her face went into a fierce and different radiation. Without warning she had seen with her own eyes a flashing nickel fall out of the man's pocket on to the ground.

"How old are you, Granny?" he was saying.

"There is no telling, mister," she said, "no telling."

Then she gave a little cry and clapped her hands, and said, "Git on away from here, dog! Look! Look at that dog!" She laughed as if in admiration. "He ain't scared of nobody. He a big black dog." She whispered, "Sick him!"

"Watch me get rid of that cur," said the man. "Sick him, Pete! Sick him!"

Phoenix heard the dogs fighting and heard the man running and throwing sticks. She even heard a gunshot. But she was slowly bending forward by that time, further and further forward, the lids stretched down over her eyes, as if she were doing this in her sleep. Her chin was lowered almost to her knees. The yellow palm of her hand came out from the fold of her apron. Her fingers slid down and along the ground under the piece of money with the grace and care they would have in lifting an egg from under a sitting hen. Then she slowly straightened up, she stood erect, and the nickel was in her apron pocket. A bird flew by. Her lips moved. "God watching me the whole time. I come to stealing."

The man came back, and his own dog panted about them. "Well, I scared him off that time," he said, and then he laughed and lifted his gun and pointed it at Phoenix.

She stood straight and faced him.

"Doesn't the gun scare you?" he said, still pointing it.

"No, sir, I seen plenty go off closer by, in my day, and for less than what I done," she said, holding utterly still.

He smiled, and shouldered the gun. "Well, Granny," he said, "you must be a hundred years old and scared of nothing. I'd give you a dime if I had any money with me But you take my advice and stay home, and nothing will happen to you."

"I bound to go on my way, mister," said Phoenix. She inclined her head in the red rag. Then they went in different directions, but she could hear the gun shooting again and again over the hill.

She walked on. The shadows hung from the oak trees to the road like curtains. Then she smelled wood-smoke, and smelled the river, and she saw a steeple and the cabins on their steep steps. Dozens of little black children whirled around her. There ahead was Natchez shining. Bells were ringing. She walked on.

In the paved city it was Christmas time. There were red and green electric lights strung and crisscrossed everywhere, and all turned on in the daytime. Old Phoenix would have been lost if she had not distrusted her eyesight and depended on her feet to know where to take her.

She paused quietly on the sidewalk, where people were passing by. A lady came along in the crowd, carrying an armful of red-, green-, and silver-wrapped presents; she gave off perfume like the red roses in hot summer, and Phoenix stopped her.

"Please, missy, will you lace up my shoe?" She held up her foot.

"What do you want, Grandma?"

"See my shoe," said Phoenix. "Do all right for out in the country, but wouldn't look right to go in a big building."

"Stand still then, Grandma," said the lady. She put her packages down carefully on the sidewalk beside her and laced and tied both shoes tightly.

"Can't lace 'em with a cane," said Phoenix. "Thank you, missy. I doesn't mind asking a nice lady to tie up my shoe when I gets out on the street."

Moving slowly and from side to side, she went into the stone building and into a tower of steps, where she walked up and around and around until her feet knew to stop.

She entered a door, and there she saw nailed up on the wall the document that had been stamped with the gold seal and framed in the gold frame which matched the dream that was hung up in her head.

"Here I be," she said. There was a fixed and ceremonial stiffness over her body.

"A charity case, I suppose," said an attendant who sat at the desk before her.

But Phoenix only looked above her head. There was sweat on her face; the wrinkles shone like a bright net.

"Speak up, Grandma," the woman said. "What's your name? We must have your history, you know. Have you been here before? What seems to be the trouble with you?"

Old Phoenix only gave a twitch to her face as if a fly were bothering her.

"Are you deaf?" cried the attendant.

But then the nurse came in.

"Oh, that's just old Aunt Phoenix," she said. "She doesn't come for herself—she has a little grandson. She makes these trips just as regular as clockwork. She lives away back off the Old Natchez Trace." She bent down. "Well, Aunt Phoenix, why don't you just take a seat? We won't keep you standing after your long trip." She pointed.

The old woman sat down, bolt upright in the chair.

"Now, how is the boy?" asked the nurse.

Old Phoenix did not speak.

"I said, how is the boy?"

But Phoenix only waited and stared straight ahead, her face very solemn and withdrawn into rigidity.

"Is his throat any better?" asked the nurse. "Aunt Phoenix, don't you hear me? Is your grandson's throat any better since the last time you came for the medicine?"

With her hand on her knees, the old woman waited, silent, erect and motionless, just as if she were in armor.

"You mustn't take up our time this way, Aunt Phoenix," the nurse said. "Tell us quickly about your grandson, and get it over. He isn't dead, is he?"

At last there came a flicker and then a flame of comprehension across her face, and she spoke.

"My grandson. It was my memory had left me. There I sat and forgot why I made my long trip."

"Forgot?" The nurse frowned. "After you came so far?"

Then Phoenix was like an old woman begging a dignified forgiveness for waking up frightened in the night. "I never did go to school—I was too old at the Surrender," she said in a soft voice. "I'm an old woman without an education. It was my memory fail me. My little grandson, he is just the same, and I forgot it in the coming."

"Throat never heals, does it?" said the nurse, speaking in a loud, sure voice to Old Phoenix. By now she had a card with something written on it, a little list. "Yes. Swallowed lye. When was it—January—two—three years ago—"

Phoenix spoke unasked now. "No, missy, he not dead, he just the same. Every little while his throat begin to close up again, and he not able to swallow. He not get his breath. He not able to help himself. So the time come around, and I go on another trip for the soothing-medicine."

"All right. The doctor said as long as you came to get it you could have it," said the nurse. "But it's an obstinate case."

"My little grandson, he sit up there in the house all wrapped up, waiting by himself," Phoenix went on. "We is the only two left in the world. He suffer and it don't seem to put him back at all. He got a sweet look. He going to last. He wear a little patch quilt and peep out, holding his mouth open like a little bird. I remembers so plain now. I not going to forget him again, no, the whole enduring time. I could tell him from all the others in creation."

"All right." The nurse was trying to hush her now. She brought her a bottle of medicine. "Charity," she said, making a check mark in a book.

Old Phoenix held the bottle close to her eyes and then carefully put it into her pocket.

"I thank you," she said.

"It's Christmas time, Grandma," said the attendant. "Could I give you a few pennies out of my purse?"

"Five pennies is a nickel," said Phoenix stiffly.

"Here's a nickel," said the attendant.

Phoenix rose carefully and held out her hand. She received the nickel and then fished the other nickel out of her pocket and laid it beside the new one. She stared at her palm closely, with her head on one side.

Then she gave a tap with her cane on the floor.

"This is what come to me to do," she said. "I going to the store and buy my child a little windmill they sells, made out of paper. He going to find it hard to believe there such a thing in the world. I'll march myself back where he waiting, holding it straight up in this hand."

She lifted her free hand, gave a little nod, turned round, and walked out of the doctor's office. Then her slow step began on the stairs, going down.

---

# THE MOURNERS
## *Bernard Malamud*

Kessler, formerly an egg candler, lived alone on social security. Though past sixty-five, he might have found well-paying work with more than one butter and egg wholesaler, for he sorted and graded with speed and accuracy, but he was a quarrelsome type and considered a trouble maker, so the wholesalers did without him. Therefore, after a time he retired, living with few wants on his old-age pension. Kessler inhabited a small cheap flat on the top floor of a decrepit tenement on the East Side. Perhaps because he lived above so many stairs, no one bothered to visit him. He was much alone, as he had been most of his life. At one time he'd had a family, but unable to stand his wife or children, always in his way, he had after some years walked out on them. He never saw them thereafter, because he never sought them, and they did not seek him. Thirty years had passed. He had no idea where they were, nor did he think much about it.

In the tenement, although he had lived there ten years, he was more or less unknown. The tenants on both sides of his flat on the fifth floor, an Italian family of three middle-aged sons and their wizened mother, and a sullen, childless German couple named Hoffman, never said hello to him, nor did he greet any of them on the way up or down the narrow wooden stairs. Others of the house recognized Kessler when they passed him in the street, but they thought he lived elsewhere on the block. Ignace, the small, bent-back janitor, knew him best, for they had several times played two-handed pinochle; but Ignace, usually the loser because he lacked skill at cards, had stopped going up after a time. He complained to his wife that he couldn't stand the stink there, that the filthy flat with its junky furniture made him sick. The janitor had spread the word about Kessler to the others on the floor, and they shunned him as a dirty old man. Kessler understood this but had contempt for them all.

One day Ignace and Kessler began a quarrel over the way the egg candler piled oily bags overflowing with garbage into the dumb-waiter, instead of using a pail. One word shot off another, and they were soon calling each other savage names, when Kessler slammed the door in the janitor's face. Ignace ran down five flights of stairs and loudly cursed out the old man to his impassive wife. It happened that Gruber, the landlord, a fat man with a consistently worried face, who wore yards of baggy clothes, was in the building, making a check of plumbing repairs, and to him the enraged Ignace related the trouble he was having with Kessler. He described, holding his nose, the smell in Kessler's flat, and called him the dirtiest person he had ever seen. Gruber knew his janitor was exaggerating, but he felt burdened by financial worries which shot his blood pressure up to astonishing heights, so he settled it quickly by saying, "Give him notice." None of the tenants in the house had held a written lease since the war, and Gruber felt confident, in case somebody asked questions, that he could easily justify his dismissal of Kessler as an undesirable tenant. It had occurred to him that Ignace could then slap a cheap coat of paint on the walls and the flat would be let to someone for five dollars more than the old man was paying.

That night after supper, Ignace victoriously ascended the stairs and knocked on Kessler's door. The egg candler opened it, and seeing who stood there, immediately slammed it shut. Ignace shouted through the door, "Mr. Gruber says to give notice. We don't want you around here. Your dirt stinks the whole house." There was silence, but Ignace waited, relishing what he had said. Although after five minutes he still heard no sound, the janitor stayed there, picturing the old Jew trembling behind the locked door. He spoke again, "You got two weeks' notice till the first, then you better move out or Mr. Gruber and myself will throw you out." Ignace watched as the door slowly opened. To his surprise he found himself frightened at the old man's appearance. He looked, in the act of opening the door, like a corpse adjusting his coffin lid. But if he appeared dead, his voice was alive. It rose terrifyingly harsh from his throat, and he sprayed curses over all the years of Ignace's life. His eyes were reddened, his cheeks sunken, and his wisp of beard moved agitatedly. He seemed to be losing weight as he shouted. The janitor no longer had any heart for the matter, but he could not bear so many insults all at once so he cried out, "You dirty old bum, you better get out and don't make so much trouble." To this the enraged Kessler swore they would first have to kill him and drag him out dead.

On the morning of the first of December, Ignace found in his letter box a soiled folded paper containing Kessler's twenty-five dollars. He showed it to Gruber that evening when the landlord came to collect the rent money. Gruber, after a minute of absently contemplating the money, frowned disgustedly.

"I thought I told you to give notice."

"Yes, Mr. Gruber," Ignace agreed. "I gave him."

"That's a helluva chuzpah," said Gruber. "Gimme the keys."

Ignace brought the ring of pass keys, and Gruber, breathing heavily, began the lumbering climb up the long avenue of stairs. Although he rested on each landing, the fatigue of climbing, and his profuse flowing perspiration, heightened his irritation.

Arriving at the top floor he banged his fist on Kessler's door. "Gruber, the landlord. Open up here."

There was no answer, no movement within, so Gruber inserted the key into the lock and twisted. Kessler had barricaded the door with a chest and some chairs. Gruber had to put his shoulder to the door and shove before he could step into the hallway of the badly-lit two and a half room flat. The old man, his face drained of blood, was standing in the kitchen doorway.

"I warned you to scram outa here," Gruber said loudly. "Move out or I'll telephone the city marshal."

"Mr. Gruber—" began Kessler.

"Don't bother me with your lousy excuses, just beat it." He gazed around. "It looks like a junk shop and it smells like a toilet. It'll take me a month to clean up here."

"This smell is only cabbage that I am cooking for my supper. Wait, I'll open a window and it will go away."

"When you go away, it'll go away." Gruber took out his bulky wallet, counted out twelve dollars, added fifty cents, and plunked the money on top of the chest. "You got two more weeks till the fifteenth, then you gotta be out or I will get a dispossess. Don't talk back talk. Get outa here and go somewhere that they don't know you and maybe you'll get a place."

"No, Mr. Gruber," Kessler cried passionately. "I didn't do anything, and I will stay here."

"Don't monkey with my blood pressure," said Gruber. "If you're not out by the fifteenth, I will personally throw you on your bony ass."

Then he left and walked heavily down the stairs.

The fifteenth came and Ignace found the twelve fifty in his letter box. He telephoned Gruber and told him.

"I'll get a dispossess," Gruber shouted. He instructed the janitor to write out a note saying to Kessler that his money was refused and to stick it under his door. This Ignace did. Kessler returned the money to the letter box, but again Ignace wrote a note and slipped it, with the money, under the old man's door.

After another day Kessler received a copy of his eviction notice. It said to appear in court on Friday at 10 A.M. to show cause why he should not be evicted for continued neglect and destruction of rental property. The official notice filled Kessler with great fright because he had never in his life been to court. He did not appear on the day he had been ordered to.

That same afternoon the marshal appeared with two brawny assistants. Ignace opened Kessler's lock for them and as they pushed their way into the flat, the janitor hastily ran down the stairs to hide in the cellar. Despite Kessler's wailing and carrying on, the two assistants methodically removed his meager furniture and set it out on the sidewalk. After that they got Kessler out, though they had to break open the bathroom door because the old man had locked himself in there. He shouted, struggled, pleaded with his neighbors to help him, but they looked on in a silent group outside the door. The two assistants, holding the old man tightly by the arms and skinny legs, carried him, kicking and moaning, down the stairs. They sat him in the street on a chair amid his junk. Upstairs, the marshal bolted the door with a lock Ignace had supplied, signed a paper which he handed to the janitor's wife, and then drove off in an automobile with his assistants.

Kessler sat on a split chair on the sidewalk. It was raining and the rain soon turned to sleet, but he still sat there. People passing by skirted the pile of his belongings. They stared at Kessler and he stared at nothing. He wore no hat or coat, and the snow fell on him, making him look like a piece of his dispossessed goods. Soon the wizened Italian woman from the top floor returned to the house with two of her sons, each carrying a loaded shopping bag. When she recognized Kessler sitting amid his furniture, she began to shriek. She shrieked in Italian at Kessler although he paid no attention to her. She stood on the stoop, shrunken, gesticulating with thin arms, her loose mouth working angrily. Her sons tried to calm her, but still she shrieked. Several of the neighbors came down to see who was making the racket. Finally, the two sons, unable to think what else to do, set down their shopping bags, lifted Kessler out of the chair, and carried him up the stairs. Hoffman, Kessler's other neighbor, working with a small triangular file, cut open the padlock, and Kessler was carried into the flat from which he had been evicted. Ignace screeched at everybody, calling them filthy names, but the three men went downstairs and hauled up Kessler's chairs, his broken table, chest, and ancient metal bed. They piled all the furniture into the bedroom. Kessler sat on the edge of the bed and wept. After a while, after the old Italian woman had sent in a soup plate full of hot macaroni seasoned with tomato sauce and grated cheese, they left.

Ignace phoned Gruber. The landlord was eating and the food turned to lumps in his throat. "I'll throw them all out, the bastards," he yelled. He put on his hat, got into his car and drove through the slush to the tenement. All the time he was thinking of his worries: high repair costs; it was hard to keep the place together; maybe the building would someday collapse. He had read of such things. All of a

sudden the front of the building parted from the rest and fell like a
breaking wave into the street. Gruber cursed the old man for taking
him from his supper. When he got to the house he snatched Ignace's
keys and ascended the sagging stairs. Ignace tried to follow, but Gruber
told him to stay the hell in his hole. When the landlord was not looking, Ignace crept up after him.

Gruber turned the key and let himself into Kessler's dark flat. He
pulled the light chain and found the old man sitting limply on the side
of the bed. On the floor at his feet lay a plate of stiffened macaroni.

"What do you think you're doing here?" Gruber thundered.

The old man sat motionless.

"Don't you know it's against the law? This is trespassing and you're
breaking the law. Answer me."

Kessler remained mute.

Gruber mopped his brow with a large yellowed handkerchief.

"Listen, my friend, you're gonna make lots of trouble for yourself. If
they catch you in here you might go to the workhouse. I'm only trying
to advise you."

To his surprise Kessler looked at him with wet, brimming eyes.

"What did I did to you?" he wept bitterly. "Who throws out of his
house a man that he lived there ten years and pays every month on
time his rent? What did I do, tell me? Who hurts a man without a
reason? Are you a Hitler or a Jew?" He was hitting his chest with his
fist.

Gruber removed his hat. He listened carefully, at first at a loss what
to say, but then answered: "Listen, Kessler, it's not personal. I own
this house and it's falling apart. My bills are sky high. If the tenants
don't take care they have to go. You don't take care and you fight
with my janitor, so you have to go. Leave in the morning, and I won't
say another word. But if you don't leave the flat, you'll get the
heave-ho again. I'll call the marshal."

"Mr. Gruber," said Kessler, "I won't go. Kill me if you want it, but
I won't go."

Ignace hurried away from the door as Gruber left in anger. The next
morning, after a restless night of worries, the landlord set out to drive
to the city marshal's office. On the way he stopped at a candy store
for a pack of cigarettes, and there decided once more to speak to Kessler. A thought had occurred to him: he would offer to get the old man
into a public home.

He drove to the tenement and knocked on Ignace's door.

"Is the old gink still up there?"

"I don't know if so, Mr. Gruber." The janitor was ill at ease.

"What do you mean you don't know?"

"I didn't see him go out. Before, I looked in his keyhole but nothing moves."

"So why don't you open the door with your key?"

"I was afraid," Ignace answered nervously.

"What are you afraid?"

Ignace wouldn't say.

A fright went through Gruber but he didn't show it. He grabbed the keys and walked ponderously up the stairs, hurrying every so often.

No one answered his knock. As he unlocked the door he broke into heavy sweat.

But the old man was there, alive, sitting without shoes on the bedroom floor.

"Listen, Kessler," said the landlord, relieved although his head pounded. "I got an idea that, if you do it the way I say, your troubles are over."

He explained his proposal to Kessler, but the egg candler was not listening. His eyes were downcast, and his body swayed slowly sideways. As the landlord talked on, the old man was thinking of what had whirled through his mind as he had sat out on the sidewalk in the falling snow. He had thought through his miserable life, remembering how, as a young man, he had abandoned his family, walking out on his wife and three innocent children, without even in some way attempting to provide for them; without, in all the intervening years—so God help him—once trying to discover if they were alive or dead. How, in so short a life, could a man do so much wrong? This thought smote him to the heart and he recalled the past without end and moaned and tore at his flesh with his fingernails.

Gruber was frightened at the extent of Kessler's suffering. Maybe I should let him stay, he thought. Then as he watched the old man, he realized he was bunched up there on the floor engaged in an act of mourning. There he sat, white from fasting, rocking back and forth, his beard dwindled to a shade of itself.

Something's wrong here—Gruber tried to imagine what and found it all oppressive. He felt he ought to run out, get away, but then saw himself fall and go tumbling down the five flights of stairs; he groaned at the broken picture of himself lying at the bottom. Only he was still there in Kessler's bedroom, listening to the old man praying. Somebody's dead, Gruber muttered. He figured Kessler had got bad news, yet instinctively knew he hadn't. Then it struck him with a terrible force that the mourner was mourning him: it was *he* who was dead.

The landlord was agonized. Sweating brutally, he felt an enormous constricted weight in him that slowly forced itself up, until his head was at the point of bursting. For a full minute he awaited a stroke; but the feeling painfully passed, leaving him miserable.

When after a while, he gazed around the room, it was clean, drenched in daylight and fragrance. Gruber then suffered unbearable remorse for the way he had treated the old man.

At last he could stand it no longer. With a cry of shame he tore the sheet off Kessler's bed, and wrapping it around his bulk, sank heavily to the floor and became a mourner.

## Study Aids: Welty

1. What do the implications of the name *Phoenix* suggest about the central character and the meaning of her journey? Why, in the broadest sense, does she make her journey, what does she seek? With what personal traits and attitudes does she make it, by what means does she manage to complete it, with what attitudes does she face its reverse sequence on the way home?
2. The path of her quest presents a number of tests or trials: the hill, the briar bush, the log over the creek, the barbed wire, the maze through the corn field, the scarecrow, the easy place, the ditch. What are the wider, symbolic significances of these, and her responses to them?
3. What is suggested by the figure of the white man who helps her from the ditch, but who has killed a bird, shoots at a dog, mocks her and lies to her?
4. What are the attitudes of the people in the clinic? What kind of contrast is achieved between their responses and the story she tells?
5. Her last poignant descriptions of her grandson and of the present she will buy him are not only complexly moving, but symbolic of the conditions of the life she faces and the means by which she endures them. What are the nature of life and the means of endurance suggested by the story?

## Study Aids: Malamud

1. How do the conditions of Kessler's apartment symbolize the conditions of his life?
2. What are Kessler's relations with his neighbors? Why do they help him back into the flat? What are the implications of these relationships?
3. What are Gruber's reasons for evicting him? What does his question on his last visit—"Is the old gink still up there?"—indicate about his attitude toward Kessler? About the attitudes of the others? About the attitude of Kessler toward them?
4. Why does Kessler refuse to leave the flat? What does it mean to him?
5. Why, at the end, is Kessler moaning and tearing at his flesh? What have the events made him see? Why does Gruber sit down and join him? What has happened to the two men? Despite the crying, in what way have they been changed?

# THE EYE
## *J. F. Powers*

All them that dropped in at Bullen's last night was talking about the terrible accident that almost happened to Clara Beck—that's Clyde Bullen's best girl. I am in complete charge of the pool tables and cigar counter, including the punchboards, but I am not in my regular spot in front, on account of Clyde has got a hot game of rotation going at the new table, and I am the only one he will leave chalk his cue. While I am chalking it and collecting for games and racking the balls I am hearing from everybody how Clara got pulled out of the river by Sleep Bailey.

He is not one of the boys, Sleep, but just a nigger that's deef and lives over in jigtown somewhere and plays the piano for dances at the Louisiana Social Parlor. They say he can't hear nothing but music. Spends the day loafing and fishing. He's fishing—is the story—when he seed Clara in the river below the Ludlow road bridge, and he swum out and saved her. Had to knock her out to do it, she put up such a fight. Anyways he saved her from drownding. That was the story everybody was telling.

Clyde has got the idee of taking up a collection for Sleep, as it was a brave deed he done and he don't have nothing to his name but a tub of fishing worms. On the other hand, he don't need nothing, being a nigger, not needing nothing. But Clara is Clyde's girl and it is Clyde's idee and so it is going over pretty big as most of the boys is trying to stay in with Clyde and the rest is owing him money and can't help themselves. I chipped in two bits myself.

Clyde is just fixing to shoot when Skeeter Bird comes in and says, "Little cold for swimming, ain't it, Clyde?"

It upsets Clyde and he has to line up the thirteen ball again. I remember it is the thirteen 'cause they ain't nobody round here that's got the eye Clyde has got for them big balls and that thirteen is his special favor-ite, says it's lucky—it and the nine. I tell you this on account of Clyde misses his shot. Looked to me and anybody else that knowed Clyde's game that what Skeeter said upset his aim.

"What's eating you?" Clyde says to Skeeter, plenty riled. I can see he don't feel so bad about the thirteen getting away as he might of, as he has left it sewed up for Ace Haskins, that claims he once took a game from the great Ralph Greenleaf. "You got something to say?" Clyde says.

"No," Skeeter says, "only—"

"Only what?" Clyde wants to know.

"Only that Bailey nigger got hisself scratched up nice, Clyde."

"So I am taking up a little collection for him," Clyde says. "Pass the plate to Brother Bird, boys."

But Skeeter, he don't move a finger, just says, "Clara got banged up some, too, Clyde. Nigger must of socked her good."

None of us knowed what Skeeter was getting at, except maybe Clyde, that once took a course in mind reading, but we don't like it. And Clyde, I can tell, don't like it. The cue stick is shaking a little in his hand like he wants to use it on Skeeter and he don't shoot right away. He straightens up and says, "Well, he hadda keep her from strangling him while he was rescuing her, didn't he? It was for her own good."

"Yeah, guess so," Skeeter says. "But they both looked like they been in a mean scrap."

"That so?" Clyde says. "Was you there?"

"No, but I heard," Skeeter says.

"You heard," Clyde says. He gets ready to drop the fifteen.

"Yeah," Skeeter says. "You know, Clyde, that Bailey nigger is a funny nigger."

"How's that?" Clyde says, watching Skeeter close. "What's wrong with him?" Clyde holds up his shot and looks right at Skeeter. "Come on, out with it."

"Oh, I don't know as they's a lot wrong with him," Skeeter says. "I guess he's all right. Lazy damn nigger is all. Won't keep a job—just wants to play on the piano and fish."

"Never would of rescued Clara if he didn't," Clyde says. "And besides what kind of job you holding down?"

Now that gets Skeeter where it hurts on account of he don't work hisself, unless you call selling rubbers work or peddling art studies work. Yeah, that's what he calls them. Art studies. Shows a girl that ain't got no clothes on, except maybe her garters, and down below it says "Pensive" or "Evening in Paris." Skeeter sells them to artists, he says—he'll tell you that to your face—but he's always got a few left over for the boys at Bullen's.

Well, Skeeter goes on up front and starts in to study the slot machines. He don't never play them, just studies them. Somebody said he's writing a book about how to beat them, but I don't think he's got the mind for it, is my opinion.

Clyde is halfway into the next game when Skeeter comes back again. He has some of the boys with him now.

"All right, all right," Clyde says, stopping his game.

"You tell him, Skeeter" the boys says.

"Yeah, Skeeter, you tell me," Clyde says.

"Oh," Skeeter says, "it's just something some of them is saying, Clyde, is all."

"Who's saying?" Clyde says. "Who's saying what?"

"Some of them," Skeeter says, "over at the Arcade."

The Arcade, in case you don't know, is the other poolhall in town. Bullen's and the Arcade don't mix, and I guess Skeeter is about the only one that shows up regular in both places, on account of he's got customers in both places. I'd personally like to keep Skeeter out of Bullen's, but Clyde buys a lot of art studies off him and I can't say nothing.

After a spell of thinking Clyde says to Skeeter, "Spill it."

"May not be a word of truth to it, Clyde," Skeeter says. "You know how folks talk. And all I know is what I hear. Course I knowed a long time that Bailey nigger is a damn funny nigger. Nobody never did find out where he come from—St. Louis, Chicago, New York, for all anybody knowed. And if he's stone deaf how can he hear to play the piano?"

"Damn the nigger," Clyde says. "What is they saying, them Arcade bastards!"

"Oh, not all of them is saying it, Clyde. Just some of them is saying it. Red Hynes, that tends bar at the El Paso, and them. Saying maybe the nigger didn't get them scratches on his face for nothing. Saying maybe he was trying something funny. That's a damn funny nigger, Clyde, I don't care what you say. And when you get right down to it, Clyde, kind of stuck up like. Anyways some of them at the Arcade is saying maybe the nigger throwed Clara in the river and then fished her out just to cover up. Niggers is awful good at covering up, Clyde."

Clyde don't say nothing to this, but I can tell he is thinking plenty and getting mad at what he's thinking—plenty. It's real quiet at Bullen's now.

"Maybe," Clyde says, "maybe they is saying what he was covering up from?"

"Yeah, Clyde," Skeeter says, "Matter of fact, they is. Yeah, some of them is saying maybe the nigger *raped* her!"

*Bang!* Clyde cracks the table with his cue stick. It takes a piece of pearl inlay right out of the apron board of the good, new table. Nobody says nothing. Clyde just stares at all the chalk dust he raised.

Then Skeeter says, "Raped her first, rescued her later, is what they is saying."

"What you going to do, Clyde?" Banjo Wheeler says.

"Clyde is thinking!" I say. "Leave him think!" But personally I never seed Clyde take that long just to think.

"Move," Clyde said.

The boys give Clyde plenty of room. He goes over to the rack and tips a little talcum in his hands. The boys is all watching him good. Then Clyde spits. I am right by the cuspidor and can see Clyde's spit floating on the water inside. Nobody says nothing. Clyde's spit is going around in the water and I am listening to hear what he is going to do. He takes the chalk out of my hand. He still don't say nothing. It is the first time he ever chalks his cue with me around to do it.

Then he says, "What kind of nigger is this Bailey nigger, Roy?"

Roy—that's me.

"Oh, just a no-good nigger, Clyde," I say. "Plays the piano at the Louisiana Social Parlor—*some* social parlor, Clyde—is about all I know, or anybody. Fishes quite a bit—just a lazy, funny, no-good nigger ..."

"But he ain't no *bad* nigger, Roy?"

"Naw, he ain't *that*, Clyde," I say. "We ain't got none of them kind left in town."

"Well," Clyde says, "just so's he ain't no *bad* nigger."

Then, not saying no more, Clyde shoots and makes the ten ball in the side pocket. I don't have to tell you the boys is all pretty disappointed in Clyde. I have to admit I never knowed no other white man but Clyde to act like that. But maybe Clyde has his reasons, I say to myself, and wait.

Well, sir, that was right before the news come from the hospital. Ace is friendly with a nurse there is how we come to get it. He calls her on the phone to find out how Clara is. She is unconscious and ain't able to talk yet, but that ain't what makes all hell break loose at Bullen's. It's—un-mis-tak-able ev-i-dence of preg-nan-cy!

Get it? Means she was knocked up. Whoa! I don't have to tell you how that hits the boys at Bullen's. Some said they admired Clyde for not flying off the handle in the first place and some said they didn't, but all of them said they had let their good natures run away with their better judgments. They was right.

I goes to Ace, that's holding the kitty we took up for the nigger, and gets my quarter back. I have a little trouble at first as some of the boys has got there in front of me and collected more than they put in—or else Ace is holding out.

All this time Clyde is in the washroom. I try to hurry him up, but he don't hurry none. Soon as he unlocks the door and comes out we all give him the news.

I got to say this is the first time I ever seed Clyde act the way he do now. I hate to say it, but—I will. Clyde, he don't act much like a man. No, he don't, not a bit. He just reaches his cue down and hands it to me.

"Chalk it," he says. "Chalk it," is all he says. Damn if I don't almost hand it back to him.

I chalk his cue. But the boys, they can't stand no more.

Ace says he is going to call the hospital again.

"Damn it, Clyde," Banjo says. "We got to do something. Else they ain't going to be no white woman safe in the streets. What they going to think of you at the Arcade? I can hear Red Hynes and them laughing."

That is the way the boys is all feeling at Bullen's, and they say so. I am waiting with the rest for Clyde to hurry up and do something, or else explain hisself. But he just goes on, like nothing is the matter, and starts up a new game. It's awful quiet. Clyde gets the nine ball on the break. It hung on the lip of the pocket like it didn't want to, but it did.

"You sure like that old nine ball, Clyde," I say, trying to make Clyde feel easy and maybe come to his senses. I rack the nine for him. My hand is wet and hot and the yellow nine feels like butter to me.

"Must be the color of the nine is what he like," Banjo says.

Whew! I thought that would be all for Banjo, but no sir, Clyde goes right on with the game, like it's a compliment.

A couple of guys is whistling soft at what Banjo got away with. Me, I guess Clyde feels sorry for Banjo, on account of they is both fighters. Clyde was a contender for the state heavy title three years back, fighting under the name of Big Boy Bullen, weighing in at two thirty-three. Poor old Banjo is a broken-down carnival bum, and when he's drinking too heavy, like last night and every night, he forgets how old and beat up he is and don't know no better than to run against Clyde, that's a former contender and was rated in *Collyer's Eye*. Banjo never was no better than a welter when he was fighting and don't tip more than a hundred fifty-five right now. What with the drink and quail he don't amount to much no more.

And then Ace comes back from calling up the hospital and says, "No change; Clara's still unconscious."

"Combination," Clyde says. "Twelve ball in the corner pocket."

That's all Clyde has got to say. We all want to do something, but Banjo wants to do it the worst and he says, "No change, still unconscious. Knocked out and knocked up—by a nigger! Combination—twelve ball in the corner pocket!"

"Dummy up!" Clyde says. He slugs the table again and ruins a cube of chalk. He don't even look at Banjo or none of us. I take the whisk broom and brush the chalk away the best I could, without asking Clyde to move.

"Thanks," Clyde says, still not seeing nobody.

I feel kind of funny on account of Clyde never says thanks for nothing before. I wonder is it the old Clyde or is he feeling sick. Then, so help me, Clyde runs the table, thirteen balls. Ace don't even get a shot that game.

But, like you guessed, the boys won't hold still for it no more and is all waiting for Clyde to do something. And Clyde don't have to be no mind reader to know it. He gets a peculiar look in his eye that I seed once or twice before and goes over to Banjo—to—guess what?—to shake his hand. Yes, sir, Clyde has got his hand out and is smiling—smiling at Banjo that said what he said.

Banjo just stands there with a dumb look on his face, not knowing what Clyde is all about, and they shake.

"So I'm yella, huh, Banjo?" That's what Clyde says to Banjo.

I don't know if Banjo means to do it, or can't help it, but he burps right in Clyde's face.

*Boom!* Clyde hits Banjo twice in the chin and mouth quick and drops him like a handkerchief. Banjo is all over the floor and his mouth is hanging open like a spring is busted and blood is leaking out the one side and he has got some bridgework loose.

"Hand me the nine, Roy," Clyde says to me. I get the nine ball and give it to Clyde. He shoves it way into Banjo's mouth that is hanging open and bleeding good.

Then Clyde lets him have one more across the jaw and you can hear the nine ball rattle inside Banjo's mouth.

Clyde says, "Now some of you boys been itching for action all night. Well, I'm here to tell you I'm just the boy to hand it out. Tonight I just feel like stringing me up a black nigger by the light of the silvery moon! Let's get gaiting!"

Now that was the old Clyde for you. A couple of guys reaches fast for cue sticks, but I am in charge of them and the tables, and I say, "Lay off them cue sticks! Get some two by fours outside!"

So we leaves old Banjo sucking on the nine ball and piles into all the cars we can get and heads down for the Louisiana Social Parlor. I am sitting next to Clyde in his car.

On the way Ace tells us when he called the hospital the second time he got connected with some doctor fella. Ace said this doctor was sore on account of Ace's girl, that's the nurse, give out information about Clara that she wasn't supposed to. But the doctor said as long as we all knowed so much about the case already he thought we ought to know it was of some months' standing, Clara's condition. Ace said he could tell from the way the doctor was saying it over and over that he was worried about what we was planning to do to the coon. Ace's girl must be copped out to him. But Ace said he thanked the doc kindly for his trouble and hung up and wouldn't give his right name when

the doc wanted to know. We all knowed about the doctor all right—
only one of them young intern fellas from Memphis or some place—
and as for the some months' standing part we all knowed in our own
minds what nigger bucks is like and him maybe burning with strong
drink on top of it. Ace said he hoped the nurse wouldn't go and lose
her job on account of the favor she done for us.

The only thing we seed when we gets to the Louisiana is one old
coon by the name of Old Ivy. He is locking up. We asks him about
Sleep Bailey, but Old Ivy is playing dumb and all he says is, "Suh?
Suh?" like he don't know what we mean.

"Turn on them there lights," we says, "so's we can see."

Old Ivy turns them on.

"Where's the crowd," we says, "that's always around?"

"Done went," Old Ivy says.

"So they's done went," Skeeter says. "Well, if they's trying to steal
that piano-playing nigger away they won't get very far."

"No, they won't get very far with that," Clyde says, "Hey, just
seeing all them bottles is got me feeling kind of dry-like."

So we gets Old Ivy to put all the liquor on the bar and us boys
refreshes ourselves. Skeeter tells Old Ivy to put some beer out for chasers.

Old Ivy says they is fresh out of cold beer.

"It don't have to be cold," Skeeter says. "We ain't proud."

Old Ivy drags all the bottled beer out on the bar with the other.
Then he goes back into the kitchen behind the bar and we don't see
him no more for a little.

"Hey, old nigger," Skeeter says. "Don't try and sneak out the back
way."

"No, suh," Old Ivy says.

"Hey, Old Ivy," Clyde says. "You got something to eat back there?"

"Suh?" He just gives us that old *suh*. "Suh?"

"You heard him," Skeeter says.

"No, suh," Old Ivy says, and we seed him in the service window.

"Guess maybe he's deaf," Skeeter says. "You old coon, I hope you
ain't blind!" And Skeeter grabs a bottle of beer and lams it at Old
Ivy's head. Old Ivy ducks and the big end of the bottle sticks in the
wall and don't break. It is just beaverboard, the wall.

All of the boys get the same idee and we starts heaving the beer bottles
through the window where Old Ivy was standing, but ain't no more.

"Hit the nigger baby!"

"Nigger in the fence!"

We keeps this up until we done run out of bottles, all except Skeeter
that's been saving one. "Hey, wait," he says. "It's all right now, Gram-
paw. Come on, old boy, you can come out now."

But Old Ivy don't show hisself. I am wondering if he got hit on a
rebound.

"Damn it, boy," Skeeter says. "Bring us some food. Or you want us to come back in there?"

"Suh?" It's that old *suh* again. "Yes, suh," Old Ivy says in the kitchen, but we don't see him.

Then we do. And Skeeter, he lets go the last bottle with all he's got. It hits Old Ivy right in the head. That was a mean thing Skeeter done, I think, but then I see it's only the cook's hat Old Ivy's got in his hand that got hit. He was holding it up like his head is inside, but it ain't.

The boys all laughs when they seed what Old Ivy done to fool Skeeter.

"Like in war when you fool the enemy," Clyde says.

"That's a smart nigger," I say.

"So that's a smart nigger, huh?" Skeeter says. "I'll take and show you what I do to smart niggers that gets smart with me!"

"Cut it out," Clyde says. "Leave him alone. He ain't hurting nothing. You just leave that old coon be." That is Clyde for you, always sticking up for somebody, even a nigger.

Clyde and me goes into the next room looking for a place to heave, as Clyde has got to. It is awful dark, but pretty soon our eyes get used to it, and we can see some tables and chairs and a juke box and some beer signs on the walls. It must be where they do their dancing. I am just standing there ready to hold Clyde's head, as he is easing hisself, when I begins to hear a piano like a radio is on low. I can just barely pick it out, a couple of notes at a time, sad music, blues music, nigger music.

It ain't no radio. It is a piano on the other side of the room. I am ready to go and look into it when Clyde says, "It ain't nothing." Ain't nothing! Sometimes I can't understand Clyde for the life of me. But I already got my own idee about the piano.

About then Skeeter and Ace comes in the room yelling for Clyde in the dark, saying the boys out front is moving on to the next place. We hear a hell of a racket out by the bar, like they broke the mirror, and then it's pretty still and we know they is almost all left.

Skeeter gives us one more yell and Ace says, "Hey, Clyde, you fall in?" They is about to leave when Skeeter, I guess it is, hears the piano just like we been hearing it. All this time Clyde has got his hand over my mouth like he don't want me to say we is there.

Skeeter calls Old Ivy and says he should turn on the lights, and when Old Ivy starts that *suh* business again Skeeter lays one on him that I can hear in the dark.

So Old Ivy turns on the lights, a lot of creepy greens, reds, and blues. Then Clyde and me both seed what I already guessed—it's the Bailey nigger playing the piano—and Skeeter and Ace seed it is him and we all seed each other.

And right then, damn if the nigger don't start in to sing a song.

Like he didn't know what was what! Like he didn't know what we come for! That's what I call a foxy nigger.

Skeeter yells at him to stop singing and to come away from the piano. He stops singing, but he don't move. So we all goes over to the piano.

"What's your name, nigger?" Skeeter says.

"Bailey," Sleep says, reading Skeeter's lips.

Old Ivy comes over and he is saying a lot of stuff like, "That boy's just a borned fool. Just seems like he got to put his foot in it some kind of way."

Sleep hits a couple of notes light on the piano that sounds nice and pretty.

"You know what we come for?" Skeeter says.

Sleep hits them same two notes again, nice and pretty, and shakes his head.

"Sure you don't know, boy?" Clyde says.

Sleep is just about to play them notes again when Skeeter hits him across the paws with a fungo bat. Then Sleep says, "I spect you after me on account of that Miss Beck I fish out of the river."

"That's right," Skeeter says. "You spect right."

"You know what they is saying uptown, Sleep?" I say.

"I heard," Sleep says.

"They is saying," I say, "you raped Clara and throwed her in the river to cover up."

"That's just a lie," Sleep says.

"Who says it's a lie?" Clyde says.

"That's just a white-folks lie," Sleep says. "It's God's truth."

"How you going to prove it?" Clyde says.

"Yeah," I say. "How you going to prove it?"

"How you going to prove it to them, son?" Old Ivy says.

"Here, ain't I?" Sleep says.

"Yeah, you's here all right, nigger," Skeeter says, "but don't you wish you wasn't!"

"If I'm here I guess I got no call to be scared," Sleep says. "Don't it prove nothing if I'm here, if I didn't run away? Don't that prove nothing?"

"Naw," Skeeter says. "It don't prove nothing. It's just a smart nigger trick."

"Wait till Miss Beck come to and talk," Sleep says. "I ain't scared."

"No," Old Ivy says, "you ain't scared. He sure ain't scared a bit, is he, Mr. Bullen? That's a good sign he ain't done nothing bad, ain't it, Mr. Bullen?"

"Well," Clyde says, "I don't know about that...."

Skeeter says, "You sure you feel all right, Clyde?"

"What you mean you don't know, Clyde?" Ace says. "Clara is knocked up and this is the bastard done it!"

"Who the hell else, Clyde?" I say. I wonder is Clyde dreaming or what.

"He ain't a bad boy like that, Mr. Bullen," Old Ivy says, working on Clyde.

"I tell you what," Clyde says.

"Aw, stop it, Clyde," Skeeter and Ace both says. "We got enough!"

"Shut up!" Clyde says and he says it like he mean it.

"Listen to what Mr. Bullen got to say," Old Ivy says.

"This is the way I seed it," Clyde says. "This ain't no open-and-shut case of rape—leastways not yet it ain't. Now the law——"

Skeeter cuts in and says, "Well, Clyde, I'll see you the first of the week." He acts like he is going to leave.

"Come back here," Clyde says. "You ain't going to tell no mob nothing till I got this Bailey boy locked up safe in the county jail waiting judgment."

"O.K., Clyde," Skeeter says. "That's different. I thought you was going to let him get away."

"Hell, no!" Clyde says. "We got to see justice did, ain't we?"

"Sure, do, Clyde," Skeeter says.

Ace says, "He'll be nice and safe in jail in case we got to take up anything with him."

I knowed what they mean and so do Old Ivy. He says, "Better let him go right now, Mr. Bullen. Let him run for it. This other way they just going to bust in the jailhouse and take him out and hang him to a tree."

"The way I seed it," Clyde says, "this case has got to be handled according to the law. I don't want this boy's blood on my hands. If he ain't to blame, I mean."

"That's just what he ain't, Mr. Bullen," Old Ivy says. "But it ain't going to do no good to put him in that old jailhouse."

"We'll see about that," Clyde says.

"Oh, sure. Hell, yes!" Skeeter says. "We don't want to go and take the law in our own hands. That ain't our way, huh, Ace?"

"Cut it out," Clyde says.

"Maybe Miss Beck feel all right in the morning, son, and it going to be all right for you," Old Ivy says to Sleep. The old coon is crying.

So we takes Sleep in Clyde's car to the county jail. We makes him get down on the floor so's we can put our feet on him and guard him better. He starts to act up once on the way, but Skeeter persuades him with the fungo bat in the right place, *conk,* and he is pretty quiet then.

Right after we get him behind bars it happens.

Like I say, Clyde is acting mighty peculiar all night, but now he blows his top for real. That's what he does all right—plumb blows it. It is all over in a second. He swings three times—one, two, three—and Skeeter and Ace is out cold as Christmas, and I am holding this fat eye. Beats me! And I don't mind telling you I laid down quick with Skeeter and Ace, like I was out, till Clyde went away. Now you figure it out.

But I ain't preferring no charges on Clyde. Not me, that's his best friend, even if he did give me this eye, and Skeeter ain't, that needs Bullen's for his business, or Ace.

What happens to who? To the jig that said he pulled Clara out of the river?

You know that big old slippery elm by the Crossing? That's the one. But that ain't how I got the eye.

---

# THIS WAY FOR THE GAS
## *Tadeusz Borowski*

Everybody is naked in the camp. Though the delousing is finished and our clothes are back from the tanks of the Ozone-2 that efficiently kills lice in clothing and humans in ovens. The heat is unbearable. The camp has been sealed off tight so that not a single prisoner, not one solitary louse, can get through the gate. All day long thousands of naked people drag themselves over the paths or lie against the walls and on the roof ledges. The women's camp is being deloused and twenty-eight thousand women have been stripped naked and chased out of their barracks. They are standing together in the yard nearby.

The heat rises, the hours are endless. There have been no new transports for several days. We are without even our usual distraction; the wide roads leading to the crematories are empty.

Several of us sit on the top bunk. We dangle our legs and slice the neat loaves of crisp, crumbly bread. It is a little coarse to the taste, the kind that stays fresh for weeks. Sent all the way from Warsaw; only a week ago my mother held this white bread in her hands . . . dear God, dear God. . . .

We unwrap the bacon, the onion, we open a can of condensed milk. Henri, the fat Frenchman, dreams out loud about French wine brought in with the transports from Strasbourg, Paris, Marseille. The sweat streams down his body.

"Listen, *mon ami,* next time we go on the loading ramp, I'll bring you real champagne. I bet you never had any, what?"

"No, but you can't smuggle it through the gate, so stop kidding.

Better try and get me some shoes, the perforated kind, you know, with a double sole, and that shirt you promised a while back."

"Patience, patience, when the new transports come in, I'll bring all you want. We'll be going on the ramp again."

"And what if there aren't any more oven transports?" I say spitefully. "Can't you see how fast things are thawing out around here— unlimited packages, no more beatings? You write letters home even. . . . All kinds of talk is going around and, dammit, they'll run out of people!"

"Stop talking nonsense." Henri's serious fat face moves rhythmically, his mouth is filled with sardines. We have been friends for a long time but I don't know his last name. "Stop talking nonsense," he repeats, swallowing hard. "They can't run out of people; we'll starve to death in this blasted camp. All of us live on what they bring."

"Not all. We have our packages. . . ."

"Yes, you and your friend and ten other friends of yours. You Poles get packages. But what about us and the Jews and the Russkis? And if we had no food, no supplies from the transports, you think you could eat those packages of yours in peace? We wouldn't let you!"

"You would, you'd starve to death like the Greeks. Around here, whoever has grub, has strength."

"Anyway, you have enough, we have enough, so why argue?"

Right, why argue. They have enough, I have enough, we eat together and we sleep on the same bunks. Henri slices the bread, he makes a tomato salad. It tastes good with mustard. Below us, the naked miserable creatures drenched in sweat plod along the narrow aisles and crowd into the lower bunks in eights and tens. They are naked and thin, stink of sweat and excrement, their cheeks are hollow. Directly underneath me, in the lowest bunk, is a rabbi; he has covered his head with a rag and is reading from a Hebrew prayer book (there's no shortage of this type of literature). He is wailing, loudly and monotonously.

"Couldn't he be shut up? He's been hollering as though he'd caught God himself by the feet."

"I don't feel like moving. Let him holler, he'll go to the oven that much sooner."

"Religion is the opium of the people," Henri, who is a Communist and a rentier, says sententiously. "If they didn't believe in God and the eternal life, they'd have torn down the crematories long ago."

"Why don't you do it then?" The question is a rhetorical one, which the Frenchman ignores. "Idiot," he says and stuffs tomato in his mouth.

Suddenly there's a commotion over by the entrance. Below us, they scurry in fright to their bunks. Our block leader walks in with a serious expression on his face.

"Canada*! *Antreten!* Hurry up! A transport is coming!"

"Good God!" yells Henri, jumping down. He swallows the tomato, grabs his coat, shouts *"Raus"* to the prisoners in the lower bunks, and runs to the door. The Canada men are leaving for the loading ramp.

"Henri, the shoes!" I call after him.

*"Keine Angst!"* he shouts back.

I proceed to put away the food. I tie a piece of rope around the suitcase, pull on my trousers, and scramble down. In the doorway I bump into Henri.

*"Allez, allez, vite, vite!"*

*"Was ist los?"*

"Want to come to the ramp with us?"

"Sure, why not?"

"Come along then, take your coat. They're short a few men. I've already spoken to the kapo," and he pushes me through the door.

We line up, someone takes our numbers, someone up ahead calls "March, march," and now we are running toward the gate, accompanied by shouts of a multilingual crowd that is already being pushed back to the barracks. Not everybody has the privilege of going on the ramp. We've almost reached the gate. *Links, zwei, drei, vier! Muetzen ab!* Erect, arms stretched stiffly down our hips, we pass through the gate briskly, smartly, almost gracefully. A sleepy SS man holding a large pad phlegmatically checks us off, marking each five men with a wave of his arm.

*"Hundert!"* he calls after we have all passed.

*"Stimmt!"* comes a hoarse shout from our front.

We march rapidly, almost at a run. All around there are guards, young men with machine guns. We pass some deserted barracks, and a clump of unfamiliar green, apple and pear trees. We burst on to the highway, and now we have arrived. A couple of yards more; there, surrounded by trees, is the ramp.

A cheerful little station, typical of many such provincial railroad stops: a small square, framed by tall chestnuts and paved with yellow gravel. Over to the side, by the road, stands a wooden shed; further along are large stacks of old rails, logs, bricks. This is where they do the loading for Birkenau: the supplies for construction in the camp, and the people for the gas ovens.

Now the guards are being posted along the rails, on the logs, in the

---

* The name (because Canada was supposed to be the land of great riches) used by the camp inmates to designate the storehouses where valuables taken from gassed prisoners were kept; the word was also used for inmates employed around this activity.

green shade of the Silesian chestnuts, forming a tight circle around the ramp. They wipe the sweat from their faces and drink from their canteens. It is unbearably hot, the sun stands motionless at its zenith.

"Disperse!"

We sit down in the narrow streaks of shade alongside the stacked rails. The hungry Greeks (several of them managed to come along, God only knows how) hunt under the rails. Someone finds a few pieces of mildewed bread, someone else a few half-rotten sardines. They eat.

"*Schweinedreck*," spits a young, tall guard with corn-colored hair and dreamy blue eyes, "soon you'll have so much food to stuff in your guts, you'll burst." He adjusts his gun, wipes his face with a handkerchief.

"Now you be careful," Henri says to me. "Don't take any money, they might be checking. Anyway, who the hell needs money, we have enough to eat. Don't take suits, either, or they'll think you plan to escape. Just get a shirt, a silk one, with a collar. And an undershirt. And if you find something to drink, don't bother calling me. I can manage for myself, but watch your step or they'll let you have it."

"They'll beat us?"

"Sure thing. You have to have eyes in your back. *Arschaugen*."

"*Was wir arbeiten?*" ask the Greeks nervously, chewing on the moldy bits of bread.

"*Niks. Transport kommen, alles Krematorium, compris?*"

"*Alles verstehen*," they answer in crematory Esperanto.

In the meantime the ramp has become more and more bustling, more and more noisy. The crews are divided into those who will open and unload the arriving freight cars and those who are to stay by the wooden steps. Motorcycles drive up, delivering SS officers, bemedaled, glittering with brass, beefy men with highly polished boots and shiny, brutal faces. Some carry briefcases, others hold thin, flexible whips. They greet each other raising an arm, Roman fashion, then shake hands cordially. Some stroll over the ramp; the silver squares glitter on their collars, the bamboo whips snap impatiently.

We lie against the rails and gaze listlessly at the men in their green uniforms, at the green trees, and at the church steeple which is visible from the distant village.

"The transport is coming," somebody says. We rise expectantly. Around the bend, one after another, the cattle cars begin rolling in: the train backs up, a conductor leans out, waves his arm, blows a whistle. The locomotive whistles back loudly, puffs, the train rolls slowly in along the ramp. Through the tiny barred windows, pale, wilted, exhausted human faces appear, tangled hair, terrified women, unshaven men. They gaze at the station in silence as the train slowly passes. But suddenly inside the cars something begins stirring and pounding.

"Water! Air!" come the monotonous, despairing cries.

Faces push at the windows, lips gasp desperately for air. The pressing faces draw a few breaths, then disappear; others come and disappear. The cries and moans get louder.

A man in a green uniform covered with more glitter than any of the others jerks up his head, his lips twist in disgust. He inhales deeply, then with a rapid gesture throws the cigarette away and signals to the guard. Slowly the guard removes the machine gun from his shoulder, aims, sends a series of shots across the train. All is quiet now. Meantime the trucks have arrived, steps are being drawn up, and Canada men stand ready at the train exits. The SS officer with the briefcase raises his hand:

"Whoever takes gold or anything besides food will be shot for stealing the property of the Reich. Understand? *Verstanden?*"

"*Jawohl!*" we answer unevenly, but eagerly.

"*Also los!* Begin!"

The bolts crack, the doors open. A wave of fresh air pours into the train. People . . . inhumanly cramped, buried under a terrifying amount of luggage, trunks, suitcases, packages, cases, bundles of every kind (they have brought everything that had been their past and was to start their future). They have been packed into a monstrous heap, have fainted from heat, have suffocated, trampled each other. Now they cluster at the open doors, breathing like fish cast out on the beach.

"Attention, get out. Take your luggage. Take everything. All the stuff must be piled up by the exits. Your coats too. It's summer. March to the left. Understand?"

"Sir, what's going to happen to us?" they jump down on to the gravel, anxious, worn out.

"Where are you from?"

"Sosnowiec, Bedzin, sir. What's going to happen to us?" they repeat the question stubbornly, gazing into our tired eyes.

"I don't know, I don't understand Polish." It's the concentration camp law that those going to their death must be deceived up to the end. This is the only permitted form of charity.

The heat has increased. The sun is directly over our heads, the white-hot sky quivers, the air vibrates, an occasional breeze feels like a sizzling, molten gust. Our lips are parched, the mouth fills with the salty taste of blood. The body is weak and heavy from lying in the sun. Water!

A huge, multicolored wave of people, loaded down with luggage, pours from the train like a wide river that tries to find a new bed. But before they have a chance to come to, before they can inhale some fresh air and look at the sky, bundles are already being snatched out of their hands, coats are pulled off their backs, women's purses and umbrellas are taken away from them.

"But sir, it's for the sun, I cannot. . . ."

"*Verboten,*" one of us barks through clenched teeth, hissing sharply. There's an SS man standing behind one's back, calm, controlled, correct.

"*Meine Herrschaften,* ladies and gentlemen, don't throw your things around, please. Show some good will," he says kindly; his hands nervously play with the slender whip.

"Certainly, certainly," many voices answer, and now they walk alongside the train a little more cheerfully. A woman bends quickly to pick up a purse. The whip flies, the woman cries out, stumbles and falls under the feet of the surging crowd. A child behind her screams: "*Mamele!*"—a very small girl with tangled black curls.

The heaps grow. Suitcases, bundles, blankets, coats, pocketbooks that open as they fall, spilling coins, gold, watches; mountains of bread pile up at the exits, jars of marmalades, jams; masses of meats, sausages; sugar spills on the gravel. Trucks, loaded with people, start up with a deafening roar amidst the wailing and screaming of women separated from their children and the stupefied silence of the men left behind. They are the ones who had been ordered to stop to the right —they are the healthy and the young who will go to the camp. In the end they will not escape the gas ovens, only first they must work.

Trucks go and come, without interruption, as on a monstrous belt. A Red Cross van goes back and forth incessantly: it transports gas, the gas that will kill these people.

The Canada men working at the trucks are not able to stop for a moment even to catch their breath. They push those going to the ovens up the steps, pack them in tightly, sixty in each truck, more or less. A young, clean-shaven gentleman, an SS man with a notebook in his hand, stands on the side; every truck gets one mark in the notebook. When sixteen trucks have gone, it makes one thousand, more or less. The gentleman is calm, precise. No truck can leave without his signal and a mark in his notebook: *Ordnung muss sein.* The marks grow into thousands, the thousands into entire transports; later the transports will be described in a word: "from Salonika," "from Strasbourg," "from Rotterdam." This one will be "Sosnowiec-Bedzin."

The train has been unloaded. A thin, pock-marked SS man composedly peers inside, shakes his head in disgust and motions toward us.

"*Rein.* Clean this up!"

We climb inside. Scattered in corners among human excrement and lost wrist watches lie smothered, trampled, squashed babies, naked little monsters with huge heads and blown-up bellies. We carry them out like chickens, holding several in each hand.

"Don't take them to the truck, pass them to the women," says the SS man lighting a cigarette. His lighter isn't working properly, he is pre-occupied with fixing it.

"Take them, for God's sake!" I blow up when the women run from me in horror, hiding their heads between their shoulders. The name of God sounds strangely pointless, since the babies will go with the women on the trucks, all will go, without exception. We know what will happen, and we look at each other with hate and horror.

"So, you don't want to take them?" says the pock-marked SS man with a note of surprise and reproach in his voice, and he reaches for his revolver.

"You mustn't shoot, I'll carry them." A tall, gray-haired woman takes the little corpses out of my hands and for an instant looks straight into my eyes. "My child, my child," she whispers and smiles. Then she walks away, stumbling on the gravel. I lean against the side of the train. I am terribly tired. Someone pulls at my sleeve.

"*En avant,* to the rails, come on!" I look up, but the face swims before my eyes, dissolves, huge and transparent, melts into the motion-less trees and the churning crowd. . . . I blink rapidly: Henri.

"Listen, Henry, are we good people?"

"That's stupid, why do you ask?"

"You see, my friend, you see, I am furious, unreasonably furious at these people—that I must be here because of them. I don't feel any pity for them, I'm not sorry that they're going to the gas. Damn them all! I could throw myself at them with my fists. It must be pathological, I can't understand. . . ."

"Ah, on the contrary, it is natural, foreseen, calculated. This job exhausts you, you rebel against it—and the easiest way to relieve your hate is to turn against someone weaker. Why, I'd even call it healthy. It's simple logic, *compris?*" He seats himself comfortably against the heap of rails. "Look at the Greeks, they know how to make the most of it! They stuff their bellies with anything they can lay their hands on; one has just consumed a whole jar of marmalade."

"Swine! Tomorrow half of them will die of the shits."

"Swine? You've been hungry."

"Swine!" I say again furiously. I close my eyes. The air is filled with ghastly noises, the earth trembles under me, I can feel a sticky mois-ture on my eyelids. My throat is utterly dry. The morbid procession streams on and on—trucks growl like mad dogs. I shut my eyes tight, but I can still see corpses dragged out of cars, trampled infants, crip-ples piled on top of the dead, wave after wave of people . . . freight cars roll in, the heaps of clothes, suitcases, and bundles grow, people get out, look at the sun, take a few breaths, beg for water, walk to the trucks, drive away. And again freight cars pull in, again people. . . . The scenes become confused in my mind; I am not sure whether all this is happening, or whether I am dreaming. There's humming inside my head, I feel that I must vomit.

Henri touches my arm. "Don't sleep, we must load up the loot."

Now all the people are gone. In the distance, the last few trucks roll along the road in clouds of dust, the train has left, several SS men promenade stiffly along the ramp, the silver glitters on their uniforms. Their boots shine, their red, beefy faces shine.

We start loading the loot. We lift heavy trunks, toss them up with an effort into the trucks. There they are arranged in stacks, packed tightly. One of the trunks falls open, suits, shirts, books drop out on the ground. . . . I pick up a small, heavy package. I unwrap it: gold, about two handfuls; bracelets, rings, pins, diamonds.

"*Gib hier,*" calmly says an SS man holding up his briefcase full of gold and colored foreign currency. The gold will go to the Reich.

It is hot, terribly hot. Our throats are dry, every word hurts. Oh, anything for a drink of water! Faster, faster, let's get it over with so we can rest. At last we are done, all the trucks have gone. Now we quickly clean up the remaining transport dirt, "so there'll be no traces left of the *Schweinerei.*" But just as the last truck disappears behind the trees and we go—finally!—to rest in the shade, a shrill whistle sounds over the bend. Slowly, terribly slowly, the train rolls in, the engine answers with a deafening shriek; weary, pale faces at the windows, flat, as though cut out of paper, with huge, feverishly burning eyes. Already trucks are pulling up, already the calm gentleman with the notebook is here, and SS men emerge from their canteen carrying briefcases for the gold and money. We open the train doors.

It is impossible to control oneself any longer. Brutally we yank suitcases from people's hands, impatiently pull off their coats. Go on, go on, vanish. They go, they vanish. Men, women, children. Some of them know.

Here's a woman—she walks quickly, but tries to appear calm. A small child, with a pink cherub's face, runs behind her and unable to catch up stretches out his little hands and cries: "Mummy! Mummy!"

"Pick up your child, woman!"

"Sir, it's not my child, it's not mine!" she shouts hysterically and runs on, covering her face with her hands. She wants to hide, she wants to get to those who will not ride the trucks, those who will go on foot, those who will live. She is young, healthy, good looking, she wants to stay alive. But the child runs after her, wailing very loudly: "Mummy, mummy, don't run away!"

"It's not mine, not mine, no!"

But she is already caught by Andrei, a sailor from Sebastopol. His eyes are glazed from vodka and the heat. With one powerful blow he knocks her off her feet, then seizes the falling woman by the hair and drags her up again. His face is distorted with fury.

"Ah you, bloody Jewess! So you're running away from your own child! I'll fix you, you whore!" His big arm chokes her, he lifts her in the air and tosses her up on the truck like a heavy sack of grain. "Here! Take this with you, bitch!" and he throws the child at her feet.

*"Gut gemacht,* good work, that's the way to deal with unnatural mothers," says the SS man standing at the foot of the truck. *"Gut, gut Ruski."*

"Shut your mouth," growls Andrei through clenched teeth and walks away. From under a pile of rags he pulls a canteen, unscrews it, takes a few deep swallows, passes it to me. The strong alcohol burns the throat. My head swims, my legs are shaky, again I feel like throwing up.

And suddenly, above the teeming crowd pushing like a river driven by an unseen power, there appears a girl. She hops lightly from the train onto the gravel, looks around inquiringly, like one who is very much surprised at something. Her soft, blond hair has fallen on her shoulders in a torrent, she throws it back impatiently. With an automatic gesture she pulls her hands along her blouse, casually straightens her skirt. She stands this way for an instant, then her gaze leaves the crowd and glides along our faces, as though searching for someone. Unconsciously I continue to stare at her until our eyes meet.

"Listen, listen, tell me, where are they taking us?"

I look at her. Here, standing before me, is a girl—a girl with enchanting blond hair, with beautiful breasts, in a little cotton blouse, with a wise, mature look in her eyes. She stands here, looking straight into my face, waiting. And over there is the gas oven: communal death, disgusting and ugly. And over there is the concentration camp: the shaved head, the heavy Soviet trousers in sweltering weather, the sickening, stale odor of dirty, damp female bodies, the animal hunger, the inhuman labor, and later the same gas oven, only an even more hideous, more terrible death. . . .

"Why did she bring it, they'll take it away from her anyway," I think to myself, noticing a lovely gold watch on her delicate wrist.

"Listen, tell me?" she repeats.

I do not answer. Her lips tighten. "I know," she says with a shade of proud contempt in her voice, tossing back her head; she walks resolutely toward the trucks. Someone tries to stop her; boldly she pushes him aside and runs up the steps. I can only catch in the distance a glimpse of her blond hair as it flies in the breeze.

I go back inside the train, I carry out babies, I unload luggage. I touch corpses, but I can't overcome the mounting, uncontrollable terror. I try to run away from them, but they are everywhere: lined up on the gravel, on the cement edge of the ramp, inside the freight cars. Infants, hideous naked women, men twisted by convulsions. I escape as far as I can go, but immediately a whip falls across my back. Out of the side of my eye I can see an SS man, swearing profusely. I stagger forward and run, lose myself in the Canada group. Now, at last, again we can rest against the stack of rails. The sun has leaned deeply over the horizon and is illuminating the ramp with a reddish glow. In the silence that settles over nature at this time of day, the human cries and groans seem to rise ever more loudly to the sky.

Only from this distance can one have a full view of the inferno on the teeming ramp. There are two human beings who have fallen to the ground locked in a last desperate embrace. The man had dug into the woman's flesh and holds on to her clothing with his teeth. She shouts hysterically, swears, cries, until at last a large boot comes down over her throat and she is silent. They are pulled apart and dragged like animals to the truck. Here are four Canada men, carrying a corpse: a huge, swollen female body. Swearing, wet from strain, they kick out of the way some stray children who have been running all over the ramp and howling like dogs. The men pick the children up by the collars, heads, arms, and toss them on the heaps in the trucks. They collect big swollen puffed-up corpses from all over the ramp, pile on top of them the invalids, the semi-smothered, the sick, the unconscious. The mountain of corpses seethes howls, growns. The driver starts the motor, the truck begins rolling.

"*Halt! Halt!*" yells an SS man. "Stop, damn you!" An old gentleman, dressed in tails and wearing a band on his arm, is being dragged toward the truck. His head knocks against the gravel and stones, he groans and wails monotonously and continually: "*Ich will mit dem Herrn Kommemdanten sprechen*—I wish to speak with the commander . . ." With senile stubbornness, he keeps repeating this all the way. Tossed up on the truck, trampled by others, choked, he moans still: "*Ich will mit dem. . . .*"

"Quiet, old man!" shouts a young SS man, laughing loudly. "In half an hour you'll be talking to the highest commander! Only don't forget to say *Heil Hitler* to him!"

Others are carrying a little girl without a leg; they hold her by the arms and the one remaining leg. Tears are running down her face, she whispers softly: "Sir, it hurts, it hurts. . . ." They throw her on the truck, on top of the corpses. She will be burned alive with them.

The evening has arrived, cool and clear. We lie against the rails—it is incredibly quiet.

"Did you get the shoes?" asks Henri.

"No."

"Why?"

"My God, man, I've enough, absolutely enough!"

"Already? After a first transport? Just think, I . . . since Christmas, at least a million people have passed through my hands. The worst are the transports from around Paris: one always meets friends."

"And what do you tell them?"

"That they're going to have a bath, and then we'll meet at the camp. What would you tell them?"

I do not answer. We drink coffee mixed with alcohol.

"Henri, what are we waiting for?"

"There'll be another transport."

"When it comes, I'm not going to unload it. I can't take any more."

"It's gotten you down, what? Nice Canada!" Henri grins amiably and disappears in the dark. In a moment he is back. "All right. Just sit here quietly. I'll try to find you your shoes."

"Don't bother me about the shoes." I want to sleep. The night is dark.

Again there's a whistle, another transport. Freight cars emerge from the darkness into a small circle of light on the ramp. Somewhere the trucks are growling. They back up to the steps, black, ghostlike. *Wasser! Luft!* The same all over again, like a late showing of the same film: a series of shots, the train is silent. But now a small girl leans out from a window and, losing her balance, falls over on the sand. She lies for a moment without moving and then rises and begins walking around in a circle, faster and faster, waving her stiff arms, breathing spasmodically and howling in a thin voice. She has lost her mind in the crowded train. This is hard on the nerves, so an SS man runs up and kicks her between the shoulders with his large boot. She falls. Holding her down with his foot he draws out a revolver, shoots once, then the second time: she remains on the ground kicking the dirt with her feet until she stiffens. The train doors are being opened.

Again I stand at the exits. A warm, sickening smell gushes from the inside. The mountain of people filling the cars, almost to the ceiling is motionless, horribly tangled, but still steaming.

*"Ausladen!"* comes the voice of an SS man who has walked into the circle of light. "Why are you standing like sheep? Start unloading!" His whip flies and falls on our backs. I seize the hand of a corpse: the fingers close tightly around mine. I pull back with a scream and stagger away. My heart pounds, jumps up to my throat. I can no longer control the nausea. Hunched under the train I begin to vomit. Then, like a man drunk, I weave over to the stack of rails.

I lie against the cool, kind metal and dream about returning to the camp to be with my friends who are not going to the gas ovens tonight. The lights on the ramp flicker with a spectral glow, the people walk on and on, endlessly, swarming, stupefied, anxious. They believe that now they must face a new life in the camp, and they prepare themselves emotionally for a hard struggle ahead. They don't know that in just a few moments they will die, that the gold, money, and diamonds which they have so prudently hidden in their clothing and on their bodies is now useless to them.

It is almost finished. The dead are being cleared off the ramp and loaded into the last truck. Canada men, carrying heavy loads of bread, marmalade, sugar, etc. are lining up to go. For a few days the whole camp will live on this transport. For a few days the whole camp will talk about the "Sosnowiec-Bedzin." The "Sosnowiec-Bedzin" has been a good, rich transport.

The stars are already beginning to pale as we walk back to the camp. The sky becomes translucent and lifts higher over our heads—it is getting light.

Great columns of smoke rise from the crematories and merge up above into a huge black river which very slowly floats through the sky over Birkenau and disappears beyond the forests in the direction of Trzebinia. The "Sosnowiec-Bedzin" transport is already burning.

We pass an SS detachment marching with machine guns to change guard. They step briskly, evenly, shoulder to shoulder, one mass, one will.

"*Und morgen die ganze Welt....*" they sing at the top of their voices.

"*Rechts ran!* To the right march!" comes a command from up ahead. We move out of their way.

## Study Aids: Powers

1. What effects of emotion, tone, and meaning does Powers achieve by his use of the first person narrator?
2. The narrator concludes by saying, "But that ain't how I got the eye." Is that true? How did he get the eye and why? What are the connections between the different kinds of violence in the story?
3. It is important to trace Clyde's motives and feelings, even though they are only indirectly presented by Roy's commentary. Explain why Clyde does some of his actions: Why does Clyde miss the shot; continue to play pool; beat up Banjo; why does he agree to lead the boys to find Sleep; not do anything when he hears Sleep playing the piano; take Sleep to the jail; why does he punch the three of them? Is Clyde the center of the story? What is revealed about him?
4. What kind of person is Skeeter? What is the significance of his being the one to arouse Clyde?
5. Why did Sleep start to play the piano?

## Study Aids: Borowski

1. With what tone and manner does the narrator describe the early parts of the story? What is suggested by his return to this tone and manner at the close? What effects are achieved by the use of the first person narrator?
2. What is the significance of the emphasis on nakedness and lice in the first paragraph?
3. What is the significance of the emphasis on such things as the white bread, the shoes, the tomato salad, the sardines?
4. Why does the narrator get angry at the people of the transport? As his emotions shift, what eventually provokes his vomiting? What are its after-effects?
5. What final implication is achieved by the last description of the SS detachment and the response to it?

---

# THE WALL
## *Jean-Paul Sartre*

They pushed us into a large white room and my eyes began to blink because the light hurt them. Then I saw a table and four fellows seated at the table, civilians, looking at some papers. The other prisoners were herded together at one end and we were obliged to cross the entire room to join them. There were several I knew, and others who must have been foreigners. The two in front of me were blond with round heads. They looked alike. I imagine they were French. The smaller one kept pulling at his trousers, out of nervousness.

This lasted about three hours. I was dog-tired and my head was empty. But the room was well-heated, which struck me as rather agreeable; we had not stopped shivering for twenty-four hours. The guards led the prisoners in one after another in front of the table. Then the four fellows asked them their names and what they did. Most of the time that was all—or perhaps from time to time they would ask such questions as: "Did you help sabotage the munitions?" or, "Where were you on the morning of the ninth and what were you doing?" They didn't even listen to the replies, or at least they didn't seem to. They just remained silent for a moment and looked straight ahead, then they began to write. They asked Tom if it was true he had served in the International Brigade. Tom couldn't say he hadn't because of the papers they had found in his jacket. They didn't ask Juan anything, but after he told them his name, they wrote for a long while.

"It's my brother José who's the anarchist," Juan said. "You know perfectly well he's not here now. I don't belong to any party. I never did take part in politics." They didn't answer.

Then Juan said, "I didn't do anything. And I'm not going to pay for what the others did."

His lips were trembling. A guard told him to stop talking and led him away. It was my turn.

"Your name is Pablo Ibbieta?"

I said yes.

The fellow looked at his papers and said, "Where is Ramon Gris?"

"I don't know."

"You hid him in your house from the sixth to the nineteenth."

"I did not."

They continued to write for a moment and the guards led me away. In the hall, Tom and Juan were waiting between two guards. We started walking. Tom asked one of the guards, "What's the idea?" "How do you mean?" the guard asked. "Was that just the preliminary questioning, or was that the trial?" "That was the trial," the guard said. "So now what? What are they going to do with us?" The guard answered drily, "The verdict will be told you in your cell."

In reality, our cell was one of the cellars of the hospital. It was terribly cold there because it was very drafty. We had been shivering all night long and it had hardly been any better during the day. I had spent the preceding five days in a cellar in the archbishop's palace, a sort of dungeon that must have dated back to the Middle Ages. There were lots of prisoners and not much room, so they housed them just anywhere. But I was not homesick for my dungeon. I hadn't been cold there, but I had been alone, and that gets to be irritating. In the cellar I had company. Juan didn't say a word; he was afraid, and besides, he was too young to have anything to say. But Tom was a good talker and knew Spanish well.

In the cellar there were a bench and four straw mattresses. When they led us back we sat down and waited in silence. After a while Tom said, "Our goose is cooked."

"I think so too," I said. "But I don't believe they'll do anything to the kid."

Tom said, "They haven't got anything on him. He's the brother of a fellow who's fighting, and that's all."

I looked at Juan. He didn't seem to have heard.

Tom continued, "You know what they do in Saragossa? They lay the guys across the road and then they drive over them with trucks. It was a Moroccan deserter who told us that. They say it's just to save ammunition."

I said, "Well, it doesn't save gasoline."

I was irritated with Tom; he shouldn't have said that.

He went on, "There are officers walking up and down the roads with their hands in their pockets, smoking, and they see that it's done right. Do you think they'd put 'em out of their misery? Like hell they do. They just let 'em holler. Sometimes as long as an hour. The Moroccan said the first time he almost puked."

"I don't believe they do that here," I said, "unless they really are short of ammunition."

The daylight came in through four air vents and a round opening that had been cut in the ceiling, to the left, and which opened directly onto the sky. It was through this hole, which was ordinarily closed by means of a trapdoor, that they unloaded coal into the cellar. Directly under the hole, there was a big pile of coal dust; it had been intended for heating the hospital, but at the beginning of the war they had evacuated the patients and the coal had stayed there unused; it even got rained on from time to time, when they forgot to close the trapdoor.

Tom started to shiver. "God damn it," he said, "I'm shivering. There, it is starting again."

He rose and began to do gymnastic exercises. At each movement, his shirt opened and showed his white, hairy chest. He lay down on his back, lifted his legs in the air and began to do the scissors movement. I watched his big buttocks tremble. Tom was tough, but he had too much fat on him. I kept thinking that soon bullets and bayonet points would sink into that mass of tender flesh as though it were a pat of butter.

I wasn't exactly cold, but I couldn't feel my shoulders or my arms. From time to time, I had the impression that something was missing and I began to look around for my jacket. Then I would suddenly remember they hadn't given me a jacket. It was rather awkward. They had taken our clothes to give them to their own soldiers and had left us only our shirts and these cotton trousers the hospital patients wore in mid-summer. After a moment, Tom got up and sat down beside me, breathless.

"Did you get warmed up?"

"Damn it, no. But I'm all out of breath."

Around eight o'clock in the evening, A Major came in with two falangists.

"What are the names of those three over there?" he asked the guard.

"Steinbock, Ibbieta and Mirbal," said the guard.

The Major put on his glasses and examined his list.

"Steinbock—Steinbock . . . Here it is. You are condemned to death. You'll be shot tomorrow morning."

He looked at his list again.

"The other two, also," he said.

"That's not possible," said Juan. "Not me."

The Major looked at him with surprise. "What's your name?"

"Juan Mirbal."

"Well, your name is here," said the Major, "and you're condemned to death."

"I didn't do anything," said Juan.

The Major shrugged his shoulders and turned toward Tom and me.

"You are both Basque?"

"No, nobody's Basque."

He appeared exasperated.

"I was told there were three Basques. I'm not going to waste my time running after them. I suppose you don't want a priest?"

We didn't even answer.

Then he said, "A Belgian doctor will be around in a little while. He has permission to stay with you all night."

He gave a military salute and left.

"What did I tell you?" Tom said. "We're in for something swell."

"Yes," I said. "It's a damned shame for the kid."

I said that to be fair, but I really didn't like the kid. His face was too refined and it was disfigured by fear and suffering, which had twisted all his features. Three days ago, he was just a kid with a kind of affected manner some people like. But now he looked like an aging fairy, and I thought to myself he would never be young again, even if they let him go. It wouldn't have been a bad thing to show him a little pity, but pity makes me sick, and besides, I couldn't stand him. He hadn't said anything more, but he had turned gray. His face and hands were gray. He sat down again and stared, round-eyed, at the ground. Tom was good-hearted and tried to take him by the arm, but the kid drew himself away violently and made an ugly face. "Leave him alone," I said quietly. "Can't you see he's going to start to bawl?" Tom obeyed regretfully. He would have liked to console the kid; that would have kept him occupied and he wouldn't have been tempted to think about himself. But it got on my nerves. I had never thought about death, for the reason that the question had never come up. But now it had come up, and there was nothing else to do but think about it.

Tom started talking. "Say, did you ever bump anybody off?" he asked me. I didn't answer. He started to explain to me that he had bumped off six fellows since August. He hadn't yet realized what we were in for, and I saw clearly he didn't *want* to realize it. I myself hadn't quite taken it in. I wondered if it hurt very much. I thought about the bullets; I imagined their fiery hail going through my body. All that was beside the real question; but I was calm, we had all night in which to realize it. After a while Tom stopped talking and I looked at him out of the corner of my eye. I saw that he, too, had turned gray and that he looked pretty miserable. I said to myself, "It's starting." It was almost dark, a dull light filtered through the air vents across the coal pile and made a big spot under the sky. Through the hole in the ceiling I could already see a star. The night was going to be clear and cold.

The door opened and two guards entered. They were followed by a blond man in a tan uniform. He greeted us.

"I'm the doctor," he said. "I've been authorized to give you any assistance you may require in these painful circumstances."

He had an agreeable, cultivated voice.

I said to him, "What are you going to do here?"

"Whatever you want me to do. I shall do everything in my power to lighten these few hours."

"Why did you come to us? There are lots of others: the hospital's full of them."

"I was sent here," he answered vaguely. "You'd probably like to smoke, wouldn't you?" he added suddenly. "I've got some cigarettes and even some cigars."

He passed around some English cigarettes and some *puros,* but we refused them. I looked him straight in the eye and he appeared uncomfortable.

"You didn't come here out of compassion," I said to him. "In fact, I know who you are. I saw you with some fascists in the barracks yard the day I was arrested."

I was about to continue, when all at once something happened to me which surprised me: the presence of this doctor had suddenly ceased to interest me. Usually, when I've got hold of a man I don't let go. But somehow the desire to speak had left me. I shrugged my shoulders and turned away. A little later, I looked up and saw he was watching me with an air of curiosity. The guards had sat down on one of the mattresses. Pedro, the tall thin one, was twiddling his thumbs, while the other one shook his head occasionally to keep from falling asleep.

"Do you want some light?" Pedro suddenly asked the doctor. The other fellow nodded, "Yes." I think he was not over-intelligent, but doubtless he was not malicious. As I looked at his big, cold, blue eyes, it seemed to me the worst thing about him was his lack of imagination. Pedro went out and came back with an oil lamp which he set on the corner of the bench. It gave a poor light, but it was better than nothing; the night before we had been left in the dark. For a long while I stared at the circle of light the lamp threw on the ceiling. I was fascinated. Then, suddenly, I came to, the light circle paled, and I felt as if I were being crushed under an enormous weight. It wasn't the thought of death, and it wasn't fear; it was something anonymous. My cheeks were burning hot and my head ached.

I roused myself and looked at my two companions. Tom had his head in his hands and only the fat, white nape of his neck was visible. Juan was by far the worst off; his mouth was wide open and his nostrils were trembling. The doctor came over to him and touched him on the shoulder, as though to comfort him; but his eyes remained cold. Then I saw the Belgian slide his hand furtively down Juan's arm to his wrist. Indifferent, Juan let himself be handled. Then, as though absentmindedly, the Belgian laid three fingers over his wrist; at the same time, he drew away somewhat and managed to turn his back to me. But I leaned over backward and saw him take out his watch and look at it a moment before relinquishing the boy's wrist. After a moment, he let the inert hand fall and went and leaned against the wall. Then, as if he had suddenly remembered something very important that had to be noted down immediately, he took a notebook from his pocket and wrote a few lines in it. "The son-of-a-bitch," I thought angrily. "He better not come and feel my pulse; I'll give him a punch in his dirty jaw."

He didn't come near me, but I felt he was looking at me. I raised my head and looked back at him. In an impersonal voice, he said, "Don't you think it's frightfully cold here?"

He looked purple with cold.

"I'm not cold," I answered him.

He kept looking at me with a hard expression. Suddenly I understood, and I lifted my hands to my face. I was covered with sweat. Here, in this cellar, in mid-winter, right in a draft, I was sweating. I ran my fingers through my hair, which was stiff with sweat; at the same time, I realized my shirt was damp and sticking to my skin. I had been streaming with perspiration for an hour, at least, and had felt nothing. But this fact hadn't escaped that Belgian swine. He had seen the drops rolling down my face and had said to himself that it showed an almost pathological terror; and he himself had felt normal and proud of it because he was cold. I wanted to get up and go punch his face in, but I had hardly started to make a move before my shame and anger had disappeared. I dropped back onto the bench with indifference.

I was content to rub my neck with my handkerchief because now I felt the sweat dripping from my hair onto the nape of my neck and that was disagreeable. I soon gave up rubbing myself, however, for it didn't do any good; my handkerchief was already wringing wet and I was still sweating. My buttocks, too, were sweating, and my damp trousers stuck to the bench.

Suddenly, Juan said, "You're a doctor, aren't you?"

"Yes," said the Belgian.

"Do people suffer—very long?"

"Oh! When . . . ? No, no," said the Belgian, in a paternal voice, "it's quickly over."

His manner was as reassuring as if he had been answering a paying patient.

"But I . . . Somebody told me—they often have to fire two volleys."

"Sometimes," said the Belgian, raising his head, "it just happens that the first volley doesn't hit any of the vital organs."

"So then they have to reload their guns and aim all over again?"

Juan thought for a moment, then added hoarsely, "But that takes time!"

He was terribly afraid of suffering. He couldn't think about anything else, but that went with his age. As for me, I hardly thought about it any more and it certainly was not fear of suffering that made me perspire.

I rose and walked toward the pile of coal dust. Tom gave a start and looked at me with a look of hate. I irritated him because my shoes squeaked. I wondered if my face was as putty-colored as his. Then I noticed that he, too, was sweating. The sky was magnificent; no light at all came into our dark corner and I had only to lift my head to see the Big Bear. But it didn't look the way it had looked before. Two days ago, from my cell in the archbishop's palace, I could see a big patch of sky and each time of day brought back a different memory. In the morning, when the sky was a deep blue, and light, I thought of beaches along the Atlantic; at noon, I could see the sun, and I remembered a bar in Seville where I used to drink manzanilla and eat anchovies and olives; in the afternoon, I was in the shade, and I thought of the deep shadow which covers half of the arena while the other half gleams in the sunlight: it really gave me a pang to see the whole earth reflected in the sky like that. Now, however, no matter how much I looked up in the air, the sky no longer recalled anything. I liked it better that way. I came back and sat down next to Tom. There was a long silence.

Then Tom began to talk in a low voice. He had to keep talking, otherwise he lost his way in his own thoughts. I believe he was talking to me, but he didn't look at me. No doubt he was afraid to look at me, because I was gray and sweating. We were both alike and worse than mirrors for each other. He looked at the Belgian, the only one who was alive.

"Say, do you understand? I don't."

Then I, too, began to talk in a low voice. I was watching the Belgian.

"Understand what? What's the matter?"

"Something's going to happen to us that I don't understand."

There was a strange odor about Tom. It seemed to me that I was more sensitive to odors than ordinarily. With a sneer, I said, "You'll understand, later."

"That's not so sure," he said stubbornly. "I'm willing to be courageous, but at least I ought to know . . . Listen, they're going to take us out into the courtyard. All right. The fellows will be standing in line in front of us. How many of them will there be?"

"Oh, I don't know. Five, or eight. Not more."

"That's enough. Let's say there'll be eight of them. Somebody will shout 'Shoulder arms!' and I'll see all eight rifles aimed at me. I'm sure I'm going to feel like going through the wall. I'll push against the wall as hard as I can with my back, and the wall won't give in. The way it is in a nightmare. . . . I can imagine all that. Ah, if you only knew how well I can imagine it!"

"Skip it!" I said. "I can imagine it too."

"It must hurt like the devil. You know they aim at your eyes and mouth so as to disfigure you," he added maliciously. "I can feel the wounds already. For the last hour I've been having pains in my head and neck. Not real pains—it's worse still. They're the pains I'll feel tomorrow morning. And after that, then what?"

I understood perfectly well what he meant, but I didn't want to seem to understand. As for the pains, I, too, felt them all through my body, like a lot of little gashes. I couldn't get used to them, but I was like him, I didn't think they were very important.

"After that," I said roughly, "you'll be eating daisies."

He started talking to himself. not taking his eyes off the Belgian, who didn't seem to be listening to him. I knew what he had come for, and that what we were thinking didn't interest him. He had come to look at our bodies, our bodies which were dying alive.

"It's like in a nightmare," said Tom. "You want to think of something, you keep having the impression you've got it, that you're going to understand, and then it slips away from you, it eludes you and it's gone again. I say to myself, afterwards, there won't be anything. But I don't really understand what that means. There are moments when I almost do—and then it's gone again. I start to think of the pains, the bullets, the noise of the shooting. I am a materialist, I swear it; and I'm not going crazy, either. But there's something wrong. I see my own corpse. That's not hard, but it's *I* who see it, with *my* eyes. I'll have to get to the point where I think—where I think I won't see anything more. I won't hear anything more, and the world will go on for the others. We're not made to think that way, Pablo. Believe me, I've already stayed awake all night waiting for something. But this is not the same thing. This will grab us from behind, Pablo, and we won't be ready for it."

"Shut up," I said. "Do you want me to call a father confessor?"

He didn't answer. I had already noticed that he had a tendency to prophesy and call me "Pablo" in a kind of pale voice. I didn't like that very much, but it seems all the Irish are like that. I had a vague impression that he smelled of urine. Actually, I didn't like Tom very much, and I didn't see why, just because we were going to die together, I should like him any better. There are certain fellows with whom it would be different—with Ramon Gris, for instance. But between Tom and Juan, I felt alone. In fact, I liked it better that way. With Ramon I might have grown soft. But I felt terribly hard at that moment, and I wanted to stay hard.

Tom kept on muttering, in a kind of absent-minded way. He was certainly talking to keep from thinking. Naturally, I agreed with him, and I could have said everything he was saying. It's not *natural* to die. And since I was going to die, nothing seemed natural any more: neither the coal pile, nor the bench, nor Pedro's dirty old face. Only it was disagreeable for me to think the same things Tom thought. And I knew perfectly well that all night long, within five minutes of each other, we would keep on thinking things at the same time, sweating or shivering at the same time. I looked at him sideways and, for the first time, he seemed strange to me. He had death written on his face. My pride was wounded. For twenty-four hours I had lived side by side with Tom, I had listened to him, I had talked to him, and I knew we had nothing in common. And now we were as alike as twin brothers, simply because we were going to die together. Tom took my hand without looking at me.

"Pablo, I wonder . . . I wonder if it's true that we just cease to exist."

I drew my hand away.

"Look between your feet, you dirty dog."

There was a puddle between his feet and water was dripping from his trousers.

"What's the matter?" he said, frightened.

"You're wetting your pants," I said to him.

"It's not true," he said furiously. "I can't be . . . I don't feel anything."

The Belgian had come closer to him. With an air of false concern, he asked, "Aren't you feeling well?"

Tom didn't answer. The Belgian looked at the puddle without comment.

"I don't know what that is," Tom said savagely, "but I'm not afraid. I swear to you, I'm not afraid."

The Belgian made no answer. Tom rose and went to the corner. He came back, buttoning his fly, and sat down, without a word. The Belgian was taking notes.

We were watching the doctor. Juan was watching him too. All three of us were watching him because he was alive. He had the gestures of a living person, the interests of a living person; he was shivering in this cellar the way living people shiver; he had an obedient, well-fed body. We, on the other hand, didn't feel our bodies any more—not the same way, in any case. I felt like touching my trousers, but I didn't dare to. I looked at the Belgian, well-planted on his two legs, master of his muscles—and able to plan for tomorrow. We were like three shadows deprived of blood; we were watching him and sucking his life like vampires.

Finally he came over to Juan. Was he going to lay his hand on the nape of Juan's neck for some professional reason, or had he obeyed a charitable impulse? If he had acted out of charity, it was the one and only time during the whole night. He fondled Juan's head and the nape of his neck. The kid let him do it, without taking his eyes off him. Then, suddenly, he took hold of the doctor's hand and looked at it in a funny way. He held the Belgian's hand between his own two hands and there was nothing pleasing about them, those two gray paws squeezing that fat red hand. I sensed what was going to happen and Tom must have sensed it, too. But all the Belgian saw was emotion, and he smiled paternally. After a moment, the kid lifted the big red paw to his mouth and started to bite it. The Belgian drew back quickly and stumbled toward the wall. For a second, he looked at us with horror. He must have suddenly understood that we were not men like himself. I began to laugh, and one of the guards started up. The other had fallen asleep with his eyes wide open, showing only the whites.

I felt tired and over-excited at the same time. I didn't want to think any more about what was going to happen at dawn—about death. It didn't make sense, and I never got beyond just words, or emptiness. But whenever I tried to think about something else I saw the barrels of rifles aimed at me. I must have lived through my execution twenty times in succession; one time I thought it was the real thing; I must have dozed off for a moment. They were dragging me toward the wall and I was resisting; I was imploring their pardon. I woke with a start and looked at the Belgian. I was afraid I had cried out in my sleep. But he was smoothing his mustache; he hadn't noticed anything. If I had wanted to, I believe I could have slept for a while. I had been awake for the last forty-eight hours, and I was worn out. But I didn't want to lose two hours of life. They would have had to come and wake me at dawn. I would have followed them, drunk with sleep, and I would have gone off without so much as "Gosh!" I didn't want it that way. I didn't want to die like an animal. I wanted to understand. Besides, I was afraid of having nightmares. I got up and began to walk up and down and, so as to think about something else, I began to think about my past life. Memories crowded in on me, helter-skelter. Some were good and some were bad—at least that was how I had thought of them *before*. There were faces and happenings. I saw the face of a little *novilero* who had gotten himself horned during the *Feria*, in Valencia. I saw the face of one of my uncles, of Ramon Gris. I remembered all kinds of things that had happened: how I had been on strike for three months in 1926, and had almost died of hunger. I recalled a night I had spent on a beach in Granada; I hadn't eaten for three days. I was nearly wild, I didn't want to give up the sponge. I had to smile. With what eagerness I had run after happiness, and women, and liberty! And to what end? I had wanted to liberate Spain, I admired Py Margall, I had belonged to the anarchist movement, I had spoken at public meetings. I took everything as seriously as if I had been immortal.

At that time I had the impression that I had my whole life before me, and I thought to myself, "It's all a god-damned lie." Now it wasn't worth anything because it was finished. I wondered how I had ever been able to go out and have a good time with girls. I wouldn't have lifted my little finger if I had ever imagined that I would die like this. I saw my life before me, finished, closed, like a bag, and yet what was inside was not finished. For a moment I tried to appraise it. I would have liked to say to myself, "It's been a good life." But it couldn't be appraised, it was only an outline. I had spent my time writing checks on eternity, and had understood nothing. Now, I didn't miss anything. There were a lot of things I might have missed: the taste of manzanilla, for instance, or the swims I used to take in summer in a little creek near Cadiz. But death had taken the charm out of everything.

Suddenly the Belgian had a wonderful idea.

"My friends," he said to us, "if you want me to—and providing the military authorities give their consent—I could undertake to deliver a word or some token from you to your loved ones...."

Tom growled, "I haven't got anybody."

I didn't answer. Tom waited for a moment, then he looked at me with curiosity. "Aren't you going to send any message to Concha?"

"No."

I hated that sort of sentimental conspiracy. Of course, it was my fault, since I had mentioned Concha the night before, and I should have kept my mouth shut. I had been with her for a year. Even as late as last night, I would have cut my arm off with a hatchet just to see her again for five minutes. That was why I had mentioned her. I couldn't help it. Now I didn't care any more about seeing her. I hadn't anything more to say to her. I didn't even want to hold her in my arms. I loathed my body because it had turned gray and was sweating—and I wasn't even sure that I didn't loathe hers too. Concha would cry when she heard about my death; for months she would have no more interest in life. But still it was I who was going to die. I thought of her beautiful, loving eyes. When she looked at me something went from her to me. But I thought to myself that it was all over; if she looked at me *now* her gaze would not leave her eyes, it would not reach out to me. I was alone.

Tom too, was alone, but not the same way. He was seated astride his chair and had begun to look at the bench with a sort of smile, with surprise, even. He reached out his hand and touched the wood cautiously, as though he were afraid of breaking something, then he drew his hand back hurriedly, and shivered. I wouldn't have amused myself touching that bench, if I had been Tom, that was just some more Irish play-acting. But somehow it seemed to me too that the different objects had something funny about them. They seemed to have grown paler, less massive than before. I had only to look at the bench, the lamp or the pile of coal dust to feel I was going to die. Naturally, I couldn't think clearly about my death, but I saw it everywhere, even on the different objects, the way they had withdrawn and kept their distance, tactfully, like people talking at the bedside of a dying person. It was *his own death* Tom had just touched on the bench.

In the state I was in, if they had come and told me I could go home quietly, that my life would be saved, it would have left me cold. A few hours, or a few years of waiting are all the same, when you've lost the illusion of being eternal. Nothing mattered to me any more. In a way, I was calm. But it was a horrible kind of calm—because of my body. My body—I saw with its eyes and I heard with its ears, but it was no longer I. It sweat and trembled independently, and I didn't recognize it any longer. I was obliged to touch it and look at it to know what was happening to it, just as if it had been someone else's body. At times I still felt it, I felt a slipping, a sort of headlong plunging, as in a falling airplane, or else I heard my heart beating. But this didn't give me confidence. In fact, everything that came from my body had something damned dubious about it. Most of the time it was silent, it stayed put and I didn't feel anything other than a sort of heaviness, a loathsome presence against me. I had the impression of being bound to an enormous vermin.

The Belgian took out his watch and looked at it.

"It's half-past three," he said.

The son-of-a-bitch! He must have done it on purpose. Tom jumped up. We hadn't yet realized the time was passing. The night surrounded us like a formless, dark mass; I didn't even remember it had started.

Juan started to shout. Wringing his hands, he implored, "I don't want to die! I don't want to die!"

He ran the whole length of the cellar with his arms in the air, then he dropped down onto one of the mattresses, sobbing. Tom looked at him with dismal eyes and didn't even try to console him any more. The fact was, it was no use; the kid made more noise than we did, but he was less affected, really. He was like a sick person who defends himself against his malady with a high fever. When there's not even any fever left, it's much more serious.

He was crying. I could tell he felt sorry for himself; he was thinking about death. For one second, one single second, I too felt like crying, crying out of pity for myself. But just the contrary happened. I took one look at the kid, saw his thin, sobbing shoulders, and I felt I was in-human. I couldn't feel pity either for these others or for myself. I said to myself, "I want to die decently."

Tom had gotten up and was standing just under the round opening looking out for the first signs of daylight. I was determined, I wanted to die decently, and I only thought about that. But underneath, ever since the doctor had told us the time, I felt time slipping, flowing by, one drop at a time.

It was still dark when I heard Tom's voice.

"Do you hear them?"

"Yes."

People were walking in the courtyard.

"What the hell are they doing? After all, they can't shoot in the dark."

After a moment, we didn't hear anything more. I said to Tom, "There's the daylight."

Pedro got up yawning, and came and blew out the lamp. He turned to the man beside him. "It's hellish cold."

The cellar had grown gray. We could hear shots at a distance.

"It's about to start," I said to Tom. "That must be in the back courtyard."

Tom asked the doctor to give him a cigarette. I didn't want any; I didn't want either cigarettes or alcohol. From that moment on, the shooting didn't stop.

"Can you take it in?" Tom said.

He started to add something, then he stopped and began to watch the door. The door opened and a lieutenant came in with four soldiers. Tom dropped his cigarette.

"Steinbock?"

Tom didn't answer. Pedro pointed him out.

"Juan Mirbal?"

"He's the one on the mattress."

"Stand up," said the Lieutenant.

Juan didn't move. Two soldiers took hold of him by the armpits and stood him up on his feet. But as soon as they let go of him he fell down.

The soldiers hesitated a moment.

"He's not the first one to get sick," said the Lieutenant. "You'll have to carry him, the two of you. We'll arrange things when we get there." He turned to Tom. "All right, come along."

Tom left between two soldiers. Two other soldiers followed, carrying the kid by his arms and legs. He was not unconscious; his eyes were wide open and tears were rolling down his cheeks. When I started to go out, the Lieutenant stopped me.

"Are you Ibbieta?"

"Yes."

"You wait here. They'll come and get you later on."

They left. The Belgian and the two jailers left too, and I was alone. I didn't understand what had happened to me, but I would have liked it better if they had ended it all right away. I heard the volleys at almost regular intervals; at each one, I shuddered. I felt like howling and tearing my hair. But instead, I gritted my teeth and pushed my hands deep into my pockets, because I wanted to stay decent.

An hour later, they came to fetch me and took me up to the first floor in a little room which smelt of cigar smoke and was so hot it seemed to me suffocating. Here there were two officers sitting in comfortable chairs, smoking, with papers spread out on their knees.

"Your name is Ibbieta?"

"Yes."

"Where is Ramon Gris?"

"I don't know."

The man who questioned me was small and stocky. He had hard eyes behind his glasses.

"Come nearer," he said to me.

I went nearer. He rose and took me by the arms. looking at me in a way calculated to make me go through the floor. At the same time he pinched my arms with all his might. He didn't mean to hurt me; it was quite a game; he wanted to dominate me. He also seemed to think it was necessary to blow his fetid breath right into my face. We stood like that for a moment, only I felt more like laughing than anything else. It take a lot more than that to intimidate a man who's about to die: it didn't work. He pushed me away violently and sat down again.

"It's your life or his," he said. "You'll be allowed to go free if you tell us where he is."

After all, these two bedizened fellows with their riding crops and boots were just men who were going to die one day. A little later than I, perhaps, but not a great deal. And there they were, looking for names among their papers, running after other men in order to put them in prison or do away with them entirely. They had their opinions on the future of Spain and on other subjects. Their petty activities seemed to me to be offensive and ludicrous. I could no longer put myself in their place. I had the impression they were crazy.

The little fat fellow kept looking at me, tapping his boots with his riding crop. All his gestures were calculated to make him appear like a spirited, ferocious animal.

"Well? Do you understand?"

"I don't know where Gris is," I said. "I thought he was in Madrid."

The other officer lifted his pale hand indolently. This indolence was also calculated. I saw through all their little tricks, and I was dumbfounded that men should still exist who took pleasure in that kind of thing.

"You have fifteen minutes to think it over," he said slowly. "Take him to the linen-room, and bring him back here in fifteen minutes. If he continues to refuse, he'll be executed at once."

They knew what they were doing. I had spent the night waiting. After that, they had made me wait another hour in the cellar, while they shot Tom and Juan, and now they locked me in the linen-room. They must have arranged the whole thing the night before. They figured that sooner or later people's nerves wear out and they hoped to get me that way.

They made a big mistake. In the linen-room I sat down on a ladder because I felt very weak, and I began to think things over. Not their proposition, however. Naturally I knew where Gris was. He was hiding in his cousins' house, about two miles outside the city. I knew, too, that I would not reveal his hiding place, unless they tortured me (but they didn't seem to be considering that). All that was definitely settled and didn't interest me in the least. Only I would have liked to understand the reasons for my own conduct. I would rather die than betray Gris. Why? I no longer liked Ramon Gris. My friendship for him had died shortly before dawn along with my love for Concha, along with my own desire to live. Of course I still admired him—he was hard. But it was not for that reason that I was willing to die in his place; his life was no more valuable than mine. No life was of any value. A man was going to be stood up against a wall and fired at till he dropped dead. It didn't make any difference whether it was I or Gris or somebody else. I knew perfectly well he was more useful to the Spanish cause than I was, but I didn't give a God damn about Spain or anarchy, either; nothing had any importance now. And yet, there I was. I could save my skin by betraying Gris and I refused to do it. It seemed more ludicrous to me than anything else; it was stubbornness.

I thought to myself, "Am I hard-headed!" And I was seized with a strange sort of cheerfulness.

They came to fetch me and took me back to the two officers. A rat darted out under our feet and that amused me. I turned to one of the falangists and said to him, "Did you see that rat?"

He made no reply. He was gloomy, and took himself very seriously. As for me, I felt like laughing, but I restrained myself because I was afraid that if I started, I wouldn't be able to stop. The falangist wore mustaches. I kept after him. "You ought to cut off those mustaches, you fool."

I was amused by the fact that he let hair grow all over his face while he was still alive. He gave me a kind of half-hearted kick, and I shut up.

"Well," said the fat officer, "have you thought things over?"

I looked at them with curiosity, like insects of a very rare species.

"I know where he is," I said. "He's hiding in the cemetery. Either in one of the vaults, or in the gravediggers' shack."

I said that just to make fools of them. I wanted to see them get up and fasten their belts and bustle about giving orders.

They jumped to their feet.

"Fine. Moles, go ask Lieutenant Lopez for fifteen men. And as for you," the little fat fellow said to me, "if you've told the truth, I don't go back on my word. But you'll pay for this, if you're pulling our leg."

They left noisily and I waited in peace. still guarded by the falangists. From time to time I smiled at the thought of the face they were going to make. I felt dull and malicious. I could see them lifting up the gravestones, or opening the doors of the vaults one by one. I saw the whole situation as though I were another person: the prisoner determined to play the hero, the solemn falangists with their mustaches and the men in uniform running around among the graves. It was irresistibly funny.

After half an hour, the little fat fellow came back alone. I thought he had come to give the order to execute me. The others must have stayed in the cemetery.

The officer looked at me. He didn't look at all foolish.

"Take him out in the big courtyard with the others," he said. "When military operations are over, a regular tribunal will decide his case."

I thought I must have misunderstood.

"So they're not—they're not going to shoot me?" I asked.

"Not now, in any case. Afterwards, that doesn't concern me."

I still didn't understand.

"But why?" I said to him.

He shrugged his shoulders without replying, and the soldiers led me away. In the big courtyard there were a hundred or so prisoners, women, children and a few old men. I started to walk around the grass plot in the middle. I felt absolutely idiotic. At noon we were fed in the dining hall. Two or three fellows spoke to me. I must have known them, but I didn't answer. I didn't even know where I was.

Toward evening, about ten new prisoners were pushed into the courtyard. I recognized Garcia, the baker.

He said to me, "Lucky dog! I didn't expect to find you alive."

"They condemned me to death," I said, "and then they changed their minds. I don't know why."

"I was arrested at two o'clock," Garcia said.

"What for?"

Garcia took no part in politics.

"I don't know," he said. "They arrest everybody who doesn't think the way they do."

He lowered his voice.

"They got Gris."

I began to tremble.

"When?"

"This morning. He acted like a damned fool. He left his cousins' house Tuesday because of a disagreement. There were any number of fellows who would have hidden him, but he didn't want to be indebted to anybody any more. He said, 'I would have hidden at Ibbieta's, but since they've got him, I'll go hide in the cemetery.' "

"In the cemetery?"

"Yes. It was the god-damnedest thing. Naturally they passed by there this morning; that had to happen. They found him in the grave-diggers' shack. They opened fire at him and they finished him off."

"In the cemetery!"

Everything went around in circles, and when I came to I was sitting on the ground. I laughed so hard the tears came to my eyes.

# THE GUEST
## *Albert Camus*

The schoolmaster was watching the two men climb toward him. One was on horseback, the other on foot. They had not yet tackled the abrupt rise leading to the schoolhouse built on the hillside. They were toiling onward, making slow progress in the snow, among the stones, on the vast expanse of the high, deserted plateau. From time to time the horse stumbled. He could not be heard yet but the breath issuing from his nostrils could be seen. The schoolmaster calculated that it would take them a half hour to get onto the hill. It was cold; he went back into the school to get a sweater.

He crossed the empty, frigid classroom. On the blackboard the four rivers of France. drawn with four different colored chalks, had been flowing toward their estuaries for the past three days. Snow had suddenly fallen in mid-October after eight months of drought without the transition of rain, and the twenty pupils, more or less, who lived in the villages scattered over the plateau had stopped coming. With fair weather they would return. Daru now heated only the single room that was his lodging, adjoining the classroom. One of the windows faced, like the classroom windows, the south. On that side the schôol was a few kilometers from the point where the plateau began to slope toward the south. In clear weather the purple mass of the mountain range where the gap opened onto the desert could be seen.

Somewhat warmed, Daru returned to the window from which he had first noticed the two men. They were no longer visible. Hence they must have tackled the rise. The sky was not so dark, for the snow had stopped falling during the night. The morning had dawned with a ditry light which had scarcely become brighter as the ceiling of clouds lifted. At two in the afternoon it seemed as if the day were merely beginning. But still this was better than those three days when the thick snow was falling amidst unbroken darkness with little gusts of wind that rattled the double door of the classroom. Then Daru had spent long hours in his room, leaving it only to go to the shed and feed the chickens or get some coal. Fortunately the delivery truck from Tadjid, the nearest village to the north, had brought his supplies two days before the blizzard. It would return in forty-eight hours.

Besides, he had enough to resist a siege, for the little room was cluttered with bags of wheat that the administration had left as a supply to distribute to those of his pupils whose families had suffered from the drought. Actually they had all been victims because they were all poor. Every day Daru would distribute a ration to the children. They had missed it, he knew, during these bad days. Possibly one of the fathers or big brothers would come this afternoon and he could supply them with grain. It was just a matter of carrying them over to the next harvest. Now shiploads of wheat were arriving from France and the worst was over. But it would be hard to forget that poverty, that army of ragged ghosts wandering in the sunlight, the plateaus burned to a cinder month after month, the earth shriveled up little by little, literally scorched, every stone bursting into dust under one's foot. The sheep had died then by thousands, and even a few men, here and there, sometimes without anyone's knowing.

In contrast with such poverty, he who lived almost like a monk, in his remote schoolhouse, had felt like a lord with his whitewashed walls, his narrow couch, his unpainted shelves, his well, and his weekly provisioning with water and food. And suddenly this snow, without warning, without the foretaste of rain. This is the way the region was, cruel to live in, even without men, who didn't help matters either. But Daru had been born here. Everywhere else, he felt exiled.

He went out and stepped forward on the terrace in front of the schoolhouse. The two men were now halfway up the slope. He recognized the horseman to be Balducci, the old gendarme he had known for a long time. Balducci was holding at the end of a rope an Arab walking behind him with hands bound and head lowered. The gendarme waved a greeting to which Daru did not reply, lost as he was in contemplation of the Arab dressed in a faded blue *jellaba,* his feet in sandals but covered with socks of heavy raw wool, his head crowned with a narrow, short *cheche.* Balducci was holding back his horse in order not to hurt the Arab, and the group was advancing slowly.

Within earshot, Balducci shouted, "One hour to do the three kilometers from El Ameur!" Daru did not answer. Short and square in his thick sweater, he watched them climb. Not once had the Arab raised his head. "Hello," said Daru when they got up onto the terrace. "Come in and warm up." Balducci painfully got down from his horse without letting go of the rope. He smiled at the schoolmaster from under his bristling mustache. His little dark eyes, deepset under a tanned forehead, and his mouth surrounded with wrinkles made him look attentive and studious. Daru took the bridle, led the horse to the shed, and came back to the two men who were now waiting for him in the school. He led them into his room. "I am going to heat up the classroom," he said. "We'll be more comfortable there."

When he entered the room again, Balducci was on the couch. He had undone the rope tying him to the Arab, who had squatted near the stove. His hands still bound, the *cheche* pushed back on his head, the Arab was looking toward the window. At first Daru noticed only his huge lips, fat, smooth, almost Negroid; yet his nose was straight, his eyes dark and full of fever. The *cheche* uncovered an obstinate forehead and, under the weathered skin now rather discolored by the cold, the whole face had a restless and rebellious look. "Go into the other room," said the schoolmaster, "and I'll make you some mint tea." "Thanks," Balducci said. "What a chore! How I long for retirement." And addressing his prisoner in Arabic, he said, "Come on, you." The Arab got up and, slowly, holding his bound wrists in front of him, went into the classroom.

With the tea, Daru brought a chair. But Balducci was already sitting in state at the nearest pupil's desk, and the Arab had squatted against the teacher's platform facing the stove, which stood between the desk and the window. When he held out the glass of tea to the prisoner, Daru hesitated at the sight of his bound hands. "He might perhaps be untied." "Sure," said Balducci. "That was for the trip." He started to get to his feet. But Daru, setting the glass on the floor, had knelt beside the Arab. Without saying anything, the Arab watched him with his feverish eyes. Once his hands were free, he rubbed his swollen wrists against each other, took the glass of tea and sucked up the burning liquid in swift little sips.

"Good," said Daru. "And where are you headed?"

Balducci withdrew his mustache from the tea. "Here, son."

"Odd pupils! And you're spending the night?"

"No. I'm going back to El Ameur. And you will deliver this fellow to Tinguit. He is expected at police headquarters."

Balducci was looking at Daru with a friendly little smile.

"What's the story?" asked the schoolmaster. "Are you pulling my leg?"

"No, son. Those are the orders."

"The orders? I'm not . . ." Daru hesitated, not wanting to hurt the old Corsican. "I mean, that's not my job."

"What! What's the meaning of that? In wartime people do all kinds of jobs."

"Then I'll wait for the declaration of war!"

Balducci nodded. "O.K. But the orders exist and they concern you too. Things are bubbling, it appears. There is talk of a forthcoming revolt. We are mobilized, in a way."

"Daru still had his obstinate look."

"Listen, son," Balducci said. "I like you and you've got to understand. There's only a dozen of us at El Ameur to patrol the whole territory of a small department and I must be back in a hurry. He couldn't be kept there. His village was beginning to stir; they wanted to take him back. You must take him to Tinguit tomorrow before the day is over. Twenty kilometers shouldn't faze a husky fellow like you. After that, all will be over. You'll come back to your pupils and your comfortable life."

Behind the wall the horse could be heard snorting and pawing the earth. Daru was looking out the window. Decidedly the weather was clearing and the light was increasing over the snowy plateau. When all the snow was melted, the sun would take over again and once more would burn the fields of stone. For days still, the unchanging sky would shed its dry light on the solitary expanse where nothing had any connection with man.

"After all," he said, turning around toward Balducci, "what did he do?" And, before the gendarme had opened his mouth, he asked, "Does he speak French?"

"No, not a word. We had been looking for him for a month, but they were hiding him. He killed his cousin."

"Is he against us?"

"I don't think so. But you can never be sure."

"Why did he kill?"

"A family squabble, I think. One owed grain to the other, it seems. It's not at all clear. In short, he killed his cousin with a billhook. You know, like a sheep, *kreezk!*"

Balducci made the gesture of drawing a blade across his throat, and the Arab, his attention attracted, watched him with a sort of anxiety. Daru felt a sudden wrath against the man, against all men with their rotten spite, their tireless hates, their blood lust.

But the kettle was singing on the stove. He served Balducci more tea, hesitated, then served the Arab again, who drank avidly a second time. His raised arms made the *jellaba* fall open, and the schoolmaster saw his thin, muscular chest.

"Thanks, son," Balducci said, "And now I'm off."

He got up and went toward the Arab, taking a small rope from his pocket.

"What are you doing?" Daru asked dryly.

Balducci, disconcerted, showed him the rope.

"Don't bother."

The old gendarme hesitated. "It's up to you. Of course, you are armed?"

"I have my shotgun."

"Where?"

"In the trunk."

"You ought to have it near your bed."

"Why? I have nothing to fear."

"You're crazy, son. If there's an uprising, no one is safe; we're all in the same boat."

"I'll defend myself. I'll have time to see them coming."

Balducci began to laugh, then suddenly the mustache covered the white teeth. "You'll have time? O.K. That's just what I was saying. You always have been a little cracked. That's why I like you; my son was like that."

At the same time he took out his revolver and put it on the desk. "Keep it; I don't need two weapons from here to El Ameur."

The revolver shone against the black paint of the table. When the gendarme turned toward him, the schoolmaster caught his smell of leather and horseflesh.

"Listen, Balducci," Daru said suddenly, "all this disgusts me, beginning with your fellow here. But I won't hand him over. Fight, yes, if I have to. But not that."

The old gendarme stood in front of him and looked at him severely.

"You're being a fool," he said slowly. "I don't like it either. You don't get used to putting a rope on a man even after years of it, and you're even ashamed—yes, ashamed. But you can't let them have their way."

"I won't hand him over," Daru said again.

"It's an order, son, and I repeat it."

"That's right. Repeat to them what I've said to you: I won't hand him over."

Balducci made a visible effort to reflect. He looked at the Arab and at Daru. At last he decided.

"No, I won't tell them anything. If you want to drop us, go ahead; I'll not denounce you. I have an order to deliver the prisoner and I'm doing so. And now you'll just sign this paper for me."

"There's no need. I'll not deny that you left him with me."

"Don't be mean with me. I know you'll tell the truth. You're from around these parts and you are a man. But you must sign; that's the rule."

Daru opened his drawer, took out a little square bottle of purple ink, the red wooden penholder with the "sergeant-major" pen he used for models of handwriting, and signed. The gendarme carefully folded the paper and put it into his wallet. Then he moved toward the door.

"I'll see you off," Daru said.

"No," said Balducci. "There's no use being polite. You insulted me."

He looked at the Arab, motionless in the same spot, sniffed peevishly, and turned away toward the door. "Good-by, son," he said. The door slammed behind him. His footsteps were muffled by the snow. The horse stirred on the other side of the wall and several chickens fluttered in fright. A moment later Balducci reappeared outside the window leading the horse by the bridle. He walked toward the little rise without turning around and disappeared from sight with the horse following him.

Daru walked back toward the prisoner, who, without stirring, never took his eyes off him. "Wait," the schoolmaster said in Arabic and went toward the bedroom. As he was going through the door, he had a second thought, went to the desk, took the revolver, and stuck it in his pocket. Then, without looking back, he went into his room.

For some time he lay on his couch watching the sky gradually close over, listening to the silence. It was this silence that had seemed painful to him during the first days here, after the war. He had requested a post in the little town at the base of the foothills separating the upper plateaus from the desert. There rocky walls, green and black to the north, pink and lavender to the south, marked the frontier of eternal summer. He had been named to a post farther north, on the plateau itself. In the beginning, the solitude and the silence had been hard for him on these wastelands peopled only by stones. Occasionally, furrows suggested cultivation, but they had been dug to uncover a certain kind of stone good for building. The only plowing here was to harvest rocks. Elsewhere a thin layer of soil accumulated in the hollows would be scraped out to enrich paltry village gardens. This is the way it was: bare rock covered three quarters of the region. Towns sprang up, flourished, then disappeared; men came by, loved one another or fought bitterly, then died. No one in this desert, neither he nor his guest, mattered. And yet, outside this desert neither of them, Daru knew, could have really lived.

When he got up, no noise came from the classroom. He was amazed at the unmixed joy he derived from the mere thought that the Arab might have fled and that he would be alone with no decision to make. But the prisoner was there. He had merely stretched out between the stove and the desk and he was staring at the ceiling. In that position, his thick lips were particularly noticeable, giving him a pouting look. "Come," said Daru. The Arab got up and followed him. In the bedroom the schoolmaster pointed to a chair near the table under the window. The Arab sat down without ceasing to watch Daru.

"Are you hungry?"

"Yes," the prisoner said.

Daru set the table for two. He took flour and oil, shaped a cake in a frying pan, and lighted the little stove that functioned on bottled gas. While the cake was cooking, he went out to the shed to get cheese, eggs, dates, and condensed milk. When the cake was done he set it on the window sill to cool, heated some condensed milk diluted with water, and beat up the eggs into an omelette. In one of his motions he bumped into the revolver stuck in his right pocket. He set the bowl down, went into the classroom, and put the revolver in his desk drawer. When he came back to the room, night was falling. He put on the light and served the Arab. "Eat," he said. The Arab took a piece of the cake, lifted it eagerly to his mouth, and stopped short.

"And you?" he asked.

"After you. I'll eat too."

The thick lips opened slightly. The Arab hesitated, then bit into the cake determinedly.

The meal over, the Arab looked at the schoolmaster. "Are you the judge?"

"No, I'm simply keeping you until tomorrow."

"Why do you eat with me?"

"I'm hungry."

The Arab fell silent. Daru got up and went out. He brought back a camp cot from the shed and set it up between the table and the stove, at right angles to his own bed. From a large suitcase which, upright in a corner, served as a shelf for papers, he took two blankets and arranged them on the cot. Then he stopped, felt useless, and sat down on his bed. There was nothing more to do or to get ready. He had to look at this man. He looked at him therefore, trying to imagine his face bursting with rage. He couldn't do so. He could see nothing but the dark yet shining eyes and the animal mouth.

"Why did you kill him?" he asked in a voice whose hostile tone surprised him.

The Arab looked away. "He ran away. I ran after him."

He raised his eyes to Daru again and they were full of a sort of woeful interrogation. "Now what will they do to me?"

"Are you afraid?"

The Arab stiffened, turning his eyes away.

"Are you sorry?"

The Arab stared at him openmouthed. Obviously he did not understand. Daru's annoyance was growing. At the same time he felt awkward and self-conscious with his big body wedged between the two beds.

"Lie down there," he said impatiently. "That's your bed."

The Arab didn't move. He cried out, "Tell me!"

The schoolmaster looked at him.

"Is the gendarme coming back tomorrow?"

"I don't know."

"Are you coming with us?"

"I don't know. Why?"

The prisoner got up and stretched out on top of the blankets, his feet toward the window. The light from the electric bulb shone straight into his eyes and he closed them at once.

"Why?" Daru repeated, standing beside the bed.

The Arab opened his eyes under the blinding light and looked at him, trying not to blink. "Come with us," he said.

In the middle of the night, Daru was not asleep. He had gone to bed after undressing completely; he generally slept naked. But when he suddenly realized that he had nothing on, he wondered. He felt vulnerable and the temptation came to him to put his clothes back on. Then he shrugged his shoulders; after all, he wasn't a child and, if it came to that, he could break his adversary in two. From his bed, he could observe him lying on his back, still motionless, his eyes closed under the harsh light. When Daru turned out the light, the darkness seemed to congeal all of a sudden. Little by little, the night came back to life in the window where the starless sky was stirring gently. The schoolmaster soon made out the body lying at his feet. The Arab was still motionless but his eyes seemed open. A faint wind was prowling about the schoolhouse. Perhaps it would drive away the clouds and the sun would reappear.

During the night the wind increased. The hens fluttered a little and then were silent. The Arab turned over on his side with his back to Daru, who thought he heard him moan. Then he listened for his guest's breathing, which had become heavier and more regular. He listened to that breathing so close to him and mused without being able to go to sleep. In the room where he had been sleeping alone for a year, this presence bothered him. But it bothered him also because it imposed on him a sort of brotherhood he refused to accept in the present circumstances; yet he was familiar with it. Men who share the same rooms, soldiers or prisoners, develop a strange alliance as if, having cast off their armor with their clothing, they fraternized every evening, over and above their differences, in the ancient community of dream and fatigue. But Daru shook himself; he didn't like such musings, and it was essential for him to sleep.

A little later, however, when the Arab stirred slightly the schoolmaster was still not asleep. When the prisoner made a second move, he stiffened, on the alert. The Arab was lifting himself slowly on his arms with almost the motion of a sleepwalker. Seated upright in bed. he waited motionless without turning his head toward Daru, as if he were listening attentively. Daru did not stir; it had just occurred to him that the revolver was still in the drawer of his desk. It was better to act at once. Yet he continued to observe the prisoner, who, with the same slithery motion, put his feet on the ground, waited again, then stood up slowly. Daru was about to call out to him when the Arab began to walk, in a quite natural but extraordinarily silent way. He was heading toward the door at the end of the room that opened into the shed. He lifted the latch with precaution and went out, pushing the door behind him but without shutting it.

Daru had not stirred. "He is running away," he merely thought. "Good riddance!" Yet he listened attentively. The hens were not fluttering; the guest must be on the plateau. A faint sound of water reached him, and he didn't know what it was until the Arab again stood framed in the doorway, closed the door carefully, and came back to bed without a sound. Then Daru turned his back on him and fell asleep. Still later he seemed, from the depths of his sleep, to hear furtive steps around the schoolhouse. "I'm dreaming! I'm dreaming!" he repeated to himself. And he went on sleeping.

When he awoke, the sky was clear; the loose window let in a cold, pure air. The Arab was asleep, hunched up under the blankets now, his mouth open, utterly relaxed. But when Daru shook him he started dreadfully, staring at Daru with wild eyes as if he had never seen him and with such a frightened expression that the schoolmaster stepped back. "Don't be afraid. It is I. You must eat." The Arab nodded his head and said yes. Calm had returned to his face, but his expression was vacant and listless.

The coffee was ready. They drank it seated together on the cot as they munched their pieces of the cake. Then Daru led the Arab under the shed and showed him the faucet where he washed. He went back into the room, folded the blankets on the cot, made his own bed, and put the room in order. Then he went through the classroom and out onto the terrace. The sun was already rising in the blue sky; a soft, bright light enveloped the deserted plateau. On the ridge the snow was melting in spots. The stones were about to reappear. Crouched on the edge of the plateau, the schoolmaster looked at the deserted expanse. He thought of Balducci. He had hurt him, for he had sent him off as though he didn't want to be associated with him. He could still hear the gendarme's farewell and, without knowing why, he felt strangely empty and vulnerable.

At that moment, from the other side of the schoolhouse, the prisoner coughed. Daru listened to him almost despite himself and then, furious, threw a pebble that whistled through the air before sinking into the snow. That man's stupid crime revolted him, but to hand him over was contrary to honor; just thinking of it made him boil with humiliation. He simultaneously cursed his own people who had sent him this

Arab and the Arab who had dared to kill and not managed to get away. Daru got up, walked in a circle on the terrace, waited motionless, and then went back into the schoolhouse.

The Arab, leaning over the cement floor of the shed, was washing his teeth with two fingers. Daru looked at him and said, "Come." He went back into the room ahead of the prisoner. He slipped a hunting jacket on over his sweater and put on walking shoes. Standing, he waited until the Arab had put on his *cheche* and sandals. They went into the classroom, and the schoolmaster pointed to the exit saying, "Go ahead." The fellow didn't budge. "I'm coming," said Daru. The Arab went out. Daru went back into the room and made a package with pieces of rusk, dates, and sugar in it. In the classroom, before going out, he hesitated a second in front of his desk, then crossed the threshold and locked the door. "That's the way," he said. He started toward the east, followed by the prisoner. But a short distance from the schoolhouse he thought he heard a slight sound behind him. He retraced his steps and examined the surroundings of the house; there was no one there. The Arab watched him without seeming to understand. "Come on," said Daru.

They walked for an hour and rested beside a sharp needle of limestone. The snow was melting faster and faster and the sun was drinking up the puddles just as quickly, rapidly cleaning the plateau, which gradually dried and vibrated like the air itself. When they resumed walking, the ground rang under their feet. From time to time a bird rent the space in front of them with a joyful cry. Daru felt a sort of rapture before the vast familiar expanse, now almost entirely yellow under its dome of blue sky. They walked an hour more, descending toward the south. They reached a sort of flattened elevation made up of crumbly rocks. From there on, the plateau sloped down—eastward toward a low plain on which could be made out a few spindly trees, and to the south toward outcroppings of rock that gave the landscape a chaotic look.

Daru surveyed the two directions. Not a man could be seen. He turned toward the Arab, who was looking at him bleakly. Daru offered the package to him. "Take it," he said. "There are dates, bread, and sugar. You can hold out for two days. Here are a thousand francs too."

The Arab took the package and the money but kept his full hands at chest level as if he didn't know what to do with what was being given him.

"Now look," the schoolmaster said as he pointed in the direction of the east, "there's the way to Tinguit. You have a two-hour walk. At Tinguit are the administration and the police. They are expecting you."

The Arab looked toward the east, still holding the package and the money against his chest. Daru took his elbow and turned him rather roughly toward the south. At the foot of the elevation on which they stood could be seen a faint path. "That's the trail across the plateau. In a day's walk from here you'll find pasturelands and the first nomads. They'll take you in and shelter you according to their law."

The Arab had now turned toward Daru, and a sort of panic was visible in his expression. "Listen," he said.

Daru shook his head. "No, be quiet. Now I'm leaving you." He turned his back on him, took two long steps in the direction of the school, looked hesitantly at the motionless Arab, and started off again. For a few minutes he heard nothing but his own step resounding on the cold ground. and he did not turn his head. A moment later, however, he turned around. The Arab was still there on the edge of the hill, his arms hanging now, and he was looking at the schoolmaster. Daru felt something rise in his throat. But he swore with impatience, waved vaguely, and started off again. He had already gone a distance when he again stopped and looked. There was no longer anyone on the hill.

Daru hesitated. The sun was now rather high in the sky and beginning to beat down on his head. The schoolmaster retraced his steps, at first somewhat uncertainly, then with decision. When he reached the little hill, he was bathed in sweat. He climbed it as fast as he could and stopped, out of breath, on the top. The rock fields to the south stood out sharply against the blue sky, but on the plain to the east a steamy heat was rising. And in that slight haze, Daru, with heavy heart, made out the Arab walking slowly on the road to prison.

A little later, standing before the window of the classroom, the schoolmaster was watching the clear light bathing the whole surface of the plateau. Behind him on the blackboard, among the winding French rivers, sprawled the clumsily chalked up words he had just read: "You handed over our brother. You will pay for this." Daru looked at the sky, the plateau, and, beyond, the invisible lands stretching all the way to the sea. In this vast landscape he had loved so much, he was alone.

## Study Aids: Sartre

1. What are the several meanings and implications of the wall? Why is it the title and central fact of the story? How does it become the story's main statement about the conditions of man's life?

2. In coming up against this wall, Pablo Ibbieta is faced with an important choice. What is his choice? What are its implications about man's life?

3. Pablo's situation produces what relationship to the others in the cell? It also causes what change of relationship between himself and his past—his actions, his ideas, his friends?

4. On what basis does he make his final choice about Ramon Gris?

5. The results of his final choice suggest what implications about the nature of man's life and choices? How are these implications related to the title and the earlier suggestions about the human condition? Why, finally, does Pablo laugh?

## Study Aids: Camus

1. The general human situation in which Daru feels he must make a choice is suggested by the characteristics of the geographic, political, and personal situation in which he finds himself. What are these characteristics and what general situation do they define?
2. Why will Daru not "hand over" the Arab as Balducci asks? What are the exact final terms of his decision? Why, for example, does he show the Arab both paths?
3. Why did the Arab prisoner not try to escape in the night? What are the reasons for and the nature of his final choice?
4. What are the consequences of Daru's choice? What do these consequences suggest about Camus' view of the conditions of man's life, his free will, his choices, his responsibility?
5. Does the final note written on the blackboard change or further develop Daru's feelings about his situation? How does it show Camus' views of the general human situation? Why?

# A HUNGER ARTIST
*Franz Kafka*

During these last decades the interest in professional fasting has markedly diminished. It used to pay very well to stage such great performances under one's own management, but today that is quite impossible. We live in a different world now. At one time the whole town took a lively interest in the hunger artist; from day to day of his fast the excitement mounted; everybody wanted to see him at least once a day; there were people who bought season tickets for the last few days and sat from morning till night in front of his small barred cage; even in the nighttime there were visiting hours, when the whole effect was heightened by torch flares; on fine days the cage was set out in the open air, and then it was the children's special treat to see the hunger artist; for their elders he was often just a joke that happened to be in fashion, but the children stood open-mouthed, holding each other's hands for greater security, marveling at him as he sat there pallid in black tights, with his ribs sticking out so prominently, not even on a seat but down among straw on the ground, sometimes giving a courteous nod, answering questions with a constrained smile, or perhaps stretching an arm through the bars so that one might feel how thin it was, and then again withdrawing deep into himself, paying no attention to anyone or anything, not even to the all-important striking of the clock that was the only piece of furniture in his cage, but merely staring into vacancy with half-shut eyes, now and then taking a sip from a tiny glass of water to moisten his lips.

Besides casual onlookers, there were also relays of permanent watchers selected by the public, usually butchers, strangely enough, and it was their task to watch the hunger artist day and night, three of them at a time, in case he should have some secret recourse to nourishment. This was nothing but a formality, instituted to reassure the masses, for the initiates knew well enough that during his fast the artist would never in any circumstances, not even under forcible compulsion, swallow the smallest morsel of food; the honor of his profession forbade it. Not every watcher, of course, was capable of understanding this, there were often groups of night watchers who were very lax in carrying out their duties and deliberately huddled together in a retired corner to play cards with great absorption, obviously intending to give the hunger artist the chance of a little refreshment, which they supposed he could draw from some private hoard. Nothing annoyed the artist more than such watchers; they made him miserable; they made his fast seem unendurable; sometimes he mastered his feebleness sufficiently to sing during their watch for as long as he could keep going, to show them how unjust their suspicions were. But that was of little use; they only wondered at his cleverness in being able to fill his mouth even while singing. Much more to his taste were the watchers who sat close up to the bars, who were not content with the dim night lighting of the hall but focused him in the full glare of the electric pocket torch given them by the impresario. The harsh light did not trouble him at all, in any case he could never sleep properly, and he could always drowse a little, whatever the light, at any hour, even when the hall was thronged with noisy onlookers. He was quite happy at the prospect of spending a sleepless night with such watchers; he was ready to exchange jokes with them, to tell them stories out of his nomadic life, anything at all to keep them awake and demonstrate to them again that he had no eatables in his cage and that he was fasting as not one of them could fast. But his happiest moment was when the morning came and an enormous breakfast was brought them, at his expense, on which they flung themselves with the keen appetite of healthy men after a weary night of wakefulness. Of course there were people who argued that this breakfast was an unfair attempt to bribe the watchers, but that was going rather too far, and when they were invited to take on a night's vigil without a breakfast, merely for the sake of the pause, they made themselves scarce, although they stuck stubbornly to their suspicions.

Such suspicions, anyhow, were a necessary accompaniment to the profession of fasting. No one could possibly watch the hunger artist continuously, day and night, and so no one could produce first-hand evidence that the fast had really been rigorous and continuous; only the artist himself could know that; he was therefore bound to be the sole completely satisfied spectator of his own fast. Yet for other reasons he was never satisfied; it was not perhaps mere fasting that had brought him to such skeleton thinness that many people had regretfully to keep away from his exhibitions, because the sight of him was too much for them, perhaps it was dissatisfaction with himself that had worn him down. For he alone knew, what no other initiate knew, how easy it was to fast. It was the easiest thing in the world. He made no secret of this, yet people did not believe him; at the best they set him down as modest, most of them, however, thought he was out for publicity, or else was some kind of cheat who found it easy to fast because he had discovered a way of making it easy, and then had the impudence to admit the fact, more or less. He had to put up with all that, and in the course of time had got used to it, but his inner dissatisfaction always rankled, and never yet, after any term of fasting—this must be granted to his credit—had he left the cage of his own free will. The longest period of fasting was fixed by his impresario at forty days, beyond that term he was not allowed to go, not even in great cities, and there was good reason for it, too. Experience had proved that for about forty days the interest of the public could be stimulated by a steadily increasing pressure of advertisement, but after that the town began to lose interest, sympathetic support began notably to fall off; there were of course local variations as between one town and another or one country and another, but as a general rule forty days marked the limit. So on the fortieth day the flower-bedecked cage was opened, enthusiastic spectators filled the hall, a military band played, two doctors entered the cage to measure the results of the fast, which were announced through a megaphone, and finally two young ladies appeared, blissful at having been selected for the honor, to help the hunger artist down the few steps leading to a small table on which was spread a carefully chosen invalid repast. And at this very moment the artist always turned stubborn. True, he would entrust his bony arms to the outstretched helping hands of the ladies bending over him but stand up he would not. Why stop fasting at this particular moment, after forty days of it? He had held out for a long time, an illimitably long time; why stop now, when he was in his best fasting form, or rather, not yet quite in his best fasting form? Why should he be cheated of the fame he would get for fasting longer, for being not only the record hunger artist of all time, which presumably he was already, but for beating his own record by a performance beyond human imagination, since he felt that there were no limits to his capacity for fasting? His public pretended to admire him so much, why should it have so little patience with him; if he could endure fasting longer, why shouldn't the public endure it? Besides, he was tired, he was comfortable sitting in the straw, and now he was supposed to lift himself to his full height and go down to a meal the very thought of which gave him a nausea that only the presence of the ladies kept him from betraying, and even that with an effort. And he looked up into the eyes of the ladies who were apparently so friendly and in reality so cruel, and shook his head, which felt too heavy on its strengthless neck. But then there happened yet again what always happened. The impresario came forward, without a word—for the band made speech impossible—lifted his arms in the air above the artist, as if inviting Heaven to look down upon its creature here in the straw, this suffering martyr, which indeed he was, although in quite another sense; grasped him round the emaciated waist, with exaggerated caution, so that the frail condition he was in might be appreciated; and committed him to the care of the blenching ladies, not without secretly giving him a shaking so that his legs and body tottered and swayed. The artist now submitted completely; his head lolled on his breast as if it had landed there by chance; his body was hollowed out; his legs in a spasm of self-preservation clung close to each other at the knees, yet scraped on the ground as if it were not really solid ground, as if they were only trying to find solid ground; and the whole weight of his body, a featherweight after all, relapsed onto one of the ladies, who, looking round for help and panting a little—this post of honor was not at all what she had expected it to be—first stretched her neck as far as she could to keep her face at least free from contact with the artist, then finding this impossible, and her more fortunate companion not coming to her aid but merely holding extended on her own trembling hand the little bunch of knucklebones that was the artist's, to the great delight of the spectators burst into tears and had to be replaced by an attendant who had long been stationed in readiness. Then came the food, a little of which the impresario managed to get between the artist's lips, while he sat in a kind of half-fainting trance, to the accompaniment of cheerful patter designed to distract the public's attention from the artist's condition; after that, a toast was drunk to the public, supposedly prompted by a whisper from the artist in the impresario's ear; the band confirmed it with a mighty flourish, the spectators melted away, and no one had any cause to be dissatisfied with the proceedings, no one except the hunger artist himself, he only, as always.

So he lived for many years, with small regular intervals of recuperation, in visible glory, honored by the world, yet in spite of that troubled in spirit, and all the more troubled because no one would take his trouble seriously. What comfort could he possibly need? What more could he possibly wish for? And if some good-natured person, feeling sorry for him, tried to console him by pointing out that his melancholy was probably caused by fasting, it could happen, especially when he had been fasting for some time, that he reacted with an outburst of fury and to the general alarm began to shake the bars of his cage like a wild animal. Yet the impresario had a way of punishing these outbreaks which he rather enjoyed putting into operation. He would apologize publicly for the artist's behavior, which was only to be excused, he admitted, because of the irritability caused by fasting; a condition hardly to be understood by well-fed people; then by natural transition he went on to mention the artist's equally incomprehensible boast that he could fast for much longer than he was doing; he praised the high ambition, the good will, the great self-denial undoubtedly implicit in such a statement; and then quite simply countered it by bringing out photographs, which were also on sale to the public, showing the artist on the fortieth day of a fast lying in bed almost dead from exhaustion. This perversion of the truth, familiar to the artist though it was, always unnerved him afresh and proved too much for him. What was a consequence of the premature ending of his fast was here presented as the cause of it! To fight against this lack of understanding, against a whole world of nonunderstanding, was impossible. Time and again in good faith he stood by the bars listening to the impresario, but as soon as the photographs appeared he always let go and sank with a groan back on to his straw, and the reassured public could once more come close and gaze at him.

A few years later when the witnesses of such scenes called them to mind, they often failed to understand themselves at all. For meanwhile the aforementioned change in public interest had set in; it seemed to happen almost overnight; there may have been profound causes for it, but who was going to bother about that; at any rate the pampered hunger artist suddenly found himself deserted one fine day by the amusement seekers, who went streaming past him to other more favored attractions. For the last time the impresario hurried him over half Europe to discover whether the old interest might still survive here and there; all in vain; everywhere, as if by secret agreement, a positive revulsion from professional fasting was in evidence. Of course it could not really have sprung up so suddenly as all that, and many premonitory symptoms which had not been sufficiently remarked or suppressed during the rush and glitter of success now came retrospectively to mind, but it was now too late to take any countermeasures. Fasting would surely come into fashion again at some future date, yet that was no comfort for those living in the present. What, then, was the hunger artist to do? He had been applauded by thousands in his time and could hardly come down to showing himself in a street booth at village fairs, and as for adopting another profession, he was not only too old for that but too fanatically devoted to fasting. So he took leave of the impresario, his partner in an unparalleled career, and hired himself to a large circus; in order to spare his own feelings he avoided reading the conditions of his contract.

A large circus with its enormous traffic in replacing and recruiting men, animals and apparatus can always find a use for people at any time, even for a hunger artist, provided of course that he does not ask too much, and in this particular case anyhow it was not only the artist who was taken on but his famous and well-known name as well; indeed considering the peculiar nature of his performance, which was not impaired by advancing age, it could not be objected that here was an artist past his prime, no longer at the height of his professional skill; seeking a refuge in some quiet corner of a circus; on the contrary, the hunger artist averred that he could fast as well as ever, which was entirely credible; he even alleged that if he were allowed to fast as he liked, and this was at once promised him without more ado, he could astound the world by establishing a record never yet achieved, a statement which certainly provoked a smile among the other professionals, since it left out of account the change in public opinion, which the hunger artist in his zeal conveniently forgot.

He had not, however, actually lost his sense of the real situation and took it as a matter of course that he and his cage should be stationed, not in the middle of the ring as a main attraction, but outside, near the animal cages, on a site that was after all easily accessible. Large and gaily painted placards made a frame for the cage and announced what was to be seen inside it. When the public came thronging out in the intervals to see the animals, they could hardly avoid passing the hunger artist's cage and stopping there for a moment, perhaps they might even have stayed longer had not those pressing behind them in the narrow gangway, who did not understand why they should be held up on their way towards the excitements of the menagerie, made it impossible for anyone to stand gazing quietly for any length of time. And that was the reason why the hunger artist, who had of course been looking forward to these visiting hours as the main achievement of his life, began instead to shrink from them. At first he could hardly wait for the intervals; it was exhilarating to watch the crowds come streaming his way, until only too soon—not even the most obstinate self-deception, clung to almost consciously, could hold out against the fact—the conviction was borne in upon him that these people, most of them, to judge from their actions, again and again, without exception, were all on their way to the menagerie. And the first sight of them from the distance remained the best. For when they reached his cage he was at once deafened by the storm of shouting and abuse that arose from the two contending factions, which renewed themselves continuously, of those who wanted to stop and stare at him—he soon began to dislike them more than the others—not out of real interest but only out of obstinate self-assertiveness, and those who wanted to go straight on to the animals. When the first great rush was past, the stragglers came along, and these, whom nothing could have prevented from stopping to look at him as long as they had breath, raced past with long strides, hardly even glancing at him, in their haste to get to the menagerie in time. And all too rarely did it happen that he had a stroke of luck, when some father of a family fetched up before him with his children, pointed a finger at the hunger artist and explained at length what the phenomenon meant, telling stories of earlier years when he himself had watched similar but much more thrilling performances, and the children, still rather uncomprehending, since neither inside nor outside school had they been sufficiently prepared for this lesson—what did they care about fasting?—yet showed by the brightness of their intent eyes that new and better times might be coming. Perhaps, said the hunger artist to himself many a time, things would be a little better if his cage were set not quite so near the menagerie. That made it too easy for people to make their choice, to say nothing of what he suffered from the stench of the menagerie, the animals' restlessness by night, the carrying past of raw lumps of flesh for the beasts of prey, the roaring at feeding times, which depressed him continually. But he did not dare to lodge a complaint with the management; after all, he had the animals to thank for the troops of people who passed his cage, among whom there might always be one here and there to take an interest in him, and who could tell where they might seclude him if he called attention to his existence and thereby to the fact that, strictly speaking, he was only an impediment on the way to the menagerie.

A small impediment, to be sure, one that grew steadily less. People grew familiar with the strange idea that they could be expected, in times like these, to take an interest in a hunger artist, and with this familiarity the verdict went out against him. He might fast as much as he could, and he did so; but nothing could save him now, people passed him by. Just try to explain to anyone the art of fasting! Anyone who has no feeling for it cannot be made to understand it. The fine placards grew dirty and illegible, they were torn down; the little notice board telling the number of fast days achieved, which at first was changed carefully every day, had long stayed at the same figure, for after the first few weeks even this small task seemed pointless to the staff; and so the artist simply fasted on and on, as he had once dreamed of doing, and it was no trouble to him, just as he had always foretold, but no one counted the days, no one, not even the artist himself, knew what records he was already breaking, and his heart grew heavy. And when once in a time some leisurely passer-by stopped, made merry over the old figure on the board and spoke of swindling, that was in its way the stupidest lie ever invented by indifference and inborn malice, since it was not the hunger artist who was cheating; he was working honestly, but the world was cheating him of his reward.

Many more days went by, however, and that too came to an end. An overseer's eye fell on the cage one day and he asked the attendants why this perfectly good stage should be left standing there unused with dirty straw inside it; nobody knew, until one man, helped out by the notice board, remembered about the hunger artist. They poked into the straw with sticks and found him in it. "Are you still fasting?" asked the overseer. "When on earth do you mean to stop?" "Forgive me, everybody," whispered the hunger artist; only the overseer, who had his ear to the bars, understood him. "Of course," said the overseer, and tapped his forehead with a finger to let the attendants know what state the man was in, "we forgive you." "I always wanted you to admire my fasting," said the hunger artist. "We do admire it," said the overseer, affably. "But you shouldn't admire it," said the hunger artist. "Well, then we don't admire it," said the overseer, "but why shouldn't we admire it?" "Because I have to fast, I can't help it," said the hunger artist. "What a fellow you are," said the overseer, "and why can't you help it?" "Because," said the hunger artist, lifting his head a little and speaking, with his lips pursed, as if for a kiss, right into the overseer's ear, so that no syllable might be lost, "because I couldn't find the food I liked. If I had found it, believe me, I should have made no fuss and stuffed myself like you or anyone else." These were his last words, but in his dimming eyes remained the firm though no longer proud persuasion that he was still continuing to fast.

"Well, clear this out now!" said the overseer, and they buried the hunger artist, straw and all. Into the cage they put a young panther. Even the most insensitive felt it refreshing to see this wild creature leaping around the cage that had so long been dreary. The panther was all right. The food he liked was brought him without hesitation by the attendants; he seemed not even to miss his freedom; his noble body, furnished almost to the bursting point with all that it needed, seemed to carry freedom around with it too; somewhere in his jaws it seemed to lurk; and the joy of life streamed with such ardent passion from his throat that for the onlookers it was not easy to stand the shock of it. But they braced themselves, crowded round the cage, and did not want ever to move away.

# THE BOUND MAN
## Ilse Aichinger

Sunlight on his face woke him, but made him shut his eyes again; it streamed unhindered down the slope, collected itself into rivulets, attracted swarms of flies, which flew low over his forehead, circled, sought to land, and were overtaken by fresh swarms. When he tried to whisk them away, he discovered that he was bound. A thick rope cut into his arms. He dropped them, opened his eyes again, and looked down at himself. His legs were tied all the way up to his thighs; a single length of rope was tied round his ankles, criss-crossed up his legs, and encircled his hips, his chest and his arms. He could not see where it was knotted. He showed no sign of fear or hurry, though he thought he was unable to move, until he discovered that the rope allowed his legs some free play and that round his body it was almost loose. His arms were tied to each other but not to his body, and had some free play too. This made him smile, and it occurred to him that perhaps children had been playing a practical joke on him.

He tried to feel for his knife, but again the rope cut softly into his flesh. He tried again, more cautiously this time, but his pocket was empty. Not only his knife, but the little money that he had on him, as well as his coat, were missing. His shoes had been pulled from his feet and taken too. When he moistened his lips he tasted blood, which had flowed from his temples down his cheeks, his chin, his neck, and under his shirt. His eyes were painful; if he kept them open for long he saw reddish stripes in the sky.

He decided to stand up. He drew his knees up as far as he could, rested his hands on the fresh grass and jerked himself to his feet. An elder branch stroked his cheek, the pain dazzled him, and the rope cut into his flesh. He collapsed to the ground again, half out of his mind with pain, and then tried again. He went on trying until the blood started flowing from his hidden weals. Then he lay still again for a long while and let the sun and the flies do what they liked.

When he awoke for the second time the elder bush had cast its shadow over him, and the coolness stored in it was pouring from between its branches. He must have been hit on the head. Then they must have laid him down carefully, just as a mother lays her baby behind a bush when she goes to work in the fields.

His chances all lay in the amount of free play allowed him by the rope. He dug his elbows into the ground and tested it. As soon as the rope tautened he stopped, and tried again more cautiously. If he had been able to reach the branch over his head he could have used it to drag himself to his feet, but he could not reach it. He laid his head back on the grass, rolled over, and struggled to his knees. He tested the ground with his toes, and then managed to stand up almost without effort.

A few paces away lay the path across the plateau, and in the grass were wild pinks and thistles in bloom. He tried to lift his foot to avoid trampling on them, but the rope round his ankles prevented him. He looked down at himself.

The rope was knotted at his ankles, and ran round his legs in a kind of playful pattern. He carefully bent and tried to loosen it, but, loose though it seemed to be, he could not make it any looser. To avoid treading on the thistles with his bare feet he hopped over them like a bird.

The cracking of a twig made him stop. People in this district were very prone to laughter. He was alarmed by the thought that he was in no position to defend himself. He hopped on until he reached the path. Bright fields stretched far below. He could see no sign of the nearest village, and if he could move no faster than this, night would fall before he reached it.

He tried walking and discovered that he could put one foot before another if he lifted each foot a definite distance from the ground and then put it down again before the rope tautened. In the same way he could actually swing his arms a little.

After the first step he fell. He fell right across the path, and made the dust fly. He expected this to be a sign for the long-suppressed laughter to break out, but all remained quiet. He was alone. As soon as the dust had settled he got up and went on. He looked down and watched the rope slacken, grow taut, and then slacken again.

When the first glow-worms appeared he managed to look up. He felt in control of himself again, and his impatience to reach the nearest village faded.

Hunger made him light-headed, and he seemed to be going so fast that not even a motorcycle could have overtaken him; alternatively he felt as if he were standing still and that the earth was rushing past him, like a river flowing past a man swimming against the stream. The stream carried branches which had been bent southward by the north wind, stunted young trees, and patches of grass with bright, long-stalked flowers. It ended by submerging the bushes and the young trees, leaving only the sky and the man above water level. The moon had risen, and illuminated the bare, curved summit of the plateau, the path, which was overgrown with young grass, the bound man making his way along it with quick, measured steps, and two hares, which ran across the hill just in front of him and vanished down the slope. Though the nights were still cool at this time of the year, before midnight the bound man lay down at the edge of the escarpment and went to sleep.

In the light of morning the animal-tamer who was camping with his circus in the field outside the village saw the bound man coming down the path, gazing thoughtfully at the ground. The bound man stopped and bent down. He held out one arm to help keep his balance and with the other picked up an empty wine-bottle. Then he straightened himself and stood erect again. He moved slowly, to avoid being cut by the rope, but to the circus proprietor what he did suggested the voluntary limitation of an enormous swiftness of movement. He was enchanted by its extraordinary gracefulness, and while the bound man looked about for a stone on which to break the bottle, so that he could use the splintered neck to cut the rope, the animal-tamer walked across the field and approached him. The first leaps of a young panther had never filled him with such delight.

"Ladies and gentlemen, the bound man!" His very first movements let loose a storm of applause, which out of sheer excitement caused the blood to rush to the cheeks of the animal-tamer standing at the edge of the arena. The bound man rose to his feet. His surprise whenever he did this was like that of a four-footed animal which has managed to stand on its hind legs. He knelt, stood up, jumped, and turned cartwheels. The spectators found it as astonishing as if they had seen a bird which voluntarily remained earthbound, and confined itself to hopping.

The bound man became an enormous draw. His absurd steps and little jumps, his elementary exercises in movement, made the rope dancer superfluous. His fame grew from village to village, but the motions he went through were few and always the same; they were really quite ordinary motions, which he had continually to practice in the daytime in the half-dark tent in order to retain his shackled freedom. In that he remained entirely within the limits set by his rope he was free of it, it did not confine him, but gave him wings and endowed his leaps and jumps with purpose; just as the flights of birds of passage have purpose when they take wing in the warmth of summer and hesitantly make small circles in the sky.

All the children of the neighborhood started playing the game of "bound man." They formed rival gangs, and one day the circus people found a little girl lying bound in a ditch, with a cord tied round her neck so that she could hardly breathe. They released her, and at the end of the performance that night the bound man made a speech. He announced briefly that there was no sense in being tied up in such a way that you could not jump. After that he was regarded as a comedian.

Grass and sunlight, tent pegs driven into the ground and then pulled up again, and on to the next village. "Ladies and gentlemen, the bound man!" The summer mounted toward its climax. It bent its face deeper over the fish ponds in the hollows, taking delight in its dark reflection, skimmed the surface of the rivers, and made the plain into what it was. Everyone who could walk went to see the bound man.

Many wanted a close-up view of how he was bound. So the circus proprietor announced after each performance that anyone who wanted to satisfy himself that the knots were real and the rope not made of rubber was at liberty to do so. The bound man generally waited for the crowd in the area outside the tent. He laughed or remained serious, and held out his arms for inspection. Many took the opportunity to look him in the face, others gravely tested the rope, tried the knots on his ankles, and wanted to know exactly how the lengths compared with the length of his limbs. They asked him how he had come to be tied up like that, and he answered patiently, always saying the same thing. Yes, he had been tied up, he said, and when he awoke he found that he had been robbed as well. Those who had done it must have been pressed for time, because they had tied him up somewhat too loosely for someone who was not supposed to be able to move and somewhat too tightly for someone who was expected to be able to move. But he did move, people pointed out. Yes, he replied, what else could he do?

Before he went to bed he always sat for a time in front of the fire. When the circus proprietor asked him why he didn't make up a better story he always answered that he hadn't made up that one, and blushed. He preferred staying in the shade.

The difference between him and the other performers was that when the show was over he did not take off his rope. The result was that every movement that he made was worth seeing, and the villagers used to hang about the camp for hours, just for the sake of seeing him get up from in front of the fire and roll himself in his blanket. Sometimes the sky was beginning to lighten when he saw their shadows disappear.

The circus proprietor often remarked that there was no reason why he should not be untied after the evening performance and tied up again next day. He pointed out that the rope dancers, for instance, did not stay on their rope overnight. But no one took the idea of untying him seriously.

For the bound man's fame rested on the fact that he was always bound, that whenever he washed himself he had to wash his clothes too and vice versa, and that his only way of doing so was to jump in the river just as he was every morning when the sun came out, and that he had to be careful not to go too far out for fear of being carried away by the stream.

The proprietor was well aware that what in the last resort protected the bound man from the jealousy of the other performers was his helplessness; he deliberately left them the pleasure of watching him groping painfully from stone to stone on the river bank every morning with his wet clothes clinging to him. When the proprietor's wife pointed out that even the best clothes would not stand up indefinitely to such treatment (and the bound man's clothes were by no means of the best), he replied curtly that it was not going to last forever. That was his answer to all objections—it was for the summer season only. But when he said this he was not being serious; he was talking like a gambler who has no intention of giving up his vice. In reality he would have been prepared cheerfully to sacrifice his lions and his rope dancers for the bound man.

He proved this on the night when the rope dancers jumped over the fire. Afterward he was convinced that they did it, not because it was midsummer's day, but because of the bound man, who as usual was lying and watching them with that peculiar smile that might have been real or might have been only the effect of the glow on his face. In any case no one knew anything about him because he never talked about anything that had happened to him before he emerged from the wood that day.

But that evening two of the performers suddenly picked him up by the arms and legs, carried him to the edge of the fire and started playfully swinging him to and fro, while two others held out their arms to catch him on the other side. In the end they threw him, but too short. The two men on the other side drew back—they explained afterward that they did so the better to take the shock. The result was that the bound man landed at the very edge of the flames and would have been burned if the circus proprietor had not seized his arms and quickly dragged him away to save the rope which was starting to get singed. He was certain that the object had been to burn the rope. He sacked the four men on the spot.

A few nights later the proprietor's wife was awakened by the sound of footsteps on the grass, and went outside just in time to prevent the clown from playing his last practical joke. He was carrying a pair of scissors. When he was asked for an explanation he insisted that he had had no intention of taking the bound man's life, but only wanted to cut his rope because he felt sorry for him. He was sacked too.

These antics amused the bound man because he could have freed himself if he wanted to whenever he liked, but perhaps he wanted to learn a few new jumps first. The children's rhyme: "We travel with the circus, we travel with the circus" sometimes occurred to him while he lay awake at night. He could hear the voices of spectators on the opposite bank who had been driven too far downstream on the way home. He could see the river gleaming in the moonlight, and the young shoots growing out of the thick tops of the willow trees, and did not think about autumn yet.

The circus proprietor dreaded the danger that sleep involved for the bound man. Attempts were continually made to release him while he slept. The chief culprits were sacked rope dancers, or children who were bribed for the purpose. But measures could be taken to safeguard against these. A much bigger danger was that which he represented to himself. In his dreams he forgot his rope, and was surprised by it when he woke in the darkness of morning. He would angrily try to get up, but lose his balance and fall back again. The previous evening's applause was forgotten, sleep was still too near, his head and neck too free. He was just the opposite of a hanged man—his neck was the only part of him that was free. You had to make sure that at such moments no knife was within his reach. In the early hours of the morning the circus proprietor sometimes sent his wife to see whether the bound man was all right. If he was asleep she would bend over him and feel the rope. It had grown hard from dirt and damp. She would test the amount of free play it allowed him, and touch his tender wrists and ankles.

The most varied rumors circulated about the bound man. Some said he had tied himself up and invented the story of having been robbed, and toward the end of the summer that was the general opinion. Others maintained that he had been tied up at his own request, perhaps in league with the circus proprietor. The hesitant way in which he told his story, his habit of breaking off when the talk got round to the attack on him, contributed greatly to these rumors. Those who still believed in the robbery-with-violence story were laughed at. Nobody knew what difficulties the circus proprietor had in keeping the bound man, and how often he said he had had enough and wanted to clear off, for too much of the summer had passed.

Later, however, he stopped talking about clearing off. When the proprietor's wife brought him his food by the river and asked him how long he proposed to remain with them, he did not answer. She thought he had got used, not to being tied up, but to remembering every moment that he was tied up—the only thing that anyone in his position could get used to. She asked him whether he did not think it ridiculous to be tied up all the time, but he answered that he did not. Such a variety of people—clowns, freaks, and comics, to say nothing of elephants and tigers—traveled with circuses that he did not see why a bound man should not travel with a circus too. He told her about the movements he was practicing, the new ones he had discovered, and about a new trick that had occurred to him while he was whisking flies from the animals' eyes. He described to her how he always anticipated the effect of the rope and always restrained his movements in such a way as to prevent it from ever tautening; and she knew that there were days when he was hardly aware of the rope, when he jumped down from the wagon and slapped the flanks of the horses in the morning as if he were moving in a dream. She watched him vault over the bars almost without touching them, and saw the sun on his face, and he told her that sometimes he felt as if he were not tied up at all. She answered that if he were prepared to be untied, there would never be any need for him to feel tied up. He agreed that he could be untied whenever he felt like it.

The woman ended by not knowing whether she was more concerned with the man or with the rope that tied him. She told him that he could go on traveling with the circus without his rope, but she did not believe it. For what would be the point of his antics without his rope, and what would he amount to without it? Without his rope he would leave them, and the happy days would be over. She would no longer be able to sit beside him on the stones by the river without arousing suspicion, and she knew that his continued presence, and her conversations with him, of which the rope was the only subject, depended on it. Whenever she agreed that the rope had its advantages, he would start talking about how troublesome it was, and whenever he started talking about its advantages, she would urge him to get rid of it. All this seemed as endless as the summer itself.

At other times she was worried at the thought that she was herself hastening the end by her talk. Sometimes she would get up in the middle of the night and run across the grass to where he slept. She wanted to shake him, wake him up and ask him to keep the rope. But then she would see him lying there; he had thrown off his blanket, and there he lay like a corpse, with his legs outstretched and his arms close together, with the rope tied round them. His clothes had suffered from the heat and the water, but the rope had grown no thinner. She felt that he would go on traveling with the circus until the flesh fell from him and exposed the joints. Next morning she would plead with him more ardently than ever to get rid of his rope.

The increasing coolness of the weather gave her hope. Autumn was coming, and he would not be able to go on jumping into the river with his clothes on much longer. But the thought of losing his rope, about which he had felt indifferent earlier in the season, now depressed him.

The songs of the harvesters filled him with foreboding. "Summer has gone, summer has gone." But he realized that soon he would have to change his clothes, and he was certain that when he had been untied it would be impossible to tie him up again in exactly the same way. About this time the proprietor started talking about traveling south that year.

The heat changed without transition into quiet, dry cold, and the fire was kept going all day long. When the bound man jumped down from the wagon he felt the coldness of the grass under his feet. The stalks were bent with ripeness. The horses dreamed on their feet and the wild animals, crouching to leap even in their sleep, seemed to be collecting gloom under their skins which would break out later.

On one of these days a young wolf escaped. The circus proprietor kept quiet about it, to avoid spreading alarm, but the wolf soon started raiding cattle in the neighborhood. People at first believed that the wolf had been driven to these parts by the prospect of a severe winter, but the circus soon became suspect. The proprietor could not conceal the loss of the animal from his own employees, so the truth was bound to come out before long. The circus people offered the burgomasters of the neighboring villages their aid in tracking down the beast, but all their efforts were in vain. Eventually the circus was openly blamed for the damage and the danger, and spectators stayed away.

The bound man went on performing before half-empty seats without losing anything of his amazing freedom of movement. During the day he wandered among the surrounding hills under the thin-beaten silver of the autumn sky, and, whenever he could, lay down where the sun shone longest. Soon he found a place which the twilight reached last of all, and when at last it reached him he got up most unwillingly from the withered grass. In coming down the hill he had to pass through a little wood on its southern slope, and one evening he saw the gleam of two little green lights. He knew that they came from no church window, and was not for a moment under any illusion about what they were.

He stopped. The animal came toward him through the thinning foliage. He could make out its shape, the slant of its neck, its tail which swept the ground, and its receding head. If he had not been bound, perhaps he would have tried to run away, but as it was he did not even feel fear. He stood calmly with dangling arms and looked down at the wolf's bristling coat under which the muscles played like his own underneath the rope. He thought the evening wind was still between him and the wolf when the beast sprang. The man took care to obey his rope.

Moving with the deliberate care that he had so often put to the test, he seized the wolf by the throat. Tenderness for a fellow creature arose in him, tenderness for the upright being concealed in the four-footed. In a movement that resembled the drive of a great bird (he felt a sudden awareness that flying would be possibly only if one were tied up in a special way) he flung himself at the animal and brought it to the ground. He felt a slight elation at having lost the fatal advantage of free limbs which causes men to be worsted.

The freedom he enjoyed in this struggle was having to adapt every movement of his limbs to the rope that tied him—the freedom of panthers, wolves, and the wild flowers that sway in the evening breeze. He ended up lying obliquely down the slope, clasping the animal's hind legs between his own bare feet and its head between his hands. He felt the gentleness of the faded foliage stroking the backs of his hands, and he felt his own grip almost effortlessly reaching its maximum, and he felt too how he was in no way hampered by the rope.

As he left the wood light rain began to fall and obscured the setting sun. He stopped for a while under the trees at the edge of the wood. Beyond the camp and the river he saw the fields where the cattle grazed, and the places where they crossed. Perhaps he would travel south with the circus after all. He laughed softly. It was against all reason. Even if he continued to put up with the sores that covered his joints and opened and bled when he made certain movements, his clothes would not stand up much longer to the friction of the rope.

The circus proprietor's wife tried to persuade her husband to announce the death of the wolf without mentioning that it had been killed by the bound man. She said that even at the time of his greatest popularity people would have refused to believe him capable of it, and in their present angry mood, with the nights getting cooler, they would be more incredulous than ever. The wolf had attacked a group of children at play that day, and nobody would believe that it had really been killed; for the circus proprietor had many wolves, and it was easy enough for him to hang a skin on the rail and allow free entry. But he was not to be dissuaded. He thought that the announcement of the bound man's act would revive the triumphs of the summer.

That evening the bound man's movements were uncertain. He stumbled in one of his jumps, and fell. Before he managed to get up he heard some low whistles and catcalls, rather like birds calling at dawn. He tried to get up too quickly, as he had done once or twice during the summer, with the result that he tautened his rope and fell back again. He lay still to regain his calm, and listened to the boos and catcalls growing into an uproar. "Well, bound man, and how did you kill the wolf?" they shouted, and: "Are you the man who killed the wolf?" If he had been one of them, he would not have believed it himself. He thought they had a perfect right to be angry: a circus at this time of year, a bound man, an escaped wolf, and all ending up with this. Some groups of spectators started arguing with others, but the greater part of the audience thought the whole thing a bad joke. By the time he had got to his feet there was such a hubbub that he was barely able to make out individual words.

He saw people surging up all round him, like faded leaves raised by a whirlwind in a circular valley at the center of which all was yet still. He thought of the golden sunsets of the last few days; and the sepulchral light which lay over the blight of all that he had built up during so many nights, the gold frame which the pious hang round dark, old pictures, this sudden collapse of everything, filled him with anger.

They wanted him to repeat his battle with the wolf. He said that such a thing had no place in a circus performance, and the proprietor declared that he did not keep animals to have them slaughtered in front of an audience. But the mob stormed the ring and forced them toward the cages. The proprietor's wife made her way between the seats to the exit and managed to get round to the cages from the other side. She pushed aside the attendant whom the crowd had forced to open a cage door, but the spectators dragged her back and prevented the door from being shut.

"Aren't you the woman who used to lie with him by the river in the summer?" they called out. "How does he hold you in his arms?" She shouted back at them that they needn't believe in the bound man if they didn't want to, they had never deserved him. Painted clowns were good enough for them.

The bound man felt as if the bursts of laughter were what he had been expecting ever since early May. What had smelt so sweet all through the summer now stank. But, if they insisted, he was ready to take on all the animals in the circus. He had never felt so much at one with his rope.

Gently he pushed the woman aside. Perhaps he would travel south with them after all. He stood in the open doorway of the cage, and he saw the wolf, a strong young animal, rise to its feet, and he heard the proprietor grumbling again about the loss of his exhibits. He clapped his hands to attract the animal's attention, and when it was near enough he turned to slam the cage door. He looked the woman in the face. Suddenly he remembered the proprietor's warning to suspect of murderous intentions anyone near him who had a sharp instrument in his hand. At the same moment he felt the blade on his wrists, as cool as the water of the river in autumn, which during the last few weeks he had been barely able to stand. The rope curled up in a tangle beside him while he struggled free. He pushed the woman back, but there was no point in anything he did now. Had he been insufficiently on his guard against those who wanted to release him, against the sympathy in which they wanted to lull him? Had he lain too long on the river bank? If she had cut the cord at any other moment it would have been better than this.

He stood in the middle of the cage, and rid himself of the rope like a snake discarding its skin. It amused him to see the spectators shrinking back. Did they realize that he had no choice now? Or that fighting the wolf now would prove nothing whatever? At the same time he felt all his blood rush to his feet. He felt suddenly weak.

The rope, which fell at its feet like a snare, angered the wolf more than the entry of a stranger into its cage. It crouched to spring. The man reeled, and grabbed the pistol that hung ready at the side of the cage. Then, before anyone could stop him, he shot the wolf between the eyes. The animal reared, and touched him in falling.

On the way to the river he heard the footsteps of his pursuers—spectators, the rope dancers, the circus proprietor, and the proprietor's wife, who persisted in the chase longer than anyone else. He hid in a clump of bushes and listened to them hurrying past, and later on streaming in the opposite direction back to the camp. The moon shone on the meadow; in that light its color was both of growth and of death.

When he came to the river his anger died away. At dawn it seemed to him as if lumps of ice were floating in the water, and as if snow had fallen, obliterating memory.

## Study Aids: Kafka

1. "A Hunger Artist" is a symbolic allegory in which both the total pattern and the specific details of the literal level have multiple associations and

meanings. Which details can be cited and arranged for a reading which stresses the condition and dilemma of the creative artist; for a reading which stresses the condition and dilemma of a holy man, a saint, a martyr; for a reading which stresses not a type of man, but aspects of man such as body and spirit, ideal and actual? What are the connections between these possible points of emphasis?

2. What are the attitudes and motivations of the artist himself? Why does he fast? Why does he find it easy, and why is he always disappointed? Why does he always want more? What does he want from the audience? Why does he beg forgiveness because he had to fast? Why did he not find the food he liked? Has he been free? Has he been successful? What do these attitudes and motivations symbolize?

3. In the first phase of his career what is the significance of such details as the incomprehension of the crowds, the permanent watchers, the attitudes of the ladies who assist him, the motives of the impresario, the shift in popular taste?

4. In the second phase of his career, what is the significance of such details as the position of his cage in the circus, the responses of children, the attitudes of the crowd, the condition of his cage, the situation of his final fast, the contrast between the hunger aritist and the panther who replaces him?

5. Why is the hunger artist in a cage throughout? What does this indicate, for example, about his relation to his society, his relation to his own vision and needs, his discovery at his death? What else does it indicate?

## Study Aids: Aichinger

1. What does the bound man's freedom consist of? What is his relationship to his bindings? How were they imposed, why could he not retie them? Why does he accept them? What might these conditions symbolize?

2. Why do others want to cut his bindings and free him?

3. Why does the proprietor's wife finally cut his bindings? What has been her attitude toward the rope previously? What was their relationship, and how was it shaped by the rope?

4. What does he feel in the fight with the wolf? Why does his performance suffer when his victory is announced?

5. What is the significance of the details of the story's climax: the audience's turning on him, his acceptance of their demand to face the wolf, the cutting of the rope, his shooting of the wolf, his flight?

# BARTLEBY, THE SCRIVENER
## *Herman Melville*

I am a rather elderly man. The nature of my avocations, for the last thirty years, has brought me into more than ordinary contact with what would seem an interesting and somewhat singular set of men, of whom, as yet, nothing, that I know of, has ever been written—I mean, the law-copyists, or scriveners. I have known very many of them, professionally and privately, and, if I pleased, could relate divers histories, at which good-natured gentlemen might smile, and sentimental souls might weep. But I waive the biographies of all other scriveners, for a few passages in the life of Bartleby, who was a scrivener, the strangest I ever saw, or heard of. While, of other law-copyists, I might write the complete life, of Bartleby nothing of that sort can be done. I believe that no materials exist, for a full and satisfactory biography of this man. It is an irreparable loss to literature. Bartleby was one of those beings of whom nothing is ascertainable, except from the original sources, and, in his case, those are very small. What my own astonished eyes saw of Bartleby, *that* is all I know of him, except, indeed, one vague report, which will appear in the sequel.

Ere introducing the scrivener, as he first appeared to me, it is fit I make some mention of myself, my *employés,* my business, my chambers, and general surroundings; because some such description is indispensable to an adequate understanding of the chief character about to be presented. Imprimis: I am a man who, from his youth upwards, has been filled with a profound conviction that the easiest way of life is the best. Hence, though I belong to a profession proverbially energetic and nervous, even to turbulence, at times, yet nothing of that sort have I ever suffered to invade my peace. I am one of those unambitious lawyers who never addresses a jury, or in any way draws down public applause; but, in the cool tranquillity of a snug retreat, do a snug

267

business among rich men's bonds, and mortgages, and title-deeds. All who know me, consider me an eminently *safe* man. The last John Jacob Astor, a personage little given to poetic enthusiasm, had no hesitation in pronouncing my first grand point to be prudence; my next, method. I do not speak it in vanity, but simply record the fact, that I was not unemployed in my profession by the late John Jacob Astor; a name which, I admit, I love to repeat; for it hath a rounded and orbicular sound to it, and rings like unto bullion. I will freely add, that I was not insensible to the late John Jacob Astor's good opinion.

Some time prior to the period at which this little history begins, my avocations had been largely increased. The good old office, now extinct in the State of New York, of a Master in Chancery, had been conferred upon me. It was not a very arduous office, but very pleasantly remunerative. I seldom lose my temper; much more seldom indulge in dangerous indignation at wrongs and outrages; but, I must be permitted to be rash here, and declare, that I consider the sudden and violent abrogation of the office of Master of Chancery, by the new Constitution, as a —— premature act; inasmuch as I had counted upon a life-lease of the profits, whereas I only received those of a few short years. But this is by the way.

My chambers were up stairs, at No. —— Wall Street. At one end, they looked upon the white wall of the interior of a spacious sky-light shaft, penetrating the building from top to bottom.

This view might have been considered rather tame than otherwise, deficient in what landscape painters call "life." But, if so, the view from the other end of my chambers offered, at least, a contrast, if nothing more. In that direction, my windows commanded an unobstructed view of a lofty brick wall, black by age and everlasting shade; which wall required no spy-glass to bring out its lurking beauties, but, for the benefit of all near-sighted spectators, was pushed up to within ten feet of my window-panes. Owing to the great height of the surrounding buildings, and my chambers being on the second floor, the interval between this wall and mine not a little resembled a huge square cistern.

At the period just preceding the advent of Bartleby, I had two copyists in my employment, and a promising lad as an office-boy. First, Turkey; second, Nippers; third, Ginger Nut. These may seem names, the like of which are not usually found in the Directory. In truth, they were nicknames, mutually conferred upon each other by my three clerks, and were deemed expressive of their respective persons or characters. Turkey was a short, pursy Englishman, of about my own age— that is, somewhere not far from sixty. In the morning, one might say, his face was of a fine florid hue, but after twelve o'clock, meridian— his dinner hour—it blazed like a grate full of Christmas coals; and continued blazing—but, as it were, with a gradual wane—till six o'clock, P.M., or thereabouts; after which, I saw no more of the proprietor of the face, which, gaining its meridian with the sun, seemed to set with it, to rise, culminate, and decline the following day, with the like regularity and undiminished glory. There are many singular coincidences I have known in the course of my life, not the least among which was the fact, that, exactly when Turkey displayed his fullest beams from his red and radiant countenance, just then, too, at that critical moment, began the daily period when I considered his business capacities as seriously disturbed for the remainder of the twenty-four hours. Not that he was absolutely idle, or averse to business, then; far from it. The difficulty was, he was apt to be altogether too energetic. There was a strange, inflamed, flurried, flighty recklessness of activity about him. He would be incautious in dipping his pen into his ink-stand. All his blots upon my documents were dropped there after twelve o'clock, meridian. Indeed, not only would he be reckless, and sadly given to making blots in the afternoon, but, some days, he went further, and was rather noisy. At such times, too, his face flamed with augmented blazonry, as if cannel coal had been heaped on anthracite. He made an unpleasant racket with his chair; spilled his sand-box; in mending his pens, impatiently split them all to pieces, and threw them on the floor in a sudden passion; stood up, and leaned over his table, boxing his papers about in a most indecorous manner, very sad to behold in an elderly man like him. Nevertheless, as he was in many ways a most valuable person to me, and at the time before twelve o'clock, meridian, was the quickest, steadiest creature, too, accomplishing a great deal of work in a style not easily to be matched—for these reasons, I was willing to overlook his eccentricities, though, indeed, occasionally, I remonstrated with him. I did this very gently, however, because, though the civilest, nay, the blandest and most reverential of men in the morning, yet, in the afternoon, he was disposed, upon provocation, to be slightly rash with his tongue—in fact, insolent. Now, valuing his morning services as I did, and resolved not to lose them—yet, at the same time, made uncomfortable by his inflamed ways after twelve o'clock—and being a man of peace, unwilling by my admonitions to call forth unseemly retorts from him, I took upon me, one Saturday noon (he was always worse on Saturdays) to hint to him, very kindly, that, perhaps, now that he was growing old, it might be well to abridge his labors; in short, he need not come to my chambers after twelve o'clock, but, dinner over, had best go home to his lodgings, and rest himself till tea-time. But no; he insisted upon his afternoon devotions. His countenance became intolerably fervid, as he oratorically assured me—gesticulating with a long ruler at the other end of the room—that if his services in the morning were useful, how indispensable, then, in the afternoon?

"With submission, sir," said Turkey, on this occasion. "I consider myself your right-hand man. In the morning I but marshal and deploy my columns; but in the afternoon I put myself at their head, and gallantly charge the foe, thus"—and he made a violent thrust with the ruler.

"But the blots, Turkey," intimated I.

"True; but, with submission, sir, behold these hairs! I am getting old. Surely, sir, a blot or two of a warm afternoon is not to be severely urged against gray hairs. Old age—even if it blot the page—is honorable. With submission, sir, we *both* are getting old."

This appeal to my fellow-feeling was hardly to be resisted. At all events, I saw that go he would not. So, I made up my mind to let him stay, resolving, nevertheless, to see to it that, during the afternoon, he had to do with my less important papers.

Nippers, the second on my list, was a whiskered, sallow, and, upon the whole, rather piratical-looking young man, of about five and twenty. I always deemed him the victim of two evil powers—ambition and indigestion. The ambition was evinced by a certain impatience of the duties of a mere copyist, an unwarrantable usurpation of strictly professional affairs, such as the original drawing up of legal documents. The indigestion seemed betokened in an occasional nervous testiness and grinning irritability, causing the teeth to audibly grind together over mistakes committed in copying; unnecessary maledictions, hissed, rather than spoken, in the heat of business; and especially by a continual discontent with the height of the table where he worked. Though of a very ingenious mechanical turn, Nippers could never get this table to suit him. He put chips under it, blocks of various sorts, bits of pasteboard, and at last went so far as to attempt an exquisite adjustment, by final pieces of folded blotting-paper. But no invention would answer. If, for the sake of easing his back, he brought the table lid at a sharp angle well up towards his chin, and wrote there like a man using the steep roof of a Dutch house for his desk, then he declared that it stopped the circulation in his arms. If now he lowered the table to his waistbands, and stooped over it in writing, then there was a sore aching in his back. In short, the truth of the matter was, Nippers knew not what he wanted. Or, if he wanted anything, it was to be rid of a scrivener's table altogether. Among the manifestations of his diseased ambition was a fondness he had for receiving visits from certain ambiguous-looking fellows in seedy coats, whom he called his clients. Indeed, I was aware that not only was he, at times, considerable of a ward-politician, but he occasionally did a little business at the Justices' courts, and was not unknown on the steps of the Tombs. I have good reason to believe, however, that one individual who called upon him at my chambers, and who, with a grand air, he insisted was his client, was no other than a dun, and the alleged title-deed, a bill. But, with all his failings, and the annoyances he caused me, Nippers, like his compatriot Turkey, was a very useful man to me; wrote a neat, swift hand; and, when he chose, was not deficient in a gentlemanly sort of deportment. Added to this, he always dressed in a gentlemanly sort of way; and so, incidentally, reflected credit upon my chambers. Whereas, with respect to Turkey, I had much ado to keep him from being a reproach to me. His clothes were apt to look oily, and smell of eating-houses. He wore his pantaloons very loose and baggy in summer. His coats were execrable; his hat not to be handled. But while the hat was a thing of indifference to me, inasmuch as his natural civility and deference, as a dependent Englishman, always led him to doff it the moment he entered the room, yet his coat was another matter. Concerning his coats, I reasoned with him; but with no effect. The truth was, I suppose, that a man with so small an income could not afford to sport such a lustrous face and a lustrous coat at one and the same time. As Nippers once observed, Turkey's money went chiefly for red ink. One winter day, I presented Turkey with a highly respectable-looking coat of my own—a padded gray coat, of a most comfortable warmth, and which buttoned straight up from the knee to the neck. I thought Turkey would appreciate the favor, and abate his rashness and obstreperousness of afternoons. But no; I verily believe that buttoning himself up in so downy and blanket-like a coat had a pernicious effect upon him—upon the same principle that too much oats are bad for horses. In fact, precisely as a rash, restive horse is said to feel his oats, so Turkey felt his coat. It made him insolent. He was a man whom prosperity harmed.

Though, concerning the self-indulgent habits of Turkey, I had my own private surmises, yet, touching Nippers, I was well persuaded that, whatever might be his faults in other respects, he was, at least, a temperate young man. But, indeed, nature herself seemed to have been his vintner, and, at his birth, charged him so thoroughly with an irritable, brandy-like disposition, that all subsequent potations were needless. When I consider how, amid the stillness of my chambers, Nippers would sometimes impatiently rise from his seat, and stooping over his table, spread his arms wide apart, seize the whole desk, and move it, and jerk it, with a grim, grinding motion on the floor, as if the table were a perverse voluntary agent, intent on thwarting and vexing him, I plainly perceive that, for Nippers, brandy-and-water were altogether superfluous.

It was fortunate for me that, owing to its peculiar cause—indigestion—the irritability and consequent nervousness of Nippers were mainly observable in the morning, while in the afternoon he was comparatively mild. So that, Turkey's paroxysms only coming on about twelve o'clock, I never had to do with their eccentricities at one time. Their fits relieved each other, like guards. When Nippers's was on, Turkey's was off; and *vice versa*. This was a good natural arrangement, under the circumstances.

Ginger Nut, the third on my list, was a lad, some twelve years old. His father was a car-man, ambitious of seeing his son on the bench instead of a cart, before he died. So he sent him to my office, as student at law, errand-boy, cleaner and sweeper, at the rate of one dollar a week. He had a little desk to himself, but he did not use it much. Upon inspection, the drawer exhibited a great array of the shells of various sorts of nuts. Indeed, to this quick-witted youth, the whole noble science of the law was contained in a nut-shell. Not the least among the employments of Ginger Nut, as well as one which he discharged with the most alacrity, was his duty as cake and apple purveyor for Turkey and Nippers. Copying law-papers being proverbially a dry, husky sort of business, my two scriveners were fain to moisten their mouths very often with Spitzenbergs, to be had at the numerous stalls nigh the Custom House and Post Office. Also, they sent Ginger Nut very frequently for that peculiar cake—small, flat, round, and very spicy—after which he had been named by them. Of a cold morning, when business was but dull, Turkey would gobble up scores of these cakes, as if they were mere wafers—indeed, they sell them at the rate of six or eight for a penny—the scrape of his pen blending with the crunching of the crisp particles in his mouth. Of all the fiery afternoon blunders and flurried rashnesses of Turkey, was his once moistening a ginger-cake between his lips, and clapping it on to a mortgage, for a seal. I came within an ace of dismissing him then. But he mollified me by making an oriental bow, and saying—

"With submission, sir, it was generous of me to find you in stationery on my own account."

Now my original business—that of a conveyancer and title hunter, and drawer-up of recondite documents of all sorts—was considerably increased by receiving the Master's office. There was now great work for scriveners. Not only must I push the clerks already with me, but I must have additional help.

In answer to my advertisement, a motionless young man one morning stood upon my office threshold, the door being open, for it was summer. I can see that figure now—pallidly neat, pitiably respectable, incurably forlorn! It was Bartleby.

After a few words touching his qualifications, I engaged him, glad to have among my corps of copyists a man of so singularly sedate an aspect, which I thought might operate beneficially upon the flighty temper of Turkey, and the fiery one of Nippers.

I should have stated before that ground-glass folding-doors divided my premises into two parts, one of which was occupied by my scriveners, the other by myself. According to my humor, I threw open these doors, or closed them. I resolved to assign Bartleby a corner by the folding-doors, but on my side of them, so as to have this quiet man within easy call, in case any trifling thing was to be done. I placed his desk close up to a small side-window in that part of the room, a window which originally had afforded a lateral view of certain grimy back-yards and bricks, but which, owing to subsequent erections, commanded at present no view at all, though it gave some light. Within three feet of the panes was a wall, and the light came down from far above, between two lofty buildings, as from a very small opening in a dome. Still further to a satisfactory arrangement, I procured a high green folding screen, which might entirely isolate Bartleby from my sight, though not remove him from my voice. And thus, in a manner, privacy and society were conjoined.

At first, Bartleby did an extraordinary quantity of writing. As if long famishing for something to copy, he seemed to gorge himself on my documents. There was no pause for digestion. He ran a day and night line, copying by sun-light and by candle-light. I should have been quite delighted with his application, had he been cheerfully industrious. But he wrote on silently, palely, mechanically.

It is, of course, an indispensable part of a scrivener's business to verify the accuracy of his copy, word by word. Where there are two or more scriveners in an office, they assist each other in this examination, one reading from the copy, the other holding the original. It is a very dull, wearisome, and lethargic affair. I can readily imagine that, to some sanguine temperaments, it would be altogether intolerable. For example, I cannot credit that the mettlesome poet, Byron, would have contentedly sat down with Bartleby to examine a law document of, say five hundred pages, closely written in a crimpy hand.

Now and then, in the haste of business, it had been my habit to assist in comparing some brief document myself, calling Turkey or Nippers for this purpose. One object I had, in placing Bartleby so handy to me behind the screen, was, to avail myself of his services on such trivial occasions. It was on the third day, I think, of his being with me, and before any necessity had arisen for having his own writing examined, that, being much hurried to complete a small affair I had in hand, I abruptly called to Bartleby. In my haste and natural expectancy of instant compliance, I sat with my head bent over the original on my desk, and my right hand sideways, and somewhat nervously extended with the copy, so that, immediately upon emerging from his retreat, Bartleby might snatch it and proceed to business without the least delay.

In this very attitude did I sit when I called to him, rapidly stating what it was I wanted him to do—namely, to examine a small paper with me. Imagine my surprise, nay, my consternation, when, without moving from his privacy, Bartleby, in a singularly mild, firm voice, replied, "I would prefer not to."

I sat awhile in perfect silence, rallying my stunned faculties. Immediately it occurred to me that my ears had deceived me, or Bartleby had entirely misunderstood my meaning. I repeated my request in the clearest tone I could assume; but in quite as clear a one came the previous reply, "I would prefer not to."

"Prefer not to," echoed I, rising in high excitement, and crossing the room with a stride. "What do you mean? Are you moon-struck? I want you to help me compare this sheet here—take it," and I thrust it towards him.

"I would prefer not to," said he.

I looked at him steadfastly. His face was leanly composed; his gray eye dimly calm. Not a wrinkle of agitation rippled him. Had there been the least uneasiness, anger, impatience or impertinence in his manner; in other words, had there been anything ordinarily human about him, doubtless I should have violently dismissed him from the premises. But as it was, I should have as soon thought of turning my pale plaster-of-paris bust of Cicero out of doors. I stood gazing at him awhile, as he went on with his own writing, and then reseated myself at my desk. This is very strange, thought I. What had one best do? But my business hurried me. I concluded to forget the matter for the present, reserving it for my future leisure. So calling Nippers from the other room, the paper was speedily examined.

A few days after this, Bartleby concluded four lengthy documents, being quadruplicates of a week's testimony taken before me in my High Court of Chancery. It became necessary to examine them. It was an important suit, and great accuracy was imperative. Having all things arranged, I called Turkey, Nippers, and Ginger Nut, from the next room, meaning to place the four copies in the hands of my four clerks, while I should read from the original. Accordingly, Turkey, Nippers, and Ginger Nut had taken their seats in a row, each with his document in his hand, when I called to Bartleby to join this interesting group.

"Bartleby! quick, I am waiting."

I heard a slow scrape of his chair legs on the uncarpeted floor, and soon he appeared standing at the entrance of his hermitage.

"What is wanted?" said he, mildly.

"The copies, the copies," said I, hurriedly. "We are going to examine them. There"—and I held towards him the fourth quadruplicate.

"I would prefer not to," he said, and gently disappeared behind the screen.

For a few moments I was turned into a pillar of salt, standing at the head of my seated column of clerks. Recovering myself, I advanced towards the screen, and demanded the reason for such extraordinary conduct.

"*Why* do you refuse?"

"I would prefer not to."

With any other man I should have flown outright into a dreadful passion, scorned all further words, and thrust him ignominiously from my presence. But there was something about Bartleby that not only strangely disarmed me, but, in a wonderful manner, touched and disconcerted me. I began to reason with him.

"These are your own copies we are about to examine. It is labor saving to you, because one examination will answer for your four papers. It is common usage. Every copyist is bound to help examine his copy. Is it not so? Will you not speak? Answer!"

"I prefer not to," he replied in a flutelike tone. It seemed to me that, while I had been addressing him, he carefully revolved every statement that I made; fully comprehended the meaning; could not gainsay the irresistible conclusion, but, at the same time, some paramount consideration prevailed with him to reply as he did.

"You are decided, then, not to comply with my request—a request made according to common usage and common sense?"

He briefly gave me to understand, that on that point my judgment was sound. Yes: his decision was irreversible.

It is not seldom the case that, when a man is browbeaten in some unprecedented and violently unreasonable way, he begins to stagger in his own plainest faith. He begins, as it were, vaguely to surmise that, wonderful as it may be, all the justice and all the reason is on the other side. Accordingly, if any disinterested persons are present, he turns to them for some reinforcement of his own faltering mind.

"Turkey," said I, "what do you think of this? Am I not right?"

"With submission, sir," said Turkey, in his blandest tone, "I think that you are."

"Nippers," said I, "what do *you* think of it?"

"I think I should kick him out of the office."

(The reader, of nice perceptions, will here perceive that, it being morning, Turkey's answer is couched in polite and tranquil terms, but Nippers replies in ill-tempered ones. Or, to repeat a previous sentence, Nipper's ugly mood was on duty, and Turkey's off.)

"Ginger Nut," said I, willing to enlist the smallest suffrage in my behalf, "what do *you* think of it?"

"I think, sir, he's a little *luny*," replied Ginger Nut, with a grin.

"You hear what they say," said I, turning towards the screen, "come forth and do your duty."

But he vouchsafed no reply. I pondered a moment in sore perplexity. But once more business hurried me. I determined again to postpone the consideration of this dilemma to my future leisure. With a little trouble we made out to examine the papers without Bartleby, though at every page or two Turkey deferentially dropped his opinion, that this proceeding was quite out of the common; while Nippers, twitching in his chair with a dyspeptic nervousness, ground out, between his set teeth, occasional hissing maledictions against the stubborn oaf behind the screen. And for his (Nippers's) part, this was the first and the last time he would do another man's business without pay.

Meanwhile Bartleby sat in his hermitage, oblivious to everything but his own peculiar business there.

Some days passed, the scrivener being employed upon another lengthy work. His late remarkable conduct led me to regard his ways narrowly. I observed that he never went to dinner; indeed, that he never went anywhere. As yet I had never, of my personal knowledge, known him to be outside of my office. He was a perpetual sentry in the corner. At about eleven o'clock though, in the morning, I noticed that Ginger Nut would advance toward the opening in Bartleby's screen, as if silently beckoned thither by a gesture invisible to me where I sat. The boy would then leave the office, jingling a few pence, and reappear with a handful of ginger-nuts, which he delivered in the hermitage, receiving two of the cakes for his trouble.

He lives, then, on ginger-nuts, thought I; never eats a dinner, properly speaking; he must be a vegetarian, then; but no! he never eats even vegetables, he eats nothing but ginger-nuts. My mind then ran on in reveries concerning the probable effects upon the human constitution of living entirely on ginger-nuts. Ginger-nuts are so called, because they contain ginger as one of their peculiar constituents, and the final flavoring one. Now, what was ginger? A hot, spicy thing. Was Bartleby hot and spicy? Not at all. Ginger, then, had no effect upon Bartleby. Probably he preferred it should have none.

Nothing so aggravates an earnest person as a passive resistance. If the individual so resisted be of a not inhumane temper, and the resisting one perfectly harmless in his passivity, then, in the better moods of the former, he will endeavor charitably to construe to his imagination what proves impossible to be solved by his judgment. Even so, for the most part, I regarded Bartleby and his ways. Poor fellow! thought I, he means no mischief; it is plain he intends no insolence; his aspect sufficiently evinces that his eccentricities are involuntary. He is useful to me. I can get along with him. If I turn him away, the chances are he will fall in with some less-indulgent employer, and then he will be rudely treated, and perhaps driven forth miserably to starve. Yes. Here I can cheaply purchase a delicious self-approval. To befriend Bartleby; to humor him in his strange willfulness, will cost me little or nothing, while I lay up in my soul what will eventually prove a sweet morsel for my conscience. But this mood was not invariable with me. The passiveness of Bartleby sometimes irritated me. I felt strangely goaded on to encounter him in new opposition—to elicit some angry spark from him answerable to my own. But, indeed, I might as well have essayed to strike fire with my knuckles against a bit of Windsor soap. But one afternoon the evil impulse mastered me, and the following little scene ensued:

"Bartleby," said I, "when those papers are all copied, I will compare them with you."

"I would prefer not to."

"How? Surely you do not mean to persist in that mulish vagary?"

No answer.

I threw open the folding-doors near by, and, turning upon Turkey and Nippers, exclaimed:

"Bartleby a second time says, he won't examine his papers. What do you think of it, Turkey?"

It was afternoon, be it remembered. Turkey sat glowing like a brass boiler; his bald head steaming; his hands reeling among his blotted papers.

"Think of it?" roared Turkey; "I think I'll just step behind his screen, and black his eyes for him!"

So saying, Turkey rose to his feet and threw his arms into a pugilistic position. He was hurrying away to make good his promise, when I detained him, alarmed at the effect of incautiously rousing Turkey's combativeness after dinner.

"Sit down, Turkey," said I, "and hear what Nippers has to say. What do you think of it, Nippers? Would I not be justified in immediately dismissing Bartleby?"

"Excuse me, that is for you to decide, sir. I think his conduct quite unusual, and, indeed, unjust, as regards Turkey and myself. But it may only be a passing whim."

"Ah," exclaimed I, "you have strangely changed your mind, then—you speak very gently of him now."

"All beer," cried Turkey; "gentleness is effects of beer—Nippers and I dined together to-day. You see how gentle *I* am, sir. Shall I go and black his eyes?"

"You refer to Bartleby, I suppose. No, not to-day, Turkey," I replied; "pray, put up your fists."

I closed the doors, and again advanced towards Bartleby. I felt additional incentives tempting me to my fate. I burned to be rebelled against again. I remembered that Bartleby never left the office.

"Bartleby," said I, "Ginger Nut is away; just step around to the Post Office, won't you? (it was but a three minutes' walk), and see if there is anything for me."

"I would prefer not to."

"You *will* not?"

"I *prefer* not."

I staggered to my desk, and sat there in a deep study. My blind inveteracy returned. Was there any other thing in which I could procure myself to be ignominiously repulsed by this lean, penniless wight? —my hired clerk? What added thing is there, perfectly reasonable, that he will be sure to refuse to do?

"Bartleby!"

No answer.

"Bartleby," in a louder tone.

No answer.

"Bartleby," I roared.

Like a very ghost, agreeable to the laws of magical invocation, at the third summons, he appeared at the entrance of his hermitage.

"Go to the next room, and tell Nippers to come to me."

"I prefer not to," he respectfully and slowly said, and mildly disappeared.

"Very good, Bartleby," said I, in a quiet sort of serenely-severe self-possessed tone, intimating the unalterable purpose of some terrible retribution very close at hand. At the moment I half intended something of the kind. But upon the whole, as it was drawing towards my dinner-hour, I thought it best to put on my hat and walk home for the day, suffering much from perplexity and distress of mind.

Shall I acknowledge it? The conclusion of this whole business was, that it soon became a fixed fact of my chambers, that a pale young scrivener, by the name of Bartleby, had a desk there; that he copied for me at the usual rate of four cents a folio (one hundred words); but he was permanently exempt from examining the work done by him, that duty being transferred to Turkey and Nippers, out of compliment, doubtless, to their superior acuteness; moreover, said Bartleby was never, on any account, to be dispatched on the most trivial errand of any sort; and that even if entreated to take upon him such a matter, it was generally understood that he would "prefer not to"—in other words, that he would refuse point-blank.

As days passed on, I became considerably reconciled to Bartleby. His steadiness, his freedom from all dissipation, his incessant industry (except when he chose to throw himself into a standing revery behind his screen), his great stillness, his unalterableness of demeanor under all circumstances, made him a valuable acquisition. One prime thing was this—*he was always there*—first in the morning, continually through the day, and the last at night. I had a singular confidence in his honesty. I felt my most precious papers perfectly safe in his hands. Sometimes, to be sure, I could not, for the very soul of me, avoid falling into sudden spasmodic passions with him. For it was exceeding difficult to bear in mind all the time those strange peculiarities, privileges, and unheard-of exemptions, forming the tacit stipulations on Bartleby's part under which he remained in my office. Now and then, in the eagerness of dispatching pressing business, I would inadvertently summon Bartleby, in a short, rapid tone, to put his finger, say, on the incipient tie of a bit of red tape with which I was about compressing some papers. Of course, from behind the screen the usual answer, "I prefer not to," was sure to come; and then, how could a human creature, with the common infirmities of our nature, refrain from bitterly exclaiming upon such perverseness—such unreasonableness. However, every added repulse of this sort which I received only tended to lessen the probability of my repeating the inadvertence.

Here it must be said, that according to the custom of most legal gentlemen occupying chambers in densely-populated law buildings, there were several keys to my door. One was kept by a woman residing in the attic, which person weekly scrubbed and daily swept and dusted my apartments. Another was kept by Turkey for convenience sake. The third I sometimes carried in my own pocket. The fourth I knew not who had.

Now, one Sunday morning I happened to go to Trinity Church, to hear a celebrated preacher, and finding myself rather early on the ground I thought I would walk around to my chambers for a while. Luckily I had my key with me; but upon applying it to the lock, I found it resisted by something inserted from the inside. Quite surprised, I called out; when to my consternation a key was turned from within; and thrusting his lean visage at me, and holding the door ajar, the apparition of Bartleby appeared, in his shirt sleeves, and otherwise in a strangely tattered deshabille, saying quietly that he was sorry, but he was deeply engaged just then, and—preferred not admitting me at present. In a brief word or two, he moreover added, that perhaps I had better walk around the block two or three times, and by that time he would probably have concluded his affairs.

Now, the utterly unsurmised appearance of Bartleby, tenanting my law-chambers of a Sunday morning, and with his cadaverously gentlemanly *nonchalance,* yet withal firm and self-possessed, had such a strange effect upon me, that incontinently I slunk away from my own door, and did as desired. But not without sundry twinges of impotent rebellion against the mild effrontery of this unaccountable scrivener. Indeed, it was his wonderful mildness chiefly, which not only disarmed me, but unmanned me as it were. For I consider that one, for the time, is a sort of unmanned when he tranquilly permits his hired clerk to dictate to him, and order him away from his own premises. Furthermore, I was full of uneasiness as to what Bartleby could possibly be doing in my office in his shirt sleeves, and in an otherwise dismantled condition of a Sunday morning. Was anything amiss going on? Nay, that was out of the question. It was not to be thought of for a moment that Bartleby was an immoral person. But what could he be doing there?—copying? Nay again, whatever might be his eccentricities, Bartleby was an eminently decorous person. He would be the last man to sit down to his desk in any state approaching to nudity. Besides, it was Sunday; and there was something about Bartleby that forbade the supposition that he would by any secular occupation violate the proprieties of the day.

Nevertheless, my mind was not pacified; and full of a restless curiosity, at last I returned to the door. Without hindrance I inserted my key, opened it, and entered. Bartleby was not to be seen. I looked round anxiously, peeped behind his screen; but it was very plain that he was gone. Upon more closely examining the place, I surmised that for an indefinite period Bartleby must have ate, dressed, and slept in my office, and that, too, without plate, mirror, or bed. The cushioned seat of a rickety old sofa in one corner bore the faint impress of a lean, reclining form. Rolled away under his desk, I found a blanket; under the empty grate, a blacking box and brush; on a chair, a tin basin, with soap and a ragged towel; in a newspaper a few crumbs of ginger-nuts and a morsel of cheese. Yes, thought I, it is evident enough that Bartleby has been making his home here, keeping bachelor's hall all by himself. Immediately then the thought came sweeping across me, what miserable friendlessness and loneliness are here revealed! His poverty is great; but his solitude, how horrible! Think of it. Of a Sunday, Wall Street is deserted as Petra; and every night of every day it is an emptiness. This building, too, which of week-days hums with industry and life, at nightfall echoes with sheer vacancy, and all through Sunday is forlorn. And here Bartleby makes his home; sole spectator of a solitude which he has seen all populous—a sort of innocent and transformed Marius brooding among the ruins of Carthage!

For the first time in my life a feeling of over-powering stinging melancholy seized me. Before, I had never experienced aught but a not unpleasing sadness. The bond of a common humanity now drew me irresistibly to gloom. A fraternal melancholy! For both I and Bartleby were sons of Adam. I remembered the bright silks and sparkling faces I had seen that day, in gala trim, swan-like sailing down the Mississippi of Broadway; and I contrasted them with the pallid copyist, and thought to myself, Ah, happiness courts the light, so we deem the world is gay; but misery hides aloof, so we deem that misery there is none. These sad fancyings—chimeras, doubtless, of a sick and silly brain—led on to other and more special thoughts, concerning the eccentricities of Bartleby. Presentiments of strange discoveries hovered round me. The scrivener's pale form appeared to me laid out, among uncaring strangers, in its shivering winding sheet.

Suddenly I was attracted to Bartleby's closed desk, the key in open sight left in the lock.

I mean no mischief, seek the gratification of no heartless curiosity, thought I; besides, the desk is mine, and its contents, too, so I will make bold to look within. Everything was methodically arranged, the papers smoothly placed. The pigeon-holes were deep, and removing  the files of documents, I groped into their recesses. Presently I felt something there, and dragged it out. It was an old bandanna handkerchief, heavy and knotted. I opened it, and saw it was a savings bank.

I now recalled all the quiet mysteries which I had noted in the man. I remembered that he never spoke but to answer; that, though at intervals he had considerable time to himself, yet I had never seen him reading—no, not even a newspaper; that for long periods he would stand looking out, at his pale window behind the screen, upon the dead brick wall; I was quite sure he never visited any refectory or eating house; while his pale face clearly indicated that he never drank beer like Turkey, or tea and coffee even, like other men; that he never went anywhere in particular that I could learn; never went out for a walk, unless, indeed, that was the case at present; that he had declined telling who he was, or whence he came, or whether he had any relatives in the world; that though so thin and pale, he never complained of ill health. And more than all, I remembered a certain unconscious air of pallid—how shall I call it?—of pallid haughtiness, say, or rather an austere reserve about him, which had positively awed me into my tame compliance with his eccentricities, when I had feared to ask him to do the slightest incidental thing for me, even though I might know, from his long-continued motionlessness, that behind his screen he must be standing in one of those dead-wall reveries of his.

Revolving all these things, and coupling them with the recently discovered fact, that he made my office his constant abiding place and home, and not forgetful of his morbid moodiness; revolving all these things, a prudential feeling began to steal over me. My first emotions had been those of pure melancholy and sincerest pity; but just in proportion as the forlornness of Bartleby grew and grew to my imagination, did that same melancholy merge into fear, that pity into repulsion. So true it is, and so terrible too, that up to a certain point the thought or sight of misery enlists our best affections; but, in certain special cases, beyond that point it does not. They err who would assert that invariably this is owing to the inherent selfishness of the human heart. It rather proceeds from a certain hopelessness of remedying excessive and organic ill. To a sensitive being, pity is not seldom pain. And when at last it is perceived that such pity cannot lead to effectual succor, common sense bids the soul to be rid of it. What I saw that morning persuaded me that the scrivener was the victim of innate and incurable disorder. I might give alms to his body; but his body did not pain him; it was his soul that suffered, and his soul I could not reach.

I did not accomplish the purpose of going to Trinity Church that morning. Somehow, the things I had seen disqualified me for the time from church-going. I walked homeward, thinking what I would do with Bartleby. Finally, I resolved upon this—I would put certain calm questions to him the next morning, touching his history, etc., and if he declined to answer them openly and unreservedly (and I supposed he would prefer not), then to give him a twenty dollar bill over and above whatever I might owe him, and tell him his services were no longer required; but that if in any other way I could assist him, I would be happy to do so, especially if he desired to return to his native place, wherever that might be, I would willingly help to defray the expenses. Moreover, if, after reaching home, he found himself at any time in want of aid, a letter from him would be sure of a reply.

The next morning came.

"Bartleby," said I, gently calling to him behind his screen.

No reply.

"Bartleby," said I, in a still gentler tone, "come here; I am not going to ask you to do anything you would prefer not to do—I simply wish to speak to you."

Upon this he noiselessly slid into view.

"Will you tell me, Bartleby, where you were born?"

"I would prefer not to."

"Will you tell me *anything* about yourself?"

"I would prefer not to."

"But what reasonable objection can you have to speak to me? I feel friendly towards you."

He did not look at me while I spoke, but kept his glance fixed upon my bust of Cicero, which, as I then sat, was directly behind me, some six inches above my head.

"What is your answer, Bartleby," said I, after waiting a considerable time for a reply, during which his countenance remained immovable, only there was the faintest conceivable tremor of the white attenuated mouth.

"At present I prefer to give no answer," he said, and retired into his hermitage.

It was rather weak in me I confess, but his manner, on this occasion, nettled me. Not only did there seem to lurk in it a certain calm disdain, but his perverseness seemed ungrateful, considering the undeniable good usage and indulgence he had received from me.

Again I sat ruminating what I should do. Mortified as I was at his behavior, and resolved as I had been to dismiss him when I entered my office, nevertheless I strangely felt something superstitious knocking at my heart, and forbidding me to carry out my purpose, and denouncing me for a villain if I dared to breathe one bitter word against this forlornest of mankind. At last, familiarly drawing my chair behind his screen, I sat down and said: "Bartleby, never mind, then, about revealing your history; but let me entreat you, as a friend, to comply as far as may be with the usages of this office. Say now, you will help to examine papers to-morrow or next day: in short, say now, that in a day or two you will begin to be a little reasonable:—say so, Bartleby."

"At present I would prefer not to be a little reasonable," was his mildly cadaverous reply.

Just then the folding-doors opened, and Nippers approached. He seemed suffering from an unusually bad night's rest, induced by severer indigestion than common. He overheard those final words of Bartleby.

"*Prefer not*, eh?" gritted Nippers—"I'd *prefer* him, if I were you, sir," addressing me—"I'd *prefer* him; I'd give him preferences, the stubborn mule! What is it, sir, pray, that he *prefers* not to do now?"

Bartleby moved not a limb.

"Mr. Nippers," said I, "I'd prefer that you would withdraw for the present."

Somehow, of late, I had got into the way of involuntarily using this word "prefer" upon all sorts of not exactly suitable occasions. And I trembled to think that my contact with the scrivener had already and seriously affected me in a mental way. And what further and deeper aberration might it not yet produce? This apprehension had not been without efficacy in determining me to summary measures.

As Nippers, looking very sour and sulky, was departing, Turkey blandly and deferentially approached.

"With submission, sir," said he, "yesterday I was thinking about Bartleby here, and I think that if he would but prefer to take a quart of good ale every day, it would do much towards mending him, and enabling him to assist in examining his papers."

"So you have got the word, too," said I, slightly excited.

"With submission, what word, sir?" asked Turkey, respectfully crowding himself into the contracted space behind the screen, and by so doing, making me jostle the scrivener. "What word, sir?"

"I would prefer to be left alone here," said Bartleby, as if offended at being mobbed in his privacy.

"*That's* the word, Turkey," said I—"*that's* it."

"Oh, *prefer*? oh yes—queer word. I never use it myself. But sir, as I was saying, if he would but prefer—"

"Turkey," interrupted I, "you will please withdraw."

"Oh, certainly, sir, if you prefer that I should."

As he opened the folding-door to retire. Nippers at his desk caught a glimpse of me, and asked whether I would prefer to have a certain paper copied on blue paper or white. He did not in the least roguishly accent the word "prefer." It was plain that it involuntarily rolled from his tongue. I thought to myself, surely I must get rid of a demented man, who already has in some degree turned the tongues, if not the heads of myself and clerks. But I thought it prudent not to break the dismission at once.

The next day I noticed that Bartleby did nothing but stand at his window in his dead-wall revery. Upon asking him why he did not write, he said that he had decided upon doing no more writing.

"Why, how now? what next?" exclaimed I, "do no more writing?"

"No more."

"And what is the reason?"

"Do you not see the reason for yourself?" he indifferently replied.

I looked steadfastly at him, and perceived that his eyes looked dull and glazed. Instantly it occurred to me, that his unexampled diligence in copying by his dim window for the first few weeks of his stay with me might have temporarily impaired his vision. 

I was touched. I said something in condolence with him. I hinted that of course he did wisely in abstaining from writing for a while; and urged him to embrace that opportunity of taking wholesome exercise in the open air. This, however, he did not do. A few days after this, my other clerks being absent, and being in a great hurry to dispatch certain letters by the mail, I thought that, having nothing else earthly to do, Bartleby would surely be less inflexible than usual, and carry these letters to the post-office. But he blankly declined. So, much to my inconvenience, I went myself. 

Still added days went by. Whether Bartleby's eyes improved or not, I could not say. To all appearance, I thought they did. But when I asked him if they did, he vouchsafed no answer. At all events, he would do no copying. At last, in reply to my urgings, he informed me that he had permanently given up copying. 

"What!" exclaimed I; "suppose your eyes should get entirely well—better than ever before—would you not copy then?"

"I have given up copying," he answered, and slid aside.

He remained as ever, a fixture in my chamber. Nay—if that were possible—he became still more of a fixture than before. What was to be done? He would do nothing in the office; why should he stay there? In plain fact, he had now become a millstone to me; not only useless as a necklace, but afflictive to bear. Yet I was sorry for him. I speak less than truth when I say that, on his own account, he occasioned me uneasiness. If he would but have named a single relative or friend, I would instantly have written, and urged their taking the poor fellow away to some convenient retreat. But he seemed alone, absolutely alone in the universe. A bit of wreck in the mid-Atlantic. At length, necessities connected with my business tyrannized over all other considerations. Decently as I could, I told Bartleby that in six days' time he must unconditionally leave the office. I warned him to take measures, in the interval, for procuring some other abode. I offered to assist him in this endeavor, if he himself would but take the first step towards a removal. "And when you finally quit me, Bartleby," added I, "I shall see that you go not away entirely unprovided. Six days from this hour, remember."

At the expiration of that period, I peeped behind the screen, and lo! Bartleby was there.

I buttoned up my coat, balanced myself; advanced slowly towards him, touched his shoulder, and said, "The time has come; you must quit this place; I am sorry for you; here is money; but you must go."

"I would prefer not," he replied, with his back still towards me.

"You *must.*"

He remained silent.

Now I had an unbounded confidence in this man's common honesty. He had frequently restored to me sixpences and shillings carelessly dropped upon the floor, for I am apt to be very reckless in such shirt-button affairs. The proceeding, then, which followed will not be deemed extraordinary.

"Bartleby," said I, "I owe you twelve dollars on account; here are thirty-two; the odd twenty are yours—Will you take it?" and I handed the bills towards him.

But he made no motion.

"I will leave them here, then," putting them under a weight on the table. Then taking my hat and cane and going to the door, I tranquilly turned and added—"After you have removed your things from these offices, Bartleby, you will of course lock the door—since every one is now gone for the day but you—and if you please, slip your key underneath the mat, so that I may have it in the morning. I shall not see you again; so good-bye to you. If, hereafter, in your new place of abode, I can be of any service to you, do not fail to advise me by letter. Good-bye, Bartleby, and fare you well."

But he answered not a word; like the last column of some ruined temple, he remained standing mute and solitary in the middle of the otherwise deserted room.

As I walked home in a pensive mood, my vanity got the better of my pity. I could not but highly plume myself on my masterly management in getting rid of Bartleby. Masterly I call it, and such it must appear to any dispassionate thinker. The beauty of my procedure seemed to consist in its perfect quietness. There was no vulgar bullying, no bravado of any sort, no choleric hectoring, and striding to and fro across the apartment, jerking out vehement commands for Bartleby to bundle himself off with his beggarly traps. Nothing of the kind. Without loudly bidding Bartleby depart—as an inferior genius might have done—I *assumed* the ground that depart he must; and upon that assumption built all I had to say. The more I thought over my procedure, the more I was charmed with it. Nevertheless, next morning, upon awakening, I had my doubts—I had somehow slept off the fumes of vanity. One of the coolest and wisest hours a man has, is just after he awakes in the morning. My procedure seemed as sagacious as ever—but only in theory. How it would prove in practice—there was the rub. It was truly a beautiful thought to have assumed Bartleby's departure; but, after all, that assumption was simply my own, and none of Bartleby's.

The great point was, not whether I had assumed that he would quit me, but whether he would prefer to do so. He was more a man of preferences than assumptions.

After breakfast, I walked down town, arguing the probabilities *pro* and *con*. One moment I thought it would prove a miserable failure, and Bartleby would be found all alive at my office as usual; the next moment it seemed certain that I should find his chair empty. And so I kept veering about. At the corner of Broadway and Canal Street, I saw quite an excited group of people standing in earnest conversation.

"I'll take odds he doesn't," said a voice as I passed.

"Doesn't go?—done!" said I, "put up your money."

I was instinctively putting my hand in my pocket to produce my own, when I remembered that this was an election day. The words I had overheard bore no reference to Bartleby, but to the success or non-success of some candidate for the mayoralty. In my intent frame of mind, I had, as it were, imagined that all Broadway shared in my excitement, and were debating the same question with me. I passed on, very thankful that the uproar of the street screened my momentary absent-mindedness.

As I had intended, I was earlier than usual at my office door. I stood listening for a moment. All was still. He must be gone. I tried the knob. The door was locked. Yes, my procedure had worked to a charm; he indeed must be vanished. Yet a certain melancholy mixed with this: I was almost sorry for my brilliant success. I was fumbling under the door mat for the key, which Bartleby was to have left there for me, when accidentally my knee knocked against a panel, producing a summoning sound, and in response a voice came to me from within—"Not yet; I am occupied."

It was Bartleby.

I was thunderstruck. For an instant I stood like the man who, pipe in mouth, was killed one cloudless afternoon long ago in Virginia, by summer lightning; at his own warm open window he was killed, and remained leaning out there upon the dreamy afternoon, till some one touched him, when he fell.

"Not gone!" I murmured at last. But again obeying that wondrous ascendancy which the inscrutable scrivener had over me, and from which ascendancy, for all my chafing, I could not completely escape, I slowly went down stairs and out into the street, and while walking round the block, considered what I should next do in this unheard-of perplexity. Turn the man out by an actual thrusting I could not; to drive him away by calling him hard names would not do; calling in the police was an unpleasant idea; and yet, permit him to enjoy his cadaverous triumph over me—this, too, I could not think of. What was to be done? or, if nothing could be done, was there anything further that I could *assume* in the matter? Yes, as before I had prospectively assumed that Bartleby would depart, so now I might retrospectively assume that departed he was. In the legitimate carrying out of this assumption, I might enter my office in a great hurry, and pretending not to see Bartleby at all, walk straight against him as if he were air. Such a proceeding would in a singular degree have the appearance of a home-thrust. It was hardly possible that Bartleby could withstand such an application of the doctrine of assumptions. But upon second thoughts the success of the plan seemed rather dubious. I resolved to argue the matter over with him again.

"Bartleby," said I, entering the office, with a quietly severe expression, "I am seriously displeased. I am pained, Bartleby. I had thought better of you. I had imagined you of such a gentlemanly organization, that in any delicate dilemma a slight hint would suffice—in short, an assumption. But it appears I am deceived. Why," I added, unaffectedly starting, "you have not even touched that money yet," pointing to it, just where I had left it the evening previous.

He answered nothing.

"Will you, or will you not, quit me?" I now demanded in a sudden passion, advancing close to him.

"I would prefer *not* to quit you," he replied, gently emphasizing the *not*.

"What earthly right have you to stay here? Do you pay any rent? Do you pay my taxes? Or is this property ours?"

He answered nothing.

"Are you ready to go on and write now? Are your eyes recovered? Could you copy a small paper for me this morning? or help examine a few lines? or step round to the post-office? In a word, will you do anything at all, to give a coloring to your refusal to depart the premises?"

He silently retired into his hermitage.

I was now in such a state of nervous resentment that I thought it but prudent to check myself at present from further demonstrations. Bartleby and I were alone. I remembered the tragedy of the unfortunate Adams and the still more unfortunate Colt in the solitary office of the latter; and how poor Colt, being dreadfully incensed by Adams, and imprudently permitting himself to get wildly excited, was at unawares hurried into his fatal act—an act which certainly no man could possibly deplore more than the actor himself. Often it had occurred to me in my ponderings upon the subject, that had that altercation taken place in the public street, or at a private residence, it would not have terminated as it did. It was the circumstance of being alone in a solitary office, up stairs, of a building entirely unhallowed by humanizing domestic associations—an uncarpeted office, doubtless, of a dusty, haggard sort of appearance—this it must have been, which greatly helped to enhance the irritable desperation of the hapless Colt.

But when this old Adam of resentment rose in me and tempted me concerning Bartleby, I grappled him and threw him. How? Why, simply by recalling the divine injunction: "A new commandment give I unto you, that ye love one another." Yes, this it was that saved me. Aside from higher considerations, charity often operates as a vastly wise and prudent principle—a great safeguard to its possessor. Men have committed murder for jealousy's sake, and anger's sake, and hatred's sake, and selfishness' sake, and spiritual pride's sake; but no man, that ever I heard of, ever committed a diabolical murder for sweet charity's sake. Mere self-interest, then, if no better motive can be enlisted, should, especially with high-tempered men, prompt all beings to charity and philanthropy. At any rate, upon the occasion in question, I strove to drown my exasperated feelings towards the scrivener by benevolently construing his conduct. Poor fellow, poor fellow! thought I, he don't mean anything; and besides, he has seen hard times, and ought to be indulged.

I endeavored, also, immediately to occupy myself, and at the same time to comfort my despondency. I tried to fancy, that in the course of the morning, at such time as might prove agreeable to him, Bartleby, of his own free accord, would emerge from his hermitage and take up some decided line of march in the direction of the door. But no. Half-past twelve o'clock came; Turkey began to glow in the face, overturn his inkstand, and become generally obstreperous; Nippers abated down into quietude and courtesy; Ginger Nut munched his noon apple; and Bartleby remained standing at his window in one of his profoundest dead-wall reveries. Will it be credited? Ought I to acknowledge it? That afternoon I left the office without saying one further word to him.

Some days now passed, during which, at leisure intervals I looked a little into "Edwards on the Will," and "Priestly on Necessity." Under the circumstances, those books induced a salutary feeling. Gradually I slid into the persuasion that these troubles of mine, touching the scrivener, had been all predestinated from eternity, and Bartleby was billeted upon me for some mysterious purpose of an all-wise Providence, which it was not for a mere mortal like me to fathom. Yes, Bartleby, stay there behind your screen, thought I; I shall persecute you no more; you are harmless and noiseless as any of these old chairs; in short, I never feel so private as when I know you are here. At last I see it, I feel it; I penetrated to the predestinated purpose of my life. I am content. Others may have loftier parts to enact; but my mission in this world, Bartleby, is to furnish you with office-room for such period as you may see fit to remain.

I believe that this wise and blessed frame of mind would have continued with me, had it not been for the unsolicited and uncharitable remarks obtruded upon me by my professional friends who visited the rooms. But thus it often is, that the constant friction of illiberal minds wears out at last the best resolves of the more generous. Though to be sure, when I reflected upon it, it was not strange that people entering my office should be struck by the peculiar aspect of the unaccountable Bartleby, and so be tempted to throw out some sinister observations concerning him. Sometimes an attorney, having business with me, and calling at my office, and finding no one but the scrivener there, would undertake to obtain some sort of precise information from him touching my whereabouts; but without heeding his idle talk, Bartleby would remain standing immovable in the middle of the room. So after contemplating him in that position for a time, the attorney would depart, no wiser than he came.

Also, when a reference was going on, and the room full of lawyers and witnesses, and business driving fast, some deeply-occupied legal gentleman present, seeing Bartleby wholly unemployed, would request him to run round to his (the legal gentleman's) office and fetch some papers for him. Thereupon, Bartleby would tranquilly decline, and yet remain idle as before. Then the lawyer would give a great stare, and turn to me. And what could I say? At least I was made aware that all through the circle of my professional acquaintance, a whisper of wonder was running round, having reference to the strange creature I kept at my office. This worried me very much. And as the idea came upon me of his possibly turning out a long-lived man, and keep occupying my chambers, and denying my authority; and perplexing my visitors; and scandalizing my professional reputation, and casting a general gloom over the premises; keeping soul and body together to the last upon his savings (for doubtless he spent but half a dime a day), and in the end perhaps outlive me, and claim possession of my office by right of his perpetual occupancy: as all these dark anticipations crowded upon me more and more, and my friends continually intruded their relentless remarks upon the apparition in my room; a great change was wrought in me. I resolved to gather all my faculties together, and forever rid me of this intolerable incubus.

Ere revolving any complicated project, however, adapted to this end, I first simply suggested to Bartleby the propriety of his permanent departure. In a calm and serious tone, I commended the idea to his careful and mature consideration. But, having taken three days to meditate upon it, he apprised me, that his original determination remained the same; in short, that he still preferred to abide with me.

What shall I do? I now said to myself, buttoning up my coat to the last button. What shall I do? what ought I to do? what does conscience say I *should* do with this man, or, rather, ghost. Rid myself of him, I must; go, he shall. But how? You will not thrust him, the poor, pale, passive mortal—you will not thrust such a helpless creature out of your door? you will not dishonor yourself by such cruelty? No, I will not, I cannot do that. Rather would I let him live and die here, and then mason up his remains in the wall. What, then, will you do? For all your coaxing, he will not budge. Bribes he leaves under your own paperweight on your table; in short, it is quite plain that he prefers to cling to you.

Then something severe, something unusual must be done. What! surely you will not have him collared by a constable, and commit his innocent pallor to the common jail? And upon what ground could you procure such a thing to be done?—a vagrant, is he? What! he a vagrant, a wanderer, who refuses to budge? It is because he will *not* be a vagrant, then, that you seek to count him *as* a vagrant. That is too absurd. No visible means of support: there I have him. Wrong again: for indubitably he *does* support himself, and that is the only unanswerable proof that any man can show of his possessing the means so to do. No more, then. Since he will not quit me, I must quit him. I will change my offices; I will move elsewhere, and give him fair notice, that if I find him on my new premises I will then proceed against him as a common trespasser.

Acting accordingly, next day I thus addressed him: "I find these chambers too far from the City Hall; the air is unwholesome. In a word, I propose to remove my offices next week, and shall no longer require your services. I tell you this now, in order that you may seek another place."

He made no reply, and nothing more was said.

On the appointed day I engaged carts and men, proceeded to my chambers, and, having but little furniture, everything was removed in a few hours. Throughout, the scrivener remained standing behind the screen, which I directed to be removed the last thing. It was withdrawn; and, being folded up like a huge folio, left him the motionless occupant of a naked room. I stood in the entry watching him a moment, while something from within me upbraided me.

I re-entered, with my hand in my pocket—and—and my heart in my mouth.

"Good-bye, Bartleby; I am going—good-bye, and God some way bless you; and take that," slipping something in his hand. But it dropped upon the floor, and then—strange to say—I tore myself from him whom I had so longed to be rid of.

Established in my new quarters, for a day or two I kept the door locked, and started at every footfall in the passages. When I returned to my rooms, after any little absence, I would pause at the threshold for an instant, and attentively listen, ere applying my key. But these fears were needless. Bartleby never came nigh me.

I thought all was going well, when a perturbed-looking stranger visited me, inquiring whether I was the person who had recently occupied rooms at No. — Wall Street.

Full of forebodings, I replied that I was.

"Then, sir," said the stranger, who proved a lawyer, "you are responsible for the man you left there. He refuses to do any copying; he refuses to do anything; he says he prefers not to; and he refuses to quit the premises."

"I am very sorry, sir," said I, with assumed tranquillity, but an inward tremor, "but, really, the man you allude to is nothing to me—he is no relation or apprentice of mine, that you should hold me responsible for him."

"In mercy's name, who is he?"

"I certainly cannot inform you. I know nothing about him. Formerly I employed him as a copyist; but he has done nothing for me now for some time past."

"I shall settle him, then—good morning, sir."

Several days passed, and I heard nothing more; and, though I often felt a charitable prompting to call at the place and see poor Bartleby, yet a certain squeamishness, of I know not what, withheld me.

All is over with him, by this time, thought I, at last, when, through another week, no further intelligence reached me. But, coming to my room the day after, I found several persons waiting at my door in a high state of nervous excitement.

"That's the man—here he comes," cried the foremost one, whom I recognized as the lawyer who had previously called upon me alone.

"You must take him away, sir, at once," cried a portly person among them, advancing upon me, and whom I knew to be the landlord of No. — Wall Street. "These gentlemen, my tenants, cannot stand it any longer; Mr. B——," pointing to the lawyer, "has turned him out of his room, and he now persists in haunting the building generally, sitting upon the banisters of the stairs by day, and sleeping in the entry by night. Everybody is concerned; clients are leaving the offices; some fears are entertained of a mob; something you must do, and that without delay."

Aghast at this torrent, I fell back before it, and would fain have locked myself in my new quarters. In vain I persisted that Bartleby was nothing to me—no more than to any one else. In vain—I was the last person known to have anything to do with him, and they held me to the terrible account. Fearful, then, of being exposed in the papers (as one person present obscurely threatened), I considered the matter, and, at length, said, that if the lawyer would give me a confidential interview with the scrivener, in his (the lawyer's) own room. I would, that afternoon, strive my best to rid them of the nuisance they complained of.

Going up stairs to my old haunt, there was Bartleby silently sitting upon the banister at the landing.

"What are you doing here, Bartleby?" said I.

"Sitting upon the banister," he mildly replied.

I motioned him into the lawyer's room, who then left us.

"Bartleby," said I, "are you aware that you are the cause of great tribulation to me, by persisting in occupying the entry after being dismissed from the office?"

No answer.

"Now one of two things must take place. Either you must do something, or something must be done to you. Now what sort of business would you like to engage in? Would you like to re-engage in copying for some one?"

"No; I would prefer not to make any change."

"Would you like a clerkship in a dry-goods store?"

"There is too much confinement about that. No, I would not like a clerkship; but I am not particular."

"Too much confinement," I cried, "why you keep yourself confined all the time!"

"I would prefer not to take a clerkship," he rejoined, as if to settle that little item at once.

"How would a bar-tender's business suit you? There is no trying of the eye-sight in that."

"I would not like it at all, though, as I said before, I am not particular."

His unwonted wordiness inspirited me. I returned to the charge.

"Well, then, would you like to travel through the country collecting bills for the merchants? That would improve your health."

"No, I would prefer to be doing something else."

"How, then, would going as a companion to Europe, to entertain some young gentleman with your conversation—how would that suit you?"

"Not at all. It does not strike me that there is anything definite about that. I like to be stationary. But I am not particular."

"Stationary you shall be, then," I cried, now losing all patience, and, for the first time in all my exasperating connection with him, fairly flying into a passion. "If you do not go away from these premises before night, I shall feel bound—indeed, I *am* bound—to—to—to quit the premises myself!" I rather absurdly concluded, knowing not with what possible threat to try to frighten his immobility into compliance. Despairing of all further efforts, I was precipitately leaving him, when a final thought occurred to me—one which had not been wholly unindulged before.

"Bartleby," said I, in the kindest tone I could assume under such exciting circumstances, "will you go home with me now—not to my office, but my dwelling—and remain there till we can conclude upon some convenient arrangement for you at our leisure? Come, let us start now, right away."

"No: at present I would prefer not to make any change at all."

I answered nothing; but, effectually dodging every one by the suddenness and rapidity of my flight, rushed from the building, ran up Wall Street towards Broadway, and jumping into the first omnibus, was soon removed from pursuit. As soon as tranquillity returned, I distinctly perceived that I had now done all that I possibly could, both in respect to the demands of the landlord and his tenants, and with regard to my own desire and sense of duty, to benefit Bartleby, and shield him from rude persecution. I now strove to be entirely care-free and quiescent; and my conscience justified me in the attempt; though, indeed, it was not so successful as I could have wished. So fearful was I of being again hunted out by the incensed landlord and his exasperated tenants, that, surrendering my business to Nippers, for a few days, I drove about the upper part of the town and through the suburbs, in my rockaway; crossed over to Jersey City and Hoboken, and paid fugitive visits to Manhattanville and Astoria. In fact, I almost lived in my rockaway for the time.

When again I entered my office, lo, a note from my landlord lay upon the desk. I opened it with trembling hands. It informed me that the writer had sent to the police, and had Bartleby removed to the Tombs as a vagrant. Moreover, since I knew more about him than any one else, he wished me to appear at that place, and make a suitable statement of the facts. These tidings had a conflicting effect upon me. At first I was indignant; but, at last, almost approved. The landlord's energetic, summary disposition, had led him to adopt a procedure which I do not think I would have decided upon myself; and yet, as a last resort, under such peculiar circumstances, it seemed the only plan.

As I afterwards learned, the poor scrivener, when told that he must be conducted to the Tombs, offered not the slightest obstacle, but, in his pale, unmoving way, silently acquiesced.

Some of the compassionate and curious bystanders joined the party; and headed by one of the constables arm in arm with Bartleby, the silent procession filed its way through all the noise, and heat, and joy of the roaring thoroughfares at noon.

The same day I received the note, I went to the Tombs, or, to speak more properly, the Halls of Justice. Seeking the right officer, I stated the purpose of my call, and was informed that the individual I described was, indeed, within. I then assured the functionary that Bartleby was a perfectly honest man, and greatly to be compassionated, however, unaccountably eccentric. I narrated all I knew, and closed by suggesting the idea of letting him remain in as indulgent confinement as possible, till something less harsh might be done—though, indeed, I hardly knew what. At all events, if nothing else could be decided upon, the almshouse must receive him. I then begged to have an interview.

Being under no disgraceful charge, and quite serene and harmless in all his ways, they had permitted him freely to wander about the prison, and, especially, in the inclosed grass-platted yards thereof. And so I found him there, standing all alone in the quietest of the yards, his face towards a high wall, while all around, from the narrow slits of the jail windows, I thought I saw peering out upon him the eyes of murderers and thieves.

"Bartleby!"

"I know you," he said, without looking round—"and I want nothing to say to you."

"It was not I that brought you here, Bartleby," said I, keenly pained at his implied suspicion. "And to you, this should not be so vile a place. Nothing reproachful attaches to you by being here. And see, it is not so sad a place as one might think. Look, there is the sky, and here is the grass."

"I know where I am," he replied, but would say nothing more, and so I left him.

As I entered the corridor again, a broad meat-like man, in an apron, accosted me, and, jerking his thumb over his shoulder, said—"Is that your friend?"

"Yes."

"Does he want to starve? If he does, let him live on the prison fare, that's all."

"Who are you?" asked I, not knowing what to make of such an unofficially speaking person in such a place.

"I am the grub-man. Such gentlemen as have friends here, hire me to provide them with something good to eat."

"Is this so?" said I, turning to the turnkey.

He said it was.

"Well, then," said I, slipping some silver into the grub-man's hands (for so they called him), "I want you to give particular attention to my friend there; let him have the best dinner you can get. And you must be as polite to him as possible."

"Introduce me, will you?" said the grub-man, looking at me with an expression which seemed to say he was all impatience for an opportunity to give a specimen of his breeding.

Thinking it would prove of benefit to the scrivener, I acquiesced; and, asking the grub-man his name, went up with him to Bartleby.

"Bartleby, this is a friend; you will find him very useful to you."

"Your sarvant, sir, your sarvant," said the grub-man, making a low salutation behind his apron. "Hope you find it pleasant here, sir; nice grounds—cool apartments—hope you'll stay with us sometime—try to make it agreeable. What will you have for dinner to-day?"

"I prefer not to dine to-day," said Bartleby, turning away. "It would disagree with me; I am unused to dinners." So saying, he slowly moved to the other side of the inclosure, and took up a position fronting the dead-wall.

"How's this?" said the grub-man, addressing me with a stare of astonishment. "He's odd, ain't he?"

"I think he is a little deranged," said I, sadly.

"Deranged? deranged is it? Well, now, upon my word, I thought that friend of yourn was a gentleman forger; they are always pale and genteel-like, them forgers. I can't help pity 'em—can't help it, sir. Did you know Monroe Edwards?" he added, touchingly, and paused. Then, laying his hand piteously on my shoulder, sighed, "he died of consumption at Sing-Sing. So you weren't acquainted with Monroe?"

"No, I was never socially acquainted with any forgers. But I cannot stop longer. Look to my friend yonder. You will not lose by it. I will see you again."

Some few days after this, I again obtained admission to the Tombs, and went through the corridors in quest of Bartleby; but without finding him.

"I saw him coming from his cell not long ago," said a turnkey, "may be he's gone to loiter in the yards."

So I went in that direction.

"Are you looking for the silent man?" said another turnkey, passing me. "Yonder he lies—sleeping in the yard there. 'Tis not twenty minutes since I saw him lie down."

The yard was entirely quiet. It was not accessible to the common prisoners. The surrounding walls, of amazing thickness, kept off all sounds behind them. The Egyptian character of the masonry weighed upon me with its gloom. But a soft imprisoned turf grew under foot. The heart of the eternal pyramids, it seemed, wherein, by some strange magic, through the clefts, grass-seed, dropped by birds, had sprung.

Strangely huddled at the base of the wall, his knees drawn up, and lying on his side, his head touching the cold stones, I saw the wasted Bartleby. But nothing stirred. I paused; then went close up to him; stooped over, and saw that his dim eyes were open; otherwise he seemed profoundly sleeping. Something prompted me to touch him. I felt his hand, when a tingling shiver ran up my arm and down my spine to my feet.

The round face of the grub-man peered upon me now. "His dinner is ready. Won't he dine to-day, either? Or does he live without dining?"

"Lives without dining," said I, and closed the eyes.

"Eh!—He's asleep, ain't he?"

"With kings and counselors," murmured I.

There would seem little need for proceeding further in this history. Imagination will readily supply the meagre recital of poor Bartleby's interment. But, ere parting with the reader, let me say, that if this little narrative has sufficiently interested him, to awaken curiosity as to who Bartleby was, and what manner of life he led prior to the present narrator's making his acquaintance, I can only reply, that in such curiosity I fully share, but am wholly unable to gratify it. Yet here I hardly know whether I should divulge one little item of rumor, which came to my ear a few months after the scrivener's decease. Upon what basis it rested, I could never ascertain; and hence, how true it is I cannot now tell. But, inasmuch as this vague report has not been without a certain suggestive interest to me, however sad, it may prove the same with some others; and so I will briefly mention it. The report was this: that Bartleby had been a subordinate clerk in the Dead Letter Office at Washington, from which he had been suddenly removed by a change in the administration. When I think over this rumor, hardly can I express the emotions which seize me. Dead letters! does it not sound like dead men? Conceive a man by nature and misfortune prone to a pallid hopelessness, can any business seem more fitted to heighten it than that of continually handling these dead letters, and assorting them for the flames? For by the cart-load they are annually burned. Sometimes from out the folded paper the pale clerk takes a ring—the finger it was meant for, perhaps, moulders in the grave; a bank-note sent in swiftest charity—he whom it would relieve, nor eats nor hungers any more; pardon for those who died despairing; hope for those who died unhoping; good tidings for those who died stifled by unrelieved calamities. On errands of life, these letters speed to death.

Ah, Bartleby! Ah, humanity!

---

# THE LONELINESS OF THE
# LONG DISTANCE RUNNER
## *Allan Sillitoe*

### I

As soon as I got to Borstal they made me a long-distance cross-country runner. I suppose they thought I was just the build for it because I was long and skinny for my age (and still am) and in any case I didn't mind it much, to tell you the truth, because running had always been made much of in our family, especially running away from the police. I've always been a good runner, quick and with a big stride as well, the only trouble being that no matter how fast I run, and I did a very fair lick even though I do say so myself, it didn't stop me getting caught by the cops after that bakery job.

You might think it a bit rare, having long-distance cross-country runners in Borstal, thinking that the first thing a long-distance runner would do when they set him loose at them fields and woods would be to run as far away from the place as he could get on a bellyful of Borstal slumgullion—but you're wrong, and I'll tell you why. The first thing is that them bastards over us aren't as daft as they most of the time look, and for another thing I am not so daft as I would look if I tried to make a break for it on my long-distance running, because to abscond and then get caught is nothing but a mug's game, and I'm not falling for it. Cunning is what counts in this life, and even that you've got to use in the slyest way you can; I'm telling you straight: they're cunning, and I'm cunning. If only 'them' and 'us' had the same ideas we'd get on like a house on fire, and they don't see eye to eye with us and we don't see eye to eye with them, so that's how it stands and how it will always stand. The one fact is that all of us are cunning, and because of this there's no love lost between us. So the thing is that they know I won't try to get away from them: they sit there like spiders in that crumbly manor house, perched like jumped-up jackdaws on the roof, watching out over the drives and fields like German generals from the tops of tanks. And even when I jog-trot on behind a wood and they can't see me anymore they know my sweeping-brush head will bob along that hedge-top in an hour's time and that I'll report to the bloke on the gate. Because when on a raw and frosty morning I get up at five o'clock and stand shivering my belly off on the stone floor and all the rest still have another hour to snooze before the bells go, I slink downstairs through all the corridors to the big outside door with a permit running-card in my fist, I feel like the first and last man on the world, both at once, if you can believe what I'm trying to say. I feel like the first man because I've hardly got a stitch on and am sent against the frozen fields in a shimmy and shorts—even the first poor bastard dropped on to the earth in midwinter knew how to make a suit of leaves, or how to skin a pterodactyl for a topcoat. But there I am, frozen stiff, with nothing to get me warm except a couple of hours' long-distance running before breakfast, not even a slice of bread-and-sheepdip. They're training me up fine for the big sports day when all the pig-faced snotty-nosed dukes and ladies—who can't add two and two together and would mess themselves like loonies if they didn't have slavies to beck-and-call—come and make speeches to us about sports being just the thing to get us leading an honest life and keep our itching finger-ends off them shop locks and safe handles and hairgrips to open gas meters. They give us a bit of blue ribbon and a cup for a prize after we've shagged ourselves out running or jumping, like race horses, only we don't get so well looked-after as race horses, that's the only thing.

So there I am, standing in the doorway in shimmy and shorts, not even a dry crust in my guts, looking out at frosty flowers on the ground.

I suppose you think this is enough to make me cry? Not likely. Just because I feel like the first bloke in the world wouldn't make me bawl. It makes me feel fifty times better than when I'm cooped up in that dormitory with three hundred others. No, it's sometimes when I stand there feeling like the *last* man in the world that I don't feel so good. I feel like the last man in the world because I think that all those three hundred sleepers behind me are dead. They sleep so well I think that every scruffy head's kicked the bucket in the night and I'm the only one left, and when I look out into the bushes and frozen ponds I have the feeling that it's going to get colder and colder until everything I can see, meaning my red arms as well, is going to be covered with a thousand miles of ice, all the earth, right up to the sky and over every bit of land and sea. So I try to kick this feeling and act like I'm the first man on earth. And that makes me feel good, so as soon as I'm steamed up enough to get this feeling in me, I take a flying leap out of the doorway, and off I trot.

I'm in Essex. It's supposed to be a good Borstal, at least that's what the governor said to me when I got here from Nottingham. "We want to trust you while you are in this establishment," he said, smoothing out his newspaper with lily-white workless hands, while I read the big words upside down: *Daily Telegraph*. "If you play ball with us, we'll play ball with you." (Honest to God, you'd have thought it was going to be one long tennis match.) "We want hard honest work and we want good athletics," he said as well. "And if you give us both these things you can be sure we'll do right by you and send you back into the world an honest man." Well, I could have died laughing, especially when straight after this I hear the barking sergeant-major's voice calling me and two others to attention and marching us off like we was Grenadier Guards. And when the governor kept saying how 'we' wanted you to do this, and 'we' wanted you to do that, I kept looking round for the other blokes, wondering how many of them there was. Of course, I knew there were thousands of them, but as far as I knew only one was in the room. And there *are* thousands of them, all over the poxeaten country, in shops, offices, railway stations, cars, houses, pubs—In-law blokes like you and them, all on the watch for Out-law blokes like me and us—and waiting to 'phone for the coppers as soon as we make a false move. And it'll always be there, I'll tell you that now, because I haven't finished making all my false moves yet, and I dare say I won't until I kick the bucket. If the In-laws are hoping to stop me making false moves they're wasting their time. They might as well stand me up against a wall and let fly with a dozen rifles. That's the only way they'll stop me, and a few million others. Because I've been doing a lot of thinking since coming here. They can spy on us all day to see if we're pulling our puddings and if we're working good or doing our "athletics" but they can't make an X-ray of our guts to find out what we're telling ourselves. I've been asking myself all sorts of questions, and thinking about my life up to now. And I like doing all this. It's a treat. It passes the time away and don't make Borstal seem half so bad as the boys in our street used to say it was. And this long-distance running lark is the best of all, because it makes me think so good that I learn things even better than when I'm on my bed at night. And apart from that, what with thinking so much while I'm running I'm getting to be one of the best runners in the Borstal. I can go my five miles round better than anybody else I know.

So as soon as I tell myself I'm the first man ever to be dropped into the world, and as soon as I take that first flying leap out into the frosty grass of an early morning when even birds haven't the heart to whistle, I get to thinking, and that's what I like. I go my rounds in a dream, turning at lane or footpath corners without knowing I'm turning, leaping brooks without knowing they're there, and shouting good morning to the early cow-milker without seeing him. It's a treat, being a long-distance runner, out in the world by yourself with not a soul to make you bad-tempered or tell you what to do or that there's a shop to break and enter a bit back from the next street. Sometimes I think that I've never been so free as during that couple of hours when I'm trotting up the path out of the gates and turning by that bare-faced, big-bellied oak tree at the lane end. Everything's dead, but good, because it's dead before coming alive, not dead after being alive. That's how I look at it. Mind you, I often feel frozen stiff at first. I can't feel my hands or feet or flesh at all, like a ghost who wouldn't know the earth was under him if he didn't see it now and again through the mist. But even though some people would call this frost-pain suffering if they wrote about it to their mams in a letter, I don't, because I know that in half an hour I'm going to be warm, that by the time I get to the main road and am turning on to the wheatfield footpath by the bus stop I'm going to feel as hot as a potbellied stove and as happy as a dog with a tin tail.

It's a good life, I'm saying to myself, if you don't give in to coppers and Borstal-bosses and the rest of them bastard-faced In-laws. Trot-trot-trot. Puff-puff-puff. Slap-slap-slap go my feet on the hard soil. Swish-swish-swish as my arms and side catch the bare branches of a bush. For I'm seventeen now, and when they let me out of this—if I don't make a break and see that things turn out otherwise—they'll try to get me in the army, and what's the difference between the army and this place I'm in now? They can't kid me, the bastards. I've seen the barracks near where I live, and if there weren't swaddies on guard outside with rifles you wouldn't know the difference between their high walls and the place I'm in now. Even though the swaddies come out at odd times a week for a pint of ale, so what? Don't I come out three mornings a week on my long-distance running, which is fifty times better than boozing. When they first said that I was to do my long-distance running without a guard pedalling beside me on a bike I couldn't believe it; but they called it a progressive and modern place, though they can't kid me because I know it's just like any other Borstal, going by the stories I've heard, except that they let me trot about like this. Borstal's Borstal no matter what they do; but anyway I moaned about it being a bit thick sending me out so early to run five miles on an empty stomach, until they talked me round to thinking it wasn't so bad—which I knew all the time—until they called me a good sport and patted me on the back when I said I'd do it and that I'd try to win them the Borstal Blue Ribbon Prize Cup For Long-Distance Cross Country Running (All England). And now the governor talks to me when he comes on his rounds, almost as he'd talk to his prize race horse, if he had one.

"All right, Smith?" he asks.

"Yes, sir," I answer.

He flicks his grey moustache: "How's the running coming along?"

"I've set myself to trot round the grounds after dinner just to keep my hand in, sir," I tell him.

The pot-bellied pop-eyed bastard gets pleased at this: "Good show. I know you'll get us that cup," he says.

And I swear under my breath: "Like boggery, I will." No, I won't get them that cup, even though the stupid tash-twitching bastard has all his hopes in me. Because what does his barmy hope mean? I ask myself. Trot-trot-trot, slap-slap-slap, over the stream and into the wood where it's almost dark and frosty-dew twigs sting my legs. It don't mean a bloody thing to me, only to him, and it means as much to him as it would mean to me if I picked up the racing paper and put my bet on a hoss I didn't know, had never seen, and didn't care a sod if I ever did see. That's what it means to him. And I'll lose that race, because I'm not a race horse at all, and I'll let him know it when I'm about to get out—if I don't sling my hook even before the race. By Christ I will. I'm a human being and I've got thoughts and secrets and bloody life inside me that he doesn't know is there, and he'll never know what's there because he's stupid. I suppose you'll laugh at this, me saying the governor's a stupid bastard when I know hardly how to write and he can read and write and add-up like a professor. But what I say is true right enough. He's stupid, and I'm not, because I can see further into the likes of him than he can see into the likes of me. Admitted, we're both cunning, but I'm more cunning and I'll win in the end even if I die in gaol at eighty-two, because I'll have more fun and fire out of my life than he'll ever get out of his. He's read a thousand books I suppose, and for all I know he might even have written a few, but I know for a dead cert, as sure as I'm sitting here, that what I'm scribbling down is worth a million to what he could ever scribble down. I don't care what anybody says, but that's the truth and can't be denied. I know when he talks to me and I look into his army mug that I'm alive and he's dead. He's as dead as a doornail. If he ran ten yards he'd drop dead. If he got ten yards into what goes on in my guts he'd drop dead as well—with surprise. At the moment it's dead blokes like him as have the whip-hand over blokes like me, and I'm almost dead sure it'll always be like that, but even so, by Christ, I'd rather be like I am—always on the run and breaking into shops for a packet of fags and a jar of jam—than have the whip-hand over somebody else and be dead from the toenails up. Maybe as soon as you get the whip-hand over somebody you do go dead. By God, to say that last sentence has needed a few hundred miles of long-distance running. I could no more have said that at first than I could have took a million-pound note from my back pocket. But it's true, you know, now I think of it again, and has always been true, and always will be true, and I'm surer of it every time I see the governor open that door and say Good-morning lads.

As I run and see my smoky breath going out into the air as if I had ten cigars stuck in different parts of my body I think more on the little speech the governor made when I first came. Honesty. Be honest. I laughed so much one morning I went ten minutes down in my timing because I had to stop and get rid of the stitch in my side. The governor was so worried when I got back late that he sent me to the doctor's for an X-ray and heart check. Be honest. It's like saying: Be dead, like me, and then you'll have no more pain of leaving your nice slummy house for Borstal or prison. Be honest and settle down in a cosy six pounds a week job. Well, even with all this long-distance running I haven't yet been able to decide what he means by this, although I'm just about beginning to—and I don't like what it means. Because after all my thinking I found that it adds up to something that can't be true about me, being born and brought up as I was. Because another thing people like the governor will never understand is that I *am* honest, that I've never been anything else but honest, and that I'll always be honest. Sounds funny. But it's true because I know what honest means according to me and he only knows what it means according to him. I think my honesty is the only sort in the world, and he thinks his is the only sort in the world as well. That's why this dirty great walled-up and fenced-up manor house in the middle of nowhere has been used to coop-up blokes like me. And if I had the whip-hand I wouldn't even bother to build a place like this to put all the cops, governors, posh whores, penpushers, army officers, Members of Parliament in; no, I'd stick them up against a wall and let them have it, like they'd have done with blokes like us years ago, that is, if they'd ever known what it means to be honest, which they don't and never will so help me God Almighty.

I was nearly eighteen months in Borstal before I thought about getting out. I can't tell you much about what it was like there because I haven't got the hang of describing buildings or saying how many crumby chairs and slatted windows make a room. Neither can I do much complaining, because to tell you the truth I didn't suffer in Borstal at all. I gave the same answer a pal of mine gave when someone asked him how much he hated it in the army. "I didn't hate it," he said. "They fed me, gave me a suit, and pocket-money, which was a bloody sight more than I ever got before, unless I worked myself to death for it, and most of the time they wouldn't let me work but sent me to the dole office twice a week." Well, that's more or less what I say. Borstal didn't hurt me in that respect, so since I've got no complaints I don't have to describe what they gave us to eat, what the dorms were like, or how they treated us. But in another way Borstal does something to me. No, it doesn't get my back up, because it's always been up, right from when I was born. What it does do is show me what they've been trying to frighten me with. They're got other things as well, like prison and, in the end, the rope. It's like me rushing up to thump a man and snatch the coat off his back when, suddenly, I pull up because he whips out a knife and lifts it to stick me like a pig if I come too close. That knife is Borstal, clink, the rope. But once you've seen the knife you learn a bit of unarmed combat. You have to, because you'll never get that sort of knife in your own hands, and this unarmed combat doesn't amount to much. Still, there it is, and you keep on rushing up to this man, knife or not, hoping to get one of your hands on his wrist and the other on his elbow both at the same time, and press back until he drops the knife.

You see, by sending me to Borstal they've shown me the knife, and from now on I know something I didn't know before: that it's war between me and them. I always knew this, naturally, because I was in Remand Homes as well and the boys there told me a lot about their brothers in Borstal, but it was only touch and go then, like kittens, like boxing-gloves, like dobbie. But now that they've shown me the knife, whether I ever pinch another thing in my life again or not, I know who my enemies are and what war is. They can drop all the atom bombs they like for all I care: I'll never call it war and wear a soldier's uniform, because I'm in a different sort of war, that they think is child's play. The war they think is war is suicide, and those that go and get killed in war should be put in clink for attempted suicide because that's the feeling in blokes' minds when they rush to join up or let themselves be called up. I know, because I've thought how good it would be sometimes to do myself in and the easiest way to do it, it occurred to me, was to hope for a big war so's I could join up and get killed. But I got past that when I knew I already was in a war of my own, that I was born into one, that I grew up hearing the sound of 'old soldiers' who'd been over the top at Dartmoor, half-killed at Lincoln, trapped in no-man's-land at Borstal, that sounded louder than any Jerry bombs. Government wars aren't my wars; they've got nowt to do with me, because my own war's all that I'll ever be bothered about. I remember when I was fourteen and I went into the country with three of my cousins, all about the same age, who later went to different Borstals, and then to different regiments, from which they soon deserted, and then to different gaols where they still are as far as I know. But anyway, we were all kids then, and wanted to go out to the woods for a change, to get away from the roads of stinking hot tar one summer. We climbed over fences and went through fields, scrumping a few sour apples on our way, until we saw the wood about a mile off. Up Colliers' Pad we heard another lot of kids talking in high-school voices behind a hedge. We crept up on them and peeped through the brambles, and saw they were eating a picnic, a real posh spread out of baskets and flasks and towels. There must have been about seven of them, lads and girls sent out by their mams and dads for the afternoon. So we went on our bellies through the hedge like crocodiles and surrounded them, and then dashed into the middle, scattering the fire and batting their tabs and snatching up all there was to eat, then running off over Cherry Orchard fields into the wood, with a man chasing us who'd come up while we were ransacking their picnic. We got away all right, and had a good feed into the bargain, because we'd been clambed to death and couldn't wait long enough to get our chops ripping into them thin lettuce and ham sandwiches and creamy cakes.

Well, I'll always feel during every bit of my life like those daft kids should have felt before we broke them up. But they never dreamed that what happened was going to happen, just like the governor of this Borstal who spouts to us about honesty and all that wappy stuff don't know a bloody thing, while I know every minute of my life that a big boot is always likely to smash any nice picnic I might be barmy and dishonest enough to make for myself. I admit that there've been times when I've thought of telling the governor all this so as to put him on his guard, but when I've got as close as seeing him I've changed my mind, thinking to let him either find out for himself or go through the same mill as I've gone through. I'm not hard-hearted (in fact I've helped a few blokes in my time with the odd quid, lie, fag, or shelter from the rain when they've been on the run) but I'm boggered if I'm going to risk being put in the cells just for trying to give the governor a bit of advice he don't deserve. If my heart's soft I know the sort of people I'm going to save it for. And any advice I'd give the governor wouldn't do him the least bit of good; it'd only trip him up sooner than if he wasn't told at all, which I suppose is what I want to happen. But for the time being I'll let things go on as they are, which is something else I've learned in the last year or two. (It's a good job I can only think of these things as fast as I can write with this stub of pencil that's clutched in my paw, otherwise I'd have dropped the whole thing weeks ago.)

By the time I'm half-way through my morning course, when after a frost-bitten dawn I can see a phlegmy bit of sunlight hanging from the bare twigs of beech and sycamore, and when I've measured my half-way mark by the short-cut scrimmage down the steep bush-covered bank and into the sunken lane, when still there's not a soul in sight and not a sound except the neighing of a piebald foal in a cottage stable that I can't see, I get to thinking the deepest and daftest of all. The governor would have a fit if he could see me sliding down the bank because I could break my neck or ankle, but I can't not do it because it's the only risk I take and the only excitement I ever get, flying flat-out like one of them pterodactyls from the "Lost World" I once heard on the wireless, crazy like a cut-balled cockerel, scratching myself to bits and almost letting myself go but not quite. It's the most wonderful minute because there's not one thought or word or picture of anything in my head while I'm going down. I'm empty, as empty as I was before I was born, and I don't let myself go, I suppose, because whatever it is that's farthest down inside me don't want me to die or hurt myself bad. And it's daft to think deep, you know, because it gets you nowhere, though deep is what I am when I've passed this half-way mark because the long-distance run of an early morning makes me think that every run like this is a life—a little life, I know—but a life as full of misery and happiness and things happening as you can ever get really around yourself—and I remember that after a lot of these runs I thought that it didn't need much know-how to tell how a life was going to end once it had got well started. But as usual I was wrong, caught first by the cops and then by my own bad brain, I could never trust myself to fly scot-free over these traps, was always tripped up sooner or later no matter how many I got over to the good without even knowing it. Looking back I suppose them big trees put their branches to their snouts and gave each other the wink, and there I was whizzing down the bank and not seeing a bloody thing.

## II

I don't say to myself: "You shouldn't have done the job and then you'd have stayed away from Borstal"; no, what I ram into my runner-brain is that my luck had no right to scram just when I was on my way to making the coppers think I hadn't done the job after all. The time was autumn and the night foggy enough to set me and my mate Mike roaming the streets when we should have been rooted in front of the telly or stuck into a plush posh seat at the pictures, but I was restless after six weeks away from any sort of work, and well you might ask me why I'd been bone-idle for so long because normally I sweated my thin guts out on a milling-machine with the rest of them, but you see, my dad died from cancer of the throat, and mam collected a cool five hundred in insurance and benefits from the factory where he'd worked, "for your bereavement," they said, or words like that.

Now I believe, and my mam must have thought the same, that a wad of crisp blue-back fivers ain't a sight of good to a living soul unless they're flying out of your hand into some shopkeeper's till, and the shopkeeper is passing you tip-top things in exchange over the counter, so as soon as she got the money, mam took me and my five brothers and sisters out to town and got us dolled-up in new clothes. Then she ordered a twenty-one-inch telly, a new carpet because the old one was covered with blood from dad's dying and wouldn't wash out, and took a taxi home with bags of grub and a new fur coat. And do you know— you wain't believe me when I tell you—she'd still near three hundred left in her bulging handbag the next day, so how could any of us go to work after that? Poor old dad, he didn't get a look in, and he was the one who'd done the suffering and dying for such a lot of lolly.

Night after night we sat in front of the telly with a ham sandwich in one hand, a bar of chocolate in the other, and a bottle of lemonade between our boots, while mam was with some fancy-man upstairs on the new bed she'd ordered, and I'd never known a family as happy as ours was in that couple of months when we'd got all the money we needed. And when the dough ran out I didn't think about anything much, but just roamed the streets—looking for another job, I told mam—hoping I suppose to get my hands on another five hundred nicker so's the nice life we'd got used to could go on and on for ever. Because it's surprising how quick you can get used to a different life. To begin with, the adverts on the telly had shown us how much more there was in the world to buy than we'd ever dreamed of when we'd looked into shop windows but hadn't seen all there was to see because we didn't have the money to buy it with anyway. And the telly made all these things seem twenty times better than we'd ever thought they were. Even adverts at the cinema were cool and tame, because now we were seeing them in private at home. We used to cock our noses up at things in shops that didn't move, but suddenly we saw their real value because they jumped and glittered around the screen and had some pasty-faced tart going head over heels to get her nail-polished grabbers on to them or her lipstick lips over them, not like the crumby adverts you saw on posters or in newspapers as dead as doornails; these were flickering around loose, half-open packets and tins, making you think that all you had to do was finish opening them before they were yours, like seeing an unlocked safe through a shop window with the man gone away for a cup of tea without thinking to guard his lolly. The films they showed were good as well, in that way, because we couldn't get our eyes unglued from the cops chasing the robbers who had satchel-bags crammed with cash and looked like getting away to spend it—until the last moment. I always hoped the would end up free to blow the lot, and could never stop wanting to put my hand out, smash into the screen (it only looked a bit of rag-screen like at the pictures) and get the copper in a half-nelson so's he'd stop following the bloke with the money-bags. Even when he'd knocked off a couple of bank clerks I hoped he wouldn't get nabbed. In fact then I wished more than ever he wouldn't because it meant the hot-chair if he did, and I wouldn't wish that on anybody no matter what they'd done, because I'd read in a book where the hot-chair worn't a quick death at all, but that you just sat there scorching to death until you were dead. And it was when these cops were chasing the crooks that we played some good tricks with the telly, because when one of them opened his big gob to spout about getting their man I'd turn the sound down and see his mouth move like a goldfish or mackerel or a minnow mimicking what they were supposed to be acting—it was so funny the whole family nearly went into fits on the brand-new carpet that hadn't yet found its way to the bedroom. It was the best of all though when we did it to some Tory telling us about how good his government was going to be if we kept on voting for them—their slack chops rolling, opening and bumbling, hands lifting to twitch moustaches and touching their buttonholes to make sure the flower hadn't wilted, so that you could see they didn't mean a word they said, especially with not a murmur coming out because we'd cut off the sound. When the governor of the Borstal first talked to me I was reminded of those times so much that I nearly killed myself trying not to laugh. Yes, we played so many good stunts on the box of tricks that mam used to call us the Telly Boys, we got so clever at it.

My pal Mike got let off with probation because it was his first job—anyway the first they ever knew about—and because they said he would never have done it if it hadn't been for me talking him into it. They said I was a menace to honest lads like Mike—hands in his pockets so that they looked stone-empty, head bent forward as if looking for half-crowns to fill 'em with, a ripped jersey and his hair falling into his eyes so that he could go up to women and ask them for a shilling because he was hungry—and that I was the brains behind the job, the guiding light when it came to making up anybody's mind, but I swear to God I worn't owt like that because really I ain't got no more brains than a gnat after hiding the money in the place I did. And I—being cranky like I am—got sent to Borstal because to tell you the honest truth I'd been to Remand Homes before—though that's another story and I suppose if ever I tell it it'll be just as boring as this one is. I was glad though that Mike got away with it, and I only hope he always will, not like silly bastard me.

So on this foggy night we tore ourselves away from the telly and slammed the front door behind us, setting off up our wide street like slow tugs on a river that'd broken their hooters, for we didn't know where the housefronts began what with the perishing cold mist all around. I was snatched to death without an overcoat: mam had forgotten to buy me on in the scrummage of shopping, and by the time I thought to remind her of it the dough was all gone. So we whistled "The Teddy Boys Picnic" to keep us warm, and I told myself that I'd get a coat soon if it was the last thing I did. Mike said he thought the same about himself, adding that he'd also get some brand-new glasses with gold rims, to wear instead of the wire frames they'd given him at the school clinic years ago. He didn't twig it was foggy at first and cleaned his glasses every time I pulled him back from a lamp-post or car, but when he saw the lights on Alfreton Road looking like octopus eyes he put them in his pocket and didn't wear them again until we did the job. We hadn't got two ha-pennies between us, and though we weren't hungry we wished we'd got a bob or two when we passed the fish and chip shops because the delicious sniffs of salt and vinegar and frying fat made our mouths water. I don't mind telling you we walked the town from one end to the other and if our eyes worn't glued to the ground looking for lost wallets and watches they was swivelling around house windows and shop doors in case we saw something easy and worth nipping into.

Neither of us said as much as this to each other, but I know for a fact that that was what we was thinking. What I don't know—and as sure as I sit here I know I'll never know—is which of us was the first bastard to latch his peepers on to that baker's backyard. Oh yes, it's all right me telling myself it was me, but the truth is that I've never known whether it was Mike or not, because I do know that I didn't see the open window until he stabbed me in the ribs and pointed it out. "See it?" he said.

"Yes," I told him, "so let's get cracking."

"But what about the wall though?" he whispered, looking a bit closer.

"On your shoulders," I chipped in.

His eyes were already up there: "Will you be able to reach?" It was the only time he ever showed any life.

"Leave it to me," I said, ever-ready. "I can reach anywhere from your ham-hock shoulders."

Mike was a nipper compared to me, but underneath the scruffy draught-board jersey he wore were muscles as hard as iron, and you wouldn't think to see him walking down the street with glasses on and hands in pockets that he'd harm a fly, but I never liked to get on the wrong side of him in a fight because he's the sort that don't say a word for weeks on end—sits plugged in front of the telly, or reads a cowboy book, or just sleeps—when suddenly BIFF—half kills somebody for almost nothing at all, such as beating him in a race for the last Football

Post on a Saturday night, pushing in before him at a bus stop, or bumping into him when he was day-dreaming about Dolly-on-the-Tub next door. I saw him set on a bloke once for no more than fixing him in a funny way with his eyes, and it turned out that the bloke was cock-eyed but nobody knew it because he'd just that day come to live in our street. At other times none of these things would matter a bit, and I suppose the only reason why I was pals with him was because I didn't say much from one month's end to another either.

He put his hands up in the air like he was being covered with a Gatling-Gun, and moved to the wall like he was going to be mowed down, and I climbed up him like he was a stile or step-ladder, and there he stood, the palms of his upshot maulers flat and turned out so's I could step on 'em like they was the adjustable jackspanner under a car, not a sound of a breath nor the shiver of a flinch coming from him. I lost no time in any case, took my coat from between my teeth, chucked it up to the glass-topped wall (where the glass worn't too sharp because the jags had been worn down by years of accidental stones) and was sitting astraddle before I knew where I was. Then down the other side, with my legs rammed up into my throat when I hit the ground, the crack coming about as hard as when you fall after a high parachute drop, that one of my mates told me was like jumping off a twelve-foot wall, which this must have been. Then I picked up my bits and pieces and opened the gate for Mike, who was still grinning and full of life because the hardest part of the job was already done. "I came, I broke, I entered," like that clever-dick Borstal song.

I didn't think about anything at all, as usual, because I never do when I'm busy, when I'm draining pipes, looting sacks, yaling locks, lifting latches, forcing my bony hands and lanky legs into making something move, hardly feeling my lungs going in-whiff and out-whaff, not realizing whether my mouth is clamped tight or gaping, whether I'm hungry, itching from scabies, or whether my flies are open and flashing dirty words like muck and spit into the late-night final fog. And when I don't know anything about all this then how can I honest-to-God say I think of anything at such times? When I'm wondering what's the best way to get a window open or how to force a door, how can I be thinking or have anything on my mind? That's what the four-eyed white-smocked bloke with the note-book couldn't understand when he asked me questions for days and days after I got to Borstal; and I couldn't explain it to him then like I'm writing it down now; and even if I'd been able to maybe he still wouldn't have caught on because I don't know whether I can understand it myself even at this moment, though I'm doing my best you can bet.

So before I knew where I was I was inside the baker's office watching Mike picking up that cash box after he'd struck a match to see where it was, wearing a tailor-made fifty-shilling grin on his square crew-cut nut as his paws closed over the box like he'd squash it to nothing. "Out," he suddenly said, shaking it so's it rattled. "Let's scram."

"Maybe there's some more," I said, pulling half a dozen drawers out of a rollertop desk.

"No," he said, like he'd already been twenty years in the game, "this is the lot," patting his tin box, "this is it."

I pulled out another few drawers, full of bills, books and letters. "How do you know, you loony sod?"

He barged past me like a bull at a gate. "Because I do."

Right or wrong, we'd both got to stick together and do the same thing. I looked at an ever-loving babe of a brand-new typewriter, but knew it was too traceable, so blew it a kiss, and went out after him. "Hang on," I said, pulling the door to, "we're in no hurry."

"Not much we aren't," he says over his shoulder.

"We've got months to splash the lolly," I whispered as we crossed the yard, "only don't let that gate creak too much or you'll have the narks tuning-in."

"You think I'm barmy?" he said, creaking the gate so that the whole street heard.

I don't know about Mike, but now I started to think of how we'd get back safe through the streets with that money-box up my jumper. Because he'd clapped it into my hand as soon as we'd got to the main road, which might have meant that he'd started thinking as well, which only goes to show how you don't know what's in anybody else's mind unless you think about things yourself. But as far as my thinking went at that moment it wasn't up to much, only a bit of fright that wouldn't budge not even with a hot blow-lamp, about what we'd say if a copper asked us where we were off to with that hump in my guts.

"What is it?" he'd ask, and I'd say: "A growth." "What do you mean, a growth, my lad?" he'd say back, narky light. I'd cough and clutch myself like I was in the most tripe-twisting pain in the world, and screw my eyes up like I was on my way to the hospital, and Mike would take my arm like he was the best pal I'd got. "Cancer," I'd manage to say to Narker, which would make his slow punch-drunk brain suspect a thing or two. "A lad of your age?" So I'd groan again, and hope to make him feel a real bully of a bastard, which would be impossible, but anyway: "It's in the family. Dad died of it last month, and I'll die of it next month by the feel of it." "What, did he have it in the guts?" "No, in the throat. But it's got me in the stomach." Groan and cough. "Well, you shouldn't be out like this if you've got cancer, you should be in the hospital." I'd get ratty now: "That's where I'm trying to go if only you'd let me and stop asking so many questions. Aren't I, Mike?" Grunt from Mike as he unslung his cosh. Then just in time the copper would tell us to get on our way, kind and considerate all of a sudden, saying that the outpatient department of the hospital closes at twelve, so hadn't he better call us a taxi? He would if we liked, he says, and he'd pay for it as well. But we tell him not to bother, that he's a good bloke even if he is a copper, that we know a short cut anyway. Then just as we're turning a corner he gets it into his big batchy head that we're going the opposite way to the hospital, and calls us back. So we'd start to run . . . if you can call all that thinking.

Up in my room Mike rips open that money-box with a hammer and chisel, and before we know where we are we've got seventy-eight pound fifteen and fourpence ha'penny *each* lying all over my bed like tea spread out on Christmas Day: cake and trifle, salad and sandwiches, jam tarts and bars of chocolate: all shared and shared alike between Mike and me because we believed in equal work and equal pay, just like the comrades my dad was in until he couldn't do a stroke anymore and had no breath left to argue with. I thought how good it was that blokes like that poor baker didn't stash all his cash in one of the big marble-fronted banks that take up every corner of the town, how lucky for us that he didn't trust them no matter how many millions of tons of concrete or how many iron bars and boxes they were made of, or how many coppers kept their blue pop-eyed peepers glued on to them, how smashing it was that he believed in money-boxes when so many shop-keepers thought it old-fashioned and tried to be modern by using a bank, which wouldn't give a couple of sincere, honest, hardworking, conscientious blokes like Mike and me a chance.

Now you'd think, and I'd think, and anybody with a bit of imagination would think, that we'd done as clean a job as could ever be done, that, with the baker's shop being at least a mile from where we lived, and with not a soul having seen us, and what with the fog and the fact that we weren't more than five minutes in the place, that the coppers should never have been able to trace us. But then, you'd be wrong. I'd be wrong, and everybody else would be wrong, no matter how much imagination was diced out between us.

Even so, Mike and I didn't splash the money about, because that would have made people think straightaway that we'd latched on to something that didn't belong to us. Which wouldn't do at all, because even in a street like ours there are people who love to do a good turn for the coppers, though I never know why they do. Some people are so mean-gutted that even if they've only got tuppence more than you and they think you're the sort that would take it if you have half the chance, they'd get you put inside if they saw you ripping lead out of a lavatory, even if it weren't their lavatory—just to keep their tuppence out of your reach. And so we didn't do anything to let on about how rich we were, nothing like going down town and coming back dressed in brand-new Teddy boy suits and carrying a set of skiffle-drums like another pal of ours who'd done a factory office about six months before. No, we took the odd bobs and pennies out and folded the notes into bundles and stuffed them up the drainpipe outside the door in the backyard. "Nobody'll ever think of looking for it here," I said to Mike. "We'll keep it doggo for a week or two, then take a few quid a week out till it's all gone. We might be thieving bastards, but we're not green."

Some days later a plain-clothes dick knocked at the door. And asked for me. I was still in bed, at eleven o'clock, and had to unroll myself from the comfortable black sheets when I heard mam calling me. "A man to see you," she said. "Hurry up, or he'll be gone."

I could hear her keeping him at the back door, nattering about how fine it had been but how it looked like rain since early this morning— and he didn't answer her except to snap out a snotty yes or no. I scrambled into my trousers and wondered why he'd come—knowing it was a copper because "a man to see you" always meant just that in our house—and if I'd had any idea that one had gone to Mike's house as well at the same time I'd have twigged it to be because of that hundred and fifty quid's worth of paper stuffed up the drainpipe outside the back door about ten inches away from that plain-clothed copper's boot, where mam still talked to him thinking she was doing me a favour, and I wishing to God she'd ask him in, though on second thoughts realizing that that would seem more suspicious than keeping him outside, because they know we hate their guts and smell a rat if they think we're trying to be nice to them. Mam wasn't born yesterday, I thought, thumping my way down the creaking stairs.

I'd seen him before: Borstal Bernard in nicky-hat, Remand Home Ronald in rowing-boat boots, Probation Pete in a pit-prop mackintosh, three-months clink in collar and tie (all this out of a Borstal skiffle-ballad that my new mate made up, and I'd tell you it in full but it doesn't belong in this story), a 'tec, who'd never had as much in his pocket as that drainpipe had up its jackses. He was like Hitler in the face, right down to the paint-brush tash, except that being six-foot tall made him seem worse. But I straightened my shoulders to look into his illiterate blue eyes—like I always do with any copper.

Then he started asking me questions, and my mother from behind said: "He's never left that television set for the last three months, so you've got nowt on him, mate. You might as well look for somebody else, because you're wasting the rates you get out of my rent and the income-tax that comes out of my pay-packet standing there like that" —which was a laugh because she'd never paid either to my knowledge, and never would, I hoped.

"Well, you know where Papplewick Street is, don't you?" the copper asked me, taking no notice of mam.

"Ain't it off Alfreton Road?" I asked him back, helpful and bright.

"You know there's a baker's half-way down on the left-hand side, don't you?"

"Ain't it next door to a pub, then?" I wanted to know.

He answered me sharp: "No, it bloody well ain't." Coppers always lose their tempers as quick as this, and more often than not they gain nothing by it. "Then I don't know it," I told him, saved by the bell.

He slid his big boot round and round on the doorstep. "Where were you last Friday night?" Back in the ring, but this was worse than a boxing match.

I didn't like him trying to accuse me of something he wasn't sure I'd done. "Was I at the baker's you mentioned? Or in the pub next door?"

"You'll get five years in Borstal if you don't give me a straight answer," he said, unbuttoning his mac even though it was cold where he was standing.

"I was glued to the telly, like mam says," I swore blind. But he went on and on with his loony questions: "Have you got a television?"

The things he asked wouldn't have taken in a kid of two, and what else could I say to the last one except: "Has the aerial fell down? Or would you like to come in and see it?"

He was liking me even less for saying that. "We know you weren't listening to the television set last Friday, and so do you, don't you?"

"P'raps not, but I was *looking* at it, because sometimes we turn the sound down for a bit of fun." I could hear mam laughing from the kitchen, and I hoped Mike's mam was doing the same if the cops had gone to him as well.

"We know you weren't in the house," he said, starting up again, cranking himself with the handle. They always say 'We' 'We', never 'I' 'I'—as if they feel braver and righter knowing there's a lot of them against only one.

"I've got witnesses," I said to him. "Mam for one. Her fancy-man, for two. Ain't that enough? I can get you a dozen more, or thirteen altogether, if it was a baker's that got robbed."

"I don't want no lies," he said, not catching on about the baker's dozen. Where do they scrape cops up from anyway? "All I want is to get from you where you put that money."

Don't get mad, I kept saying to myself, don't get mad—hearing mam setting out cups and saucers and putting the pan on the stove for bacon. I stood back and waved him inside like I was a butler. "Come and search the house. If you've got a warrant."

"Listen, my lad," he said, like the dirty bullying jumped-up bastard he was, "I don't want too much of your lip, because if we get you down to the Guildhall you'll get a few bruises and black-eyes for your trouble." And I knew he wasn't kidding either, because I'd heard about all them sort of tricks. I hoped one day though that him and all his pals would be the ones to get the black-eyes and kicks; you never knew. It might come sooner than anybody thinks, like in Hungary. "Tell me where the money is, and I'll get you off with probation."

"What money?" I asked him, because I'd heard that one before as well.

"You know what money."

"Do I look as though I'd know owt about money?" I said, pushing my fist through a hole in my shirt.

"The money that was pinched, that you know all about," he said. "You can't trick me, so it's no use trying."

"Was it three-and-eightpence ha'penny?" I asked.

"You thieving young bastard. We'll teach you to steal money that doesn't belong to you."

I turned my head around: "Mam," I called out, "get my lawyer on the blower, will you?"

"Clever, aren't you?" he said in a very unfriendly way, "but we won't rest until we clear all this up."

"Look," I pleaded, as if about to sob my socks off because he'd got me wrong, "it's all very well us talking like this, it's like a game almost, but I wish you'd tell me what it's all about, because honest-to-God I've just got out of bed and here you are at the door talking about me having pinched a lot of money, money that I don't know anything about."

He swung around now as if he'd trapped me, though I couldn't see why he might think so. "Who said anything about money? I didn't. What made you bring money into this little talk we're having?"

"It's you," I answered, thinking he was going barmy and about to start foaming at the chops, "you've got money on the brain, like all policemen. Baker's shops as well."

He screwed his face up. "I want an answer from you: where's that money?"

But I was getting fed-up with all this. "I'll do a deal."

Judging by his flash-bulb face he thought he was suddenly on to a good thing. "What sort of a deal?"

So I told him: "I'll give you all the money I've got, one and four-pence ha'penny, if you stop this third-degree and let me go in and get my breakfast. Honest, I'm clambed to death. I ain't had a bite since yesterday. Can't you hear my guts rollin'?"

His jaw dropped, but on he went, pumping me for another half hour. A routine check-up, as they say on the pictures. But I knew I was winning on points.

Then he left, but came back in the afternoon to search the house. He didn't find a thing, not a French farthing. He asked me questions again and I didn't tell him anything except lies, lies, lies, because I can go on doing that forever without batting an eyelid. He'd got nothing on me and we both of us knew it, otherwise I'd have been down at the Guildhall in no time, but he kept on keeping on because I'd been in a Remand Home for a high-wall job before; and Mike was put through the same mill because all the local cops knew he was my best pal.

When it got dark me and Mike were in our parlour with a low light on and the telly off, Mike taking it easy in the rocking chair and me slouched out on the settee, both of us puffing a packet of Woods. With the door bolted and curtains drawn we talked about the dough we'd crammed up the drainpipe. Mike thought we should take it out and both of us do a bunk to Skegness or Cleethorpes for a good time in the arcades, living like lords in a boarding house near the pier, then at least we'd both have had a big beano before getting sent down.

"Listen, you daft bleeder," I said, "we aren't going to get caught at all, *and* we'll have a good time, later." We were so clever we didn't even go out to the pictures, though we wanted to.

In the morning old Hitler-face questioned me again, with one of his pals this time, and the next day they came, trying as hard as they could to get something out of me, but I didn't budge an inch. I know I'm showing off when I say this, but in me he'd met his match, and I'd never give in to questions no matter how long it was kept up. They searched the house a couple of times as well, which made me think they thought they really had something to go by, but I know now that they hadn't, and that it was all buckshee speculation. They turned the house upside down and inside out like an old sock, went from top to bottom and front to back but naturally didn't find a thing. The copper even poked his face up the front-room chimney (that hadn't been used or swept for years) and came down looking like Al Jolson so that he had to swill himself clean at the scullery sink. They kept tapping and pottering around the big aspidistra plant that grandma had left to mam, lifting it up from the table to look under the cloth, putting it aside so's they could move the table and get at the boards under the rug—but the big headed stupid ignorant bastards never once thought of emptying the soil out of the plant pot, where they'd have found the crumpled-up money-box that we'd buried the night we did the job. I suppose it's still there, now I think about it, and I suppose mam wonders now and again why the plant don't prosper like it used to—as if it could with a fistful of thick black tin wrapped around its guts.

The last time he knocked at our door was one wet morning at five minutes to nine and I was sleep-logged in my crumby bed as usual. Mam had gone to work that day so I shouted for him to hold on a bit, and then went down to see who it was. There he stood, six-feet tall and sopping wet, and for the first time in my life I did a spiteful thing I'll never forgive myself for: I didn't ask him to come in out of the rain, because I wanted him to get double pneumonia and die. I suppose he could have pushed by me and come in if he'd wanted, but maybe he'd got used to asking questions on the doorstep and didn't want to be put off by changing his ground even though it was raining. Not that I don't like being spiteful because of any barmy principle I've got, but this bit of spite, as it turned out, did me no good at all. I should have treated him as a brother I hadn't seen for twenty years and dragged him in for a cup of tea and a fag, told him about the picture I hadn't seen the night before, asked him how his wife was after her operation and whether they'd shaved her moustache off to make it, and then sent him happy and satisfied out by the front door. But no, I thought, let's see what he's got to say for himself now.

He stood a little to one side of the door, either because it was less wet there, or because he wanted to see me from a different angle, perhaps having found it monotonous to watch a bloke's face always telling lies from the same side. "You've been identified," he said, twitching raindrops from his tash. "A woman saw you and your mate yesterday and she swears blind you are the same chaps she saw going into that bakery."

I was dead sure he was still bluffing, because Mike and I hadn't even seen each other the day before, but I looked worried. "She's a menace then to innocent people, whoever she is, because the only bakery I've been in lately is the one up our street to get some cut-bread on tick for mam."

He didn't bite on this. "So now I want to know where the money is"—as if I hadn't answered him at all.

"I think mam took it to work this morning to get herself some tea in the canteen." Rain was splashing down so hard I thought he'd get washed away if he didn't come inside. But I wasn't much bothered, and went on: "I remember I put it in the telly-vase last night—it was my only one-and-three and I was saving it for a packet of tips this morning —and I nearly had a jibbering black fit just now when I saw it had gone. I was reckoning on it for getting me through today because I don't think life's worth living without a fag, do you?"

I was getting into my stride and began to feel good, twigging that this would be my last pack of lies, and that if I kept it up for long enough this time I'd have the bastards beat: Mike and me would be off to the coast in a few weeks time having the fun of our lives, playing at penny football and latching on to a couple of tarts that would give us all they were good for. "And this weather's no good for picking-up fag-ends in the street," I said, "because they'd be sopping wet. Course, I know you could dry 'em out near the fire, but it don't taste the same you know, all said and done. Rainwater does summat to 'em that don't bear thinkin' about: it turns 'em back into hoss-tods without the taste though."

I began to wonder, at the back of my brainless eyes, why old copper-lugs didn't pull me up sharp and say he hadn't got time to listen to all this, but he wasn't looking at me anymore, and all my thoughts about Skegness went bursting to smithereens in my sludgy loaf. I could have dropped into the earth when I saw what he'd fixed his eyes on.

He was looking at *it*, an ever-loving fiver, and I could only jabber:

"The one thing is to have some real fags because new hoss-tods is always better than stuff that's been rained on and dried, and I know how you feel about not being able to find money because one-and-three's one-and-three in anybody's pocket, and naturally if I see it knocking around I'll get you on the blower tomorrow straightaway and tell you where you can find it."

I thought I'd go down in a fit: three green-backs as well had been washed down by the water, and more were following, lying flat at first after their fall, then getting tilted at the corners by wind and rainspots as if they were alive and wanted to get back into the dry snug drainpipe out of the terrible weather, and you can't imagine how I wished they'd be able to. Old Hitler-face didn't know what to make of it but just kept staring down and down, and I thought I'd better keep on talking, though I knew it wasn't much good now.

"It's a fact, I know, that money's hard to come by and half-crowns don't get found on bus seats or in dustbins, and I didn't see any in bed last night because I'd 'ave known about it, wouldn't I? You can't sleep with things like that in the bed because they're too hard, and anyway at first they're . . ." It took Hitler-boy a long time to catch on; they were beginning to spread over the yard a bit, reinforced by the third colour of a ten-bob note, before his hand clamped itself on to my shoulder.

## III

The pop-eyed potbellied governor said to a pop-eyed potbellied Member of Parliament who sat next to his pop-eyed potbellied whore of a wife that I was his only hope for getting the Borstal Blue Ribbon Prize Cup For Long-Distance Cross-Country Running (all England), which I was, and it set me laughing to myself inside, and I didn't say a word to any potbellied pop-eyed bastard that might give them real hope, though I knew the governor anyway took my quietness to mean he'd got that cup already stuck on the bookshelf in his office among the few other mildewed trophies.

"He might take up running in a sort of professional way when he gets out," and it wasn't until he'd said this and I'd heard it with my own flap-tabs that I realized it might be possible to do such a thing, run for money, trot for wages on piece work at a bob a puff rising bit by bit to a guinea a gasp and retiring through old age at thirty-two because of lace-curtain lungs, a football heart, and legs like varicose beanstalks. But I'd have a wife and car and get my grinning long-distance clock in the papers and have a smashing secretary to answer piles of letters sent by tarts who'd mob me when they saw who I was as I pushed my way into Woolworth's for a packet of razor blades and a cup of tea. It was something to think about all right, and sure enough the governor knew he'd got me when he said, turning to me as if I would at any rate have to be consulted about it all: "How does this matter strike you, then, Smith, my lad?"

A line of potbellied pop-eyes gleamed at me and a row of goldfish mouths opened and wiggled gold teeth at me, so I gave them the answer they wanted because I'd hold my trump card until later. "It'd suit me fine, sir," I said.

"Good lad. Good show. Right spirit. Splendid."

"Well," the governor said, "get that cup for us today and I'll do all I can for you. I'll get you trained so that you whack every man in the Free World." And I had a picture in my brain of me running and beating everybody in the world, leaving them all behind until only I was trot-trotting across a big wide moor alone, doing a marvellous speed as I ripped between boulders and reed-clumps, when suddenly: CRACK! CRACK!—bullets that can go faster than any man running, coming from a copper's rifle planted in a tree, winged me and split my gizzard in spite of my perfect running, and down I fell.

The potbellies expected me to say something else. "Thank you, sir," I said.

Told to go, I trotted down the pavilion steps, out on to the field because the big cross-country was about to begin and the two entries from Gunthorpe had fixed themselves early at the starting line and were ready to move off like white kangaroos. The sports ground looked a treat: with big tea-tents all round and flags flying and seats for families—empty because no mam or dad had known what opening day meant—and boys still running heats for the hundred yards, and lords and ladies walking from stall to stall, and the Borstal Boys Brass Band in blue uniforms; and up on the stands the brown jackets of Hucknall as well as our own grey blazers, and then the Gunthorpe lot with shirt sleeves rolled. The blue sky was full of sunshine and it couldn't have been a better day, and all of the big show was like something out of Ivanhoe that we'd seen on the pictures a few days before.

"Come on, Smith," Roach the sports master called to me, "we don't want you to be late for the big race, eh? Although I dare say you'd catch them up if you were." The others cat-called and grunted at this, but I took no notice and placed myself between Gunthorpe and one of the Aylesham trusties, dropped on my knees and plucked a few grass blades to suck on the way round. So the big race it was, for them, watching from the grandstand under a fluttering Union Jack, a race for the governor, that he had been waiting for, and I hoped he and all the rest of his pop-eyed gang were busy placing big bets on me, hundred to one to win, all the money they had in their pockets, all the wages they were going to get for the next five years, and the more they placed the happier I'd be. Because here was a dead cert going to die on the big name they'd built for him, going to go down dying with laughter whether it choked him or not. My knees felt the cool soil pressing into them, and out of my eye's corner I saw Roach lift his hand. The Gunthorpe boy twitched before the signal was given; somebody cheered too soon; Medway bent forward; then the gun went, and I was away.

We went once around the field and then along a half-mile drive of elms, being cheered all the way, and I seemed to feel I was in the lead as we went out by the gate and into the lane, though I wasn't interested enough to find out. The five-mile course was marked by splashes of whitewash gleaming on gateposts and trunks and stiles and stones, and a boy with a waterbottle and bandage-box stood every half-mile waiting for those that dropped out or fainted. Over the first stile, without trying, I was still nearly in the lead but one; and if any of you want tips about running, never be in a hurry, and never let any of the other runners know you are in a hurry even if you are. You can always overtake on long-distance running without letting the others smell the hurry in you; and when you've used your craft like this to reach the two or three up front then you can do a big dash later that puts everybody else's hurry in the shade because you've not had to make haste up till then. I ran to a steady jog-trot rhythm, and soon it was so smooth that I forgot I was running, and I was hardly able to know that my legs were lifting and falling and my arms going in and out, and my lungs didn't seem to working at all, and my heart stopped that wicked thumping I always get at the beginning of a run. Because you see I never race at all; I just run, and somehow I know that if I forget I'm racing and only jog-trot along until I don't know I'm running I always win the race. For when my eyes recognize that I'm getting near the end of the course—by seeing a stile or cottage corner—I put on a spurt, and such a fast big spurt it is because I feel that up till then I haven't been running and that I've used up no energy at all. And I've been able to do this because I've been thinking; and I wonder if I'm the only one in the running business with this system of forgetting that I'm running because I'm too busy thinking; and I wonder if any of the other lads are on the same lark, though I know for a fact that they aren't. Off like the wind along the cobbled footpath and rutted lane, smoother than the flat grass track on the field and better for thinking because it's not too smooth, and I was in my element that afternoon knowing that nobody could beat me at running but intending to beat myself before the day was over. For when the governor talked to me of being honest when I first came in he didn't know what the word meant or he wouldn't have had me here in this race, trotting along in shimmy and shorts and sunshine. He'd have had me where I'd have had him if I'd been in his place: in a quarry breaking rocks until he broke his back. At least old Hitler-face the plain-clothes dick was honester than the governor, because he at any rate had had it in for me and I for him, and when my case was coming up in court a copper knocked at our front door at four o'clock in the morning and got my mother out of bed when she was paralytic tired, reminding her she had to be in court at dead on half past nine. It was the finest bit of spite I've ever heard of, but I would call it honest, the same as my mam's words were honest when she really told that copper what she thought of him and called him all the dirty names she'd ever heard of, which took her half an hour and woke the terrace up.

I trotted on along the edge of a field bordered by the sunken lane, smelling green grass and honeysuckle, and I felt as though I came from a long line of whippets trained to run on two legs, only I couldn't see a toy rabbit in front and there wasn't a collier's cosh behind to make me keep up the pace. I passed the Gunthorpe runner whose shimmy was already black with sweat and I could just see the corner of the fenced-up copse in front where the only man I had to pass to win the race was going all out to gain the half-way mark. Then he turned into a tongue of trees and bushes where I couldn't see him anymore, and I couldn't see anybody, and I knew what the loneliness of the long-distance runner running across country felt like, realizing that as far as I was concerned this feeling was the only honesty and realness there was in the world and I knowing it would be no different ever, no matter what I felt at odd times, and no matter what anybody else tried to tell me. The runner behind me must have been a long way off because it was so quiet, and there was even less noise and movement than there had been at five o'clock of a frosty winter morning. It was hard to understand, and all I knew was that you had to run, run, run, without knowing why you were running, but on you went through fields you didn't understand and into woods that made you afraid, over hills without knowing you'd been up and down, and shooting across streams that would have cut the heart out of you had you fallen into them. And the winning post was no end to it, even though crowds might be cheering you in, because on you had to go before you got your breath back, and the only time you stopped really was when you tripped over a tree trunk and broke your neck or fell into a disused well and stayed dead in the darkness forever. So I thought: they aren't going to get me on this racing lark, this running and trying to win, this jog-trotting for a bit of blue ribbon, because it's not the way to go on at all, though they swear blind that it is. You should think about nobody and go your own way, not on a course marked out for you by people holding mugs of water and bottles of iodine in case you fall and cut yourself so that they can pick you up—even if you want to stay where you are—and get you moving again.

On I went, out of the wood, passing the man leading without knowing I was going to do so. Flip-flap, flip flap, jog-trot, jog-trot, crunch-slap-crunchslap, across the middle of a broad field again, rhythmically running in my greyhound effortless fashion, knowing I had won the race though it wasn't half over, won it if I wanted it, could go on for ten or fifteen or twenty miles if I had to and drop dead at the finish of it, which would be the same, in the end, as living an honest life like the governor wanted me to. It amounted to: win the race and be honest, and on trot-trotting I went, having the time of my life, loving my progress because it did me good and set me thinking which by now I liked to do, but not caring at all when I remembered that I had to win this race as well as run it. One of the two, I had to win the race or run it, and I knew I could do both because my legs had carried me well in front—now coming to the short cut down the bramble bank and over the sunken road—and would carry me further because they seemed made of electric cable and easily alive to keep on slapping at those ruts and roots, but I'm not going to win because the only way I'd see I came in first would be if winning meant that I was going to escape the coppers after doing the biggest bank job of my life, but winning means the exact opposite, no matter how they try to kill or kid me, means running right into their white-gloved wall-barred hands and grinning mugs and staying there for the rest of my natural long life of stone-breaking anyway, but stone-breaking in the way I want to do it and not in the way they tell me.

Another honest thought that comes is that I could swing left at the next hedge of the field, and under its cover beat my slow retreat away from the sports ground winning post. I could do three or six or a dozen miles across the turf like this and cut a few main roads behind me so's they'd never know which one I'd taken; and maybe on the last one when it got dark I could thumb a lorry-lift and get a free ride north with somebody who might not give me away. But no, I said I wasn't daft didn't I? I won't pull out with only six months left, and besides there's nothing I want to dodge and run away from; I only want a bit of my own back on the In-laws and Potbellies by letting them sit up there on their big posh seats and watch me lose this race, though as sure as God made me I know that when I do lose I'll get the dirtiest crap and kitchen jobs in the months to go before my time is up. I won't be worth a threpp'ny-bit to anybody here, which will be all the thanks I get for being honest in the only way I know. For when the governor told me to be honest it was meant to be in his way not mine, and if I kept on being honest in the way he wanted and won my race for him he'd see I got the cushiest six months still left to run; but in my own way, well, it's not allowed, and if I find a way of doing it such as I've got now then I'll get what-for in every mean trick he can set his mind to. And if you look at it in my way, who can blame him? For this is war—and ain't I said so?—and when I hit him in the only place he knows he'll be sure to get his own back on me for not collaring that cup when his heart's been set for ages on seeing himself standing up at the end of the afternoon to clap me on the back as I take the cup from Lord Earwig or some such chinless wonder with a name like that. And so I'll hit him where it hurts a lot, and he'll do all he can to get his own back, tit for tat, though I'll enjoy it most because I'm hitting first, and because I planned it longer. I don't know why I think these thoughts are better than any I've ever had, but I do, and I don't care why. I suppose it took me a long time to get going on all this because I've had no time and peace in all my bandit life, and now my thoughts are coming pat and the only trouble is I often can't stop, even when my brain feels as if it's got cramp, frostbite and creeping paralysis all rolled into one and I have to give it a rest by slap-dashing down through the brambles of the sunken lane. And all this is another upper-cut I'm getting in first at people like the governor, to show how—if I can—his races are never won even though some bloke always comes unknowingly in first, how in the end the governor is going to be doomed while blokes like me will take the pickings of his roasted bones and dance like maniacs around his Borstal's ruins. And so this story's like the race and once again I won't bring off a winner to suit the governor; no, I'm being honest like he told me to, without him knowing what he means, though I don't suppose he'll ever come in with a story of his own, even if he reads this one of mine and knows who I'm talking about.

I've just come up out of the sunken lane, kneed and elbowed, thumped and bramble-scratched, and the race is two-thirds over, and a voice is going like a wireless in my mind saying that when you've had enough of feeling good like the first man on earth of a frosty morning and you've known how it is to be taken bad like the last man on earth on a summer's afternoon, then you get at last to being like the only man on earth and don't give a bogger about either good or bad, but just trot on with your slippers slapping the good dry soil that at least would never do you a bad turn. Now the words are like coming from a crystal-set that's broken down, and something's happening inside the shell-case of my guts that bothers me and I don't know why or what to blame it on, a grinding near my ticker as though a bag of rusty screws is loose inside me and I shake them up every time I trot forward. Now and again I break my rhythm to feel my left shoulder-blade by swinging a right hand across my chest as if to rub the knife away that has some-how got stuck there. But I know it's nothing to bother about, that more likely it's caused by too much thinking that now and again I take for worry. For sometimes I'm the greatest worrier in the world I think (as you twigged I'll bet from me having got this story out) which is funny anyway because my mam don't know the meaning of the word so I don't take after her; though dad had a hard time of worry all his life up to when he filled his bedroom with hot blood and kicked the bucket that morning when nobody was in the house. I'll never forget it, straight I won't, because I was the one that found him and I often wished I hadn't. Back from a session on the fruit-machines at the fish-and-chip shop, jingling my three-lemon loot to a nail-dead house, as soon as I got in I knew something was wrong, stood leaning my head against the cold mirror above the mantelpiece trying not to open my eyes and see my stone-cold clock—because I knew I'd gone as white as a piece of chalk since coming in as if I'd been got at by a Dracula-vampire and even my penny-pocket winnings kept quiet on purpose.

Gunthorpe nearly caught me up. Birds were singing from the briar hedge, and a couple of thrushies flew like lightning into some thorny bushes. Corn had grown high in the next field and would be cut down soon with scythes and mowers; but I never wanted to notice much while running in case it put me off my stroke, so by the haystack I decided to leave it all behind and put on such a spurt, in spite of nails in my guts, that before long I'd left both Gunthorpe and the birds a good way off; I wasn't far now from going into that last mile and a half like a knife through margarine, but the quietness I suddenly trotted into between two pickets was like opening my eyes underwater and looking at the pebbles on a stream bottom, reminding me again of going back that morning to the house in which my old man had croaked, which is funny because I hadn't thought about it at all since it happened and even then I didn't brood much on it. I wonder why? I suppose that since I started to think on these long-distance runs I'm liable to have anything crop up and pester at my tripes and innards, and now that I see my bloody dad behind each grass-blade in my barmy runner-brain I'm not so sure I like to think and that it's such a good thing after all. I choke my phlegm and keep on running anyway and curse the Borstal-builders and their athletics—flappity-flap, slop-slop, crunch-slap-crunchslap-crunchslap—who've maybe got their own back on me from the bright beginning by sliding magic-lantern slides into my head that never stood a chance before. Only if I take whatever comes like this in my runner's stride can I keep on keeping on like my old self and beat them back; and now I've thought on this far I know I'll win, in the crunchslap end. So anyway after a bit I went upstairs one step at a time not thinking anything about how I should find dad and what I'd do when I did. But now I'm making up for it by going over the rotten life mam led him ever since I can remember, knocking-on with different men even when he was alive and fit and she not caring whether he knew it or not, and most of the time he wasn't so blind as she thought and cursed and roared and threatened to punch her tab, and I had to stand up to stop him even though I knew she deserved it. What a life for all of us. Well, I'm not grumbling, because if I did I might just as well win this bleeding race, which I'm not going to do, though if I don't lose speed I'll win it before I know where I am, and then where would I be?

Now I can hear the sportsground noise and music as I head back for the flags and the lead-in drive, the fresh new feel of underfoot gravel going against the iron muscles of my legs. I'm nowhere near puffed despite that bag of nails that rattles as much as ever, and I can still give a big last leap like gale-force wind if I want to, but everything is under control and I know now that there ain't another long-distance cross-country running runner in England to touch my speed and style. Our doddering bastard of a governor, our half-dead gangrened gaffer is hollow like an empty petrol drum, and he wants me and my running life to give him glory, to put in him blood and throbbing veins he never had, wants his potbellied pals to be his witnesses as I gasp and stagger up to his winning post so's he can say: "My Borstal gets that cup, you see. I win my bet, because it pays to be honest and try to gain the prizes I offer to my lads, and they know it, have known it all along. They'll always be honest now, because I made them so." And his pals will think: "He trains his lads to live right, after all; he deserves a medal but we'll get him made a Sir"—and at this very moment as the birds come back to whistling I can tell myself I'll never care a sod what any of the chinless spineless In-laws think or say. They've seen me and they're cheering now and loudspeakers set around the field like elephant's ears are spreading out the big news that I'm well in the lead, and can't do anything else but stay there. But I'm still thinking of the Out-law death my dad died, telling the doctors to scat from the house when they wanted him to finish up in hospital (like a bleeding guinea-pig, he raved at them). He got up in bed to throw them out and even followed them down the stairs in his shirt though he was no more than skin and stick. They tried to tell him he'd want some drugs but he didn't fall for it, and only took the pain-killer that mam and I got from a herb seller in the next street. It's not till now that I know what guts he had, and when I went into the room that morning he was lying on his stomach with the clothes thrown back, looking like a skinned rabbit, his grey head resting just on the edge of the bed, and on the floor must have been all the blood he'd had in his body, right from his toenails up, for nearly all of the lino and carpet was covered in it, thin and pink.

And down the drive I went, carrying a heart blocked up like Boulder Dam across my arteries, the nail-bag clamped down tighter and tighter as though in a woodwork vice, yet with my feet like birdwings and arms like talons ready to fly across the field except that I didn't want to give anybody that much of a show, or win the race by accident. I smell the hot dry day now as I run towards the end, passing a mountain-heap of grass emptied from cans hooked on to the fronts of lawnmowers pushed by my pals; I rip a piece of tree-bark with my fingers and stuff it in my mouth, chewing wood and dust and maybe maggots as I run until I'm nearly sick, yet swallowing what I can of it just the same because a little birdie whistled to me that I've got to go on living for at least a bloody

sight longer yet but that for six months I'm not going to smell that
grass or taste that dusty bark or trot this lovely path. I hate to have to
say this but something bloody-well made me cry, and crying is a thing
I haven't bloody-well done since I was a kid of two or three. Because
I'm slowing down now for Gunthorpe to catch me up, and I'm doing it
in a place just where the drive turns into the sportsfield—where they
can see what I'm doing, especially the governor and his gang from the
grandstand, and I'm going so slow I'm almost marking time. Those on
the nearest seats haven't caught on yet to what's happening and are
still cheering like mad ready for when I make that mark, and I keep
on wondering when the bleeding hell Gunthorpe behind me is going
to nip by on to the field because I can't hold this up all day, and I think
Oh Christ it's just my rotten luck that Gunthorpe's dropped out and
that I'll be here for half an hour before the next bloke comes up, but
even so, I say, I won't budge, I won't go for that last hundred yards if
I have to sit down cross-legged on the grass and have the governor and
his chinless wonders pick me up and carry me there, which is against
their rules so you can bet they'd never do it because they're not clever
enough to break the rules—like I would be in their place—even though
they are their own. No, I'll show him what honesty means if it's the
last thing I do, though I'm sure he'll never understand because if he
and all them like him did it'd mean they'd be on my side which is impossible. By God I'll stick this out like my dad stuck out his pain and
kicked them doctors down the stairs: if he had guts for that then I've
got guts for this and here I stay waiting for Gunthorpe or Aylesham to
bash that turf and go right slap-up against that bit of clothes-line
stretched across the winning post. As for me, the only time I'll hit that
clothes-line will be when I'm dead and a comfortable coffin's been got
ready on the other side. Until then I'm a long-distance runner, crossing
country all on my own no matter how bad it feels.

The Essex boys were shouting themselves blue in the face telling me
to get a move on, waving their arms, standing up and making as if to
run at that rope themselves because they were only a few yards to the
side of it. You cranky lot, I thought, stuck at that winning post, and yet
I knew they didn't mean what they were shouting, were really on my
side and always would be, not able to keep their maulers to themselves, in and out of copshops and clink. And there they were now having the time of their lives letting themselves go in cheering me which
made the governor think they were heart and soul on his side when he
wouldn't have thought any such thing if he'd had a grain of sense.
And I could hear the lords and ladies now from the grandstand, and
could see them standing up to wave me in: "Run!" they were shouting
in their posh voices. "Run!" But I was deaf, daft and blind, and stood
where I was, still tasting the bark in my mouth and still blubbing like a
baby, blubbing now out of gladness that I'd got them beat at last.

Because I heard a roar and saw the Gunthorpe gang throwing their coats up in the air and I felt the pat-pat of feet on the drive behind me getting closer and closer and suddenly a smell of sweat and a pair of lungs on their last gasp passed me by and went swinging on towards that rope, all shagged out and rocking from side to side, grunting like a Zulu that didn't know any better, like the ghost of me at ninety when I'm heading for that fat upholstered coffin. I could have cheered him myself: "Go on, go on, get cracking. Knot yourself up on that piece of tape." But he was already there, and so I went on, trot-trotting after him until I got to the rope, and collapsed, with a murderous sounding roar going up through my ears while I was still on the wrong side of it.

It's about time to stop; though don't think I'm not still running, because I am, one way or another. The governor at Borstal proved me right; he didn't respect my honesty at all; not that I expected him to, or tried to explain it to him, but if he's supposed to be educated then he should have more or less twigged it. He got his own back right enough, or thought he did, because he had me carting dustbins about every morning from the big full-working kitchen to the garden-bottoms where I had to empty them, and in the afternoon I spread out slops over spuds and carrots growing in the allotments. In the evenings I scrubbed floors, miles and miles of them. But it wasn't a bad life for six months, which was another thing he could never understand and would have made it grimmer if he could, and it was worth it when I look back on it, considering all the thinking I did, and the fact that the boys caught on to me losing the race on purpose and never had enough good words to say about me, or curses to throw out (to themselves) at the governor.

The work didn't break me; if anything it made me stronger in many ways, and the governor knew, when I left, that his spite had got him nowhere. For since leaving Borstal they tried to get me in the army, but I didn't pass the medical and I'll tell you why. No sooner was I out, after that final run and six-months hard, than I went down with pleurisy, which means as far as I'm concerned that I lost the governor's race all right, and won my own twice over, because I know for certain that if I hadn't raced my race I wouldn't have got this pleurisy, which keeps me out of khaki but doesn't stop me doing the sort of work my itchy fingers want to do.

I'm out now and the heat's switched on again, but the rats haven't got me for the last thing I pulled. I counted six hundred and twenty-eight pounds and am still living off it because I did the job all on my own, and after it I had the peace to write all this, and it'll be money enough to keep me going until I finish my plans for doing an even bigger snatch, something up my sleeve I wouldn't tell to a living soul. I worked out my systems and hiding-places while pushing scrubbing-brushes around them Borstal floors, planned my outward life of innocence and honest work, yet at the same time grew perfect in the razor-edges of my craft for what I knew I had to do once free; and what I'll do again if netted by the poaching coppers.

In the meantime (as they say in one or two books I've read since, useless though because all of them ended on a winning post and didn't teach me a thing) I'm going to give this story to a pal of mine and tell him that if I do get captured again by the coppers he can try and get it put into a book or something, because I'd like to see the governor's face when he reads it, if he does, which I don't suppose he will; even if he did read it though I don't think he'd know what it was all about. And if I don't get caught the bloke I give this story to will never give me away; he's lived on our terrace for as long as I can remember, and he's my pal. That I do know.

## Study Aids: Melville

1. What are the characteristics of the various walls described in the story? What do they symbolize about the condition of Bartleby's life and the lives of the others?
2. How do the nature of the job and the nature of the way in which the other three clerks do their work further define the conditions of Bartleby's life?
3. Why does Bartleby "prefer not to"? What is he doing? What are the stages in the development of this course of action?
4. Why is the discovery of Bartleby's former job at the Dead Letter Office the final clue to the reasons for Bartleby's course of action? How is this job related to the conditions of his last job?
5. What connection to Bartleby does the lawyer feel? What are the stages of his feelings toward Bartleby? What does he recognize with his last statement: "Ah, Bartleby! Ah, humanity!"?

## Study Aids: Sillitoe

1. What are the different meanings (literal and symbolic) attached to the word *running* throughout the story? What values are attached to them? What is the difference between *running* and *racing?* What are the meanings of his *loneliness?* In what ways is running the race connected to the whole pattern of his life?
2. What are the two kinds of honesty? How do they determine the outcome of the race? What is the nature of the honesty he feels while running the race?
3. The runner several times discusses *spite.* What part does spite play in his decision to lose? What part does it play in his arrest? In his general defiance? After the race, he comments that the Governor's spite had got him nowhere. How is that comment connected to the author's view of the runner himself, to his winning only by losing, and to the ending of the story?
4. The runner insists he "will go on making false moves." Why? How does

he see the conditions of his life? What is the basis of his definition of those conditions, especially the two sides; what is the basis of his hostility? What does he oppose and defy?

5. How do the details at the beginning of section II define the social causes of the crime the runner commits?

# PART THREE

*Stories—For Further Comparison*

# THE OVAL PORTRAIT

*Edgar Allan Poe*

The chateau into which my valet had ventured to make forcible entrance, rather than permit me, in my desperately wounded condition, to pass a night in the open air, was one of those piles of commingled gloom and grandeur which have so long frowned among the Appennines, not less in fact than in the fancy of Mrs. Radcliffe. To all appearance it had been temporarily and very lately abandoned. We established ourselves in one of the smallest and least sumptuously furnished apartments. It lay in a remote turret of the building. Its decorations were rich, yet tattered and antique. Its walls were hung with tapestry and bedecked with manifold and multiform armorial trophies, together with an unusually great number of very spirited modern paintings in frames of rich golden arabesque. In these paintings, which depended from the walls not only in their main surfaces, but in very many nooks which the bizarre architecture of the chateau rendered necessary—in these paintings my incipient delirium, perhaps, had caused me to take deep interest; so that I bade Pedro to close the heavy shutters of the room—since it was already night,—to light the tongues of a tall candelabrum which stood by the head of my bed, and to throw open far and wide the fringed curtains of black velvet which enveloped the bed itself. I wished all this done that I might resign myself, if not to sleep, at least alternately to the contemplation of these pictures, and the perusal of a small volume which had been found upon the pillow, and which purported to criticise and describe them.

Long, long I read—and devoutly, devoutly I gazed. Rapidly and gloriously the hours flew by and the deep midnight came. The position of the candelabrum displeased me, and outreaching my hand with difficulty, rather than disturb my slumbering valet, I placed it so as to throw its ray more fully upon the book.

But the action produced an effect altogether unanticipated. The rays of the numerous candles (for there were many) now fell within a niche of the room which had hitherto been thrown into deep shade by one of the bedposts. I thus saw in vivid light a picture all unnoticed before. It was the portrait of a young girl just ripening into womanhood. I glanced at the painting hurriedly, and then closed my eyes. Why I did this was not at first apparent even to my own perception. But while my lids remained thus shut, I ran over in my mind my reason for so shutting them. It was an impulsive movement to gain time for thought—to make sure that my vision had not deceived me—to calm and subdue my fancy for a more sober and more certain gaze. In a very few moments I again looked fixedly at the painting.

That I now saw aright I could not and would not doubt; for the first flashing of the candles upon that canvas had seemed to dissipate the dreamy stupor which was stealing over my senses, and to startle me at once into waking life.

The portrait, I have already said, was that of a young girl. It was a mere head and shoulders, done in what is technically termed a *vignette* manner; much in the style of the favorite heads of Sully. The arms, the bosom, and even the ends of the radiant hair melted imperceptibly into the vague yet deep shadow which formed the background of the whole. The frame was oval, richly gilded and filigreed in *Moresque*. As a thing of art nothing could be more admirable than the painting itself. But it could have been neither the execution of the work, nor the immortal beauty of the countenance, which had so suddenly and so vehemently moved me. Least of all, could it have been that my fancy, shaken from its half slumber, had mistaken the head for that of a living person. I saw at once that the peculiarities of the design, of the *vignetting,* and of the frame, must have instantly dispelled such idea—must have prevented even its momentary entertainment. Thinking earnestly upon these points, I remained, for an hour perhaps, half sitting, half reclining with my vision riveted upon the portrait. At length, satisfied with the true secret of its effect, I fell back within the bed. I had found the spell of the picture in an absolute *life-likeliness* of expression, which, at first startling, finally confounded, subdued, and appalled me. With deep and reverent awe I replaced the candelabrum in its former position. The cause of my deep agitation being thus shut from view, I sought eagerly the volume which discussed the paintings and their histories. Turning to the number which designated the oval portrait, I there read the vague and quaint words which follow:

"She was a maiden of rarest beauty, and not more lovely than full of glee. And evil was the hour when she saw, and loved, and wedded the painter. He, passionate, studious, austere, and having already a bride in his Art; she a maiden of rarest beauty, and not more lovely than full of glee; all light and smiles, and frolicsome as the young fawn;

loving and cherishing all things; hating only the Art which was her rival; dreading only the pallet and brushes and other untoward instruments which deprived her of the countenance of her lover. It was thus a terrible thing for this lady to hear the painter speak of his desire to portray even his young bride. But she was humble and obedient, and sat meekly for many weeks in the dark, high turret-chamber where the light dripped upon the pale canvas only from overhead. But he, the painter, took glory in his work, which went on from hour to hour, and from day to day. And he was a passionate, and wild, and moody man, who became lost in reveries; so that he *would* not see that the light which fell so ghastly in that lone turret withered the health and the spirits of his bride, who pined visibly to all but him. Yet she smiled on and still on, uncomplainingly, because she saw that the painter (who had a high renown) took a fervid and burning pleasure in his task, and wrought day and night to depict her who so loved him, yet who grew daily more dispirited and weak. And in sooth some who beheld the portrait spoke of its resemblance in low words, as of a mighty marvel, and a proof not less of the power of the painter than of his deep love for her whom he depicted so surpassingly well. But at length, as the labor drew nearer to its conclusion, there were admitted none into the turret; for the painter had grown wild with the ardor of his work, and turned his eyes from the canvas rarely, even to regard the countenance of his wife. And he *would* not see that the tints which he spread upon the canvas were drawn from the cheeks of her who sat beside him. And when many weeks had passed, and but little remained to do, save one brush upon the mouth and one tint upon the eye, the spirit of the lady again flickered up as the flame within the socket of the lamp. And then the brush was given, and then the tint was placed; and, for one moment, the painter stood entranced before the work which he had wrought; but in the next, while he yet gazed, he grew tremulous and very pallid, and aghast, and crying with a loud voice, 'This is indeed *Life* itself!' turned suddenly to regard his beloved:— *She was dead!*"

---

# THE LAMENT
*Anton Chekhov*

It is twilight. A thick wet snow is slowly twirling around the newly lighted street lamps, and lying in soft thin layers on roofs, on horses' backs, on people's shoulders and hats. The cabdriver Iona Potapov is quite white, and looks like a phantom; he is bent double as far as a human body can bend double; he is seated on his box; he never makes a move. If a whole snowdrift fell on him, it seems as if he would not find it necessary to shake it off. His little horse is also quite white, and remains motionless; its immobility, its angularity, and its straight wooden-looking legs, even close by, give it the appearance of a gingerbread horse worth a *kopek*. It is, no doubt, plunged in deep thought. If you were snatched from the plow, from your usual gray surroundings, and were thrown into this slough full of monstrous lights, unceasing noise, and hurrying people, you too would find it difficult not to think.

Iona and his little horse have not moved from their place for a long while. They left their yard before dinner, and up to now, not a fare. The evening mist is descending over the town, the white lights of the lamps replacing brighter rays, and the hubbub of the street getting louder. "Cabby for Viborg way!" suddenly hears Iona. "Cabby!"

Iona jumps, and through his snow-covered eyelashes sees an officer in a greatcoat, with his hood over his head.

"Viborg way!" the officer repeats. "Are you asleep, eh? Viborg way!"

With a nod of assent Iona picks up the reins, in consequence of which layers of snow slip off the horse's back and neck. The officer seats himself in the sleigh, the cabdriver smacks his lips to encourage his horse, stretches out his neck like a swan, sits up, and, more from habit than necessity, brandishes his whip. The little horse also stretches its neck, bends its wooden-looking legs, and makes a move undecidedly.

"What are you doing, werewolf!" is the exclamation Iona hears from the dark mass moving to and fro, as soon as they have started.

"Where the devil are you going! To the r-r-right!"

"You do not know how to drive. Keep to the right!" calls the officer angrily.

A coachman from a private carriage swears at him; a passerby, who has run across the road and rubbed his shoulder against the horse's nose, looks at him furiously as he sweeps the snow from his sleeve. Iona shifts about on his seat as if he were on needles, moves his elbows as if he were trying to keep his equilibrium, and gapes about like someone suffocating, who does not understand why and wherefore he is there.

"What scoundrels they all are!" jokes the officer; "one would think they had all entered into an agreement to jostle you or fall under your horse."

Iona looks round at the officer, and moves his lips. He evidently wants to say something, but the only sound that issues is a snuffle.

"What?" asks the officer.

Iona twists his mouth into a smile, and with an effort says hoarsely: "My son, *barin*, died this week."

"Hm! What did he die of?"

Iona turns with his whole body toward his fare, and says:

"And who knows! They say high fever. He was three days in the hospital, and then died. . . . God's will be done."

"Turn round! The devil!" sounds from the darkness. "Have you popped off, old doggie, eh? Use your eyes!"

"Go on, go on," says the officer, "otherwise we shall not get there by tomorrow. Hurry up a bit!"

The cabdriver again stretches his neck, sits up, and, with a bad grace, brandishes his whip. Several times again he turns to look at his fare, but the latter has closed his eyes, and apparently is not disposed to listen. Having deposited the officer in the Viborg, he stops by the tavern, doubles himself up on his seat, and again remains motionless, while the snow once more begins to cover him and his horse. An hour, and another. . . . Then, along the footpath, with a squeak of galoshes, and quarreling, come three young men, two of them tall and lanky, the third one short and humpbacked.

"Cabby, to the Police Bridge!" in a cracked voice calls the humpback. "The three of us for two *griveniks!*"

Iona picks up his reins, and smacks his lips. Two *griveniks* is not a fair price, but he does not mind whether it is a *rouble* or five *kopeks*— to him it is all the same now, so long as they are fares. The young men, jostling each other and using bad language, approach the sleigh, and all three at once try to get onto the seat; then begins a discussion as to which two shall sit and who shall be the one to stand. After wrangling, abusing each other, and much petulance, it is at last decided that the humpback shall stand, as he is the smallest.

"Now then, hurry up!" says the humpback in a twanging voice, as he takes his place and breaths in Iona's neck. "Old furry! Here, mate, what a cap you have! There is not a worse one to be found in all Petersburg! . . ."

"He-he!—he-he!" giggles Iona. "Such a . . ."

"Now you, 'such a,' hurry up, are you going the whole way at this pace? Are you? . . . Do you want it in the neck?"

"My head feels like bursting," says one of the lanky ones. "Last night at the Donkmasovs, Vaska and I drank the whole of four bottles of cognac."

"I don't understand what you lie for," says the other lanky one angrily; "you lie like a brute."

"God strike me, it's the truth!"

"It's as much the truth as that a louse coughs!"

"He, he," grins Iona, "what gay young gentlemen!"

"Pshaw, go to the devil!" says the humpback indignantly.

"Are you going to get on or not, you old pest? Is that the way to drive? Use the whip a bit! Go on, devil, go on, give it to him well!"

Iona feels at his back the little man wriggling, and the tremble in his voice. He listens to the insults hurled at him, sees the people, and little by little the feeling of loneliness leaves him. The humpback goes on swearing until he gets mixed up in some elaborate six-foot oath, or chokes with coughing. The lankies begin to talk about a certain Nadejda Petrovna. Iona looks round at them several times; he waits for a temporary silence, then, turning round again, he murmurs:

"My son ... died this week."

"We must all die," sighs the humpback, wiping his lips after an attack of coughing. "Now, hurry up, hurry up! Gentlemen, I really cannot go any farther like this! When will he get us there?"

"Well, just you stimulate him a little in the neck!"

"You old pest, do you hear, I'll bone your neck for you! If one treated the like of you with ceremony one would have to go on foot! Do you hear, old serpent Gorinytch! Or do you not care a spit?"

Iona hears rather than feels the blows they deal him.

"He, he," he laughs. "They are gay young gentlemen, God bless 'em!"

"Cabby, are you married?" asks a lanky one.

"I? He, he, gay young gentlemen! Now I have only a wife and the moist ground ... he, ho, ho ... that is to say, the grave. My son has died, and I am alive....A wonderful thing, death mistook the door ... instead of coming to me, it went to my son...."

Iona turns round to tell them how his son died, but at this moment, the humpback, giving a little sigh, announces, "Thank God, we have at last reached our destination," and Iona watches them disappear through the dark entrance. Once more he is alone, and again surrounded by silence. . . . His grief, which has abated for a short while, returns and rends his heart with greater force. With an anxious and hurried look, he searches among the crowds passing on either side of the street to find whether there may be just one person who will listen to him. But the crowds hurry by without noticing him or his trouble. Yet it is such an immense, illimitable grief. Should his heart break and the grief pour out, it would flow over the whole earth, so it seems, and yet no one sees it. It has managed to conceal itself in such an insignificant shell that no one can see it even by day and with a light.

Iona sees a hall porter with some sacking, and decides to talk to him.

"Friend, what sort of time is it?" he asks.

"Past nine. What are you standing here for? Move on."

Iona moves on a few steps, doubles himself up, and abandons himself to his grief. He sees it is useless to turn to people for help. In less than five minutes he straightens himself, holds up his head as if he felt some sharp pain, and gives a tug at the reins; he can bear it no longer. "The stables," he thinks, and the little horse, as if it understands, starts off at a trot.

About an hour and a half later Iona is seated by a large dirty stove. Around the stove, on the floor, on the benches, people are snoring; the air is thick and suffocatingly hot. Iona looks at the sleepers, scratches himself, and regrets having returned so early.

"I have not even earned my fodder," he thinks. "That's what's my trouble. A man who knows his job, who has had enough to eat, and his horse too, can always sleep peacefully."

A young cabdriver in one of the corners half gets up, grunts sleepily, and stretches towards a bucket of water.

"Do you want a drink?" Iona asks him.

"Don't I want a drink?"

"That's so? Your good health! But listen, mate—you know, my son is dead. . . . Did you hear? This week, in the hospital. . . . It's a long story."

Iona looks to see what effect his words have, but sees none—the young man has hidden his face and is fast asleep again. The old man sighs, and scratches his head. Just as much as the young one wants to drink, the old man wants to talk. It will soon be a week since his son died, and he has not been able to speak about it properly to anyone. One must tell it slowly and carefully; how his son fell ill, how he suffered, what he said before he died, how he died. One must describe every detail of the funeral, and the journey to the hospital to fetch the dead son's clothes. His daughter Anissia has remained in the village— one must talk about her too. Is it nothing he has to tell? Surely the listener would gasp and sigh, and sympathize with him? It is better, too, to talk to women; although they are stupid, two words are enough to make them sob.

"I'll go and look after my horse," thinks Iona; "there's always time to sleep. No fear of that!"

He puts on his coat, and goes to the stables to his horse; he thinks of the corn, the hay, the weather. When he is alone, he dares not think of his son; he can speak about him to anyone, but to think of him, and picture him to himself, is unbearably painful.

"Are you tucking in?" Iona asks his horse, looking at its bright eyes; "go on, tuck in, though we've not earned our corn, we can eat hay. Yes! I am too old to drive—my son could have, not I. He was a first-rate cabdriver. If only he had lived!"

Iona is silent for a moment, then continues:

"That's how it is, my old horse. There's no more Kuzma Ionitch. He has left us to live, and he went off pop. Now let's say, you had a foal, you were the foal's mother, and suddenly, let's say, that foal went and left you to live after him. It would be sad, wouldn't it?"

The little horse munches, listens, and breathes over its master's hand. . . .

Iona's feelings are too much for him, and he tells the little horse the whole story.

# THE UPTURNED FACE
## *Stephen Crane*

"What will we do now?" said the adjutant, troubled and excited.

"Bury him," said Timothy Lean.

The two officers looked down close to their toes where lay the body of their comrade. The face was chalk-blue; gleaming eyes stared at the sky. Over the two upright figures was a windy sound of bullets, and on top of the hill Lean's prostrate company of Spitzbergen infantry was firing measured volleys.

"Don't you think it would be better—" began the adjutant. "We might leave him until tomorrow."

"No," said Lean. "I can't hold that post an hour longer. I've got to fall back, and we've got to bury old Bill."

"Of course," said the adjutant, at once. "Your men got entrenching tools?"

Lean shouted back to his little line, and two men came slowly, one with a pick, one with a shovel. They started in the direction of the Rostina sharpshooters. Bullets cracked near their ears. "Dig here," said Lean gruffly. The men, thus caused to lower their glances to the turf, became hurried and frightened, merely because they could not look to see whence the bullets came. The dull beat of the pick striking the earth sounded amid the swift snap of close bullets. Presently the other private began to shovel.

"I suppose," said the adjutant slowly, "we'd better search his clothes for—things."

Lean nodded. Together in curious abstraction they looked at the body. Then Lean stirred his shoulders suddenly, arousing himself.

"Yes," he said, "we'd better see what he's got." He dropped to his knee, and his hands approached the body of the dead officer. But his hands wavered over the buttons of the tunic. The first button was brick-red with drying blood, and he did not seem to dare to touch it.

"Go on," said the adjutant, hoarsely.

Lean stretched his wooden hand, and his fingers fumbled the blood-stained buttons. At last he rose with ghastly face. He had gathered a watch, a whistle, a pipe, a tobacco-pouch, a handkerchief, a little case of cards and papers. He looked at the adjutant. There was a silence. The adjutant was feeling that he had been a coward to make Lean do all the grisly business.

"Well," said Lean, "that's all, I think. You have his sword and revolver?"

"Yes," said the adjutant, his face working, and then he burst out in a sudden strange fury at the two privates. "Why don't you hurry up with that grave? What are you doing, anyhow? Hurry, do you hear? I never saw such stupid—"

Even as he cried out in his passion, the two men were laboring for their lives. Ever overhead the bullets were spitting.

The grave was finished. It was not a masterpiece—a poor little shallow thing. Lean and the adjutant again looked at each other in a curious silent communication.

Suddenly the adjutant croaked out a weird laugh. It was a terrible laugh which had its origin in that part of the mind which is first moved by the singing of the nerves. "Well," he said humorously to Lean, "I suppose we had best tumble him in."

"Yes," said Lean. The two privates stood waiting, bent over their implements. "I suppose," said Lean, "it would be better if we laid him in ourselves."

"Yes," said the adjutant. Then, apparently remembering that he had made Lean search the body, he stooped with great fortitude and took hold of the dead officer's clothing. Lean joined him. Both were particular that their fingers should not feel the corpse. They tugged away; the corpse lifted, heaved, toppled, flopped into the grave, and the two officers, straightening, looked again at each other—they were always looking at each other. They sighed with relief.

The adjutant said, "I suppose we should—we should say something. Do you know the service, Tim?"

"They don't read the service until the grave is filled in," said Lean, pressing his lips to an academic expression.

"Don't they?" said the adjutant, shocked that he had made the mistake. "Oh well," he cried, suddenly, "let us—let us say something —while he can hear us."

"All right," said Lean. "Do you know the service?"

"I can't remember a line of it," said the adjutant.

Lean was extremely dubious. "I can repeat two lines, but—"

"Well, do it," said the adjutant. "Go as far as you can. That's better than nothing. And the beasts have got our range exactly."

Lean looked at his two men. "Attention," he barked. The privates came to attention with a click, looking much aggrieved. The adjutant lowered his helmet to his knee. Lean, bareheaded, stood over the grave. The Rostina sharpshooters fired briskly.

"O Father, our friend has sunk in the deep waters of death, but his spirit has leaped toward Thee as the bubble arises from the lips of the drowning. Perceive, we beseech, O Father, the little flying bubble, and—"

Lean, although husky and ashamed, had suffered no hesitation up to this point, but he stopped with a hopeless feeling and looked at the corpse.

The adjutant moved uneasily. "And from Thy superb heights," he began, and then he too came to an end.

"And from Thy superb heights," said Lean.

The adjutant suddenly remembered a phrase in the back of the Spitzbergen burial service, and he exploited it with the triumphant manner of a man who has recalled everything, and can go on.

"O God, have mercy—"

"O God, have mercy—" said Lean.

"Mercy," repeated the adjutant, in quick failure.

"Mercy," said Lean. And then he was moved by some violence of feeling, for he turned upon his two men and tigerishly said, "Throw the dirt in."

The fire of the Rostina sharpshooters was accurate and continuous.

One of the aggrieved privates came forward with his shovel. He lifted his first shovel-load of earth, and for a moment of inexplicable hesitation it was held poised above this corpse which from its chalk-blue face looked keenly out from the grave. Then the soldier emptied his shovel on—on the feet.

Timothy Lean felt as if tons had been swiftly lifted from off his forehead. He had felt that perhaps the private might empty the shovel on—on the face. It had been emptied on the feet. There was a great point gained there—ha, ha!—the first shovelful had been emptied on the feet. How satisfactory!

The adjutant began to babble. "Well, of course—a man we've messed with all these years—impossible—you can't, you know, leave your intimate friends rotting on the field. Go on, for God's sake, and shovel, you."

The man with the shovel suddenly ducked, grabbed his left arm with his right hand, and looked at his officer for orders. Lean picked the shovel from the ground. "Go to the rear," he said to the wounded man. He also addressed the other private. "You get under cover, too; I'll finish this business."

The wounded man scrambled hard for the top of the ridge without devoting any glances to the direction from whence the bullets came, and the other man followed at an equal pace; but he was different, in that he looked back anxiously three times.

This is merely the way—often—of the hit and unhit.

Timothy Lean filled the shovel, hesitated, and then, in a movement which was like a gesture of abhorrence, he flung the dirt into the grave, and as it landed it made a sound—plop. Lean suddenly stopped and mopped his brow—a tired laborer.

"Perhaps we have been wrong," said the adjutant. His glance wavered stupidly. "It might have been better if we hadn't buried him just at this time. Of course, if we advance tomorrow the body would have been—"

"Damn you," said Lean, "shut your mouth." He was not the senior officer.

He again filled the shovel and flung the earth. Always the earth made that sound—plop. For a space, Lean worked frantically, like a man digging himself out of danger.

Soon there was nothing to be seen but the chalk-blue face. Lean filled the shovel. "Good God," he cried to the adjutant. "Why didn't you turn him somehow when you put him in? This—" Then Lean began to stutter.

The adjutant understood. He was pale to the lips. "Go on, man," he cried, beseechingly, almost in a shout.

Lean swung back the shovel. It went forward in a pendulum curve. When the earth landed it made a sound—plop.

---

# IN ANOTHER COUNTRY
## *Ernest Hemingway*

In the fall the war was always there, but we did not go to it any more. It was cold in the fall in Milan and the dark came very early. Then the electric lights came on, and it was pleasant along the streets looking in the windows. There was much game hanging outside the shops, and the snow powdered in the fur of the foxes and the wind blew their tails. The deer hung stiff and heavy and empty, and small birds blew in the wind and the wind turned their feathers. It was a cold fall and the wind came down from the mountains.

We were all at the hospital every afternoon, and there were different ways of walking across the town through the dusk to the hospital. Two of the ways were alongside canals, but they were long. Always, though, you crossed a bridge across a canal to enter the hospital. There was a choice of three bridges. On one of them a woman sold roasted chestnuts. It was warm, standing in front of her charcoal fire, and the chestnuts were warm afterward in your pocket. The hospital was very old and very beautiful, and you entered through a gate and walked across a courtyard and out a gate on the other side. There were usually funerals starting from the courtyard. Beyond the old hospital were the new brick pavilions, and there we met every afternoon and were all very polite and interested in what was the matter, and sat in the machines that were to make so much difference.

The doctor came up to the machine where I was sitting and said: "What did you like best to do before the war? Did you practice a sport?"

I said: "Yes, football."

"Good," he said. "You will be able to play football again better than ever."

My knee did not bend and the leg dropped straight from the knee to the ankle without a calf, and the machine was to bend the knee and make it move as in riding a tricycle. But it did not bend yet, and instead the machine lurched when it came to the bending part. The doctor said: "That will all pass. You are a fortunate young man. You will play football again like a champion."

In the next machine was a major who had a little hand like a baby's. He winked at me when the doctor examined his hand, which was between two leather straps that bounced up and down and flapped the stiff fingers, and said: "And will I too play football, captain-doctor?" He had been a very great fencer, and before the war the greatest fencer in Italy.

The doctor went to his office in a back room and brought a photograph which showed a hand that had been withered almost as small as the major's, before it had taken a machine course, and after was a little larger. The major held the photograph with his good hand and looked at it very carefully. "A wound?" he asked.

"An industrial accident," the doctor said.

"Very interesting, very interesting," the major said, and handed it back to the doctor.

"You have confidence?"

"No," said the major.

There were three boys who came each day who were about the same age I was. They were all three from Milan, and one of them was to be a lawyer, and one was to be a painter, and one had intended to be a soldier, and after we were finished with the machines, sometimes we walked back together to the Cafe Cova, which was next door to the Scala. We walked the short way through the communist quarter because we were four together. The people hated us because we were officers, and from a wineshop someone called out, "A basso gli ufficiale!" as we passed. Another boy who walked with us sometimes and made us five wore a black silk handkerchief across his face because he had no nose then and his face was to be rebuilt. He had gone out to the front from the military academy and been wounded within an hour after he had gone into the front line for the first time. They rebuilt his face, but he came from a very old family and they could never get the nose exactly right. (He went to South America and worked in a bank.) But this was a long time ago, and then we did not any of us know how it was going to be afterward. We only knew then that there was always the war, but that we were not going to it any more.

We all had the same medals, except the boy with the black silk bandage across his face, and he had not been at the front long enough to get any medals. The tall boy with a very pale face who was to be a lawyer had been a lieutenant of Arditi and had three medals of the sort we each had only one of. He had lived a very long time with death and was a little detached. We were all a little detached, and there was nothing that held us together except that we met every afternoon at the hospital. Although, as we walked to the Cova through the tough part of town, walking in the dark with light and singing coming out of the wineshops, and sometimes having to walk into the street when the men and women would crowd together on the sidewalk so that we would have had to jostle them to get by, we felt held together by there being something that had happened that they, the people who disliked us, did not understand.

We ourselves all understood the Cova, where it was rich and warm and not too brightly lighted, and noisy and smoky at certain hours, and there were always girls at the tables and the illustrated papers on a rack on the wall. The girls at the Cova were very patriotic, and I found that the most patriotic people in Italy were the cafe girls—and I believe they are still patriotic.

The boys at first were very polite about my medals and asked me what I had done to get them. I showed them the papers, which were written in very beautiful language and full of *fratellanza* and *abnegazione,* but which really said, with the adjectives removed, that I had been given the medals because I was an American. After that their manner changed a little toward me, although I was their friend against outsiders. I was a friend, but I was never really one of them after they had read the citations, because it had been different with them and they had done very different things to get their medals. I had been wounded, it was true; but we all knew that being wounded, after all, was really an accident. I was never ashamed of the ribbons, though, and sometimes, after the cocktail hour, I would imagine myself having done all the things they had done to get their medals; but walking home at night through the empty streets with the cold wind and all the shops closed, trying to keep near the street lights, I knew that I would never have done such things, and I was very much afraid to die, and often lay in bed at night by myself, afraid to die and wondering how I would be when I went back to the front again.

The three with the medals were like hunting-hawks; and I was not a hawk, although I might seem a hawk to those who had never hunted; they, the three, knew better and so we drifted apart. But I stayed good friends with the boy who had been wounded his first day at the front, because he would never know now how he would have turned out; so he could never be accepted either, and I liked him because I thought perhaps he would not have turned out to be a hawk either.

The major, who had been the great fencer, did not believe in bravery, and spent much time while we sat in the machines correcting my grammar. He had complimented me on how I spoke Italian, and we talked together very easily. One day I had said that Italian seemed such an easy language to me that I could not take a great interest in it; everything was so easy to say. "Ah, yes," the major said. "Why, then, do you not take up the use of grammar?" So we took up the use of grammar, and soon Italian was such a difficult language that I was afraid to talk to him until I had the grammar straight in my mind.

The major came very regularly to the hospital. I do not think he ever missed a day, although I am sure he did not believe in the machines. There was a time when none of us believed in the machines, and one day the major said it was all nonsense. The machines were new then and it was we who were to prove them. It was an idiotic idea, he said, "a theory, like another." I had not learned my grammar, and he said I was a stupid impossible disgrace, and he was a fool to have bothered with me. He was a small man and he sat straight up in his chair with his right hand thrust into the machine and looked straight ahead at the wall while the straps thumped up and down with his fingers in them.

"What will you do when the war is over if it is over?" he asked me. "Speak grammatically!"

"I will go to the States."

"Are you married?"

"No, but I hope to be."

"The more of a fool you are," he said. He seemed very angry. "A man must not marry."

"Why, Signor Maggiore?"

"Don't call me 'Signor Maggiore.' "

"Why must not a man marry?"

"He cannot marry. He cannot marry," he said angrily. "If he is to lose everything, he should not place himself in a position to lose that. He should not place himself in a position to lose. He should find things he cannot lose."

He spoke very angrily and bitterly, and looked straight ahead while he talked.

"But why should he necessarily lose it?"

"He'll lose it," the major said. He was looking at the wall. Then he looked down at the machine and jerked his little hand out from between the straps and slapped it hard against his thigh. "He'll lose it," he almost shouted. "Don't argue with me!" Then he called to the attendant who ran the machines. "Come and turn this damned thing off."

He went back into the other room for the light treatment and the massage. Then I heard him ask the doctor if he might use his telephone and he shut the door. When he came back into the room, I was sitting in another machine. He was wearing his cape and had his cap on, and he came directly toward my machine and put his arm on my shoulder.

"I am so sorry," he said, and patted me on the shoulder with his good hand. "I would not be rude. My wife has just died. You must forgive me."

"Oh—" I said, feeling sick for him. "I am so sorry."

He stood there biting his lower lip. "It is very difficult," he said. "I cannot resign myself."

He looked straight past me and out through the window. Then he began to cry. "I am utterly unable to resign myself," he said and choked. And then crying, his head up looking at nothing, carrying himself straight and soldierly, with tears on both his cheeks and biting his lips, he walked past the machines and out the door.

The doctor told me that the major's wife, who was very young and whom he had not married until he was definitely invalided out of the war, had died of pneumonia. She had been sick only a few days. No one expected her to die. The major did not come to the hospital for three days. Then he came at the usual hour, wearing a black band on the sleeve of his uniform. When he came back, there were large framed photographs around the wall, of all sorts of wounds before and after they had been cured by the machines. In front of the machine the major used were three photographs of hands like his that were completely restored. I do not know where the doctor got them. I always understood we were the first to use the machines. The photographs did not make much difference to the major because he only looked out of the window.

# A LITTLE CLOUD
## *James Joyce*

Eight years before he had seen his friend off at the North Wall and wished him godspeed. Gallaher had got on. You could tell that at once by his travelled air, his well-cut tweed suit, and fearless accent. Few fellows had talents like his and fewer still could remain unspoiled by such success. Gallaher's heart was in the right place and he had deserved to win. It was something to have a friend like that.

Little Chandler's thoughts ever since lunch-time had been of his meeting with Gallaher, of Gallaher's invitation and of the great city London where Gallaher lived. He was called Little Chandler because, though he was but slightly under the average stature, he gave one the idea of being a little man. His hands were white and small, his frame was fragile, his voice was quiet and his manners were refined. He took the greatest care of his fair silken hair and moustache and used perfume discreetly on his handkerchief. The half-moons of his nails were perfect and when he smiled you caught a glimpse of a row of childish white teeth.

As he sat at his desk in the King's Inns he thought what changes those eight years had brought. The friend whom he had known under a shabby and necessitous guise had become a brilliant figure on the London Press. He turned often from his tiresome writing to gaze out of the office window. The glow of a late autumn sunset covered the grass plots and walks. It cast a shower of kindly golden dust on the untidy nurses and decrepit old men who drowsed on the benches; it flickered upon all the moving figures—on the children who ran screaming along the gravel paths and on everyone who passed through the gardens. He watched the scene and thought of life; and (as always happened when he thought of life) he became sad. A gentle melancholy took possession of him. He felt how useless it was to struggle against fortune, this being the burden of wisdom which the ages had bequeathed to him.

He remembered the books of poetry upon his shelves at home. He had bought them in his bachelor days and many an evening, as he sat in the little room off the hall, he had been tempted to take one down from the bookshelf and read out something to his wife. But shyness had always held him back; and so the books had remained on their shelves. At times he repeated lines to himself and this consoled him.

When his hour had struck he stood up and took leave of his desk and of his fellow-clerks punctiliously. He emerged from under the feudal arch of the King's Inns, a neat modest figure, and walked swiftly down Henrietta Street. The golden sunset was waning and the air had grown sharp. A horde of grimy children populated the street. They stood or ran in the roadway or crawled up the steps before the gaping doors or squatted like mice upon the thresholds. Little Chandler gave them no thought. He picked his way deftly through all that minute vermin-like life and under the shadow of the gaunt spectral mansions in which the old nobility of Dublin had roystered. No memory of the past touched him, for his mind was full of a present joy.

He had never been in Corless's but he knew the value of the name. He knew that people went there after the theatre to eat oysters and drink liqueurs; and he had heard that the waiters there spoke French and German. Walking swiftly by at night he had seen cabs drawn up before the door and richly dressed ladies, escorted by cavaliers, alight and enter quickly. They wore noisy dresses and many wraps. Their faces were powdered and they caught up their dresses, when they touched earth, like alarmed Atalantas. He had always passed without turning his head to look. It was his habit to walk swiftly in the street even by day and whenever he found himself in the city late at night he hurried on his way apprehensively and excitedly. Sometimes, however, he courted the causes of his fear. He chose the darkest and narrowest streets and, as he walked boldly forward, the silence that was spread about his footsteps troubled him, the wandering, silent figures troubled him; and at times a sound of low fugitive laughter made him tremble like a leaf.

He turned to the right towards Capel Street. Ignatius Gallaher on the London Press! Who would have thought it possible eight years before? Still, now that he reviewed the past, Little Chandler could remember many signs of future greatness in his friend. People used to say that Ignatius Gallaher was wild. Of course, he did mix with a rakish set of fellows at that time, drank freely and borrowed money on all sides. In the end he had got mixed up in some shady affair, some money transaction: at least, that was one version of his flight. But nobody denied him talent. There was always a certain . . . something in Ignatius Gallaher that impressed you in spite of yourself. Even when he was out at elbows and at his wits' end for money he kept up a bold face. Little Chandler remembered (and the remembrance brought a slight flush of pride to his cheek) one of Ignatius Gallaher's sayings when he was in a tight corner:

"Half time now, boys," he used to say lightheartedly. "Where's my considering cap?"

That was Ignatius Gallaher all out; and, damn it, you couldn't but admire him for it.

Little Chandler quickened his pace. For the first time in his life he felt himself superior to the people he passed. For the first time his soul revolted against the dull inelegance of Capel Street. There was no doubt about it: if you wanted to succeed you had to go away. You could do nothing in Dublin. As he crossed Grattan Bridge he looked down the river towards the lower quays and pitied the poor stunted houses. They seemed to him a band of tramps, huddled together along the river-banks, their old coats covered with dust and soot, stupefied by the panorama of sunset and waiting for the first chill of night to bid them arise, shake themselves and begone. He wondered whether he could write a poem to express his idea. Perhaps Gallaher might be able to get it into some London paper for him. Could he write something original? He was not sure what idea he wished to express but the thought that a poetic moment had touched him took life within him like an infant hope. He stepped onward bravely.

Every step brought him nearer to London, farther from his own sober inartistic life. A light began to tremble on the horizon of his mind. He was not so old—thirty-two. His temperament might be said to be just at the point of maturity. There were so many different moods and impressions that he wished to express in verse. He felt them within him. He tried to weigh his soul to see if it was a poet's soul. Melancholy was the dominant note of his temperament, he thought, but it was a melancholy tempered by recurrences of faith and resignation and simple joy. If he could give expression to it in a book of poems perhaps men would listen. He would never be popular: he saw that. He could not sway the crowd but he might appeal to a little circle of kindred minds. The English critics, perhaps, would recognize him as one of the Celtic school by reason of the melancholy tone of his poems; besides that, he would put in allusions. He began to invent sentences and phrases from the notice which his book would get. *"Mr. Chandler has the gift of easy and graceful verse."* . . . *"A wistful sadness pervades these poems."* . . . *"The Celtic note."* It was a pity his name was not more Irish-looking. Perhaps it would be better to insert his mother's name before the surname: Thomas Malone Chandler, or better still: T. Malone Chandler. He would speak to Gallaher about it.

He pursued his revery so ardently that he passed his street and had to turn back. As he came near Corless's his former agitation began to overmaster him and he halted before the door in indecision. Finally he opened the door and entered.

The light and noise of the bar held him at the doorways for a few moments. He looked about him, but his sight was confused by the shining of many red and green wine-glasses. The bar seemed to him to be full of people and he felt that the people were observing him curiously. He glanced quickly to right and left (frowning slightly to make his errand appear serious), but when his sight cleared a little he saw that nobody had turned to look at him: and there, sure enough, was Ignatius Gallaher leaning with his back against the counter and his feet planted far apart.

"Hallo, Tommy, old hero, here you are! What is it to be? What will you have? I'm taking whisky: better stuff than we get across the water. Soda? Lithia? No mineral? I'm the same. Spoils the flavour. . . . Here, *garçon,* bring us two halves of malt whiskey, like a good fellow. . . . Well, and how have you been pulling along since I saw you last? Dear God, how old we're getting! Do you see any signs of aging in me—eh, what? A little grey and thin on the top—what?"

Ignatius Gallaher took off his hat and displayed a large closely cropped head. His face was heavy, pale and cleanshaven. His eyes, which were of bluish slate-colour, relieved his unhealthy pallor and shone out plainly above the vivid orange tie he wore. Between these rival features the lips appeared very long and shapeless and colourless. He bent his head and felt with two sympathetic fingers the thin hair at the crown. Little Chandler shook his head as a denial. Ignatius Gallaher put on his hat again.

"It pulls you down," he said, "Press life. Always hurry and scurry, looking for copy and sometimes not finding it: and then, always to have something new in your stuff. Damn proofs and printers, I say, for a few days. I'm deuced glad, I can tell you, to get back to the old country. Does a fellow good, a bit of a holiday. I feel a ton better since I landed again in dear dirty Dublin.... Here you are, Tommy. Water? Say when."

Little Chandler allowed his whiskey to be very much diluted.

"You don't know what's good for you, my boy," said Ignatius Gallaher. "I drink mine neat."

"I drink very little as a rule," said Little Chandler modestly. "An odd half-one or so when I meet any of the old crowd: that's all."

"Ah, well," said Iagnatius Gallaher, cheerfully, "here's to us and to old times and old acquaintance."

They clinked glasses and drank the toast.

"I met some of the old gang to-day," said Ignatius Gallaher. "O'Hara seems to be in a bad way. What's he doing?"

"Nothing," said Little Chandler. "He's gone to the dogs."

"But Hogan has a good sit, hasn't he?"

"Yes; he's in the Land Commission."

"I met him one night in London and he seemed to be very flush.... Poor O'Hara! Boose, I suppose?"

"Other things, too," said Little Chandler shortly. Ignatius Gallaher laughed.

"Tommy," he said, "I see you haven't changed an atom. You're the very same serious person that used to lecture me on Sunday mornings when I had a sore head and a fur on my tongue. You'd want to knock about a bit in the world. Have you never been anywhere even for a trip?"

"I've been to the Isle of Man," said Little Chandler.

Ignatius Gallaher laughed.

"The Isle of Man!" he said. "Go to London or Paris: Paris, for choice. That'd do you good."

"Have you seen Paris?"

"I should think I have! I've knocked about there a little."

"And is it really so beautiful as they say?" asked Little Chandler.

He sipped a little of his drink while Ignatius Gallaher finished his boldly.

"Beautiful?" said Ignatius Gallaher, pausing on the word and on the flavour of his drink. "It's not so beautiful, you know. Of course, it is beautiful.... But it's the life of Paris; that's the thing. Ah, there's no city like Paris for gaiety, movement, excitement...."

Little Chandler finished his whisky and, after some trouble, succeeded in catching the barman's eye. He ordered the same again.

"I've been to the Moulin Rouge," Ignatius Gallaher continued when the barman had removed their glasses, "and I've been to all the Bohemian cafes. Hot stuff! Not for a pious chap like you, Tommy."

Little Chandler said nothing until the barman returned with two glasses: then he touched his friend's glass lightly and reciprocated the former toast. He was beginning to feel somewhat disillusioned. Gallaher's accent and way of expressing himself did not please him. There was something vulgar in his friend which he had not observed before. But perhaps it was only the result of living in London amid the bustle and competition of the Press. The old personal charm was still there under this new gaudy manner. And, after all, Gallaher had lived, he had seen the world. Little Chandler looked at his friend enviously.

"Everything in Paris is gay," said Ignatius Gallaher. "They believe in enjoying life—and don't you think they're right? If you want to enjoy yourself properly you must go to Paris. And, mind you, they've a great feeling for the Irish there. When they heard I was from Ireland they were ready to eat me, man."

Little Chandler took four or five sips from his glass.

"Tell me," he said, "is it true that Paris is so . . . immoral as they say?"

Ignatius Gallaher made a catholic gesture with his right arm.

"Every place is immoral," he said. "Of course you do find spicy bits in Paris. Go to one of the students' balls, for instance. That's lively, if you like, when the *cocottes* begin to let themselves loose. You know what they are, I suppose?"

"I've heard of them," said Little Chandler.

Ignatius Gallaher drank off his whisky and shook his head.

"Ah," he said, "you may say what you like. There's no woman like the Parisienne—for style, for go."

"Then it is an immoral city," said Little Chandler, with timid insistence—"I mean, compared with London or Dublin?"

"London!" said Ignatius Gallaher. "It's six of one and half-a-dozen of the other. You ask Hogan, my boy. I showed him a bit about London when he was over there. He'd open your eye. . . . I say, Tommy, don't make punch of that whisky: liquor up."

"No, really. . . ."

"O, come on, another one won't do you any harm. What is it? The same again, I suppose?"

"Well . . . all right."

"*François,* the same again. . . . Will you smoke, Tommy?"

Ignatius Gallaher produced his cigar-case. The two friends lit their cigars and puffed at them in silence until their drinks were served.

"I'll tell you my opinion," said Ignatius Gallaher, emerging after some time from the clouds of smoke in which he had taken refuge, "it's a rum world. Talk of immorality! I've heard of cases—what am I saying?—I've known them: cases of . . . immorality. . . ."

Ignatius Gallaher puffed thoughtfully at his cigar and then, in a calm historian's tone, he proceeded to sketch for his friend some pictures of the corruption which was rife abroad. He summarised the vices of many capitals and seemed inclined to award the palm to Berlin. Some things he could not vouch for (his friends had told him), but of others he had had personal experience. He spared neither rank nor caste. He revealed many of the secrets of religious houses on the Continent and described some of the practices which were fashionable in high society and ended by telling, with details, a story about an English duchess—a story which he knew to be true. Little Chandler was astonished.

"Ah, well," said Ignatius Gallaher, "here we are in old jog-along Dublin where nothing is known of such things."

"How dull you must find it," said Little Chandler, "after all the other places you've seen!"

"Well," said Ignatius Gallaher, "it's a relaxation to come over here, you know. And, after all, it's the old country, as they say, isn't it? You can't help having a certain feeling for it. That's human nature.... But tell me something about yourself. Hogan told me you had ... tasted the joys of connubial bliss. Two years ago, wasn't it?"

Little Chandler blushed and smiled.

"Yes," he said. "I was married last May twelve months."

"I hope it's not too late in the day to offer my best wishes," said Ignatius Gallaher. "I didn't know your address or I'd have done so at the time."

He extended his hand, which Little Chandler took.

"Well, Tommy," he said, "I wish you and yours every joy in life, old chap, and tons of money, and may you never die till I shoot you. And that's the wish of a sincere friend, an old friend. You know that?"

"I know that," said Little Chandler.

"Any youngsters?" said Ignatius Gallaher.

Little Chandler blushed again.

"We have one child," he said.

"Son or daughter?"

"A little boy."

Ignatius Gallaher slapped his friend sonorously on the back.

"Bravo," he said, "I wouldn't doubt you, Tommy."

Little Chandler smiled, looked confusedly at his glass and bit his lower lip with three childishly white front teeth.

"I hope you'll spend an evening with us," he said, "before you go back. My wife will be delighted to meet you. We can have a little music and—"

"Thanks awfully, old chap," said Ignatius Gallaher, "I'm sorry we didn't meet earlier. But I must leave tomorrow night."

"To-night. perhaps . . . ?"

"I'm awfully sorry, old man. You see I'm over here with another fellow, clever young chap he is too, and we arranged to go to a little card party. Only for that . . ."

"O, in that case. . . ."

"But who knows?" said Ignatius Gallaher considerately. "Next year

I may take a little skip over here now that I've broken the ice. It's only a pleasure deferred."

"Very well," said Little Chandler, "the next time you come we must have an evening together. That's agreed now, isn't it?"

"Yes, that's agreed," said Ignatius Gallaher. "Next year if I come, *parole d'honneur.*"

"And to clinch the bargain," said Little Chandler, "we'll just have one more now."

Ignatius Gallaher took out a large gold watch and looked at it.

"Is it to be the last?" he said. "Because you know, I have an a.p."

"O, yes, positively," said Little Chandler.

"Very well, then," said Ignatius Gallaher, "let us have another one as a *deoc an doruis*—that's good vernacular for a small whisky, I believe."

Little Chandler ordered the drinks. The blush which had risen to his face a few moments before was establishing itself. A trifle made him blush at any time: and now he felt warm and excited. Three small whiskies had gone to his head and Gallaher's strong cigar had confused his mind, for he was a delicate and abstinent person. The adventure of meeting Gallaher after eight years, of finding himself with Gallaher in Corless's surrounded by lights and noise, of listening to Gallaher's stories and of sharing for a brief space Gallaher's vagrant and triumphant life, upset the equipoise of his sensitive nature. He felt acutely the contrast between his own life and his friend's, and it seemed to him unjust. Gallaher was his inferior in birth and education. He was sure that he could do something better than his friend had ever done, or could ever do, something higher than mere tawdry journalism if he only got the chance. What was it that stood in his way? His unfortunate timidity! He wished to vindicate himself in some way, to assert his manhood. He saw behind Gallaher's refusal of his invitation. Gallaher was only patronising him by his friendliness just as he was patronising Ireland by his visit.

The barman brought their drinks. Little Chandler pushed one glass towards his friend and took up the other boldly.

"Who knows?" he said, as they lifted their glasses. "When you come next year I may have the pleasure of wishing long life and happiness to Mr. and Mrs. Ignatius Gallaher."

Ignatius Gallaher in the act of drinking closed one eye expressively over the rim of his glass. When he had drunk he smacked his lips decisively, set down his glass and said:

"No blooming fear of that, my boy. I'm going to have my fling first and see a bit of life and the world before I put my head in the sack—if I ever do." .

"Some day you will," said Little Chandler calmly.

Ignatius Gallaher turned his orange tie and slate-blue eyes full upon his friend.

"You think so?" he said.

"You'll put your head in the sack," repeated Little Chandler stoutly, "like everybody else if you can find the girl."

He had slightly emphasized his tone and he was aware that he had betrayed himself but, though the colour had heightened in his cheek, he did not flinch from his friend's gaze. Ignatius Gallaher watched him for a few moments and then said:

"If ever it occurs, you may bet your bottom dollar there'll be no mooning and spooning about it. I mean to marry money. She'll have a good fat account at the bank or she won't do for me."

Little Chandler shook his head.

"Why, man alive," said Ignatius Gallaher, vehemently, "do you know what it is? I've only to say the word and to-morrow I can have the woman and the cash. You don't believe it? Well, I know it. There are hundreds—what am I saying?—thousands of rich Germans and Jews, rotten with money, that'd only be too glad. . . . You wait a while, my boy. See if I don't play my cards properly. When I go about a thing I mean business. I tell you. You just wait."

He tossed his glass to his mouth, finished his drink and laughed loudly. Then he looked thoughtfully before him and said in a calmer tone:

"But I'm in no hurry. They can wait. I don't fancy tying myself to one woman, you know."

He imitated with his mouth the act of tasting and made a wry face.

"Must get a bit stale, I should think," he said.

.    .    .    .    .    .

Little Chandler sat in the room off the hall, holding a child in his arms. To save money they kept no servant but Annie's young sister Monica came for an hour or so in the morning and an hour or so in the evening to help. But Monica had gone home long ago. It was a quarter to nine. Little Chandler had come home late for tea and, moreover, he had forgotten to bring Annie home the parcel of coffee from Bewley's. Of course she was in a bad humour and gave him short answers. She said she would do without any tea but when it came near the time at which the shop at the corner closed she decided to go out herself for a quarter of a pound of tea and two pounds of sugar. She put the sleeping child deftly in his arms and said:

"Here. Don't waken him."

A little lamp with a white china shade stood upon the table and its light fell over a photograph which was enclosed in a frame of crumpled horn. It was Annie's photograph. Little Chandler looked at it, pausing at the thin tight lips. She wore the pale blue summer blouse which he had brought her home as a present one Saturday. It had cost him ten and elevenpence; but what an agony of nervousness it had cost him! How he had suffered that day, waiting at the shop door until the shop was empty, standing at the counter and trying to appear at his ease while the girl piled ladies' blouses before him, paying at the desk and forgetting to take up the odd penny of his change, being called back by the cashier, and finally, striving to hide his blushes as he left the shop by examining the parcel to see if it was securely tied. When he brought the blouse home Annie kissed him and said it was very pretty and stylish; but when she heard the price she threw the blouse on the table and said it was a regular swindle to charge ten and elevenpence for it. At first she wanted to take it back but when she tried it on she was delighted with it, especially with the make of the sleeves, and kissed him and said he was very good to think of her.

Hm! . . .

He looked coldly into the eyes of the photograph and they answered coldly. Certainly they were pretty and the face itself was pretty. But he found something mean in it. Why was it so unconscious and ladylike? The composure of the eyes irritated him. They repelled him and defied him: there was no passion in them, no rapture. He thought of what Gallaher had said about rich Jewesses. Those dark Oriental eyes, he thought, how full they are of passion, of voluptuous longing! . . . Why had he married the eyes in the photograph?

He caught himself up at the question and glanced nervously round the room. He found something mean in the pretty furniture which he had bought for his house on the hire system. Annie had chosen it herself and it reminded him of her. It too was prim and pretty. A dull resentment against his life awoke within him. Could he not escape from his little house? Was it too late for him to try to live bravely like Gallaher? Could he go to London? There was the furniture still to be paid for. If he could only write a book and get it published, that might open the way for him.

A volume of Byron's poems lay before him on the table. He opened it cautiously with his left hand lest he should waken the child and began to read the first poem in the book:

> *"Hushed are the winds and still the evening gloom,*
> *Not e'en a zephyr wanders through the grove,*
> *Whilst I return to view my Margaret's tomb*
> *And scatter flowers on the dust I love."*

He paused. He felt the rhythm of the verse about him in the room. How melancholy it was! Could he, too, write like that, express the melancholy of his soul in verse? There were so many things he wanted to describe: his sensation of a few hours before on Grattan Bridge, for example. If he could get back again into that mood. . . .

The child awoke and began to cry. He turned from the page and tried to hush it: but it would not be hushed. He began to rock it to and fro in his arms but its wailing cry grew keener. He rocked it faster while his eyes began to read the second stanza:

> *"Within this narrow cell reclines her clay,*
> *That clay where once . . ."*

It was useless. He couldn't read. He couldn't do anything. The wailing of the child pierced the drum of his ear. It was useless, useless! He was a prisoner for life. His arms trembled with anger and suddenly bending to the child's face he shouted:

"Stop!"

The child stopped for an instant, had a spasm of fright and began to scream. He jumped up from his chair and walked hastily up and down the room with the child in his arms. It began to sob piteously, losing its breath for four or five seconds, and then bursting out anew. The thin walls of the room echoed the sound. He tried to soothe it but it sobbed more convulsively. He looked at the contracted and quivering face of the child and began to be alarmed. He counted seven sobs without a break between them and caught the child to his breast in fright. If it died! . . .

The door was burst open and a young woman ran in, panting.

"What is it? What is it?" she cried.

The child, hearing its mother's voice, broke out into a paroxysm of sobbing.

"It's nothing, Annie . . . it's nothing. . . . He began to cry . . ."

She flung her parcels on the floor and snatched the child from him.

"What have you done to him?" she cried, glaring into his face.

Little Chandler sustained for one moment the gaze of her eyes and his heart closed together as he met the hatred in them. He began to stammer:

"It's nothing. . . . He . . . he began to cry. . . . I couldn't . . . I didn't do anything. . . . What?"

Giving no heed to him she began to walk up and down the room, clasping the child tightly in her arms and murmuring:

"My little man! My little mannie! Was 'ou frightened, love? . . . There now, love! There now! . . . Lamba-baun! Mamma's little lamb of the world . . . . There now!"

Little Chandler felt his cheeks suffused with shame and he stood back out of the lamplight. He listened while the paroxysm of the child's sobbing grew less and less; and tears of remorse started to his eyes.

# WINE
## *Doris Lessing*

A man and woman walked toward the boulevard from a little hotel in a side street.

The trees were still leafless, black, cold; but the fine twigs were swelling toward spring, so that looking upward it was with an expectation of the first glimmering greenness. Yet everything was calm, and the sky was a calm, classic blue.

The couple drifted slowly along. Effort, after days of laziness, seemed impossible; and almost at once they turned into a café and sank down, as if exhausted, in the glass-walled space that thrust forward into the street.

The place was empty. People were seeking the midday meal in the restaurants. Not all: that morning crowds had been demonstrating, a procession had just passed, and its straggling end could still be seen. The sounds of violence, shouted slogans and singing, no longer absorbed the din of Paris traffic; but it was these sounds that had roused the couple from sleep.

A waiter leaned at the door, looking after the crowds, and he reluctantly took an order for coffee.

The man yawned; the woman caught the infection; and they laughed with an affectation of guilt and exchanged glances before their eyes, without regret, parted. When the coffee came, it remained untouched. Neither spoke. After some time the woman yawned again; and this time the man turned and looked at her critically, and she looked back. Desire asleep, they looked. This remained; that while everything which drove them slept, they accepted from each other a sad irony; they could look at each other without illusion, steady-eyed.

And then, inevitably, the sadness deepened in her till she consciously resisted it; and into him came the flicker of cruelty.

"Your nose needs powdering," he said.

"You need a whipping boy."

But always he refused to feel sad. She shrugged, and, leaving him to it, turned to look out. So did he. At the far end of the boulevard there was a faint agitation, like stirred ants, and she heard him mutter, "Yes, and it still goes on. . . ."

Mocking, she said, "Nothing changes, everything always the same. . . ."

But he had flushed. "I remember," he began, in a different voice. He stopped, and she did not press him, for he was gazing at the distant demonstrators with a bitterly nostalgic face.

Outside drifted the lovers, the married couples, the students, the old people. There the stark trees; there the blue, quiet sky. In a month the trees would be vivid green; the sun would pour down heat; the people would be brown, laughing, bare-limbed. No, no, she said to herself, at this vision of activity. Better the static sadness. And, all at once, unhappiness welled up in her, catching her throat, and she was back fifteen years in another country, She stood in blazing tropical moonlight, stretching her arms to a landscape that offered her nothing but silence; and then she was running down a path where small stones glinted sharp underfoot, till at last she fell spent in a swathe of glistening grass. Fifteen years.

It was at this moment that the man turned abruptly and called the waiter and ordered wine.

"What," she said humorously, "already?"

"Why not?"

For the moment she loved him completely and maternally, till she suppressed the counterfeit and watched him wait, fidgeting, for the wine, pour it, and then set the two glasses before them beside the still-brimming coffee cups. But she was again remembering that night, envying the girl ecstatic with moonlight, who ran crazily through the trees in an unsharable desire for—but that was the point.

"What are you thinking of?" he asked, still a little cruel.

"Ohhh," she protested humorously.

"That's the trouble, that's the trouble." He lifted his glass, glanced at her, and set it down. "Don't you want to drink?"

"Not yet."

He left his glass untouched and began to smoke.

These moments demanded some kind of gesture—something slight, even casual, but still an acknowledgment of the separateness of those two people in each of them; the one seen, perhaps, as a soft-staring never-closing eye, observing, always observing, with a tired compassion; the other, a shape of violence that struggled on in the cycle of desire and rest, creation and achievement.

He gave it her. Again their eyes met in the grave irony, before he turned away, flicking his fingers irritably against the table; and she turned also, to note the black branches where the sap was tingling.

"I remember," he began; and again she said, in protest, "Ohhh!"

He checked himself. "Darling," he said drily, "you're the only woman I've ever loved." They laughed.

"It must have been this street. Perhaps this café—only they change so. When I went back yesterday to see the place where I came every summer, it was a *pâtisserie*, and the woman had forgotten me. There was a whole crowd of us—we used to go around together—and I met a girl here, I think, for the first time. There were recognized places for contacts; people coming from Vienna or Prague, or wherever it was, knew the places—it couldn't be this café, unless they've smartened it up. We didn't have the money for all this leather and chromium."

"Well, go on."

"I keep remembering her, for some reason. Haven't thought of her for years. She was about sixteen, I suppose. Very pretty—no, you're quite wrong. We used to study together. She used to bring her books to my room. I liked her, but I had my own girl, only she was studying something else, I forget what." He paused again, and again his face was twisted with nostalgia, and involuntarily she glanced over her shoulder down the street. The procession had completely disappeared, not even the sounds of singing and shouting remained.

"I remember her because. . . ." And, after a preoccupied silence: "Perhaps it is always the fate of the virgin who comes and offers herself, naked, to be refused."

"What!" she exclaimed, startled. Also, anger stirred in her. She noted it, and sighed. "Go on."

"I never made love to her. We studied together all that summer. Then, one weekend, we all went off in a bunch. None of us had any money, of course, and we used to stand on the pavements and beg lifts, and meet up again in some village. I was with my own girl, but that night we were helping the farmer get in his fruit, in payment for using his barn to sleep in, and I found this girl Marie was beside me. It was moonlight, a lovely night, and we were all singing and making love. I kissed her, but that was all. That night she came to me. I was sleeping up in the loft with another lad. He was asleep. I sent her back down to the others. They were all together down in the hay. I told her she was too young. But she was no younger than my own girl." He stopped; and after all these years his face was rueful and puzzled. "I don't know," he said. "I don't know why I sent her back." Then he laughed. "Not that it matters, I suppose."

"Shameless hussy," she said. The anger was strong now. "You had kissed her, hadn't you?"

He shrugged. "But we were all playing the fool. It was a glorious night—gathering apples, the farmer shouting and swearing at us because we were making love more than working, and singing and drinking wine. Besides, it was that time: the youth movement. We regarded faithfulness and jealousy and all that sort of thing as remnants of bourgeois morality." He laughed again, rather painfully. "I kissed her. There she was, beside me, and she knew my girl was with me that weekend."

"You kissed her." she said accusingly.

He fingered the stem of his wineglass, looking over at her and grinning. "Yes, darling," he almost crooned at her. "I kissed her."

She snapped over into anger. "There's a girl all ready for love. You

make use of her for working. Then you kiss her. You know quite
well. . . ."

"What do I know quite well?"

"It was a cruel thing to do."

"I was a kid myself. . . ."

"Doesn't matter." She noted, with discomfort, that she was almost
crying. "Working with her! Working with a girl of sixteen, all summer!"

"But we all studied very seriously. She was a doctor afterward, in
Vienna. She managed to get out when the Nazis came in, but. . . ."

She said impatiently, "Then you kissed her, on *that* night. Imagine
her, waiting till the others were asleep, then she climbed up the ladder
to the loft, terrified the other man might wake up, then she stood
watching you sleep, and she slowly took off her dress and. . . ."

"Oh, I wasn't asleep. I pretended to be. She came up dressed. Shorts
and sweater—our girls didn't wear dresses and lipstick—more bourgeois morality. I watched her strip. The loft was full of moonlight. She
put her hand over my mouth and came down beside me." Again, his
face was filled with rueful amazement. "God knows, I can't understand it myself. She was a beautiful creature. I don't know why I remember it. It's been coming into my mind the last few days." After a
pause, slowly twirling the wineglass: "I've been a failure in many
things, but not with. . . ." He quickly lifted her hand, kissed it, and
said sincerely: "I don't know why I remember it now, when. . . ." Their
eyes met, and they sighed.

She said slowly, her hand lying in his: "And so you turned her away."

He laughed. "Next morning she wouldn't speak to me. She started a
love affair with my best friend—the man who'd been beside me that
night in the loft, as a matter of fact. She hated my guts, and I suppose
she was right."

"Think of her. Think of her at that moment. She picked up her
clothes, hardly daring to look at you. . . ."

"As a matter of fact, she was furious. She called me all the names
she could think of; I had to keep telling her to shut up, she'd wake the
whole crowd."

"She climbed down the ladder and dressed again, in the dark. Then
she went out of the barn, unable to go back to the others. She went
into the orchard. It was still brilliant moonlight. Everything was silent
and deserted, and she remembered how you'd all been singing and
laughing and making love. She went to the tree where you'd kissed her.
The moon was shining on the apples. She'll never forget it, never,
never!"

He looked at her curiously. The tears were pouring down her face.

"It's terrible," she said. "Terrible. Nothing could ever make up to
her for that. Nothing, as long as she lived. Just when everything was
most perfect, all her life, she'd suddenly remember that night, standing

alone, not a soul anywhere, miles of damned empty moonlight. . . ."

He looked at her shrewdly. Then, with a sort of humorous, deprecating grimace, he bent over and kissed her and said: "Darling, it's not my fault; it just isn't my fault."

"No," she said.

He put the wineglass into her hands; and she lifted it, looked at the small crimson globule of warming liquid, and drank with him.

---

# TICKETS, PLEASE
## *D. H. Lawrence*

There is in the Midlands a single-line tramway system which boldly leaves the country town and plunges off into the black, industrial countryside, up hill and down dale, through the long, ugly villages of workmen's houses, over canals and railways, past churches perched high and nobly over the smoke and shadows, through stark, grimy, cold little market-places, tilting away in a rush past cinemas and shops down to the hollow where the collieries are, then up again, past a little rural church, under the ash trees, on in a rush to the terminus, the last little ugly place of industry, the cold little town that shivers on the edge of the wild, gloomy country beyond. There the green and creamy colored tram-car seems to pause and purr with curious satisfaction. But in a few minutes—the clock on the turret of the Co-operative Wholesale Society's Shops gives the time—away it starts once more on the adventure. Again there are the reckless swoops downhill, bouncing the loops: again the chilly wait in the hill-top market-place: again the breathless slithering round the precipitous drop under the church: again the patient halts at the loops, waiting for the outcoming car: so on and on, for two long hours, till at last the city looms beyond the fat gas-works, the narrow factories draw near, we are in the sordid streets of the great town, once more we sidle to a standstill at our terminus, abashed by the great crimson and cream-coloured city cars, but still perky, jaunty, somewhat dare-devil, green as a jaunty sprig of parsley out of a black colliery garden.

To ride on these cars is always an adventure. Since we are in war-time, the drivers are men unfit for active service: cripples and hunchbacks. So they have the spirit of the devil in them. The ride becomes a steeplechase. Hurray! we have leapt in a clear jump over the canal bridges—now for the four-lane corner. With a shriek and a trail of sparks we are clear again. To be sure, a tram often leaps the rails—but what matter! It sits in a ditch till other trams come to haul it out. It is quite common for a car, packed with one solid mass of living people, to come to a dead halt in the midst of unbroken blackness, the heart of nowhere on a dark night, and for the driver and the girl conductor to call, "All get off—car's on fire!" Instead, however, of rushing out in a panic, the passengers stolidly reply: "Get on—get on! We're not coming out. We're stopping where we are. Push on, George." So till flames actually appear.

The reason for this reluctance to dismount is that the nights are howlingly cold, black, and windswept, and a car is a haven of refuge. From village to village the miners travel, for a change of cinema, of girl, of pub. The trams are desperately packed. Who is going to risk himself in the black gulf outside to wait perhaps an hour for another tram, then to see the forlorn notice "Depot Only," because there is something wrong! or to greet a unit of three bright cars all so tight with people that they sail past with a howl of derision. Trams that pass in the night.

This, the most dangerous tram-service in England, as the authorities themselves declare, with pride, is entirely conducted by girls, and driven by rash young men, a little crippled, or by delicate young men, who creep forward in terror. The girls are fearless young hussies. In their ugly blue uniform, skirts up to their knees, shapeless old peaked caps on their heads, they have all the sang-froid of an old non-commissioned officer. With a tram packed with howling colliers, roaring hymns downstairs and a sort of antiphony of obscenities upstairs, the lasses are perfectly at their ease. They pounce on the youths who try to evade their ticket-machine. They push off the men at the end of their distance. They are not going to be done in the eye—not they. They fear nobody —and everybody fears them.

"Hello, Annie!"

"Hello, Ted!"

"Oh, mind my corn, Miss Stone. It's my belief you've got a heart of stone, for you've trod on it again."

"You should keep it in your pocket," replies Miss Stone, and she goes sturdily upstairs in her high boots.

"Tickets, please."

She is peremptory, suspicious, and ready to hit first. She can hold her own against ten thousand. The step of that tram-car is her Thermopylæ.

Therefore, there is a certain wild romance aboard these cars—and in the sturdy bosom of Annie herself. The time for soft romance is in the morning, between ten o'clock and one, when things are rather slack: that is, except market-day and Saturday. Thus Annie has time to look about her. Then she often hops off her car and into a shop where she has spied something, while the driver chats in the main road. There is very good feeling between the girls and the drivers. Are they not companions in peril, shipments aboard this careering vessel of a tram-car, for ever rocking on the waves of a stormy land.

Then, also, during the easy hours, the inspectors are most in evidence. For some reason, everybody employed in this tram-service is young: there are no grey heads. It would not do. Therefore the inspectors are of the right age, and one, the chief, is also good-looking. See him stand on a wet, gloomy morning, in his long oilskin, his peaked cap well down over his eyes, waiting to board a car. His face is ruddy, his small brown moustache is weathered, he has a faint impudent smile. Fairly tall and agile, even in his waterproof, he springs aboard a car and greets Annie.

"Hello, Annie! Keeping the wet out?"

"Trying to."

There are only two people in the car. Inspecting is soon over. Then for a long and impudent chat on the footboard, a good, easy, twelve-mile chat.

The inspector's name is John Thomas Raynor—always called John Thomas, except sometimes, in malice, Coddy. His face sets in fury when he is addressed, from a distance, with this abbreviation. There is considerable scandal about John Thomas in half a dozen villages. He flirts with the girl conductors in the morning and walks out with them in the dark night, when they leave their tram-car at the depot. Of course, the girls quit the service frequently Then he flirts and walks out with the newcomer: always providing she is sufficiently attractive, and that she will consent to walk. It is remarkable, however, that most of the girls are quite comely, they are all young, and this roving life aboard the car gives them a sailor's dash and recklessness. What matter how they behave when the ship is in port. Tomorrow they will be aboard again.

Annie, however, was something of a Tartar, and her sharp tongue had kept John Thomas at arm's length for many months. Perhaps, therefore, she liked him all the more: for he always came up smiling, with impudence. She watched him vanquish one girl, then another. She could tell by the movement of his mouth and eyes, when he flirted with her in the morning, that he had been walking out with this lass, or the other, the night before. A fine cock-of-the-walk he was. She could sum him up pretty well.

In this subtle antagonism they knew each other like old friends, they were as shrewd with one another almost as man and wife. But Annie had always kept him sufficiently at arm's length. Besides, she had a boy of her own.

The Statutes fair, however, came in November, at Bestwood. It happened that Annie had the Monday night off. It was a drizzling ugly night, yet she dressed herself up and went to the fair ground. She was alone, but she expected soon to find a pal of some sort.

The roundabouts were veering round and grinding out their music, the side shows were making as much commotion as possible. In the cocoanut shies there were no cocoanuts, but artificial war-time substi-

tutes, which the lads declared were fastened into the irons. There was a
sad decline in brilliance and luxury. None the less, the ground was
muddy as ever, there was the same crush, the press of faces lighted up
by the flares and the electric lights, the same smell of naphtha and a
few fried potatoes, and of electricity.

Who should be the first to greet Miss Annie, on the show ground,
but John Thomas. He had a black overcoat buttoned up to his chin, and
a tweed cap pulled down over his brows, his face between was ruddy
and smiling and handy as ever. She knew so well the way his mouth
moved.

She was very glad to have a "boy." To be at the Statutes without a
fellow was no fun. Instantly, like the gallant he was, he took her on the
Dragons, grim-toothed, roundabout switchbacks. It was not nearly so
exciting as a tram-car actually. But, then, to be seated in a shaking green
dragon, uplifted above the sea of bubble faces, careering in a rickety
fashion in the lower heavens, whilst John Thomas leaned over her, his
cigarette in his mouth, was after all the right style. She was a plump,
quick, alive little creature. So she was quite excited and happy.

John Thomas made her stay on for the next round. And therefore
she could hardly for shame repulse him when he put his arm round her
and drew her a little nearer to him, in a very warm and cuddly manner.
Besides, he was fairly discreet, he kept his movement as hidden as
possible. She looked down and saw that his red, clean hand was out of
sight of the crowd. And they knew each other so well. So they warmed
up to the fair.

After the dragons they went on the horses. John Thomas paid each
time, so she could but be complaisant. He, of course, sat astride on the
outer horse—named "Black Bess"—and she sat sideways, towards him,
on the inner horse—named "Wildfire." But of course John Thomas
was not going to sit discreetly on "Black Bess," holding the brass bar.
Round they spun and heaved, in the light. And round he swung on his
wooden steed, flinging one leg across her mount, and perilously tipping
up and down, across the space, half lying back, laughing at her. He
was perfectly happy; she was afraid her hat was on one side, but she
was excited.

He threws quoits on a table and won for her two large, pale-blue
hatpins. And then, hearing the noise of the cinemas, announcing another performance, they climbed the boards and went in.

Of course, during these performances pitch darkness falls from time
to time, when the machine goes wrong. Then there is a wild whooping,
and a loud smacking of simulated kisses. In these moments John
Thomas drew Annie towards him. After all, he had a wonderfully warm,
cosy way of holding a girl with his arm, he seemed to make such a nice
fit. And after all, it was pleasant to be so held: so very comforting and
cosy and nice. He leaned over her and she felt his breath on her hair;

she knew he wanted to kiss her on the lips. And after all, he was so warm and she fitted in to him so softly. After all, she wanted him to touch her lips.

But the light sprang up; she also started electrically, and put her hat straight. He left his arm lying nonchalantly behind her. Well, it was fun, it was exciting to be at the Statutes with John Thomas.

When the cinema was over they went for a walk across the dark, damp fields. He had all the arts of love-making. He was especially good at holding a girl, when he sat with her on a stile in the black, drizzling darkness. He seemed to be holding her in space, against his own warmth and gratification. And his kisses were soft and slow and searching.

So Annie walked out with John Thomas, though she kept her own boy dangling in the distance. Some of the tram-girls chose to be huffy. But there, you must take things as you find them, in this life.

There was no mistake about it, Annie liked John Thomas a good deal. She felt so rich and warm in herself whenever he was near. And John Thomas really liked Annie more than usual. The soft, melting way in which she could flow into a fellow, as if she melted into his very bones, was something rare and good. He fully appreciated this.

But with a developing acquaintance there began a developing intimacy. Annie wanted to consider him a person, a man; she wanted to take an intelligent interest in him, and to have an intelligent response. She did not want a mere nocturnal presence. which was what he was so far. And she prided herself that he could not leave her.

Here she made a mistake. John Thomas intended to remain a nocturnal presence; he had no idea of becoming an all-round individual to her. When she started to take an intelligent interest in him and his life and his character, he sheered off. He hated intelligent interest. And he knew that the only way to stop it was to avoid it. The possessive female was aroused in Annie. So he left her.

It is no use saying she was not surprised. She was at first startled, thrown out of her count. For she had been so *very* sure of holding him. For a while she was staggered, and everything became uncertain to her. Then she wept with fury, indignation, desolation, and misery. Then she had a spasm of despair. And then, when he came, still impudently, on to her car, still familiar, but letting her see by the movement of his head that he had gone away to somebody else for the time being and was enjoying pastures new, then she determined to have her own back.

She had a very shrewd idea what girls John Thomas had taken out. She went to Nora Purdy. Nora was a tall, rather pale, but well-built girl, with beautiful yellow hair. She was rather secretive.

"Hey!" said Annie, accosting her; then softly, "Who's John Thomas on with now?"

"I don't know," said Nora.

"Why tha does," said Annie, ironically lapsing into dialect. "Tha knows as well as I do."

"Well, I do, then," said Nora. "It isn't me, so don't bother."

"It's Cissy Meakin, isn't it?"

"It is, for all I know."

"Hasn't he got a face on him!" said Annie. "I don't half like his cheek. I could knock him off the footboard when he comes round at me."

"He'll get dropped-on one of these days," said Nora.

"Ay, he will when somebody makes up their mind to drop it on him. I should like to see him taken down a peg or two, shouldn't you?"

"I shouldn't mind," said Nora.

"You've got quite as much cause to as I have," said Annie. "But we'll drop on him one of these days, my girl. What? Don't you want to?"

"I don't mind," said Nora.

But as a matter of fact, Nora was much more vindictive than Annie.

One by one Annie went the round of the old flames. It so happened that Cissy Meakin left the tramway service in quite a short time. Her mother made her leave. Then John Thomas was on the qui-vive. He cast his eyes over his old flock. And his eyes lighted on Annie. He thought she would be safe now. Besides, he liked her.

She arranged to walk home with him on Sunday night. It so happened that her car would be in the depot at half-past nine: the last car would come in at ten-fifteen. So John Thomas was to wait for her there.

At the depot the girls had a little waiting-room of their own. It was quite rough, but cosy, with a fire and an oven and a mirror, and table and wooden chairs. The half dozen girls who knew John Thomas only too well had arranged to take service this Sunday afternoon. So, as the cars began to come in, early, the girls dropped into the waiting-room. And instead of hurrying off home, they sat around the fire and had a cup of tea. Outside was the darkness and lawlessness of war-time.

John Thomas came on the car after Annie, at about a quarter to ten. He poked his head easily into the girls' waiting-room.

"Prayer-meeting?" he asked.

"Ay," said Laura Sharp. "Ladies only."

"That's me!" said John Thomas. It was one of his favourite exclamations.

"Shut the door, boy," said Muriel Baggaley.

"On which side of me?" said John Thomas.

"Which tha likes," said Polly Birkin.

He had come in and closed the door behind him. The girls moved in their circle, to make a place for him near the fire. He took off his greatcoat and pushed back his hat.

"Who handles the teapot?" he said.

Nora Purdy silently poured him out a cup of tea.

"Want a bit o' my bread and drippin'?" said Muriel Baggaley to him.

"Ay, give us a bit."

And he began to eat his piece of bread.

"There's no place like home, girls," he said.

They all looked at him as he uttered this piece of impudence. He seemed to be sunning himself in the presence of so many damsels.

"Especially if you're not afraid to go home in the dark," said Laura Sharp.

"Me! By myself I am."

They sat till they heard the last tram come in. In a few minutes Emma Houselay entered.

"Come on, my old duck!" cried Polly Birkin.

"It *is* perishing," said Emma, holding her fingers to the fire.

"But—I'm afraid to, go home in, the dark," sang Laura Sharp, the tune having got into her mind.

"Who're you going with tonight, John Thomas?" asked Muriel Baggaley, coolly.

"Tonight?" said John Thomas. "Oh, I'm going home by myself tonight—all on my lonely-O."

"That's me!" said Nora Purdy, using his own ejaculation.

The girls laughed shrilly.

"Me as well, Nora," said John Thomas.

"Don't know what you mean," said Laura.

"Yes, I'm toddling," said he, rising and reaching for his overcoat.

"Nay," said Polly. "We're all here waiting for you."

"We've got to be up in good time in the morning," he said in the benevolent official manner.

They all laughed.

"Nay," said Muriel. "Don't leave us all lonely, John Thomas. Take one!"

"I'll take the lot, if you like," he responded gallantly.

"That you won't, either," said Muriel. "Two's company; seven's too much of a good thing."

"Nay—take one," said Laura. "Fair and square, all above board, and say which."

"Ay," cried Annie, speaking for the first time. "Pick, John Thomas; let's hear thee."

"Nay," he said. "I'm going home quiet tonight. Feeling good, for once."

"Whereabouts?" said Annie. "Take a good un, then. But tha's got to take one of us!"

"Nay, how can I take one," he said, laughing uneasily. "I don't want to make enemies."

"You'd only make *one*," said Annie.

"The chosen *one,*" added Laura.

"Oh, my! Who said girls!" exclaimed John Thomas, again turning, as if to escape. "Well—good-night."

"Nay, you've got to make your pick," said Muriel. "Turn your face to the wall and say which one touches you. Go on—we shall only just touch your back—one of us. Go on—turn your face to the wall, and don't look, and say which one touches you."

He was uneasy, mistrusting them. Yet he had not the courage to break away. They pushed him to a wall and stood him there with his face to it. Behind his back they all grimaced, tittering. He looked so comical. He looked around uneasily.

"Go on!" he cried.

"You're looking—you're looking!" they shouted.

He turned his head away. And suddenly, with a movement like a swift cat, Annie went forward and fetched him a box on the side of the head that set his cap flying and himself staggering. He started round.

But at Annie's signal they all flew at him, slapping him, pinching him, pulling his hair, though more in fun than in spite or anger. He, however, saw red. His blue eyes flamed with strange fear as well as fury, and he butted through the girls to the door. It was locked. He wrenched at it. Roused, alert, the girls stood round and looked at him. He faced them, at bay. At that moment they were rather horrifying to him, as they stood in their short uniforms. He was distinctly afraid.

"Come on, John Thomas! Come on! Choose!" said Annie.

"What are you after? Open the door," he said.

"We sha'n't—not till you've chosen!" said Muriel.

"Chosen what?" he said.

"Chosen the one you're going to marry," she replied.

He hesitated a moment.

"Open the blasted door," he said, "and get back to your senses." He spoke with official authority.

"You've got to choose!" cried the girls.

"Come on!" cried Annie, looking him in the eye. "Come on! Come on!"

He went forward, rather vaguely. She had taken off her belt, and swinging it, she fetched him a sharp blow over the head with the buckle end. He sprang and seized her. But immediately the other girls rushed upon him, pulling and tearing and beating him. Their blood was now thoroughly up. He was their sport now. They were going to have their own back, out of him. Strange, wild creatures, they hung on him and rushed at him to bear him down. His tunic was torn right up the back, Nora had hold at the back of his collar, and was actually strangling him. Luckily, the button burst. He struggled in a wild frenzy of fury and terror, almost mad terror. His tunic was simply torn off his back, his shirt-sleeves were torn away, his arms were naked. The girls rushed at him, clenched their hands on him and pulled at him: or they rushed at him and pushed him, butted him with all their might: or they struck him wild blows. He ducked and cringed and struck sideways. They became more intense.

At last he was down. They rushed on him, kneeling on him. He had neither breath nor strength to move. His face was bleeding with a long scratch, his brow was bruised.

Annie knelt on him, the other girls knelt and hung on to him. Their faces were flushed, their hair wild, their eyes were all glittering strangely. He lay at last quite still, with face averted, as an animal lies when it is defeated and at the mercy of the captor. Sometimes his eye glanced back at the wild faces of the girls. His breast rose heavily, his wrists were torn.

"Now, then, my fellow!" gasped Annie at length. "Now then— now——"

At the sound of her terrifying, cold triumph, he suddenly started to struggle as an animal might, but the girls threw themselves upon him with unnatural strength and power, forcing him down.

"Yes—now, then!" gasped Annie at length.

And there was a dead silence, in which the thud of heart-beating was to be heard. It was a suspense of pure silence in every soul.

"Now you know where you are," said Annie.

The sight of his white, bare arm maddened the girls. He lay in a kind of trance of fear and antagonism. They felt themselves filled with supernatural strength.

Suddenly Polly started to laugh—to giggle wildly—helplessly—and Emma and Muriel joined in. But Annie and Nora and Laura remained the same, tense, watchful, with gleaming eyes. He winced away from these eyes.

"Yes," said Annie, in a curious low tone, secret and deadly. "Yes! You've got it now! You know what you've done, don't you? You know what you've done."

He made no sound nor sign, but lay with bright, averted eyes, and averted, bleeding face.

"You ought to be *killed*, that's what you ought," said Annie tensely. "You ought to be *killed*." And there was a terrifying lust in her voice.

Polly was ceasing to laugh, and giving long-drawn oh-h-hs and sighs as she came to herself.

"He's got to choose," she said vaguely.

"Oh, yes, he has," said Laura, with vindictive decision.

"Do you hear—do you hear?" said Annie. And with a sharp movement that made him wince, she turned his face to her.

"Do you hear?" she repeated, shaking him.

But he was quite dumb. She fetched him a sharp slap on the face.

He started, and his eyes widened. Then his face darkened with defiance, after all.

"Do you hear?" she repeated.

He only looked at her with hostile eyes.

"Speak!" she said, putting her face devilishly near his.

"What?" he said, almost overcome.

"You've got to *choose!*" she cried, as if it were some terrible menace, and as if it hurt her that she could not exact more.

"What?" he said in fear.

"Choose your girl, Coddy. You've got to choose her now. And you'll get your neck broken if you play any more of your tricks, my boy. You're settled now."

There was a pause. Again he averted his face. He was cunning in his overthrow. He did not give in to them really—no, not if they tore him to bits.

"All right, then," he said, "I choose Annie." His voice was strange and full of malice. Annie let go of him as if he had been a hot coal.

"He's chosen Annie!" said the girls in chorus.

"Me!" cried Annie. She was still kneeling, but away from him. He was still lying prostrate, with averted face. The girls grouped uneasily around.

"Me!" repeated Annie, with a terrible bitter accent.

Then she got up, drawing away from him with strange disgust and bitterness.

"I wouldn't touch him," she said.

But her face quivered with a kind of agony, she seemed as if she would fall. The other girls turned aside. He remained lying on the floor, with his torn clothes and bleeding, averted face.

"Oh, if he's chosen——" said Polly.

"I don't want him—he can choose again," said Annie, with the same rather bitter hopelessness.

"Get up," said Polly, lifting his shoulder. "Get up."

He rose slowly, a strange, ragged, dazed creature. The girls eyed him from a distance, curiously, furtively, dangerously.

"Who wants him?" cried Laura roughly.

"Nobody," they answered with contempt. Yet each one of them waited for him to look at her, hoped he would look at her. All except Annie, and something was broken in her.

He, however, kept his face closed and averted from them all. There was a silence of the end. He picked up the torn pieces of his tunic, without knowing what to do with them. The girls stood about uneasily, flushed, panting, tidying their hair and their dress unconsciously, and watching him. He looked at none of them. He espied his cap in a corner and went and picked it up. He put it on his head, and one of the girls burst into a shrill, hysteric laugh at the sight he presented. He, however, took no heed but went straight to where his overcoat hung on a peg. The girls moved away from contact with him as if he had been an electric wire. He put on his coat and buttoned it down. Then he rolled his tunic-rags into a bundle, and stood before the locked door, dumbly.

"Open the door, somebody," said Laura.

"Annie's got the key," said one.

Annie silently offered the key to the girls. Nora unlocked the door.

"Tit for tat, old man," she said. "Show yourself a man, and don't bear a grudge."

But without a word or sign he had opened the door and gone, his face closed, his head dropped.

"That'll learn him," said Laura.

"Coddy!" said Nora.

"Shut up, for God's sake!" cried Annie fiercely, as if in torture.

"Well, I'm about ready to go, Polly. Look sharp!" said Muriel.

The girls were all anxious to be off. They were tidying themselves hurriedly, with mute, stupefied faces.

---

# A DILL PICKLE
## *Katherine Mansfield*

And then, after six years, she saw him again. He was seated at one of those little bamboo tables decorated with a Japanese vase of paper daffodils. There was a tall plate of fruit in front of him, and very carefully, in a way she recognized immediately as his "special" way, he was peeling an orange.

He must have felt that shock of recognition in her for he looked up and met her eyes. Incredible! He didn't know her! She smiled; he frowned. She came towards him. He closed his eyes an instant, but opening them his face lit up as though he had struck a match in a dark room. He laid down the orange and pushed back his chair, and she took her little warm hand out of her muff and gave it to him.

"Vera!" he exclaimed. "How strange. Really, for a moment I didn't know you. Won't you sit down? You've had lunch? Won't you have some coffee?"

She hesitated, but of course she meant to.

"Yes, I'd like some coffee." And she sat down opposite him.

"You've changed. You've changed very much," he said, staring at her with that eager, lighted look. "You look so well. I've never seen you look so well before."

"Really?" She raised her veil and unbuttoned her high fur collar. "I don't feel very well. I can't bear this weather, you know."

"Ah, no. You hate the cold...."

"Loathe it." She shuddered. "And the worst of it is that the older one grows..."

He interrupted her. "Excuse me," and tapped on the table for the waitress. "Please bring some coffee and cream." To her: "You are sure you won't eat anything? Some fruit, perhaps. The fruit here is very good."

"No, thanks. Nothing."

"Then that's settled." And smiling just a hint too broadly he took up the orange again. "You were saying—the older one grows—"

"The colder," she laughed. But she was thinking how well she remembered that trick of his—the trick of interrupting her—and of how it used to exasperate her six years ago. She used to feel then as though he, quite suddenly, in the middle of what she was saying, put his hand over her lips, turned from her, attended to something different, and then took his hand away, with just the same slightly too broad smile, gave her his attention again.... Now we are ready. That is settled.

"The colder!" He echoed her words, laughing too. "Ah, ah. You still say the same things. And there is another thing about you that is not changed at all—your beautiful voice—your beautiful way of speaking." Now he was very grave; he leaned towards her, and she smelled the warm, stinging scent of the orange peel. "You have only to say one word and I would know your voice among all other voices. I don't know what it is—I've often wondered—that makes your voice such a —haunting memory.... Do you remember that first afternoon we spent together at Kew Gardens? You were so surprised because I did not know the names of any flowers. I am still just as ignorant for all your telling me. But whenever it is very fine and warm, and I see some bright colors—it's awfully strange—I hear your voice saying: 'Geranium, marigold and verbena.' And I feel those three words are all I recall of some forgotten, heavenly language.... You remember that afternoon?"

"Oh, yes, very well." She drew a long, soft breath, as though the paper daffodils between them were almost too sweet to bear. Yet, what had remained in her mind of that particular afternoon was an absurd scene over the tea table. A great many people taking tea in a Chinese pagoda, and he behaving like a maniac about the wasps—waving them away, flapping at them with his straw hat, serious and infuriated out of all proportion to the occasion. How delighted the sniggering tea drinkers had been. And how she had suffered.

But now, as he spoke, that memory faded. His was the truer. Yes, it had been a wonderful afternoon, full of geranium and marigold and verbena, and—warm sunshine. Her thoughts lingered over the last two words as though she sang them.

In the warmth, as it were, another memory unfolded. She saw herself sitting on a lawn. He lay beside her, and suddenly, after a long silence, he rolled over and put his head in her lap.

"I wish," he said, in a low, troubled voice, "I wish that I had taken poison and were about to die—here now!"

At that moment a little girl in a white dress, holding a long, dripping water lily, dodged from behind a bush, stared at them, and dodged back again. But he did not see. She leaned over him.

"Ah, why do you say that? I could not say that."

But he gave a kind of soft moan, and taking her hand he held it to his cheek.

"Because I know I am going to love you too much—far too much. And I shall suffer so terribly, Vera, because you never, never, will love me."

He was certainly far better looking now than he had been then. He had lost all that dreamy vagueness and indecision. Now he had the air of a man who has found his place in life, and fills it with a confidence and an assurance which was, to say the least, impressive. He must have made money, too. His clothes were admirable, and at that moment he pulled a Russian cigarette case out of his pocket.

"Won't you smoke?"

"Yes, I will." She hovered over them. "They look very good."

"I think they are. I get them made for me by a little man in St. James's Street. I don't smoke very much. I'm not like you—but when I do, they must be delicious, very fresh cigarettes. Smoking isn't a habit with me; it's a luxury—like perfume. Are you still so fond of perfumes? Ah, when I was in Russia . . ."

She broke in: "You've really been to Russia?"

"Oh, yes. I was there for over a year. Have you forgotten how we used to talk of going there?"

"No, I've not forgotten."

He gave a strange half laugh and leaned back in his chair. "Isn't it curious. I have really carried out all those journeys that we planned. Yes, I have been to all those places that we talked of, and stayed in them long enough to—as you used to say, 'air oneself' in them. In fact, I have spent the last three years of my life traveling all the time. Spain, Corsica, Siberia, Russia, Egypt. The only country left is China, and I mean to go there, too, when the war is over."

As he spoke, so lightly, tapping the end of his cigarette against the ashtray, she felt the strange beast that had slumbered so long within her bosom stir, stretch itself, yawn, prick up its ears, and suddenly bound to its feet, and fix its longing, hungry stare upon those far away places. But all she said was, smiling gently: "How I envy you."

He accepted that. "It has been," he said, "very wonderful—especially Russia. Russia was all that we had imagined, and far, far more. I even spent some days on a river boat on the Volga. Do you remember that boatman's song that you used to play?"

"Yes." It began to play in her mind as she spoke.

"Do you ever play it now?"

"No, I've no piano."

He was amazed at that. "But what has become of your beautiful piano?"

She made a little grimace. "Sold. Ages ago."

"But you were so fond of music," he wondered.

"I've no time for it now," said she.

He let it go at that. "That river life," he went on, "is something quite special. After a day or two you cannot realize that you have ever known another. And it is not necessary to know the language—the life of the boat creates a bond between you and the people that's more than sufficient. You eat with them, pass the day with them, and in the evening there is that endless singing."

She shivered, hearing the boatman's song break out again loud and tragic, and seeing the boat floating on the darkening river with melancholy trees on either side. . . . "Yes, I should like that," said she, stroking her muff.

"You'd like almost everything about Russian life," he said warmly. "It's so informal, so impulsive, so free without question. And then the peasants are so splendid. They are such human beings—yes, that is it. Even the man who drives your carriage has—has some real part in what is happening. I remember the evening a party of us, two friends of mine and the wife of one of them, went for a picnic by the Black Sea. We took supper and champagne and ate and drank on the grass. And while we were eating the coachman came up. 'Have a dill pickle,' he said. He wanted to share with us. That seemed to me so right, so— you know what I mean?"

And she seemed at that moment to be sitting on the grass beside the mysteriously Black Sea, black as velvet, and rippling against the banks in silent, velvet waves. She saw the carriage drawn up to one side of the road, and the little group on the grass, their faces and hands white in the moonlight. She saw the pale dress of the woman outspread and her folded parasol, lying on the grass like a huge pearl crochet hook. Apart from them, with his supper in a cloth on his knees, sat the coachman. "Have a dill pickle," said he, and although she was not certain what a dill pickle was, she saw the greenish glass jar with a red chili like a parrot's beak glimmering through. She sucked in her cheeks; the dill pickle was terribly sour. . . .

"Yes, I know perfectly what you mean," she said.

In the pause that followed they looked at each other. In the past when they had looked at each other like that they had felt such a boundless understanding between them that their souls had, as it were, put their arms round each other and dropped into the same sea, content to be drowned, like mournful lovers. But now, the surprising thing was that it was he who held back. He who said:

"What a marvellous listener you are. When you look at me with those wild eyes I feel that I could tell you things that I would never breathe to another human being."

Was there just a hint of mockery in his voice or was it her fancy? She could not be sure.

"Before I met you," he said, "I had never spoken of myself to anybody. How well I remember one night, the night that I brought you the little Christmas tree, telling you all about my childhood. And of how I was so miserable that I ran away and lived under a cart in our yard for two days without being discovered. And you listened, and your eyes shone, and I felt that you had even made the little Christmas tree listen too, as in a fairy story."

But of that evening she had remembered a little pot of caviare. It had cost seven and sixpence. He could not get over it. Think of it—a tiny jar like that costing seven and sixpence. While she ate it he watched her, delighted and shocked.

"No, really, that is eating money. You could not get seven shillings into a little pot that size. Only think of the profit they must make...." And he had begun some immensely complicated calculations.... But now good-bye to the caviare. The Christmas tree was on the table, and the little boy lay under the cart with his head pillowed on the yard dog.

"The dog was called Bosun," she cried delightedly.

But he did not follow. "Which dog? Had you a dog? I don't remember a dog at all."

"No, no. I mean the yard dog when you were a little boy." He laughed and snapped the cigarette case to.

"Was he? Do you know I had forgotten that. It seems such ages ago. I cannot believe that it is only six years. After I had recognized you to-day—I had to take such a leap—I had to take a leap over my whole life to get back to that time. I was such a kid then." He drummed on the table. "I've often thought how I must have bored you. And now I understand so perfectly why you wrote to me as you did—although at the time that letter nearly finished my life. I found it again the other day, and I couldn't help laughing as I read it. It was so clever—such a true picture of me." He glanced up. "You're not going?"

She had buttoned her collar again and drawn down her veil.

"Yes, I am afraid I must," she said, and managed a smile. Now she knew that he had been mocking.

"Ah, no, please," he pleaded. "Don't go just for a moment," and he caught up one of her gloves from the table and clutched at it as if that would hold her. "I see so few people to talk to nowadays, that I have turned into a sort of barbarian," he said. "Have I said something to hurt you?"

"Not a bit," she lied. But as she watched him draw her glove through his fingers, gently, gently, her anger really did die down, and besides, at the moment he looked more like himself of six years ago. . . .

"What I really wanted then," he said softly, "was to be a sort of carpet—to make myself into a sort of carpet for you to walk on so that you need not be hurt by the sharp stones and the mud that you hated so. It was nothing more positive than that—nothing more selfish. Only I did desire, eventually, to turn into a magic carpet and carry you away to all those lands you longed to see."

As he spoke she lifted her head as though she drank something; the strange beast in her bosom began to purr. . . .

"I felt that you were more lonely than anybody else in the world," he went on, "and yet, perhaps, that you were the only person in the world who was really, truly alive. Born out of your time," he murmured, stroking the glove, "fated."

Ah, God! What had she done! How had she dared to throw away her happiness like this. This was the only man who had ever understood her. Was it too late? Could it be too late? *She* was that glove that he held in his fingers. . . .

"And then the fact that you had no friends and never had made friends with people. How I understood that, for neither had I. Is it just the same now?"

"Yes," she breathed. "Just the same. I am as alone as ever."

"So am I," he laughed gently, "just the same."

Suddenly with a quick gesture he handed her back the glove and scraped his chair on the floor. "But what seemed to me so mysterious then is perfectly plain to me now. And to you, too, of course. . . . It simply was that we were such egoists, so self-engrossed, so wrapped up in ourselves that we hadn't a corner in our hearts for anybody else. Do you know," he cried, naive and hearty, and dreadfully like another side of that old self again, "I began studying a Mind System when I was in Russia, and I found that we were not peculiar at all. It's quite a well known form of . . ."

She had gone. He sat there, thunder-struck, astounded beyond words. . . . And then he asked the waitress for his bill.

"But the cream has not been touched," he said. "Please do not charge me for it."

# HARRISON BERGERON
*Kurt Vonnegut, Jr.*

The year was 2081, and everybody was finally equal. They weren't only equal before God and the law. They were equal every which way. Nobody was smarter than anybody else. Nobody was better looking than anybody else. Nobody was stronger or quicker than anybody else. All this equality was due to the 211th, 212th, and 213th Amendments to the Constitution, and to the unceasing vigilance of agents of the United States Handicapper General.

Some things about living still weren't quite right, though. April, for instance, still drove people crazy by not being springtime. And it was in that clammy month that the H-G men took George and Hazel Bergeron's fourteen-year-old son, Harrison, away.

It was tragic, all right, but George and Hazel couldn't think about it very hard. Hazel had a perfectly average intelligence, which meant she couldn't think about anything except in short bursts. And George, while his intelligence was way above normal, had a little mental handicap radio in his ear. He was required by law to wear it at all times. It was tuned to a government transmitter. Every twenty seconds or so, the transmitter would send out some sharp noise to keep people like George from taking unfair advantage of their brains.

George and Hazel were watching television. There were tears on Hazel's cheeks, but she'd forgotten for the moment what they were about.

On the television screen were ballerinas.

A buzzer sounded in George's head. His thoughts fled in panic, like bandits from a burglar alarm.

"That was a real pretty dance, that dance they just did," said Hazel.

"Huh?" said George.

"That dance—it was nice," said Hazel.

"Yup," said George. He tried to think a little about the ballerinas. They weren't really very good—no better than anybody else would have been, anyway. They were burdened with sash-weights and bags of birdshot, and their faces were masked, so that no one, seeing a free and graceful gesture or a pretty face, would feel like something the cat drug in. George was toying with the vague notion that maybe dancers shouldn't be handicapped. But he didn't get very far with it before another noise in his ear radio scattered his thoughts.

George winced. So did two out of the eight ballerinas.

Hazel saw him wince. Having no mental handicap herself, she had to ask George what the latest sound had been.

"Sounded like somebody hitting a milk bottle with a ball peen hammer," said George.

"I'd think it would be real interesting, hearing all the different sounds," said Hazel, a little envious. "All the things they think up."

"Um," said George.

"Only, if I was Handicapper General, you know what I would do?" said Hazel. Hazel, as a matter of fact, bore a strong resemblance to the Handicapper General, a woman named Diana Moon Glampers. "If I was Diana Moon Glampers," said Hazel, "I'd have chimes on Sunday—just chimes. Kind of in honor of religion."

"I could think, if it was just chimes," said George.

"Well—maybe make 'em real loud," said Hazel. "I think I'd make a good Handicapper General."

"Good as anybody else," said George.

"Who knows better'n I do what normal is?" said Hazel.

"Right," said George. He began to think glimmeringly about his abnormal son who was now in jail, about Harrison, but a twenty-one-gun salute in his head stopped that.

"Boy!" said Hazel, "that was a doozy, wasn't it?"

It was such a doozy that George was white and trembling, and tears stood on the rims of his red eyes. Two of the eight ballerinas had collapsed to the studio floor, were holding their temples.

"All of a sudden you look so tired," said Hazel. "Why don't you stretch out on the sofa, so's you can rest your handicap bag on the pillows, honeybunch." She was referring to the forty-seven pounds of birdshot in a canvas bag, which was padlocked around George's neck. "Go on and rest the bag for a little while," she said. "I don't care if you're not equal to me for a while."

George weighed the bag with his hands. "I don't mind it," he said. "I don't notice it any more. It's just a part of me."

"You been so tired lately—kind of wore out," said Hazel. "If there was just some way we could make a little hole in the bottom of the bag, and just take out a few of them lead balls. Just a few."

"Two years in prison and two thousand dollars fine for every ball I took out," said George. "I don't call that a bargain."

"If you could just take a few out when you came home from work," said Hazel. "I mean—you don't compete with anybody around here. You just set around."

"If I tried to get away with it," said George, "then other people'd get away with it—and pretty soon we'd be right back to the dark ages again, with everybody competing against everybody else. You wouldn't like that, would you?"

"I'd hate it," said Hazel.

"There you are," said George. "The minute people start cheating on laws, what do you think happens to society?"

If Hazel hadn't been able to come up with an answer to this question, George couldn't have supplied one. A siren was going off in his head.

"Reckon it'd fall apart," said Hazel.

"What would?" said George blankly.

"Society," said Hazel uncertainly. "Wasn't that what you just said?"

"Who knows?" said George.

The television program was suddenly interrupted for a news bulletin. It wasn't clear at first as to what the bulletin was about, since the announcer, like all announcers, had a serious speech impediment. For about half a minute, and in a state of high excitement, the announcer tried to say, "Ladies and gentlemen—"

He finally gave up, handed the bulletin to a ballerina to read.

"That's all right—" Hazel said of the announcer, "he tried. That's the big thing. He tried to do the best he could with what God gave him. He should get a nice raise for trying so hard."

"Ladies and gentlemen—" said the ballerina, reading the bulletin. She must have been extraordinarily beautiful, because the mask she wore was hideous. And it was easy to see that she was the strongest and most graceful of all the dancers, for her handicap bags were as big as those worn by two-hundred-pound men.

And she had to apologize at once for her voice, which was a very unfair voice for a woman to use. Her voice was a warm, luminous, timeless melody. "Excuse me—" she said, and she began again, making her voice absolutely uncompetitive.

"Harrison Bergeron, age fourteen," she said in a grackle squawk, "has just escaped from jail, where he was held on suspicion of plotting to overthrow the government. He is a genius and an athlete, is underhandicapped, and should be regarded as extremely dangerous."

A police photograph of Harrison Bergeron was flashed on the screen —upside down, then sideways, upside down again, then right side up. The picture showed the full length of Harrison against a background calibrated in feet and inches. He was exactly seven feet tall.

The rest of Harrison's appearance was Halloween and hardware. Nobody had ever borne heavier handicaps. He had outgrown hindrances faster than the H-G men could think them up. Instead of a little ear radio for a mental handicap, he wore a tremendous pair of earphones, and spectacles with thick wavy lenses. The spectacles were intended to make him not only half blind, but to give him whanging headaches besides.

Scrap metal was hung all over him. Ordinarily, there was a certain symmetry, a military neatness to the handicaps issued to strong people, but Harrison looked like a walking junkyard. In the race of life, Harrison carried three hundred pounds.

And to offset his good looks, the H-G men required that he wear at all times a red rubber ball for a nose, keep his eyebrows shaved off, and cover his even white teeth with black caps at snaggle-tooth random.

"If you see this boy," said the ballerina, "do not—I repeat, do not —try to reason with him."

There was the shriek of a door being torn from its hinges.

Screams and barking cries of consternation came from the television set. The photograph of Harrison Bergeron on the screen jumped again and again, as though dancing to the tune of an earthquake.

George Bergeron correctly identified the earthquake, and well he might have—for many was the time his own home had danced to the same crashing tune. "My God—" said George, "that must be Harrison!"

The realization was blasted from his mind instantly by the sound of an automobile collision in his head.

When George could open his eyes again, the photograph of Harrison was gone. A living, breathing Harrison filled the screen.

Clanking, clownish, and huge, Harrison stood in the center of the studio. The knob of the uprooted studio door was still in his hand. Ballerinas, technicians, musicians, and announcers cowered on their knees before him, expecting to die.

"I am the Emperor!" cried Harrison. "Do you hear? I am the Emperor! Everybody must do what I say at once!" He stamped his foot and the studio shook.

"Even as I stand here—" he bellowed, "crippled, hobbled, sickened —I am a greater ruler than any man who ever lived! Now watch me become what I *can* become!"

Harrison tore the straps of his handicap harness like wet tissue paper, tore straps guaranteed to support five thousand pounds.

Harrison's scrap-iron handicaps crashed to the floor.

Harrison thrust his thumbs under the bar of the padlock that secured his head harness. The bar snapped like celery. Harrison smashed his headphones and spectacles against the wall.

He flung away his rubber-ball nose, revealed a man that would have awed Thor, the god of thunder.

"I shall now select my Empress!" he said, looking down on the cowering people. "Let the first woman who dares rise to her feet claim her mate and her throne!"

A moment passed, and then a ballerina arose, swaying like a willow.

Harrison plucked the mental handicap away from her ear, snapped off her physical handicaps with marvellous delicacy. Last of all, he removed her mask.

She was blindingly beautiful.

"Now—" said Harrison, taking her hand, "shall we show the people the meaning of the word dance? Music!" he commanded.

The musicians scrambled back into their chairs, and Harrison stripped them of their handicaps, too. "Play your best," he told them, "and I'll make you barons and dukes and earls."

The music began. It was normal at first—cheap, silly, false. But Harrison snatched two musicians from their chairs, waved them like batons as he sang the music as he wanted it played. He slammed them back into their chairs.

The music began again and was much improved.

Harrison and his Empress merely listened to the music for a while—listened gravely, as though synchronizing their heartbeats with it.

They shifted their weights to their toes.

Harrison placed his big hands on the girl's tiny waist, letting her sense the weightlessness that would soon be hers.

And then, in an explosion of joy and grace, into the air they sprang!

Not only were the laws of the land abandoned, but the law of gravity and the laws of motion as well.

They reeled, whirled, swiveled, flounced, capered, gamboled, and spun.

They leaped like deer on the moon.

The studio ceiling was thirty feet high, but each leap brought the dancers nearer to it.

It became their obvious intention to kiss the ceiling.

They kissed it.

And then, neutralizing gravity with love and pure will, they remained suspended in air inches below the ceiling, and they kissed each other for a long, long time.

It was then that Diana Moon Glampers, the Handicapper General, came into the studio with a double-barreled ten-gauge shotgun. She fired twice, and the Emperor and the Empress were dead before they hit the floor.

Diana Moon Glampers loaded the gun again. She aimed it at the musicians and told them they had ten seconds to get their handicaps back on.

It was then that the Bergerons' television tube burned out.

Hazel turned to comment about the blackout to George. But George had gone out into the kitchen for a can of beer.

George came back in with the beer, paused while a handicap signal shook him up. And then he sat down again. "You been crying?" he said to Hazel.

"Yup," she said.

"What about?" he said.

"I forget," she said. "Something real sad on television."

"What was it?" he said.

"It's all kind of mixed up in my mind," said Hazel.

"Forget sad things," said George.

"I always do," said Hazel.

"That's my girl," said George. He winced. There was the sound of a riveting gun in his head.

"Gee—I could tell that one was a doozy," said Hazel.

"You can say that again," said George.

"Gee—" said Hazel, "I could tell that one was a doozy."

---

# RANSOME AT SUBLIMITY
*Donald Monroe*

## Chapter 1: IS THERE AN ART TO BEING AGNES?

*"Aggh," shouts Agnes, "grab some Kleenex. Your stuff's running out of me all over the floor."*

I first met Agnes at the Art and Architecture Department picnic at the beach. She was sliding down an eighty-foot mountain of sand drinking wine from a canteen. Later, she gave her piece of bread to four scrawny kittens someone had abandoned in the park and she scared four Boy Scouts away from her campsite by making faces at them, because they had been chasing the kittens through the woods. That night she cried about it.

"They'll be all right," I said.

"No they won't," she said. "No they won't."

Agnes types my letters for me.

I write:

Dear Edward,

Enjoying your sabbatical? How're things over in Belfast? Is the killing and destruction as bad as it reads in the papers? My neighbors have a flock of noisy domesticated peacocks that keep me awake all night. Say hello to May from Agnes and me.

Agnes types:

Dear Edward,

Enjoying your sabbatical? My neighbors are a flock of noisy, domesticated peacocks that keep me awake all night. Say hello to May from Agnes and me.

I let it stand. Agnes knows me better than I do. Fuck politics.

## Chapter 2: ON THE NATURE OF DREAMS

Agnes, I dreamed my father died. I went home to clean the barn.

In it, mice had jumped into an iron pot of garden sulphur. Five of them. Their bodies lay in the form of a cross, chemically burned, or as if by napalm or an atomic blast. Above them, flower pots, umber as the faces of Indians who touched and drew roots and herbs, food and magic from this ground a hundred years ago, line the shelves of the tack room like skulls.

These pots are filled with fur pulled by the mice from a threadbare Chinese rug stored beneath; and now these threads, made soft by their chewing, shelter a smell (years after their small deaths) toxic as the rot of larger corpses: like battlefields of the dead, though fainter; a suggestion of youth or the war.

And in this small barn, beneath a home-fire-brigade water pump (the black hose of which crumbles in my hand), beneath my father's old white civil defense hard hat with the emblem on it, which he carried to meetings once a week (too old for the killing itself), beneath also a noncombatant gas mask in which, where the nose of a man should go, mice have gathered another small home; beneath all of this I discovered what seemed at first only a pine cupboard with a brass handle at each end.

I dragged it squealing across the brown floor, down two steps into the sun, and I saw that it had once been painted carnival yellow with red piping. Inside, the shelves were bright as they must have been forty years ago, the small cupboard new; though the outside had faded even locked away in the dark barn.

The top of this picnic-buffet is oak, and can, I discover, be lifted off. Beneath it, on a hidden molding, someone about six years old has written in pencil, "ELISabETH." My mother cannot remember any friends or relatives with that name. In the summer, my mother explained, my two uncles would carry the cupboard among the trees and the women would fill it with sturdy china and steel tableware, and on certain special, warm evenings the family would walk down the yew alley from the porch like a processional, with hot dishes wrapped in white cloths; and they would sit, the ten of them, around the stump-and-beam table and pretend to have come miles to this woods beyond the garden. The children played the barn was their ruin; the indifferent, munching sheep became unicorns, and the broken sulky, a chariot.

## Chapter 3: ON THE NATURE OF THE MUSEUM

1. I WILL PUT OUT MY CIGARETTE BEFORE I LEAVE THE MUSEUM.
2. I WILL TURN OFF THE HOTPLATE BEFORE I LEAVE THE MUSEUM.
3. I WILL MAKE SURE ALL THE DOORS AND WINDOWS ARE LOCKED BEFORE I LEAVE THE MUSEUM.
4. I WILL TURN ON THE BURGLAR ALARM BEFORE I LEAVE THE MUSEUM.

While Edward Shackleton is on sabbatical, I am Acting Director of the Museum. Mrs. Beremy is the office secretary. She was also, I think, the Museum's first accession.

"Mrs. Beremy?"

"Yes?"

"Let's take down that goddam sign."

"Mr. Grove put that sign up," she says, "in nineteen twenty-seven."
Mr. Grove has been dead for fifteen years now.

"Do you smoke?"

"No, Mr. Ransome."

"Then why is it necessary to remind you to put out your cigarette?
And you're the one who always closes up. You know about the alarms."

"That sign's been there a long time, Mr. Ransome."

"It's had a long, happy life," I say, taking it from the wall. "Let its
passage be easy."

"I like that sign!" she says. "But Mr. Shackleton didn't like it either."

The "either" sounds ominous, as if Edward had suddenly disappeared after objecting to the sign.

"You know," she says, "maybe we ought to wait until Mr. Shackleton comes back. After all, he *is* the Director."

"Five," I murmur, carrying the sign toward the trash. "I will put a
gun to my head before leaving the Museum."

"What did you say, Mr. Ransome?"

She waited weeks to get even. Then one morning she walked into my
office and laid a paper on my desk.

"The University Press sent this back. It was supposed to go in the
*Monthly Newsletter,* under 'Recent Accessions,' but they think there's
been some mistake."

She turned and walked away. I looked down.

> 1 white shirt
> 4 cl.        "
> 2 sheets
> 2 pl. cs.
> 7 hanks.
> NO STARCH PLEASE
> J. Ransome

## Chapter 4: ON THE POSSIBILITY OF AESTHETIC IMPROPRIETY

Agnes, my drawing student Eva McKenna rides her bicycle down by
the campus. She wears jeans, a bright green sweater, and her long hair
is the color of dark red earth, or of some of the old bricks in my parents' garden wall. I am driving my car. I wave at her as I pass. She
recognizes me and waves back. Somehow, I alone in my car, she on
her bike—it is the closest we may ever come, going the same direction.
Closer than in class, surrounded by all the others.

"McKenna," I said to her one day after class. "What a beautiful name."

"Married it and divorced it!" she said. She is funny and free of bitterness.

"But you kept the name?"

"Better than my old one."

"And what was that?"

"Stickel. 'Eva Stickel is a pickle, Eva Stickel is a pickle.' I got so sick of my name when I was a little girl I used to think maybe it was something I got for being bad."

"Were you?"

She laughed.

"Yes."

"Would it be all right," said Eva McKenna one day that spring, "if I missed your class for about a month? My daughter has to have heart surgery and I need to take care of her."

"Certainly."

Eva McKenna, you go to the very best corner I keep hidden in the back of my mind. Agnes Day is there, and several other women. I think you will like them. The first went there when I was five. I had been sick and was recovering at my great-aunt's small cottage in Carmel. The first day I was allowed outside was in March, cold and sunny. On the porch of the house next door was a woman who must have been, I now realize, about ten years older than your twenty-eight. She had long brown hair and long hands and she was drawing an acacia which stood in her front yard. "She's a real Countess," my great-aunt said. "She escaped, with no money." I stood in the yard, looking at her over the coreopsis. She must have heard our murmuring above the light wind, for she turned and looked at me, longer than just a glance; then, as if nothing had happened, she continued drawing. I went back into the house and lay down. I never saw her again, yet I remember her face better than any I have ever seen. Go with her, Eva McKenna; I believe I have always known at once those I could love.

## Chapter 5: ON THE CORRECTION OF AESTHETIC IMPROPRIETY

*"Aggh," shouts Agnes, "grab some Kleenex. Your stuff's running out of me all over the floor."*

I love only Agnes Day. She taught me how to walk on the beach at night, to hear each wave winding higher in pitch as it nears the sand. Then, in the morning, beneath the swell of a dune, she laced a vine with flowers, half buried it, and thrust a daisy upright in the center.

"There," she said.

"What is it?"

"You don't know?"

"No," I said.

"It's an elf trap."

"An elf trap."

"Yes, you see the elf's attracted by the daisy and when he steps in the noose to get it, you trap him."

"Ah-*ha*."

Later that day, beside a stream so clear the water seemed only a glaze on the pebbles beneath, she made me a fishing pole. I had found some leader hooked on a rock. She broke off a sapling, tied the leader to it, and to the leader she attached a sprig of blueberries.

"There," she said.

"But what can I do with it?" I said.

"You can fish."

"But what will I catch with berries?"

"An Ondine," she said. "Spirit of the water."

And so I caught her, or she, me, and I learned to throw on seasons with a free hand, to eat full, cold winter crab and parsleyed sole in warmer months. And life seemed to go as slow and magically as swimming beneath the sea, one's breath held—my own breath held that life would not sweep out of her fragile, coved body like a tide.

"Aggh," shouts Agnes, "grab some Kleenex. Your stuff's running out of me all over the floor."

"Let it."

"But it'll make a spot on your rug."

"Let it!"

"Oh, come here, you. . . ."

## Chapter 6: IN THE MUSEUM

*Would it be all right if I missed your class for about a month? My daughter has to have heart surgery and I need to take care of her.*

*Certainly.*

Drawing class meets on Tuesday afternoon. Eva McKenna has been absent for a week, taking her daughter to surgery. On Monday, in another state, at another university, four students were shot to death by National Guardsmen. My students are setting up their drawing equipment. I am sitting on the window ledge. Through the window, I can see fifty or so people walking silently down Chandler Street past the Humanities Building three blocks away, a daylight vigil.

"Want to hold class today?" I say. I'm surprised how very flat and tired my voice sounds. "Do you want to?" No one answers or gestures, only a few look up. Everyone is very, very quiet.

"You know what?" says Mr. D. quietly, from the back of the room. "I feel like when Kennedy got shot." I say nothing and nod. Mr. D.

looks around, his features a faded fresco on the dusty air. No one is going to speak. I think to myself: Mr. D., Eva McKenna, the Greenberg girl—they teach my class. I only read aloud from their eyes.

"Let's talk about the war," says Mr. D.

"What," I say, "do you want to say about it?"

"Do you know how many people were killed in it yesterday?" he says louder. "Not *us* and *them* figures, but how many *people?*"

"How many people died here in town yesterday," I say, sliding down from the window ledge.

"What do you mean?"

"I mean, how many people died here in town yesterday? Ten? Twelve?"

"That's different," he says. "I'm talking about killing."

"Ten or twelve people died here in town yesterday . . ."

"But we can *stop* the war and we can't stop people getting old and dying."

Good. He's getting mad at me.

"How about some more comments?" I say. I glance around. Everyone is very, very quiet. What is there to say? We are all so much the same.

"Come on," I say. "I'll show you something."

I'm out in the hall before people start trailing along. Mr. D. catches up with me.

"Where we going?" he says.

"The Museum."

It's closed. I use my key. We go in. It was built in 1912 to house a large collection of Oriental art donated to the University. We walk to the second floor, past cabinets of jade urns, past ebony thrones, past scrolls, hangings, and the implements of war. Then, in a side room, we arrive at the tomb statues, half a dozen of them, in a small glass case. Beneath each is a card stating the fragment's age, where it came from, and the words "Anonymous Modeler."

"See," I say. "Same guy did all of them."

Mr. D. Snorts, then looks puzzled.

"He's dead," I say. "The 'Anonymous Modeler' has been dead from eight to twelve hundred years. Even the corpses from the graves these things were on have been gone for a thousand years. *But here are the works.*"

Mr. D.: "*Sure, but of course it wasn't even just one guy and we don't even know their names and it was just chance all this stuff wasn't smashed.*"

Perfect quiet for a real, full second.

"Good. Now, you think about that."

I turn and walk away.

Stopping by the Art Department, I open my mailbox. There are two ads from textbook companies, which I throw in a trash can down the hall. A note from the department chairman about fouled-up registration which I look at while opening the door to the stairwell. And going down the stairs, I see the unfamiliar return address, the strange handwriting on the envelope. I rip it open. Out the basement door, beneath the serriform clouds: the single sheet is yellow, torn from a small notebook.

Dear Mr. Ransome,
My daughter died Friday morning. The surgery went well but there were complications.
I guess no more drawings for a while.

Eva McKenna

## Chapter 7: ON THE NATURE OF JOHN BLACK'S FARM AT SUBLIMITY, OREGON

The same day. Night, and a full moon. I should be writing a letter to Miss McKenna explaining how sorry I am to hear about her daughter dying—no, not that I am sorry to hear about it, but that I am sorry it happened. That her daughter died. *I am sorry that your daughter died.* Elaborate that. I don't feel like writing the letter. I don't feel like doing anything. I get in my car and drive out toward John Black's place. He teaches what I teach.

John lives on a small farm twelve miles out. I drive up the Coast Highway about six miles and turn off to the right, up Orchard Road, negotiating a rather steep hill. At the top of that hill, on one side of the road, stretch fields enough to make ten families rich (if no sons want to move to town), fields gray in the cold light. The road is gravel with deep ruts, though not rough enough to need a jeep. I bounce a little. Only ten miles an hour, the gravel crunching underneath. I stop for some reason.

After I get out, I think for a moment: my car's in the middle of the road. But, hell, nobody drives out here and there are only a couple of houses and you can see miles. I think, too, of leaving my headlights on, but don't. I open the trunk and take out a big bottle of wine, drink some, and stick it back among the old clothes, hatchet, flashlight, beat-up charred pans, roll of toilet paper, rain slicker, yellow newspapers, couple of prestologs, sleeping bag, tarp, rope, copy of Russell's *History of Western Philosophy,* and a transistor radio that hasn't worked for three or four years.

Nothing. Silence. I sit on the hood. I have been outside a half hour and I can see pretty well: the valley, its colors dying for rain, muted toward the perfect dark, the black at the base of trees, hidden in grass, far off.

I get back in and start the engine. I do not turn on the headlights. It is as if I can see in the dark—no, not see in the dark—I can see the dark itself and what it does not cover, see how far it goes. And hear the darkness at the edge of the road, beside the wheels; for there *is* darkness there, a fall of two hundred feet or so, down through jack pine. The gravel is thicker at the edge of the road and as I approach the drop I can hear the heavier rock hitting the underside of the car.

Strange, not to give a good goddam about going over the edge here; or, perhaps, this is a car-driver's thought. Surely my great-grandfather drove a wagon at night, guided only under the moon, the ruts as intelligible as runes beneath an archeologist's fingers; and perhaps Indians walked on the trail which became this road, without fear—how silly even to think of it—of falling into the shallow valley.

Up ahead I see a curve where John's driveway is, turn toward the house, sound "shave-and-a-haircut" on the horn.

I take the wine out of the trunk. The house itself seems a darker dark than the road outside, though there are lights at the windows and loud rock, music almost thick enough to float on, washing from the front door.

"Hey, come on in!" says John.

Here are people. About ten. Mr. D., my painting and drawing student, is here. He nods at me. So are a bunch of other people I know, men and women. They are sitting around on the big braid rug, passing a pipe. I go sit down next to Mr. D. after he motions me over.

"Give me a pull on that, will you?" he says. I hand him the bottle. I get the pipe and pass it on without using it. "Go ahead," he says.

"Maybe later."

"No, go ahead."

I look at him very seriously. I whisper, loud as I can, "I'm afraid of getting busted."

Somebody's voice on the other side of the room says, "Ransome's drunk out of his mind."

Mr. D. looks at me very seriously. He says, "But Mr. Ransome, don't you see? If we get busted, so will you, just for being here."

"But," I say, "it's the *principle* of the thing." I smile. He smiles. And we both start laughing.

After a few minutes he says, "That Kent State shit, that's bad shit." I watch him. "Man I don't think you got," he says. "I don't think you got what I meant today." He studies me. "See, I meant, if we don't . . . *change* . . . we're going to kill our fucking selves and everybody else."

I can't say anything.

"See," he says, "that's all I meant. I don't think you understand. It's people dying man, dying, you know?"

I look away. John comes over and crouches down. (John: calls Agnes "Supermind" because she speaks so many languages, loves her

like he was her brother. She calls him "The Devil's Cherub" because
he's a little fat. John's wife is Chinese and her name is Victoria.)

"You look deader than usual," John says. "What happened?"

"Nothing."

"Here, take a joint and go up on the roof. Nice night out there."
He slaps me on the shoulder like a friendly bear.

"I think I *will* go out and walk around a little."

"Good. Make some noise when you come in so we know it's you."

"Okay."

"I'm getting paranoid," says John.

"Me too." I stand up. "Here," I say to Mr. D., handing him the
wine. "See you later." I stick the joint in the cuff of my sweater.

The screen door closes behind me. I don't want to go up on the roof.
I don't want to go home. I don't want to go anyplace. I laugh at myself. I'll sleep around here, I think; get out my sleeping bag and sleep
around here.

There is a barn about a hundred yards behind the house. Before
John bought it, the place was a working farm. That is where I will
sleep, in the barn. I open the trunk of my car and grab the bag—and
something else, a pencil and my tablet. I will write to Miss McKenna.

## Chapter 8: DEFECTS THAT MILITATE AGAINST JOHN'S FARM AT SUBLIMITY

Death. Death here. The smell of dead sheep which, living, greased the
fold beneath where I will sleep. A faint smell of birds. Even their
skeletons have flown to purer air. Nothing here was born after I was,
even the dust.

I unroll my sleeping bag. A few feet away is a workbench with no
tools, some child's perhaps. Between the handle of the small vise and
the top of the workbench is a skein of cobwebs. The windows are
opaque with dirt. Moonlight enters only around two jagged, splintered
panes near the roof. I lie down and there is not one sound moving
anywhere around me.

Here is where I should write to Eva McKenna but I can't because I
feel too tired. (I must be too tired because I can't think of a thing to
say.) So, I will go to sleep.

Hours later, through my sleep, John's first yell is a mumble. The
second one's clearer:

"Wake up, you mother!" John's laughing between shouts. "Wake
up up there!" He pounds on the wall. "What the fuck you doing to
my barn?"

"Shut up. I'm asleep. Go away."

Other voices: "What's happening? Oh, nothing. He's freaked out in
the barn. No shit?"

"I'm asleep, goddamit! Go away!"

"Hey, leave him alone John, he sounds mad."

"Shit, he's not mad, he's just *irritated*. Ransome, you mother, don't light any matches up there because this thing's condemned and I don't care if you burn yourself up but I don't want to lose this barn. You hear me?"

"Go fuck your wife!"

"You go fuck my wife!"

"Everybody else maybe, but not me!"

"Come on people, let's go back to the house. He's okay."

"You sure he's okay?"

"Oh, hell yes. It's when he shuts up I start worrying about him."

## Chapter 9: LOFT

It is growing lighter. Here is where I will begin.

Dear Eva McKenna, now I know why I paint. The sun is almost coming up and the boards over my head in the barn where I have slept have become a dozen differing shades of brown, like a section of the earth, dug into deeply. This barn, I think, was built from other barns or other, earlier buildings, for each board shows a different age, a different degree of dark weathering. How could words explain this? Have we enough in the names of colors; and what of the mixtures? Let me, then, call all these slowly brightening strips, these solid ribbons of wood, brown. *Brown.* I think I could paint it, the dim, rich colors above my head, but instead I will give you only, as I can give only at the moment, the word: *brown. Brownnnnnnnn. Brown.*

Dear Eva McKenna, I don't know why I or anybody else is crazy enough to paint. It doesn't do a damn thing for your health and it isn't real. Throw away all your equipment and go sleep in a barn.

(Love. Love? *Love?* We do not act, or write letters, on love. It would be too hurtful. We must be kind. *Oh, let me be kind, to not leave someone I may not love for someone I may love . . . to be as good as the hot muffins Agnes makes on Saturday morning . . . to not thunder off on some sudden infatuation. I left another woman to come to Agnes on just such an intuition . . . and it was right.* Life makes no sense. *I promise to be kind.* Life must be, at least, kind.)

I remember how, in a loft, the loft of a warehouse, a flop, two doors from the Rescue Mission, that I was awakened in the night by sounds like the shrieks of braked freights; that, barely awake, I became aware that they were the sounds of a man. And finally, that they were my own sounds; and I felt arms and hands beneath my own arms and hands and was carried upward and away to a room nearby that was very white. From a window in that room came, after days of perfect silence, the sounds of the big trains starting up slowly once again. I can remember those first sounds well and now I realize that it is no accident that they resemble the sounds of your name: Eva McKenna Eva McKenna Eva McKennaEvaMcKennaEvaMcKennaEvaMcKenna.

Somebody going out of his head is supposed to see his penis turn into a serpent; what really drives a man crazy is finding his penis has turned into a monkey wrench, which he proceeds to throw into the best-ordered aspects of his life.

Agnes, I love you.

Dear Eva McKenna, somewhere in space all deaths are past facts. I am told that if the sun were to burn out, shattered as the Mazda bulb above my head in this barn has been shattered, by some random or aimed shot, if the sun were to cease giving light, we would not know it for an unimaginable length of time. And so too, I would say, for each of us a sun has already flamed and died somewhere. This darkness walks toward us, slow as the speed of light.

Dear Eva McKenna, cosmology is no cure for death, neither is painting. In fact, it is not even my own death itself I fear so much as the suggestion of it, like pissing blood. . . .

## Chapter 10: THE PRICE OF SUBLIMITY

The phone rang. I took off my coat then answered it.

"Where have you been?" said Agnes.

"John Black's barn."

"John's barn?" I don't think she believes me.

"I took my sleeping bag up in the loft of John's barn. Then he came in and woke me up shouting at about three and I couldn't go back to sleep and about five I went to the all-night and had some eggs and coffee."

"But why would you sleep in his barn?"

"I was thinking."

"I still don't understand."

"I can't explain it. I'm tired."

"You slept in John's barn."

"No, I went out and screwed fourteen different women." I sound unpleasant but it is only the tiredness.

"All right, all right." She believes me about the barn now. "I was up all night. I didn't know where you were."

"Why didn't you call John or Bill? You could have figured I would have been at one of their places."

"Oh. . . ." Sigh.

"Oh, I'm sorry. I understand. You don't want to be calling around for me in the middle of the night like some distraught housewife. Look, I'm terribly tired. I have to try and sleep now. I have to."

"I'm worried about you."

"I understand. It was terrible of me not to call and let you know where I was. I'm terribly sorry." *Dear Eva McKenna, I'm terribly sorry...*

"Well, I still can't understand this."

"We'll talk about it later." *I'm terribly sorry to hear of your daughter's death... I'm terribly sorry to hear of your loss...I...*

"All right. Try to go to sleep."

"Really I'm terribly sorry." *I am terribly sorry about the loss of your...I am terribly sorry to learn of...I am terribly sorry to...*

"Jack, are you crying?"

"Yes."

## Chapter 11: ON THE NATURE OF DREAMS, PART TWO

When I fell asleep I dreamed I was looking from my parents' dining room window into the large, sunken rose garden. I was ten. It had been raining for several days. The brick wall around the back of the garden was dark red between patches of brown moss. The grass was thick and uncut, as it was late fall. It was a dark day, though the darkness made the green lawn seem bright against the dark green boxwood borders. Down in the rose garden, twenty yards from me, two people were throwing a plastic ball, like a beach ball, back and forth. One was my student, Eva McKenna, the other her daughter, who, as I had guessed, had red hair like her mother's. And as they threw the ball back and forth, the mother lightly to the child, the child with effort, laughing, I realized that Eva McKenna's daughter must be named Elizabeth.

"Elizabeth," I said, knocking on the window. "Elizabeth, come inside, it's raining out." And it was raining. Elizabeth's hair, like her mother's, clung in ropes of burnt umber. With my tapping, the child turned and, hesitating for her mother's approval, she walked toward me, across the grass and up the brick steps.

I smiled at her and she at me, and she flattened her hand against the window. I, on the other side, placed my hand over it and felt the chill glass slowly warming.

## Chapter 12: ON THE CORRECTNESS AND NECESSITY OF THE PERFECTLY IMPROPER

"Here!"

*"No," says Agnes.*

"Right here!"

*"It's not right. Not on your parents' property."*

"Ohhh..."

*"Oh," she says, touching me, "we just* did *yesterday and we'll be home again tomorrow. Just... not here."*

*We had carried glasses of brandy, glasses with pictures of horses on them, horses going over hedges after hounds and foxes, carried these glasses into the arboretum. And suddenly we had been sitting on the rough grass of the hillside, looking at the mountains sixty miles across the valley, and I had wanted to make love to her.*

"*Just not here,*" she says.

"*Yes, but that's just it.*" *I look at her.* "*It has to be here. Now.*"

Now. All this happened a year ago. The picnic-buffet is still in the barn, which I cleaned. Eva McKenna's daughter is dead and in the ground. The arboretum has been sold and cut into small lots.

> Dear Miss McKenna,
> What can I say?
> Jack Ransome

Oh, Agnes, I say: it must be here. Now.

## Chapter 13: FRAGMENTS AND THE WHOLE

Eva, I have tried to paint a picture of you and the effort has died in embers the color of your hair. You have lost your child and I have lost only, sadly, an idea: the idea of yourself, of myself perhaps and the Indians, the house, the ground; nothing lost to me as real as your child, her thin legs running through the mind's unburnt fields. I cannot scorch that blight. I cannot even offer you my transient hands. There is no difference in fidelity to the dead or to the living. Someone loves me, someone (at least one) loves you. Only the moment finds my lover alive, your loving child gone.

The darkness is walking toward us. And this light.

---

# SAINT MANUEL BUENO, MARTYR
## *Miguel de Unamuno*

> If in this life only we have hope in Christ, we are of all
> men most miserable.        *Saint Paul: I Cor. 15:19*

Now that the bishop of the diocese of Renada, to which this my beloved village of Valverde de Lucerna belongs, is said to be urging the process of beatification of our Don Manuel, or rather, Saint Manuel Bueno, who was parish priest here, I want to put in writing, by way of confession (although to what end only God, and not I can say), all that I know and remember about that matriarchal man who pervaded the most secret life of my soul, who was my true spiritual father, the father of my spirit, the spirit of myself, Angela Carballino.

The other, my flesh-and-blood temporal father, I scarcely knew, for he died when I was still very young. I know that he came to Valverde de Lucerna from elsewhere—that he was a stranger to the place—and that he settled here when he married my mother. He had brought a number of books with him: *Don Quixote,* some classical plays, some novels, a few histories, the *Bertoldo,* a veritable grab bag. These books (practically the only ones in the entire village), set me daydreaming, and I was devoured by my daydreams. My dear mother told me very little about the words or the deeds of my father. For the words and deeds of Don Manuel, whom she worshiped, of whom she was enamored, in common with all the rest of the village—in an exquisitely chaste manner, of course—had obliterated all memory of the words and deeds of her husband whom she fervently commended to God, as she said her daily rosary.

I remember Don Manuel as if it were yesterday, from the time when I was a girl of ten, just before I was taken to the convent school in the cathedral city of Renada. At that time Don Manuel, our saint, must have been about thirty-seven years old. He was tall, slim; he carried himself erect, his head the way our Buitre Peak carries its crest, and his eyes had all the blue depth of our lake. As he walked he commanded all eyes, and not only the eyes but the hearts of all; gazing round at us he seemed to look through our flesh as through glass and penetrate our hearts. We all loved him, especially the children. And the things he said to us! The villagers could scent the odor of sanctity, they were intoxicated with it.

It was at this time that my brother Lázaro, who was in America, from where he regularly sent us money with which we lived in decent comfort, had my mother send me to the convent school, so that my education might be completed outside the village; he suggested this move despite the fact that he had no special fondness for the nuns. "But, since, as far as I know," he wrote us, "there are no lay schools there yet—especially not for young ladies—we will have to make use of the ones that do exist. The important thing is for Angelita to receive some polish and not be forced to continue among village girls." And so I entered the convent school. At one point I even thought of becoming a teacher; but pedagogy soon palled.

At school I met girls from the city and I made friends with some of them. But I still kept in touch with people in our village, and I received frequent news from them and sometimes a visit. And the fame of the parish priest even reached the school, for he was beginning to be talked of in the cathedral city. And the nuns never tired of asking me about him.

Ever since I was a child I had been endowed, I don't really know why, with a large degree of curiosity and uneasiness, due in part at least to that jumble of books which my father had collected, and at school these qualities were stimulated, especially in the course of a friendship I developed with a girl who grew excessively attached to me. At times she suggested that we enter the same convent together, swearing to an everlasting "sisterhood"—and even that we seal the oath in blood. At other times she talked to me, with half-closed eyes, of sweethearts and marriage adventures. Strangely enough, I have never heard anything of her since, nor of what became of her, despite the fact that whenever our Don Manuel was mentioned, or when my mother wrote me something about him in her letters—which happened in almost every letter —and I read it to her, the girl would cry out ecstatically: "What a lucky girl you are to be able to live near a saint like that, a living saint, of flesh and blood, and to be able to kiss his hand; when you go back to your village write to me a lot and tell me lots of things about him."

I spent five years at school, five years which have now evanesced in memory like a dream at dawn, and when I was fifteen I returned to my own Valverde de Lucerna. By now everything there revolved around Don Manuel: Don Manuel, the lake, and the mountain. I arrived home anxious to know him, to place myself in his care, and hopeful that he would set me on my path in life.

It was rumored that he had entered the seminary to become a priest so that he might thus look after the children of a recently widowed sister and provide for them in place of their father; that in the seminary his keen mind and his talents had distinguished him and that he had subsequently turned down opportunities of a brilliant career in the Church because he wanted to remain exclusively a part of his Valverde de Lucerna, of his remote village which lay like a brooch between the lake and the mountain reflected in it.

How he loved his people! He spent his life salvaging wrecked marriages, forcing unruly children to submit to their parents, or reconciling parents to their children, and, above all, he consoled the embittered and weary in spirit and helped everyone to die well.

I recall, among other incidents, the occasion when the unfortunate daughter of old Aunt Rabona returned to our town. She had been living in the city and lost her virtue there; now she returned unmarried and abandoned, and she brought back a little son. Don Manuel did not rest until he had persuaded an old sweetheart, Perote by name, to marry the poor girl and, moreover, to legitimize the infant with his own name. Don Manuel told Perote:

"Come now, give this poor waif a father, for he hasn't got one except in heaven."

"But, Don Manuel, it's not my fault...!"

"Who knows, my son, who knows...! And in any case, it's not a question of guilt."

And today, poor old Perote, inspired on that occasion to saintliness by Don Manuel, and now a paralytic and invalid, has the support and consolation of his life in the son he accepted as his own when the boy was not his at all.

On Midsummer's Night, the shortest night of the year, it was, and still is, a local custom here for all the old crones, and a lot of old men, who thought they were possessed or bewitched—they were, in fact, hysterical for the most part, and in some cases epileptics—to flock to the lake. Don Manuel undertook to fulfill the same function as the lake, to serve as a pool of healing, to treat his people and even, if possible, to cure them. And such was the effect of his presence, of his gaze, and above all of his voice—his miraculous voice!—and the infinitely sweet authority of his words, that he actually did achieve some remarkable cures. Whereupon his fame increased, drawing all the sick of the environs to our lake and our priest. And yet, once, when a mother came to ask for a miracle on behalf of her son, he answered her with a sad smile:

"Ah, but I don't have my bishop's permission to perform miracles."

He was particularly interested in seeing that all the villagers kept themselves clean. If he chanced upon someone with a torn garment he would say: "Go and see the sacristan, and let him mend that tear." The sacristan was a tailor. And when, on the first day of the year, everyone went to congratulate the priest on his saint's day—his holy patron was Our Lord Jesus Himself—it was Don Manuel's wish that everyone should appear in a new shirt, and those that had none received the present of a new one from Don Manuel himself.

He treated everyone with the greatest kindness; if he favored anyone, it was the most unfortunate, and especially those who rebelled. There was a congenital idiot in the village, the fool Blasillo, and it was toward him that Don Manuel chose to show the greatest love and concern; as a consequence he succeeded in miraculously teaching him things which had appeared beyond the idiot's comprehension. The fact was that the embers of understanding feebly glowing in the idiot were kindled whenever, like a pitiable monkey, he imitated his Don Manuel.

The marvel of the man was his voice; a divine voice which brought one close to weeping. Whenever he officiated at Solemn High Mass and intoned the Preface, a tremor ran through the congregation and all who heard his voice were moved to the depths of their being. The sound of his chanting, overflowing the church, went on to float over the lake and settle at the foot of the mountain. And when on Good Friday he chanted, "My God, My God, why hast Thou forsaken me?" a profound shudder swept through the multitude, like the lash of the northeast wind across the waters of the lake. It was as if these people heard Our Lord Jesus Christ Himself, as if the voice sprang from the ancient crucifix, at the foot of which generations of mothers had offered up their sorrows. And it happened that on one occasion when his mother heard him, she was unable to contain herself, and cried out to him right in the church, "My son!" And the entire congregation was visibly affected, tears pouring down every cheek. It was as if the mother's cry had issued from the half-open lips of the Mater Dolorosa —her heart transfixed by seven swords—which stood in one of the side chapels. Afterwards, the fool Blasillo went about piteously repeating, like an echo, "My God, my God, why hast Thou forsaken me?" with such effect that everyone who heard him was moved to tears, to the great satisfaction of the fool, who prided himself on this triumph of imitation.

The priest's effect on people was such that no one ever dared to tell him a lie, and everyone confessed to him without need of a confessional. So true was this that one day, after a revolting crime had been committed in a neighboring village, the judge—a dull fellow who badly misunderstood Don Manuel—called on the priest and said:

"Let's see if *you*, Don Manuel, can get this bandit to admit the truth."

"So that *you* may punish him afterwards?" asked the saintly man. "No, Judge, no; I will not extract from any man a truth which could be the death of him. That is a matter between him and his God. ... Human justice is none of my affair. 'Judge not that ye be not judged,' said our Lord."

"But the fact is, Father, that I, a judge..."

"I understand. You, Judge, must render unto Caesar that which is Caesar's, while I shall render unto God that which is God's."

And, as Don Manuel departed, he gazed at the suspected criminal and said:

"Make sure, only, that God forgives you, for that is all that matters."

Everyone in the village went to Mass, even if it were only to hear him and see him at the altar, where he appeared to be transfigured, his countenance lit from within. He introduced one holy practice into popular worship; it consisted in assembling the whole town inside the church, men and women, old and young, about a thousand souls; there we recited the Creed, in unison, so that it sounded like a single voice: "I believe in God, the Father almighty, creator of heaven and earth ..." and all the rest. It was not a chorus, but a single voice, all the voices blending into one forming a kind of mountain, whose peak, lost at times in the clouds, was Don Manuel. As we reached the section "I believe in the resurrection of the flesh and eternal life," Don Manuel's voice was submerged, drowned in the voice of the populace as in a lake. In truth, he was silent. And I could hear the bells of the city which is said hereabouts to be at the bottom of the lake—bells which are said also to be audible on Midsummer's Night—the bells of the city which is submerged in the spiritual lake of our people. I was hearing the voice of our dead, resurrected in us by the communion of saints. Later, when I had learned the secret of our saint, I understood that it was as if a caravan crossing the desert lost its leader as they approached the goal of their trek, whereupon his people lifted him up on their shoulders to bring his lifeless body into the promised land.

When it came to dying themselves, most of the villagers refused to die unless they were holding onto Don Manuel's hand, as if to an anchor chain.

In his sermons he never inveighed against unbelievers, Freemasons, liberals, or heretics. What for, when there were none in the village? Nor did it occur to him to speak out against the wickedness of the press. On the other hand, one of his most frequent themes was the sinfulness of gossip. As he himself forgave everything and everyone, he would not accept the existence of forked tongues.

"Envy," he liked to repeat, "is nurtured by those who prefer to think they are envied, and most persecutions are the result of a persecution complex rather than of an impulse to persecute."

"But Don Manuel, just listen to what that fellow was trying to tell me. . . ."

"We should concern ourselves less with what people are trying to tell us than with what they tell us without trying. . . ."

His life was active rather than contemplative, and he constantly fled from idleness, even from leisure. Whenever he heard it said that idleness was the mother of all vices, he added: "And also of the greatest vice of them all, which is to think idly." Once I asked him what he meant and he answered: "Thinking idly is thinking as a substitute for doing, or thinking too much about what is already done instead of about what must be done. What's done is done and over with, and one must go on to something else, for there is nothing worse than remorse without possible solution." Action! Action! Even in those early days I had already begun to realize that Don Manuel fled from being left to think in solitude, and I sensed that some obsession haunted him.

And so it was that he was always busy, sometimes even busy looking for things to do. He wrote very little on his own, so that he scarcely left us anything in writing, not even notes; on the other hand, he acted as scribe for everyone else, especially composing letters for mothers to their absent children.

He also worked with his hands, pitching in to help with some of the village tasks. At threshing time he reported to the threshing floor to flail and winnow, meanwhile teaching and entertaining the workers by turn. Sometimes he took the place of a worker who had fallen sick. One bitter winter's day he came upon a child half-dead with cold. The child's father had sent him into the woods to bring back a calf that had strayed.

"Listen," he said to the child, "you go home and get warm, and tell your father that I am bringing back the calf." On the way back with the animal he ran into the father, who had come out to meet him, thoroughly ashamed of himself.

In winter he chopped wood for the poor. When a certain magnificent walnut tree died—"that matriarchal walnut," he called it, a tree under whose shade he had played as a boy and whose nuts he had eaten for so many years—he asked for the trunk, carried it to his house and, after he had cut six planks from it, which he kept at the foot of his bed, he made firewood of the rest to warm the poor. He also was in the habit of making handballs for the boys and many toys for the younger children.

Often he used to accompany the doctor on his rounds, and stressed the importance of following the doctor's orders. Most of all he was interested in maternity cases and the care of children; it was his opinion that the old wives' sayings "from the cradle to heaven" and the other one about "little angels belong in heaven" were nothing short of blasphemy. The death of a child moved him deeply.

"A stillborn child, or one who dies soon after birth are, like suicides, the most terrible mystery to me," I once heard him say. "Like a child crucified!"

And once, when a man had taken his own life and the father of the suicide, an outsider, asked Don Manuel if his son could be buried in consecrated ground, the priest answered:

"Most certainly, for at the last moment, in the very last throes, he must surely have repented. There is no doubt of it whatsoever in my mind."

Often he would visit the local school too, to help the teacher, to teach alongside him—and not only the catechism. The simple truth was that he fled relentlessly from idleness and from solitude. He went so far in this desire of his to mingle with the villagers, especially the young people and the children, that he even attended the village dances. And more than once he played the drum to keep time for the youths and girls dancing; this kind of activity, which in another priest would have seemed like a grotesque mockery of his calling, in him somehow took on the appearance of a divine office. When the Angelus rang out, he would put down the drum and sticks, take off his hat (all the others doing the same) and pray: "The angel of the Lord declared unto Mary: Hail Mary . . ." and afterwards: "Now let us rest until tomorrow."

"The most important thing," he would say, "is for the people to be happy; everyone must be happy just to be alive. To be satisfied with life is of first importance. No one should want to die until it is God's will."

"I want to die now," a recently widowed woman once told him, "I want to follow my husband. . . ."

"But why?" he asked. "Stay here and pray God for his soul."

Once he commented at a wedding: "Ah, if I could only change all the water in our lake into wine, into a gentle little wine which, no matter how much of it one drank, would always make one joyful without making one drunk . . . or, if it made one drunk, would make one joyfully tipsy."

One day a band of poor circus people came through the village. Their leader—who arrived with a gravely ill and pregnant wife and three children to help him—played the clown. While he was in the village square making all the children, and even some of the adults, laugh with glee, his wife suddenly fell desperately ill and had to leave; she went off accompanied by a look of anguish from the clown and a howl of laughter from the children. Don Manuel hurried after her, and a little later, in a corner of the inn's stable, he helped her give up her soul in a state of grace. When the performance was over and the villagers and the clown learned of the tragedy, they came to the inn, and there the poor, bereaved clown, in a voice overcome with tears, said to Don Manuel, as he took his hand and kissed it: "They are quite right, Father, when they say you are a saint." Don Manuel took the clown's hand in his and replied in front of everyone:

"It is you who are the saint, good clown. I watched you at your work and understood that you do it not only to provide bread for your own children, but also to give joy to the children of others. And I tell you now that your wife, the mother of your children, whom I sent to God while you worked to give joy, is at rest in the Lord, and that you will join her there, and that the angels, whom you will make laugh with happiness in heaven, will reward you with their laughter."

And everyone present wept, children and adults alike, as much from sorrow as from a mysterious joy in which all sorrow was drowned. Later, recalling that solemn hour, I came to realize that the imperturbable happiness of Don Manuel was merely the temporal, earthly form of an infinite, eternal sadness which the priest concealed from the eyes and ears of the world with heroic saintliness.

His constant activity, his ceaseless intervention in the tasks and diversions of his flock, had the appearance of a flight from himself, a flight from solitude. He confirmed this suspicion: "I have a fear of solitude," he would say. And still, from time to time he would go off by himself, along the shores of the lake, to the ruins of the abbey where the souls of pious Cistercians seem still to repose, although history has long since buried them in oblivion. There, the cell of the so-called Father-Captain can still be found, and it is said that the drops of blood spattered on the walls as he flagellated himself can still be seen. What thoughts occupied our Don Manuel as he walked there? I remember a conversation we held once when I asked him, as he was speaking of the abbey, why it had never occurred to him to enter a monastery, and he answered me:

"It is not at all because my sister is a widow and I have her children and herself to support—for God looks after the poor—but rather because I simply was not born to be a hermit, an anchorite; the solitude would crush my soul; and, as far as a monastery is concerned, my monastery is Valverde de Lucerna. I was not meant to live alone, or die alone. I was meant to live for my village, and die for it too. How should I save my soul if I were not to save the soul of my village as well?"

"But there have been saints who were hermits, solitaries...," I said.

"Yes, the Lord gave them the grace of solitude which He has denied me, and I must resign myself. I must not throw away my village to win my soul. God made me that way. I would not be able, alone, to carry the cross of birth...."

I trust that these recollections, which keep my faith alive, will portray our Don Manuel as he was when I, a young girl of almost sixteen, returned from the convent of Renada to our "monastery of Valverde de Lucerna," to kneel once more at the feet of our "abbot."

"Well, here is Simona's daughter," he said as soon as he saw me, "quite a young woman, and knowing French, and how to play the piano, and embroider, and heaven knows what else besides! Now you must get ready to give us a family. And your brother Lázaro; when is he coming back? Is he still in the New World?"

"Yes, Father, he is still in America."

"The New World! And we in the Old. Well then, when you write to him, tell him from me, on behalf of the parish priest, that I should like to know when he is returning from the New World to the Old, to bring us the latest from over there. And tell him that he will find the lake and the mountain as he left them."

When I first went to him for confession, I became so confused that I could not enunciate a word. I recited the "Forgive me, Father, for I have sinned," in a stammer, almost sobbing. And he, observing this, said:

"Good heavens, my dear, what are you afraid of, or of whom are you afraid? Certainly you're not trembling under the weight of your sins, nor in fear of God. No, you're trembling because of me, isn't that so?"

At this point I burst into tears.

"What have they been telling you about me? What fairy tales? Was it your mother, perhaps? Come, come, please be calm; you must imagine you are talking to your brother...."

At this I plucked up courage and began to tell him of my anxieties, doubts, and sorrows.

"Bah! Where did you read all this, Miss Bluestocking? All this is literary nonsense. Don't believe everything you read just yet, not even Saint Teresa. If you want to amuse yourself, read the *Bertoldo,* as your father before you did."

I came away from my first confession to that holy man deeply consoled. The initial fear—simple fright more than respect—with which I had approached him, turned into a profound pity. I was at that time a very young woman, almost a girl still; and yet, I was beginning to be a woman, in my innermost being I felt the maternal instinct, and when I found myself in the confessional at the side of the saintly priest, I sensed a kind of unspoken confession on his part in the soft murmur of his voice. And I remembered how when he had chanted in the church the words of Jesus Christ: "My God, my God, why hast Thou forsaken me?" his own mother had cried out in the congregation: "My son!"; and I could hear the cry that had rent the silence of the temple. And I went to him again for confession—and to comfort him.

Another time in the confessional I told him of a doubt which assailed me, and he responded:

"As to that, you know what the catechism says. Don't question me about it, for I am ignorant; in Holy Mother Church there are learned doctors of theology who will know how to answer you."

"But you are the learned doctor here."

"Me? A learned doctor? Not even in my dreams! I, my little theologian, am only a poor country priest. And those questions. . . . do you know who whispers them into your ear? Well . . . the Devil does!"

Then, making bold. I asked him point-blank:

"And suppose he were to whisper these questions to you?"

"Who? To me? The Devil? No, we don't even know each other, my child, we haven't even met."

"But if he did whisper them? . . ."

"I wouldn't pay any attention. And that's enough of that; let's get on, for there are some sick people, some really sick people, waiting for me."

I went away thinking, I don't know why, that our Don Manuel, so famous for curing the bedeviled, didn't really believe in the Devil. As I started home, I ran into the fool Blasillo, who had probably been hovering outside; as soon as he saw me, and by way of treating me to a display of his virtuosity, he began repeating—and in what a manner!—"My God, my God, why has Thou forsaken me?" I arrived home utterly saddened and locked myself in my room to cry, until finally my mother arrived.

"With all these confessions, Angelita, you will end up going off to a nunnery."

"Don't worry, Mother," I answered her. "I have plenty to do here; the village is my convent."

"Until you marry."

"I don't intend to," I rejoined.

The next time I saw Don Manuel I asked him, looking him straight in the eye:

"Is there really a Hell, Don Manuel?"

And he, without altering his expression, answered:

"For you, my child, no."

"For others, then?"

"Does it matter to you, if you are not to go there?"

"It matters to me for the others. Is there a Hell?"

"Believe in Heaven, the Heaven we can see. Look at it there"—and he pointed to the heavens above the mountain, and then down into the lake, to the reflection.

"But we are supposed to believe in Hell as well as in Heaven," I said.

"Yes, that's true. We must believe everything that our Holy Mother Church believes and teaches, our Holy Mother Church, Catholic, Apostolic, and Roman. And now, that's enough of that!"

I thought I read a deep sadness in his eyes, eyes as blue as the waters of the lake.

Those years went by as if in a dream. Within me, a reflected image of Don Manuel was unconsciously taking form. He was an ordinary enough man in many ways, as everyday as the daily bread we asked for in our Paternoster. I helped him whenever I could with his tasks, visiting his sick, our sick, the girls at school, and helping too, with the church linen and the vestments; I served in the role, as he said, of his deaconess. Once I was invited to the city for a few days by an old schoolfriend, but I had to hurry back home, for the city stifled me— something was missing, I was thirsty for a sight of the waters of the lake, hungry for a sight of the peaks of the mountain; and even more, I missed my Don Manuel, as if he were calling me, as if he were en- dangered by my being so far away, as if he were in need of me. I began to feel a kind of maternal affection for my spiritual father; I longed to help him bear the cross of birth.

My twenty-fourth birthday was approaching when my brother Lá- zaro came back from America with the small fortune he had saved up. He came back to Valverde de Lucerna with the intention of taking me and my mother to live in a city, perhaps even in Madrid.

"In the country," he said, "in these villages, a person becomes dull, brutalized, and spiritually impoverished." And he added: "Civiliza- tion is the very opposite of everything countrified. The idiocy of coun- try life! No, that's not for us; I didn't have you sent away to school so that afterwards you might go to waste here, among these ignorant peasants."

I said nothing, though I was ready to oppose any idea of moving.

But our mother, already past sixty, took a firm stand from the start: "Change pastures at my age?" she demurred at once. A little later she made it quite clear that she could not live away from her lake, her mountain, and above all, her Don Manuel.

"You are both of you like those cats that get attached to houses," my brother kept saying.

When he realized the extent of the sway exercised over the entire village—especially over my mother and myself—by the saintly priest, my brother began to resent him. He saw in this situation an example of the obscurantist theocracy which, according to him, smothered Spain. And he began to spout the old anticlerical commonplaces, to which he added antireligious and "progressive" propaganda brought back from the New World.

"In this Spain of useless, easy-going men, the priests manipulate the women, and the women manipulate the men. Not to mention the idiocy of the country, and this feudal backwater!"

"Feudal," to him, meant something frightful. "Feudal" and "medieval" were the epithets he employed to condemn something out of hand.

The absolute failure of his diatribes to move us and their lack of effect upon the village—where they were listened to with respectful indifference—disconcerted him no end. "The man does not exist who could move these clods." But he soon began to understand—for he was an intelligent man, and therefore a good one—the kind of influence exercised over the village by Don Manuel, and he came to appreciate the effect of the priest's work in the village.

"This priest is not like the rest of them," he announced. "He is, in fact, a saint."

"How do you know what the rest of them are like?" I asked him, and he replied:

"I can imagine."

Even so, he did not set foot inside the church nor did he miss an opportunity to parade his lack of belief—though he always exempted Don Manuel from his scornful accusations. In the village, an unconscious expectancy began to build up, the anticipation of a kind of duel between my brother Lázaro and Don Manuel—in short, it was expected that Don Manuel would convert my brother. No one doubted but that in the end the priest would bring him into the fold. On his side, Lázaro was eager (he told me so himself, later) to go and hear Don Manuel, to see and hear him in the church, to get to know him and to talk with him, so that he might learn the secret of his spiritual sway over our souls. And he let himself be coaxed to this end, so that finally —"out of curiosity," as he said—he went to hear the preacher.

"Now, this is something else again," he told me as soon as he came back from hearing Don Manuel for the first time. "He's not like the others; still, he doesn't fool me, he's too intelligent to believe everything he has to teach."

"You mean you think he's a hypocrite?"

"A hypocrite . . . no! But he has to live by his job."

As for me, my brother was determined I should read the books he brought me, and others which he urged me to buy.

"So your brother Lázaro wants you to read," Don Manuel declared. "Well read, my child, read and make him happy. I know you will only read worthy books. Read, even if you only read novels; they are as good as histories which claim to be 'true.' You are better off reading than concerning yourself with village gossip and old wives' tales. Above all, though, you will do well to read some devotional books which will bring you contentment in life, a quiet, gentle contentment, and peace."

And he, did he enjoy such contentment?

It was about this time that our mother fell mortally sick and died. In her last days her one wish was that Don Manuel should convert Lázaro, whom she hoped to see again in heaven, in some little corner among the stars from where they could see the lake and the mountain of Valverde de Lucerna. She felt she was going there now, to see God.

"You are not going anywhere," Don Manuel kept telling her; "you are staying right here. Your body will remain here, in this earth, and your soul also, in this house, watching and listening to your children though they will not see or hear you."

"But, Father," she said, "I am going to see God."

"God, my daughter, is all around us, and you will see Him from here, right from here. And all of us in Him, and He in all of us."

"God bless you," I whispered to him.

"The peace in which your mother dies will be her eternal life," he told me.

And, turning to my brother Lázaro: "Her heaven is to go on seeing you, and it is at this moment that she must be saved. Tell her you will pray for her."

"But . . ."

"But what? . . . Tell her you will pray for her, to whom you owe your life. And I know that once you promise her, you *will* pray, and I know that once you pray . . ."

My brother, with tears in his eyes, went up to our dying mother and gave her his solemn promise to pray for her.

"And I, in heaven will pray for you, for all of you," my mother replied. And then, kissing the crucifix and fixing her eyes on Don Manuel, she gave up her soul to God.

"Into Thy hands I commend my spirit," prayed the priest.

My brother and I stayed on in the house alone. What had happened at the time of my mother's death had established a bond between Lázaro and Don Manuel. The latter seemed even to neglect some of his charges, his patients, and his other needy to look after my brother. In the afternoons, they would go for a walk together, beside the lake or toward the ivy-covered ruins of the old Cistercian abbey.

"He's an extraordinary man," Lázaro told me. "You know the story they tell of how there is a city at the bottom of the lake, submerged beneath the water, and that on Midsummer's Night at midnight the sound of its church bells can be heard...."

"Yes, a city 'feudal and medieval'..."

"And I believe," he went on, "that at the bottom of Don Manuel's soul there is a city, submerged and drowned, and that sometimes the sound of its bells can be heard...."

"Yes.... And this city submerged in Don Manuel's soul, and per- haps—why not?—in yours as well, is certainly the cemetery of the souls of our ancestors, the ancestors of our Valverde de Lucerna... 'feudal and medieval'!"

Eventually my brother began going to Mass. He went regularly to hear Don Manuel. When it became known that he was prepared to comply with his annual duty of receiving Communion, that he would receive Communion when the others did, an inner joy ran through the town, which felt that by this act he was restored to his people. The re- joicing was so simple and honest, that Lázaro never did feel that he had been "vanquished" or "overcome."

The day of his Communion arrived; of Communion before and with the entire village. When my brother's turn came, I saw Don Manuel— white as the January snow on the mountain, and moving like the sur- face of the lake when it is stirred by the northeast wind—come up to him with the holy wafer in his hand, trembling violently as he reached out to Lázaro's mouth; at that moment the priest shook so that the wafer dropped to the ground. My brother himself recovered it and placed it in his mouth. The people saw the tears on Don Manuel's cheeks, and everyone wept, saying: "How he loves him!" And then, because it was dawn, a cock crowed.

On returning home I shut myself in with my brother; alone with him I put my arms around his neck and kissed him.

"Lázaro, Lázaro, what joy you have given us all today; the entire village, the living and the dead, especially our mother. Did you see how Don Manuel wept for joy? What joy you have given us all!"

"That's why I did it," he answered me.

"Is that why? Just to give us pleasure? Surely you did it for your own sake, because you were converted."

And then Lázaro, my brother, grew as pale and tremulous as Don

Manuel when he was giving Communion, and bade me sit down, in the chair where our mother used to sit. He took a deep breath, and, in the intimate tone of a family confession, he told me:

"Angelita, it is time for me to tell you the truth, the absolute truth, and I shall tell it, because I must, because I cannot and ought not to conceal it from you, and because sooner or later, you are bound to find it out anyway, if only halfway—which would be worse."

Thereupon, serenely and tranquilly, in a subdued voice, he recounted a tale that cast me into a lake of sorrow. He told me how Don Manuel had begged him, particularly during the walks to the ruins of the old Cistercian abbey, to set a good example, to avoid scandalizing the townspeople, to take part in the religious life of the community, to feign belief even if he did not feel any, to conceal his own ideas—all this without attempting in any way to catechize him, to instruct him in religion, or to effect a true conversion.

"But is it possible?" I asked in consternation.

"Very possible and absolutely true. When I said to him: 'Is it really you, the priest, who suggests that I pretend?' he replied, hesitatingly: 'Pretend? Not at all! It would not be pretending. "Dip your fingers in holy water, and you will end by believing," as someone said.' And I, gazing into his eyes, asked him: 'And you, by celebrating the Mass, have you ended up by believing?' He looked away and stared out at the lake, until his eyes filled with tears. And it was in this way that I came to understand his secret."

"Lázaro!" I moaned.

At that moment the fool Blasillo came along our street, crying out his: "My God, my God, why hast Thou forsaken me?" And Lázaro shuddered, as if he had heard the voice of Don Manuel, or even that of Christ.

"It was then," my brother at length continued, "that I really understood his motives and his saintliness; for a saint he is, sister, a true saint. In trying to convert me to his holy cause—for it is a holy cause, a most holy cause—he was not attempting to score a triumph, but rather was doing it to protect the peace, the happiness, the illusions, perhaps, of his flock. I understood that if he thus deceives them—if it *is* deceit—it is not for his own advantage. I submitted to his logic—and that was my conversion. And I shall never forget the day on which I said to him: 'But, Don Manuel, the truth, the truth, above all!'; and he, all a-tremble, whispered in my ear—though we were all alone in the middle of the countryside—'The truth? The truth, Lázaro, is perhaps something so unbearable, so terrible, something so deadly, that simple people could not live with it!'

"'And why do you allow me a glimpse of it now, here, as if we were in the confessional?' I asked. And he said: 'Because if I did not, I would be so tormented by it, so tormented that I would finally shout it in the middle of the plaza, which I must never, never, never do. . . . I am put here to give life to the souls of my charges, to make them happy, to make them dream they are immortal—and not to destroy them. The important thing is that they live undisturbed, in concord with one another—and with the truth, with my truth, they could not live at all. Let them live. That is what the Church does, it lets them live. As for true religion, all religions are true insofar as they give spiritual life to the people who profess them, insofar as they console them for having been born only to die. And for each race the truest religion is their own, the religion that made them. . . . And mine? Mine consists in consoling myself by consoling others, even though the consolation I give them is not ever mine.' I shall never forget his words."

"But then this Communion of yours has been a sacrilege," I dared interrupt, regretting my words as soon as I said them.

"Sacrilege? What about the priest who gave it to me? And his Masses?"

"What martyrdom!" I exclaimed.

"And now," said my brother, "there is one more person to console the people."

"To deceive them, you mean?" I said.

"Not at all." he replied, "but rather to confirm them in their faith."

"And they, the people, do you think they really believe?"

"As to that, I know nothing! . . . They probably believe without trying, from force of habit, tradition. The important thing is not to stir them up. To let them live on the thin diet of their emotions rather than acquiring the torments of luxury. Blessed are the poor in spirit!"

"So that is what you have learned from Don Manuel. . . . And tell me, do you feel you have carried out your promise to our mother on her deathbed, when you promised to pray for her?"

"Do you think I could fail her? What do you take me for, sister? Do you think I would go back on my word, my solemn promise made at the hour of death to a mother?"

"I don't know. . . . You might have wanted to deceive her so she could die in peace."

"The fact is, though, that if I had not lived up to my promise, I would be totally miserable."

"And . . ."

"I have carried out my promise and I have never neglected for a single day to pray for her."

"Only for her?"

"Well, for whom else?"

"For yourself! And now, for Don Manuel."

We parted and each went to his room, I to weep through the night, praying for the conversion of my brother and of Don Manuel. And Lázaro, to what purpose, I know not.

From that day on I was nervous about finding myself alone with Don Manuel, whom I continued to help in his pious works. And he seemed to sense my inner state and to guess at its cause. When at last I approached him in the confessional's penitential tribunal (who was the judge, and who the offender?) the two of us, he and I, bowed our heads in silence and began to weep. It was Don Manuel who finally broke the silence, with a voice that seemed to issue from a tomb:

"Angelita, you have the same faith you had when you were ten, don't you? You believe, don't you?"

"Yes, I believe, Father."

"Then go on believing. And if doubts come to torment you, suppress them utterly, even to yourself. The main thing is to live. . . ."

I summoned up my courage, and dared to ask, trembling:

"But, Father, do you believe?"

For a brief moment he hesitated, and then, taking hold of himself, he said:

"I believe!"

"In what, Father, in what? Do you believe in the life hereafter? Do you believe that when we die, we do not die altogether? Do you believe that we will see each other again, that we will love each other in the next world? Do you believe in the next life?"

The poor saint was sobbing.

"My child, leave off, leave off!"

Now, as I write this memoir, I ask myself: Why did he not deceive me? Why did he not deceive me as he deceived the others? Why did he torture himself? Why could he not deceive himself, or why could he not deceive me? And I prefer to think that he was tormented because he could not deceive himself into deceiving me.

"And now," he said, "pray for me, for your brother, and for yourself —for all of us. We must go on living. And giving life."

And, after a pause:

"Angelita, why don't you marry?"

"You know why."

"No, no; you must marry. Lázaro and I will find you a suitor. For it would be good for you to marry, and rid yourself of these obsessions."

"Obsessions, Don Manuel?"

"I know what I am saying. You should not torment yourself for the sake of others, for each of us has more than enough to do answering for himself."

"That it should be you, Don Manuel, saying this! That you should advise me to marry and answer for myself alone and not suffer over others! That it should be you!"

"Yes, you are right, Angelita. I am no longer sure of what I am saying since I began to confess to you. Only, one must go on living. Yes! One must live!"

And when I rose to leave the church, he asked me:

"Now, Angelita, in the name of the people, do you absolve me?"

I felt pierced by a mysterious and priestly prompting and said:

"In the name of the Father, the Son, and the Holy Ghost, I absolve you, Father."

We left the church, and as I went out I felt the quickening of maternal feelings within me.

My brother, now totally devoted to the work of Don Manuel, had become his closest and most zealous collaborator and companion. They were bound together, moreover, by their common secret. Lázaro accompanied the priest on his visits to the sick, and to schools, and he placed his fortune at the disposition of the saintly man. And he nearly learned to help celebrate Mass. All the while he was sounding deeper the unfathomable soul of the priest.

"What an incredible man!" he exclaimed to me once. "Yesterday, as we were walking along beside the lake he said: 'There lies my greatest temptation.' When I interrogated him with my eyes, he went on: 'My poor father, who was close to ninety when he died, was tormented all his life, as he himself confessed to me, by a temptation to commit suicide, by an instinct toward self-destruction, which had come to him from a time before memory—from birth, from his *nation,* as he said— and he was forced to fight against it always. And this struggle grew to be his life. So as not to succumb to this temptation he was forced to take precautions, to guard his life. He told me of terrible episodes. His urge was a form of madness—and I have inherited it. How that water beckons me with its deep quiet! . . . an apparent serenity reflecting the sky like a mirror—and beneath it the hidden current! My life, Lázaro, is a kind of continual suicide, or a struggle against suicide, which is the same thing. . . . Just so long as our people go on living!' And then he added: 'Here the river eddies to form a lake, so that later, flowing down the plateau, it may form cascades, waterfalls, and torrents, hurling itself through gorges and chasms. Thus life eddies in the village; and the temptation to commit suicide is greater beside the still waters which at night reflect the stars, than it is beside the crashing falls which drive one back in fear. Listen, Lázaro, I have helped poor villagers to die well, ignorant, illiterate villagers, who had scarcely ever been out of their village, and I have learned from their own lips, or sensed it when they were silent, the real cause of their sickness unto death, and there at their deathbed I have been able to see into the black abyss of their life-weariness. A weariness a thousand times worse than hunger! For our part, Lázaro, let us go on with our kind of suicide working for the people, and let them dream their lives as the lake dreams the heavens.'

"Another time," said my brother, "as we were coming back, we caught sight of a country girl, a goatherd, standing tall, on the crest of the mountain slope overlooking the lake and she was singing in a voice fresher than the waters. Don Manuel stopped me, and pointing to her said: 'Look, it's as though time had stopped, as though this country girl had always been there just as she is, singing the way she is, and it's as though she would always be there, as she was before my consciousness began, as she will be when it is past. That girl is a part of nature —not of history—along with the rocks, the clouds, the trees, and the water.' He has such a subtle feeling for nature, he infuses it with feeling! I shall never forget the day when snow was falling and he asked me: 'Have you ever seen a greater mystery, Lázaro, than the snow falling, and dying, in the lake, while a headdress is laid upon the mountain?' "

Don Manuel had to moderate and temper my brother's zeal and his neophyte's rawness. As soon as he heard that Lázaro was going about inveighing against some of the popular superstitions he told him firmly:

"Leave them alone! It's difficult enough making them understand where orthodox belief leaves off and where superstition begins. And it's even harder for us. Leave them alone, then, as long as they get some comfort. . . . It's better for them to believe everything, even things that contradict one another, than to believe nothing. The idea that someone who believes too much ends up not believing anything is a Protestant notion. Let us not protest! Protestation destroys contentment and peace."

My brother told me, too, about one moonlit night when they were returning to the village along the lake, whose surface was being stirred by a mountain breeze, so that the moonbeams topped the white-crested waves, and Don Manuel turned to him and said:

"Look, the water is reciting the litany and saying: *ianua caeli, ora pro nobis;* gate of heaven, pray for us."

And two tears fell from his lashes to the grass, where the light of the full moon shone upon them like dew.

And time sped by, and my brother and I began to notice that Don Manuel's spirits were failing, that he could no longer control completely the deep-rooted sadness which consumed him; perhaps some treacherous illness was undermining his body and soul. In an effort to arouse his interest, Lázaro spoke to him of the good effect the organization of something like a Catholic agrarian syndicate in the Church would have.

"A syndicate?" Don Manuel replied sadly. "A syndicate? And what is that? The Church is the only syndicate I know of. And you have certainly heard 'My kingdom is not of this world.' Our kingdom, Lázaro, is not of this world. . . ."

"And of the other?"

Don Manuel bowed his head:

"The other is here. Two kingdoms exist in this world. Or rather, the other world.... Ah, I don't really know what I am saying. But as for the syndicate, that's a carry-over from your radical days. No, Lázaro, no; religion does not exist to resolve the economic or political conflicts of this world, which God handed over to men for their disputes. Let men think and act as they will, let them console themselves for having been born, let them live as happily as possible in the illusion that all this has a purpose. I don't propose to advise the poor to submit to the rich, nor to suggest to the rich that they submit to the poor; but rather to preach resignation in everyone, and charity toward everyone. For even the rich man must resign himself—to his riches, and to life; and the poor man must show charity—even to the rich. The Social Question? Ignore it, for it is none of our business. So, a new society is on the way, in which there will be neither rich nor poor, in which wealth will be justly divided, in which everything will belong to everyone—and so, what then? Won't this general well-being and comfort lead to even greater tedium and weariness of life? I know well enough that one of those leaders of what they call the Social Revolution said that religion is the opium of the people. Opium ... Opium ... Yes, opium it is. We should give them opium, and help them sleep, and dream. I, myself, with my mad activity am giving myself opium. And still I don't manage to sleep well, let alone dream well.... What a fearful nightmare! ... I, too, can say, with the Divine Master: 'My soul is exceedingly sorrowful, even unto death.' No, Lázaro, no; no syndicates for us. If *they* organize them, well and good—they would be distracting themselves in that way. Let them play at syndicates, if that makes them happy."

The entire village began to realize that Don Manuel's spirit was weakening, that his strength was waning. His very voice—that miracle of a voice—acquired a kind of tremor. Tears came into his eyes at the slightest provocation—or without provocation. Whenever he spoke to people about the next world, about the next life, he was forced to pause at frequent intervals, and he would close his eyes. "It is a vision," people would say, "he has a vision of what lies ahead." At such moments the fool Blasillo was the first to burst into tears. He wept copiously these days, crying now more than he laughed, and even his laughter had the sound of tears.

The last Easter Week which Don Manuel was to celebrate among us, in this world, in this village of ours, arrived, and all the village sensed that the tragedy was coming to an end. And how those words struck home when for the last time Don Manuel cried out before us: "My God, my God, why hast Thou forsaken me?" And when he repeated the words of the Lord to the Good Thief—"all thieves are good," Don Manuel used to tell us—: "Today shalt thou be with me in paradise." And then, the last general Communion which our saint was to give! When he came to my brother to give him the Host—his hand steady this time—just after the liturgical "... *in vitam aeternam*," he bent down and whispered to him: "There is no other life than this, no life more eternal ... let them dream it eternal ... let it be eternal for a few years...." And when he came to me he said: "Pray, my child, pray for us all." And then, something so extraordinary happened that I carry it now in my heart as the greatest of mysteries: he leant over and said, in a voice which seemed to belong to the other world: "... and pray, too, for our Lord Jesus Christ."

I stood up weakly like a sleepwalker. Everything around me seemed dreamlike. And I thought: "Am I to pray, too, for the lake and the mountain?" And next: "Am I bedeviled, then?" Home at last, I took up the crucifix my mother had held in her hands when she had given up her soul to God, and, gazing at it through my tears and recalling the "My God, my God, why hast Thou forsaken me?" of our two Christs, the one of this earth and the other of this village, I prayed: "Thy will be done on earth as it is in heaven," and then, "And lead us not into temptation. Amen." After this I turned to the statue of the Mater Dolorosa—her heart transfixed by seven swords—which had been my poor mother's most sorrowful comfort, and I prayed again: "Holy Mary, Mother of God, pray for us sinners, now and at the hour of our death. Amen." I had scarcely finished the prayer, when I asked myself: "Sinners? Us, sinners? And what is our sin, what is it?" And all day I brooded over the question.

The next day I went to see Don Manuel—now in the full sunset of his magnificent religiosity—and I said to him:

"Do you remember, my Father, years ago when I asked you a certain question you answered: 'That is a question you must not ask me; for I am ignorant; there are learned doctors of the Holy Mother Church who will know how to answer you'?"

"Do I remember? ... Of course, I do. And I remember I told you those were questions put to you by the Devil."

"Well, then, Father, I have come again, bedeviled, to ask you another question put to me by my Guardian Devil."

"Ask it."

"Yesterday, when you gave me Communion, you asked me to pray for all of us, and even for ..."

"That's enough! ... Go on."

"I arrived home and began to pray; when I came to the part 'Pray for us sinners, now and at the hour of our death,' a voice inside me asked: 'Sinners? Us, sinners? And what is our sin?' What is our sin, Father?"

"Our sin?" he replied. "A great doctor of the Spanish Catholic
Apostolic Church has already explained it; the great doctor of *Life
Is a Dream* had written 'The greatest sin of man is to have been born.'
That, my child, is our sin; to have been born."

"Can it be atoned, Father?"

"Go away and pray again. Pray once more for us sinners, now and at
the hour of our death.... Yes, at length the dream is atoned... at
length life is atoned... at length the cross of birth is expiated and
atoned, and the drama comes to an end.... And as Calderón said, to
have done good, to have feigned good, even in dreams, is something
which is not lost."

The hour of his death arrived at last. The entire village saw it come.
And he made it his finest lesson. For he did not want to die alone or at
rest. He died preaching to his people in the church. But first, before
being carried to the church—his paralysis made it impossible for him
to move—he summoned Lázaro and me to his bedside. Alone there, the
three of us together, he said:

"Listen to me: watch over my poor flock; find some comfort for
them in living, and let them believe what I could not. And Lázaro,
when your hour comes, die as I die, as Angela will die, in the arms of
the Holy Mother Church, Catholic, Apostolic, and Roman; that is to
say, the Holy Mother Church of Valverde de Lucerna. And now farewell; until we never meet again, for this dream of life is coming to an
end...."

"Father, Father," I cried out.

"Do not grieve, Angela, only go on praying for all sinners, for all
who have been born. Let them dream, let them dream.... Oh, how I
long to sleep, to sleep, to sleep without end, to sleep for all eternity,
and never dream! Forgetting this dream!... When they bury me, let
it be in a box made from the six planks I cut from the old walnut tree
—poor old tree!—in whose shade I played as a child, when I began
the dream.... In those days, I really did believe in life everlasting.
That is to say, it seems to me now that I believed. For a child, to believe
is the same as to dream. And for a people too ... You'll find those six
planks I cut at the foot of the bed."

He was seized by a sudden fit of choking, and then, feeling better,
he went on:

"You will recall that when we prayed together, animated by a common sentiment, a community of spirit, and we came to the final verse
of the Creed, you will remember that I would fall silent.... When
the Israelites were coming to the end of their wandering in the desert,
the Lord told Aaron and Moses that because they had not believed in
Him they would not set foot in the Promised Land with their people;
and he bade them climb the heights of Mount Hor, where Moses or-

dered Aaron to be stripped of his garments, so that Aaron died there, and then Moses went up from the plains of Moab to Mount Nebo, to the top of Pisgah, looking into Jericho, and the Lord showed him all of the land promised to His people, but He said to him: 'Thou shalt not go over thither.' And there Moses died, and no one knew his grave. And he left Joshua to be chief in his place. You, Lázaro, must be my Joshua, and if you can make the sun stand still, make it stop, and never mind progress. Like Moses, I have seen the face of God—our supreme dream—face to face, and as you already know, and as the Scriptures say, he who sees God's face, he who sees the eyes of the dream, the eyes with which He looks at us, will die inexorably and forever. And therefore, do not let our people, so long as they live, look into the face of God. Once dead, it will no longer matter, for then they will see nothing. . . ."

"Father, Father, Father," I cried again.

And he said:

"Angela, you must pray always, so that all sinners may go on dreaming, until they die, of the resurrection of the flesh and life everlasting. . . ."

I was expecting "and who knows it might be . . ." but instead, Don Manuel had another choking fit.

"And now," he finally went on, "and now, at the hour of my death, it is high time to have me taken, in this very chair, to the church, so that I may take leave there of my people, who are waiting for me."

He was carried to the church and taken, in his armchair, into the chancel, to the foot of the altar. In his hands he held a crucifix. My brother and I stood close to him, but the fool Blasillo wanted to stand even closer. He wanted to grasp Don Manuel by the hand, so that he could kiss it. When some of the people nearby tried to stop him, Don Manuel rebuked them and said:

"Let him come closer. . . . Come, Blasillo, give me your hand."

The fool cried for joy. And then Don Manuel spoke:

"I shall say very few words, my children; I scarcely have strength except to die. And I have nothing new to tell you either. I have already said everything I have to say. Live together in peace and happiness, in the hope that we will all see each other again some day, in that other Valverde de Lucerna up there among the stars of the night, the stars which the lake reflects over the image of the reflected mountain. And pray, pray to the Most Blessed Virgin, and to our Lord. Be good . . . that is enough. Forgive me whatever wrong I may have done you inadvertently or unknowingly. After I give you my blessing, let us pray together, let us say the Paternoster, the Ave Maria, the Salve, and the Creed."

Then he gave his blessing to the whole village, with the crucifix held in his hand. while the women and children cried and even some of the men wept softly. Almost at once the prayers were begun. Don Manuel listened to them in silence, his hand in the hand of Blasillo the fool, who was falling asleep to the sound of the praying. First the Paternoster, with its "Thy will be done on earth as it is in heaven," then the Ave Maria, with its "Pray for us sinners, now and at the hour of our death"; followed by the Salve, with its "mourning and weeping in this vale of tears"; and finally, the Creed. On reaching "The resurrection of the flesh and life everlasting" the people sensed that their saint had yielded up his soul to God. It was not necessary to close his eyes even, for he died with them closed. When we tried to wake up Blasillo, we found that he, too, had fallen asleep in the Lord forever. So that later there were two bodies to be buried.

The whole village immediately went to the saint's house to carry away holy relics, to divide up pieces of his garments among themselves, to carry off whatever they could find as a memento of the blessed martyr. My brother kept his breviary, between the pages of which he discovered a carnation, dried as in a herbarium and mounted on a piece of paper, and upon the paper a cross and a certain date.

No one in the village seemed willing to believe that Don Manuel was dead; everyone expected to see him—perhaps some of them did—taking his daily walk along the shore of the lake, his figure mirrored in the water, or silhouetted against the background of the mountain. They continued to hear his voice, and they all visited his grave, around which a veritable cult grew up: old women "possessed by devils" came to touch the walnut cross, made with his own hands from the tree which had given the six planks of his coffin. And the ones least willing to believe in his death were my brother and I.

Lázaro carried on the tradition of the saint, and he began to compile a record of the priest's work. Some of the conversations in this account of mine were made possible by his notes.

"It was he," said my brother, "who made me into a new man. I was a true Lazarus whom he raised from the dead. He gave me faith."

"Faith? . . ." I interrupted.

"Yes, faith, faith in life itself, faith in life's consolations. It was he who cured me of my delusion of 'progress,' of my belief in its political implications. For there are, Angela, two types of dangerous and harmful men: those who, convinced of life beyond the grave, of the resurrection of the flesh, torment other people—like the inquisitors they are—so that they will despise this life as a transitory thing and work for the other life; and then, there are those who, believing only in this life . . ."

"Like you, perhaps . . ."

"Yes, and like Don Manuel. Believing only in this world, this second group looks forward to some vague future society and exerts every effort to prevent the populace from finding consolation in the belief in another world. . . ."

"And so . . ."

"The people should be allowed to live with their illusion."

The poor priest who came to replace Don Manuel found himself overwhelmed in Valverde de Lucerna by the memory of the saint, and he put himself in the hands of my brother and myself for guidance. He wanted only to follow in the footsteps of the saint. And my brother told him: "Very little theology, Father, very little theology. Religion, religion, religion." Listening to him, I smiled to myself, wondering if this were not a kind of theology, too.

And at this time I began to fear for my poor brother. From the time of Don Manuel's death it could scarcely be said that he lived. He went to the priest's tomb daily; he stood gazing into the lake for hours on end. He was filled with nostalgia for deep, abiding peace.

"Don't stare into the lake so much," I begged him.

"Don't, worry. It's not this lake which draws me, nor the mountain. Only, I cannot live without his help."

"And the joy of living, Lázaro, what about the joy of living?"

"That's for others. Not for those of us who have seen God's face, those of us on whom the Dream of Life has gazed with His eyes."

"What; are you preparing to go and see Don Manuel?"

"No, sister, no. Here at home now, between the two of us, the whole truth—bitter as it may be, bitter as the sea into which the sweet waters of our lake flow—the whole truth for you, who are so set against it . . ."

"No, no, Lázaro. You are wrong. Your truth is not the truth."

"It's my truth."

"Yours, perhaps, but surely not . . ."

"His, too."

"No, Lázaro. Not now, it isn't. Now, he must believe otherwise; now he must believe . . ."

"Listen, Angela, once Don Manuel told me that there are truths which, though one reveals them to oneself, must be kept from others; and I told him that telling me was the same as telling himself. And then he said, he confessed to me, that he thought that more than one of the great saints, perhaps the very greatest himself, had died without believing in the other life."

"It's not possible!"

"All too possible! And now, sister, you must be careful that, here, among the people, no one even suspects our secret. . . ."

"Suspect it!" I cried out in amazement. "Why, even if I were to try, in a fit of madness, to explain it to them, they wouldn't understand it. The people do not understand your words, they have only understood your actions. To try and explain all this to them would be like reading some pages from Saint Thomas Aquinas to eight-year old children, in Latin!"

"All the better. In any case, when I am gone, pray for me and for him and for all of us."

At length, his own hour came. A sickness which had been eating away at his robust constitution seemed to flare up with the death of Don Manuel.

"I don't so much mind dying," he said to me in his last days, "as the fact that with me another piece of Don Manuel dies too. The remainder of him must live on with you. Until, one day, even we dead will die forever."

When he lay in the throes of death, the people, as is customary in our villages, came to bid him farewell and they commended his soul to the care of Don Manuel—Saint Manuel Bueno, Martyr. My brother said nothing to them; he had nothing more to say. He had already said everything there was to say. He had become a link between the two Valverdes de Lucerna—the one at the bottom of the lake and the one reflected on its surface. He was already one more of us who had died of life, and, in his way, one more of our saints.

I was disconsolate, more than disconsolate; but I was, at least, among my own people, in my own village. Now, having lost my Saint Manuel, the father of my soul, and my own Lázaro, my more than flesh and blood brother, my spiritual brother, it is now that I realize that I have aged. But have I really lost them then? Have I grown old? Is my death approaching?

Life must go on! And he taught me to live, he taught us to live, to feel life, to feel the meaning of life, to merge with the soul of the mountain, with the soul of the lake, with the soul of the village, to lose ourselves in them so as to remain in them forever. He taught me by his life to lose myself in the life of the people of my village, and I no longer felt the passing of the hours, and the days, and the years, any more than I felt the passage of the water in the lake. It began to seem that my life would always be like this. I no longer felt myself growing old. I no longer lived in myself, but in my people, and my people lived in me. I tried to speak as they spoke, as they spoke without trying. I went into the street—it was the one highway—and, since I knew everyone, I lived in them and forgot myself (while, on the other hand, in Madrid, where I went once with my brother, I had felt a terrible loneliness, since I knew no one, and had been tortured by the sight of so many unknown people).

Now, as I write this memoir, this confession of my experience with saintliness, with a saint, I am of the opinion that Don Manuel the Good, my Don Manuel, and my brother, too, died, believing they did not believe, but that, without believing in their belief, they actually believed, in active, resigned desolation.

But why, I have asked myself repeatedly, did not Don Manuel attempt to convert my brother through deception, pretending to be a believer himself without being one? And I have finally come to the conclusion that Don Manuel realized he would not be able to delude him, that with him a fraud would not do, that only through the truth, with his truth, would he be able to convert him; that he knew he would accomplish nothing if he attempted to enact the comedy—the tragedy, rather—which he played out for the benefit of the people. And so, he won him over to his pious fraud; he won him over to the cause of life with the truth of death. And thus did he win me, and I never permitted anyone to see through his divine, his most saintly, game. For I believed then, and I believe now, that God—as part of I know not what sacred and inscrutable purpose—caused them to believe they were unbelievers. And that at the moment of their passing, perhaps, the blindfold was removed.

And I, do I believe?

As I write this—here in my mother's old house, and I past my fiftieth year and with my memories growing as dim and faded as my hair—outside it is snowing, snowing upon the lake, snowing upon the mountain, upon the memory of my father, the stranger, upon the memory of my mother, my brother Lázaro, my people, upon the memory of my Saint Manuel, and even on the memory of the poor fool Blasillo, my Saint Blasillo—and may he help me in heaven! The snow effaces corners and blots out shadows, for even in the night it shines and illuminates. Truly, I do not know what is true and what is false, nor what I saw and what I merely dreamt—or rather, what I dreamt and what I merely saw—nor what I really knew or what I merely believed to be true. Neither do I know whether or not I am transferring to this paper, white as the snow outside, my awareness, for it to remain in writing, leaving me without it. But why cling to it any longer?

Do I really understand any of it? Do I really believe in any of it? What I am writing about here, did it actually take place, and did it take place in just the way I am telling it? Can such things really happen? Can all this be more than a dream dreamed within another dream? Can it be that I, Angela Carballino, a woman in her fifties, am the only one in this village to be assailed by these far-fetched thoughts, thoughts unknown to everyone else? And the others, those around me, do they believe? At least they go on living. And now they believe in Saint Manuel Bueno, Martyr, who, with no hope of immortality for himself, preserved that hope in them.

It appears that our most illustrious bishop, who set in motion the process of beatifying our saint from Valverde de Lucerna, is intent on writing an account of Don Manuel's life, something which would serve as a guide for the perfect parish priest, and with this end in mind he is gathering information of every sort. He has repeatedly solicited information from me; he has come to see me more than once; and I have supplied him with all sorts of facts and details. But I have never revealed the tragic secret of Don Manuel and my brother. And it is curious that he has never suspected anything. I trust that what I have set down here will never come to his knowledge. For, all temporal authorities are to be feared; I distrust all authorities on this earth— even when they are Church authorities.

And here I end this memoir. Let its fate be what it will. . . .

How, you may ask, did this document, this memoir of Angela Carballino, fall into my hands? That, dear reader, is something I must keep secret. I have transcribed it for you just as it was written, with only a few, a very few editorial emendations. Does it remind you of other things I have written? This fact does not gainsay its objectivity nor its reality. Moreover, for all I know, perhaps I created real, actual beings, independent of me, beyond my control, characters with immortal souls. For all I know, Augusto Pérez in my novel *Mist* was right when he claimed to be more real, more objective than I am, I who thought I had invented him. As for the reality of this Saint Manuel the Good, Martyr—as he is revealed to me by his disciple and spiritual daughter, Angela Carballino—it has not occurred to me to doubt his reality. I believe in it more than the saint himself did. I believe in it more than I do in my own reality.

And now, before I bring this epilogue to a close, I wish to remind you, patient reader, of the ninth verse of the Epistle of the forgotten Apostle, Saint Jude—what power in a name!—where we are told how my heavenly patron, Saint Michael Archangel (Michael means "Who such as God?" and archangel means arch-messenger) disputed with the Devil (Devil means accuser, prosecutor) over the body of Moses, and would not allow him to carry it off as a prize, to damnation. Instead, he told the Devil: "May the Lord rebuke thee." And may he who wishes to understand, understand!

I should like also, since Angela Carballino introduced her own feelings into the story—I don't know how it could have been otherwise—to comment on her statement to the effect that if Don Manuel and his disciple Lázaro had confessed their convictions to the people, they, the people, would not have understood. Nor, I should like to add, would they have believed the two of them. They would have believed in their works and not in their words. And works stand by themselves, and need no words to back them up. In a village like Valverde de Lucerna one makes one's confession by one's conduct.

And as for faith, the people scarcely know what it is, and care less.

I am well aware of the fact that no action takes place in this narrative, this *novelistic* narrative, if you will—the novel is, after all, the most intimate, the truest history, so that I scarcely understand why some people are outraged to have the Gospels called a novel, when such a designation actually sets it above some mere chronicle or other. In short, nothing happens. But I hope that this is because everything in it remains, remains forever like the lakes and the mountains and the blessed simple souls, who, beyond faith and despair, the blessed souls who, in the lakes and the mountains, outside history, took refuge in a divine novel.

# PART FOUR
---
*Writing About Fiction*

Writing about fiction requires alert and productive reading and understanding of a story, yet careful reading does not necessarily produce clear and convincing writing. This section can serve you as a brief guide to the other skills needed for criticizing literature, partly with its general comments on the nature and purposes of writing about fiction, and partly with its suggestions and examples of strategies to follow in writing the most useful kinds of criticism.

Writing about literature—literary criticism—can take two basic forms, although these, in practice, are often mixed. The writer can try to judge a work to evaluate its merits and worth; or he can interpret a work to analyze its possible meanings. Both are valid forms of literary criticism, but for the beginning writer and critic the practice of interpretive criticism is not only the most likely method of producing an effective paper, but also the best method of insuring a sound basis for eventual value judgments. The formula: *Understanding precedes appreciation.*

The writing of an interpretive critical paper is a job that has its own technical requirements, but it is also a means to further understanding. A work of fiction, through its active shaping, ordering, and unifying of life, its making connections, can be experienced as a way of finding a meaning in life. The critical interpretation, through its more analytical ordering and unifying, its making connections in the work of fiction, can be a way to clarify the living experience of literature, for oneself and one's fellow readers.

The primary tool of interpretation is analysis. Analysis separates or breaks up a whole into its parts to find out their nature, function and relationship, so that—and this final step should not be forgotten—it can put the parts back together into a more meaningful whole. Literary analysis is an intellectual, logical process. Yet it must also take into account and rely on intuitions and emotions, even hunches, as a means to the discovery of the basic germ of an interpretation. In this it is essentially the same as scientific analysis. Literary interpretation flows in this sequence: response and discovery, analysis, hypothesis, and proof.

## Strategies for Writing About Fiction

The strategy of writing an effective paper must begin with the reader-writer's response to significant details, significant evidence in the work. This leads him to a discovery of his topic, and, in turn, the limiting of that topic. He then determines a thesis statement about that limited topic, subdivides that thesis into logical parts, and collects and organizes evidence as a countercheck and development of that thesis and its subdivisions.

*1. The Topic.* The discovery of the topic for a literary paper can be the result of a sudden insight, a special interest, or a logical examination of the details of the work. But whether you decide suddenly, *this* is what sticks out for me, or whether you deliberately attempt to apply Freudian psychology, or slowly conclude that the evidence points to *this,* you must still take the trouble to focus your topic clearly. A writer must countercheck his discovery against the actual terms of the story to see if his discovery does truly fit the evidence, and then proceed further to *limit* that discovery to a more precise and controlling subject than its first vague intimations.

*Limiting a topic* is reducing the area of subject matter to be covered, or to put it another way, sharpening the focus to examine a more limited area in detail. In verbal terms, limiting the topic may mean lowering the level of abstraction or the level of generality, so the subject can be seen less broadly, but in more concrete detail. A limited topic shows a more restricted area of concern, but an examination of this area reveals additional connections among the modifying and qualifying details; some important connections can be observed more carefully and described more accurately. For example, to reduce the area of meaning, the level of abstraction, of the simple general noun *boy,* connect it to another quality by adding a modifier: *tall boy.* The more modifiers—or connected points—that we add, the more we take away, the more we reduce and limit the area of meaning: *the tall, thin, freckle-faced boy.* We might apply this procedure first to a potential subject for a non-literary paper: "Engineering." A better and more limited topic would be "Electrical Engineering." Better or more limited still: "Career Opportunities in Electrical Engineering." Or equally limited but going in another direction of limitation: "Educational Requirements for a Career in Electrical Engineering."

Now let's apply this procedure to literary subjects. Whenever the assignment allows (and it usually does), you should try to form a topic by putting two things together. Not just "Women in Hemingway's Work," but "The Subservience of Women in Hemingway's Work." Not just "The Joad Family in *Grapes of Wrath*," but "The Sources of Strength in the Joad Family," or better still, "Love of Family vs. Brotherhood of Man in *Grapes of Wrath*." Take your subject a step further, add a qualifying, modifying point of connection that limits your topic to something more manageable, pointed, controlling. Talk about A in terms of B. Not just, "I will talk about A," but "I will show that A is B, or A does B, A causes B, A is a part of B, is in opposition to B. . . ."

Here are some examples that show contrast between a focus on vague, broad topics, as against topics that are a little more limited in scope:

*Ibsen's* Doll's House—*a story of the battle of the sexes. vs.* Doll's House —*a study of the struggle for domination in marriage.*

*Hemingway's* Farewell to Arms—*a novel of pessimism about life vs.* Farewell to Arms—*a dramatization of the forces in life that make permanent happiness impossible.*

*Shakespeare's* Hamlet—*a man overwhelmed by inescapable tragic destiny vs.* Hamlet—*a man too clever to keep himself alive.*

*2. The Thesis.* Just as an empty house is not a home until it has been given purpose and meaning by the life within it, so a topic, even a well-defined topic, is not a paper. It, too, is an empty framework until it has been given purpose, meaning and direction by a thesis statement about it. The thesis, the controlling and directing idea, of any kind of paper is a *statement about* a subject. "Career Opportunities in Electrical Engineering" is a limited topic. "With the dawn of the space age, career opportunities in electrical engineering *have increased immensely.*"—this is a thesis *about* a topic (if not a very interesting one). The thesis statement is a further step in the process of limiting scope, connecting ideas, and committing the writer to a course of discovery.

The thesis of a paper about literature, however, has a further unique characteristic. It is a specific, limited statement by the writer about the specific, limited statement (or method) of another writer: a thesis, in many cases, about a thesis, or theme. Thus the critic must be sure he has logically and accurately determined the original author's statement, or some aspect of it, even before he makes sure of his own statement about it. In exploring the basis for understanding fiction, we find that a hypothesis about the possible theme of a story should fulfill five requisites: It should be complete enough to take into account all of the details of a story; even if not all are actually mentioned, it cannot blink away conspicuous details that are not consistent with it. On the other hand, a hypothesis about a theme should be as simple, pointed, and limited as possible, while still being complete. It should follow inevitably and relevantly—with probability—from the actual details of the material. It should take into account the author's probable intentions and judgments. And it should take into account the emotional complexities and effects of the story.

As for the critic's side of the thesis statement, it should not be a random association or mere summary, but a meaningful, connected comment about the theme or method of the author. And the sharper the leading or argumentative edge, the better. As an example: "I am going to discuss Hemingway's treatment of women in his fiction" does not produce the clear, definitive focus of this thesis statement: "The women in Hemingway's novels merely serve as passive extensions of the egos of the men, and as objects for the pleasures of these men." Even if this is not *completely* true, it has the sharp, biting edge of the kind of thesis that produces a good—and even an interesting—paper.

Here are three examples—from bad to good—of a thesis about a more limited topic:

*In this paper I will discuss the point of view in Ring Lardner's "Ex Parte."*

*In Ring Lardner's "Ex Parte" there is a close relationship between point of view and the meaning of the story.*

*In Ring Lardner's "Ex Parte" the point of view is one of the author's chief means of revealing the destruction of self and others that blind self-regard can produce.*

3. *Development.*    Effectiveness in developing a thesis is controlled by the incisive, logical limits of that thesis, but there are also a number of considerations within the development itself that determine its effectiveness.

The *beginning* may profitably contain some broader references to provide a helpful perspective or orientation, but it should get down to business as soon as possible—without such postponements and evasions as this:

*William Faulkner is one of the most famous stylists in our literature. Many critics have commented on the uniqueness of his personal style. It is very emotional for the reader to read it, and must have been very difficult for Mr. Faulkner to develop it. This paper will be concerned with the subject of the style of Mr. Faulkner's novel* The Sound and the Fury. *This is a novel that has created a great deal of controversy and . . .*

Similarly, it should not dally with a misused mosaic of critical or historical gleanings:

*D. H. Lawrence was a forerunner of the modern novelist in the Twentieth Century. His work was a rebellion against the restraints of Victorian and Edwardian society. It introduced many of the Freudian concepts of the unconscious drives of man, the id, and the primal energies that have....*

The beginning can employ a paraphrase or even the direct quotation of the remarks of a critic or scholar as a starting point, but it must go on to apply these remarks in a statement that focuses on the specific uniqueness of the work under consideration, and the critic's specific personal claim about that work.

It must, then, shape the direction that the paper is going to take by including (most profitably at the beginning or end of the opening paragraph or set of paragraphs) a specific, controlling thesis. Not a statement like "Melville's *Billy Budd* is an example of many ideas about justice." Rather, a statement like "Melville's *Billy Budd* depicts the dilemma of justice that arises when the demands of a society clash with the interests of the individual." The latter example sets a direction for the paper by introducing the determining word *dilemma* and by suggesting the two sides of the dilemma—the demands of the society and the interests of the individual—that will be the basis for grouping subsequent details into logical subdivisions.

The *body*, or middle, of the paper, takes its direction from the logic and directness of the beginning. But in developing the body of a paper, you must be sure to keep the focus constantly on the thesis and not suddenly digress or broaden the discussion into something else. The best method of organizing the development is by analyzing the thesis and dividing it into sub-topics. These sub-topics should then form the basis of the organization of the paper, possibly, for example, as the topic sentences of each paragraph or set of paragraphs. In this way the paper is organized on the basis of what you have to say about the story, not on the basis of the chronology of the story, a random list of its characters, or a checklist of separate points based on the elements of a short story.

Of course, the body of the paper must refer to the details of the work. But these references—summaries, paraphrases, quotations—should be used as evidence in defense of your own assertions, always with the assumption that the reader of the paper has also read the story. This use of evidence (and particularly quotations) means more than alternating a statement of yours with a paraphrase or quotation from the story. It means actively interpreting the evidence as you use it, relating it back to each generality in more specific, limited terms. The evidence must be thorough enough for clarity, but should not ramble on and on with such sequences as "And then he did this and then he did that and then...." The use of evidence should take into account details from a story's resolution and ending, toward which the whole work is usually pointed. And it must place details in context and not distort them in a way the author had never intended to have them viewed.

In general, the body should develop appropriate proportions for its parts. It should make clear the relationships between these parts and maintain a constant relationship of the parts to the opening thesis claim. For example, if in writing about *Billy Budd,* you want to use a paragraph on Billy's past, that paragraph should make clear how those details are related to the thesis element of the interests of the individual, which you would earlier have established as one major side in the controlling claim of a dilemma of justice. This clarity of relationship is often achieved by actual repetition of key terms or variations on them; standard grammatical and rhetorical devices for achieving clear transitions between paragraphs and continuity between sentences are also a part of keeping relationships clear.

The possible use of secondary sources is usually determined by your instructor, but in any case they should be used with honesty and active application to the material. All such uses—in summary, paraphrase, or quotation—must be adequately footnoted. The use of footnote references to the stories themselves is determined by individual instructors, although it is often not necessary in limited student papers.

Little need be said, finally, about the *ending* of a paper, beyond the obvious remark that it should mark a definite conclusion and résumé of the thesis in terms of what now has been said about it, and should not dwindle away into details of the ending of a plot, excuses, complaints, unanswered questions, or arguments with the assignment.

*4. Style.*    A brief warning. A paper on literature demands a balancing of your ideas, vocabulary, and sentence structure with the often unfamiliar and complex ideas and expressions of an author, and possibly, with the unfamiliar thinking and style of a literary critic, as well. The result is often a severe strain on the stylistic equilibrium of a student writer. Beware, then, the pitfalls of undigested and faulty paraphrase; the misappropriation, misuse and misunderstanding of terminology; the over-extension of sentence structure into unwieldy and confusing length and subordination; the general bloat of the would-be high and philosophic style.

## Tactics for Papers and Assignments

In this section we turn to a check list of some of the most common types of literary papers and assignments, and to some suggestions for approaching and developing each type.

*1. Comparison and Contrast.*    One of the most frequent and useful assignments in writing about literature is the paper of comparison of similarities (and distinctions) between equal items or the contrast of differences between opposing but equal items. The logical process of comparison is a means of developing meaningful connections between items by showing a more general category to which two or more items belong (or in which they can be placed), but showing as well the differentiations of each from the other member (or members) of the category. Thus, you might develop the relationship between a Cadillac and a Suzuki motor scooter by showing their connections as members of the category *motor vehicles*, but differentiations in terms of attributes, advantages, disadvantages, etc.

In the study of literature, the comparison can be made in a number of ways. You can compare several works by one author with the works of another author on the basis of certain thematic ideas or methods. You can compare a single work by an author with a single work by another author, or one work by an author with another by himself, again in terms of a basic common thematic idea or a method. You can focus on common themes or methods in the works of several authors. You can compare characters, within a single work or in separate works, that have something in common or distinct opposition. You can compare specific elements—setting, point of view, style—in two separate works. You can compare resolutions of similar conflicts, or treatment of a common general subject, such as marriage.

In each instance, you need to find a common basis of comparison—a link, a likeness—and then go on to qualify that likeness by reference to specific details of character, situation, description, or event in each. The significance or moral evaluation of a character may be broadened by finding a like character in another story and showing the general character problem both are part of—say, inability to communicate—and then showing the different ways these problems are developed and resolved in the two stories: one retreats further into isolation, the other, through the sharing of suffering, makes the beginning of a connection to others.

Here is a sample opening paragraph that establishes the specific point of connection between two stories and suggests as well the direction of the differences that are to be distinguished between them:

*The journeys of Robin through the darkness of the "crooked and narrow streets" of the town and Kay through the cold, dark night on a decaying railroad car are both journeys into the dark complexity of a deeper truth of reality. From this perspective, Hawthorne's "My Kinsman, Major Molineux" and Capote's "A Tree of Night" are both stories of initiation. In both, naive, innocent, and self-assured youth is faced with a new, strange, and unmanageable experience; in both the meaning of that experience is finally brought into inarticulate but significant focus. That meaning, in somewhat different form in each story, is the existence and the complex nature of evil in the world. Both of the young people are changed by their recognition of evil, although the change in Robin's consciousness goes beyond that of Kay's.*

As the paragraph illustrated, you should begin a comparison by focusing on and defining the exact point of connection between the items. Your thesis should be a statement about both (or all) of the items of the comparison, rather than a statement about only one of them at a time, or merely a statement that you are going to compare them. Here is another effective opening thesis for a comparison of two characters:

*In the lives of Paul Morel in* Sons and Lovers *and Holden Caulfield in* The Catcher in the Rye, *their emotional development—particularly the development of their relationships with others—is blocked by their relationships with their parents. Yet the reasons are exactly the opposite: too much love for Paul, no love for Holden.*

Once the connecting thesis is established, you can then organize the development of the paper by subdividing the thesis. The pattern would look like this for the Morel-Caulfield comparison:

*Thesis: Point of Connection in Both (See above)*

   I.   *Sub-Theme One: Relations with Mothers*
        A.   *In Work One: Paul*
        B.   *In Work Two: Holden*
  II.   *Sub-Theme Two: Relations with Fathers*
        A.   *In Work One: Paul*
        B.   *In Work Two: Holden*
 III.   *Sub-Theme Three: Effect on Development*
        A.   *In Work One: Paul*
             1.   *Paul and Miriam*
             2.   *Paul and Clara*
        B.   *In Work Two: Holden*
             1.   *Holden and boys*
             2.   *Holden and girls*
             3.   *Holden and adults*
             4.   *Holden and Phoebe*
  IV.   *Sub-Theme Four: Changes in Development*
        A.   *In Work One: Paul*
        B.   *In Work Two: Holden*

In this pattern, the works are not taken up completely, one at a time; rather, references to the works are placed within a controlling claim about a sub-theme, or subdivision, of the original thesis.

It is possible to organize a comparison paper on the basis of the works themselves, but in this pattern you should beware of mere sum-

mary of plot in chronological order. Instead, details should be selected
to illustrate a sequence of sub-themes, first in one work and then the
other. The outline would look like this:

*I.*   *Paul in* Sons and Lovers
    *A.*   *Relations with mother*
    *B.*   *Relations with father*
    *C.*   *Effect on development*
    *D.*   *Changes in development*
*II.*   *Holden in* Catcher in the Rye
    *A.*   *Relations with mother*
    *B.*   *Relations with father*
    *C.*   *Effect on development*
    *D.*   *Changes in development*

To make the comparisons more precise and emphatic, during the discussion of Holden in the second part, references should be made to
what had earlier been said about Paul regarding the same sub-theme.

A possible variation on this pattern would be to discuss each character in terms of the first three sub-themes. And then in a final section,
the important resolutions in both works would be dealt with together
at a climactic point of the paper: both Paul and Holden in terms of
the changes in their development.

In cases where the details are not so completely opposed as in the
case of Holden and Paul, you can present the details from each work
organized on the basis of similarities and then differences under each
sub-theme. For example:

*I.*   *Sub-Theme One: Failure of Relations with Bosses*

    *A.*   *Similarities: John and Fred*
    *B.*   *Differences: John and Fred*

In cases where the similarities are very strong, this next overall pattern might be used, although it is, generally speaking, a less effective
method of organization:

*Thesis on both:*

  *I.*   *Similarity One*
    *A.*   *Work One*
    *B.*   *Work Two*
 *II.*   *Similarity Two*
    *A.*   *Work One*
    *B.*   *Work Two*
*III.*   *Differentiation*
    *A.*   *Work One*
    *B.*   *Work Two*

Any of these patterns (or others that might be developed to fit specific situations) can be extended to include more than two items. They can also be used as a possible method of organization in some of the further types of papers discussed.

2. *Thematic Idea.* Equally common and effective as a basis of a paper or assignment is the analysis of one of the central thematic ideas of a single story. For this paper you need first to discover and isolate the idea that will be the premise of your interpretation, your definition of at least one of the meanings of the story. You then go on to develop and prove your definition by showing how the idea is dramatized and revealed in the concrete terms of the story. The formula: What it is and how it is revealed.

In determining this thematic idea or statement, you can be guided by (as we have seen in more detail earlier) direct statements by the author, the title, the characters' thoughts and dialogue, the character types the characters represent, the nature of the central conflict, prominent actions, setting, and any of the other elements of the story. You should be sure to counter-check your thematic hypothesis against the evidence and should be sure, as well, that your final formulation of it is as limited and direct as possible. Again: "This story is a prime illustration of D. H. Lawrence's interest in the problems of love" is not limited enough. But this statement of a thematic idea is: "This story convincingly demonstrates D. H. Lawrence's contention that fulfilled love demands the harmonious balance of both the emotional and intellectual, the sensual and spiritual elements in mankind."

You develop and organize your paper by showing how the thematic idea is revealed in the story. Your organization should not be based on the mere chronology of the story, but on sub-topics that you develop by analyzing your statement of the central thematic idea. Often these sub-topics may well be an expansion of the key terms that were part of your opening thesis: *balance—emotional* and *intellectual, sensual and spiritual.* Here is a pattern for development on the basis of sub-topics:

*Thesis: "The story shows how fulfilled love demands a balance of emotional and intellectual, sensual and spiritual elements in mankind."*

I.  *Sub-Theme One: Need for balance*
    A.  *Citation of characters and actions*
        1.  *Those who fail*
        2.  *Those who succeed*
    B.  *Citation of parallel in setting*
        1.  *The City*
        2.  *The Country*
II. *Sub-Theme Two: One kind of balance*

    A.  *Citation of character and action*
    B.  *Citation of parallel in style*
*III.*  *Sub-Theme Three: Second kind of balance*
    A.  *Citation of character and action*
    B.  *Citation of climax and resolution*

The following pattern is organized on the basis of elements of the story, but still refers them to the same sub-topics:

*Thesis: "Love demands a balance of emotional and intellectual, sensual and spiritual elements."*

  *I.*  *Parallel One: Character and action*
    A.  *Reveals Sub-Theme One*
    B.  *Reveals Sub-Theme Two*
 *II.*  *Parallel Two: Setting*
    A.  *Also reveals Sub-Theme Two*
    B.  *Reveals Sub-Theme Four (which is minor)*
*III.*  *Parallel Three: Resolution*
    A.  *Also reveals Sub-Theme One and Two*
    B.  *Emphasizes Sub-Theme Three*

This opening paragraph of an analysis of Melville's "Bartleby" sets the key term, *meaninglessness*, connects it to the relationship of the individual and his society, and defines the course of the actions pursued by the protagonist.

*Herman Melville's "Bartleby The Scrivener" is a tragi-comic study of meaninglessness. Bartleby, isolated in an unfeeling society, seems "absolutely alone in the universe," with only one course of action that can preserve any sense of himself: a pathetic, strangely heroic, whimsically humorous kind of passive defiance. Only through rejection and refusal can he still act; only by destroying himself can he save anything of value.*

In developing one sub-division of this theme, this paragraph traces the function and meaning of one of the story's key symbols, the walls, in relation to the central thematic claim of meaninglessness:

*For Bartleby, life is a series of walls—between man and society, man and other men, man and the meaning of his own life. These walls that isolate, block, and deaden are, in part, the trap of an impersonal, sterile society. The office that has become the whole of Bartleby's existence is located on Wall Street, the center of the business society. Out one window, the inhabitants of the office can see the inner white wall of an airshaft. Out the other window all that they can see, some ten feet away, is the blackened wall of another building. But for Bartleby the wall outside is only three feet away! And at the story's close the walls of the society's prison are even closer. After his last position in life, "fronting the dead wall," Bartleby finally lies "huddled at the base of the wall," "his head touching the cold stone."*

*3. Character Analysis.*   One of the most common and effective ways of writing about fiction is through an analysis of principal characters in a story. This approach allows many possible points of emphasis and methods of organization.

A writer can define the character's central trait or constellation of traits—i.e. egoistic self-absorption—and then go on to develop such sub-themes as insensitivity, pride, cruelty. Each point will be substantiated with a citation from the story concerning the character's actions, dialogue, or thoughts.

While a fully substantiated definition of character might stand by itself as a critical paper, the analysis would be more complete, and the thesis more pointed and informative, if the paper went on to develop an argument for what was the author's apparent attitude toward the character and his actions. For instance, the thesis could point to a cause-and-effect pattern of how characteristics lead to certain consequences, with an indication of the author's evaluation of those consequences. Or similarly, the paper could seek to prove that certain basic character types have been set up by the author for moral judgment. The stress would fall not only on what the character's type is, but why the author has given it a special significance.

On the other hand, a paper might focus on the forces and influences that shape a character and seem to cause him to be as he is. Details from the story would substantiate both the traits of character to be defined and the forces and influences that shape them. Again, the paper can point to the author's moral judgment of the characters and the influences.

Another possible variation is the emphasis upon the development or change—for better or worse—in the course of the story: what the character is and what he becomes, what causes him to change, and with what final result. Here is a sample opening of a character analysis of this type, applied to two stories:

*At different points in their marriages—Little Chandler within two years, Francis Weed after many years—the central characters in James Joyce's "A Little Cloud" and John Cheever's "The Country Husband" suddenly feel that their lives, and particularly the routine domesticity of marriage, have become a deadening defeat. Their submerged romantic natures rebel; each finds a glowing dream to fulfill his yearnings. But each dream is shattered, and the romantic rebels surrender, to different degrees and in different ways, to their realities. In Chandler's world, romance is forever lost; in Francis' it may still make occasional forays in the night.*

The emphasis can also be changed by focusing on the methods the author uses to reveal his character's traits: direct statement, dialogue, revealing actions, thoughts, etc.

In this same vein, you can make an evaluation of the author's methods and his results: obviousness or subtlety of the methods, simplicity or complexity of the result, and its credibility.

It is possible to use several characters: two or more who are variations on a similar trait or examples of opposing traits; two or more whose relationship to each other is seen as more important or significant than what each is separately.

And, finally, you might even use a minor character or several to show how, even though they are minor, they contribute to the story in terms of plot, contrast, setting, symbol, etc.

Whatever the variation, you will note the basic job of defining the character's traits and providing evidence from the story itself to prove and develop your contentions. You will note as well that none of the variations calls for the mere summary of a plot from start to finish as the way of explaining a character.

Here are some outline patterns that would apply to many of the above possibilities. In the first group, the basic method of subdivision is by traits of character, although the method of developing the subdivision varies according to the purpose:

I. *Sub-Theme One: Trait One*
   A. *Citation of action or method*
   B. *Citation of action or method*
II. *Sub-Theme Two: Trait Two*

I. *Sub-Theme One: Trait One*
   A. *Initial stage*
   B. *Developed stage*
II. *Sub-Theme Two: Trait Two*

I. *Sub-Theme One: Trait One*
   A. *Examples of it*
      1. *With wife*
      2. *With daughter*
   B. *Final consequences*
II. *Sub-Theme Two: Trait Two*

I. *Sub-Theme One: Trait One*
   A. *Cause of it*
   B. *Result of it*
II. *Sub-Theme Two: Trait Two*

These next patterns indicate the way in which other aspects of the story could be the basis of the setting up and developing the subdivisions:

I.   *Sub-Theme One: Influence One*
   A.   *Evidence*
   B.   *Resulting trait*
II.  *Sub-Theme Two: Influence two*
III. *Sub-Theme Three: Author's attitude*
       *or*
III. *Sub-Theme Three: Total consequences*

I.   *Sub-Theme One: Relationship to John*
   A.   *Initial*
   B.   *Final*
II.  *Sub-Theme Two: Relationship to Betty*
   A.   *Initial*
   B.   *Final*
III. *Sub-Theme Three: Significance*

*4. Point of view.* An analysis of the point of view of a story is primarily concerned with the *function* of the point of view in producing the emotional and intellectual effect of the story. To make this function clear, you need to go beyond merely defining what the point of view is technically and what character (if any) is "speaking" or "seeing" the events. You will almost certainly need to define the reliability of this character's narration. But finally, you must try to discover what effect this kind of narration produces on the reader. You must ask what emphasis or focus, what revelations of character, what revelations of author's attitude, what emotional response in the reader, even what intentional distortions are produced. For the student, point-of-view papers are probably most useful in treating stories with first person narrators, especially when there is an ironic tone.

The following sample of an opening paragraph immediately establishes a workable thesis concerning point of view; it clearly states a relationship between the nature of the narrating character and the story's theme:

*The plural in the title of Cesare Pavese's "Suicides" refers not only to the two deaths that the narrator has indirectly caused, but also to the living death that he himself still endures. The three are interrelated, for the nature of his own living death has contributed to the literal deaths of the others. The nature of that death-in-life is given its full emotional impact and definitive shape by Pavese's use of the first person point of view and narration. His method is not full, but subtly partial irony; with that irony he exposes the destructive partial awareness of the narrator and the coldness of his frozen emotional life.*

*5. Conflict and Resolution.* An examination of the conflict and resolution of a story, while usually used as material for developing papers on theme or character, can also become the central focus of a paper aimed at clarifying the basic patterns of ideas in a story. In order to become the center of a worthwhile paper, however, the conflict and resolution must be examined considerably beyond the depth of the literal plot level. A recitation of the plot from start to finish is *not* a critical paper. Rather, an analysis of the dynamics of plot, conflict, and resolution, should lead conclusively to an opinion about the generalized significance of the story, usually in terms of its characters or theme.

*6. Plot.* An effective analysis of plot must go beyond chronological summary, but it should also go beyond simple definitions or narrow classifications of plot "types." To make a discussion that clarifies the experience of reading the plot, you can take a number of different approaches.

*Structure.* The study of structure is concerned with defining the organization and emphasis of the sequence of events as a means of clarifying emotional or thematic effects. This approach, often very useful in longer stories and novels, can be used for a story of any length. It can focus on such considerations as the subdivisions or sections in the work and their relationships, their relative lengths and weights. For example, the organization of the novel *Sons and Lovers* can be first defined in terms of four sections: Family Background, with emphasis on Paul and Mother; One Type of Love, with emphasis on Paul and Miriam; Second Type of Love, with emphasis on Paul and Clara; Final Relationships with Mother, Miriam, and Clara. The function of these sections in Lawrence's examination of the problems of love would then be established as the thesis of the paper. Other considerations are the balance between events summarized and events dramatized in scenes, the juxtaposition of events, the emphasis or lack of emphasis on certain events.

*Time.* The sense of time developed in a story, the shortening or lengthening or slowing of events, and the possible shifts in time or flashbacks, can make a valuable focus for discussing how the plot places emphasis on the main features of the theme.

*Significance of the actions* in the plot can be discussed either as a revelation of a character's traits or as a development in the story's symbolism. The former is similar to a character analysis, with the emphasis reversed to show character revealed specifically by plot. The latter is an interpretation of the symbolic implications of single acts, a sequence of acts, or even certain types of acts: acts of accident, coincidence, bad luck, violence, passivity.

*Motivation.* An analysis of the motivation behind plot actions also involves much of the same materials as for character analysis, but here the emphasis is on the actions of a character or characters and on the motives and causes both in character and in situation, that led to them. In some cases it is worthwhile to stress the apparent lack of motive or cause.

*Evaluation.* If the material warrants, you can present a judgment of the actions of the plot, in terms of such points as coincidence, inevitability, plausibility, and of the motivations of the characters in terms of credibility and degree of complexity.

*Scene or Single Act.* In a part-to-whole study of a single plot episode you may show how a part—a single act, a scene, a particular confrontation of characters, for example—is representative and is used to illustrate the author's overall ideas, methods, or style. Or perhaps you may show how the part is significant for the total development of the story's plot and/or the theme. Here is a pattern of organization for a study of the function of a scene:

*Thesis: Paul Morel's fight with Clara Dawe's husband, Baxter, produces a cleansing catharsis or purge for the emotions of both men and thus becomes a turning point in their emotional development.*

I.  *Emotions they bring to the fight*
    A.  *Paul*
        1.  *Guilt*
        2.  *Dissatisfaction*
        3.  *Sense of Insufficiency*
    B.  *Baxter*
        1.  *Sense of Insufficiency*
        2.  *Guilt*
        3.  *Aimlessness*
II.  *Reasons fight purges emotions of each*
III.  *After-effects of fight show it as turning point for each*

A possible variation in the organization of the opening:

I.  *Emotions they bring to the fight*
    A.  *Similar emotions*
        1.  *Guilt*
        2.  *Insufficiency*
    B.  *Different emotions*
        1.  *Paul's dissatisfaction*
        2.  *Baxter's aimlessness*

7. *Setting.* In a study of setting, the characters of a *part* of the setting—a room, a valley in the country, the assembly line of a factory —or the whole *pattern* of the setting—nature vs. the factory—should be connected to a further point of thematic significance. You can, for one example, define the general atmosphere and mood of the slum environ-

ment of a character, show the details that create this atmosphere, and show the effects of the atmosphere on the emotions and understanding of the reader. For another example, you can explain the influence, the psychological effects of the setting on a character and his actions. Or, you can interpret the symbolic parallels of the setting. In this latter study you can treat the setting separately and show its relationship to thematic ideas or you can treat its relations to a character—the kind of setting a character is associated with (in Steinbeck's "Flight," Pepe and nature, the hunters and the city) or the kind of setting in which certain actions of a character occur (love scenes in the mountains, scenes of violence on the plains).

*8. Style and Tone.*   It is possible to define the characteristics of a style and tone—ironic, solemn, understated, exuberant, sentimental, formal, angry, etc.—and provide evidence for the definition. But it is probably better to go one step further and show the contribution the style makes to the emotional and thematic whole of the story. In either case, avoid lengthy reproductions and directly analyze the samples used, rather than merely pasting them in without close comment.

One useful approach is to use a single short passage only, closely analyze it, and thus show its way of representing the whole. Of course, you can also keep the whole of the story in focus, and select samples from different passages as evidence for your definition and interpretation.

An interesting variation would be to examine the unique style of the dialogue, or even the description of a character's thought processes, to show the relation of the author's style of speaking and thinking to that of his character.

If the story employs a first person narrator, the style and tone of his entire discourse then become a means of revealing the narrator's character and his way of looking at the events.

*9. Symbolism.*   Much of what has been said about the other types of papers involves the uses of the symbolic implications of various parts of a story. The symbolic element of a story can also be the central focus of a critical paper.

One approach is to emphasize as the central topic of the thesis a particular kind or pattern of imagery that has a consistent symbolic meaning throughout the story: flowers in association with innocence; rain in association with death; the countryside in contrast to the factory, in constant association with the basic conflict of the theme.

On the other hand, an image—such as the cruel granite rock at the end of Steinbeck's "Flight"—that appears only once in a story can be connected to the actions, characters and meanings of that particular moment.

In a like manner, a single action or a general kind of action, or a character can be used to draw up a thesis that stresses the specific symbolic use of the action or character.

In all cases, you must be sure to "read" the symbol in context and discuss it without distorting the pattern in which the author has placed it.

*10. Evaluation.* The evaluation, the judgment of what is good or bad, worthy or not, is one of the basic forms of literary criticism. But in the thoughtless or careless critic's hands it is often a deadly weapon that blows up in his face. The right to hold opinions is no guarantee that those opinions—whether original, stereotyped, or courageous—will be valid or valuable. There are, however, some criteria and methods of applying them that can help not only to increase the chances of a valid evaluation, but also make of that evaluation an act of growth, of change, of learning, rather than a reflex of habit and bias.

*Truth.* Aristotle said that art is an imitation of reality, and critics have been arguing over what he meant by "imitation" ever since. Certainly the details of a story should be credible, believable, accurate, and should have the ring of truth. But the critic should keep in mind the possible limitations of his own ability to know that truth of reality, and keep in mind, too, the many ways in which that truth appears in the eyes of others—especially characters in the story. Precise, photographic realism of appearance, action, speech is not the only kind of realism and, indeed, may even be used as a false front to conceal underlying realities or to create an image of people and life that is limited and distorted. On the other hand, the fundamental truth of a situation may be portrayed within a style or convention whose details are intentionally nonrealistic or at least only partially realistic: fantasy, the exaggerations of myth, or of comedy, particularly satirical, critical comedy. The wild events of Joseph Heller's savagely funny *Catch 22* certainly never occurred, nor are they likely to occur in just that way; yet for many the book provides a deep insight into the essential truths of a world at war. Thus, you need to be careful in defining what you mean by truth and careful to take into account the author's conventions and intentions when you attempt to evaluate the truth of his work.

One helpful scale to employ as either a part or the whole of a judgment of truth is that of complexity vs. simplification. For example, a story may employ a realistic surface convention and yet so oversimplify the characters, and reduce the credibility, the inevitability of their actions and motivations, that it fails to show the complexity of truth in actual human beings.

*Moral Truth or Didacticism.* These terms refer to the meanings that the author seems to draw from his material—the comments, criticisms, attitudes, judgments, beliefs that his themes suggest. This is, of course, a much more difficult kind of truth to evaluate than the truth of specific actions or speech or even motivation. You—or any other critic, for that matter—should tread with humility in judging an author's ideas, but here too the complexity-simplification scale is often a good basis for a start. You need not, of course, agree with an author's ideas to allow their possible validity. However, an important criterion for you to determine is the question of whether these ideas seem to follow inevitably from the probabilities of the character or situation, or whether they seem imposed on it. It is important to keep in mind one further point of departure as well: the difference between questions and answers. Quite often an author's ideas are part of an insight into the questions, the problems, even the dilemmas, humans face; he should not necessarily be judged for the answers he envisions or supplies. As a matter of fact, the specific answers that authors sometimes provide— often wrenching their material to do so—turn out frequently to be the least important, and possibly least valid, part of their contribution.

One last but most crucial caution on a different level: be sure not to misread the ideas of a character, or even all of the characters, as necessarily the ideas of the author. When F. Scott Fitzgerald portrays a man who thinks that money is so important that he doesn't even care what happens to people, that doesn't mean that F. Scott Fitzgerald agrees with his character.

*Unity.* The criterion of unity involves appropriateness: the kind of order imposed on the material; the relationship of all the parts to a central effect or idea; the appropriate balance and differences of emphasis between parts; the appropriateness of each element in context with the others; the degree of complexity maintained within the unifying pattern; the economy and inevitability of the means used to produce its effects. On all these questions you establish responsible judgments.

*Beauty.* This is probably the most difficult term to deal with, particularly in reference to the whole of a story, since in this matter you would again be concerned with the unity, the balance, the harmony between the parts. It might be more practical to focus on the beauty of specific passages, in terms of the grace or emotion of a style, the quality of a description.

*Impact.* An important value of a short story is its emotional impact, the force with which it can affect the reader, the power with which it can engage his imagination, draw his empathy, even produce in him a kind of emotional crisis and catharsis. There is a danger here, however, in valuing only the obvious kind of impact that can be achieved by violent or sensational material. To deal maturely with the emotional effects of a story, you need to appraise the kind of impact it achieves, the means it uses to achieve its effects, and to develop the ability to respond to a variety of emotional effects, including the more subtle, quiet, sensitive kind.

*Originality.* Evaluation on the basis of the author's originality requires definition and judgment of the story's freshness of insight in emotions and ideas, as well as of its inventiveness in methods and style.

*Honesty.* Evaluating the author's honesty would bring into question not only his basic attitude toward his subject, but his way of using the materials of that subject, with special attention to a possible twisting of what would appear to be the inevitable course of the material for the sake of plot, emotional effect, or theme.

*11. Author Study.* An author's work usually develops a number of consistent patterns of subject, theme, or method, although these patterns will still include much change, development, or variation. Your critical paper can approach these overall patterns of an author's work in several ways:

You can focus on one work and have as your thesis the unique relationship of this work to the author's constant concerns or methods. You can show why it is typical of certain techniques or subjects, how it illustrates a certain basic theme, making clear as well its uniqueness, its specific variation on the central theme. To do this you need to refer to a wider context than the one work itself, including references to other works. This contextual information might be gained from lectures, secondary sources, or the actual reading of other works.

Similarly, you can focus on two or more works equally, comparing them as to their variations on some central theme, subject, or method.

The other approaches involve a broader focus on the overall pattern itself. You can trace a technique or device, a subject or theme, through a number of works. You can organize this approach on the basis of a series of equal and distinct variations, or on the basis of a certain direction of growth, change, or development.

*12. Historical Study.* An author's work—a single story or the body of his work—is, at least in some degree, both a mirror of his times and a product of his times. A critical paper, then, might effectively approach that work on either of these two bases: (1) what the author's work reveals of the historical, political, economic, social, intellectual, religious currents and problems of its time, or (2) how these can be shown to have influenced the methods or themes of the work. This kind of study might require your use of secondary sources for the background material. In developing the historical paper, you must be sure to avoid irrelevant blocks of background material, or an imbalance between the background material and the work. Most of all, your treatment of a story as an artifact of history must never overlook its most important feature—its artistic arrangement and re-creation of the experience of living.

*13. Source and Influence Study.*   The historical study can lead into a more specialized area of criticism, but one that can be valuable and instructive. In a source study, on the basis of your reading in primary or secondary sources, or both, you determine a thesis to show how a story's plot, or characters, or thematic ideas are, to some degree, derived from the author's experience or his reading of a previously written source or sources—for example, Melville's use of Thomas Carlyle's concept of "The Everlasting Nay" in *Moby Dick*. The development of your thesis would illustrate changes and even contrasts, as well as similarities.

The influence study can go both ways: it can show the literary influences that at least helped to shape both the form and content of a work, or it can show how the work under consideration became an influence on the form and content of subsequent works. In either case, you would not show a complete correlation (since you would not expect to be proving total plagiarism), but rather a partial connection on the basis of certain specific elements of the work.

*14. Research in Criticism.*   A source paper on the critical background of a piece of fiction differs from the research papers previously mentioned, for it requires a double load of very careful interpretation. In research on criticism, the first part of the task is to arrive at your own careful reading of the fiction, your own interpretation, and perhaps your own tentative thesis about a controversial point of artistic technique in the story. The second phase is locating and reading some critics whose discussion bears significantly on the aspect of the story you wish to discuss. In general, the critics are probably more experienced in careful reading and interpretation of fiction than you; yet you will undoubtedly find considerable disagreement among them, if not downright contradiction.

Your problem, then, is to try to decide what is the range of legitimate disagreement among serious critics, including yourself, and to decide where your own interpretation stands. Eventually you must formulate a thesis for your paper based on what interpretive evidence you can supply to support or contradict some of the criticism. You may decide to treat the critics objectively and descriptively, giving a straight account of what seem to be the key points of variation in critical interpretation, and explaining why these points seem crucial to your judgment of the story. Or perhaps you will take sides, with one party and against another, or, with extreme care and deliberation, against all the critics on certain points of controversy. Whatever your strategy, it is important that you make your own analysis of the story a prominent feature of what you have to say, even when the focus of the source paper is on criticism.

*15. Examinations.* Solid preparation—accurate, thoughtful, responsive reading and disciplined review—is of course essential in taking examinations. But this preparation can be put to more fruitful use if some attention is also paid to the characteristics and requirements of the common types of written examination questions.

*Identification.* When presented with a character, a place, an action, a title, a quotation, etc., you should briefly answer in terms of the *significance* of the item: Not merely who or what it is, where it is, or what happened, but also what that illustrates or represents in a work, the author's work in general, a historical period, or form of literature.

*Analytical.* A longer essay question might be one that asks you to analyze the importance of a single item of literary material (a character, a plot, a particular story) as related to a larger or more general context or idea (an entire novel, the rise of social criticism in American fiction, the theme of lost innocence in American stories). You may be asked to relate a single story to the author's work as a whole, for instance, or to literature in that period, or to a form of literature, such as tragedy.

The point of the analytical question is always that you show how specific features of the literary material are related to those of the general concept. Sometimes you are left to determine for yourself what larger or more general concept should be developed from the evidence of a single item or items ("How would you typify the character of Ahab in *Moby Dick?*"). In any case, you should not waste time summarizing or pharaphrasing the features of the item to be discussed; you should comment on the specific features which show a relationship to the general concept (i.e. how Ahab challenges fate in the manner of the heroes of Greek tragedy).

The analytical question may also call for a comparison and/or contrast between two equal items. These items may in turn have to be related to some larger context, as variations within it; but frequently you need only draw connections between them. The point of the connection may be given to you: Compare and contrast the treatment of love in Story A and Story B. Or it may be left open: Compare and contrast Story A and Story B. Do not merely summarize each separately; draw specific connections between them and refer to both items in discussing each point of connection. Use specific differences and variations as well as similarities; these are often more valuable than general similarities.

*General.* A general question starts from the top down; you supply the specific works, characters, etc., as evidence. The question is most frequently a directed one, in which you are asked to discuss a particular problem: "Discuss the Alienated Hero or 'Anti-hero' in American Fiction of the Sixties," or, "What Were the Dominant Characteristics of the Hero in American Fiction of the Sixties?" Notice that the second example gives you a direction for your answer, but a less specific one than does the first. A question can also involve a comparison and/or contrast: "Compare and contrast political concerns in American Fiction of the Thirties and Sixties," or, "Compare American Fiction of the Thirties and Sixties." Notice again the differences between the degree of direction of the examples.

Occasionally the general question will be completely nondirected, or apparently so, as in a quotation (perhaps a passage from a story or poem; perhaps a quotation from the opinion of a critic) or as in some form of controversial statement presented without comment (i.e.—Ahab's struggle is not tragic, in the Greek sense of the word, since he had a foreboding of his doom). In these situations you are expected to determine the relevance of the statement to the literary material you have been studying. Since the statement is usually fairly sharply pointed, your task is to state the prominent points of connection between it and the significance you see in your literary material, usually in the form of some specific thesis supported by examples from your reading.

In summary, in dealing with all types of questions, think and organize first. Analyze the question carefully for its key words and emphasis, its thesis. Directly respond to this thesis. Follow the direction the question wants you to take; do not wander off onto some random association, standard definition, or factual background that was not asked for. Organize your answer into a thesis sentence and topic sentences for sub-themes. Be sure to refer to specific details (not necessarily quotations) of the works, for a question about literature is finally a question about the reading and comprehension of specific works. But *use* these specific references for what they represent, illustrate, signify. Do not merely be a name, passage, character, action or title dropper.

# PART FIVE

*Assignments in*
*Criticism—Five Models*

The following five essays (excerpts from which appear in Part Four of the text) provide models for several types of analytical, interpretive papers. They are, in order, concerned with (1) comparison and contrast on several levels, (2) character analysis, (3) point-of-view criticism and how it is related to the theme, (4) comparison of thematic ideas concerning a particular philosophy, and (5) character and symbolism of setting and how they pertain to the thematic idea of a single story.

## 1. Journeys Into the Dark: "My Kinsman, Major Molineux" and "A Tree of Night."

The journeys of Robin through the darkness of the "crooked and narrow streets" of the town and Kay through the cold, dark night on a decaying railroad car are both journeys into the dark complexity of a deeper truth of reality. From this perspective, Hawthorne's "My Kinsman, Major Molineux" and Capote's "A Tree of Night" are both stories of initiation. In both, naive, innocent, and self-assured youth is faced with a new, strange, and unmanageable experience; in both the meaning of that experience is finally brought into inarticulate but significant focus. That meaning, in somewhat different form in each story, is the existence and the complex nature of evil in the world. Both of the young people are changed by their recognition of evil, although the change in Robin's consciousness goes beyond that of Kay's.

Although both Robin and Kay begin their journeys in the youthful state of innocence and illusion, their goals differ, and this difference can be seen as reflecting a difference in their stages of maturation. Robin is at a consciously transitional point in his life. He is definitely leaving one stage behind and seeking a new life in the city. He knows he is making a new beginning. Kay, on the other hand, has just brushed by an experience with death without truly responding to it and is returning to the pattern of her old life of college and family. Although these two old patterns of life differ, they carry the same symbolic implications. Thus Robin's background of the country and family and Kay's of the city and family both represent a limited, secure, protected form of life which has insulated the two from the harsher edges of reality. Robin's world of illusion has been that of rustic and religious simplicity; paradoxically, Kay's has been that of surface sophistication.

Despite Robin's more conscious intention of beginning a new life and making his way to fame and fortune in the city, he comes to his trial of initiation no better prepared than does Kay to her unexpected test. Both employ the mannerisms of habit. With the oaken cudgel he has brought with him from the country, Robin is ready to physically beat those who cross him. Kay tries reading her magazine, smoking a cigarette, talking with polite coldness: "Oh, I should love to." Both have magical slogans that should be the key to all: Robin's constantly repeated "my kinsman, Major Molineux," Kay's "and tomorrow we'll be in Atlanta and I'm nineteen and I'll be twenty in August and I'm a sophomore . . ." But neither Robin's password nor his kinsman himself can any longer help him find his way. Nor can Kay's complacent veneer of social assurance any longer insulate her from the reality that even her uncle's funeral had not brought to true experience for her.

The reality that both encounter is conveyed in terms of a nightmarish grotesquerie, a mysterious unreality that is an appropriate vehicle for the complexities of experience that lie beyond the reaches of cool rationality or social grace. Robin first encounters a man who threatens to put him in the stocks when the youth asks about the Major. In a like manner, he is chased from an inn for asking the same. He then mistakes a harlot for his kinsman's housekeeper, is threatened again with the stocks, and encounters the man with the parti-colored face of red and black. Waiting in front of a church, he thinks of home and its securities but wakes from his daydream in a quandry: "Am I here or there?" Suddenly he wonders if his kinsman might be dead. Less arrogant now, he meets the first kindly stranger he has come across, who advises him to wait. The wild, frightening parade finally arrives and reveals the core of its terrors—the tarred and feathered Major Molineux.

This, then, is a world in which the church is empty, home left behind; a world in which death is possible, and irrational cruelty present; a world in which the moorings of one's life are loosened, the keys to all the doors destroyed. Harlot or housekeeper, benefactor or victim, friend or enemy—the truth is ambiguous; and the old answers don't fit the new questions. In this world, man's face has its horrors, and so does his soul. Evil and violence form one of the colors of his existence. And in this hard-visaged world one must muddle through himself. He cannot rely on his Major Molineux: his assumptions and dogmas, his easy solutions, his familial securities. Even these are not immune to the tar and feather of evil and violence.

A face is also the central sign of the world of reality into which Kay is led. In a decaying old railroad car, amid 'dead smoke, stale odors, garbage, and water leaking from a cooler, she must sit opposite the short woman with the huge head, and the man with the "wide, hairless face [that] had no real expression." The woman wants to talk and Kay cannot evade her, is forced as well to take a drink of terrible gin. While the woman is getting cups, the man leans forward and touches Kay's cheek; later he sees her pour the gin in her guitar and she seeks his aid. The woman's intimidations continue as she tells of their act of bringing the man back from the dead—causing Kay to think of her dead uncle's face—and tries to get her to buy a love charm. Kay flees to the observation platform, but the "harmless, vapid face" follows her, reminding her of a childhood terror of the wizard man. After one last attempt at evasion with the magazine, she succumbs, collapsing before them as they steal her purse.

The face of this world is the face of death, the "secret stillness" of the face of her dead uncle and of the meekly intimidating deaf mute in the railroad car. While death was only a minor element in the reality that Robin encountered, it is the core of the reality that assaults Kay against her will. But it is not the whole of that reality, for this is a world of living terrors as well, of mystery and vague, sordid evil. It is the adult world in which the fantasies of childhood are made manifest: "He lived everywhere, the wizard man, and everywhere was danger." In contrast to the situation of Robin, Kay's experience does validate at least one aspect of the world of childhood—not its innocence, but its terrors. These become a part of the new life, but the childhood means of coping with them are no longer effective. The quiet, deathlike evil of the old railroad car is overpowering.

Both Robin and Kay first respond to their encounters with pride—in their manner of doing things, in their connections and status. Both feel capable of handling the situation, feel anger and disgust at those whom they meet. But their assurance soon gives way to perplexity and confusion and finally—despite last thoughts of the simple, stable world they have left—to the terror of recognition. At this point, the resolutions of the stories differ.

Kay, after recognizing that the terrors of childhood have now materialized in other forms, tries to effect some compromise, but then crumbles. She has seen the face of reality, but can do nothing with it, is hypnotized by it and sinks down before it, her own face covered with the raincoat "like a shroud." Robin's story, on the other hand, is taken further past the point of climax. His first response to "the foul disgrace of a head grown gray with honor" is to tremble with "pity and terror," sharing with his kinsman the suffering of the moment. But the experience is too much for him, and the irrationality of mankind that he has now experienced is revealed in him, first in "a sort of mental inebriety" and then in a wild "shout of laughter" that echoes louder than all the rest of the "senseless uproar." It is a strange response, a part of the experience of the ambiguity of reality, now within himself. But Hawthorne takes him even further through the ritual of initiation. For we see that with the aid of the kind stranger, he may yet learn to make his way in the world without the magic formulas of the world of innocence he has had to leave behind.

## 2. The Buried Life: "A Little Cloud" and "The Country Husband."

At different points in their marriages—Little Chandler within two years, Francis Weed after many years—the central characters in James Joyce's "A Little Cloud" and John Cheever's "The Country Husband" suddenly feel that their lives, and particularly the routine domesticity of marriage, have become a deadening defeat. Their submerged romantic natures rebel; each finds a glowing dream to fulfill his yearnings. But each dream is shattered, and the romantic rebels surrender, to different degrees and in different ways, to their realities. In Chandler's world, romance is forever lost; in Francis' it may still make occasional forays in the night.

Chandler is a timid, passive, ineffectual man, a man who appears smaller than he is. Francis is much more successful, active, and outgoing, yet he too has lost his spirit and his independence to "the patterns he had chosen." Both feel trapped in the routines of their lives. For Chandler the furnishings of his small apartment seem too prim and pretty, dead—a part of the world of his wife, who is the main source of his defeat. Her eyes, he feels, are cold and mean; there is no passion in them. "Why," he thinks, "had he married the eyes in the photograph?" His child is a burden and, moreover, a successful rival for the affections of his wife. His work is empty and repetitious.

Francis is far less oppressed and certainly less dominated and victimized. On the surface, at least, he is a success. His defeat is far more subtle, less painful and complete. His house is large, its furnishings tidy and lovely, in the best taste; but the house, the furnishings, the good taste mirror for him the affluent vacuum of the suburban community. He is less alienated from his wife, and yet he is disappointed in what their relationship has become: "... I would like to be as we were—sweet and bawdy and dark—but now there are too many people." He is irritated at her tantrums and especially at her overriding concern for their social position and that of their children. His relationship with his children is snarled in the details and confusions of rearing a family of four. A talk with his daughter Helen about the crash landing gets shunted aside by an argument over her reading *True Romances*. His work, from all we see, gives no center to his life; it is merely something he commutes to and from. It pays for the country life he is living.

The habitual relation of each to the routine of his life is shattered by an external stimulus. The return of his old friend Gallaher from "the great city of London" and his dinner with him ignite envy in Chandler, a resentment at his own manner of living, and an illusory hope of changing that life. Gallaher is a man of the world, a successful literary man, a man familiar with, even part of, the romance, even the romantic immorality, of the capitals of Europe. For Francis Weed, there is a sequence of disturbing and awakening events. The emergency crash landing—"a brush with death" which ironically still did not keep him from taking his regular commuting train home—breaks through the surface of his habitual responses. It stirs him, makes him more sensitive to the limitations of his life that was almost suddenly snuffed out. His disturbance is heightened by his inability to break through the family routines to tell anybody about the event and its significance to him. His recognition of the maid at a dinner party as the girl he had seen punished in France at the end of the war further sensitizes him to the existence of a world other than that tidy suburban world he is caught in. When the lovely sitter, in whose beautiful face he had seen "a direct appeal for love," cries in his arms over her drunken father, he is swept into his wild dream of romance regained.

It is indicative of the differences in the two men and their situations that Chandler's romantic yearnings are purely mental and illusory, while Francis' are more active, actual, and possible—if finally illusory, too. Chandler, although he has never written a poem, daydreams of becoming a successful poet and even imagines the critical response to the poems he only dreams of writing. The pathetic extent of his fulfilling his dream is to begin to read a poem by Lord Byron. Francis' yearnings take the more active form of falling in love with the sitter, with whom he feels as though he is returning to a submerged memory of his youth. He thinks of her constantly, thinks he sees her on the commuting train, buys her a bracelet, kisses her twice, and writes her a love letter which he knows he will never mail. As a consequence of his sudden love, he does recognize his loss of independence and seeks to assert it anew by insulting Mrs. Wrightson.

Chandler's balloon of romance, typically, is deflated even before he gets it fully rounded. He is disillusioned by Gallaher's vulgarity, although he still envies his life and feels the injustice of their respective positions. When submerged again in the domesticity of his apartment, he finds that even his *reading* of a poem is interrupted: "It was useless, useless! He was a prisoner for life." In anger, he shouts at the crying child; but this only intensifies the child's screaming, frightens Chandler, and further defeats his dream, his wish "to vindicate himself in some way, to assert his manhood." The completeness of the defeat is revealed in the story's final action. The pattern of poor Chandler's life has hardened and set. His wife intimidates him and turns her love to the child; it is the child, not Chandler, who is her "little man," her "love." Chandler feels shame and remorse not only for the frightening of the child, but for the loss of the possibility of fulfilling any dreams, a loss made irretrievable by his life and his own weakness.

The explosion of Francis' dream also produces an angry response initially. After young Clayton—tall and homely with horn-rimmed glasses—tells Francis "I think people ought to be able to dream big dreams," he demolishes Francis' dream with the announcement of his engagement to Anne Murchison, the sitter. In the "dingy light" of his spirit, Francis then fights with his wife and hits her. Her threatened leaving averted, he nonetheless commits a more destructive act of revenge: ruining Clayton's chances of getting a job by calling him worthless, even a thief. Facing the "wickedness of what he has done," Francis still has the ability to know he must make a choice. He does. He relinquishes romance and chooses adjustment. With mocking, yet bittersweet irony, Cheever has Francis seek a psychiatrist's aid (as would and probably did many others in his suburbia) for his illness of being in love. The therapy is again ironic. In his do-it-yourself workshop (and we can imagine it as one of many in Shady Hill) Francis is keeping himself busy with something practical, making a coffee table —one more piece of furniture to fit into the tidy, and tight, pattern of his country life. Unlike Chandler, he is happy in his adjustment. Though something is gone from his life.

Still, romance is not completely dead in the world of Shady Hill, as it is and always will be in the "poor stunted houses" of Chandler's Dublin. In the night at Shady Hill a husband pursues his wife, naked, across their terrace. Jupiter, the retriever—independent, high-spirited, irrepressible—still "prances through the tomato vines" as unadjusted as ever. In the dark night, romance still lingers—"kings in golden suits ride elephants over the mountains"—even though forsaken as impractical by Francis Weed.

## 3. The Limitations of Awareness: "Suicides."

The plural in the title of Cesare Pavese's "Suicides" refers not only to the two deaths that the narrator has indirectly caused, but also to the living death that he himself still endures. The three are interrelated, for the nature of his own living death has contributed to the literal deaths of the others. The nature of that death-in-life is given its full emotional impact and definitive shape by Pavese's use of the first person point of view and narration. His method is not full, but subtly partial irony; with that irony he exposes the destructive partial awareness of the narrator and the coldness of his frozen emotional life.

It is a life of isolation, of the aloneness that the narrator repeatedly insists on and even derives pleasure from. It is a life without real connection or communication, relationship or love—a life in which the isolated self can only use others for its own satisfaction, yet knows that very process of use, of objectifying others, ends up objectifying the self and deadening the sources of any satisfaction or fulfillment.

The coldness of this life of frozen, deadened, emptied emotion is dramatized of course by the narrator's treatment of Carlotta (to which we will return in detail later). But it is captured as well in the manner and tone of his narration. In referring to his mother, he speaks of "the old lady who calls herself my mother." The single phrase suggests not only the nature of the family relationship that helped shape him, but also the damaging result of that relationship which now perpetuates itself through just such distancing and denial of the full existence of others. For the narrator, others are *things,* not people—in this case an object of scorn.

His first description of Carlotta is typical of this same dehumanizing perspective: "She was one of those transparently simple souls—pitiful women—who become irritating if they cease for only an instant being themselves and attempt subterfuge or flirtation." After he first hurts her, he merely reports that "I did not return for three days; and when I did I addressed her formally. Thereupon another ridiculous courtship began . . ." Even in a description of a relatively pleasant time, his tone is degrading: "The evening we went to the movies I shut her up with a kiss." And the whole chilling negativism of the only kind of relationship he can allow is caught in a single statement of his description when she hugs him the next morning: "I did not repulse her."

His descriptions of her appearance and the comparisons he uses in describing her intensify the impact of his callousness, especially as his irritation over being trapped in the relationship increases. She is a "sponge" he uses to cleanse himself. He scans "her as one scans the pages of local news in the paper." She "looked at me like a whipped dog." When he causes her to suffer, he responds, "But she was too simple a soul to turn it to her gain. Rather, as happens to those who really suffer, it made her ugly. I was sorry, but I would have to have done with her, I felt." When he returns to her once more, he "disliked her damp face."

The man who responds to people in this way is caught by the author in a complex, but partial state of awareness of his condition. He *is* aware of the kind of thing he is doing, yet never penetrates the full truth of his situation. He even admits that he has "not fathomed, even yet," his feelings and behavior. Yet even his partial awareness becomes another means of self protection, another block to any human connection. It is a subtle delineation, and a profound insight into the ambiguities of human consciousness, conveyed ironically by the statements of the character himself.

One of the most significant of his interpretations of his life has to do with his suffering. By the fourth paragraph he is talking of how he has "suffered keen stabs of disappointment and regret." Further on he talks of the "cause" of his present state of estrangement and pain, his previous lover who had tormented him, not recognizing, of course, that his pattern of behavior and response is a much deeper part of his own character than something caused by an immediate disappointment in love. In the same way, his story of his friend's unintentional "suicide" produces feelings of pity for himself as he comments that love always leads to thoughts of killing oneself—again his obsessive concern with his own emotions only, his own suffering.

He does, however, realize his guilt, and speaks of this several times, but again (in an interesting insight) stresses the suffering this causes him. He recognizes, for example, that he is repaying Carlotta for the actions of the other woman, yet rationalizes this in terms of the pain *he* must endure. He says that his "stupid cruelty," unlike that of others, is merely stumbled into unintentionally. He feels, in fact, an inevitability in the pattern of his relationships that is beyond his control. "I would have to have done with her," he feels when her suffering begins to bother him, and, significantly, the actual break with her is then quickly passed over by him, with only a brief explanation that he was annoyed with her continuing interest in her husband.

He interprets his boredom and disinterest as the result of the limitations of this specific relationship, not of some general malaise of his own. When he awakes in the morning with her, he images "an altogether different waking and another mate." He feels "degraded" by the claims *she* places upon him. These dissatisfactions are, in turn, related to the pleasure he feels in being alone—without the recognition of the selfish isolation that pleasure is a part of and serves to reinforce.

The coldness and the distorting partial awareness conveyed by the ironies of language and interpretation in the narrative point of view are further dramatized in the irony of his actions toward Carlotta. Each time that he leaves her suddenly after making love to her, he explains it only by his desire to be alone. When she mentions divorce, he "shuts her up" by shouting or by kissing her—whatever his feelings at the time. When she talks of love, he decides to "avoid her for weeks on end." He becomes constantly irritated at the "enslavement" of their relationship, and the more this irritation hurts her, the more it grows. He refuses to take her seriously. If she is jealous, it is merely an act, and he is amused. When she tries to explain her relationship to her husband, the attempt at intimacy is ironically reversed: he stops seeing her. And in the story's final irony, when he feels desire for *her* again, he manages to overcome it—while she has already killed herself as a result of just this kind of refusal to accept her and deal with her as a human being, not merely as an object of his desire, irritation or self-pleasing cruelty.

The narrator does not comment on her death at the story's close. The story itself is that comment. He knows his responsibility, and yet —as the subtle ironies of the narrative point of view serve to dramatize —that knowledge reinforces the suffering of his own death in life and the suffering of others that such deadening refusal of true human connection continues to produce.

## 4. Choice and Absurdity: "The Wall" and "The Guest."

Pablo in Jean-Paul Sartre's "The Wall" and Daru in Albert Camus' "The Guest" are both concerned with performing a decent, honorable act; and in both stories the nature of their acts, as well as the general problem of moral choice and action, can best be understood from the perspective of some of the ideas of the philosophy of Existentialism. For in both cases, the situation in which the choices are made, the basis of the choices, and the results and value of the choices are defined by the authors in terms of the view of the nature of human existence suggested by this important and influential contemporary philosophy.

Camus himself has used the term *Absurd* to define the situation in which man finds himself. To the existentialist, the world is Absurd, first of all, because neither the life of man nor the universe has an essence, a meaningful total purpose and pattern. Moreover, not only must man face this nothingness, this universe with no all-encompassing, defining, transcendent principles; but he must face the constant orneriness of existence—that is, the constant, and usually ironic, overturning of any glimpses of order he might obtain. Of all the affronts to hope and meaning, death is probably the most significant symptom of the unreasonable, ultimately unfair nature of man's existence.

In the face of this situation, the existentialist poses the separate, subjective consciousness of each man as the basis of all meaning and value. Each man is isolated, alone and aimless, in a world that no longer seems to "work" in a reasonable fashion. All he can know of reality, of truth or purpose, is what he projects for himself. In the phrase of Soren Kierkegaard, each man must make his own "bloody truths."

Yet this predicament is also man's challenge and glory. For he is seen as having a free existence, not determined by some essence, pattern, or end. He can choose to make himself what he will be, and in this choice he fulfills his freedom. Although man's choice is hedged in and limited, confounded by circumstance, accident, and irrationality, it is the basis of value in his existence. The act of choosing is an act of definition; by it he shapes—until his next choice—the meaning of his life. But by his choice he is also made responsible, for his life and for others; he is creating an ethic. Thus, if faced honestly, his lonely, uncharted, unsupported freedom of choice is a challenging but awesome responsibility.

It is more than coincidence, then, that both Pablo and Daru face their lives in solitude—reduced to the bare essentials of their subjectivity and freedom. Faced with the sentence of death—the wall that marks the limits of life for all of us—Pablo feels himself separated from the rest of mankind, from the things of the world, even from his own body. People no longer matter to him; nor do causes, the sky, his own skin and bones. "I am alone," he thinks, knowing finally the irreducible, isolated core of his consciousness. And Tom, he thinks, Tom is alone, too. We all are—facing death. Daru, in "The Guest," is also seen in the bedrock extremity of his solitude long before the story's final summation of his condition: "he was alone." He is all alone in the cold schoolhouse; he is in an isolated region that further dramatizes his separateness. He is caught, alone, between the two sides of the civil war in Algeria. He is left, alone, within the incomprehensibility of the minds and decisions of others.

In "The Wall" the physical fact of death is, of course, the major element of the absurd external world that the isolated consciousness of Pablo must face. It is not the pain of death that is its chief threat; it is what happens after. What does it mean not to be alive? As Tom says, "And after that, then what?" It is this threat of death that sets the inescapable pattern within which a man must still exert his freedom. "It didn't make sense," Pablo thinks—of the death itself, but also of the life that is now seen, felt, within a different perspective. It was all an "emptiness," once the fact of impending death could no longer be evaded, was finally and truly experienced as *there*. But death is not the only element of the absurdity of existence in the story. There is injustice in the shooting of the men, particularly the nonpolitical Juan. And even more important there is the ludicrous absurdity of accident and coincidence, the unreasonable turns of life that confound the attempts of men to impose a personal pattern on it. In defiance and honor, Pablo names the most unlikely place he can think of when asked about the hiding place of Ramon Gris. Yet—by a meaningfully ridiculous coincidence—that is just the place Ramon Gris has chosen to hide, after all.

The ambiguous absurdity of life also confounds the decision of Daru, but in this case Camus places greater stress on the irrational reactions of men which produce the quicksands of meaning in which men must make their moral choices. The Arab prisoner does not escape in the night when Daru does nothing while he quietly slips out. Nor will he take advantage of Daru's final offer to seek out the Bedouins instead of the police at Tinguit. Out of his own strange honor and pride—and ironically because of Daru's allowing him his free choice—he chooses captivity and death. Equally unreasonably—and yet similarly within a code of honor—the Arab's brother will retaliate for Daru's attempted kindness by killing him. The external situation parallels the human dilemma. Daru cannot take sides in the warfare that splits his homeland; the land itself is inhospitable, forbidding, cruel, isolating; and yet—like the world in which man must live—it is the only home Daru feels he can have.

Unfair—absurd—as these predicaments are, they do not deter Pablo or Daru from their acts of choosing; rather, they prod them into making the only kind of choice that is valuable—that which is meaningful personally to them, for whatever reasons, with whatever outcome. They become responsible for their choices, and the consequences. Unlike Juan and Tom, Pablo has the will and strength to examine the reality of his death sentence with lucidity (to use a favorite term of Camus'). He realizes that what he must do must be done for himself—despite the overpowering presence of his mortality—not for the sake of some future, or some cause, or even for the sake of another man. The life of Ramon is no more valuable than his own, he decides. His decision to help Ramon becomes a significant act in the shaping of his own life; that is where its importance lies. And in his predicament, his life will take its shape from the manner in which he can die. "I didn't want to die like an animal," he thinks. "I wanted to understand." He wants to remain "hard"—in control of himself—before the fact of his death, and that means following a moral code that is meaningful to himself: "I wanted to die decently." Helping Ramon Gris feels decent to him—in terms of the choice itself, not in terms of pity or usefulness.

The context of Daru's decision does not have the sharp definition that the waiting wall of death gives Pablo's. His own position is much more ambiguous. He is alienated from both sides of the conflict, whereas even Pablo's withdrawal had not left him neutral between the two sides of the Spanish Civil War. "Listen, Balducci," Daru says, "all this disgusts me, beginning with your fellow here. But I won't hand him over." Thus, he will not comply with the order to take the prisoner to the police at Tinguit out of personal—and undefined—motives; not out of a decision of social loyalty. "Come with us," the Arab says to him, sensing his possible assistance. But Daru will not do that, either.

Still, Daru does not tell the Arab to escape. When he thinks he is running away in the night, he thinks, "Good riddance!" but gives him no direct offer. In the morning, he still feels himself trapped between "his own people who had sent him this Arab and the Arab who had dared kill but had not managed to get away." And so his final decision to show him the path to the south—and freedom—as well as the path to the east and the police is based on his personal sense of honor: "to hand him over was contrary to honor." Even in his final decision, Daru's position, and emotions, are ambiguous. He does not directly offer escape; he offers only the chance of a free choice for the Arab. His own choice is not to commit himself, out of honor. And so he leaves possible the Arab's choice of the police station, out of *his* sense of honor.

Neither choice—Pablo's or Daru's—produces any useful consequences for those whom they were aiding. By coincidence, Pablo's causes the death by Ramon Gris. Because of the unfathomable ambiguities of the human mind and emotions, Daru's allows the death of the Arab prisoner. The ironic reversals are further compounded, although differently, in the lives of the two protagonists. Pablo's death sentence is commuted (or in the broader sense, at least postponed). He will live on. Daru's life is threatened. He, at the end, is faced with the death sentence Pablo faced at the beginning. The absurdity will continue; the choices have made no difference in that. But both men have acted with the only kind of freedom and responsibility the existentialist sees is possible, and both have recognized the complex nature of their freedom to choose. Both now know they are alone.

## 5. Against the Walls: "Bartleby, the Scrivener."

Herman Melville's "Bartleby" is a tragi-comic study of meaninglessness. In it the absence of life-giving meaning in society and the difficulty, if not impossibility, of determining meaning on a personal basis leave the isolated scrivener, "absolutely alone in the universe," with only one course of action that can preserve any sense of himself: a pathetic, strangely heroic, whimsically humorous kind of passive defiance. For only through rejection and refusal can he still act. Only by destroying himself can he save anything of value.

For Bartleby, life is a series of walls—between man and society, man and other men, man and the meaning of his own life. These walls that isolate, block, and deaden are, in part, the trap of an impersonal, sterile society. The office that has become the whole of Bartleby's existence is located on Wall Street, the center of the business society. Out one window, the inhabitants of the office can see the inner white wall of an airshaft. Out the other window all that they can see, some ten feet away, is the blackened wall of another building. All but Bartleby: the wall outside of his window is only three feet away! And at the story's close the walls of the society's prison are even closer. After his last position in life, "fronting the dead wall," Bartleby finally lies "huddled at the base of the wall," "his head touching the cold stone."

But the walls that trap and block fulfillment, that shut out the light of life's meaning, are not only social. They are also the failure of connection and communication between persons, individuals. The lawyer shuts the ground-glass folding doors between himself and the scriveners. Bartleby is split from the other scriveners by these doors, but also split from the lawyer by the high green folding screen that is placed around him. Yet these are only the visible parallels to the more intangible kind of walls that block any communication with, any understanding of the existence of another person. In this world any communication of sympathy, encouragement, hope, or salvation is always too late, always goes astray, and ends being burned in the dead letter office.

Yet the isolation seems also to have a further extention, an inner dimension. For the men are also blocked from any full understandnig of themselves. The lawyer, "an eminently safe man," loses himself in the voluminous details of his work; he too has no significant life outside of his office. The scriveners, caught in the endless, deadly impersonal copying of the legal documents of the business society, are only half men: Turkey, able to work only in the mornings, and then losing himself in drink. The anxious, uneasy Nipper, wanting something he cannot understand, never able to settle down to work till afternoon. The young Ginger Nut, reduced even further to being merely the errand boy for the treats with which the other two distract themselves from the condition of their lives. It is only Bartleby that can see more clearly. He has at least faced the true nature of the problem, but now he knows there is no solution. He can understand only that there is nothing left that he can understand, nothing that can give meaning to his life.

Bartleby, then, sees the walls, and in the face of them, he has decided to withdraw with honor. If the walls will isolate him, he will isolate himself even further. If they will destroy him, he will destroy himself first. Though muted, and always polite, his "I would prefer not to" is a deep and spiritually resounding defiance of the conditions of his life on the only terms which he can still conceive. He, like Melville's more passionate seekers of meaning, has awakened to the true terrors at the core of his life. Unlike Captain Ahab, he is not allowed to shout his "No!" in thunder to maintain the honor and value of the "queenly personality" that resides in him. But wryly, with a grotesque whimsy, Melville does allow him to maintain his dignity and integrity. Bartleby prefers not to.

In tracing the deepening course of his refusals, we need to keep in mind the revelation that is kept to the end of the story: the penetration to the truth that his last job at the dead letter office had provided. After this, no compromise is possible. The "motionless young man" (as the lawyer first describes him) is committed to deeper and deeper immobility, to a dogged "passive resistance" (a term used by the narrator) against the forces that oppress him.

Bartleby first limits his acceptances to the precise job required of him. He will copy, but he would prefer not to examine the copies with the others, go to the post office, or go in the other office to get Nipper. At this same time, he limits his whole life to the office and when the lawyer comes by on a weekend, would "prefer" not to let him in. Nor will he share any of the facts of his life with the lawyer. He next takes a much more decisive step: he will not do any work at all. Rejecting copying, he rejects the whole basis of any kind of working relationship with society. He will only stare at the wall he knows is there. He will not be fired, he will not leave the office. When forced out by the new tenants, he will not leave the hallway. When asked to come home with him by the lawyer, he prefers "not to make any change at all." He will take no further action to give his life meaning. Yet even in prison, even as he rejects eating to keep himself alive, he does not blink away the truth of his existence. "I know where I am" he tells the lawyer. To his dying moment, he continues to stare at the wall.

For Melville, Bartleby, in the extreme form of a symbolic hyperbole, is humanity. And the story's theme of the isolation and meaninglessness of humanity's existence is also embodied in less extreme form in the life of the narrator.

Surrounded by walls, blocked by his ground-glass folding doors, caught in the routine of his work and secure position, the lawyer too is one of Melville's isolated men. With all of his limitations, nonetheless, he maintains a humaneness, if not the means to fulfill it. If anything might be Bartleby's last chance, it is he: and he seems to know this, and know as well the importance of Bartleby to him. For Bartleby may well be *his* last chance. Yet for reasons both within and beyond his control, he fails Bartleby. And himself. He cannot break through the wall.

Still, the lawyer recognizes his tie to Bartleby: that they shared "the bond of a common humanity," "A fraternal melancholy!" These phrases occur to him after he discovers, in Bartleby's living in the office, his "miserable friendlessness and loneliness," "his solitude." And, we might infer, his own. He recognizes, too, that Bartleby's strange behavior is a threat, a vague but troubling questioning of his own way of life and assumptions: that "the easiest way of life is the best."

As he tries to understand and help Bartleby, the lawyer's pity turns to repulsion and anger at the hopelessness of the task. Still, he treats him with care and is willing to accept the cross of Bartleby as his mission in the world. At this point the pressures of society became too great for him, and he gives in to the prodding of his professional acquaintances, but at the sacrifice of his own office so as not to violate Bartleby. When the new tenants complain, he entreats Bartleby to leave. Too late, he now offers to take Bartleby to his home. But the chance has already been lost and he next abdicates all responsibility for Bartleby, feeling the relief of at last being "care-free." In the prison he insists, "It was not I that brought you here," but is troubled by Bartleby's implication of his complicity. Too late again, after Bartleby's death, the lawyer for the first time reaches out and touches him.

Inevitably, it seems, and yet also as a result of human limitations, his concern has been one more dead letter, speeding, on an errand of life, to death. Human communication, sympathetic connection have not been established; and the lawyer is left more isolated than ever to face his deepened sense of the meaninglessness of his existence.